Lecture Notes in Computer Science 6664

Commenced Publication in 1973
Founding and Former Series Editors:
Gerhard Goos, Juris Hartmanis, and Jan van Leeuwen

Michael Butler   Wolfram Schulte (Eds.)

FM 2011:
Formal Methods

17th International Symposium on Formal Methods
Limerick, Ireland, June 20-24, 2011
Proceedings

 Springer

Volume Editors

Michael Butler
University of Southampton, Electronics and Computer Science
Highfield, Southampton SO17 1BJ, UK
E-mail: mjb@ecs.soton.ac.uk

Wolfram Schulte
Microsoft Research
One Microsoft Way, Redmond, WA 98052-6399, USA
E-mail: schulte@microsoft.com

ISSN 0302-9743   e-ISSN 1611-3349
ISBN 978-3-642-21436-3   e-ISBN 978-3-642-21437-0
DOI 10.1007/978-3-642-21437-0
Springer Heidelberg Dordrecht London New York

Library of Congress Control Number: 2011928375

CR Subject Classification (1998): D.2, F.3, D.3, D.1, J.1, K.6, F.4

LNCS Sublibrary: SL 2 – Programming and Software Engineering

Typesetting: Camera-ready by author, data conversion by Scientific Publishing Services, Chennai, India

Printed on acid-free paper

Springer is part of Springer Science+Business Media (www.springer.com)

Preface

The FM 2011 Symposium was held in Limerick during June 20–24, 2011. FM 2011 was the 17th in a series of symposia organized by Formal Methods Europe, an independent association whose aim is to stimulate the use of, and research on, formal methods for software development.

The FM 2011 Symposium had the goal of highlighting and celebrating advances and maturity in formal methods research, education, and deployment via tool support and industrial best practice, and their role in a variety of industries and domains. The call for papers invited contributions covering the use of formal methods in practice, tools for formal methods, the role of formal methods in software and systems engineering, theoretical foundations for formal methods and teaching of formal methods.

There were 101 submissions in total for FM 2011. After thorough review and discussion, including a rebuttal phase where authors were invited to submit a short response to the reviews, the committee decided to accept 29 papers based on originality, technical soundness, presentation and relevance to the themes of FM 2011.

The papers accepted covered a range of topics including the use of formal methods for analysis of cyber-physical systems and secure systems. Several papers on reasoning about concurrency and about dynamic structures were selected as well as papers addressing process algebra. On the tools front, there were papers on tools for model checking, runtime verification and program compilation and transformation. There were also papers on verification experiments and on formal methods education. The authors of the submitted papers represented 36 different countries

The symposium included three exciting and challenging presentations from invited speakers. Janos Sztipanovits gave a talk on modelling and cyber-physical systems, David Harel gave a talk on behavioral programming and Jasmin Fisher gave a talk on executable biology.

We wish to thank the members of the Program Committee and the numerous sub-reviewers for their work. Lero, the Irish Software Engineering Research Centre, at the University of Limerick, hosted the conference. Thanks to Mike Hinchey and other Lero members for managing the local organization and to FME for their strong support of the symposium. The Easychair system was used for management of the submission and reviewing process. Thanks to Springer for publication of the proceedings.

April 2011

Michael Butler
Wolfram Schulte

Organization

General Chair	Mike Hinchey, Lero
Program Chairs	Michael Butler, University of Southampton Wolfram Schulte, Microsoft Research
Workshop Chairs	Emil Vassev, Lero David Sinclair, Lero
Tutorials Chair	Nico Plat, West Consulting
Industry Day Chairs	Andrew Butterfield, Trinity College Dublin Thierry Lecomte, ClearSy
Doctoral Chair	Norah Power, Lero
Publicity Chair	Jonathan P. Bowen, Museophile Limited

Program Committee

Farhad Arbab	CWI and Leiden University, The Netherlands
Jos Baeten	TUE
Anindya Banerjee	IMDEA Software Institute, Spain
David Basin	ETH Zurich, Switzerland
Eerke Boiten	University of Kent, UK
Jonathan P. Bowen	Museophile Limited, UK
Michael Butler	University of Southampton, UK
Andrew Butterfield	Trinity College Dublin, Ireland
Ana Cavalcanti	University of York, UK
Byron Cook	Microsoft Research
Jin Song Dong	National University of Singapore
Colin Fidge	Queensland University of Technology, Australia
Bernd Finkbeiner	Saarland University, Germany
John Fitzgerald	Newcastle University, UK
Marc Frappier	University of Sherbrooke, Canada
Dimitra Giannakopoulou	Carnegie Mellon / NASA Ames, USA
Stefania Gnesi	ISTI-CNR Pisa, Italy
Reiner Hahnle	Chalmers University of Technology, Sweden
Klaus Havelund	Jet Propulsion Laboratory, California Institute of Technology, USA

Additional Reviewers

Aguirre, Nazareno
Ahrendt, Wolfgang
Ait Ameur, Yamine
Alglave, Jade
Alkassar, Eyad
Andres, Cesar
André, Étienne
Bendisposto, Jens
Bertolini, Cristiano
Bherer, Hans
Boström, Pontus
Broda, Sabine
Bryans, Jeremy W.
Bubel, Richard
Böhme, Sascha
Bøgholm, Thomas
Castro, Pablo
Cazorla, Diego
Chen, Chunqing
Cornelio, Marcio
Crocker, Paul
Daum, Matthias
Degerlund, Fredrik
Demasi, Ramiro
Dimitrova, Rayna
Donaldson, Alastair
Ehlers, Rüdiger
Ellison, Chucky
Fantechi, Alessandro
Ferrari, Alessio
Genaim, Samir
Gervais, Frederic
Gopinath, Divya
Greenaway, David
Gregorio-Rodríguez, Carlos
Griesmayer, Andreas
Haller, Leopold
Hansen, Helle Hvid
He, Nannan
Hoang, Thai Son
Homeier, Peter
Ilic, Dubravka
Jacobs, Bart

Ji, Ran
Jonker, Hugo
Jost, Steffen
Kaiser, Alexander
Kamali, Maryam
Khalek, Shadi
Kozyura, Vitaly
Kumar Mohalik, Swarup
Li, Qin
Lin, Shang-Wei
Liu, Yang
Llana, Luis
Malkis, Alexander
Mammar, Amel
Mariano, Georges
Markovski, Jasen
Marriott, Chris
Mazzanti, Franco
Mehlhorn, Kurt
Meinicke, Larissa
Meredith, Patrick
Moreira, Nelma
Morgan, Carroll
Mota, Alexandre
Murray, Toby
Myreen, Magnus O.
Møller, Mikael H.
Naumann, David
Nishihara, Hideki
Nogueira, Sidney
Nokhbeh, Razieh
Olesen, Mads Chr.
Olszewska Plaska, Marta
Pang, Jun
Patcas, Lucian
Pereira, David
Peter, Hans-Jörg
Plagge, Daniel
Qiu, Zongyan
Rabe, Markus
Reniers, Michel
Rinetzky, Noam
Rodrigues, Vitor Gabriel

Rosa, Fernando
Ruemmer, Philipp
Rungta, Neha
Ryan, Mark
Satpathy, Manoranjan
Schlatte, Rudolf
Schmidt, Benedikt
Schäf, Martin
Serbanuta, Traian
Siddiqui, Junaid
Sprenger, Christoph
Stefanescu, Andrei
Steffen, Martin

Stolz, Volker
Sun, Jun
Tapia Tarifa, Silvia Lizeth
Tautschnig, Michael
Vain, Juri
Valarcher, Pierre
Van De Mortel-Fronczak, Asia
Varpaaniemi, Kimmo
Wei, Wei
Westerholm, Jan
Winwood, Simon
Yang, Guowei
Yatsu, Hirokazu

Table of Contents

Experience

Program Compilation and Transformation

Security

Process Algebra

Education

Concurrency

Dynamic Structures

Model Checking

Model Integration and Cyber Physical Systems:
A Semantics Perspective

Janos Sztipanovits

Institute for Software Integrated Systems, Vanderbilt University, P.O. Box 1829 Sta. B.
Nashville, TN 37235, USA
janos.sztipanovits@vanderbilt.edu

Abstract. Recent attention to Cyber Physical Systems (CPS) is driven by the need for deeper integration of design disciplines that dominate physical and computational domains. Consequently, heterogeneity is the norm as well as the main challenge in CPS design: components and systems are modeled using multiple physical, logical, functional and non-functional modeling aspects. The scope of relevant design domains includes (1) physical domains, such as structure, mechanical dynamics, thermal, propulsion, fluid, electrical, acoustics/vibration and (2) computational/networking domains, such as system control, sensors, health management, mission management, communication. However, the practice of multi-modeling – using established domain-specific modeling languages and tools independently in the design process – is insufficient. Modeling and analyzing cross-domain interactions among physical and computational/networking domains and understanding the effects of heterogeneous abstraction layers in the design flow are fundamental part of CPS design theories. I will cast this challenge as a model integration problem and discuss solutions for capturing interdependencies across the modeling domains using constructs for meta-model composition and integration.

M. Butler and W. Schulte (Eds.): FM 2011, LNCS 6664, p. 1, 2011.

Some Thoughts on Behavioral Programming

David Harel

Dept. of Computer Science and Applied Mathematics
The Weizmann Institute of Science
Rehovot 76100, Israel

Abstract. The talk starts from a dream/vision paper I published in 2008, whose title is a play on that of John Backus' famous Turing Award Lecture (and paper). I will propose that — or rather ask whether — programming can be made a lot closer to the way we humans think about dynamics, and the way we somehow manage to get others (e.g., our children, our employees, etc.) to do what we have in mind. Technically, the question is whether we can liberate programming from its three main straightjackets: (1) having to directly produce a precise artifact in some language; (2) having actually to produce two separate artifacts (the program and the requirements) and having then to pit one against the other; (3) having to program each piece/part/object of the system separately. The talk will then get a little more technical, providing some evidence of feasibility of the dream, via LSCs and the play-in/play-out approach to scenario-based programming, and its more recent Java variant. The entire body of work around these ideas can be framed as a paradigm, which we call behavioral programming.

M. Butler and W. Schulte (Eds.): FM 2011, LNCS 6664, p. 2, 2011.

The Only Way Is Up

Jasmin Fisher[1], Nir Piterman[2], and Moshe Y. Vardi[3]

[1] Microsoft Research Cambridge, UK
[2] University of Leicester, UK
[3] Rice University, USA

Abstract. We draw an analogy between biology and computer hardware systems and argue for the need of a tower of abstractions to tame complexity of living systems. Much like in hardware design, where engineers use a tower of abstractions to produce the most complex man-made systems, we stress that in reverse engineering of biological systems; only by using a tower of abstractions we would be able to understand the "program of life".

1 Introduction

System-level approaches in biology have gained mainstream attention in the past decade, in an effort to better understand biological complexity. An important activity in system biology is the development of mathematical and computational models. Abstraction is well understood to be a key to modeling complex systems in general, and biological systems in particular, where by "abstraction" we refer to a model at a certain level of description, suppressing lower-level details in a principled way. All models used in system biology employ abstraction, but they vary in their level of abstraction from low-level differential equations all the way to Boolean logic. Today's systems biology offers a tool set of many different types of abstraction, but without an overall organizing principle. Furthermore, the overwhelming majority of cellular models focus on the levels of genes, proteins, and metabolites, as well as metabolic or regulatory networks. Our claim is that abstraction alone is unlikely to be sufficient as a tool to understand biological systems; what is needed, we believe, is a *tower of abstractions*; that is, a sequence of models of increasing degree of abstraction, each level building on the level below it. Biology, we believe, must "climb up the ladder of tower of abstractions."

To show how a tower of abstractions can be used to tame complexity, it is useful to draw an analogy between biological systems and computing hardware systems. We note that, in recent years, many tools and formalisms that were originally designed for the development and analysis of computing systems have been successfully used for modeling biological systems [14,10,24]. Perhaps the most striking resemblance between biology and hardware is the ability to do concurrent computation. Biological systems operate with inherent concurrency events (e.g., biochemical reactions, intercellular signaling, and the like) do not occur one after the other, but rather concurrently in different compartments over the entire organism just as the logical elements in computing hardware execute

M. Butler and W. Schulte (Eds.): FM 2011, LNCS 6664, pp. 3–11, 2011.

concurrently. In order for computing hardware to make sequential progress, for example, to sum up a vector of numbers, one has to add to the hardware memory elements, referred to as registers, which make it possible to transfer values from one machine cycle to the next. Analogously, in a cell, the accumulation of a certain protein may serve as a memory device and triggers events that depend on it. It is exactly this concurrency, however, that makes it difficult to understand the behavior of hardware and biological systems.

Our thesis is that in order to better understand complex biological behaviors, which will hopefully (and eventually) help us understand how genotype gives rise to phenotype, one must think of multiple useful levels of abstraction, similar to the tower of abstractions used by computer scientists and engineers in designing computing hardware. The argument is that to tame biological complexity we must find the right levels of abstraction to model biological systems, and that without such a tower of abstractions it would probably be impossible to understand the machinery behind complex living systems. Furthermore, the analysis through multi-leveled abstraction can serve to identify emergent behaviors of biological systems. A computer cannot be understood by pondering the behavior of transistors, or logic gates; similarly, the behavior of a cell cannot be predicted by understanding its chemistry at a molecular level. In order to understand the protocols employed by biological systems, which Caste and Doyle have suggested will give the necessary tools to reason about biological systems [8], we have to first identify the right levels of abstraction.

2   The Process of Hardware Design

To pursue the analogy of biology and hardware, it is useful to give a short (and rather simplified) overview of the process of hardware design [29]. The most notable feature of the design process is that it is a top-down process. Hardware design starts with the *formulation of requirements*, typically provided in a natural-language document. The next stage is the development of a *software model* of the intended system. This software model is intended to serve as an initial prototype for the system, which ultimately is implemented in hardware. The software model is an executable model, which can be experimented with, modified, and tuned.

The second design stage is a *transformation* of the software model into a hardware-description language (HDL). Such a language is essentially a programming language for hardware; it includes specialized features that talk about clocks and concurrency. While traditional software programming languages are designed to produce procedural code, executed one command at a time, HDLs assume that everything happens concurrently. An HDL model describes the behavior of the hardware in terms of signal flow and data transfer between registers (memory elements) and the operations performed on these signals and data. Note that the HDL model is not meant to run the software model; the software model and the HDL model are both models of the same system, but at different levels of abstraction.

The next stage is called *logic synthesis*; it converts the HDL model into a gate-level model, which describes the design implementation in terms logic gates and their connectivity. The conversion uses a predefined library of logic gates (e.g., AND gate with 2, 3, 4, or 8 inputs, etc.) that serve as elementary building blocks. Logic synthesis is typically an automated process, which implies that the two different descriptions (HDL and logic gates) should have exactly the same functionality.

The next stage is called *physical design*; here the logic has to be mapped to its physical implementation, in terms of components, component locations, component wiring, and the like. Here one deals with transistors and wires rather than with logic gates. While previously the main constraints were functional, here they are mainly physical. Length of wires, width of transistors, capacity, power consumption, and timing are the primary concerns. Ultimately, this design phase ends with a photomask, to be used in photolithography. Finally, the transistors and wires are actually printed on silicon.

Let us now illustrate this with a concrete example. We start with a software-level definition of integer multiplication, which can be described by K=I*J.

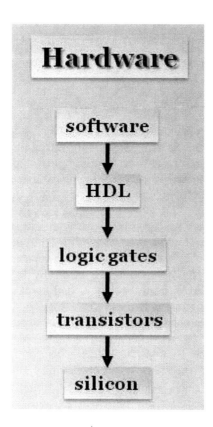

Fig. 1. The process of hardware design

At the HDL level, we choose (for the sake of this example) to implement multiplication via iterated addition. We need registers for I, J, and K (initially 0). We now iterate, at each iteration decrementing I and adding J to K. We stop when I reaches 0. At the gate level, we represent I, J, and K as 32-bit-vectors, that is, arrays of bits, each of length 32. We now need to implement bit-level decrementation and addition in terms of AND, OR, and NOT gates, and replicate that circuit 32 times. Finally, at the transistor level, we need to implement logic gates and registers using transistors. The final device will have thousands of transistors.

What is the point of this detailed description of computing hardware design? It is to emphasize the importance of having multiple levels of abstractions. Abstraction is the hardware designer's primary tool in dealing with complexity. The designers of the first microprocessor, in 1974, were able to work directly at the level of its 2300 transistors, but a modern microprocessor can have over two billion transistors. Today's tower of abstractions in hardware design (see Figure 1)software, HDL, logic-gates, transistors, silicon has emerged from close to 50 years of experience in hardware design. Hardware designers realized not only that abstraction is necessary for taming complexity, but also that several levels of abstraction are actually necessary.

3   Hardware and Wetware

It is important to note that the description above refers to the design of digital hardware systems, which have discrete behavior and form the basis for most computing systems. In continuous (analog) hardware systems, such as amplifiers, regulators, and filters, the focus is much more in the physical attributes of the devices, such as gain, power, and resistance. Which approach, discrete or continuous, is more appropriate for viewing biological systems? Many researchers believe that biology is completely continuous, doubting whether discrete abstractions can be found at all. This view, in our opinion misses an important point. Even digital computer systems are ultimately continuous systems, implemented in terms of transistors and wires. The value of discrete models is in their utility; they enable us to abstract away from the low-level continuous details. Thus, in hardware design continuous models are used only at the lowest level of abstraction, with higher levels, from logic gates and above, using discrete models. Discrete models are also extremely useful in biology. Indeed, the genetic code is discrete. Similarly, the opening and closing gating of ion channels in response to specific stimuli allowing cells to control their internal environment is just like having discrete switches. Biologists have been using discrete models, such as Boolean networks, since the 1960s [17]. For example, Boolean models correctly capture network motifs such as forward loops and dual-positive feedback loops [4,19] and lead to better understanding of the Drosophila segment polarity gene network resilience [2,7].

Clearly, biological systems are the "hardware of life", referred to as "wetware" by Rudy Rucker in his 1988 science-fiction novel [26]. The description above of the hardware-design process reveals, however, fundamental differences between hardware and wetware. Most fundamentally, computing hardware systems are designed by an intelligent designer, while biological systems are the result of billions of years of evolution. Furthermore, while hardware design proceeds in a sequence of distinct well-defined modelssoftware, HDL, logic gates, transistors, and silicon biology provides us with only the final 'model', so to speak, the living organism. What then is the value of the hardware-wetware analogy?

To understand the value of this analogy we need to remember that the biologist is not a designer, but rather a reverse engineer, with the task of uncovering, given a device, the functionality of that device and its principles of operation. Consider now a hardware engineer who is given a hardware device with the task of reverse engineering it. That task can be quite difficult. Take the device described above for integer multiplication. An inspection of a semiconductor chip may reveal an intricate network of thousands of transistors, but may say nothing about the functionality of the device. The reverse-engineering process is helped enormously by the reverse engineer's understanding of the (forward engineering) design process. Understanding that the transistor network implements logic gates, which implement HDL, which implements software, is critical to the success of reverse engineering a hardware device. We believe that the main value of the hardware-wetware analogy is in its showing that abstraction, and multiple levels of it, are absolutely crucial to handling biological complexity.

The importance of abstraction has been implicitly understood for quite some time. As stated by Brenner, "while the genome sequence is central, it is a level of abstraction that is too cryptic to be used for the organization of data and derivation of theoretical models." [6] Boolean gene networks are an example of an abstract model, whose value is that it is much easier to work with than the network of differential equations that it approximates. When Bornholdt says "Less Is More in Modeling Large Genetic Networks" [4], he is pointing out to the value of abstract models. In our view, Biology needs to go beyond mere abstraction and develop its own tower of abstractions. Note that we are not referring here to the fact that biology requires models at different scales (e.g., molecular, cellular, organ), rather, even a single scale requires multiple levels of abstraction, just as hardware designers apply multiple levels of abstraction during the design process at the same scale, for example, multiplication can be performed in terms of iterated addition. In biology, one can also observe different level of abstraction at the same scale. For example, the process of cell-fate determination in the earthworm *C. elegans* can be observed at different levels of abstraction. On the low-level, we can look at signal transduction and describe gene-expression levels [30] and the change in protein quantities over time [11,20], or, at a higher level of abstraction, we can observe the cell acquiring a specific cell fate according to morphology, cell division, or position of its daughter cells [28,27]. The cellular module of circadian clocks, constructed from genes and proteins involved in interlocking feedback loops [13], is an example of functional module that is best considered at a higher level of abstraction than that of regulatory, or metabolic pathways, which in turn are at a higher level of abstraction than that of genes, proteins, and metabolites [22]. The segmentation clock, a transcriptional oscillator that is responsible for vertebrate somitogenesis, is, in turn, an ensemble of numerous cellular oscillators [15].

One may argue that because biological systems are evolved rather than engineered, unlike hardware, they are unlikely to be amenable to hierarchical modeling. We argue otherwise. Evolution selects by fitness, and fitness is determined by phenotype. It is the very high-level attributes and traits of an organism that determine its fitness. Precisely because evolution typically works via reuse and modification of biological modules [16,18], we should expect a tower of abstractions to bridge the large gap between the genotype and phenotype. The brain is another complex system that is the result of evolution. While at the lowest level, brain functionality is driven by neurons, a full understanding of the brain requires it to be understood in terms of systems, subsystems, and sub-subsystems [23]; one would expect this to also be the case in cellular biology. As an example, let us consider bacterial chemotaxis, whereby bacteria migrate towards chemical attractants and away from chemical repellents. Chemotaxis is a behavior that contributed to fitness and is therefore selected for by evolution. The molecular mechanisms underlying chemotaxis are a subject of ongoing research, which shows that these mechanisms vary among different bacterial species [25]. The process of chemotaxis is very amenable to hierarchical modeling. Low level models consider the configuration of the molecules in the base of a flagellum and how changes in their phosphorylation leads to the binary choice of clockwise or anti-clockwise rotation [3]. The change in conformation is abstracted in the signaling network model of Rao et al., which includes the sensing (through ligand binding) and rotation-direction decision (through phosphorylation of controller). Higher-level models could, for example, abstract away the signaling network and connect directly sensing and motion.

While hardware is based on a well-defined and well understood tower of abstractions, a standard abstraction tower for biology has yet to emerge, see Figure 2 for a putative tower (of course, a biological tower of abstraction may not be as neat and orderly as the computing hardware tower). Even at the most basic level, we do not have a biological analogy to the most fundamental fact of hardware design, which is that transistors implement logic gates. Searching for the fundamental "bio-logic gates" [10] is a highly active research area. Brandman et al. [5] describe several general building blocks in genetic networks, such as excitatory feedback loop, inhibitory feedback loop, and the like. Nurse [21] calls for a program of describing and cataloguing cellular "logic circuits". In the context of synthetic biology, which is concerned with designing artificial biological systems, Endy [9] has argued for using functional modules and in turn to use these modules to create systems. In essence, these calls are for the development of a "bio-logic gate-level model" (obviously, in a biological setting the components are much more fluid than in an engineering setting, often performing different tasks in different contexts). While the development of such a model would constitute a significant step forward in system biology, we should remember that in hardware design the gate-level model is still a fairly low-level model. The reverse engineer who has

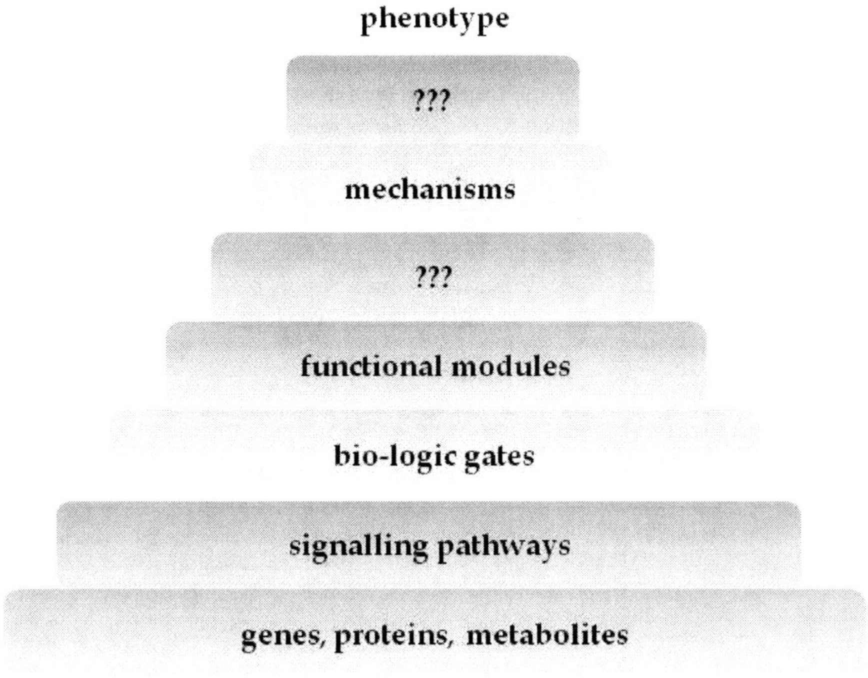

phenotype

???

mechanisms

???

functional modules

bio-logic gates

signalling pathways

genes, proteins, metabolites

Fig. 2. Tower of abstractions in biology

uncovered the gate-level model of the multiplication device described above is still far from realizing that the device performs integer multiplication. Similarly, we must define models that are more abstract and higher-level than the "bio-logic gate-level model." The segmentation clock [15], mentioned above, which is an ensemble of numerous cellular oscillators seems to be an example of a functional module that is best considered at a level above that of "bio-logic gates."

4   The Software of Life

In the tower of abstractions of hardware design, the highest level was the software level, which describes the behavior of the hardware device. What is then the software of life? Let us go back to the example above. The software of the device we described above is the equation $Z=X*Y$. This equation is not directly represented in the silicon; nevertheless, the silicon implements it. Thus, $Z=X*Y$ *emerges* from the simple and local interaction of the thousands of transistors that constitute the circuit. It follows that the software of hardware can be viewed as an *emergent behavior* of the hardware. This behavior is the top level in our tower of abstractions; see [1] for a discussion of emergence and multi-levelled abstraction in science. Analogously, the "software of life" is an emergent behavior of biological systems (e.g., chemotaxis). To understand how genotype leads to behavior, we need to identify first the tower of abstractions bridging genotype and behavior. In genetics, the central dogma provides us with the appropriate level of abstraction, referring to the DNA-to-protein transfer. While system biology researchers are largely aware of the importance of abstraction, system biology has concentrated its efforts in models of the gene/protein/metabolite and regulatory network levels. We believe that biological models should have multiple levels of abstraction, starting from molecular-level models, going through bio-logic-gate models, and eventually getting to behavioral models, relating to the "software of life". Identifying these levels of abstraction is, in our opinion, one of the central challenges of system biology; and quoting a recent piece on systems biology theory by Gunawardena [12], "Molecular biology was reductionism's finest hour. Now, there is nowhere left to go but up."

References

1. Abott, R.: Emergence explained-abstractions. Complexity 12(1), 13–26 (2006)
2. Albert, R., Othmer, H.G.: The topology of the regulatory interactions predicts the expression pattern of the segment polarity genes in drosophila melanogaster. J. Theor. Biol. 223(1), 1–18 (2003)
3. Bai, F., Branch, R.W., Nicolau Jr., D.V., Pilizota, T., Steel, B.C., Maini, P.K., Berry, R.M.: Conformational spread as a mechanism for cooperativity in the bacterial flagellar switch. Science 327(5966), 685–689 (2010)
4. Bornholdt, S.: Systems biology. less is more in modeling large genetic networks. Science 310(5747), 449–451 (2005)
5. Brandman Jr., O., Ferrell, J.E., Li, R., Meyer, T.: Interlinked fast and slow positive feedback loops drive reliable cell decisions. Science 310(5747), 496–498 (2005)
6. Brenner, S.: Sequences and consequences. Philos. Trans. R Soc. Lond. B Biol. Sci. 365(1537), 207–212 (2010)
7. Chaves, M., Albert, R., Sontag, E.D.: Robustness and fragility of boolean models for genetic regulatory networks. J. Theor. Biol. 235(3), 431–449 (2005)
8. Csete, M.E., Doyle, J.C.: Reverse engineering of biological complexity. Science 295(5560), 1664–1669 (2002)
9. Endy, D.: Foundations for engineering biology. Nature 438(7067), 449–453 (2005)
10. Fisher, J., Henzinger, T.A.: Executable cell biology. Nat. Biotechnol. 25(11), 1239–1249 (2007)
11. Grant, B.D., Wilkinson, H.A.: Functional genomic maps in caenorhabditis elegans. Curr. Opin. Cell Biol. 15(2), 206–212 (2003)
12. Gunawardena, J.: Systems biology. biological systems theory. Science 328(5978), 581–582 (2010)
13. Hardin, P.E.: The circadian timekeeping system of drosophila. Curr. Biol. 15(17), R714–R722 (2005)
14. Harel, D.: On comprehensive and realistic modeling: some ruminations on the what, the how and the why. Clin. Invest. Med. 28(6), 334–337 (2005)
15. Horikawa, K., Ishimatsu, K., Yoshimoto, E., Kondo, S., Takeda, H.: Noise-resistant and synchronized oscillation of the segmentation clock. Nature 441(7094), 719–723 (2006)

16. Kashtan, N., Alon, U.: Spontaneous evolution of modularity and network motifs. Proc. Natl. Acad. Sci. U S A 102(39), 13773–13778 (2005)

17. Kauffman, S.A.: Metabolic stability and epigenesis in randomly constructed genetic nets. J. Theor. Biol. 22(3), 437–467 (1969)

18. Kitano, H.: Biological robustness. Nat. Rev. Genet. 5(11), 826–837 (2004)

19. Klemm, K., Bornholdt, S.: Topology of biological networks and reliability of information processing. Proc. Natl. Acad. Sci. U S A 102(51), 18414–18419 (2005)

20. Long, F., Peng, H., Liu, X., Kim, S.K., Myers, E.: A 3d digital atlas of c. elegans and its application to single-cell analyses. Nat. Methods 6(9), 667–672 (2009)

21. Nurse, P.: Life, logic and information. Nature 454(7203), 424–426 (2008)

22. Oltvai, Z.N., Barabasi, A.L.: Systems biology. life's complexity pyramid. Science 298(5594), 763–764 (2002)

23. Perus, M.: Multi-level synergetic computation in brain. Nonlinear Phenomena in Complex Systems 4(2), 157–193 (2001)

24. Priami, C.: Algorithmic systems biology. Communications of the ACM 52(5), 80–88 (2009)

25. Rao, C.V., Kirby, J.R., Arkin, A.P.: Design and diversity in bacterial chemotaxis: a comparative study in escherichia coli and bacillus subtilis. PLoS Biol. 2(2), E49 (2004)

26. Rudy, V.B.: Rucker and Copyright Paperback Collection (Library of Congress). Wetware. Avon Books, New York (1988)

27. Sternberg, P.W., Felix, M.A.: Evolution of cell lineage. Curr. Opin. Genet. Dev. 7(4), 543–550 (1997)

28. Sulston, J.E.: C. elegans: the cell lineage and beyond. Biosci. Rep. 23(2-3), 49–66 (2003)

29. Wakerly, J.F.: Digital Design: Principles and Practices, 4th edn. Pearson Education, London (2008)

30. Wang, M., Sternberg, P.W.: Pattern formation during c. elegans vulval induction. Curr. Top Dev. Biol. 51, 189–220 (2001)

Does It Pay to Extend the Perimeter of a World Model?[*]

Werner Damm[1] and Bernd Finkbeiner[2]

[1] Carl von Ossietzky Universität Oldenburg
[2] Universität des Saarlandes

Abstract. Will the cost for observing additional real-world phenomena in a world model be recovered by the resulting increase in the quality of the implementations based on the model? We address the quest for optimal models in light of industrial practices in systems engineering, where the development of control strategies is based on combined models of a system and its environment. We introduce the notion of remorsefree dominance between strategies, where one strategy is preferred over another if it outperforms the other strategy in comparable situations, even if neither strategy is guaranteed to achieve all objectives. We call a world model optimal if it is sufficiently precise to allow for a remorsefree dominating strategy that is guaranteed to remain dominant even if the world model is refined. We present algorithms for the automatic verification and synthesis of dominant strategies, based on tree automata constructions from reactive synthesis.

1 Introduction

What constitutes a good model? We revisit this fundamental question using concepts and algorithms from reactive synthesis, which allow us to construct and compare different strategies for achieving a given collection of objectives. A key challenge rests in the identification of the perimeter of the model: given a (physical) system S under development, what real-world aspects could potentially impact S in a way that endangers its proper functioning? Examples of systems of interest are aircrafts, cars, nuclear power plants, defibrillators, production plants, or in general what is often referred to as cyber-physical systems, i.e., systems where both software and hardware components play key roles in realizing the system's functionality.

1.1 A Motivating Example

Suppose we wish to develop a driver assistance system that maintains, whenever possible, a safe distance to objects ahead on the same lane, such as another car or some obstacle on the road. The starting point for the development is the world model shown in Figure 1(a), which specifies how environment disturbances like

---

[*] This research was partially supported by the German Science Foundation within the Transregional Collaborative Research Center TR14 AVACS.

M. Butler and W. Schulte (Eds.): FM 2011, LNCS 6664, pp. 12–26, 2011.

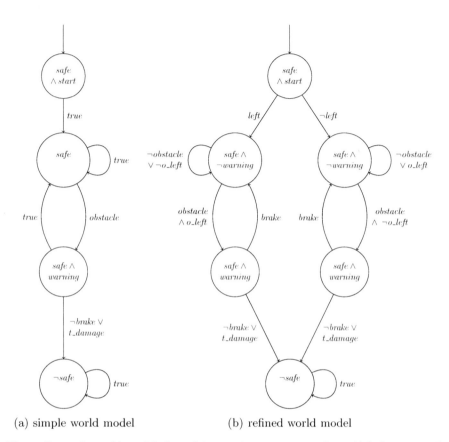

(a) simple world model   (b) refined world model

Fig. 1. Example world models for a driver assistance system. Sets of labels are specified using logical formulas: for example, the edges marked with *true* are labeled with all subsets of {*obstacle*, *o_left*, *t_damage*, *left*, *brake*}.

the appearance of obstacles (*obstacle*) or a sudden tire damage (*t_damage*), and controllable system actions, such as braking (*brake*), result in transitions on the world states.

In the initial state the world is *safe*. Once an obstacle appears somewhere ahead, we observe (through some distance sensor) a *warning* signal, as indicated in the middle state; at this point, the world may transition into the unsafe bottom state. Braking will prevent the unsafe state unless a rare event such as a sudden tire damage (*t_damage*) causes the transition to the unsafe state. Clearly, this world model is very simple; in particular, we have not modeled the lane in which our car is traveling and the lane where the obstacle appears. As a result, the effect of a decision not to brake is nondeterministic: after not braking in the *warning* state, the next state will either be *safe*, if the obstacle was indeed on the same lane as the car and we thus avoided the obstacle by changing the lane, or the bottom unsafe state, if the obstacle was in fact on the other lane. The nondeterminism can be eliminated in a refined world model, such as the one shown in Figure 1(b): this world model extends the perimeter to additionally include the concept of lanes. In this example, there is a left and a right lane (for the same direction of travel). The states on the left correspond to the case that the car is on the left lane, the states on the right to the case that the car is on the right lane. In the initial state, the car chooses one of the two lanes, we assume that there is no further possibility to change lanes. The refined world model in Figure 1(b) is larger and more detailed than the simple world model in Figure 1(a). But does the extension pay?

Let us assume that the primary objective of our driver assistance system is to maintain safety, i.e., to ensure that *safe* is always true, and that an additional, secondary, objective is to avoid braking, i.e., to ensure that *brake* is always false. Consider the following three example control strategies: Strategy 1 never brakes. Strategy 2 brakes if and only if a *warning* has occurred. Strategy 3 brakes all the time. In both world models it is clear that none of the three strategies guarantees that the objectives are met in all situations: irrespectively of the strategy, the occurrence of an obstacle followed by tire damage will always cause a transition to the unsafe state, violating the primary objective. A more meaningful comparison of the strategies is therefore to see how they perform on particular sequences of disturbances.

Strategy 3 is clearly not dominant, because it brakes, and, hence, violates the secondary objective, even in the middle *safe* state, where there is no danger that the primary objective might be violated. Strategies 1 and 2 avoid this unnecessary braking. Because of the nondeterminism in the simple world model, it is, however, also impossible to identify one of the two strategies as remorsefreely dominant. If, starting from the *warning* state, the assistance system does not brake, following Strategy 1, then there is the possibility that the unsafe state is reached and, hence, the primary objective is violated. It would thus have been preferable to brake, as suggested by Strategy 2. On the other hand, if the assistance system does brake, following Strategy 2, then there is also the possibility that not braking would have led to a transition to the *safe* state, in which case the secondary objective was violated unnecessarily.

The simple world model thus does not allow us to choose a dominant strategy. Let us analyze the same situation in the refined world model of Figure 1(b). Strategy 2 still dominates Strategies 1 and 3, because Strategy 1 may violate the primary objective in the *warning* state, and Strategy 3 may violate the secondary objective in middle *safe* state. As before, Strategy 3 never performs better than Strategy 2. Unlike in the simple model, however, the same holds for Strategy 1: In the *warning* state it is now always better to brake, as suggested by Strategy 2, because the nondeterministic possibility to return to the middle *safe* state without braking has been eliminated. Hence, the payoff of the refinement of the world model is that we can identify Strategy 2 as dominant.

1.2   From Correctness to Dominance

As the example illustrates, cyber-physical systems should not be expected to always guarantee their functional requirements – the system is likely to exhibit failures when exposed to a physical environment outside the perimeter of the employed world model. Since the concept of an all encompassing complete model is of philosophical interest only, the notion of "correctness" has to be revisited and replaced by notions addressing the inherent incompleteness of verification approaches induced from modeling boundaries.

In this paper, we propose such a new notion of correctness based on a comparison of the available strategies. We call the strategic dominance described in the example (for each sequence of disturbances, the dominating strategy achieves at least the same priority as the dominated strategy) *remorsefree dominance*. Remorsefree dominance allows us to compare two strategies even if both strategies violate some objectives. Intuitively, remorsefree dominance means that one never feels "remorse" about a decision, because, in retrospect, after having seen a sequence of disturbances, the other strategy would appear preferable.

We compare the strategic capabilities when extending the perimeter of the world model: does it pay to extend the perimeter of a world model from from a set V of real-world phenomena to a set $V \cup \{e\}$ – i.e., can strategies which are aware about the real-world phenomenon e avoid violations of the system requirements more often than strategies which are only aware about real-world phenomena contained in V?

We must be careful to distinguish the unavailability of information about a phenomenon due to an incomplete observation of the world through a limited sensor system on the one hand from a complete absence of the phenomenon in the world model on the other. In systems engineering, this distinction corresponds to the following two different design questions. The first question is that of *sensor completeness:* Relative to a given perimeter of the world model, will adding certain sensors strengthen the strategic capabilities to achieve the given objectives? For example, in the driver assistance system, it is irrelevant whether we directly observe the occurrence of an *obstacle* as long as we observe the *warning* signal. The second question refers to the *perimeter of the model:* Will extending the perimeter of the model add strategic capabilities?

To answer the first question, we study strategy classes that are indexed by the available observables: The strategy class $\mathcal{S}_I$ consists of all strategies that determine the system actions based on observations from I. We are interested in finding strategies from one class $\mathcal{S}_I$ that remorsefreely dominate all strategies from another class $\mathcal{S}_J$ with more ($I \subset J$) or even full information.

To answer the second question, we search for strategies that remain dominant under all possible refinements of the world model. A simple (but correct) model hides the impact of certain phenomena with nondeterminism; whether or not this imprecision has an impact on the existence of a dominating strategy depends on how relevant the phenomenon is for the objectives under consideration. We thus have a formal characterization of what constitutes an optimal world model: A world model is *optimal* if the description of the relevant phenomena is sufficiently precise to guarantee the existence of a dominating strategy that remains dominant in all possible refinements of the model.

1.3   Verification and Synthesis

An algorithmic treatment of these questions combines aspects of verification (which objectives are achieved?) with aspects of synthesis (is there a better strategy?). The algorithmic approach of the paper is therefore based on constructions on automata over infinite trees, similar to those used in the automata-theoretic synthesis of reactive systems [1,2,3,4,5]. We characterize remorsefree dominance as a language on infinite trees by providing a tree automaton that accepts all dominating strategies. This automaton can be used to verify that a given strategy is dominant (it is dominant iff it is accepted by the automaton) and to synthesize a dominant strategy iff such a strategy exists (it exists iff the language of the automaton is nonempty). We also give analogous constructions for the set of strategies that remain dominant over all refinements of the world model.

The paper thus provides a conceptual and algorithmic framework for what could be called a new relativized theory of correctness, which accepts that systems may fail and replaces absolute guarantees (all objectives are guaranteed to be achieved) with the relative notions of dominance and optimality.

2   Foundations

2.1   World Models

We study the interaction of a system with its environment. Let $\mathcal{V}_S$ be a finite set of system variables, modeling actions under the system's control, such as the setting of actuators, and $\mathcal{V}_E$ be an arbitrary set of *environment variables*, in the context of control theory corresponding to the variables of the plant model. We assume that the environment variables are partitioned into disjoint sets of *disturbances* $\mathcal{V}_D$, modeling uncontrollable environment observations, and *controllable environment variables* $\mathcal{V}_C$, modeling phenomena in the environment, i.e., actions and observations which can be influenced by the system through the system variables. For the purposes of this paper, we assume that all values can be finitely encoded, and thus, without loss of generality, assume all variables to be of Boolean type.

We formalize the possible interactions between the system and its environment using labeled graphs, which we call *world models*. Nodes represent the states of a plant. Transitions between nodes then represent the effect of a given setting of the system variables and a given disturbance on the current state of the plant. The actual choice of settings of system variables will be determined by (control-) strategies discussed below.

We consider world models that restrict only a finite subset $V_E \subseteq \mathcal{V}_E$ of the environment variables. We call this subset the *perimeter* of the world model. As made formal in the definition below, models with restricted perimeter can be understood as full models by assigning arbitrary valuations to the environment variables outside the perimeter of the model. We denote, for a valuation[1] $\sigma \subseteq V_E$ of environment variables V_E, the set of valuations of $\mathcal{V}_E$ obtained by assigning arbitrary valuations to environment variables outside the perimeter by $\mathcal{E}(\sigma) = \{\sigma \cup r \,|\, r \subseteq (\mathcal{V}_E \smallsetminus V_E)\}$.

A *world model* $M = (V_E, N, n_0, E, L_N, L_E)$ is a labeled directed graph, where $V_E \subseteq \mathcal{V}_E$ is the subset of environment variables observed by the model, N is a possibly infinite set of nodes, $n_0 \in N$ is an initial node, $E \subseteq N \times N$ is a set of edges, and $L_N : N \to 2^{2^{\mathcal{V}_C}}, L_E : E \to 2^{2^{\mathcal{V}_S \cup \mathcal{V}_D}}$ is a pair of labeling functions that assign to each node a set of valuations of the controllable environment variables and to each edge a set of valuations of the system variables and the disturbances.

We denote by $V_C = V_E \cap \mathcal{V}_C$ and $V_D = V_E \cap \mathcal{V}_D$ the finite sets of controllable environment variables and disturbances, respectively, within the perimeter of the world model. We assume L_N and L_E to be induced from valuations of environment variables within the perimeter, e.g., L_N to be induced by a labeling function $L'_N : N \to 2^{2^{V_C}}$ such that $L_N(n) = \bigcup_{\sigma \in L'_N(n)} \mathcal{E}(\sigma)$, and, similarly, L_E to be induced by a function $L'_E : E \to 2^{2^{V_S \cup V_D}}$ such that $L_E(e) = \bigcup_{\sigma \in L'_E(E)} \mathcal{E}(\sigma)$. We furthermore assume that the world models are *total*, i.e., for each node $n \in N$, each valuation σ_S of the system variables, and each valuation σ_D of the disturbances there exists a node $m \in N$ such that $\sigma_S \cup \sigma_E \in L'_E(n, m)$.

As an example, consider the world models of Figure 1. The models refer to the system variables $\mathcal{V}_S = \{brake, left\}$, the disturbances $\mathcal{V}_D = \{obstacle, o\_left, t\_damage\}$ and the controllable environment variables $\mathcal{V}_C = \{safe, start, warning\}$. The perimeter of the simple world model, $V_E = \{obstacle, t\_damage, safe, start, warning\}$, is a subset of the perimeter of the refined world model, $V'_E = V_E \cup \{left, o\_left\}$.

The purpose of the world model is to predict the consequences of system actions. Because each model only considers a finite number of phenomena, however, it typically abstracts from some relevant phenomena with nondeterminism: We call a world model *nondeterministic* if there exist two edges $(n, m_1), (n, m_2)$ such that the edge labels are not disjoint, $L'_E(n, m_1) \cap L'_E(n, m_2) \neq \emptyset$, and the union of the target node labels is not singleton $|L'_N(m_1) \cup L'_N(m_2)| \geq 1$. Otherwise, we call the world model *deterministic*[2].

It is often possible to reduce the nondeterminism by extending the perimeter of the world model. While the models may differ in their precision, they model the same reality. We therefore expect them to be consistent in the sense that the *more concrete* (or *refined*) model must be simulated by the *more abstract* model.

A concrete world model $M_1 = (V_{E_1}, N_1, n_{0_1}, E_1, L_{E_1}, L_{N_1})$ *is simulated by* an abstract world model $M_2 = (V_{E_2}, N_2, n_{0_2}, E_2, L_{E_2}, L_{N_2})$ with $V_{E_2} \subseteq V_{E_1}$ iff there exists a *simulation relation* $R \subseteq \{(n_1, n_2) \in N_1 \times N_2 \mid L_{N_1}(n_1) \subseteq L_{N_2}(n_2)\}$ such that

---

[1] All variables are of Boolean type. A variable is evaluated to true iff it is an element of σ.

[2] Note that a deterministic model may still have multiple runs due to different evaluations of the system and disturbance variables.

1. $(n_{0_1}, n_{0_2}) \in R$ and
2. for all $(n_1, n_2) \in R, (n_1, m_1) \in E_1$, and $\sigma \in L_{E_1}(n_1, m_1)$
   there exists a pair $(n_2, m_2) \in E_2$ such that $\sigma \in L_{E_2}$ and $(m_1, m_2) \in R$.

For example, the world model in Figure 1(a) simulates the world model in Figure 1(b). The simulation relation relates two nodes from the two wolds models whenever they are depicted horizontally next to each other, i.e., the initial nodes are related, the nodes labeled *safe* $\land \neg warning$ are related to the node labeled *safe*, etc.

2.2   Strategic Objectives

We use linear-time temporal logic (LTL) [6] to specify strategic objectives. Let $\mathcal{V} = \mathcal{V}_S \cup \mathcal{V}_E$. We interpret LTL formulas over *computations*, which are infinite sequences $\sigma = \sigma_0 \sigma_1 \sigma_2 \ldots \in (2^{\mathcal{V}})^\omega$ of variable valuations. We denote restrictions of a computation σ or other sequences of variables to a subset $X \subseteq \mathcal{V}$ of the variables by $\sigma|_X = \sigma_0 \cap X \, \sigma_1 \cap X, \ldots$. The satisfaction of an LTL formula φ on a computation σ is denoted by $\sigma \models \varphi$.

An *objective specification* $\varphi = (\mathcal{O}, p)$ consists of a set $\mathcal{O}$ of LTL formulas, called *objectives*, and a *priority function* $p : \mathcal{O} \to \{1, \ldots, |\mathcal{O}|\}$, which identifies the priority of each objective as a positive number, where 1 is the most important priority.

In the driver assistance system, the objectives consist of two invariants, the invariant $\Box safe$ with priority two, and the invariant $\Box \neg brake$ with priority two.

We say that a computation σ *satisfies priorities up to* n if n is the greatest nonnegative number $n \in \mathbb{N}_{\geq 0}$ such that $\sigma \models \phi$ for all $\phi \in \mathcal{O}$ and $p(\phi) \leq n$. A set of computations $\mathcal{C}$ *satisfies priorities up to* n if n is the greatest nonnegative number $n \in \mathbb{N}_{\geq 0}$ such that $\sigma \models \phi$ for all $\varphi \in \mathcal{O}$, $p(\phi) \leq n$, and $\sigma \in \mathcal{C}$. If a strategy s or a set $\mathcal{S}$ of strategies satisfies priorities up to 0, i.e., none of the priorities are met, we say that s or $\mathcal{S}$, respectively, *completely violates* $(\mathcal{O}, p)$.

2.3   Strategy Classes

Let $M = (V_E, N, n_0, d_0, E, L_N, L_E)$ be a world model over V_E, modeling the influence of a valuation of the system variables $\mathcal{V}_S$ and the disturbances V_D on the controllable environment variables. Let $V = V_E \cup \mathcal{V}_S$.

A *control strategy* (or short: *strategy*) for M selects the valuation of the system variables dependent on the sequence of valuations of the environment variables V_E as observed through a finite set of *observables* $I \subseteq V_E$. Formally, a control strategy over observables I is a function $s : (2^I)^* \to 2^{\mathcal{V}_S}$.

A control strategy s and a sequence of disturbances $\sigma_D \in (2^{V_D})^\omega$ determine jointly the following set of computations $C_M(\sigma_D, s)$ in the world model M: $C_M(\sigma_D, s) = \{\sigma_0 \sigma_1 \ldots \in (2^V)^\omega \mid \exists n_0 n_1 \ldots \in N^\omega . \sigma_0 = L'_N(n_0) \cup d_0 \cup s(\epsilon) \land \forall j > 0 . (n_{j-1}, n_j) \in E \, L'_E(n_{j-1}, n_j) = (\sigma_S, \sigma_D) \land \sigma_j = \sigma_S \cup \sigma_D \cup L'_N(n_j)\}$, where $\sigma_S = s(\sigma_0 \cap I \, \ldots \, \sigma_{j-1} \cap I)$.

We call the class of such strategies s_I the *I-observation strategy class*, denoted by $\mathcal{S}_I$. The special case $I = V_E$ is called the *full-observation class*. We use the term *partial observation strategies* for strategies in some I-observation strategy class with $I \subsetneq V_E$.

2.4   Winning Strategies

We call the set $C_M(s) = \bigcup_{\sigma_D \in (2^{V_D})^\omega} C_M(\sigma_D, s)$ of computations that result from combining a strategy s with sequences of disturbances the *computations of s*. We say that strategy s is *winning up to priority* n if every computation in $C_M(s)$ satisfies the objective specification up to priority n. This induces a partial order $\sqsubseteq$ on strategies: a strategy s is *dominated by* a strategy t, denoted by $s \sqsubseteq_M t$, if s is winning up to priority n, t is winning up to priority m, and $n \leq m$.

3   Remorsefree Dominance

As discussed in the introduction, it is often unrealistic to expect a strategy to enforce an objective for *every* possible environment behavior. For example, in the driver assistance system, a tire damage can always cause a transition to the unsafe state. If even the full-observation strategies violate the objective specification completely, then the $\sqsubseteq$-hierarchy collapses: all strategies violate the objective specification completely.

We now introduce a finer dominance order that allows us to distinguish strategies even if none of the objectives can be guaranteed. Remorsefree dominance refers to individual computations rather than full strategies. We say a computation σ *is dominated by* a computation η, denoted by $\sigma \sqsubseteq \eta$, if σ satisfies the objective specification up to priority m, η up to priority n, and $m \leq n$.

A strategy s *is remorsefreely dominated* (in world model M) by a strategy t, denoted by $s \preceq_M t$, iff for every sequence of disturbances $\sigma_D \in (2^{V_D})^\omega$ and every computation $c \in C_M(\sigma_D, t)$ there is a computation $c' \in C_M(\sigma_D, s)$ such that c dominates c'.

To motivate the "for every ... there is" quantification in the above definition, consider the following two variations of the same scenario: An aircraft is approaching the airport under strong shear winds. In variation 1, the aircraft is not equipped with a shear wind sensor, and the autopilot (unaware of the shear wind) initiates an approach. In this variation, an uncontrollable nondeterminism will decide over life and death, i.e., whether by chance the aircraft is still able to land, or whether the shear wind will cause the aircraft to crash on the ground. In variation 2, the aircraft is equipped with a shear wind sensor, and the autopilot tests for the velocity and changes of the shear wind and automatically initiates an abort of the approach. In variation 1, there is thus an uncontrollable chance that both the primary objective (safety) and the secondary objective (landing) is achieved. However, at the uncontrollable risk of violating the primary objective. In variation 2, by contrast, safety is guaranteed at the price of excluding the possibility of achieving the secondary objective. In such a situation, we argue that the more informed strategy should be considered remorsefreely dominating.

Comparing remorsefree dominance $\preceq_M$ to the notion of dominance defined in Section 3, it is easy to see that $s \preceq_M t$ implies $s \sqsubseteq t$:

Theorem 1. *For two strategies s and t, $s \preceq_M t$ implies $s \sqsubseteq_M t$.*

Proof. Assume, by way of contradiction, that $s \preceq_M t$ and $s \not\sqsubseteq_M t$. Since $s \not\sqsubseteq_M t$, there exists a priority n such that all computations in $\mathcal{C}_M(s)$ satisfy the objective specification up to priority n but there exists a computation $c \in \mathcal{C}(t)$ that violates priority n. Let σ_D be the sequence of disturbances in c. No computation in $\mathcal{C}_M(\sigma_D, s)$ is dominated by c, which is in $\mathcal{C}_M(\sigma_D, t)$. This contradicts the assumption that $s \preceq_M t$. □

The converse does not hold: suppose, for example, that strategies s_1 and s_2 both completely violate the objective specification, but s_1 achieves some objective for some specific sequence of disturbances, while s_2 achieves no objective, no matter what the environment does; then $s_1 \sqsubseteq_M s_2$, but not $s_1 \preceq_M s_2$.

In addition to comparing strategies with strategies, we are also interested in comparing strategy classes with strategies: A strategy class $\mathcal{S}$ is *remorsefully dominated* by a specific strategy $t \in \mathcal{T}$ from some strategy class $\mathcal{T}$, denoted by $\mathcal{S} \preceq_M t$, iff for every strategy $s \in \mathcal{S}$, it holds that $s \preceq_M t$.

4   An Automata-Theoretic Characterization of Remorsefree Dominance

The remainder of the paper is devoted to the algorithmic analysis of remorsefree dominance. We start, in this section, by constructing an automaton over infinite trees that characterizes the set of remorsefreely dominating strategies in a particular strategy class. This automaton can be used to verify that a strategy is dominant and to synthesize dominant strategies.

4.1   Preliminaries: Automata over Infinite Words and Trees

We assume familiarity with automata over infinite words and trees. In the following we only give a quick summary of the standard terminology, the reader is referred to [7] for a full exposition.

A (full) *tree* is given as the set Υ^* of all finite words over a given set of directions Υ. For given finite sets Σ and Υ, a Σ-*labeled* Υ-*tree* is a pair $\langle \Upsilon^*, l \rangle$ with a labeling function $l : \Upsilon^* \to \Sigma$ that maps every node of Υ^* to a letter of Σ.

An *alternating tree automaton* $\mathcal{A} = (\Sigma, \Upsilon, Q, q_0, \delta, \alpha)$ runs on Σ-labeled Υ-trees. Q is a finite set of states, $q_0 \in Q$ a designated initial state, δ a transition function $\delta : Q \times \Sigma \to \mathbb{B}^+(Q \times \Upsilon)$, where $\mathbb{B}^+(Q \times \Upsilon)$ denotes the positive Boolean combinations of $Q \times \Upsilon$, and α is an acceptance condition. Intuitively, disjunctions in the transition function represent nondeterministic choice; conjunctions start an additional branch in the run tree of the automaton, corresponding to an additional check that must be passed by the input tree. A run tree on a given Σ-labeled Υ-tree $\langle \Upsilon^*, l \rangle$ is a $Q \times \Upsilon^*$-labeled tree where the root is labeled with $(q_0, l(\varepsilon))$ and where for a node n with a label (q, x) and a set of children $child(n)$, the labels of these children have the following properties:

- for all $m \in child(n)$: the label of m is $(q_m, x \cdot v_m)$, $q_m \in Q, v_m \in \Upsilon$ such that (q_m, v_m) is an atom of $\delta(q, l(x))$, and
- the set of atoms defined by the children of n satisfies $\delta(q, l(x))$.

A run tree is *accepting* if all its paths fulfill the acceptance condition. A *parity condition* is a function α from Q to a finite set of colors $C \subset \mathbb{N}$. A path is accepted if the highest color appearing infinitely often is even. The *safety condition* is the special case of the parity condition where all states are colored with 0. The *Büchi condition* is the special case of the parity condition where all states are colored with either 1 or 2. A Σ-labeled Υ-tree is *accepted* if it has an accepting run tree. The set of trees accepted by an alternating automaton $\mathcal{A}$ is called its *language* $\mathcal{L}(\mathcal{A})$. An automaton is empty iff its language is empty.

A *nondeterministic* automaton is a special alternating automaton where the image of δ consists only of such formulas that, when rewritten in disjunctive normal form, contain exactly one element of $Q \times \{v\}$ in every disjunct. A *deterministic* automaton is a special nondeterministic automaton where the image of δ contains no disjunctions.

A *word automaton* is the special case of a tree automaton where the set Υ of directions is singleton. For word automata, we omit the direction in the transition function.

4.2 Dominant Computations

A strategy dominates another if, for every sequence of disturbances, each computation that is produced by the first strategy dominates some computation produced by the second. We begin our construction with a word automaton that checks for dominance between computations. In order to relate two computations that result from the same sequence of disturbances, we duplicate the variables in $\mathcal{V}_S$ and $\mathcal{V}_C$, i.e., we consider sequences over the alphabet $2^{\mathcal{V}_D \cup \mathcal{V}_S \cup \mathcal{V}_C \cup \mathcal{V}'_S \cup \mathcal{V}'_C}$, where $\mathcal{V}'_S$ and $\mathcal{V}'_C$ are sets of fresh "primed" variables duplicating the variables in $\mathcal{V}_S$ and $\mathcal{V}_C$, respectively. We write $primed(X)$ for the set of primed variables corresponding to the variables in a set X, and, for two sequences $\sigma \in (2^{\mathcal{V}_D \cup \mathcal{V}_S \cup \mathcal{V}_C})^\omega$ and $\eta \in (2^{\mathcal{V}_D \cup \mathcal{V}'_S \cup \mathcal{V}'_C})^\omega$, we write $[\sigma, \eta]$ for the sequence $((\sigma_0[V \mapsto V']) \cup \eta_0)((\sigma_1[V \mapsto V']) \cup \eta_1)\ldots$, where $[V \mapsto V']$ indicates that each variable from V is replaced by the corresponding primed variable in V'.

Lemma 1. *Let $\varphi = (\mathcal{O}, p)$ be an objective specification, let $V = V_D \cup \mathcal{V}_S \cup V_C$, $\mathcal{V}'_S = primed(\mathcal{V}_S), V'_C = primed(V_C)$, and $V' = V_D \cup \mathcal{V}'_S \cup V'_C$. There exists a deterministic parity word automaton $\mathcal{A}_\varphi$ over $V \cup V'$ such that $[\sigma, \eta]$ is accepted by $\mathcal{A}_\varphi$ iff $\sigma \sqsubseteq \eta$.*

Proof. We define an LTL formula ψ for the desired property as follows:

$$\psi = \bigwedge_{n \in \{1,\ldots,|\mathcal{O}|\}} \left(\bigwedge_{\phi \in \mathcal{O}, p(\phi) \leq n} \phi[V \mapsto V'] \rightarrow \bigwedge_{\phi \in \mathcal{O}, p(\phi) \leq n} \phi \right).$$

We translate ψ to a deterministic parity word automaton using a standard construction (cf. [8]). □

The definition of dominant strategies compares different computations of a particular world model M. In preparation for the construction of the automaton for dominant strategies in the next subsection, we condition $\mathcal{A}_\varphi$ with respect to M.

Lemma 2. *Let M be a model, $\varphi = (\mathcal{O}, p)$ an objective specification, and let $V = V_D \cup V_S \cup V_C$, $V'_S = primed(V_S)$, $V'_C = primed(V_C)$, and $V' = V_D \cup V'_S \cup V'_C$. There exists a parity word automaton $\mathcal{B}_{M,\varphi}$ over $V \cup V'$ such that the sequence $[\sigma, \eta]$ is accepted by $\mathcal{B}_{M,\varphi}$ iff (1) $\sigma \sqsubseteq \eta$ and σ is a computation of M or (2) η is not a computation of M.*

Proof. We start by translating the world model M into a safety word automaton $\mathcal{A}_M$ over the alphabet $2^{V_D \cup V_C \cup V_S}$, which accepts the sequences of variable evaluations allowed by M. Let $\mathcal{A}'_M$ be the same automaton as $\mathcal{A}_M$, but over the alphabet $2^{V_D \cup V'_C \cup V'_S}$ with the variables in V_C and V_S replaced by their counterparts in V'_C and V'_S, respectively. We represent condition (1) by building the product of $\mathcal{A}'_M$ with $\mathcal{A}_\varphi$. We represent condition (2) by complementing $\mathcal{A}_M$. $\mathcal{B}_{M,\varphi}$ is an automaton that accepts the language union of the two automata. □

4.3   Dominant Strategies

We now construct a tree automaton that recognizes the subset of strategies in $\mathcal{S}_{I_1}$ that dominate a strategy class $\mathcal{S}_{I_2}$ in a given world model M. We assume that $I_1 \subseteq I_2$, i.e., the reference strategy class $\mathcal{S}_{I_2}$ has the larger set of observable variables. A first observation is that we can, without loss of generality, assume that $V_D \subseteq I_2$. As explained in the following lemma, this is due to the fact that the definition of remorsefree dominance refers to individual sequences of disturbances. If some strategy in $\mathcal{S}_{I_2 \cup V_D}$ is not dominated, then this is due to some individual computation; however, there exists a strategy in $\mathcal{S}_{I_2}$ that behaves exactly as the strategy in $\mathcal{S}_{I_2 \cup V_D}$ on that particular computation.

Lemma 3. *Let M be a world model and let $\mathcal{S}_{I_1}$ and $\mathcal{S}_{I_2}$ be two strategy classes with $I_1 \subseteq I_2$. For every $t \in \mathcal{S}_{I_1}$ it holds that $\mathcal{S}_{I_2} \preceq_M t$ iff $\mathcal{S}_{I_2 \cup V_D} \preceq_M t$.*

Proof. The "if" direction is obvious, because $\mathcal{S}_{I_2} \subseteq \mathcal{S}_{I_2 \cup V_D}$. For the "only if" direction, suppose, by way of contradiction, that $\mathcal{S}_{I_2} \preceq_M t$ but $\mathcal{S}_{I_2 \cup V_D} \npreceq_M t$. Since $\mathcal{S}_{I_2 \cup V_D} \npreceq_M t$, there exists a sequence of disturbances $\sigma_D \in (2^{V_D})^\omega$ and a computation $c \in C_M(\sigma_D, t)$ such there exists an alternative strategy $t' \in \mathcal{S}_{I_2 \cup V_D}$ where for all $c' \in C_M(\sigma_D, t')$ it holds that $c' \nprec c$. There exists, however, the strategy $t'' \in \mathcal{S}_{I_2}$ with $t''(\sigma_0 \sigma_1 \ldots \sigma_k) = t'((\sigma_0 \cup \sigma_{D,0})(\sigma_1 \cup \sigma_{D,1}) \ldots (\sigma_k \cup \sigma_{D,k}))$, which has the same set $C_M(\sigma_D, t'') = C_M(\sigma_D, t')$ of strictly better computations. This contradicts the assumption that $\mathcal{S}_{I_2} \preceq_M t$. □

The construction of the tree automaton in the following theorem uses the conjunctive branching available in alternating automata to compare against all possible strategies in $\mathcal{S}_{I_2}$.

Theorem 2. *Let M be a world model, φ an objective specification, and $\mathcal{S}_{I_1}$ and $\mathcal{S}_{I_2}$ two strategy classes with $I_1 \subseteq I_2$. Then there exists an alternating parity tree automaton $\mathcal{C}_{M,\varphi,I_1,I_2}$ that recognizes the subset of strategies in $\mathcal{S}_{I_1}$ that dominate the strategy class $\mathcal{S}_{I_2}$ in M.*

Proof. We construct a tree automaton that reads a strategy of $\mathcal{S}_{I_1}$ as its input tree and simulates all possible reference strategies in $\mathcal{S}_{I_2}$ in its run tree. Since $I_1 \subseteq I_2$, the reference strategy may have more branches than the input tree. These additional branches are simulated by the transition function as follows: The part due to V_D is simulated by conjunction, since the computation of the input strategy must dominate the computation of the reference strategy for all possible sequences of disturbances. Applying Lemma 3, we assume that $V_D \subseteq I_2$. The reference strategy therefore branches according to (at least) V_D.

The part due to $I_2 \smallsetminus V_D$ is simultated by disjunction, because we may choose the computation of the reference strategy. The part due to $V_C \smallsetminus I_2$ is chosen by projection: we choose a computation of the reference strategy for every computation of the input strategy; unlike the part due to I_2, however, the reference strategy does not branch according to these choices. We therefore project and determinize the word automaton $\mathcal{B}_{M,\varphi}$ accordingly.

Let $\mathcal{B}_{M,\varphi}$ be as defined in Lemma 2. Let $\mathcal{B}' = (2^{V_D \cup \mathcal{I}_1 \cup \mathcal{V}_S \cup I_2' \cup \mathcal{V}_S'}, \{\emptyset\}, Q, q_0, \delta, \alpha)$ be the determinization of the universal projection with respect to $V_C \smallsetminus I_1$ of the existential projection with respect to $V_C' \smallsetminus I_2'$ of $\mathcal{B}_{M,\varphi}$. We construct the alternating parity tree automaton $\mathcal{C}_{M,\varphi,I_1,I_2} = (2^{\mathcal{V}_S}, 2^{I_1}, Q, q_0, \delta', \alpha)$ with transition function

$$\delta'(q, W_S) = \bigwedge_{W_D \subseteq V_D} \bigwedge_{W_1 \subseteq I_1 \smallsetminus V_D} \bigvee_{W_2' \subseteq I_2' \smallsetminus V_D'} \bigwedge_{W_S' \subseteq \mathcal{V}_S'} \\ (\delta(q, W_S \cup W_D \cup W_1 \cup W_2' \cup W_S'), (W_D \cup W_1) \cap I_1).$$

□

5   Verifying and Synthesizing Dominant Strategies

With the tree automaton $\mathcal{C}_{M,\varphi,I_1,I_2}$ constructed in the previous section, we can check if a given strategy is dominant (iff it is accepted by $\mathcal{C}_{M,\varphi,I_1,I_2}$) and if the strategy class $\mathcal{S}_{I_1}$ contains a strategy that dominates $\mathcal{S}_{I_2}$ (iff $\mathcal{C}_{M,\varphi,I_1,I_2}$ is nonempty).

Theorem 3. *Let M be a world model, φ an objective specification and $\mathcal{S}_{I_1}$ and $\mathcal{S}_{I_2}$ two strategy classes with $I_1 \subseteq I_2$. We can automatically check whether a given strategy in $\mathcal{S}_{I_1}$ (given as a safety word automaton) dominates $\mathcal{S}_{I_2}$, and whether $\mathcal{S}_{I_1}$ contains a strategy that remorsefreely dominates $\mathcal{S}_{I_2}$.*

Proof. To check whether a given strategy (represented as a safety word automaton T) is accepted by $\mathcal{C}_{M,\varphi,I_1,I_2}$, we solve the parity game that results from combining T and $\mathcal{C}_{M,\varphi,I_1,I_2}$ (cf. [9]). To check whether there exists a strategy that is accepted by $\mathcal{C}_{M,\varphi,I_1,I_2}$, we translate the alternating automaton into an equivalent nondeterministic automaton. Language emptiness of the nondeterministic automaton can be checked by solving a parity game on its state graph. If the language is non-empty, an accepted tree can be extracted.   □

6 Towards Optimal World Models

We now address the fundamental question whether a given world model is optimal: does it pay to refine the model?

For a given objective specification and strategy class, we say that a world model is *optimal* if the current strategy class already contains a strategy that dominates all strategies in the same class for any refined model. For example, the simple world model from Figure 1(a) is not optimal because there is no dominant strategy; the refined world model from Figure 1(b) is optimal due to the dominating Strategy 2 (brake if and only if a *warning* has occurred).

In the automata-theoretic analysis, we can safely restrict our attention to refined world models that are deterministic. In a deterministic model, a sequence of disturbances and a strategy determine a unique computation. Remorsefree dominance in the deterministic models thus implies remorsefree dominance in nondeterministic models, where it suffices to dominate some computation from a set of possible computations.

In the following, we describe the necessary adaptations of our constructions. When comparing the computations of two strategies in an unknown but deterministic refinement of a world model M, we must ensure that variations in V_C may only occur if there was a previous variation in V_S. The following lemma adapts Lemma 2 accordingly:

Lemma 4. *Let M be a deterministic world model, let $\varphi = (\mathcal{O}, p)$ be an objective specification, and let $V = V_D \cup V_S \cup V_C$, $V'_S = primed(V_S), V'_C = primed(V_C)$, and $V' = V_D \cup V'_S \cup V'_C$. There exists a parity word automaton $\mathcal{E}_{M,\varphi}$ over $V \cup V'$ such that $[\sigma, \eta]$ is accepted by $\mathcal{E}_{M,\varphi}$ iff (1) $\sigma \sqsubseteq \eta$ and σ is a computation of M and the valuation of the variables in V_C differs in σ and η only if there was a previous difference in the valuation of the variables in V_S or (2) η is not a computation of M.*

Proof. The construction of $\mathcal{E}_{M,\varphi}$ is analogous to the construction of $\mathcal{B}_{M,\varphi,I_2}$ in Lemma 2. For the modified condition (1), we add a memory bit to the state of the automaton that records whether a deviation in the valuation of the variables in V_S has occurred. If a deviation in the valuation of the variables in V_C occurs before the bit has been set, the automaton enforces condition (2).   □

The following theorem is an adaptation of Theorem 2 that checks for dominance in all deterministic refinements of the world model.

Theorem 4. *Let M be a world model with environment variables V_E, φ an objective specification, and $\mathcal{S}_I$ a strategy class. There exists an alternating parity tree automaton $\mathcal{F}_{M,\varphi,I}$ that recognizes the subset of strategies in $\mathcal{S}_I$ that dominate a strategy class $\mathcal{S}_I$ in every deterministic model M' such that M simulates M'.*

Proof. The construction of $\mathcal{F}_{M,\varphi,I}$ is analogous to the construction of $\mathcal{C}_{M,\varphi,I_1,I_2}$ in Theorem 2. Let $\mathcal{E}_{M,\varphi}$ be the parity word automaton from Lemma 4 and let $\mathcal{E}' = (2^{V_D \cup V_S \cup V'_S \cup V_C \cup V'_C}, \{\emptyset\}, Q, q_0, \delta, \alpha)$ be the determinization of the universal projection with respect to $(V_C \smallsetminus I) \cup (V_C' \smallsetminus I')$ of $\mathcal{B}_{M,\varphi}$. We construct the alternating parity tree automaton $\mathcal{F}_{M,\varphi,I} = (2^{V_S}, 2^I, Q, q_0, \delta', \alpha)$ with transition function

$$\delta'(q, W_S) = \bigwedge_{W_D \subseteq V_D} \bigwedge_{W_1 \subseteq I \smallsetminus V_D} \bigwedge_{W_2' \subseteq I' \smallsetminus V_D'} \bigwedge_{W_S' \subseteq V_S'} (\delta(q, W_D \cup W_1 \cup W_2' \cup W_S'), (W_D \cup W_1) \cap I).$$

The difference to the construction in Theorem 2 is that the valuation of the variables in $V_C' \smallsetminus V_D'$ is chosen conjunctively, rather than disjunctively: if the world model is deterministic, then the set of computations corresponding to the reference strategy is singleton.   □

Using the tree automaton from Theorem 4, we can check if our world model is optimal: M is optimal iff there exists a strategy that dominates the strategies of the same class in all deterministic refinements of M, which is the case iff $\mathcal{F}_{M,\varphi,I}$ is nonempty.

Theorem 5. *Let M be a world model, φ an objective specification and $\mathcal{S}_I$ a strategy class. We can automatically check whether M is optimal for φ and $\mathcal{S}_I$ and, in case of a positive answer, synthesize a remorsefreely dominating strategy.*

Proof. To check whether there exists a strategy that is accepted by $\mathcal{F}_{M,\varphi,I}$ and to obtain such a strategy, we proceed as in the proof of Theorem 3: we translate the alternating automaton into an equivalent nondeterministic automaton and solve the resulting emptiness game.   □

7   Conclusions

One of the paradoxical challenges in bringing formal methods to practice is that detecting errors is most useful when done early, at a point in the design process when it is still inexpensive to make a change; but how can one apply formal verification if there is no system yet to analyze?

Arguably, the approach presented in this paper brings formal methods to the earliest possible point in the design process, when the developer has not even started with the design, but rather tries to understand the environment in which the planned system is to achieve its objectives. Our constructions allow the designer to optimize the world model to ensure that no objective will be missed because too few real-world phenomena have been considered.

Since the verification of remorsefree dominance must not only analyze the given strategy, but also search through an entire class of strategies for an alternative, our algorithms are more complex than typical verification algorithms and are, in fact, closer to synthesis [1,2,3,4,5] than to standard verification. Recently, there has been a lot of interest in efficient implementation techniques for synthesis algorithms (such as bounded synthesis [5] and GR(1) synthesis [4]), for which the analysis of world models should provide an interesting new application domain.

A fundamental difference to both the classical verification and synthesis problems is, however, that we do not necessarily expect our strategies to meet all objectives and instead only demand optimality with respect to remorsefree dominance. While such a relative notion of correctness is very unusual in formal verification and synthesis, it is an established concept in general decision theory: Regret minimization [10], for example, is a model of choice under uncertainty, where the player minimizes the difference between the payoff of the chosen strategy and the payoff that would have been obtained with a different course of action.

References

1. Pnueli, A., Rosner, R.: On the synthesis of a reactive module. In: Proc. of POPL, pp. 179–190 (1989)
2. Kupferman, O., Vardi, M.Y.: Synthesis with incomplete informatio. In: Proc. of ICTL (1997)
3. Finkbeiner, B., Schewe, S.: Uniform distributed synthesis. In: Proc. of LICS, pp. 321–330 (2005)
4. Piterman, N., Pnueli, A., Sa'ar, Y.: Synthesis of reactive(1) designs. In: Proc. of VMCAI, pp. 364–380 (2006)
5. Finkbeiner, B., Schewe, S.: SMT-based synthesis of distributed systems. In: Proc. of AFM (2007)
6. Manna, Z., Pnueli, A.: The Temporal Logic of Reactive and Concurrent Systems: Specification. Springer, New York (1991)
7. Grädel, E., Thomas, W., Wilke, T. (eds.): Automata, Logics, and Infinite Games. LNCS, vol. 2500. Springer, Heidelberg (2002)
8. Vardi, M.Y., Wilke, T.: Automata: from logics to algorithms. In: Flum, J., Grädel, E., Wilke, T. (eds.) Logic and Automata: History and Perspectives, pp. 629–736 (2007)
9. Jurdziński, M.: Small progress measures for solving parity games. In: Proc. STACS, pp. 290–301 (2000)
10. Loomes, G., Sugden, R.: Regret theory: An alternative theory of rational choice under uncertainty. Economic Journal 92, 805–824 (1982)

System Verification through Program Verification[*]

Daniel Dietsch, Bernd Westphal, and Andreas Podelski

Albert-Ludwigs Universität Freiburg, Freiburg, Germany
{dietsch,westphal,podelski}@informatik.uni-freiburg.de

Abstract. We present an automatable approach to verify that a system satisfies its requirements by verification of the program that controls the system. The approach can be applied if the interaction of the program with the system hardware can be faithfully described by a table relating domain phenomena and program variables. We show the applicability of the approach with a case study based on a real-world system.

1 Introduction

When software for systems that interact with a physical environment is to be developed, the requirements are typically *system requirements*. That is, requirements stated in terms of *domain phenomena* observable in the physical environment. For instance, when a software shall realise the monitoring of a backup battery of a system, one requirement could be

"For each point in time, the battery-low warning light is on if and only if the battery is low, i.e. the current battery voltage is below 6.6 V",

or, formalised using LTL (cf. Section 2)

$$\varphi_{batt} : \mathsf{G}(\textit{battery-low warning light is on} \iff \textit{battery is low } (V_{batt} < 6.6V)).$$

Here, "battery-low warning light is on" and "battery is low" are domain phenomena. Whether such a phenomenon is present or absent in a given point in time can be measured in the physical environment.

There is a need to assess whether a given program P is correct, that is, whether the system S executing P satisfies the requirements φ. Even battery monitoring can be safety critical, for instance if it is the backup battery of a fire alarm system. An undetected battery failure can cause undetected fires in case of power outage, a false indication of battery failure causes unnecessary costs.

Tests can falsify correctness. If the program P is executed on the system hardware and if measurements in the physical environment show a violation of a requirement φ, then P is clearly not correct. But to establish that P is correct without executing it on S (for instance because S is not yet built), we

---

[*] Partly funded by the Ministry of Science and Culture (MWK) Baden-Württemberg in project "Verbundprojekt Salomo" (www.salomo-projekt.de).

M. Butler and W. Schulte (Eds.): FM 2011, LNCS 6664, pp. 27–41, 2011.

face the problem that the program only operates on program variables, not on domain phenomena. On programs, we can only evaluate and analyse *software specifications*, i.e. properties of the evolution of program variables over time, but not system requirements. In this situation, we need a software specification $f(\varphi)$ such that P satisfies $f(\varphi)$ if and only if S executing P satisfies φ.

Closely related to this problem is the work in [18], which provides a general framework to derive software specifications from system requirements. There, the authors explain how the transition from requirements to specifications can be done in a structured way by introducing additional domain assumptions ("breadcrumbs") that shift single requirements closer to the software. A sequence of breadcrumbs gives a so-called crumbtrail from requirements to specifications.

In the example, one helpful domain assumption would be that the battery-low warning light is attached to an output pin on the system hardware which is accessed via memory-mapped I/O by the variable SCL in the program and that the light is on if and only if $SCL = 1$.

[18] defines the correctness of breadcrumbs, but does not describe an automatable procedure to obtain them. In general, providing breadcrumbs is a highly creative act which involves insight into properties of the domain and the system design. For example, the breadcrumbs of the treatment control system or the two-way traffic light in [18] are clearly not obvious.

At the end of a crumbtrail, we find a software specification. In [18], the corresponding software is given in form of a high-level Alloy program which is then analyzed. In this paper, the software specification refers not to an Alloy program but to C code which will be executed by a system. This raises the additional challenge of dealing with real C code running on controller boards, such as the delay between reading inputs and providing outputs due to the computation phase.

In this work, we observe that there is a special class of systems and domain phenomena where breadcrumbs simply make explicit the relations between domain phenomena and program variables that can be assumed to be known by the programmer. For this class, we significantly ease the creation of the last breadcrumbs in the crumbtrail.

We identify premises under which we can conclude the satisfaction of the system requirements from results of model-checking the program against a software specification, which is obtained by transforming the system requirements. We argue that these premises are met at least by a certain common pattern of C programs and demonstrate the application on a case study employing a C verification tool.

Our approach allows for a high degree of automation. Except for providing the system requirements and the program, only the relation between domain phenomena and software observables is needed. The rest of the analysis can be carried out automatically.

We believe that especially small and medium-sized enterprises (SMEs) concerned with the development of safety-critical systems can benefit from this work. They typically cannot afford the high entry costs – in terms of training as well as tool licenses – for the introduction of formal methods [8, 19]. Our approach reduces those costs while, at the same time, it allows for a gradual introduction of formal methods to development processes in SME.

The remainder of this document is organized as follows. Section 2 introduces the formal prerequisites of our approach, namely syntax and semantics of LTL with respect to Kripke structures. Section 3 details the formal foundation of the approach, Section 4 discusses its application to C programs of a certain form running on system hardware with memory mapped I/O or special function registers. In Section 5 we present the verification of an excerpt of a real world system, a radio-based fire alarm system, with the Verifying C Compiler [6, 21] as a case study. Section 6 discusses the related work and Section 7 summarises our contributions and names future work.

2   Preliminaries

2.1   Kripke Structure

A *Kripke structure* M over a set of variables *Var* is a tuple $M := (S, s_{init}, \rightarrow, \mu)$, where

- S is a finite set of states,
- $s_{init} \in S$ is an initial state,
- $\rightarrow \subseteq S \times S$ is the transition relation, and
- $\mu : S \rightarrow (Var \rightarrow \mathcal{D}(Var))$ labels each state with a valuation of the variables, i.e. with a function which assigns each variable in *Var* a value from the domain $\mathcal{D}(Var)$.

A *path* π in M is a sequence of states $s_0 s_1 s_2 \ldots$ such that $(s_i, s_{i+1}) \in \rightarrow$ for all $i \in \mathbb{N}_0$. We write $\pi(n)$ to denote the n-th state s_n of π.

Furthermore, $\Pi_M(s)$ denotes the set of paths in M with $s_0 = s$, i.e. all paths that start in s and $\Pi(M) := \Pi_M(s_{init})$ denotes the set of paths of the Kripke structure M.

2.2   LTL Syntax

Let $Expr_{\mathbb{B}}(Var)$ be a set of boolean expressions over variables *Var*. The set of LTL formulas over $Expr_{\mathbb{B}}(Var)$ is inductively defined as follows.

$$\varphi ::= expr \mid \neg\varphi_1 \mid \varphi_1 \wedge \varphi_2 \mid \mathsf{X}\,\varphi_1 \mid \varphi_1\,\mathsf{U}\,\varphi_2 \mid \varphi_1\,\overset{\leftarrow}{\mathsf{U}}\,\varphi_2$$

where $expr \in Expr_{\mathbb{B}}(Var)$ and φ_1, φ_2 are LTL formulas.

2.3   LTL Semantics

Let M be a Kripke structure over *Var* and φ an LTL formula over $Expr_{\mathbb{B}}(Var)$. Let $\mathcal{I}[\![expr]\!](\beta) \in \{\top, \bot\}$ be the interpretation of boolean expression $expr \in Expr_{\mathbb{B}}(Var)$ under valuation $\beta : Var \rightarrow \mathcal{D}(Var)$. We say that $M \models \varphi$ iff $\pi, 0 \models \varphi$ for all paths $\pi \in \Pi(M)$. The satisfaction relation $\pi, n \models \varphi$, $n \in \mathbb{N}_0$, is inductively defined as follows.

$\pi, n \models expr$ iff $\mathcal{I}[\![expr]\!](\mu(\pi(n))) = \top$.

$\pi, n \models \neg\varphi_1$ iff $\pi, n \not\models \varphi_1$.

$\pi, n \models \varphi_1 \wedge \varphi_2$ iff $\pi, n \models \varphi_1$ and $\pi, n \models \varphi_2$.

$\pi, n \models X\,\varphi_1$ iff $\pi, n+1 \models \varphi_1$.

$\pi, n \models \varphi_1 \, U \, \varphi_2$ iff there exists $j \geq n$ such that $\pi, j \models \varphi_2$ and $\pi, i \models \varphi_1$ for all $n \leq i < j$.

$\pi, n \models \varphi_1 \, \overset{\leftarrow}{U} \, \varphi_2$ iff there exists $j \leq n$ such that $\pi, j \models \varphi_2$ and $\pi, i \models \varphi_1$ for all $j < i \leq n$.

3   The Interface between Requirements and Software

We consider programs to be Kripke structures over the program variables. We assume that there is a dedicated boolean program variable v_{sn} which the programmer sets in the program whenever she considers the last inputs to be fully processed, where the outputs are stable, and where new inputs are read. For instance, the points in time where computed results are written into the memory-mapped I/O region or into special function registers to control output pins and where values of input pins are obtained via such addresses or registers (cf. Section 4).

Definition 1 (Program). *Let $Var \supseteq \{v_{sn}\}$ be a set of variables called* program variables. *The variable v_{sn} is called* snapshot variable.

A program *over Var is a Kripke structure $P = (S_P, s_{init\,_P}, \rightarrow_P, \mu_P)$ over $Var \cup \{{}^\bullet v \mid v \in Var\}$ where the snapshot variable is a boolean flag which holds in the initial state, i.e. for each $s \in S_P$, $\mu_P(s, v_{sn}) \in \{\top, \bot\}$ and $\mu_P(s_{init}, v_{sn}) = \top$.*

For simplicity, we assume that the valuation of ${}^\bullet v$ in a state s provides the value of v at the last snapshot state visited before s. We write $[expr]_{@pre}$ to denote the expression obtained from $expr$ by syntactically substituting each variable v by ${}^\bullet v$, i.e. the expression $expr[v := {}^\bullet v \mid v \in Var]$.

Given a set of program variables Var, an LTL formula over $Expr_{\mathbb{B}}(Var)$ is called *(software) specification.*

For us, a system S is a hardware such as a controller board with inputs and outputs to which switches, sensors, etc. or lights, actuators, etc. can be connected, and a micro-processor which can execute programs. The named sensors and actuators interact with the environment which we consider not to be part of the system. For instance, a sensor can measure the voltage of a battery and an actuator can automatically dial a phone number to inform service personnel about power problems. Following Jackson et al. [18], the controller board, the sensors, and the voltage as well as the photons emitted by the light are part of the domain. A *domain phenomenon* is a phenomenon observable in the domain which is either present or absent. Such as the battery being low or the power warning light being on. Each domain phenomenon dp is either *controlled* by the system or *uncontrolled.* For example, the voltage of the battery is uncontrolled (an input to the system) while the warning light is controlled (an output of the system).

Given a set of domain phenomena DP, an LTL formula over DP as atomic propositions (that is, by assuming that DP is the set of variables, i.e. $Var := DP$, and that the set of expressions over these variables only provides the variable names itself, no logical connectives or functions, etc., i.e. $Expr_{\mathbb{B}}(Var) := Var$) is called *requirement*. Unless otherwise noted, from now on we assume that sets of domain phenomena DP and boolean expressions $Expr_{\mathbb{B}}(Var)$ over program variables are disjoint.

Let $S(P)$ denote the behaviour of a system which is executing program P in the considered domain, that is, $S(P)$ includes the evolution of domain phenomena over time. In general, $S(P)$ does not directly satisfy a requirement like the faithfulness of low battery warnings because the system in reality takes time to process the inputs. Such systems can in reality not process inputs in zero time. For example, there may be short periods in time where we can observe in $S(P)$ that the battery has recovered to a voltage above the critical threshold, that is, the domain phenomenon "battery low" is not observed, but that the warning light is still on because the program is currently processing the inputs. For the reasons given above, these violations cannot and should not be "blamed" on the program. So we consider a program P to be correct if $S(P)$ already satisfies the requirements admitting a reasonable processing time to the program.

Instead of $S(P)$ we thus consider $S_{\varepsilon}(P)$ as representation of the system executing P, a Kripke structure which is (conceptually) obtained by observing $S(P)$ and noting down the presence or absence of controlled (output) domain phenomena and the presence or absence of uncontrolled (input) domain phenomena *at the last relevant point in time* according to some sampling procedure ε. Such a sampling procedure may depend on such various criteria as changes of the domain phenomena, the clock of the hardware board, or the current program counter. For example, if we use a predicate over the program counter as sampling procedure, we can separate the actual processing time of the program from the functional properties of the requirements. If necessary, techniques like worst case execution time analysis can be used to determine the actual time between the sampling points in the program and thus to conclude a time bound. Altogether, ε ensures that in the states of $S_{\varepsilon}(P)$ we see the reaction of the system together with the last uncontrolled domain phenomena, on which the system reacted. Thereby, we can leave the formula from Section 1 unchanged and uncluttered by details of the (orthogonal) observation procedure. Over $S_{\varepsilon}(P)$, the example requirement φ_{batt} correctly expresses that the warning light shall be on now if and only if the previous measurement of battery voltage found the battery to be low.

Definition 2 (System). *Let DP be a set of boolean variables called* domain phenomena *and P a program. A* system *controlled by program P and observed according to sampling procedure ε is a Kripke structure $S_{\varepsilon}(P)$ over DP.*

We say a program P correctly realises the requirements φ on hardware S if and only if $S_{\varepsilon}(P) \models \varphi$.

Definition 3 (*IRS*). *Let DP be a set of domain phenomena and* $Expr_\mathbb{B}(Var)$
a set of boolean expressions over Var. A function

$$IRS : DP \rightarrow Expr_\mathbb{B}(Var)$$

is called interface between requirements and software *(or IRS-table, for short).*

Each row of an *IRS*-table is a *domain assumption* in the sense of [18]. It states
the assumption that domain phenomenon $dp \in DP$ is observable if and only if
$IRS(dp)$ holds for a valuation of program variables. Intuitively, it makes explicit
the programmer's assumption how, i.e. by which (expressions over) program
variables, the program controls or obtains domain phenomena.

   Note that $S_\varepsilon(P)$ is conceptually obtained by observing the running system so
this structure is not directly available for analysis, in contrast to the program
itself. Yet for the program, we cannot directly evaluate a requirement because a
requirement is a formula over domain phenomena and a program only provides
valuations of program variables.

   Recall from the definition of programs that there is the dedicated snapshot
variable v_{sn} which indicates that the software has completely processed the last
set of inputs. So we can apply the *IRS*-table backwards at each state of the
program where v_{sn} holds to obtain a system $\triangleright_{IRS}$, i.e. a Kripke structure over
domain phenomena. The program states where v_{sn} does not hold are removed
as they do not influence the environment and disregard the current environment
situation. In the resulting $\triangleright_{IRS}$, corresponding acceleration transitions are introduced between states s and s' if and only if there is a consecutive finite sequence
of states $s = s_0 s_1 \ldots s_n = s'$ in the program where v_{sn} holds for s and s' but not
in between.

Definition 4 ($\triangleright_{IRS}$). *Let* $P = (S_P, s_{init_P}, \rightarrow_P, \mu_P)$ *be a program over Var,*
DP a set of domain phenomena, and IRS an IRS-table relating DP and Var.
   Then $\triangleright_{IRS}(P)$ *is the Kripke structure* $(S, s_{init}, \rightarrow, \mu)$ *over DP with*

- $S = \{s \in S_P \mid \mu_P(s, v_{sn}) = \top\}$,
- $s_{init} = s_{init_P}$,
- $\rightarrow = \{(s, s') \in S \times S \mid \exists s_0, s_1, \ldots, s_n \in S.s_0 = s \wedge s_n = s' \wedge$
  $\forall 0 \le i < n.(s_i, s_{i+1}) \in \rightarrow_P \wedge \forall 0 < i < n.\mu_P(s_i, v_{sn}) = \bot\}$, *and*
- $\forall s \in S, dp \in DP.\mu(s, dp) = \mathcal{I}[\![IRS(dp)]\!](\mu_P(s))$.

We say program P satisfies requirements φ if and only if $\triangleright_{IRS}(P) \models \varphi$.

   Instead of applying Definition 4 in a constructive fashion, that is, constructing
the Kripke structure $\triangleright_{IRS}$ and checking requirement φ on it, we want a software
specification that is satisfied by a program if and only if the system executing
the program satisfies the requirements. Given such a software specification, any
program analysis procedure or tool able to decide whether the given formula
holds for the program becomes directly applicable for deciding whether the program satisfies the requirements. In Definition 5 we give a procedure to construct
such a software specification from a requirement, Lemma 1 states that the software specifications yielded by Definition 5 indeed characterises satisfaction of
requirements.

Definition 5 ($f_{IRS}^{v_{sn}}$). *Let P be a program over Var, DP a set of domain phenomena, and IRS an IRS-table relating DP and Var.*

Let φ be a requirement, i.e. an LTL formula over DP. Then $f_{IRS}^{v_{sn}}(\varphi)$ denotes the software specification inductively defined as follows.

$$f_{IRS}^{v_{sn}}(\varphi) := \begin{cases} \neg v_{sn} \overleftarrow{\mathsf{U}} (v_{sn} \wedge IRS(dp)) & \textit{iff } \varphi = dp \ \textit{(controlled)} \\ \neg v_{sn} \overleftarrow{\mathsf{U}} (v_{sn} \wedge [IRS(dp)]_{@\text{pre}}) & \textit{iff } \varphi = dp \ \textit{(uncontrolled)} \\ \neg f_{IRS}^{v_{sn}}(\varphi_1) & \textit{iff } \varphi = \neg \varphi_1 \\ f_{IRS}^{v_{sn}}(\varphi_1) \wedge f_{IRS}^{v_{sn}}(\varphi_2) & \textit{iff } \varphi = \varphi_1 \wedge \varphi_2 \\ \mathsf{X}(\neg v_{sn} \mathsf{U} (v_{sn} \wedge f_{IRS}^{v_{sn}}(\varphi_1))) & \textit{iff } \varphi = \mathsf{X}\varphi_1 \\ f_{IRS}^{v_{sn}}(\varphi_1) \mathsf{U} f_{IRS}^{v_{sn}}(\varphi_2) & \textit{iff } \varphi = \varphi_1 \mathsf{U} \varphi_2 \\ f_{IRS}^{v_{sn}}(\varphi_1) \overleftarrow{\mathsf{U}} f_{IRS}^{v_{sn}}(\varphi_2) & \textit{iff } \varphi = \varphi_1 \overleftarrow{\mathsf{U}} \varphi_2 \end{cases}$$

Lemma 1. *Let P be a program over Var, DP a set of domain phenomena, φ a requirement, and IRS an IRS-table relating DP and Var. Then*

$$P \models f_{IRS}^{v_{sn}}(\varphi) \iff \triangleright_{IRS}(P) \models \varphi.$$

Proof. By induction over the structure of φ show the contraposition. □

By the following theorem, we can conclude from properties of the program P to properties of the system $S_\varepsilon(P)$ if we employ a *valid* IRS-table, that is, an IRS-table which faithfully represents the dependencies between domain phenomena and program variables as observed when executing P on a system S. In the particular case we consider here for simplicity, validity of IRS implicitly requires that the observation procedure ε corresponds to the processing of inputs as indicated by the snapshot variable.

Definition 6. *Let P be a program over Var, DP a set of domain phenomena, and IRS an IRS-table relating DP and Var. Let S be a system and ε an observation procedure.*

The IRS-table IRS is called valid *if and only if $\triangleright_{IRS}(P) = S_\varepsilon(P)$.*

Theorem 1. *Let P be a program over Var, DP a set of domain phenomena, S be a system, and ε an observation procedure. Let IRS be a valid IRS-table relating DP and Var.*

Then for each requirement φ over DP,

$$S_\varepsilon(P) \models \varphi \iff P \models f_{IRS}^{v_{sn}}(\varphi).$$

Proof. Lemma 1. □

4 The Class of Memory-Mapped Systems

Memory-mapped systems are characterized by a close and direct interaction between input and output ports of the hardware and the memory the microcontroller provides to the program running on it. Typically there is a dedicated area of memory (e.g. the first 512 bytes) where the program can read values that directly correspond to the applied voltage at an input port. In the same fashion there is a dedicated area of memory for the output ports of the hardware.

Furthermore, many memory-mapped systems operate in three phases. First, they read values from the input ports (read inputs), then they process the obtained data (process data) and finally they write the resulting values to the output ports (write outputs). After such a cycle, the system has reacted to changes in its environment and is stable again. Here we can observe if it adheres to its requirements or not and thus any sampling procedure ε for such a system has to be interested in observing those stable states of the system. Naturally, an observation during the cycle, for example right after an input value has been read, would prohibit the system from exhibiting the correct reaction to the read input value and result in the system's failure to adhere to its requirements. More generally, systems can never react immediately (*atomic*) to changes in the environment because every system needs some time to calculate the reaction. Furthermore, the actual input values can change during the process-data phase or even during the write-outputs phase, again resulting in a mismatch between desired and observed system reaction.

Let us recall the battery measurement example from Section 1. There is a system with a backup battery. It has to routinely measure its battery to ensure it is operational in case of an emergency. The system reads the input providing the current battery voltage, calculates if this voltage is already too low and decides if it has to switch on the battery-low warning light and finally writes the actual reaction to the output variable. The sampling procedure ε observes the state of the domain phenomena at the end of the cycle, compares the value read by the program (i.e. the memorized input value) to the defined battery-low threshold and observes if the light is on or not.

Now let us assume that our example system is controlled by a C program. Let us further assume that the hardware is such that the memory address 0xFF14 is mapped to the input port representing the battery voltage and the fourth bit of the word starting at 0xFF00 is mapped to the output port controlling the battery-low warning light. Then, we expect to see variable declarations similar to the ones shown in Figure 1.

Figure 2 shows the main function of the C program that together with the variable declarations from Figure 1 and the aforementioned hardware constitutes

```
1   // . . .
2   sfr  P0 = 0xFF00;
3   // . . .
4   sfrp ADCR = 0xFF14;
5   // . . .
6   bool SCL = P0.3;
7   // . . .
```

Fig. 1. An example of the declaration of memory-mapped in- and outputs for an 8-bit microprocessor in a real-world C program. **sfr** and **sfrp** are compiler-specific keywords that indicate special function registers.

the system. The function is divided into two parts. First, all local variables are declared and initialized. Then the main loop follows, where the program progresses through the three phases, namely reading inputs, calculating a response to those inputs and finally writing outputs. After writing outputs, the program becomes stable and then the whole cycle starts again. Here the snapshot variable v_{sn} evaluates to $\top$. Note here that the first evaluation of v_{sn} to $\top$ is the initial state of the program P, thus we omit the initialization and the first execution of the loop body from our considerations.

Because the program completely controls the system, the three phases are exactly those we can observe when looking at the system. As we said, ε samples the system at the end of every cycle. In the program, this is at the end of the while-loop, thus at the same point in time where v_{sn} evaluates to $\top$. Therefore, we check for the desired behavior in the system as well as in the program at the same point in time, thus carrying the assumption $\rhd_{IRS}(P) = S_\varepsilon(P)$ from Definition 6 by ensuring that the sets of states of $\rhd_{IRS}(P)$ and $S_\varepsilon(P)$ have the same size. Although the identification of the three phases in general may be not as easy as in our example, a large class of programs, namely PLC programs (cf. IEC 61131 [9]), exhibits exactly those.

Another important aspect concerns the validity of the IRS-table. The variables in the program have to be bound to the "right" hardware addresses, that is, if the IRS-table states that the light is on if SCL == 1, SCL has to be bound to the output port controlling that light such that it is on if and only if SCL is set to 1. If this is the case can be easily validated by someone familiar with the hardware of the system. Consider a relation between program variables and hardware addresses, similar to the IRS-table (or the variable declaration shown in Figure 1). With such a relation and a description of the hardware, e.g. the data sheet of the microcontroller, one can formulate the relation between domain phenomena and hardware in terms of in- and output ports. This relation then states when a domain phenomenon is observable in terms of hardware in- and output ports.

To sum up, we say that if a system consists of a memory-mapping hardware and a program adhering to the three phases described above, and if the program variables used in the IRS-table are bound to the hardware addresses that correspond to the right domain phenomena, we fulfill the assumption $\rhd_{IRS}(P) = S_\varepsilon(P)$, which in turn enables the use of Theorem 1 to check the system requirement φ directly on the program.

5   Case Study

Recall the requirement from Section 1:

$$\varphi_{batt} : \mathsf{G}(\textit{battery-low warning light is on} \iff \textit{battery is low } (< 6.6V))$$

We want to verify if the system described in Section 4 satisfies φ_{batt}. That system is actually an excerpt from the central unit F.BZ 100, which is embedded in the cc100 system, a radio-based fire alarm system which consists of F.BZ 100 itself, different sensors and input/output devices as well as repeaters, all interconnected via high-frequency radio. In order to verify the system, we first need an *IRS*-table for the program shown in Figure 2. Figure 3 shows that *IRS*-table. Now we can apply the function $f_{IRS}^{v_{sn}}$ to φ_{batt}, which yields the following software specification:

$$\sigma_1 : G\left(\left(\neg sn \overset{\leftarrow}{U} (sn \wedge \texttt{SCL} == 1)\right) \Longleftrightarrow \left(\neg sn \overset{\leftarrow}{U} (sn \wedge \texttt{ADCR} < 33152)\right)\right)$$

Since we already know that our system belongs to the class of memory-mapped systems, thus operates in three phases, we only need to show that our program adheres to the specification σ_1 to invoke Theorem 1 and be confident that the whole system satisfies φ_{batt}.

For our case we chose Microsoft's *Verifying C Compiler* (VCC) [6,21] as sound code-level analysis method. Because VCC has to handle the complexity of a low-level program with considerable size (Hyper-V [16] has approximately 100.000 LOC), we expected it to be usable for smaller system code as well. Besides a high level of automation and scalability, VCC also provides a tight integration in Microsoft Visual Studio [22], a commonly used integrated development environment (IDE). This integration allows an easy reporting of verification errors, comparable to the error messages provided by compilers [1].

The input to VCC is C code extended with annotations, which consist of function pre- and post-conditions, assertions, type invariants and specification code [6]. For VCC, we need to transform the software specification to annotations of the C program. This transformation depends in general on the form of

```
1   void main(void)
2   {
3       // init
4       bool led = 0;
5       unsigned int battery = 0;
6
7       // main loop
8       while(1)
9       {
10          // read inputs
11          battery = ADCR;
12
13          // calculate
14          led = (battery < 33152);
15
16          // write outputs
17          SCL = led;
18      }
19  }
```

Fig. 2. A program controlling a battery-low warning light. The variable ADCR is bound to the input port monitoring the battery voltage while the variable SCL is bound to the output port controlling the battery-low warning light.

DP	$Expr_{\mathbb{B}}(Var)$
battery low warning light is on	SCL == 1
battery low (<6.6V)	ADCR < 33152

Fig. 3. The IRS-table for the requirement φ_{batt}

```
1   #include <vcc.h>
2
3   bool SCL;
4   volatile unsigned int ADCR;
5
6   void main(void)
7   writes(set_universe())
8   maintains(program_entry_point())
9   {
10    // init
11    bool led = 0;
12    unsigned int battery = 0;
13
14    spec(bool dp;)
15
16    // main loop
17    while(1)
18    {
19      // read inputs
20      battery = ADCR;
21      spec(dp = ADCR < 33152;)
22
23      // calculate
24      led = (battery < 33152);
25
26      // write outputs
27      SCL = led;
28
29      //check
30      assert(SCL <==> dp);
31    }
32  }
```

Fig. 4. The program from Figure 2 after preparing it for the code-level analysis by VCC. The highlighted parts are new annotations.

the software specification as VCC is not supporting LTL directly. For our experiments, we exploited the fact that the requirement is a simple global invariant.

A manual transformation of the specification yielded the program shown in Figure 4. In the following, we describe the important aspects of those annotations:

- In line 4 we declared the input variable ADCR as volatile. This causes VCC to interpret the variable as non-deterministic, i.e. it can assume every value its type allows regardless of the last write to the variable observed in the program, thereby representing all values the corresponding domain phenomena can assume. Also, note that because of this we could not use the variable declarations from Figure 1 but rather re-declared SCL and ADCR.
- In line 14 we declare a ghost variable dp, which is used in line 21 to memorize the value of the boolean expression $ADCR < 33152$ – representing the input domain phenomena "battery-low warning light is on" – directly after the read-access to ADCR occurred. This is done because, like in the real system, every access to ADCR could yield different values, but later in our check we want to use the value that actually determined the output. In this example dp corresponds to the ghost variables $\bullet v$ from Definition 1.
- Finally, in line 30 we check if our specification holds. This is the only place where the last input is fully processed and therefore the snapshot variable v_{sn} evaluates to $\top$. Here we place the assert-statement, thus synchronizing on the sampling procedure ε of the system. We use that v_{sn} evaluates to $\top$, so we can assert $SCL == 1 \iff ADCR < 33152$ to represent the software specification σ_1. We also substitute the memorized value for $ADCR < 33152$ from line 21 (dp) and get $SCL \iff dp$ as the actual condition that has to be checked.

Additionally we had to include the various VCC macros in line 1, declare that the function main may write and read every global variable (line 7) and that function main is the program entry point (line 8).

VCC reports that the assert-statement in line 30 holds, and with Theorem 1 and Section 4 we conclude that the system satisfies the requirement φ_{batt}.

6   Related Work

Constructive formal methods like RAISE [20], VDM [13] or the B-Method [15] have successfully been applied in industrial settings to construct correct systems (for a recent survey see [24]). They are centered around the stepwise-refinement paradigm [14], that is, the development starts by formulating high level requirements in a formal language and continues with the stepwise refinement of these. Every iteration adds more details to the formal representation and requires a new check for correctness. The process is repeated until the formal representation is detailed enough to allow a code generator to generate executable code. A tool that supports this activity is for example SCADE [7], which generates C or ADA code from the high-level language LUSTRE [5]. In contrast to our work, they employ a model-based development approach, which requires extensive knowledge for e.g. choosing the right abstractions. Such refinement-based approaches typically require SMEs to restructure their whole software development process and to perform intensive training of the participating engineers.

Notably, the RAISE method provides a new approach to software engineering as a whole, namely domain engineering [4, 3, 2]. In domain engineering, one tries to formalize the important parts of the domain to define the bridge between domain and software automatically. Like our approach, it is concerned with the relation between domain phenomena and software representations, but instead of relying on the implicit domain knowledge of the developer manifesting in form of the IRS-table, it demands an explicit formalization of this knowledge. This, again, requires much effort and training from the user, but promises great benefits through the automatic detection of errors in the transition from the domain to the software. A recent example for the application of domain engineering can be found in [17].

The approach presented in this paper relates directly to previous work on the transformation of system requirements to software specifications, in particular [12] and [18]. In [12], conditions are given under which a transformation from requirements to specifications can be successful; the automation of the transformation is not considered. An extension of those considerations is presented in [18] in form of an iterative process called requirement progression. Its goal is to obtain a specification in terms of the to-be-specified software from requirements represented as problem frames [11]. There, domain assumptions – called breadcrumbs – are used to create a new requirement from an old one that talks about domain phenomena. In each iteration new breadcrumbs are introduced until the new requirement only talks about phenomena known to the software. In a sense, our IRS function represents a special form of those breadcrumbs. We have for each domain phenomenon dp an entry in the IRS, namely $dp \iff Expr_{\mathbb{B}}(Var)$. While this allows even untrained programmers to create such a function, it also prohibits the direct use in more complex systems, where a single domain phenomenon is not directly relatable to the software. Contrary to our approach, they do not consider C code which is still widely found in practice, thus their approach does not directly apply there.

7   Conclusion

We have presented an approach to verify that a program correctly realises system requirements by verification of the program code itself. The approach can be applied if the interaction of the program with the system hardware can faithfully be described by an IRS-table. The basic variant presented here already covers the huge class of systems where C code with dedicated read/process/write phases is executed on memory mapped I/O hardware and where domain phenomena are closely related to inputs and outputs of the system.

Given the system requirements, our approach requires nothing but the IRS-table and a C model-checker, in particular there is no need for a changed development process. We assume every programmer capable of developing software as discussed here is capable of creating an IRS-table because he or she is necessarily already familiar with the domain phenomena in order to be able to develop the software.

Furthermore, we do not assume that system requirements are complete in any sense. Thus our approach can also be applied to only some, possibly most relevant system requirements giving control over the overall costs. By these advantages, our approach is in particular appealing for small or medium sized companies (SMEs), which on the one hand are often concerned with the class of systems we consider here but on the other hand cannot afford the high entry costs associated with formal methods or significant changes in the development process. Our approach provides for a gradual introduction of formal methods.

Furthermore, capturing the domain assumptions of the programmer in form of an IRS-table is a contribution towards dependability [10]. The IRS-table is an artifact which can be validated by domain experts. Additionally, the IRS-table defines a clear boundary of the responsibilities of the programmer. By providing the IRS-table, the programmer describes how sensors and actors have to be connected to, e.g., input and output pins of the system hardware. If the connection is according to the IRS-table, then the system will satisfy the system requirements. If the system malfunctions due to incorrect connections, this is clearly the responsibility of the party deploying the software.

The latter aspect is in particular relevant for sub-contracting software development. In addition to clearly limiting the responsibility of the programmer, it opens the possibility to decide the fulfillment of the contract by software model-checking tools [23].

Further work consists of a generalisation of the theory to more involved systems, e.g. where inputs and outputs have certain characteristics. For example, inputs may be constrained by environmental assumptions or can be fed back into the system directly or indirectly (such that there are dependencies between inputs and outputs). Also, outputs may not immediately change the environment but only after a certain delay.

Another important aspect is the automation and extension of C code annotations as described in Section 5, in particular covering the whole class of safety requirements in addition to the shown global invariant.

Acknowledgments. We would like to thank the anonymous reviewers for their many suggestions which helped us improving our work.

References

1. Barnett, M., Chang, B.Y.E., DeLine, R., Jacobs, B., Leino, K.R.M.: Boogie: A Modular Reusable Verifier for Object-Oriented Programs. In: de Boer, F.S., Bonsangue, M.M., Graf, S., de Roever, W.-P. (eds.) FMCO 2005. LNCS, vol. 4111, pp. 364–387. Springer, Heidelberg (2006)
2. Bjørner, D.: Domains as a prerequisite for requirements and software domain perspectives and facets, requirements aspects and software views. In: Broy, M., Rumpe, B. (eds.) RTSE 1997. LNCS, vol. 1526, pp. 1–41. Springer, Heidelberg (1998)

3. Bjørner, D.: Domain engineering: A software engineering discipline in need of research. In: Hlaváč, V., Jeffery, K.G., Wiedermann, J. (eds.) SOFSEM 2000. LNCS, vol. 1963, pp. 1–17. Springer, Heidelberg (2000)
4. Bjørner, D.: Domain engineering: a "Radical innovation" for software and systems engineering? A biased account. In: Dershowitz, N. (ed.) Verification: Theory and Practice. LNCS, vol. 2772, pp. 100–144. Springer, Heidelberg (2004)
5. Caspi, P., Pilaud, D., Halbwachs, N., Plaice, J.: Lustre: A declarative language for programming synchronous systems. In: POPL, pp. 178–188 (1987)
6. Cohen, E., Dahlweid, M., Hillebrand, M.A., Leinenbach, D., Moskal, M., Santen, T., Schulte, W., Tobies, S.: VCC: A Practical System for Verifying Concurrent C. In: Berghofer, S., Nipkow, T., Urban, C., Wenzel, M. (eds.) TPHOLs 2009. LNCS, vol. 5674, pp. 23–42. Springer, Heidelberg (2009)
7. Halbwachs, N., Raymond, P., Ratel, C.: Generating Efficient Code From Data-Flow Programs. In: PLILP, vol. 22, pp. 207–218 (1991); special Issue on WOFACS 1998
8. Hall, A.: Realising the benefits of formal methods. J. UCS 13(5), 669–678 (2007)
9. IEC 61131 Programmable controllers, www.iec.ch
10. Jackson, D.: A Direct Path to Dependable Software. Commun. ACM 52(4), 78–88 (2009)
11. Jackson, M.: Software Requirements & Specifications: A Lexicon of Practice, Principles and Prejudices. ACM Press/Addison-Wesley Publishing Co., New York, NY, USA (1995)
12. Jackson, M., Zave, P.: Deriving specifications from requirements: An example. In: ICSE, pp. 15–24 (1995)
13. Jones, C.B.: Systematic software development using VDM. Prentice Hall International (UK) Ltd., Hertfordshire (1986)
14. Kant, E., Barstow, D.R.: The refinement paradigm: The interaction of coding and efficiency knowledge in program synthesis. IEEE Trans. Software Eng. 7(5), 458–471 (1981)
15. Lano, K.: The B Language and Method: A Guide to Practical Formal Development. Springer, New York (1996)
16. Leinenbach, D., Santen, T.: Verifying the microsoft hyper-V hypervisor with VCC. In: Cavalcanti, A., Dams, D. (eds.) FM 2009. LNCS, vol. 5850, pp. 806–809. Springer, Heidelberg (2009)
17. Nami, M.R., Tehrani, M.S., Sharifi, M.: Applying domain engineering using raise into a particular banking domain. SIGSOFT Softw. Eng. Notes 32(2), 1–6 (2007)
18. Seater, R., Jackson, D., Gheyi, R.: Requirement Progression in Problem Frames: Deriving Specifications from Requirements. Requir. Eng. 12(2), 77–102 (2007)
19. Snook, C.F., Harrison, R.: Practitioners' views on the use of formal methods: an industrial survey by structured interview. Information & Software Technology 43(4), 275–283 (2001)
20. The RAISE Method Group: The RAISE Development Method. The BCS Practitioners Series, Prentice-Hall International, Englewood Cliffs (1995)
21. The Verifying C Compiler at Codeplex, http://vcc.codeplex.com/
22. Microsoft Visual Studio at MSDN, http://msdn.microsoft.com/en-us/vstudio/default.aspx
23. Westphal, B., Dietsch, D., Podelski, A., Pahlow, L.: Successful software subcontracting by system verification (submitted)
24. Woodcock, J., Larsen, P.G., Bicarregui, J., Fitzgerald, J.: Formal methods: Practice and experience. ACM Comput. Surv. 41(4), 1–36 (2009)

Adaptive Cruise Control:
Hybrid, Distributed, and Now Formally Verified[*]

Sarah M. Loos, André Platzer, and Ligia Nistor

Carnegie Mellon University, Computer Science Department, Pittsburgh, PA, USA
{sloos,aplatzer,lnistor}@cs.cmu.edu

Abstract. Car safety measures can be most effective when the cars on a street coordinate their control actions using distributed cooperative control. While each car optimizes its navigation planning locally to ensure the driver reaches his destination, all cars coordinate their actions in a distributed way in order to minimize the risk of safety hazards and collisions. These systems control the physical aspects of car movement using cyber technologies like local and remote sensor data and distributed V2V and V2I communication. They are thus cyber-physical systems. In this paper, we consider a distributed car control system that is inspired by the ambitions of the California PATH project, the CICAS system, SAFESPOT and PReVENT initiatives. We develop a formal model of a distributed car control system in which every car is controlled by adaptive cruise control. One of the major technical difficulties is that faithful models of distributed car control have both distributed systems and hybrid systems dynamics. They form distributed hybrid systems, which makes them very challenging for verification. In a formal proof system, we verify that the control model satisfies its main safety objective and guarantees collision freedom for arbitrarily many cars driving on a street, even if new cars enter the lane from on-ramps or multi-lane streets. The system we present is in many ways one of the most complicated cyber-physical systems that has ever been fully verified formally.

1 Introduction

Because of its societal relevance, many parts of car control have been studied before [1–18]. Major initiatives have been devoted to developing next generation individual ground transportation solutions, including the California PATH project, the SAFESPOT and PReVENT initiatives, and the CICAS-V system. Chang et al. [1], for instance, propose CICAS-V in response to a report that crashes at intersections in the US cost $97 Billion in the year 2000. The promise is tempting. Current uncontrolled car traffic is inefficient and has too many safety risks, which are caused, e.g., by traffic jams behind curves, reduced vision at night, inappropriate reactions to difficult driving conditions, or sleepy drivers. Next generation car control aims to solve these problems by

---

[*] This material is based upon work supported by National Science Foundation under NSF CA-REER Award CNS-1054246 and Grant Nos. CNS-0926181, CNS-0931985, CNS-1035800, CNS-1035813, and ONR N00014-10-1-0188. The first author was supported by an NSF Graduate Research Fellowship. For proofs and interactive car system simulations, see http://www.ls.cs.cmu.edu/dccs/ online.

M. Butler and W. Schulte (Eds.): FM 2011, LNCS 6664, pp. 42–56, 2011.
© Springer-Verlag Berlin Heidelberg 2011

using advanced sensing, wireless V2V (vehicle to vehicle) and V2I (vehicle to roadside infrastructure) communication, and (semi)automatic driver assistance technology that prevents accidents and increases economical and ecological efficiency.

Yet, there are several challenges that still need to be solved to make next generation car control a reality. The most interesting challenge for us is that it only makes sense to introduce any of these systems after its correct functioning and reliability has been ensured. Otherwise, the system might do more harm than good. This is the formal verification problem for distributed car control, which we consider in this paper.

What makes this problem particularly exciting is its practical relevance. What makes it particularly challenging is its complicated dynamics. Distributed car control follows a hybrid dynamics, because cars move continuously along differential equations and their behavior is affected by discrete control decisions like when and how strongly to brake or to accelerate and to steer. It is in the very nature of distributed car control, however, to go beyond that with *distributed* traffic agents that interact by local sensing, broadcast communication, remote sensor data, or cooperative networked control decisions. This makes distributed car control systems prime examples of what are called *distributed hybrid systems*. In fact, because they form distributed cyber-physical multi-agent systems, the resulting systems are distributed hybrid systems regardless of whether they are built using explicitly distributed V2V and V2I network communication infrastructure or just rely on the distributed effects of sensor readings about objects traveling at remote locations (e.g., laser-range sensors measuring the distance to the car in front).

Cars reach maneuvering decisions locally in a distributed way. Is the global dynamics that emerges from the various local choices safe? What can a car assume about other cars in its maneuver planning? How do we ensure that multiple maneuvers that make sense locally do not cause conflicts or collisions globally? Formal verification of distributed hybrid systems had been an essentially unsolved challenge until recently [19].

Our main contribution is that we develop a distributed car control system and a formal proof that this system is collision-free for arbitrarily many cars, even when new cars enter or leave a multi-lane highway with arbitrarily many lanes. Another contribution is that we develop a proof structure that is strictly modular. We reduce the proof to modular stages that can be verified without the details in lower levels of abstraction. We believe the principles behind our modular structure and verification techniques are useful for other systems beyond the automotive domain. Further contributions are:

- This is the first case study in distributed hybrid systems to be verified with a generic and systematic verification approach that is not specific to the particular problem.
- We identify a simple invariant that all cars have to obey and show that it is sufficient for safety, even for emergent behavior of multiple distributed car maneuvers.
- We identify generic and static constraints on the input output parameters that any controller must obey to ensure that cars always stay safe.
- We demonstrate the feasibility of distributed hybrid systems verification.

2 Related Work

Car control is a deep area that has been studied by a number of different communities. The societal relevance of vehicle cooperation for CICAS intersection collision avoidance [11] and for automated highway systems [5,8] has been emphasized. Horowitz et al. [10] proposed a lane change maneuver within platoons. Varaiya [13] outlines the key features of an IVHS (Intelligent Vehicle/Highway System). A significant amount of work has been done in the pioneering California PATH Project. Our work is strongly inspired by these systems, but it goes further and sets the groundwork for the modeling and formal verification of their reliability and safety even in distributed car control.

Dao et al. [3,4] developed an algorithm and model for lane assignment. Their simulations suggest [3] that traffic safety can be enhanced if vehicles are organized into platoons, as opposed to having random space between them. Our approach considers an even more general setting: we not only verify safety for platoon systems, but also when cars are driving on a lane without following platooning controllers. Hall et al. [6] also used simulations to find the best strategy of maximizing traffic throughput. Chee et al. [15] showed that lane change maneuvers can be achieved in automated highway systems using the signals available from on-board sensors. Jula et al. [9] used simulations to study the conditions under which accidents can be avoided during lane changes and merges. They have only tested safety partially. In contrast to [3,4,6,9,15], we do not use simulation but formal verification to validate our hypotheses.

Hsu et al. [7] propose a control system for IVHS that organizes traffic in platoons of closely spaced vehicles. They specify this system by interacting finite state machines. Those cannot represent the actual continuous movement of the cars. We use differential equations to model the continuous dynamics of the vehicles and thus consider more realistic models of the interactions between vehicles, their control, and their movement.

Stursberg et al. [12] applied counterexample-guided verification to a cruise control system with two cars on one lane. Their technique can not scale to an arbitrary number of cars. Althoff et al. [17] use reachability analysis to prove the safety of evasive maneuvers with constant velocity. They verify a very specific situation: a wrong way driver threatens two autonomously driving vehicles on a road with three lanes.

Wongpiromsarn et al. [14] verify safety of the planner-controller subsystem of a single autonomous ground vehicle. Their verification techniques restrict acceleration changes to fixed and perfect polling frequency, while our model of an arbitrary number of cars allows changes in acceleration at any point in time, with irregular sensor updates.

Damm et al. [2] give a verification rule that is specialized to collision freedom of traffic agents. To show that two cars do not collide, they need to manually prove eighteen verification conditions. Lygeros and Lynch [20] prove safety only for one deceleration strategy for a string of vehicles: the leading vehicle applies maximum deceleration until it stops, while at the same time, the cars following it in the string decelerate to a stop. The instantaneous, globally synchronized reaction of the cars is an unrealistic assumption that we do not make in our case study. Dolginova and Lynch [21] verify that no collisions with big relative velocity can occur when two adjacent platoons do a merge maneuver. This does not prove the absence of small relative velocity collisions, nor the behavior of 3 platoons or when not merging. In contrast to the manual semantic reasoning of [2,20,21], our techniques follow a formal proof calculus [19], which can be mechanized. In the case studies analyzed by [20,21] safety is proved only for a particular scenario, while our modular formal proofs deal with the general case. In our case study, the cars have more flexibility and an arbitrary number of control choices.

Unlike [2,12,14,17], we prove safety for an arbitrary number of cars. Our techniques and results are more general than the case-specific approaches [2,12,14,17,20,21], as we prove collision-freedom for any number of cars driving on any finite number of lanes. None of the previously cited papers have proved safety for distributed car control in which cars can dynamically enter the highway system, change lanes, and exit.

3   Preliminaries: Quantified Differential Dynamic Logic

Distributed car control systems are distributed hybrid systems, which we model by *quantified hybrid programs* (QHPs) [19]. QHPs are defined by the grammar (α, β are QHPs, θ a term, i a variable, f a function symbol, and H a formula of first-order logic):

$$\alpha, \beta \ ::= \ \forall i:C \ f(i) := \theta \mid \forall i:C \ f(i)' = \theta \& H \mid f(i) := * \mid ?H \mid \alpha \cup \beta \mid \alpha; \beta \mid \alpha^*$$

The effect of *quantified assignment* $\forall i:C \ f(i) := \theta$ is an instantaneous discrete jump assigning θ to $f(i)$ simultaneously for all objects i of type C. Usually i occurs in θ. The effect of *quantified differential equation* $\forall i:C \ f(i)' = \theta \& H$ is a continuous evolution where, for all objects i of type C, all differential equations $f(i)' = \theta$ hold *and* (written $\&$ for clarity) formula H holds throughout the evolution (the state remains in the region described by H). Usually, i occurs in θ. Here $f(i)'$ is intended to denote the derivative of the interpretation of the term $f(i)$ over time during continuous evolution, not the derivative of $f(i)$ by its argument i. For $f(i)'$ to be defined, we assume f is an $\mathbb{R}$-valued function symbol. The effect of the random assignment $f(i) := *$ is to non-deterministically pick an arbitrary number or object (of type the type of $f(i)$) as the value of $f(i)$.

The effect of *test* $?H$ is a *skip* (i.e., no change) if formula H is true in the current state and *abort* (blocking the system run by a failed assertion), otherwise. *Non-deterministic choice* $\alpha \cup \beta$ is for alternatives in the behavior of the distributed hybrid system. In the *sequential composition* $\alpha; \beta$, QHP β starts after α finishes (β never starts if α continues indefinitely). *Non-deterministic repetition* α^* repeats α an arbitrary number of times ≥ 0.

For stating and proving properties of QHPs, we use *quantified differential dynamic logic* Qd$\mathcal{L}$ [19] with the grammar:

$$\phi, \psi \ ::= \ \theta_1 = \theta_2 \mid \theta_1 \geq \theta_2 \mid \neg\phi \mid \phi \wedge \psi \mid \forall i:C \ \phi \mid \exists i:C \ \phi \mid [\alpha]\phi \mid \langle\alpha\rangle\phi$$

In addition to all formulas of first-order real arithmetic, Qd$\mathcal{L}$ allows formulas of the form $[\alpha]\phi$ with a QHP α and a formula ϕ. Formula $[\alpha]\phi$ is true in a state ν iff ϕ is true in all states that are reachable from ν by following the transitions of α; see [19] for details.

4   The Distributed Car Control Problem

Our approach to proving safety of a distributed car control system is to break the verification into modular pieces. In this way, we simplify what would otherwise be a very large and complex proof. The ultimate result of this paper is a formally verified model of any straight stretch of highway on which each car is following adaptive cruise control. On any highway, there will be an arbitrary number of lanes and an arbitrary number of cars, and the system will change while it runs when cars enter and leave the highway.

This would be an incredibly complex system to verify if we were to tackle it at this level. Each lane has a group of cars driving on it. This group is constantly changing as cars weave in and out of surrounding traffic. Each car has a position, velocity, and acceleration, and must obey the laws of physics. On top of that, in order to ensure complete safety of the system, every car must be certain at all times that its control choices will not cause a collision anywhere else in the system at any time in the future.

These issues are compounded by the limits of the sensory and communications networks. On a highway that stretches hundreds of miles, we could not hope for any car to collect and analyze real-time data from every other car on the interstate. Instead, we must assume each car is making decisions based on its local environment, e.g., within the limitations of sensors, V2V and V2I communication, and real-time computation.

Fig. 1. Emergent highway collision risk

Additionally, once you split your system into reasonably local models, it is still difficult to reason about how these local groups of cars interact. For example, consider a local group of three cars for a lane change maneuver: the car changing lanes, and the two cars that will be ahead and behind it. It is tempting to signal the car ahead to speed up and the car behind to slow down in order to make space for the car changing lanes. This is perfectly reasonable on the local level; however, Fig. 1 demonstrates a problem that appears when we attempt to compose these seemingly safe local cases into a global system. Two cars are attempting safe and legal lane changes simultaneously, but the car which separates the merging cars is at risk. The car in the middle simultaneously receives requests to slow down and speed up. It cannot comply, which could jeopardize the safety of the entire system.

To avoid complex rippling cases that could result in a situation similar to the one in Fig. 1, we organize our system model as a collection of hierarchical modular pieces. The smallest piece consists of only two cars on a single lane. We present a verification of this model in Sect. 5 and build more complex proofs upon it throughout the paper.

In Sect. 6, we prove that a lane with an arbitrary number of cars driven by any distributed homogeneous adaptive cruise control system is safe, assuming the system has been proved safe for two cars. We generate our own verified adaptive cruise control model for this system, but, due to the modular proof structure, it can be substituted with *any* implementation-specific control system which has been proved safe for two cars.

The verification of this one lane system, as well as the verification we present in Sect. 8 for a highway with multiple lanes, will hold independently with respect to the adaptive cruise control specifications. In Sect. 7, we look at the local level of a multi-lane highway system. We verify the adaptive cruise control for a single lane, where cars are allowed to merge in and out of the lane. Finally in Sect. 8, we compose the lane systems verified in Sect. 7 to provide a full verification of the highway system.

5 Local Lane Control

The local car dynamics problem that we are solving is: we have two cars on a straight lane that can accelerate, coast or brake and we want to prove that they will not collide.

This system contains complex physical controls as well as discrete and continuous dynamics, thus, is a hybrid system. Once the model for the local problem is verified, we will use it in a compositional fashion to prove safety for more complicated scenarios, such as multiple cars driving on a lane or on parallel lanes. We can apply modular composition because we have structured the models in a hierarchical order, we have found the right decomposition of the sub-problems and we have identified the right invariants.

Modeling. We develop a formal model of the local car dynamics as a QHP. Each car has state variables that determine how it operates: position, velocity, and acceleration. For follower car f, x_f represents its position, v_f its velocity, and a_f its acceleration (similarly for leader car ℓ).

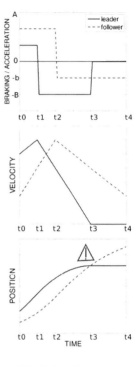

The continuous dynamics for f are described by the following differential equation system: $x'_f = v_f$, $v'_f = a_f$. This is the ideal-world dynamics that is adequate for a kinematic model of longitudinal lane maneuvers. The rate with which the position of the car changes is given by x'_f, i.e., the velocity. The velocity itself changes continuously according to the current acceleration a_f. We do not assume permanent control over the acceleration, but tolerate delays since sensor readings are not available continuously, control decisions may need time, and actuators may take time to react. For simplicity, though, we still assume that, once set, the acceleration a_f takes instant effect. We assume a global limit for the maximum acceleration and we denote it by $A \geq 0$. We assume that all cars have an emergency brake with a braking power between a maximum value B and a minimum value b, where $B \geq b > 0$. The two values have to be positive, otherwise the cars cannot brake. They may be different, however,

Fig. 2. Local car crash

because we cannot expect all cars to realize exactly the same emergency braking power and it would be unrealistic to build a system based on the assumption that all reactions are equal.

In Fig. 2, we see that leader ℓ brakes unexpectedly at time $t1$ with its maximum braking power, $-B$. Unfortunately, f did not follow ℓ at a safe distance, and so when sensor and network data finally inform f at time $t2$ that ℓ is braking, it is already too late for f to prevent a collision. Although f applies its full braking power, $-b$, at time $t2$, the cars will inevitably crash at time $t3$. The same problem can happen if ℓ brakes with $-b$ and f brakes with $-B$. This example shows that control choices which look good early on can cause problems later. Adding cars to the system amplifies these errors.

We present the entire specification of the local lane control (llc), consisting of the discrete control and the continuous dynamics, in Model 1. This system evolves over time, which is measured by a clock, i.e., variable t changing with slope $t' = 1$ as in (8). The differential equation system (8) formalizes the physical laws for movement, which are restricted to the evolution domain (9). Neither human drivers nor driver assistance

---

Model 1. Local lane control (llc)

$$llc \equiv (ctrl; dyn)^* \tag{1}$$

$$ctrl \equiv \ell_{ctrl} \parallel f_{ctrl}; \tag{2}$$

$$\ell_{ctrl} \equiv (a_\ell := *; \ ?(-B \leq a_\ell \leq A)) \tag{3}$$

$$f_{ctrl} \equiv (a_f := *; \ ?(-B \leq a_f \leq -b)) \tag{4}$$

$$\cup \ (?\mathbf{Safe}_\varepsilon; \ a_f := *; \ ?(-B \leq a_f \leq A)) \tag{5}$$

$$\cup \ (?(v_f = 0); \ a_f := 0) \tag{6}$$

$$\mathbf{Safe}_\varepsilon \equiv x_f + \frac{v_f^2}{2b} + \left(\frac{A}{b} + 1\right)\left(\frac{A}{2}\varepsilon^2 + \varepsilon v_f\right) < x_\ell + \frac{v_\ell^2}{2B} \tag{7}$$

$$dyn \equiv (t := 0; \ x_f' = v_f, \ v_f' = a_f, \ x_\ell' = v_\ell, \ v_\ell' = a_\ell, t' = 1 \tag{8}$$

$$v_f \geq 0 \ \wedge \ v_\ell \geq 0 \ \wedge \ t \leq \varepsilon) \tag{9}$$

---

technology are able to react immediately and each vehicle or driver will have a specific reaction time. Therefore we have a constant parameter, ε, which serves as an upper bound on the reaction time for all vehicles. We verify car control for arbitrary values of ε. Cars can react as quickly as they want, but they can take no longer than ε.

The leading car is not restricted by the car behind, so it may accelerate, coast, or brake at will. In Model 1, a_ℓ is first randomly assigned a real value, non-deterministically through (3). The model continues if a_ℓ is within the physical limits of the car's brakes and engine, i.e. between -B and A. On the other hand, f depends on the distance to ℓ and has a more restrictive set of possible moves. Car f can take some choices only if certain safety constraints about the distance and velocities are met.

Braking is allowed at all times, so a human driver may always override the automated control to brake in an emergency. In fact, braking is the only option if there is not enough distance between the cars for f to maintain its speed or accelerate. This is represented in (4), where there is no precondition for any force between $-B$ and $-b$.

The second possibility, (5), is that there is enough distance between the two cars for f to take any choice. This freedom is only given when (7) is satisfied. If (7) holds, then ℓ will still be safely in front of f until the controllers can react again (i.e., after they drive for up to ε time units), no matter how ℓ accelerates or brakes. This distance is greater than the minimum distance required for safety if they both brake simultaneously. The ε terms in (7) add this extra distance to account for the possibility that f accelerates for time ε even when ℓ decides to brake, which f may not notice until the next sensor update. These terms represent the distance traveled during one maximum reaction cycle of ε time units with worst-case acceleration A, including the additional distance needed to reduce the speed down to v_f again after accelerating with A for ε time units.

Now the third possibility. If f had previously chosen to brake by $a_f = -b$ then the continuous evolution dyn cannot continue with the current acceleration choices below velocity $v_f = 0$ due to constraint (9). Thus, we add the choice (6) saying that the car may always choose to stand still at its position if its velocity is 0 already.

The two cars can repeatedly choose from the range of legal accelerations. This non-deterministic repetition is represented by operator * in (1). The controllers of the two cars operate in parallel as seen in (2). Notice that the controllers are independent with respect to read and write variables (which also makes sense for implementation purposes), so in this case, parallel ($\|$) is equivalent to sequential composition (;).

Verification. To verify the local lane control problem modeled in Sect. 5, we use a formal proof calculus for QdL [19]. In the local lane control problem, we want f to be safely behind ℓ at all times. To verify that a collision is not possible, we show that there is always a reasonable distance between ℓ and f; enough distance that if both cars brake instantly, the cars would not collide. We verify this property for all times and under any condition which the system can run, so if a car can come so close to another car that even instant braking would not prevent a crash, the system is already unsafe.

For two cars f and ℓ, we have identified the following crucial relation ($f \ll \ell$), i.e., follower f is *safely behind* leader ℓ:

$$(f \ll \ell) \equiv (x_f \leq x_\ell) \wedge (f \neq \ell) \rightarrow \left(x_f < x_\ell \wedge x_f + \frac{v_f^2}{2b} < x_\ell + \frac{v_\ell^2}{2B} \wedge v_f \geq 0 \wedge v_\ell \geq 0\right)$$

If ($f \ll \ell$) is satisfied, then f has a safe distance from ℓ. The formula states that, if ℓ is the leading car (i.e., $x_f \leq x_\ell$ for different cars $f \neq \ell$), then the leader must be strictly ahead of the follower, and there must be enough distance between them such that the follower can stop when the leader is braking. Also both cars must be driving forward.

The safe distance formula ($f \ll \ell$) is the most important invariant. The system must satisfy it at all times to be verified. This is not to be confused with the definition of **Safe**$_\varepsilon$ in the control, which must foresee the impact of control decisions for the future of ε time. For simplicity, these formulas do not allow cars to have non-zero length; however, adding the car length to x_f would eliminate this requirement.

Proposition 1 (Safety of local lane control llc). *If car f is safely behind car ℓ initially, then the cars will never collide while they follow the* llc *control model; therefore, safety of* llc *is expressed by the provable formula:* $(f \ll \ell) \rightarrow [\texttt{llc}](f \ll \ell)$

We proved Proposition 1 using KeYmaera, a theorem prover for hybrid systems (proof files available online [22]). A proof sketch is presented in [23, Appendix A.1].

6   Global Lane Control

Fig. 3. Lane risk

In Sect. 5 we show that a system of two cars is safe, which gives a local version of the problem to build upon. However, our goal is to prove safety for a whole highway of high-speed vehicles. The next step toward this goal is to verify safety for a single lane of n cars, where n is arbitrary and finite, and the ordering of the cars is fixed (i.e., no car can pass another). Each car follows the same control we proved safe for two cars in Sect. 5, but adding cars to the system and making it distributed has introduced new risks. It is now necessary to show, for example, if you are driving along and the car in front of you slows while the car behind simultaneously accelerates, you won't be left sandwiched between with no way to avoid a collision (as in Fig. 3).

Model 2. Global lane control (`glc`)

$$\text{glc} \equiv (ctrl''; dyn'')^* \tag{10}$$

$$ctrl'' \equiv \forall i : C\ (ctrl(i)) \tag{11}$$

$$ctrl(i) \equiv (a(i) := *;\ ?(-B \le a(i) \le -b)) \tag{12}$$

$$\cup\ (?\mathbf{Safe}_\varepsilon(i);\ a(i) := *;\ ?(-B \le a(i) \le A)) \tag{13}$$

$$\cup\ (?(v(i) = 0);\ a(i) := 0) \tag{14}$$

$$\mathbf{Safe}_\varepsilon(i) \equiv x(i) + \frac{v(i)^2}{2b} + \left(\frac{A}{b} + 1\right)\left(\frac{A}{2}\varepsilon^2 + \varepsilon v(i)\right) < x(L(i)) + \frac{v(L(i))^2}{2B} \tag{15}$$

$$dyn'' \equiv (t := 0;\ \forall i : C\ (dyn(i)), t' = 1, t \le \varepsilon) \tag{16}$$

$$dyn(i) \equiv x'(i) = v(i), v'(i) = a(i), v(i) \ge 0 \tag{17}$$

Modeling. Because we are now looking at a lane of cars, our model will require additional features. First, we must represent the position, velocity, and acceleration of each car. If these variables were represented as primitives, the number of variables would be large and difficult to handle. Using only primitive variables, we cannot verify a system for any arbitrary number of cars, i.e., we could verify for, say, 5 cars, but not for any n cars. Therefore, we give each car an index, i, and use first-order variables $x(i)$, $v(i)$, and $a(i)$ to refer to the position, velocity and acceleration of car i. With these first-order variables, our verification applies to a lane of any number of cars.

Of course, the cars are all driving along the road at the same time, so we evolve the positions of the cars simultaneously along their differential equations. The acceleration, $a(i)$, of all cars is also set simultaneously in the control. We need notation for this parallel execution, so we use the universal quantifier ($\forall$) in the definition of the overall control and continuous dynamics (see (11) and (16) in Model 2). The control of all cars in the system is defined by $ctrl''$ (11). This says that for each car i, we execute $ctrl(i)$. This control is exactly the control defined in Sect. 5 - under *any* conditions the car may brake (12); if the car is safely following its leader, it may choose any valid acceleration between $-b$ and A (13); and if the car is stopped, it may remain stopped (14). There are only two distinctions between the control introduced in `glc` and the control used in `llc` described in Sect. 5. First, we change primitive variables to first-order variables. Second, with so many cars in the system, we have to determine which car is our leader.

It is vital that every car be able to identify, through local sensors or V2V/V2I communication networks, which car is directly in front of it. It is already assumed that the sensor and communication network is guaranteed to give accurate updates to every car within time ε. We now also make the reasonable assumption that with each update, every car is able to identify which car is directly ahead of it in its lane. This may be a bit tricky if the car only has sensor readings to guide it, but this assumption is reasonable if all cars are broadcasting their positions (and which lane they occupy in the case of multiple lanes). For some car i, we call the car directly ahead of it $L(i)$, or the *leader of car i*. More formally, we assume the following properties about $L(i)$:

$$L(i) = j \equiv x(i) < x(j) \wedge \forall k : C\backslash\{i, j\}\ (x(k) < x(i) \vee x(j) < x(k))$$

$$(i \ll L(i)) \equiv \forall j : C((L(i) = j) \rightarrow (i \ll j))$$

The equation $L(i) = j$ is expanded to mean that the position of j must be ahead of the position of i, and there can be no cars between. The second formula states that for a car, i, to be safely behind its leader, denoted $(i \ll L(i))$, we require that i should be safely behind any car which fulfills the requirements of the first equation. Each car will have at most one leader at any given time. At the end of the finite length lane, we position a stationary car. This car has no leader and therefore will never move.

The constraint $\textbf{Safe}_\varepsilon$ from Sect. 5 has been updated to a first-order variable as well (15). It now uses $L(i)$ to identify which car is directly ahead of car i, and then determines if i is following safely enough to accelerate for ε time. This constraint is applied to all cars in the system when the individual controls set acceleration.

The continuous dynamics are the same as those described in Sect. 5, but with the added dynamics of the other cars in the system (16). Once $a(i)$ has been set for all cars by $ctrl^n$ (11), each car evolves along the dynamics of the system for no more than ε time (maximum reaction time). The position of each car evolves as the second derivative of the acceleration set by the control (17). The model requires that the cars never move backward by adding the constraint $v(i) \geq 0$. We still have a global time variable, t, that is introduced in the definition of dyn^n (16). Since $t' = 1$, all cars evolve along their respective differential equations in an absolute timeframe. Note that t is never read by the controller, thus, $\texttt{glc}$ has no issues with local clock drift.

We model all cars in the system as repeatedly setting their accelerations as they synchronously receive sensor updates (11) and following the continuous dynamics (16). When put together and repeated non-deterministically with the * operator, these QHPs form the $\texttt{glc}$ model (10) for global lane control. The $\texttt{glc}$ model is easy to implement since each car relies on local information about the car directly ahead. Our online supplementary material shows a demo of an implementation of this model [22].

Verification. Now that we have a suitable model for a system of n cars in a single lane, we identify a suitable set of requirements and prove that our model never violates them. In Sect. 5, since there were only two cars on the road, it was sufficient to show that the follower car was safely behind its leader at all times. However, in this model it is not enough to only ensure safety for each car and its direct leader. We must also verify that a car is safely following all cars ahead – each car has to be safely behind its leader, and the leader of its leader, and the car in front of that car, and so on.

For example, suppose there were a long line of cars following each other very closely (they could, for instance, be in a platoon). If the first car brakes, then one-by-one the cars behind each react to the car directly in front of them and apply their brakes. In some models, it would be possible for these reaction delays to add up and eventually result in a crash [24]. Our model is not prone to this fatal error, because our controllers are explicitly designed to tolerate reaction delays. Each car is able to come to a full stop no matter what the behavior of the cars in front of it (so long as all cars behave within the physical limits of their engines and brakes). To show this, we must verify that under the system controls every car is always safely behind all cars ahead until the lane ends. We do this by first defining *transitive leaders*, $L^*(i)$ as follows:

$$(i \ll L^*(i)) \equiv [k := i; (k := L(k))^*](i \ll k)$$

The QHP, $k := i; (k := L(k))^*$, continually redefines k to be the next car in the lane (until the lane ends). Because this QHP is encapsulated in $[\ ]$, all states that are reachable in the program must satisfy the formula ($i \ll k$). In other words, starting with ($k := i$), we check that i is safely behind k, or ($i \ll i$). Next, $k := L(k)$, so $k := L(i)$, and we prove that i is safely behind k: ($i \ll L(i)$). Then we redefine k to be its leader again ($k := L(k)$), and we check that i is safely behind k: ($i \ll L(L(i))$). This check is continued indefinitely: ($i \ll L(L(... L(i))))$. Hence the notation, ($i \ll L^*(i)$).

Proposition 2 (Safety of global lane control glc). *For every configuration of cars in which each car is safely following the car directly in front of it, all cars will remain in a safe configuration (i.e., no car will ever collide with another car) while they follow the distributed control. This is expressed by the following provable formula:*
$$\forall i : C(i \ll L(i)) \;\rightarrow\; [\texttt{glc}](\forall i : C(i \ll L^*(i)))$$
This means that as the cars move along the lane, every car in the system is safely following all of its transitive leaders.

Using Gödel's generalization rule, our proof for a lane of cars splits immediately into two branches: one which relies on the verification of the control and dynamics in the local, two car case, and one which verifies the rest of the system. These two branches are independent, and furthermore, the control and dynamics of the cars are only expanded in the verification of the local model. This is good news for two reasons. First, it keeps the resulting proof modular, which makes it possible to verify larger and more complex systems. Second, if the control or dynamics of the model are modified, only an updated verification of safety for two cars will be needed to verify the new model for the whole system. Proof details are available in [23, Appendix A.2].

7   Local Highway Control

In Sect. 6, we verified an automated control system for an arbitrary, but constant, number of cars on a lane. Later, we will put lots of these lanes together to model highway traffic. In our full highway model, cars will be able to pass each other, change lanes, and enter or leave the highway. We first study how this full system behaves from the perspective of a single lane. When a car changes into or out of that lane, it will look like a car is appearing or disappearing in the middle of the lane: in front of and behind existing cars. It is crucial to show that these appearances and disappearances are safe.

   If a new car cuts into the lane without leaving enough space for the car behind it, it could cause an accident. Furthermore, when two cars enter the lane simultaneously, if there are several cars between them, we must prove that there will not be a ripple effect which causes those cars between to crash (also see Fig. 1). Faithful verification must apply to all kinds of complex maneuvers and show safety for all cars in the system, not just those involved locally in one maneuver.

   Our verification approach proves separate, modular properties. This allows us to compose these modular proofs and verify collision freedom for the entire system for any valid maneuver, no matter how complex, even multiple maneuvers at different places.

Modeling. We have additional challenges in modeling this new system where cars can appear and disappear dynamically. First of all, in previous sections we have used $\forall i : C$ to mean "for all cars in the system." We will now abuse this notation and take it to mean

---

Model 3. Local highway control ($\mathtt{lhc}$)

$$\mathtt{lhc} \equiv (delete^*; create^*; ctrl''; dyn'')^* \tag{18}$$

$$create \equiv n := new; \; ?((F(n) \ll n) \wedge (n \ll L(n))) \tag{19}$$

$$(n := new) \equiv n := *; \; ?(E(n) = 0); \; E(n) := 1 \tag{20}$$

$$(F(n) \ll n) \equiv \forall j : C \; (L(j) = n \rightarrow (j \ll n)) \tag{21}$$

$$delete \equiv n := *; \; ?(E(n) = 1); \; E(n) := 0 \tag{22}$$

"for all cars which currently exist on this lane." (In our formal proof we use an actualist quantifier to distinguish between these situations. This technique is described in detail in another paper [19].) Secondly, our model must represent what physical conditions in the lane must be met before a car may disappear or appear safely. And finally, the model must be robust enough to allow disappearances and appearances to happen throughout the evolution of the system (i.e., a car may enter or leave the lane at any time).

Recall that a car, n, has three real values: position, velocity and acceleration. Now that cars can appear and disappear, we add a fourth element: existence. The existence field is just a bit that we flip on ($E(n) := 1$) when the car appears and flip off ($E(n) := 0$) when the car disappears.

When we create a new car, n, we start by allowing the car to be anything. This can be written in dynamic logic as a random assignment $n := *$. Of course, when we look at the highway system as a whole, we won't allow cars to pop out of thin air onto the lane. This definition can be restricted to cars which already exist on an adjacent lane. However, since the choice of $*$ is non-deterministic, we are verifying our model for all possible values of n. This means that the verification required for an entire highway system will be a subset of the cases covered by this model of a single lane. Because $n := *$ allows n to be any car, one that exists on the lane or one that doesn't, we first must check that this "new" car isn't already on the lane. If it doesn't exist, i.e. $?(E(n) = 0)$, then we can flip our existence bit to on and it will join the existing cars on this lane (20).

Now that we have defined appearance, we can define its dual: disappearance. We delete cars by choosing a car, n, non-deterministically, checking that it exists, and then flipping that bit so that it no longer exists on this lane (22). After a delete, notice that while the car ceases to exist physically on our lane, we are still able to refer to it in our model and verification as car n – a car that used to be in the lane.

A car may leave the lane at any time (assuming there is an adjacent lane which it can move into safely), but it should only be allowed to enter the lane if it is safely between the car that will be in front of it and the car that will be behind it. Because of this, when creating a car in the lane, our model will check that the car is safely between the car in front and behind. If we have a test which follows a creation of a new car, as in our definition of *create* in (19), a new car will only appear if the test succeeds. The formula $(F(i) \ll i)$ evaluates to true if car i is safely ahead of the car behind it. This is the dual of $(i \ll L(i))$. We define this formally in terms of $(i \ll L(i))$ as shown in (21).

The $\mathtt{lhc}$ model is identical to the $\mathtt{glc}$ model in Sect. 6, but at the beginning of each control cycle it includes zero or more car *delete*s or *create*s as shown by *delete** and *create** in (18). It is important to note that the verification will include interleaving and simultaneous *creates* and *deletes* since the continuous dynamics (dyn^n) are allowed to evolve for zero time and start over immediately with another *delete* and *create* cycle.

Verification. Now that we have a model for local highway control, we have to describe a set of requirements that we want the model to satisfy in order to ensure safety. These requirements will be identical to the requirements necessary in the global lane control. We want to show that every car is a safe distance from its transitive leaders: $\forall i : C(i \ll L^*(i))$. Because these requirements are identical to those presented in Proposition 2, the statement of Proposition 3 is identical except for the updated model.

Proposition 3 (Safety of local highway control lhc). *Assuming the cars start in a controllable state (i.e. each car is a safe distance from the car in front of it), the cars may move, appear, and disappear as described in the (lhc) model, then no cars will ever collide. This is expressed by the following provable formula:*

$$\forall i : C(i \ll L(i)) \;\rightarrow\; [\mathtt{lhc}]\forall i : C(i \ll L^*(i))$$

We keep the proof of Proposition 3 entirely modular just as we did in the previous section for Proposition 2. The proof is presented in [23, Appendix A.3].

8   Global Highway Control

So far, we have verified an automated car control system for cars driving on one lane. A highway consists of multiple lanes, and cars may change from one lane to the other. Just because a system is safe on one lane does not mean that it would operate safely on multiple lanes. When a car changes lanes, it might change from a position that used to be safe for its previous lane over to another lane where that position becomes unsafe. Lane change needs to be coordinated and not chaotic. We have to ensure that multiple local maneuvers cannot cause global inconsistencies and follow-up crashes; see Fig. 1.

Modeling. The first aspect we need to model is which lane is concerned. The quantifier $\forall i : C$, which in Sect. 7 quantified over "all cars which exist on the lane", now needs to be parametrized by the lane that it is referring to. We use the notation $\forall i : C_l$ to quantify over all cars on lane l. Likewise, instead of the existence function $E(i)$, we now use $E(i, l)$ to say whether car i exists on lane l. A car could exist on some l but not on others. A car can exist on multiple lanes at once if its wheels are on different lanes (e.g., when crossing dashed lines). We use subscripted $ctrl_l^n, dyn_l^n, L_l(i), L_l^*(i)$ etc. to denote variants of $ctrl^n, dyn^n, L(i), L^*(i)$ in which all quantifiers refer to lane l. Similarly, we write $\forall l : L\ ctrl_l^m$ for the QHP running the controllers of all cars on all lanes at once.

In addition to whatever a car may do in terms of speeding up or slowing down, lane change corresponds to a sequence of changes in existence function $E(i, l)$. A model for an instant switch of car i from lane l to lane l' would correspond to $E(i, l) := 0$; $E(i, l') := 1$, i.e., disappearance from l and subsequent appearance on l'. This is mostly for adjacent lanes $l' = l \pm 1$, but we allow arbitrary lanes l, l' to capture highways with complex topology. Real cars do not change lanes instantly, of course. They gradually move from one lane over to the other while (partially) occupying both lanes simultaneously for some period of time. This corresponds to the same car existing on multiple lanes for some time (studying the actual local curve dynamics is beyond the scope of this paper, but benefits from our modular hierarchical proof structure).

Gradual lane change is modeled by an appearance of i on the new lane ($E(i, l') := 1$) when the lane change starts, then a period of simultaneous existence on both lanes while the car is in the process of moving over, and then, eventually, disappearance from the old lane ($E(i, l) := 0$) when the lane change has been completed and the car occupies no part of the old lane anymore. Consequently, gradual lane change is over-approximated by a series of deletes from all lanes ($\forall l : L\ delete_l^*$) together with a series of appearances on all lanes ($\forall l : L\ new_l^*$). Global highway control with multiple cars moving on multiple lanes and non-deterministic gradual lane changing can be modeled by QHP:

$$\mathsf{ghc} \equiv (\forall l : L\ delete_l^*;\ \forall l : L\ new_l^*;\ \forall l : L\ ctrl_l^n;\ \forall l : L\ dyn_l^n)^*$$

Verification. Global highway control ghc is safe, i.e., guarantees collision freedom for multi-lane car control with arbitrarily many lanes, cars, and gradual lane changing.

Theorem 1 (Safety of global highway control ghc). *The global highway control system (ghc) for multi-lane distributed car control is collision-free. This is expressed by the provable formula:*

$$\forall l : L \forall i : C_l(i \ll L_l(i)) \rightarrow$$
$$[(\forall l : L\ delete_l^*; \forall l : L\ new_l^*; \forall l : L\ ctrl_l^n; \forall l : L\ dyn_l^n)^*] \forall l : L \forall i : C_l(i \ll L_l^*(i))$$

For the proof see [23, Appendix A.4]. Note that the constraints on safe lane changing coincide with those identified in Sect. 7 for safe appearance on a lane.

9   Conclusion and Future Work

Distributed car control has been proposed repeatedly as a solution to safety and efficiency problems in ground transportation. Yet, a move to this next generation technology, however promising it may be, is only wise when its reliability has been ensured. Otherwise the cure would be worse than the disease. Distributed car control has been out of scope for previous formal verification techniques. We have presented formal verification results guaranteeing collision freedom in a series of increasingly complex settings, culminating in a safety proof for distributed car control despite an arbitrary and evolving number of cars moving between an arbitrary number of lanes. Our research is an important basis for formally assured car control. The modular proof structure we identify in this paper generalizes to other scenarios, e.g., variations in local car dynamics or changes in system design. Future work includes mechanizing the proof and addressing time synchronization, sensor inaccuracy, curved lanes, and asynchronous sensors.

References

1. Chang, J., Cohen, D., Blincoe, L., Subramanian, R., Lombardo, L.: CICAS-V research on comprehensive costs of intersection crashes. Technical Report 07-0016, NHTSA (2007)
2. Damm, W., Hungar, H., Olderog, E.R.: Verification of cooperating traffic agents. International Journal of Control 79, 395–421 (2006)

3. Dao, T.S., Clark, C.M., Huissoon, J.P.: Distributed platoon assignment and lane selection for traffic flow optimization. In: IEEE IV 2008, pp. 739–744 (2008)
4. Dao, T.S., Clark, C.M., Huissoon, J.P.: Optimized lane assignment using inter-vehicle communication. In: IEEE IV 2007, pp. 1217–1222 (2007)
5. Hall, R., Chin, C., Gadgil, N.: The automated highway system / street interface: Final report. PATH Research Report UCB-ITS-PRR-2003-06, UC Berkeley (2003)
6. Hall, R., Chin, C.: Vehicle sorting for platoon formation: Impacts on highway entry and troughput. PATH Research Report UCB-ITS-PRR-2002-07, UC Berkeley (2002)
7. Hsu, A., Eskafi, F., Sachs, S., Varaiya, P.: Design of platoon maneuver protocols for IVHS. PATH Research Report UCB-ITS-PRR-91-6, UC Berkeley (1991)
8. Ioannou, P.A.: Automated Highway Systems. Springer, Heidelberg (1997)
9. Jula, H., Kosmatopoulos, E.B., Ioannou, P.A.: Collision avoidance analysis for lane changing and merging. PATH Research Report UCB-ITS-PRR-99-13, UC Berkeley (1999)
10. Horowitz, R., Tan, C.W., Sun, X.: An efficient lane change maneuver for platoons of vehicles in an automated highway system. PATH Research Report UCB-ITS-PRR-2004-16, UC Berkeley (2004)
11. Shladover, S.E.: Effects of traffic density on communication requirements for Cooperative Intersection Collision Avoidance Systems (CICAS). PATH Working Paper UCB-ITS-PWP-2005-1, UC Berkeley (2004)
12. Stursberg, O., Fehnker, A., Han, Z., Krogh, B.H.: Verification of a cruise control system using counterexample-guided search. Control Engineering Practice 38, 1269–1278 (2004)
13. Varaiya, P.: Smart cars on smart roads: problems of control. IEEE Trans. Automat. Control 38, 195–207 (1993)
14. Wongpiromsarn, T., Mitra, S., Murray, R.M., Lamperski, A.: Periodically controlled hybrid systems: Verifying a controller for an autonomous vehicle. In: Majumdar, R., Tabuada, P. (eds.) HSCC 2009. LNCS, vol. 5469, pp. 396–410. Springer, Heidelberg (2009)
15. Chee, W., Tomizuka, M.: Vehicle lane change maneuver in automated highway systems. PATH Research Report UCB-ITS-PRR-94-22, UC Berkeley (1994)
16. Johansson, R., Rantzer, A. (eds.): Nonlinear and Hybrid Systems in Automotive Control. Society of Automotive Engineers Inc. (2003)
17. Althoff, M., Althoff, D., Wollherr, D., Buss, M.: Safety verification of autonomous vehicles for coordinated evasive maneuvers. In: IEEE IV 2010, pp. 1078–1083 (2010)
18. Berardi, L., Santis, E., Benedetto, M., Pola, G.: Approximations of maximal controlled safe sets for hybrid systems. In: Johansson, R., Rantzer, A. (eds.) Nonlinear and Hybrid Systems in Automotive Control, pp. 335–350. Springer, Heidelberg (2003)
19. Platzer, A.: Quantified Differential Dynamic Logic for Distributed Hybrid Systems. In: Dawar, A., Veith, H. (eds.) CSL 2010. LNCS, vol. 6247, pp. 469–483. Springer, Heidelberg (2010)
20. Lygeros, J., Lynch, N.: Strings of vehicles: Modeling safety conditions. In: Henzinger, T.A., Sastry, S.S. (eds.) HSCC 1998. LNCS, vol. 1386, pp. 273–288. Springer, Heidelberg (1998)
21. Dolginova, E., Lynch, N.: Safety verification for automated platoon maneuvers: A case study. In: Maler, O. (ed.) HART, pp. 154–170. Springer, Heidelberg (1997)
22. Electronic Proof and Demo, http://www.ls.cs.cmu.edu/dccs/
23. Loos, S.M., Platzer, A., Nistor, L.: Adaptive cruise control: Hybrid, distributed, and now formally verified. Technical Report CMU-CS-11-107, Carnegie Mellon University (2011)
24. Germann, S.: Modellbildung und Modellgestützte Regelung der Fahrzeuglängsdynamik. Fortschrittsberichte VDI, Reihe 12, Nr. 309, VDI Verlag (1997)

TRACECONTRACT: A Scala DSL for Trace Analysis[*]

Howard Barringer[1] and Klaus Havelund[2]

[1] School of Computer Science, University of Manchester, UK
Howard.Barringer@manchester.ac.uk
[2] Jet Propulsion Laboratory, California Institute of Technology, USA
Klaus.Havelund@jpl.nasa.gov

Abstract. In this paper we describe TRACECONTRACT, an API for trace analysis, implemented in the SCALA programming language. We argue that for certain forms of trace analysis the best weapon is a high level programming language augmented with constructs for temporal reasoning. A trace is a sequence of events, which may for example be generated by a running program, instrumented appropriately to generate events. The API supports writing properties in a notation that combines an advanced form of data parameterized state machines with temporal logic. The implementation utilizes SCALA's support for defining internal Domain Specific Languages (DSLs). Furthermore SCALA's combination of object oriented and functional programming features, including partial functions and pattern matching, makes it an ideal host language for such an API.

1 Introduction

The trace analysis problem consists of determining whether a trace, a sequence of events, satisfies a formalized property. One challenge is to find convenient and expressive languages for expressing such trace properties. We present in this paper an API, named TRACECONTRACT, in the SCALA programming language [2] for performing trace analysis (runtime verification). It supports writing temporal properties about traces and can be used for analyzing log files produced as a result of program executions or for monitoring systems executing online. The contribution of the paper is a convenient and very expressive specification notation, which can be perceived as a hybrid between state machines and temporal logic, but formulated as an API in a high level programming language. This allows a mixture of temporal specification and high level programming, a combination we find very attractive for practical purposes. The implementation of the API benefits from SCALA's support for defining domain specific languages and from its functional programming features. This includes specifically the use of partial functions and pattern matching over parameterized events to model state transitions, which is very similar to the way to the `receive` function in SCALA's `Actor` class is implemented to model an actor's reception of messages from other concurrently running actors. The API and SCALA have been chosen for analysis of command

---

[*] Part of the research described in this publication was carried out at Jet Propulsion Laboratory, California Institute of Technology, under a contract with the National Aeronautics and Space Administration.

M. Butler and W. Schulte (Eds.): FM 2011, LNCS 6664, pp. 57–72, 2011.
© Springer-Verlag Berlin Heidelberg 2011

sequences for NASA's LADEE (Lunar Atmosphere and Dust Environment Explorer) mission [1].

A large number of formalisms have been proposed in recent years for supporting trace analysis, see for example [13,9,12,10,3,15,8]. Examples are temporal logics, including past time as well as future time, regular expressions, state machines, context free grammars, real-time logics, and statistics gathering logics. Most have been implemented as what are often referred to as *external DSLs* (Domain Specific Languages), external to the programming language they are implemented in, and parsed with a specialized parser. Our own work includes several such systems, most of which put emphasis on expressiveness, in order to be able to capture the many different logics provided in other systems. Amongst these systems are EAGLE [4] — based on recursive definitions of temporal predicates; RULER [7] — a rule-based framework providing the same level of formal expressivity as EAGLE but with a simpler and more efficient step-wise monitoring algorithm; and LOGSCOPE [5] — a state machine-like subset of RULER with the addition of a temporal logic. From these experiences, we observe two key points: (i) once a DSL is defined, it is laborious to change/extend it later; and (ii) users often ask for additional features, some of which are best handled by a general purpose programming language. We propose here instead to write trace monitors in a high level programming language, SCALA, augmented with support for temporal specification. Our solution is what is referred to as an *internal DSL*, internal to (embedded in) the programming language it is developed in. Stolz and Huch describe in [16] an embedding of LTL in HASKELL. Our framework differs in two major ways. First, we handle data parameterization by re-using SCALA's built-in notion of partial functions and pattern matching. Second, we introduce a new formalism which is a hybrid between state machines and temporal logic.

TRACECONTRACT is really just an API, formulated using the host language's primitives. It does, however, have the flavor of a DSL due to SCALA's special support for defining internal DSLs, and due to the fact that SCALA supports functional as well as object oriented programming. We shall use the terms API and DSL interchangeably. The DSL is a *shallow* embedding, meaning that we are making the host language's constructs part of the DSL. This is in contrast to a *deep embedding*, as in [16], where a separate internal representation is made of the DSL (an abstract syntax), which is then interpreted or compiled as in the case of an external DSL. See [11] for a recent discussion of shallow vs. deep embeddings. Generally, the arguments *for* a shallow internal DSL are: limited implementation effort (leading to adaptability), feature richness through the host language, and tool inheritance. The arguments *against* are: lack of analyzability — which can have consequences for performance and reporting to users, and full exposure of the implementation language (the user has to be a programmer, in this case a SCALA programmer). The groundwork for a theoretical study of the characteristics of the approach, such as soundness, completeness, and expressiveness, has been done during our previous work on EAGLE and RULER. However, a full theoretical presentation of TRACECONTRACT, including a formal semantics, is planned.

The rest of the paper is organized as follows. Section 2 presents the API and examples of its use. Section 3 outlines how the API is implemented. Section 4 concludes the paper.

2 The TraceContract DSL

A trace contract conceptually represents a predicate on execution traces, where an execution trace is a finite sequence of events. TRACECONTRACT is parameterized with the event type, which may be any type. To illustrate, we shall consider a simplified planetary rover scenario (to be our on-going example), similar to the example used in [5][1]. A rover is controlled from ground via commands emitted to it. Commands can either fail or succeed. Events are commonly modeled as objects (instances) of certain classes. The following SCALA classes define the type Event of events, and three specific kinds of events we are interested in monitoring:

Listing 1.1. Type Event

```
1  abstract class Event
2  case class COMMAND(name: String, nr: Int) extends Event
3  case class SUCCESS(name: String, nr: Int) extends Event
4  case class FAIL(name: String, nr: Int) extends Event
```

The class Event is defined as abstract, meaning that it has to be subclassed. Each kind of event is defined as a subclass of class Event. Each event class is furthermore defined as a **case** class, which enables pattern matching over members of the type (this we be illustrated below). Each subclass in this scenario is parameterized with data (the constructor parameters), which must be provided when creating an object of the class. Note that in SCALA constructor parameters can be provided in the class definition without having to define an explicit constructor inside the class as in JAVA. All of the events here have two parameters: a command name of type String and a command number of type Int. Success and fail events have the command number corresponding to the command they stem from. With the above definitions, the following is an example of a trace of four events:

```
val trace: List[Event] = List(
  COMMAND("STOP_DRIVING", 1), SUCCESS("STOP_DRIVING", 1),
  COMMAND("TAKE_PICTURE", 2), FAIL("TAKE_PICTURE", 2))
```

The **val** keyword introduces a constant, in this case trace of type List[Event], defined as the list returned by the list constructor call: List($event_1$, $event_2$,...). Each element in the list is an event, an object of one of the event classes. For example, the first list element COMMAND("STOP_DRIVING", 1) is an object of class COMMAND. Due to the fact that the event classes are defined as **case** classes, objects can be conveniently created without use of the **new** keyword. Such a trace can for example be constructed by parsing a log file produced by the rover software. Note, however, that events can be processed one by one as well, they do not need to come as part of a pre-computed trace.

2.1 The DSL and a First Example

The main two classes are Monitor, offering functions for writing properties, and Formula, representing the type of temporal formulas used to define properties. A class

---

[1] This example is inspired from the Mars Science Laboratory (MSL) rover mission.

FactOps offers additional functions on recorded facts (to model past time temporal logic). The API interfaces of these three classes are shown in code listings 1.2 and 1.3 respectively. These, and other listings will be referred to using references of the form: ⟨*listing-id*:*line-number*⟩ (one line), or: ⟨*listing-id*:*line-number*$_1$-*line-number*$_2$⟩ (a range of lines).

Listing 1.2. Class Monitor

```
1    class Monitor[Event] {
2      def property(name: Symbol)(formula: Formula): Unit
3      def invariant(name: Symbol)(block: Block): Unit
4      def monitor(monitors: Monitor[Event]*): Unit
5      def verify(event: Event): Unit
6      def end(): Unit
7      def verify(trace: List[Event]): Unit
8      def finish(): Unit
9      def getMonitorResult: MonitorResult[Event]
10
11     // state logic:
12     type Block = PartialFunction[Event, Formula]
13     def always(block: Block): Formula
14     def state(block: Block): Formula
15     def hot(block: Block): Formula
16     def step(block: Block): Formula
17     def strong(block: Block): Formula
18     def weak(block: Block): Formula
19     def error(message: String): Formula
20     def error: Formula
21     def ok(message: String): Formula
22     def ok: Formula
23
24     // future time temporal logic:
25     def matches(predicate: PartialFunction[Event, Boolean]): Formula
26     def not(formula: Formula): Formula
27     def globally(formula: Formula): Formula
28     def eventually(formula: Formula): Formula
29     def strongnext(formula: Formula): Formula
30     def within(time: Int)(formula: Formula): Formula
31
32     // past time temporal logic:
33     abstract class Fact
34     implicit def convFact2FactOps(fact: Fact): FactOps
35     def factExists(pred: PartialFunction[Fact,Boolean]): Boolean
36
37     // implicit conversions to Formula:
38     implicit def convEvent2Formula(event: Event): Formula
39     implicit def convBoolean2Formula(cond: Boolean): Formula
40     implicit def convUnitToFormula(unit: Unit): Formula
41   }
```

Listing 1.3. Classes Formula and FactOps

```scala
abstract class Formula {
  // propositional and future time temporal logic:
  def and(that: Formula): Formula
  def or(that: Formula): Formula
  def implies(that: Formula): Formula
  def until(that: Formula): Formula
  def unless(that: Formula): Formula

  // sequential, causal and hierarchical composition:
  def then(that: Formula): Formula
  def causes(that: Formula): Formula
  def except(block: Block): Formula
}

class FactOps(fact: Fact) {
  def + : Unit
  def - : Unit
  def ? : Boolean
  def ~ : Boolean
}
```

The public functions in each class are here represented by their signatures, each introduced with the **def** keyword (the associated bodies are not shown here). Most of these functions will be explained in the following. The class Monitor is parameterized with the event type, which must be provided at instantiation time. A user-defined monitor representing one or more trace properties must extend class Monitor to get access to the functions defined therein. Consider as an example the following requirements: R_1: *"Whenever a command is issued, it should eventually succeed with no failure occurring before then"*, and R_2: *"A command must not succeed more than once"*. These requirements can be formulated as the TRACECONTRACT monitor in Listing 1.4. The monitor is defined as a class named CommandRequirements, which extends the class Monitor. In SCALA, the body of a class can contain statements (in addition to definitions), which will get executed when an object is constructed (the body of the class works as the constructor). Each of the two requirements is defined by a call of the function property ⟨1.2:2⟩ from the Monitor API. It is a curried function, which as first argument takes the name of the property, and as second argument takes the formula to be checked. The function returns no value of importance (return type is Unit), but has as side effect to add the formula to the list of formulas being checked.

Consider the formalization of the first requirement R_1. The first argument to the property function is the name of the property, in this case the symbol 'R1 of type Symbol. SCALA's Symbol type contains quoted names, which are convenient to type instead of strings, such as "R1". The second argument to the property function is a formula ⟨1.4:4-10⟩ of the form: always{...}. The formula is the result of a call of the always function ⟨1.2:13⟩, which takes as argument a partial function from events to formulas, called a *block* ⟨1.2:12⟩. A partial function f of type PartialFunction[A, B]

is associated with a function `isDefinedAt(x: A):Boolean` where `f.definedAt(v)` returns true if and only if the partial function `f` is defined at v. A partial function is typically defined with a sequence of **case** statements, each defining a subset of *A* for which it is defined. In the above case, the argument to the `always` function is the partial function defined only on `COMMAND` objects (there is only one **case** statement ⟨1.4:5⟩):

```
{case COMMAND(name, number) => hot { ... }}
```

When the function is applied to a value *v*, the value is matched against the patterns in the **case** statements, in a left to right manner, until a match occurs (an exception is thrown in case a match does not occur). In the above example, the value *v* is matched against the pattern `COMMAND(name, number)`. In case *v* is a command the match succeeds, the identifiers `name` and `number` are bound to the actual corresponding values in *v*, and the result is the value of the expression to the right of the `=>` symbol. It is the fact that the event classes `COMMAND`, `SUCCESS` and `FAIL` are defined as **case** classes (Listing 1.1) that allows us to perform pattern matching as above. The intuition is that the `always` function creates a state (a kind of formula), in which the monitor will wait until an event arrives for which the partial function is defined. When this happens, the partial function is applied to obtain a new formula, namely the right hand side of `=>`, in this case a new state *H* produced by the `hot` function ⟨1.4:6⟩. The net result is the conjunction of the original `always{...}` formula and this new state *H*: `always{...}` $\land$ *H* - to reflect the fact that we will keep checking the body of the `always` function.

Listing 1.4. Formalization of Requirements R_1 and R_2

```
1   \vspace*{1mm}
2   class CommandRequirements extends Monitor[Event] {
3     property('R1) {
4       always {
5         case COMMAND(name, number) =>
6           hot {
7             case FAIL('name', 'number') => error
8             case SUCCESS('name', 'number') => ok
9           }
10      }
11    }
12
13    property('R2) {
14      always {
15        case SUCCESS(_, number) =>
16          state {
17            case SUCCESS(_, 'number') => error
18          }
19      }
20    }
21  }
```

The hot function ⟨1.2:15⟩ similarly takes a partial function (*block*) as argument. As before, a hot state will remain waiting until an event arrives for which the partial function is defined. However, when such an event arrives, the net result is the value of the body – that is, there is no repetition as in the case of always. The hot state is also signified by causing an error in case it has not been left before the end of the trace. The partial function occurring as argument to the hot function ⟨1.4:7-8⟩ contains patterns which contain quoted variable names: `name` and `number`. The meaning of such patterns is that the incoming value must equal the value of these variables, instead of being bound to them. In this example, the monitor is waiting for failure or success of the command previously observed (same name and number). Finally, the formulas error ⟨1.2:20⟩ and ok ⟨1.2:22⟩ are special formulas, essentially representing False and True respectively. These functions also exist in overloaded forms taking a message as argument, ⟨1.2:19⟩ and ⟨1.2:21⟩, which is printed to standard out.

The property R_2 ⟨1.4:13-20⟩ states that a success with a certain number should never be followed by another success with the same number. The underscore ('_') is the wild-card pattern that always matches, and is here used to model that the command name is not of importance to this requirement. The state function ⟨1.2:14⟩ takes, as before, a partial function (*block*) as argument, and creates a state where the monitor will wait until an event arrives for which the partial function is defined, in which case an error is emitted in this example. In contrast to a hot state, however, no error is issued if a monitor remains in such a state at the end of the trace. state states are hence used to model *safety properties*, whereas hot states are used to model *liveness properties* (see [6] for a discussion of safety and liveness properties on finite traces).

2.2   State Machines

The API contains other kinds of states, produced by functions that take partial functions as arguments, such as step ⟨1.2:16⟩, strong ⟨1.2:17⟩, and weak ⟨1.2:18⟩ states. A step state evaluates to true if it does not trigger in the next step (this corresponds to ignoring this branch). A strong state evaluates to false if it does not trigger in the next step (some event *must* happen in the next step). A weak state, like a strong state, evaluates to false if it does not trigger in the next step, provided there is a next step.

In the example shown in Listing 1.4, properties have a flavor of temporal logic in the sense that intermediate states are not explicitly named. For example, in property 'R1, the right hand side of the transition '**case** COMMAND(name, number) => hot{...}' is a hot state that is not explicitly named, corresponding to a use of the diamond (eventually) operator ◇ in temporal logic. TRACECONTRACT also, however, naturally supports naming of states using SCALA's already built-in function concept, and consequently supports definition of state machines. The two styles (named states and inlined states as in Listing 1.4) can furthermore be mixed freely, which is the main characteristic of the TRACECONTRACT DSL. Consider the requirement R_3: *"Consecutive command numbers should increase by exactly 1, and a command (name) should not be re-issued with a new number until a success has occurred"*. In addition, let's collect the names of the commands issued and store them in a set for later printing. The property is presented in Listing 1.5, including the definition of two functions (increaseCmdNumber and holdCmd), each representing a parameterized named state. Instead of a call of

the form: property(*name*){always{*block*}}, here we use the invariant function
⟨1.2:3⟩, giving rise to the abbreviated form: invariant(*name*){*block*}. That is:

```
def invariant(name: Symbol)(block: Block) = property(name){always{block}}
```

Listing 1.5. A State Machine

```
1  \vspace*{2mm}
2  var commands: Set[String] = Set()
3
4  invariant('R3) {
5    case COMMAND(name, number) =>
6      commands += name
7      increaseCmdNumber(number) and holdCmd(name, number)
8  }
9
10 def increaseCmdNumber(number: Int) =
11   state {
12     case COMMAND(_, number2) => number2 == number+1
13   }
14
15 def holdCmd(name: String, number: Int) =
16   state {
17     case COMMAND('name', number2) if number2 != number => error
18     case SUCCESS('name', 'number') => ok
19   }
```

The property illustrates a number of features. Line ⟨1.5:2⟩ declares the monitor
local updatable variable commands (keyword **var**) of type Set[String], initialized
to the empty set. This variable is updated in line ⟨1.5:6⟩ by adding the command
name to the set. The variable update is followed in line ⟨1.5:7⟩ by a formula, which
is the conjunction of two states. TRACECONTRACT allows conjunction as well as disjunction of states corresponding to AND/OR automata. These two lines illustrate how
side-effects elegantly can be combined with logic. The two states are themselves the result of applying the two functions increaseCmdNumber and holdCmd, defined after the
property. Line ⟨1.5:12⟩ illustrates how a Boolean expression (number2 == number+1)
appears as a formula (it is lifted to a formula by an implicit function ⟨1.2:39⟩). Line
⟨1.5:17⟩ illustrates a conditional transition: the transition is only taken if the pattern
COMMAND('name', number2) matches, and the expression number2 != number evaluates to true.

2.3   Future Time Temporal Logic

TRACECONTRACT offers, as an alternative, a set of functions supporting writing
properties in Linear Temporal Logic (LTL). This includes propositional logic ⟨1.2:26⟩,
⟨1.3:3-5⟩, and temporal operators ⟨1.2:27-29⟩, ⟨1.3:6-7⟩. As an example, the requirement R_1 from above can alternatively be stated as in Listing 1.6, in a notation similar to
LTL.

The right hand side of the transition is an LTL formula constructed as follows. First, the events FAIL(name, number) and SUCCESS(name, number) are each converted to a formula via the implicit conversion function convEvent2Formula ⟨1.2:38⟩. Generally, the implicit functions ⟨1.2:38-40⟩ automatically convert values of the argument type into values of the result type. Whenever a SCALA expression fails to type check, the SCALA compiler will consult the implicit functions in scope and determine whether the application of a such will make the expression type check, and in this case the compiler will insert an application of the function (there can be no more than one such implicit conversion function, otherwise the SCALA compiler will complain). These functions allow us to write events, Boolean expressions, and code blocks returning Unit as formulas. Second, the formula obtained from the FAIL(name, number) event is negated with the not function ⟨1.2:26⟩, resulting in a new formula. Listing 1.3 shows the functions callable on formulas, including the until function ⟨1.3:6⟩. SCALA permits to write calls of functions on objects without dot-notation and without parentheses around arguments (as required in JAVA). That is, given an object o of a class defining a function m, instead of: $o.m(a)$, we are allowed to write: o m a. This technique is used to write the above LTL formula composing two formulas with the infix until operator. The formula is equivalent to: not(FAIL(name, number)).until(SUCCESS(name, number)).

Listing 1.6. An LTL Formula

```
1  \vspace*{1mm}
2  invariant('R4) {
3    case COMMAND(name, number) =>
4      not(FAIL(name, number)) until SUCCESS(name, number)
5  }
```

As we can see, we have here mixed pattern matching with LTL. In support for handling pattern matching, the API furthermore offers the matches function ⟨1.2:25⟩, which returns a formula that will be true or false on an event, depending on whether the partial function argument (a predicate) to matches is defined, and furthermore returns true on the event. Note that in this case no binding of values takes place, it is purely a predicate. Amongst other combinators we can mention:- Sequential composition – f_1 then f_2 ⟨1.3:10⟩: evaluates f_1 until (and if) it becomes true whereupon f_2 is evaluated; Cause and effect – f_1 causes f_2 ⟨1.3:11⟩: whenever f_1 evaluates to true, f_2 is evaluated (similar to message sequence diagrams); Bounds– f except{$block$} ⟨1.3:12⟩: f is evaluated unless the partial function $block$ becomes defined for an incoming event, in which case it is applied and its result becomes the new formula. Several other forms of formula are offered, including formulas counting events, for example that some event must happen within n steps.

2.4 Past Time Temporal Logic

Consider the requirement: R_5: *"A failure should only occur if a command (same name and number) has been observed in the past, and no success has been observed so far since then."*. This requirement expresses a past time property. TRACECONTRACT offers a set of constructs for writing past time properties. The general idea is to support recording of facts in a database, which can then be queried later, i.e. in the future. The API provides an abstract class Fact ⟨1.2:33⟩, which the user can extend in order to define facts. An implicit function ⟨1.2:34⟩ converts facts into objects of class FactOps ⟨1.3:15⟩, which offers a collection of functions on facts (applied using post-fix notation): a function for adding a fact to the database (+), a function for deleting a fact (-), and functions for querying whether a fact is in the database (?) or not (˜). There is also a function factExists ⟨1.2:35⟩ for checking whether a fact exists that satisfies a predicate. Requirement R_5 can be formulated as in Listing 1.7.

Listing 1.7. Reasoning About the Past

```
1  case class Commanded(name: String, number: Int) extends Fact
2
3  invariant('R5) {
4    case COMMAND(name, number) => Commanded(name, number) +
5    case SUCCESS(name, number) => Commanded(name, number) -
6    case FAIL(name, number) if Commanded(name, number) ˜ => error
7  }
```

A class Commanded is defined ⟨1.7:1⟩ extending class Fact. An object Commanded(n,x) of this class is meant to represent the fact that a command with name n and number x has been observed. By defining it as a **case** class, objects can be conveniently created without using the **new** keyword. The property then updates the database in the first two transitions ⟨1.7:4-5⟩, by adding respectively deleting a fact, and in the third transition ⟨1.7:6⟩ by testing for the absence of the fact (absence is an error). This specification style is very close to the way such past time properties are specified in RULER and LOGSCOPE. Indeed, [7] presents a translation scheme from future and past time LTL to RULER, the past time part of which can be fully mimicked to obtain a formal translation of past time LTL into TRACECONTRACT. Essentially, there is one key difference between the two. In RULER, memory is encoded by rules that are not persistent, i.e. they exist for the next moment only, whereas, here for TRACECONTRACT, facts are persistent by default and must be forcibly removed. Theoretical results about the separation of any LTL formula into pure past, present and pure future parts then enables us to claim, similar to our result for RULER, that any temporal logic property can be embedded/encoded in TRACECONTRACT.

We observe, however, that it is possible, as an alternative to the above, to declare variables in a monitor that maintains such a database and one may then find, because of SCALA's convenient syntax, the incurred effort is not too burdensome.

2.5 Using Monitors

Properties can be written in different monitors and composed in a hierarchical manner by calls of the monitor(monitors: Monitor[Event]*):Unit function ⟨1.2:4⟩. This is a function with a variable length argument list, indicated by '*', taking zero or more monitors as arguments. The example in Listing 1.8 illustrates how two sets of requirements are composed into a new monitor AllRequirements ⟨1.8:1-3⟩. This class is then instantiated to an object ⟨1.8:7⟩, upon which the verify function is called ⟨1.8:9⟩. In this case a trace is read from a log file and the verify function ⟨1.2:7⟩ that takes a trace as argument is called. This function will check the events in the trace against the provided properties. In some scenarios, events may be provided in a step-wise manner, for example during online monitoring of a running system, or if the log file is too large to be represented as a SCALA list. In such cases the alternative verify(event: Event) function ⟨1.2:5⟩ can be called on each incoming event. Such a sequence of calls has to be ended with a call of the end function ⟨1.2:6⟩. The user can in the monitor override the finish function ⟨1.2:8⟩ (for example to compute and print some statistics), which will be called when end is called.

Listing 1.8. Using a Monitor

```
1   class AllRequirements extends Monitor[Event] {
2     monitor(new CommandRequirements, new RadioRequirements)
3   }
4
5   object TraceAnalysis {
6     def main(args: Array[String]) {
7       val monitor = new AllRequirements
8       val trace = readLog()
9       monitor.verify(trace)
10    }
11  }
```

3   Implementation

In this section we shall briefly outline how the combinators described above have been implemented. We shall leave out non-essential details.

3.1   Formulas and Linear Temporal Logic

Requirements to be monitored are expressed as formulas. Formulas are objects of subclasses of the abstract class in Listing 1.9.

Listing 1.9. Class Formula

```
1   abstract class Formula {
2     def apply(event: Event): Formula
3     def reduce(): Formula = this
4     def and(that: Formula): Formula = And(this, that).reduce()
5     def until(that: Formula): Formula = Until(this, that).reduce()
6     ...
7   }
```

Each kind of formula is represented by a specific subclass of this class. A number of functions are defined on all formulas, four of which are shown here. The apply function takes an event and returns a new formula, either unchanged in case the event is not relevant, or a changed to reflect the impact of the event. The apply function is special in SCALA in that for a given formula f, it allows us to write f(e) instead of f.apply(e). The function is defined as abstract and is overridden by the different subclasses of Formula.

The apply function is invoked as follows. A monitor consists in principle of a collection of formulas to be monitored. The verify function ⟨1.2:7⟩ applied to a trace will traverse the trace, and will for each event e call verify(e) ⟨1.2:5⟩, which in turn will apply each formula f in the monitor to the event: $f(e)$, resulting in either True, False, an unchanged formula, or a changed formula different from True and False. At the end of the trace (when the end function ⟨1.2:6⟩ is called) all formulas are evaluated to either true (if they represent safety properties) or false (if they represent liveness properties).

The Formula class furthermore contains all infix operators on formulas, including Boolean logic operators, such as and, as well as temporal operators such as until. For example, given two formulas f_1 and f_2, the function and allows us to write: f_1 and f_2 (instead of the more classical also allowed: f_1.and(f_2)). The result is an object of class And, which is one of the many subclasses of class Formula, see Listing 1.10.

When composing Boolean logic expressions, it is necessary to simplify them. For example, for a formula f: *true* $\land f$ can be reduced to: f. The reduce function will perform this rewriting according to the classical Boolean axioms for each formula resulting during monitoring. By default the function is defined to leave the formula unchanged, but may be overridden in subclasses of Formula.

The atomic formulas are True, False, and Now(e), for some event e. The latter formula is true if the current event is equal to e. These atomic combinators are defined as subobjects/classes of Formula. A term such as And(f_1, f_2) is evaluated by evaluating its subformulas, and subsequently calling reduce to perform Boolean logic reduction, as shown in Listing 1.10.

Here reduce is defined with a **match** statement: the tuple (formula1, formula2) is matched against the patterns (False, _), (_, False), etc., until there is a match, and the formula on the right hand side of the corresponding => symbol is returned. The formulas corresponding to the classical LTL operators $\square$ (globally) and $\lozenge$ (eventually) are defined using the classical rewrite rules '$\square p = p \land \bigcirc \square p$' and '$\lozenge p = p \lor \bigcirc \lozenge p$', as shown in Listing 1.11.

We have mentioned that events, Booleans and the unit value are automatically transformed to formulas. This is achieved through the definitions in Listing 1.12. The conversion from the unit value to True allows us to write a block of code in the place of a formula, which can be useful when writing state machines.

3.2 State-Oriented Constructs

The most common specification style in TRACECONTRACT is to use (anonymous or named) states, The formula classes of some of these are shown in Listing 1.13. Common for all states is that they consist of a block ⟨1.2:12⟩, which is a partial function from events to formulas. States differ in how they evaluate when the partial function is not defined for an event. That is, whether they become True, False, or stay unchanged (**this**).

Listing 1.10. Class And

```
1  case class And(formula1: Formula, formula2: Formula) extends Formula {
2    override def apply(event: Event): Formula =
3      And(formula1(event), formula2(event)).reduce()
4
5    override def reduce(): Formula = {
6      (formula1, formula2) match {
7        case (False, _) => False
8        case (_, False) => False
9        case (True, _) => formula2
10       case (_, True) => formula1
11       case (f1, f2) if f1 == f2 => f1
12       case _ => this
13     }
14   }
15 }
```

Listing 1.11. Classes Globally and Eventually

```
1  case class Globally(formula: Formula) extends Formula {
2    override def apply(event: Event): Formula =
3      And(formula(event), this).reduce()
4  }
5
6  case class Eventually(formula: Formula) extends Formula {
7    override def apply(event: Event): Formula =
8      Or(formula(event), this).reduce()
9  }
```

Listing 1.12. Implicit Functions

```
1  implicit def convEvent2Formula(event: Event): Formula = Now(event)
2  implicit def convBoolean2Formula(cond: Boolean): Formula =
3    if (cond) True else False
4  implicit def convUnitToFormula(unit: Unit): Formula = True
```

States, and other formulas, also differ in the way they evaluate at the end of the trace. Some formulas will evaluate to true (representing safety properties: nothing unexpected happened), while others will evaluate to false (representing liveness properties: something expected did not happen). For example, for any formula f, at the end the formula Globally(f) evaluates to true whereas Eventually(f) evaluates to false. Likewise, for any block b, State(b) evaluates to true whereas Hot(b) evaluates to false.

3.3 Properties, Formulas, and Error Traces

A monitor technically contains a collection of properties. A property is a named formula. A property also maintains an error trace candidate for the formula. Whenever the formula changes due to a new incoming event, that event is recorded in the error trace.

This way an error trace for a formula reflects only those events that are important to the evolution of the formula. If the formula at some point is violated, that error trace can be printed to the user. However, formulas of the form always$\{f\}$, for some formula f, are treated differently than other formulas at the top level in order to provide the user with informative error traces. That is, in case such a formula occurs and f changes to f' different from True or False, then a new property is created specifically for the new f', with a new error trace initialized to contain the event that caused the formula change. The original always$\{f\}$ continues to be monitored as well, reflecting the semantics: $\Box p = p \wedge \bigcirc \Box p$. Consider as an example the formula always$\{$**case** e => eventually(q) $\}$. Each time e matches an incoming event, a new property monitoring eventually(q) is created, tracking the error trace only for this particular scenario.

Listing 1.13. States

```
1   case class State(block: Block) extends Formula {
2     override def apply(event: Event): Formula =
3       if (block.isDefinedAt(event)) block(event) else this
4   }
5
6   case class Hot(block: Block) extends Formula {
7     override def apply(event: Event): Formula =
8       if (block.isDefinedAt(event)) block(event) else this
9   }
10
11  case class Step(block: Block) extends Formula {
12    override def apply(event: Event): Formula =
13      if (block.isDefinedAt(event)) block(event) else True
14  }
15
16  case class Strong(block: Block) extends Formula {
17    override def apply(event: Event): Formula =
18      if (block.isDefinedAt(event)) block(event) else False
19  }
```

4   Conclusion

TRACECONTRACT is implemented as an API in SCALA, also referred to as a *shallow internal* DSL. Internal since it extends the host language (SCALA) and shallow since it is defined relying heavily on SCALA's already existing language constructs, such as function definitions, partial functions and pattern matching. An immediate consequence is that, in contrast to RULER, TRACECONTRACT is close to an order of magnitude smaller in code size, even though it offers greater functionality and easier adaptability. Previously, we have had many discussions as to how to integrate temporal logic into the RULER and LOGSCOPE systems. The internal DSL surprisingly provides many of these concepts with very little effort. Using SCALA as a host language can, however, potentially in some contexts be considered as a drawback instead of a virtue, depending on who the user is. Flight missions at NASA are for example more often manned with system/hardware engineers than with software engineers. One cannot expect a system engineer to use a programming language such as SCALA. A system engineer is more likely to pick up an external DSL with limited scope and limited potential for introducing programming errors. This dilemma is a subject for further research.

Our approach with TRACECONTRACT in SCALA has led to a very expressive and convenient DSL, but at the cost of analyzability. That is, a piece of specification is a SCALA fragment, and SCALA does not offer enough reflexive capabilities to allow one to analyze such a fragment, unless one interferes with the SCALA compiler. Amongst the things that become difficult is to provide the user with detailed information about the specification, such as visualizing state machines, or showing the progress of monitoring. It might also become a challenge to maximally optimize the implementation.

TRACECONTRACT was initially developed for analysis of log files produced from running software. For this purpose we believe that the solution is very powerful and convenient. The system can, however, also be used for online monitoring. Indeed, online monitoring of SCALA programs is a natural application, and future work includes extending Odersky's design by contract [14] with TRACECONTRACT.

References

1. NASA's LADEE (Lunar Atmosphere and Dust Environment Explorer) mission, http://www.nasa.gov/mission_pages/LADEE/main
2. The Scala programming language, http://www.scala-lang.org
3. Allan, C., Avgustinov, P., Christensen, A.S., Hendren, L., Kuzins, S., Lhoták, O., de Moor, O., Sereni, D., Sittamplan, G., Tibble, J.: Adding trace matching with free variables to AspectJ. In: OOPSLA 2005. ACM Press, New York (2005)
4. Barringer, H., Goldberg, A., Havelund, K., Sen, K.: Rule-based runtime verification. In: Steffen, B., Levi, G. (eds.) VMCAI 2004. LNCS, vol. 2937, pp. 44–57. Springer, Heidelberg (2004)
5. Barringer, H., Groce, A., Havelund, K., Smith, M.: Formal analysis of log files. Journal of Aerospace Computing, Information, and Communication 7(11), 365–390 (2010)
6. Barringer, H., Havelund, K., Rydeheard, D., Groce, A.: Rule systems for runtime verification: A short tutorial. In: Bensalem, S., Peled, D.A. (eds.) RV 2009. LNCS, vol. 5779, pp. 1–24. Springer, Heidelberg (2009)
7. Barringer, H., Rydeheard, D.E., Havelund, K.: Rule systems for run-time monitoring: from EAGLE to RULER. J. Log. Comput. 20(3), 675–706 (2010)
8. Chen, F., Roşu, G.: MOP: An efficient and generic runtime verification framework. In: Object-Oriented Programming, Systems, Languages and Applications, OOPSLA 2007 (2007)
9. Drusinsky, D.: The temporal rover and the ATG rover. In: Havelund, K., Penix, J., Visser, W. (eds.) SPIN 2000. LNCS, vol. 1885, pp. 323–330. Springer, Heidelberg (2000)
10. Finkbeiner, B., Sankaranarayanan, S., Sipma, H.: Collecting statistics over runtime executions. Formal Methods in System Design 27(3), 253–274 (2005)
11. Garillot, F., Werner, B.: Simple types in type theory: Deep and shallow encodings. In: Schneider, K., Brandt, J. (eds.) TPHOLs 2007. LNCS, vol. 4732, pp. 368–382. Springer, Heidelberg (2007)
12. Havelund, K., Rosu, G.: Monitoring programs using rewriting. In: 16th ASE conference, San Diego, CA, USA, pp. 135–143 (2001)

13. Lee, I., Kannan, S., Kim, M., Sokolsky, O., Viswanathan, M.: Runtime assurance based on formal specifications. In: PDPTA, pp. 279–287. CSREA Press (1999)
14. Odersky, M.: Contracts for scala. In: Barringer, H., Falcone, Y., Finkbeiner, B., Havelund, K., Lee, I., Pace, G., Roşu, G., Sokolsky, O., Tillmann, N. (eds.) RV 2010. LNCS, vol. 6418, pp. 51–57. Springer, Heidelberg (2010)
15. Stolz, V., Bodden, E.: Temporal assertions using AspectJ. In: Proc. of the 5th Int. Workshop on Runtime Verification (RV 2005). ENTCS, vol. 144(4), pp. 109–124. Elsevier, Amsterdam (2006)
16. Stolz, V., Huch, F.: Runtime verification of concurrent Haskell programs. In: Proc. of the 4th Int. Workshop on Runtime Verification (RV 2004). ENTCS, vol. 113, pp. 201–216. Elsevier, Amsterdam (2005)

Using Debuggers to Understand
Failed Verification Attempts

Peter Müller and Joseph N. Ruskiewicz

ETH Zurich, Switzerland
{peter.mueller,joseph.ruskiewicz}@inf.ethz.ch

Abstract. Automatic program verification allows programmers to detect program errors at compile time. When an attempt to automatically verify a program fails the reason for the failure is often difficult to understand. Many program verifiers provide a counterexample of the failed attempt. These counterexamples are usually very complex and therefore not amenable to manual inspection. Moreover, the counterexample may be invalid, possibly misleading the programmer. We present a new approach to help the programmer understand failed verification attempts by generating an executable program that reproduces the failed verification attempt described by the counterexample. The generated program (1) can be executed within the program debugger to systematically explore the counterexample, (2) encodes the program semantics used by the verifier, which allows us to detect errors in specifications as well as in programs, and (3) contains runtime checks for all specifications, which allows us to detect spurious errors. Our approach is implemented within the Spec# programming system.

1   Introduction

A common approach to automatic program verification is to compute *verification conditions*, logical formulas whose validity entails the correctness of the program. The verification conditions are then passed to an automatic theorem prover, typically an SMT solver such as Simplify [7] or Z3 [6]. If the prover can establish the validity of the verification condition then verification succeeds; otherwise verification fails for one of the following reasons:

1. The program is incorrect, that is, the program does not satisfy its specification, and the *specification* expresses what the programmer intended. A typical example is a runtime error such as division by zero.
2. The specification is incorrect or incomplete, that is, the program does not satisfy its specification, and the *program* expresses what the programmer intended. A typical example is a loop invariant that is too weak.
3. The prover was too weak to validate the condition, that is, the verification error is a false positive, called a *spurious error*.

All three causes occur frequently in program verification; in particular, incorrect and incomplete specifications are as common as errors in programs. Spurious errors are less common, but are more difficult to understand when they do occur.

M. Butler and W. Schulte (Eds.): FM 2011, LNCS 6664, pp. 73–87, 2011.

```
class IntList {                          class SortedList {
  int[] Elements;                          IntList list;
  int Count;
                                           // The list is sorted
  void Add (int value)                     invariant Sorted (list.Elements);
    modifies Count, Elements, Elements[*];
    ensures Contains (Elements, value)     void AddSorted (int value)
  { ... }                                    modifies list.Count, list.Elements[*];
                                             ensures Contains (list.Elements,value);
  void Sort ()                             {
    modifies Elements[*];                    list.Add (value);
    ensures Sorted (Elements);               list.Sort ();
  { ... }                                  }
}                                        }
```

Fig. 1. Spec# is unable to verify `AddSorted`. The notation `Sorted`(a) abbreviates the condition that array a is sorted and `Contains`(a,v) abbreviates that v is contained in a. Both conditions can be expressed in Spec# via quantification over the indices of a. The modifies-clauses specify frame properties by listing the locations a method is allowed to modify. For brevity, we omit the method bodies in class `IntList`, access modifiers, as well as Spec#'s ownership and non-null annotations.

Consider the small Spec# [11] program in Fig. 1. The method `AddSorted` of class `SortedList` adds the `value` parameter to the list of integers and then sorts the list. The specification requires that after the execution of `AddSorted`, the list be sorted (by an object invariant) and that it contains `value` (by a postcondition). Verifying the method with the Spec# program verifier fails. A modular verifier such as Spec# verifies each method individually and reasons about method calls in terms of the callee's specification, not its implementation. The specification of `Sort` states only that the elements of the list will be sorted, not that they will be preserved. Consequently, the verifier is unable to prove that `value` is still contained in `list.Elements` after the call to `list.Sort` and, thus, that the postcondition of `AddSorted` holds. We will discuss a second verification error related to `AddSorted`'s modifies clause in Sec. 5.

A programmer who may not understand the cause of this failure from the program text can query the program verifier for a counterexample. The counterexample essentially contains a value for each variable in each state—a trace leading to the failing specification. For programs with non-trivial states (in particular, heap data structures) these counterexamples can be magnitudes larger than the program. For our example, the counterexample is over 1,200 lines of text. It is therefore not amenable to manual inspection and provides little benefit to the programmer. Moreover, due to the limitations of automatic proving, the counterexample may be invalid and not representative of a valid execution, thus misleading the programmer.

Using the initial state from the counterexample to construct a unit test for the failing method is helpful only if the error is in the program; errors caused by incorrect or incomplete specifications cannot be reproduced by a unit test. For example, a test that executes `AddSorted` with the initial state from the counterexample and then asserts the postcondition will succeed because the implementation does satisfy its postcondition. It is the incomplete specification of `list.Sort` that causes the verification to fail, not the implementation. So successful tests are inconclusive about the presence and cause of verification errors.

In this paper, we present a technique that enables programmers to use standard debuggers to inspect program verification and counterexamples just as they use debuggers to inspect program executions and execution states. Our technique enables programmers to step through the verification of a method, check the validity of assertions, and observe the evolution of the state described by the counterexample. It detects verification failures caused by all three reasons mentioned in the introduction and notifies the programmer of invalid counterexamples. This tool support allows programmers to understand, locate, and fix verification errors more easily. We believe that applying a familiar tool for this task is crucial for making program verification more efficient and for increasing acceptance among practitioners. Our approach is implemented within the Spec# programming system. The tool, examples, and a demo video are available online at `http://www.pm.inf.ethz.ch/publications/cee`.

Outline. In Sec. 2 we give an overview of our approach. We explain how we reproduce counterexample states in Sec. 3. Sec. 4 describes how we rewrite the program to simulate its verification semantics and to reproduce the execution described by the counterexample. In Sec. 5 we extend the runtime assertion checker to handle all relevant specifications and show how it can be used to check the validity of the verification failure in Sec. 6. We discuss experiences using our approach and give a debugging procedure in Sec. 7. We present related work in Sec. 8 and conclude with Sec. 9.

2 Approach

Given a Spec# program and a counterexample produced by Z3, we construct an executable .NET program that simulates the verification semantics and reproduces states given by the counterexample. The constructed program can be executed in a program debugger, allowing the programmer to systematically and efficiently explore the counterexample. By executing the constructed program, we are able to detect spurious errors and validate failed verification attempts. The three key features of our approach are as follows:

(1) The constructed program *simulates the verification semantics* of the program as defined by the verifier rather than the concrete execution semantics as defined by the .NET platform. The semantics used by a program verifier is typically an abstraction of the execution semantics. Loops are typically verified via loop invariants rather than by considering the actual iterations, and modular verifiers reason about method calls in terms of method specifications rather than the implementation of the called method. By simulating the verification semantics rather than the execution semantics, we can detect verification errors caused by incorrect or incomplete specifications.

(2) The constructed program *reproduces the states given by the counterexample*. We execute the constructed program in the initial state described by the counterexample. For each statement whose verification semantics differs from

the execution semantics, we reproduce the effect of executing the statement by creating a program stub that alters the state as described by the counterexample. This allows programmers to use the debugger to explore and navigate through the counterexample.

(3) The constructed program *contains runtime checks for specifications* that are relevant for the verification error. For those specifications that generally cannot be checked efficiently at runtime (for instance, frame specifications, which universally quantify over all allocated objects), we use the counterexample to determine which objects are relevant for the verification error and focus the runtime checks on those. Moreover, checking the relevant specifications at runtime allows us to determine whether or not a verification error is spurious. This is the case if the constructed program terminates without a runtime error or specification violation.

Our approach enables the programmer to understand the failed verification attempt in method `AddSorted` as follows: We extract the initial state from the counterexample and construct a program driver that will create a `SortedList` object that contains an `IntList` object (in field `list`) with a list containing the elements, say, 0 and 1. We then rewrite the body of `AddSorted` so that it simulates Spec#'s verification semantics. That is, we replace the calls to `Add` and `Sorted` with program stubs that change the program state to the state given by the counterexample. The stub for the call to `Add` changes `list.Elements` to contain the elements `[0,1,-3]`[1]. The stub for the call to `Sort` updates the state of `list.Elements` to some sorted array, say `[7,7,7]`. We finish by constructing a runtime check for the invariant of `SortedList` and the postcondition (and modifies clause) of `AddSorted`. For each step in the construction, we insert debugger directives that allow the programmer to control the execution of the of the *original* program, but observe the states of the *constructed* program.

A programmer using our approach is presented with the original implementation of `AddSorted` highlighted by the program debugger. The programmer can either use the debugger to inspect the initial (counterexample) state or execute the method until either the runtime assertion checker notifies them of a failing assertion or the method terminates, notifying the programmer of a spurious error. In our example, the runtime assertion checker will notify the programmer of the failing postcondition `AddSorted`, thus confirming the verification failure. The programmer can then inspect the post-state of the method and observe the value `[7,7,7]` for `list.Elements`. However, the initial state contained the state `[0,1]` for `list.Elements` and `-3` for `value`. The programmer can now single-step through the body of `AddSorted` inspecting the (counterexample) state of each step. Stepping over the call to `list.Add` adds `value` to `list.Elements`, as expected. Stepping over the call to `list.Sort` changes `list.Elements` to `[7,7,7]`. This unexpected change points the programmer to the cause of the verification failure, namely the incomplete specification of `Sort`. Note that it is the simulation of the verification semantics that enables us to identify the

---

[1] Given the weak specification of `Add`, the counterexample could provide any array that contains the initial value of `value`, which we assume here to be `-3`.

incomplete specification as the cause of this verification error. Using the execution semantics, for instance in a test case, could exhibit only errors in the code.

3   State Construction

To simulate the verification semantics of the failing method, we replace each statement whose verification semantics differs from the execution semantics by a program stub that alters the state as prescribed by the counterexample. Both for this purpose and to set up the initial state of the method execution, we extract information from the counterexample and construct the corresponding state.

A counterexample contains values for all local variables in each execution state; we use those to extract the method arguments. Moreover, it contains function interpretations, in particular, for the select and store functions that are used to encode the heap; we use those to extract field values. The extraction is relatively simple and works for all counterexamples.

In this section we describe the construction of *mock types* that replace the original types in the program with versions that enable flexible initialization, of *program stubs* that construct the state given by the counterexample, and of the entry point to the failing method, the *driver*.

3.1   Type Mocking

For variables of built-in types such as primitive types and arrays, the state construction consists of straightforward assignments. For variables of user-defined types such as classes and interfaces, the state construction involves the creation of objects and the initialization of their fields according to the state given in the counterexample. Object creation is not possible for abstract types; initialization is difficult for types that do not provide a suitable constructor.

To address these issues we replace each user-defined type in the program by a mock type—a concrete class—that contains: (1) a parameterless constructor with empty body, which allows the program stubs to instantiate the class; (2) a declaration for each field that is accessible to the failing method or that is mentioned in a specification; if the field is of a user-defined type, we replace it by the corresponding mock type. We declare all fields of mock types public, which allows the program stubs to initialize them according to the counterexample via field assignments. Mock types do not contain any methods, except for the method that simulates the verification semantics of the failing method as we describe in Sec. 4.

In our example, we construct mock types for SortedList and IntList. Class SortedList contains a field list, which is accessed in the body of AddSorted. The type of this field is the mock type for IntList. All the fields of IntList are of built-in types. The type mocking is performed on the .NET level and transparent to the programmer.

3.2 Program Stubs

We replace each statement s whose verification semantics differs from the execution semantics by a program stub. This stub simulates the verification semantics of s by constructing the state after the execution of s as described by the counterexample. For this purpose, we extract the state before and after the execution of s from the counterexample. For each variable or field in which these two states differ, the program stub contains an assignment that updates the variable to reflect the state change.

When updating variables of reference types, we must preserve any alias properties contained in the counterexample, that is, when two variables contain the same symbolic reference in the counterexample, they must also contain the same reference in the constructed state. So when we update a variable of a reference type, we first check if we have already constructed an object for the symbolic reference in the counterexample. If so, we assign a reference to that object. If not, we create and initialize a new object, making use of the type mocking.

3.3 Driver

To begin executing the failing method we have to generate a *driver*, which constructs the initial state, attaches itself to the program debugger, and then calls the failing method. The initial state consists of values for the receiver, the method arguments, and all objects reachable from them (an extension to global data is straightforward). Its construction is a special case of the state construction described in the previous subsection; the only difference is that the driver constructs the entire state and not just the changes since a previous state. The programmer does not see the driver, but only the effects the driver produces.

```
// Construct the array for IntList.Elements
int[] Elements = new int[2];
Elements[0] = 0;
Elements[1] = 1;

// Construct an instance of IntList
IntList list = new IntList ();
list.Elements = Elements;
list.Count = 2;

// Construct receiver of failing method
SortedList rcvr = new SortedList ();
rcvr.list = list;
```

```
// Attach to the program debugger
Debugger.Launch ();

// Set the first step of the debugger
Debugger.Step ("rcvr.AddSorted (-3)");

// Call the failing method
rcvr.AddSorted (-3);
```

Fig. 2. The driver for our example first constructs the initial state, then launches the debugger, and finally calls the failing method. The types `IntList` and `SortedList` denote the mock types generated for the classes with the same names, which declare parameterless constructors and public fields.

The driver for our example creates the initial state for the failing method `AddSorted`, in particular, the receiver of type `SortedList` (Fig. 2, left column). In order to initialize this object, it first constructs and initializes an `IntList` object that will be assigned to the receiver's `list` field. For this purpose, we create an integer array of the length given in the counterexample (2) and directly initialize its elements with the values from the counterexample ([0,1]). We use this array to initialize the new `IntList` object. After the initialization of the `IntList` object, the driver creates and initializes the receiver of the failing method.

After the initial state construction, the driver launches the debugger, and then calls the failing method `AddSorted` on the constructed receiver with the argument value from the counterexample, -3 (Fig. 2, right column).

4   Verification Semantics

Program verifiers such as Spec# reason about a program using a verification semantics, which abstracts from the execution semantics. The two main abstractions are to reason about method calls in terms of the method's specification rather than its implementation (for the sake of modularity) and to reason about loops in terms of a loop invariant rather than actual iterations (to avoid impractical fixpoint computations). To help the programmer detect verification errors caused by incorrect or incomplete specifications, we replace in the failing method all method calls and loops by program stubs that simulate the verification semantics. The counterexample indicates which path through the failing method lead to the verification error; we use this information to eliminate all branches, jumps, and loops from the failing method. The resulting method body contains only straight-line code.

Although we rewrite the body of the failing method, the program debugger displays the original method body; the rewriting is transparent to the programmer. We achieve this effect by injecting debugger directives (in the form of calls to `Debugger.Step`) into the program stubs. These directives highlight the code in the original method body and allow the programmer to control the execution of the stubs from the original method body.

4.1   Method Calls

The verification semantics of a call to a method m is (1) to assert m's precondition, (2) to assign arbitrary values to all memory locations that may be changed by m (according to its modifies clause), and then (3) to assume m's postcondition. To simulate this semantics, we replace each call to a method m in the failing method, including recursive calls and constructor calls, with a program stub that contains: (1) a runtime check for m's precondition (2) code that updates the state of the program to reflect the state given by the counterexample as described in Sec. 3.2, and (3) a runtime check for m's postcondition; the motivation for this check will be explained in Sec. 6.

Method `AddSorted` contains calls to `list.Add` and `list.Sort`. For each call the counterexample contains a state describing the effect of the call. We replace these method calls with the stubs in Fig. 3. The stub for the call to `list.Add` (left column) constructs the state as prescribed by the counterexample. In the counterexample, `Elements` contains a new symbolic reference; so we construct a

```
// Step over the method list.Add
Debugger.Step (list.Add);

// Construct the poststate of list.Add
int[] Elements = new int[3];
Elements[0] = 0;
Elements[1] = 1;
Elements[2] = -3;
list.Elements = Elements;
list.Count = 3;

// Check postcondition of list.Add
... // See Sec. 6.2
```

```
// Step over the method list.Sort
Debugger.Step (list.Sort);

// Construct the poststate of list.Sort
list.Elements[0] = 7;
list.Elements[1] = 7;
list.Elements[2] = 7;

// Check postcondition of list.Sort
... // See Sec. 6.2
```

Fig. 3. The program stubs replacing the calls to list.Add and list.Sort in the failing method AddSorted. The debugger directives instruct the program debugger to highlight the calls. The stubs construct the post-states of the calls given by the counterexample.

new Elements array. The list field has not changed since the pre-state of the call, so we update only the state of the referenced object with the new values given by the counterexample. The stub then checks the postcondition of method Add, which we discuss in Sec. 6.

The stub for the call to list.Sort (right column) is analogous; however, we do not update list.Elements because the counterexample does not contain a value that is different from the pre-state (because the modifies clause of Sort does not permit modifications of the field Elements, only of the elements within the array). Note that the two stubs do not contain precondition checks because neither of the two methods has a precondition.

Specification languages such as Spec# allow specifications to contain calls to side-effect free (*pure*) methods. The verification semantics of such calls is to encode the pure method as a mathematical function that is axiomatized based on the specification of the pure method and not on its implementation [5]. Calls to pure methods in specifications are then encoded as applications of these mathematical functions. To simulate this semantics, we replace all occurrences of a pure method within a specification with the result value contained in the counterexample. Since pure methods are not allowed to change the heap, this simple replacement is sufficient to capture the effects of the pure method.

4.2 Loops

The verification semantics of a loop is: (1) to assert the loop invariant before the loop, (2) to simulate the state after an arbitrary number of (possibly zero) loop iterations by assigning arbitrary values to all locations that may be modified by the loop and assuming that the resulting state again satisfies the loop invariant. The verification semantics then considers two possibilities to continue the execution: (3) an arbitrary execution of the loop body by assuming that the condition of the loop holds, executing the loop body, and asserting that the loop invariant holds again after the body, or (4) exiting the loop by assuming that the condition of the loop does not hold and proceeding to the statement after the loop. Checking an arbitrary iteration of the loop suffices to ensure that any execution of the loop preserves the loop invariant.

To simulate this semantics we replace each loop with a program stub that contains: (1) a runtime check for the loop invariant, and (2) code that updates the state of the program to reflect the state given by the counterexample as described in Sec. 3.2 and another runtime check for the loop invariant, which we discuss in Sec. 6. From the counterexample, we know whether the verification error occurred on the path that contains the arbitrary loop iteration (branch (3)) or the path that exits the loop (branch (4)). In case (3), the stub contains a runtime check for the loop condition (see Sec. 6), the loop body (replacing any method calls or inner loops), another runtime check for the loop invariant, and then terminates the execution of the method. In case (4), the stub just contains a runtime check for the negation of the loop condition (see Sec. 6) and then proceeds with the code following the loop.

As we mentioned above, a programmer using our approach will not see the program stubs, but only the effect they have on the state of the program. If the error is located in the loop body, the execution as presented to the programmer enters the loop body; upon entry, the programmer will observe a sudden change of the state to the arbitrary state prescribed by the counterexample (satisfying the loop invariant and the loop condition). If the error is located after the loop, execution skips the loop entirely, also with a sudden change of the state (to an arbitrary state that satisfies the loop invariant and the negation of the loop condition).

5   Extended Runtime Checking

We rely on the runtime assertion checker to reproduce failed verification attempts. An execution of the rewritten failing method that does not lead to an assertion violation indicates a spurious error. To be conclusive about a verification failure, the runtime checker must be able to check any failing assertion.

Most assertions in Spec# programs are executable. In particular, quantifiers that range over finite integer intervals, such as array indices, are checked by iterating over the range. However, the verification semantics of Spec# also makes use of assertions that quantify over possibly unbounded sets, for instance, over all allocated objects in the assertions for modifies clauses and object invariants. Such assertions cannot be checked efficiently at runtime.

Nevertheless, we can generate useful runtime checks for most *failed* quantified assertions. When an assertion with a *universal* quantifier fails to verify, the counterexample contains instantiations of the quantified variables for which the assertion does not hold. In order to check whether a verification error is spurious, it is sufficient to generate a runtime check for those specific instantiations, which is straightforward. For unbounded *existential* quantifiers, the counterexample does not contain useful information because one would have to check all values of the unbounded set, not just one. However, automatic program verifiers avoid unbounded existential quantifiers because they are not handled well by SMT solvers. Therefore, not checking them at runtime is not a limitation in practice.

In our example, method `AddSorted` does not satisfy its modifies clause because the call to `list.Add` may modify `list.Elements` but `AddSorted` must not.

Therefore, the static verification of `AddSorted` leads to a second verification error. The counterexample for this error contains instantiations for the quantified variables in the assertion for `AddSorted`'s modifies clause. Here, these instantiations indicate that the `Elements` field of the object `list` is being modified without permission by the modifies clause. Using this information, we generate code that stores the initial value of `list.Elements` upon entry to `AddSorted` and then checks that `list.Elements` has not been modified upon termination of the method. Since the program stub for the call to `list.Add` changes the value of `list.Elements` (see Fig. 3), this runtime check fails and confirms the verification error.

The programmer debugging this verification failure can localize the error efficiently by attaching a data breakpoint to `list.Elements`. If a statement then modifies `list.Elements`, the debugger stops the execution notifying the programmer of the modification; in our example, at the call to `list.Add`. The programmer, now aware of the location of the failure, can fix the error by weakening the modifies clause of `AddSorted`.

6   Error Validation

In this section we explain how our approach detects spurious errors and invalid counterexamples.

6.1   Spurious Errors

Since the validity of verification conditions is undecidable, SMT solvers cannot always determine whether a verification condition is valid or not. Whenever the SMT solver does not provide a conclusive result, a sound verifier needs to be conservative and report a verification error, which is possibly spurious. Spurious errors occur frequently in automatic program verification, for instance, when specifications include quantifiers or non-linear arithmetic.

By extending the runtime assertion checker to handle *all relevant* failing assertions in Spec#, we are able to validate verification failures. If the execution of the rewritten failing method terminates without a failed runtime assertion check, we can safely conclude that the error is spurious and notify the programmer; who can now address the problem by rephrasing the specification, rather than spending time determining the cause of an error that does not exist.

6.2   Invalid Counterexamples

A counterexample is supposed to satisfy all assumptions that are being made in the verification semantics of a program. For instance, the initial state in a counterexample is supposed to satisfy the precondition of the failing method. However, if the assumptions contain formulas that are beyond the capabilities of the prover, it might construct an invalid counterexample that contradicts the assumptions. For example, most automatic provers do not fully support non-linear arithmetic and might produce an initial state such as -563 for x and 4 for y for the precondition x / y > 0. Simulating the execution described by an invalid counterexample and, in particular, checking assertions in states extracted from an invalid counterexample, is not helpful to understand verification errors.

We extract states from the counterexample in three cases: (1) to set up the initial state in the driver, (2) to reproduce the state changes made by a method call, (3) and to reproduce the state changes made by a loop iteration. For these cases, the verification semantics of Spec# makes the following assumptions about the expected state: (1) the precondition of the failing method, (2) the postcondition and modifies clause of a called method, and (3) the loop invariant and the loop condition. To guard against invalid counterexamples, we introduce runtime checks for each of these assumptions. When such a runtime check fails, it indicates that the counterexample state does not satisfy the assumption and, thus, the counterexample is invalid.

The failing method `AddSorted` of our example assumes its precondition as well as the postconditions and modifies clauses of the called methods `Add` and `Sort`. The assumption for the precondition would be part of the driver, which extracts the initial state from the counterexample, but is omitted in Fig. 2 because `AddSorted` has no precondition. The assumptions for the postconditions are part of the program stubs that replace the calls. To the stubs in Fig. 3, we append the checks `assert Contains(list.Elements,value)` and `assert Sorted(list.Elements)`, respectively.

Our approach checks most assumptions in the verification semantics at runtime, but not all of them. Assumptions that are not checked include for instance the modifies clause of a called method, which contains an unbounded universal quantification; the extended runtime checking described in Sec. 5 does not apply here, because this check does not correspond to a failed assertion and, therefore, the counterexample does not provide instantiations for the quantifier. Therefore, our approach might theoretically miss some invalid counterexamples, but that has not happened in any of the examples we have tried so far.

7   Experience

We have applied our approach in debugging the various verification failures found in examples from the Spec# tutorial [11], the Spec# test suite (see http://specsharp.codeplex.com), and our own test suite[2]. In this section, we outline a systematic procedure that we have found to be effective for using our approach to locate the cause of verification failures. We also summarize and evaluate our experiences using this procedure.

The main observations of our experiments are: (1) Our approach is helpful for understanding most of the verification failures in the examples. In particular, we were able to effectively and efficiently detect bugs in the implementation as well as incorrect or incomplete specifications. The examples where our approach did not provide any benefit were fairly obvious errors in small methods. For those

---

[2] Also included in the download of our tool.

verification failures, the error message provided by Spec# was sufficient to localize and fix the error. (2) Our set of examples contained very few spurious errors and invalid counterexamples because we took them mostly from the Spec# tutorial and test suite, both of which focus on examples that are handled well by the verifier. Nevertheless, our runtime checks identified all of the spurious errors and invalid counterexamples. (3) Most verification failures can be debugged systematically with a simple procedure, which we outline below.

These initial results are very promising. However, our evaluation may be biased in two ways. Firstly, the examples were written for Spec# demonstrations and might not be representative of real application code. Secondly, the evaluation was performed by people who are familiar with Spec#'s program verifier; it is possible that programmers might struggle with issues that are obvious to us. Nevertheless, we are confident that our positive experience will be confirmed by programmers working on application code.

Debugging Procedure. We have found the following steps to be an efficient way to localize and understand the cause of a verification failure. If the verifier reports several errors for the same method, we debug them in the order of their source location.

1. Use the error message to check the method for obvious errors. For very simple programs and specifications our approach usually requires more effort than simply inspecting the failing method. This is often the case for programs that contain neither method calls nor loops, which reduces the likelihood that the verification failure is caused by an incorrect or incomplete specification.

2. Run the rewritten program in the debugger and observe the failure. Before attempting to localize the error, one should first confirm that the verifier has found a valid error by running the rewritten program in the debugger. This run will either result in an assertion violation (confirming the validity of the error), in a failed assumption check (indicating an invalid counterexample), or in a message that suggests that the error is spurious. In the latter two cases, the programmer needs to find an alternative way of expressing the program or its specification and re-verify the program. In the former case, the debugging procedure continues with the next step.

3. Inspect the state in which the assertion failed. The runtime check for an assertion fails either because the assertion is incorrect or because the assertion was checked in a state the programmer did not expect. We recommend to inspect the assertion and the state in which the runtime check failed to determine which case applies. If the assertion is incorrect, we can fix it and re-verify the method. If the state contains unexpected values, we determine their origin in the next step.

4. Step through the rewritten program and observe changes to the relevant variables. From step 3, we know which assertion fails. It is helpful to track the values of the variables in this assertions to detect unexpected values, for instance, caused by a weak precondition or loop invariant. This tracking is best performed by adding these variables to the variable watch window of the debugger and then single-stepping through the rewritten method. Unexpected initial values point us to a weak precondition; unexpected modifications during a single step require further investigation, described in step 5. Single-stepping through the method is also likely to reveal errors in the code such as incorrect control flow or the absence of a necessary assignment.

A variation of step 4 is more efficient when the failing assertion contains only a small number of variables, such as the runtime check for a modifies clause which focuses on only one heap location (see Sec. 5). In this case, one can avoid the single-stepping and instead add data breakpoints for the relevant variables. We can then run the rewritten method in the debugger and get notified whenever a variable of interest gets updated.

5. Analyze unexpected modifications. Step 4 determines where a variable receives an unexpected value. If this happens during a method call or in a loop, we have identified the method's specification or the loop invariant as the cause of the unexpected value and can amend them. If the unexpected value comes from an assignment then we may also need to track the variables in the right-hand side expression by adding them to the watch window and repeating from step 4.

8   Related Work

The literature contains several proposals for extracting useful information from counterexamples, but in the context of deductive program verification, these proposals are generally not sufficient to understand the verification failure. In particular, they do not support the programmer in detecting incomplete specifications, spurious errors, and invalid counterexamples.

Some verifiers such as Spec# apply heuristics to extract those parts of a counterexample that are likely to be relevant for the verification error. However, it is difficult to tune the heuristics such that they provide all necessary information without swamping the programmer with irrelevant details. For instance, Spec# filters too aggressively for the method `AddSorted` and it provides only the following excerpt from the counterexample, which does not point us in the direction of the error: (`initial value of: value`) `== -3`.

Trace and distance based techniques [1,8,3] have been applied successfully in the context of model checking to localize program errors. They compare successful program executions against failing executions to determine which branches of the program lead to the error. Narrowing down the location of the error is useful, but may not suffice to determine the actual cause of the error. For instance, since the method body of `AddSorted` does not contain branches, these techniques will not provide any benefit. They also do not assist the programmer in detecting spurious errors. Another localization technique is program slicing [14], which systematically removes statements that are not relevant for the validity of the failed verification condition. In practice, however, program slicers do not effectively reduce the size of programs (and counterexamples) with heap data structures and specifications containing quantifiers. Slicing the body of `AddSorted` will not result in a smaller program because both statements affect the state of `list`, which is relevant for the failing postcondition.

Another approach is to construct a test case from a failed verification attempt, using the initial state of the counterexample as test input [4,2,13]. This approach is only helpful if the test leads to a runtime error or if the violated specification can be found by a runtime assertion checker. However, when static verification fails because of incomplete specifications, or when the violated specification is not checked at runtime (for instance, when the specification contains unbounded quantification over objects), or when the error is spurious, the test case will succeed and, thus, not help the programmer to determine the cause of the verification error and might even mislead the programmer into believing that the error does not exist [4].

Verification techniques based on symbolic execution assist the programmer in understanding failed verification attempts by presenting the programmer with the symbolic states used during the verification process [9,10]. Inspecting a symbolic state is very helpful to a verification expert who is familiar with the symbolic representation of the program, whereas our approach seems more appropriate for programmers. Moreover, it is not clear to what extent symbolic states help in detecting spurious errors.

Alternative techniques based on visualizing the counterexample, such as those based on graph visualization [12,15], are limited by the size of the state presented and do not help in identifying spurious errors and invalid counterexamples.

9 Conclusions

We have presented our approach to help programmers to understand failed verification attempts. We generate an executable program that reproduces the verification error by encoding the verification semantics of the program and by using variable values from a counterexample. We extend the runtime assertion checker to reproduce all relevant verification errors, identify spurious errors, and detect invalid counterexamples. Executing the generated program inside a debugger allows the programmer to systematically and efficiently explore the counterexample; which is crucial for understanding, localizing, and fixing the verification failure. The generation of the executable program is entirely automatic and is transparent to the programmer.

We have implemented our approach in Spec#, but it is applicable to all program verifiers based on automatic provers that provide counterexamples. Our experience using our approach is very promising; we are able to understand and fix verification errors effectively and efficiently. As an additional benefit, we have found our approach useful to debug the encoding of Spec#. We have indeed found an error in the Spec# verifier; when inspecting a counterexample in our tool, we noticed that a variable of type `uint` contained a negative value, which pointed us to an omission in the encoding of Spec# programs.

The main direction for future work is to combine our approach with counterexample-based dynamic program slicing to further reduce the time for localizing and fixing verification errors. Slicing will in particular allow us to automate step 5 of our debugging procedure.

Acknowledgments. We are grateful to the reviewers for their insightful comments. We would like to thank Christoph M. Wintersteiger for the various discussions on the internals of SMT solvers. We are also indebted to Jürg Billeter for the initial implementation of the tool and Christoph Studer for adding additional support for pure methods and modifies clauses.

References

1. Ball, T., Naik, M., Rajamani, S.K.: From symptom to cause: Localizing errors in counterexample traces. In: POPL, pp. 97–105. ACM, New York (2003)
2. Beyer, D., Chlipala, A.J., Henzinger, T.A., Jhala, R., Majumbar, R.: Generating tests from counterexamples. In: ICSE, pp. 326–335. IEEE, Los Alamitos (2004)
3. Clarke, E.M., Kroening, D., Lerda, F.: A tool for checking ANSI C programs. In: Jensen, K., Podelski, A. (eds.) TACAS 2004. LNCS, vol. 2988, pp. 168–176. Springer, Heidelberg (2004)
4. Csallner, C., Smaragdakis, Y.: Check 'n' Crash: Combining static checking and testing. In: ICSE, pp. 422–431. ACM, New York (2005)
5. Darvas, Á., Müller, P.: Reasoning about method calls in interface specifications. Journal of Object Technology 5(5), 59–85 (2006)
6. de Moura, L., Bjørner, N.: Z3: An efficient SMT solver. In: Ramakrishnan, C.R., Rehof, J. (eds.) TACAS 2008. LNCS, vol. 4963, pp. 337–340. Springer, Heidelberg (2008)
7. Detlefs, D., Nelson, G., Saxe, J.B.: Simplify: A theorem prover for program checking. Technical Report HPL-2003-148, HP Laboratories, Palo Alto (2003)
8. Groce, A.: Error explanation with distance metrics. In: Jensen, K., Podelski, A. (eds.) TACAS 2004. LNCS, vol. 2988, pp. 108–122. Springer, Heidelberg (2004)
9. Hähnle, R., Baum, M., Bubel, R., Rothe, M.: A visual interactive debugger based on symbolic execution. In: ASE, pp. 143–146. ACM, New York (2010)
10. Hall, R.J., Zisman, A.: Validating personal requirements by assisted symbolic behavior browsing. In: ASE, pp. 56–66. IEEE, Los Alamitos (2004)
11. Leino, K.R.M., Müller, P.: Using the spec# language, methodology, and tools to write bug-free programs. In: Müller, P. (ed.) LASER Summer School 2007/2008. LNCS, vol. 6029, pp. 91–139. Springer, Heidelberg (2010)
12. Rayside, D., Chang, F.S.-H., Dennis, G., Seater, R., Jackson, D.: Automatic visualization of relational logic models. ECEASST 7 (2007)
13. Tillman, N., Schulte, W.: Mock-object generation with behavior. In: ASE, pp. 365–368. IEEE, Los Alamitos (2006)
14. Tip, F.: A survey of program slicing techniques. Journal of Programming Languages 3(3) (1995)
15. Zeller, A., Lütkehaus, D.: DDD—a free graphical front-end for UNIX debuggers. SIGPLAN Notices 31(1), 22–27 (1996)

Sampling-Based Runtime Verification

Borzoo Bonakdarpour, Samaneh Navabpour, and Sebastian Fischmeister

Department of Electrical and Computer Engineering
University of Waterloo
200 University Avenue West
Waterloo, Ontario, Canada, N2L 3G1
{borzoo,snavabpo,sfischme}@ece.uwaterloo.ca

Abstract. The literature of runtime verification mostly focuses on *event-triggered* solutions, where a monitor is invoked by every change in the state of the system and evaluates properties of the system. This constant invocation introduces two major drawbacks to the system under scrutiny at run time: (1) significant *overhead* and (2) *unpredictability*. To circumvent the latter drawback, in this paper, we introduce a *time-triggered* approach, where the monitor frequently takes samples from the system to analyze the system's health. We propose formal semantics of sampling-based monitoring and discuss how to optimize the sampling period using minimum auxiliary memory. We show that such optimization is NP-complete and consequently introduce a mapping to *Integer Linear Programming*. Experiments on benchmark applications show that our approach introduces bounded overhead and effectively reduces involvement of the monitor at run time using negligible auxiliary memory.

Keywords: Runtime verification, monitoring, time-triggered, predictability.

1 Introduction

Runtime verification [2, 3, 4, 8, 21] is a complementary technique to exhaustive verification methods such as model checking and theorem proving, as well as incomplete solutions such as testing. Roughly speaking, in runtime verification, the objective is to ensure that at run time, a system satisfies its desirable properties; i.e., the system under inspection is observed and analyzed by a decision procedure called the *monitor*.

In the literature of runtime verification, constructing a monitor involves synthesizing an automaton that realizes the properties that the system under scrutiny must satisfy [17]. Then, by composing the monitor with the system, the monitor observes the occurrence of each transition and decides whether the specification has been met, violated, or impossible to tell. Thus, the monitor is invoked by each event (e.g., change of value of a variable) triggered in the system. We call this type of monitoring *event-triggered*. The main drawback of event-triggered runtime verification is twofold: the monitor (1) imposes *unpredictable overhead*

M. Butler and W. Schulte (Eds.): FM 2011, LNCS 6664, pp. 88–102, 2011.

and (2) may introduce *bursts* of interruptions to the system at run time. This can lead to undesirable transient overload situations in time-sensitive systems.

With this motivation, in this paper, we propose an alternative approach for runtime verification of *sequential* systems where the monitor is *time-triggered*. The idea is that the monitor takes samples from the system with a *constant* frequency to analyze the system's soundness. This way, the involvement of the monitor is time-bounded and predictable. However, the main challenge in this mechanism is accurate reconstruction of the system's state between two samples; i.e., if the value of a variable of interest changes more than once between two samples, the monitor may fail to detect violations of some properties. Hence, the problem boils down to finding the longest possible sampling period that allows state reconstruction.

We calculate the sampling period through building the system's control-flow graph. Then, we employ this sampling period to define the formal semantics of sampling-based runtime verification using the timed automata formalism. The sampling period extracted from control-flow graphs tend to be short and, hence, precipitates highly frequent involvement of the monitor even in branches of the program that do not require monitoring. To tackle this problem, we propose a method for increasing the sampling period by incorporating auxiliary memory, where we store a history of state changes. Obviously, we face a tradeoff between minimizing the size of auxiliary memory versus maximizing the sampling period. We show that the corresponding optimization problem is NP-complete.

In order to cope with the exponential complexity of the optimization problem, we map the problem onto *Integer Linear Programming* (ILP). We have developed a tool chain that takes C programs as input, instruments the program to build optimal history, and constructs a monitor that takes samples with the optimal sampling period. Our experimental results show encouraging results. Firstly, the size of ILP models for benchmark applications are manageable. Secondly, we observe that in event-triggered implementations, the system suffers from bursts of monitor involvement, whereas our sampling-based monitor adds bounded and, hence, predictable overhead. Finally, we observe that the memory usage overhead is negligible and our method effectively increases the sampling period, which results in adding less overall overhead at run time and in some cases obtaining faster execution of the system as compared to event-triggered methods.

2   Preliminaries

Definition 1. *The* control-flow graph *of a program P is a weighted directed simple graph $CFG_P = \langle V, v^0, A, w \rangle$, where:*

- *V: is a set of vertices, each representing a basic block of P. Each basic block consists of a sequence of instructions in P.*
- *v^0: is the initial vertex with indegree 0, which represents the initial basic block of P.*
- *A: is a set of arcs (u, v), where $u, v \in V$. An arc (u, v) exists in A, if and only if the execution of basic block u can immediately lead to the execution of basic block v.*

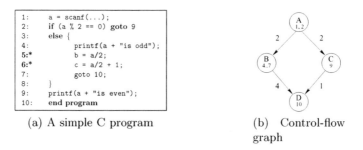

```
1:      a = scanf(...);
2:      if (a % 2 == 0) goto 9
3:      else {
4:          printf(a + "is odd");
5:*         b = a/2;
6:*         c = a/2 + 1;
7:          goto 10;
8:      }
9:      printf(a + "is even");
10:     end program
```

(a) A simple C program   (b)   Control-flow
                                    graph

Fig. 1. A C program and its control-flow graph

- *w: is a function $w : A \to \mathbb{N}$, which defines a* weight *for each arc in A. The weight of an arc is the* best-case execution time *(BCET) of the source basic block.* ☐

Notation: Since the weight of all outgoing arcs from a vertex v are equal, $w(v)$ denotes the weight of the arcs that originate from v.

For example, consider the C program in Figure 1(a). If each instruction takes one time unit to execute, the resulting control-flow graph will be as shown in Figure 1(b). Vertices of the graph in Figure 1(b) are annotated by the corresponding line numbers of the C program in Figure 1(a).

Timed automata.   Let Σ be an alphabet. A *timed word* over Σ is a sequence $(a_0, t_0), (a_1, t_1) \cdots (a_k, t_k)$, where each $a_i \in \Sigma$ and each t_i is in non-negative real numbers $\mathbb{R}_{\geq 0}$ and the occurrence times increase monotonically. Let X be a set of *clock variables.* A *clock constraint* over X is a Boolean combination of formulae of the form $x \preceq c$ or $x - y \preceq c$, where $x, y \in X$, $c \in \mathbb{Z}_{\geq 0}$, and $\preceq$ is either $<$ or $\leq$. We denote the set of all clock constraints over X by $\Phi(X)$. A *clock valuation* is a function $\nu : X \to \mathbb{R}_{\geq 0}$ that assigns a real value to each clock variable. For $\tau \in \mathbb{R}_{\geq 0}$, we write $\nu + \tau$ to denote $\nu(x) + \tau$ for every clock variable x in X. Also, for $\lambda \subseteq X$, $\nu[\lambda := 0]$ denotes the clock valuation that assigns 0 to each $x \in \lambda$ and agrees with ν over the rest of the clock variables in X.

Definition 2.   *A timed automaton [1] is a tuple $\mathcal{A} = \langle L, L^0, X, \Sigma, E, I \rangle$, where*

- *L is a finite set of* locations.
- *$L^0 \subseteq L$ is a set of* initial locations.
- *X is a finite set of* clock variables.
- *Σ is a finite set of* labels.
- *$E \subseteq (L \times \Sigma \times 2^X \times \Phi(X) \times L)$ is a set of* switches. *A switch $\langle l, a, \lambda, \varphi, l' \rangle$ represents a transition from location l to location l' labelled by a, under clock constraint φ. The set $\lambda \subseteq X$ gives the clocks to be reset with this switch.*
- *$I : L \to \Phi(X)$ assigns* delay invariants *to locations.* ☐

The semantics of a timed automaton $\mathcal{A}$ is as follows. A *state* is a pair (l, ν), where $l \in L$ and ν is a clock valuation for X. A state (l, ν) is an initial state, if $l \in L^0$ and $\nu(x) = 0$ for all $x \in X$. There are two types of *transitions*:

1. *Location switches* are of the form $\langle l, a, \lambda, \varphi, l' \rangle$ such that ν satisfies φ, $(l, \nu) \xrightarrow{a} (l', \nu[\lambda := 0])$, and $\nu[\lambda := 0]$ satisfies $I(l')$.
2. *Delay transitions* are of the form $(l, \nu) \xrightarrow{\tau} (l, \nu + \tau)$, which preserves the location l for time duration $\tau \in \mathbb{R}_{\geq 0}$, such that for all $0 \leq \tau' \leq \tau$, $\nu + \tau'$ satisfies the invariant $I(l)$.

For a timed word $w = (a_0, t_0), (a_1, t_1) \cdots (a_k, t_k)$, a *run* over w is a sequence

$$q_0 \xrightarrow{t_0} q_0' \xrightarrow{a_0} q_1 \xrightarrow{t_1 - t_0} q_1' \xrightarrow{a_1} q_2 \xrightarrow{t_2 - t_1} q_2' \xrightarrow{a_2} q_3 \rightarrow \cdots \xrightarrow{a_k} q_{k+1}$$

such that q_0 is an initial state.

Let $\mathcal{A}_1 = \langle L_1, L_1^0, X_1, \Sigma_1, E_1, I_1 \rangle$ and $\mathcal{A}_2 = \langle L_2, L_2^0, X_2, \Sigma_2, E_2, I_2 \rangle$ be two timed automata, where $X_1 \cap X_2 = \emptyset$. The *parallel composition* of $\mathcal{A}_1$ and $\mathcal{A}_2$ is $\mathcal{A}_1 \| \mathcal{A}_2 = \langle L_1 \times L_2, L_1^0 \times L_2^0, X_1 \cup X_2, \Sigma_1 \cup \Sigma_2, E, I \rangle$, where $I(l_1, l_2) = I(l_1) \wedge I(l_2)$, and E is defined by:

1. for $a \in \Sigma_1 \cap \Sigma_2$, for every $\langle l_1, a, \lambda_1, \varphi_1, l_1' \rangle$ in E_1, and $\langle l_2, a, \lambda_2, \varphi_2, l_2' \rangle$ in E_2, E contains $\langle (l_1, l_2), a, \lambda_1 \cup \lambda_2, \varphi_1 \wedge \varphi_2, (l_1', l_2') \rangle$.
2. for $a \in \Sigma_1 \backslash \Sigma_2$, for every $\langle l, a, \lambda, \varphi, l' \rangle$ in E_1, and every $m \in L_2$, E contains $\langle (l, m), a, \lambda, \varphi, (l', m) \rangle$.
3. for $a \in \Sigma_2 \backslash \Sigma_1$, for every $\langle l, a, \lambda, \varphi, l' \rangle$ in E_2, and every $m \in L_1$, E contains $\langle (m, l), a, \lambda, \varphi, (m, l') \rangle$.

3   Formal Semantics of Sampling-Based Monitoring

Given a program P, we describe the semantics of sampling-based monitoring in two steps: (1) identifying the minimum sampling period and (2) constructing and composing a sampling-based monitor with P.

3.1   Calculating the Sampling Period

Let P be a program and Π be a logical property (e.g., in LTL), where P is expected to satisfy Π. Let $\mathcal{V}_\Pi$ denote the set of variables that participate in Π. In our idea of sampling-based monitoring, the monitor wakes up with some sampling period, reads the value of variables in $\mathcal{V}_\Pi$ and evaluates Π. The main challenge in this mechanism is accurate reconstruction of the state of P between two samples; i.e., if the value of a variable in $\mathcal{V}_\Pi$ changes more than once between two samples, the monitor may fail to detect violations of Π.

To handle value changes accurately, we modify CFG_P as follows. In the first step, we ensure that each *critical instruction* (i.e., an instruction that modifies a variable in $\mathcal{V}_\Pi$) is in a basic block that contains no other instructions. We refer to such a basic block as *critical basic block* or *critical vertex*. Formally, let $inst_v = \langle v^1 \cdots v^n \rangle$ denote the sequence of instructions in a basic block v of CFG_P. Let v^i, where $1 < i < n$, be a critical instruction. We split vertex v into three vertices v_1, v_2, and v_3, such that $inst_{v_1} = \langle v_1^1 \cdots v_1^{i-1} \rangle$, $inst_{v_2} = \langle v_2^i \rangle$, and $inst_{v_3} = \langle v_3^{i+1} \cdots v_3^n \rangle$. Incoming arcs to v now enter v_1. We add arc (v_1, v_2),

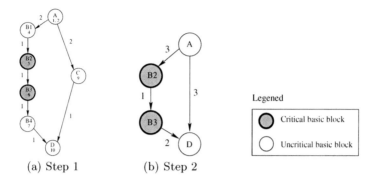

(a) Step 1   (b) Step 2

Fig. 2. Obtaining a critical CFG and calculating the sampling period

where $w(v_1, v_2)$ is equal to the best-case execution time of $\langle v_1^1 \cdots v_1^{i-1} \rangle$. We also add arc (v_2, v_3), where $w(v_2, v_3)$ is equal to the best-case execution time of $\langle v_2^i \rangle$. Outgoing arcs from v now leave v_3 with weight equal to the best-case execution time of $\langle v_3^{i+1} \cdots v_3^n \rangle$. Obviously, if $i = 1$ or $i = n$, we split v into two vertices. We continue this procedure until each critical instruction is in one basic block. For example, in the program in Figure 1(a), if variables b and c are of interest for verifying a property at run time, then instructions 5 and 6 will be critical and we will obtain the control-flow graph in Figure 2(a).

Since only critical vertices play a role in determining the sampling period, in the second step, we collapse uncritical vertices as follows. Let $CFG = \langle V, v^0, A, w \rangle$ be a control-flow graph. *Transformation* $T(CFG, v)$, where $v \in V \backslash \{v^0\}$ and out-degree of v is positive, obtains $CFG' = \langle V', v^0, A', w' \rangle$ via the following ordered steps:

1. Let A'' be the set $A \cup \{(u_1, u_2) \mid (u_1, v), (v, u_2) \in A\}$. Observe that if an arc (u_1, u_2) already exists in A, then A'' will contain parallel arcs (such arcs can be distinguished by a simple indexing or renaming scheme). We eliminate the additional arcs in Step 3.
2. For each arc $(u_1, u_2) \in A''$,

$$w'(u_1, u_2) = \begin{cases} w(u_1, u_2) & \text{if } (u_1, u_2) \in A \\ w(u_1, v) + w(v, u_2) & \text{if } (u_1, u_2) \in A'' \backslash A \end{cases}$$

3. If there exist parallel arcs from vertex u_1 to u_2, we only include the one with minimum weight in A''.
4. Finally, $A' = A'' \backslash \{(u_1, v), (v, u_2) \mid u_1, u_2 \in V\}$ and $V' = V \setminus \{v\}$.

We clarify a special case of the above transformation, where u and v are two uncritical vertices with arcs (u, v) and (v, u) between them. Deleting one of the vertices, e.g., u, results in a self-loop (v, v), which we can safely remove. This is simply because a loop that contains no critical instructions does not affect the sampling period.

We apply the above transformation on all uncritical vertices. We call the result a *critical control-flow graph*. Such a graph includes (1) an uncritical initial basic block, (2) possibly an uncritical vertex with outdegree zero (if the program is terminating), and (3) a set of critical vertices. Figure 2(b) shows the critical CFG of the graph in Figure 2(a).

Definition 3. *Let* $CFG = \langle V, v^0, A, w \rangle$ *be a critical control-flow graph. The minimum sampling period for CFG is* $MSP_{CFG} = \min\{w(v_1, v_2) \mid (v_1, v_2) \in A \wedge v_1 \text{ is a critical vertex}\}$. $\qquad\qquad\square$

Intuitively, minimum sampling period is the minimum amount of time that two variables in V_Π get changed. For example the minimum sampling period of the control-flow graph in Figure 2(b) is $MSP = 1$. Later in this section, we will show that by applying this sampling period, no property violations can be overlooked.

3.2   Constructing and Composing Sampling-Based Monitor

We now explain the semantics of sampling-based monitoring using timed automata. Transformation of a control-flow graph $CFG = \langle V, v^0, A, w \rangle$ into a timed automaton $\mathcal{A}_{CFG} = \langle L, L^0, X, \Sigma, E, I \rangle$, where $X = \{t\}$ and $\Sigma = \{a, s\}$, is as follows:

- $L = \{l_v \mid v \in V\}$
- $L^0 = \{l_{v^0}\}$
- $E = \{\langle l_v, a, \{t\}, t \geq w(v, v'), l_{v'}\rangle \mid (v, v') \in A\} \cup \{\langle l_v, s, \{\}, true, l_v\rangle \mid v \in V\}$.
- $I(l_v)$ – worst-case execution time of basic block $v \in V$.

Intuitively, $\mathcal{A}_{CFG}$ works as follows. Each location of $\mathcal{A}_{CFG}$ corresponds to one and only one vertex of *CFG*. The initial location corresponds to the initial basic block of *CFG*. Each location is associated with a delay invariant; the execution can stay in a location no longer than the worst-case execution time of the corresponding basic block. $\mathcal{A}_{CFG}$ has two types of switches. The first set of switches (labelled by a) change location. Each such switch takes place when the execution of the corresponding basic block is complete. Obviously, this can happen not earlier than the best-case execution time of the basic block. The other set of switches (labelled by s) are self-loops and are meant to synchronize with the sampling-based monitor. The timed automaton obtained from the control-flow graph in Figure 1(b) is shown in Figure 3(a), where the worst-case execution time of each instruction is 2.

The relation between execution of a program P and runs of timed automaton $\mathcal{A}_{CFG_P}$ is as follows. Intuitively, a delay transition in $\mathcal{A}_{CFG_P}$ corresponds to execution of a set of instructions in P. Formally, let $q = (l, t = 0)$ be a state of $\mathcal{A}_{CFG_P}$, where location l hosts instructions $\{l^1 \cdots l^n\}$. An outgoing transition from this state with delay τ reaches a state $(l, t + \tau)$ which leads to executing zero or more instructions. Thus, starting from $(l, t = 0)$, a run of $\mathcal{A}_{CFG_P}$ is of the form:

$$(l, t = 0) \xrightarrow{\tau_1} (l^i, t + \tau_1) \xrightarrow{\tau_2} (l^j, t + \tau_1 + \tau_2) \xrightarrow{\tau_3} \cdots \xrightarrow{\tau_m} (l^n, t + \sum_{k=1}^{m} \tau_k) \xrightarrow{a} (l', t = 0),$$

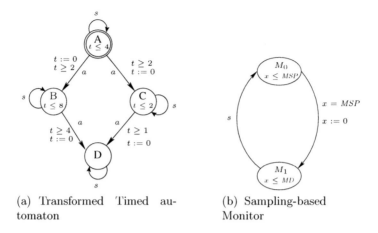

(a) Transformed Timed automaton

(b) Sampling-based Monitor

Fig. 3. Formal semantics of sampling-based monitoring

such that $i \leq j \leq m$, $l \neq l'$, $(l^i, t + \tau_1)$ denotes the fact that instructions $\langle l^1 \cdots l^i \rangle$ have been executed within τ_1 time units, $\sum_{k=1}^{m} \tau_k \geq w(l, l')$ in CFG_P, and $\sum_{k=1}^{m} \tau_k$ satisfies $I(l)$. Note that an s-transition may occur in such a run, but such transitions obviously do not change the current location or the value of t.

A sampling-based monitor $\mathcal{M}_P$ for program P works as follows (see Figure 3(b)). From the initial location M_0 the only outgoing switch is enabled when the sampling period is complete (i.e., $x = MSP_{CFG_P}$). The monitor may remain in location M_1 for at most MD time units, where MD is the maximum delay that can occur in execution of an instruction. Such delays are normally caused by pipeline stalls, I/O operations, etc. From location M_1, the monitor synchronizes with $\mathcal{A}_{CFG_P}$ on the switch labelled by s in order to read the variables of interest for evaluating properties. Thus, the parallel composition $\mathcal{A}_{CFG_P} || \mathcal{M}_P$ constructs the entire system. For example, the following is a run of the automaton in Figure 3(a) composed with a monitor with sampling period $MSP = 1$ and $MD = 0$:

$$AM_0 \xrightarrow{1} A^1 M_1 \xrightarrow{s} A^1 M_0 \xrightarrow{1} A^2 M_1 \xrightarrow{s} A^2 M_0 \xrightarrow{a} BM_0 \xrightarrow{1} B^4 M_1 \xrightarrow{s} B^4 M_0 \xrightarrow{1} B^5 M_1 \rightarrow \cdots,$$

Assumption 1. *We assume that $MD \leq MSP$.*   □

Theorem 1. *Let P be a program and $w = (a_0, t_0), (a_1, t_1) \cdots$ be a timed word of $\mathcal{A}_{CFG_P} || \mathcal{M}_P$. For all i and j, where $i < j$, $a_i = a_j = s$, and there does not exist an s-transition between a_i and a_j in w, no run over w contains delay transitions between a_i and a_j that includes two critical instructions.*   □

4   Optimizing Sampling Period and Its Complexity

To reduce the sampling points, we use auxiliary memory to build a history of critical state changes between two samples. More specifically, let (u, v) be an arc and v be a vertex in a critical control-flow graph CFG, where $inst_v = \langle i \rangle$ and i changes the value of a variable, say a. We apply transformation $T(CFG, v)$ introduced in Subsection 3.1 and add an instruction $i' : a' \leftarrow a$, where a' is an auxiliary memory location. Thus, we obtain $inst_u = inst_u.\langle i, i' \rangle$. We call this process *instrumenting transformation* and denote it by $IT(CFG, v)$. Observe that adding the extra instruction does not affect the calculation of the sampling period. This is due to the fact that adding instrumentation only increases the best case execution time of a basic block and by maintaining the calculated sampling period, we are guaranteed that no critical instruction is overlooked.

Unlike uncritical vertices, the issue of loops involving critical vertices need to be handled differently. Suppose u and v are two critical vertices with arcs (u, v) and (v, u) between them and we intend to delete u through the use of auxiliary memory. This results in a self-loop (v, v), where $w(v, v) = w(u, v) + w(v, u)$. Since we do not know how many times the loop may iterate at run time, it is impossible to determine the upperbound on the size of auxiliary memory needed to collapse vertex v. Hence, to ensure correctness, we do not allow applying transformation IT on critical vertices that have self-loops.

Given a critical control-flow graph, our goal is to optimize two factors through a set of IT transformations: (1) minimizing auxiliary memory, and (2) maximizing sampling period. We now analyze the complexity of such optimization.

Instance. A critical control-flow graph $CFG = \langle V, v^0, A, w \rangle$ and positive integers X and Y.

Transformation optimization decision problem (TO). Does there exist a set $U \subseteq V$, such that after applying transformation $IT(CFG, u)$ for all $u \in U$, we obtain a critical control-flow graph $CFG' = \langle V', v^0, A', w' \rangle$, where $|U| \leq Y$ and for all arcs $(u, v) \in A'$, $w'(u, v) \geq X$?

Theorem 2. *TO is NP-complete.*   □

5   Mapping to Integer Linear Programming

The *Integer Linear Programming* (ILP) problem is of the form:

$$\begin{cases} \text{Minimize} \quad c.\mathbf{z} \\ \\ \text{Subject to } A.\mathbf{z} \geq \mathbf{b} \end{cases}$$

where A (a rational $m \times n$ matrix), c (a rational n-vector), and $\mathbf{b}$ (a rational m-vector) are given, and, $\mathbf{z}$ is an n-vector of integers to be determined. In other words, we try to find the minimum of a linear function over a feasible set defined by a finite number of linear constraints. It can be shown that a problem with linear equalities and inequalities can always be put in the above form, implying that this formulation is more general than it might look.

We now describe how we map the optimization problem described in Section 4 to ILP. Our mapping takes the critical control-flow graph $CFG = \langle V, v^0, A, w \rangle$

of a given source code and a desired sampling period SP as input. Our objective is to find the minimum number of vertices that must be removed from V.

Integer variables. Our ILP model employs the following sets of variables:

1. $\mathbf{x} = \{x_v \mid v \in V\}$, where each x_v is a binary integer variable: if $x_v = 1$, then vertex v is removed from V, whereas $x_v = 0$ means that v remains in V.
2. $\mathbf{a} = \{a_v \mid v \in V\}$: where each a_v is an integer variable which represents the weight of arcs originating from vertex v. Recall that all the outgoing arcs of a vertex have the same weight in CFG. This variable is needed to store the new weight of an arc created by merging a sequence of arcs. For example, in Figure 2(b), initially, variable $a_{B_2} = 1$. However, if $x_{B_3} = 1$ (i.e., vertex B_3 is removed), then $a_{B_2} = 3$.
3. $\mathbf{y} = \{y_v, y_v' \mid v \in V\}$, called *choice variables*, where each y_v and y_v' is an integer variable. The application of this set is described later in this section.

Constraints for the initial basic block. Since we always want a sample at the beginning of the program to extract the initial value of variables, we add the following constraints:

$$x_{v^0} = 0 \tag{1}$$
$$a_{v^0} = w(v^0) \tag{2}$$

Constraints for arc weights and internal vertices. Since our goal is to ensure that the weight of all arcs become at least SP, if there exists an arc of weight less than SP, then the target vertex of the arc must be removed from the graph. Thus, for every arc $(u, v) \in A$, we add the following constraint:

$$a_u + SP.x_v \geq SP \tag{3}$$

Next, we add constraints for calculating the new weights of arcs when vertices are deleted from CFG. We distinguish two cases:

- **Case 1:** If $x_v = 0$, for some $v \in V$, then $a_v = w(v)$.
- **Case 2:** If $x_v = 1$, then $a_v = w(v) + w(u)$, where $(u, v) \in A$. Note that in this case, although vertex v is removed, for simplicity, we use variable a_v as the weight of the newly created arc. Also note that in this case, outgoing arcs from u automatically satisfy Constraint 3.

To make these cases mutually exclusive in ILP, we use the choice variables with the following properties:

- **Prop. 1:** The values of y_v and y_v' are such that one of them is zero and the other is a_u. This property enforces mutual exclusiveness of the above cases.
- **Prop. 2:** If $x_v = 1$, then $y_v = a_u$ and $y_v' = 0$. On the contrary, if $x_v = 0$, then $y_v = 0$ and $y_v' = a_u$.

To enforce Prop. 1, we use a special data structure implemented in our ILP solver called *Special Ordered Set Type 1*, where at most one variable can take a positive value while all others must have a value of zero. The following constraints enforce Prop. 1 and 2:

$$y_v + y'_v = a_u \qquad (4)$$
$$sos_1(y_v, y'_v) \qquad (5)$$
$$1 \le x_v + y'_v \le a_u \qquad (6)$$

The following constraints implement Case 1 and 2, respectively:

$$w(v) + a_u - y'_v = a_v \qquad (7)$$
$$y_v + w(v) = a_v \qquad (8)$$

For example, if v is deleted (i.e., $x_v = 1$), then we have $y_v = 0$ and $y'_v = a_u$ by Constraints 4-6. Moreover, when v is deleted, the weight of the newly created arc a_v will be $a_u + w(v)$. This is ensured by Constraints 7 and 8.

Now, we duplicate Constraints 4-8 for each incoming arc to vertex v. More specifically, for arcs $(u_1, v), (u_2, v) \cdots (u_n, v)$, we instantiate Constraints 4-8 with variables $a_{u_1}, a_{u_2} \cdots a_{u_n}$ and $a_v^{u_1}, a_v^{u_2} \cdots a_v^{u_n}$. We note that existence of multiple incoming arcs in a control-flow graph is due to the existence of conditional and *goto* statements in the input program. Since the depth of nested conditional statements is not normally high, we do not expect to encounter an explosion in the number of a-variables in our ILP model.

Handling loops.   Recall that in Section 4, we argued that vertices with self-loops cannot be removed. Self-loops are created when we apply the *IT* transformation on vertices of a cycle in a control-flow graph. To ensure that self-loops are not removed, we add a constraint to our ILP model, such that from each cycle $v_1 \to v_2 \to \cdots \to v_n \to v_1$, only $n - 1$ vertices can be deleted:

$$\sum_{i=1}^{n} x_{v_i} \le n - 1 \qquad (9)$$

We note that cycles can be identified when we construct *CFG* and there is no need for graph exploration to enumerate them.

Objective function.   Finally, we state our objective function, where we aim at minimizing the set of vertices removed from *CFG*:

$$\text{Minimize} \sum_{v \in V} x_v \qquad (10)$$

6   Experimental Results

In this section, we present the results of our experiments using the following tool chain. First, we generate the control-flow graph of a given C program using the tool CIL [19]. Next, we generate the critical control-flow graph and transform it into an ILP model. The model is given to the tool lp_solve [18] to obtain the

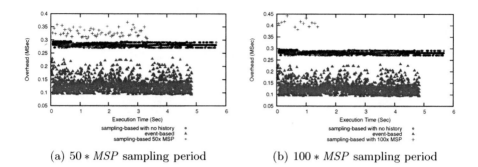

(a) $50 * MSP$ sampling period   (b) $100 * MSP$ sampling period

Fig. 4. Experimental results for Dijktra

optimal sampling period and the size of auxiliary memory. We use the breakpoint mechanism of gdb [7] to implement monitors. Finally, a Python script controls gdb and handles possible exceptions.

Our case studies are from the MiBench [9] benchmark suite:

1. Blowfish: This benchmark has 745 lines of code, which results in a CFG of 169 vertices and 213 arcs. We take 20 variables for monitoring.
2. Dijkstra: This benchmark has 171 lines of code, which results in a CFG of 65 vertices and 78 arcs. We take 8 variables for monitoring.

All experiments are conducted on a Mac Book Pro with 2.26GHz Intel Core 2 Duo and 2GB main memory. We consider the following different settings:

– **Event-based:** gdb extracts the new value of variables of interest whenever they get changed throughout the program execution.
– **Sampling-based with no history:** gdb is invoked every MSP time units (see Subsection 3.1) to extract the value of all the variables of interest.
– **Sampling-based with history:** This setting incorporates our ILP optimization. Thus, whenever gdb is invoked, it extracts the value of variables of interest as well as the history.

In the event-based setting (see Figures 4(a) and 5(a)), since the monitor interrupts the program execution irregularly, unequal bursts in the overhead can be seen. Moreover, the overhead caused by each data extraction is proportional to the data type. Hence, the data extraction overhead varies considerably from one interruption to another. Thus, the monitor introduces probe-effects, which in turn may create unpredictable and even incorrect behaviour. This anomaly is, in particular, unacceptable for real-time embedded and mission-critical systems.

On the contrary, since the sampling-based monitor interrupts the program execution on a regular basis, the overhead introduced by data extraction is not subject to any bursts and, hence, remains consistent and bounded (see Figures 4(a) and 5(a)). Consequently, the monitored program exhibits a predictable behaviour. Obviously, the sampling-based monitor may potentially increase the

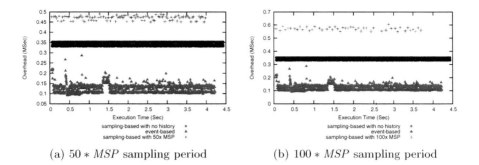

(a) $50 * MSP$ sampling period   (b) $100 * MSP$ sampling period

Fig. 5. Experimental results for Blowfish

overhead, which extends the overall execution time. Nonetheless, in many commonly considered applications, designers prefer predictability at the cost of larger overhead.

Regarding the third setting, recall that we prohibited deletion of self-loops from critical control-flow graphs. Hence, if some variables get updated in loops, the minimum sampling period of loops, can determine the optimal sampling period. For example, in both case studies, since the majority of the variables of interest are updated in loops, we cannot increase the sampling period beyond $4 * MSP$. In such a situation, employing the new sampling period and history does not achieve much. To overcome this problem, we devise a simple heuristic that makes a conservative estimate of the size of a buffer needed to build the history for loops. By incorporating this heuristic, we allow deletion of self-loops. For example, in both case studies, the ILP solver can increase the sampling period up to $100 * MSP$.

Figures 4(a) and 5(a) show the results of our experiments for sampling period of $50 * MSP$. As can be seen, increasing the sampling period results in larger overhead. This is because the monitor needs to read a larger amount of data formed by the history. However, the increase in overhead is considerably small (less than twice the original overhead). Having said that, the other side of the coin is that by increasing the sampling period, the program is subject to less monitoring interrupts. This results in significant decrease in the overall execution time of the programs. This is indeed advantageous for monitoring hard real-time programs. Although adding history causes variability in data extraction overhead, the system behavior is still highly predictable as compared to the event-based setting.

The above observations are valid for the case, where we increase the sampling period by $100 * MSP$ as well (see Figures 4(b) and 5(b)). Observe that the reduction in execution time of Blowfish is less than Dijkstra, as the overhead of data extraction in Blowfish is proportionally larger than Dijkstra. This is due to the fact that in Blowfish more and larger variables are stored in the history between two samples. On the other hand, overhead variability in Blowfish is less than Dijkstra, as the number of variables stored in the history from one sample to another does not significantly vary in Blowfish.

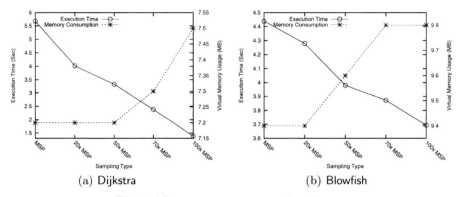

Fig. 6. Memory usage vs. execution time

Finally, we discuss the tradeoff between execution time and the added memory consumption when the sampling period is increased (see Figure 6). As can be seen, as we increase the sampling period, the system requires negligible extra memory. Also, one can clearly observe the proportion of increase in memory usage versus the reduction in the execution time. In other words, by employing small amount of auxiliary memory, one can achieve considerable speedups.

7   Related Work

From the logical and language point of view, runtime verification has mostly been studied in the context of Linear Temporal Logic (LTL) properties [2, 8, 10, 11, 12, 23] and in particular safety properties [13, 22]. Other languages and frameworks have also been developed for facilitating specification of temporal properties [15, 16, 24]. Runtime verification of ω-languages was considered in [5].

In [6], the authors introduce a sampling-based program monitoring technique. They propose a framework that allows quantitative reasoning about issues involved in sampling-based techniques. They also discuss how to optimally instrument a program by a set of *markers*, such that different execution paths reachable from the same state are distinguishable. In the same context, in [20], the authors propose the language Capilot for developing hard real-time monitors. The aim of this language is to develop programs where the monitor (1) does not change the functionality and schedule of the program, and (2) adds minimal overhead to the program. We, however, take a different approach by focusing on designing a method where predictable monitors are added to observe the behaviour of existing programs. We also present optimization techniques and experimental evidence on the effectiveness of our approach. Finally, in [14], the authors propose a method to control the overhead of software monitoring using control theory for discrete event systems. In this work, overhead control is achieved by temporarily disabling involvement of monitor, thus avoiding the overhead to pass a user-defined threshold.

8   Conclusion

We investigated a sampling-based approach for runtime verification. We explored the problem by defining it in formal terms and then showed that the optimization problem for using minimum auxiliary memory to maximize the sampling period is NP-complete. As a practical solution, we encoded our problem in Integer Linear Programming (ILP). Our approach is implemented in a tool chain that takes a C program as input and (1) constructs a time-triggered monitor with an optimal sampling period, and (2) instruments the input program in order to build a history of optimal size. Experimental results show that sampling-based monitoring provides a predictive overhead on the system. Moreover, using negligible auxiliary memory, one can increase the sampling period, which results in less overall overhead and faster execution of the system under scrutiny.

For future work, we are considering several research directions. We are currently working on adaptive monitoring, where the monitor adapts its sampling period based upon the structure of the input program. Also, one may consider developing hybrid monitors that take advantage of both event-triggered as well as time-triggered techniques.

Acknowledgement

This research was supported in part by NSERC DG 357121-2008, ORF RE03-045, ORE RE-04-036, and ISOP IS09-06-037.

References

1. Alur, R., Dill, D.: A theory of timed automata. Theoretical Computer Science 126(2), 183–235 (1994)
2. Bauer, A., Leucker, M., Schallhart, C.: Runtime Verification for LTL and TLTL. ACM Transactions on Software Engineering and Methodology, TOSEM (2009) (in press)
3. Bauer, A., Leucker, M., Schallhart, C.: Comparing LTL Semantics for Runtime Verification. Journal of Logic and Computation 20(3), 651–674 (2010)
4. Colin, S., Mariani, L.: Run-Time Verification. In: Broy, M., Jonsson, B., Katoen, J.-P., Leucker, M., Pretschner, A. (eds.) Model-Based Testing of Reactive Systems. LNCS, vol. 3472, pp. 525–555. Springer, Heidelberg (2005)
5. D'Amorim, M., Roşu, G.: Efficient Monitoring of omega-Languages. In: Etessami, K., Rajamani, S.K. (eds.) CAV 2005. LNCS, vol. 3576, pp. 364–378. Springer, Heidelberg (2005)
6. Fischmeister, S., Ba, Y.: Sampling-based Program Execution Monitoring. In: ACM International conference on Languages, compilers, and tools for embedded systems (LCTES), pp. 133–142 (2010)
7. GNU debugger, http://www.gnu.org/software/gdb/
8. Giannakopoulou, D., Havelund, K.: Automata-Based Verification of Temporal Properties on Running Programs. Automated Software Engineering (ASE), pp. 412–416 (2001)

9. Guthaus, M.R., Ringenberg, J.S., Ernst, D., Austin, T.M., Mudge, T., Brown, R.B.: MiBench: A free, commercially representative embedded benchmark suite. In: IEEE International Workshop on In Workload Characterization (WWC), pp. 3–14 (2001)
10. Havelund, K., Rosu, G.: Monitoring Java Programs with Java PathExplorer. Electronic Notes in Theoretical. Computer Science 55(2) (2001)
11. Havelund, K., Rosu, G.: Monitoring Programs Using Rewriting. Automated Software Engineering (ASE), 135–143 (2001)
12. Havelund, K., Roşu, G.: Synthesizing Monitors for Safety Properties. In: Katoen, J.-P., Stevens, P. (eds.) TACAS 2002. LNCS, vol. 2280, pp. 342–356. Springer, Heidelberg (2002)
13. Havelund, K., Rosu, G.: Efficient Monitoring of Safety Properties. Software Tools and Technology Transfer (STTT) 6(2), 158–173 (2004)
14. Huang, X., Seyster, J., Callanan, S., Dixit, K., Grosu, R., Smolka, S.A., Stoller, S.D., Zadok, E.: Software monitoring with controllable overhead. Software tools for technology transfer, STTT (2011) (to appear)
15. Kim, M., Lee, I., Sammapun, U., Shin, J., Sokolsky, O.: Monitoring, Checking, and Steering of Real-Time Systems. Electronic. Notes in Theoretical Computer Science 70(4) (2002)
16. Kim, M., Viswanathan, M., Kannan, S., Lee, I., Sokolsky, O.: Java-MaC: A Run-Time Assurance Approach for Java Programs. Formal Methods in System Design (FMSD) 24(2), 129–155 (2004)
17. Kupferman, O., Vardi, M.Y.: Model Checking of Safety Properties. In: Halbwachs, N., Peled, D.A. (eds.) CAV 1999. LNCS, vol. 1633, pp. 172–183. Springer, Heidelberg (1999)
18. ILP solver lp_solve, http://lpsolve.sourceforge.net/5.5/
19. Necula, G.C., McPeak, S., Rahul, S., Weimer, W.: CIL: Intermediate language and tools for analysis and transformation of c programs. In: Proceedings of Conference on Compiler Construction (2002)
20. Pike, L., Goodloe, A., Morisset, R., Niller, S.: Copilot: A hard real-time runtime monitor. In: Barringer, H., Falcone, Y., Finkbeiner, B., Havelund, K., Lee, I., Pace, G., Roşu, G., Sokolsky, O., Tillmann, N. (eds.) RV 2010. LNCS, vol. 6418, pp. 345–359. Springer, Heidelberg (2010)
21. Pnueli, A., Zaks, A.: PSL model checking and run-time verification via testers. In: Misra, J., Nipkow, T., Karakostas, G. (eds.) FM 2006. LNCS, vol. 4085, pp. 573–586. Springer, Heidelberg (2006)
22. Roşu, G., Chen, F., Ball, T.: Synthesizing monitors for safety properties: This time with calls and returns. In: Leucker, M. (ed.) RV 2008. LNCS, vol. 5289, pp. 51–68. Springer, Heidelberg (2008)
23. Stolz, V., Bodden, E.: Temporal Assertions using Aspectj. Electronic Notes in Theoretical Computer Science 144(4) (2006)
24. Zhou, W., Sokolsky, O., Loo, B.T., Lee, I.: MaC: Distributed Monitoring and Checking. In: Bensalem, S., Peled, D.A. (eds.) RV 2009. LNCS, vol. 5779, pp. 184–201. Springer, Heidelberg (2009)

Specifying and Verifying the SYNERGY Reconfiguration Protocol with LOTOS NT and CADP

Fabienne Boyer[1], Olivier Gruber[1], and Gwen Salaün[2]

[1] UJF-Grenoble 1, INRIA, France
{Fabienne.Boyer,Olivier.Gruber}@inria.fr
[2] Grenoble INP, INRIA, France
Gwen.Salaun@inria.fr

Abstract. Dynamic software systems that provide the ability to reconfigure themselves seem to be reaching a complexity that suggests the use of formal methods in the design process, helping system designers master that complexity, better understand their systems, find and correct bugs rapidly, and ultimately build strong confidence in the correctness of their systems. As an illustration of this trend, this paper reports on our experience with the co-design and specification of the reconfiguration protocol of a component-based platform, intended as the foundation for building robust dynamic systems. We wrote the specification in LOTOS NT, whose evolution from the E-LOTOS standard proved especially suited to this work. We extensively verified the protocol using the CADP toolbox. This formal analysis helped to detect several issues which enabled us to correct various parts of the protocol. The protocol is implemented in the SYNERGY virtual machine, the prototype of an ongoing research programme on reconfigurable and robust component-aware virtual machines.

1 Introduction

A major factor in the complexity of modern software systems is their ability to reconfigure themselves as directed by changing circumstances. This ability often relies on the component paradigm where software is understood as an assembly of components that can be reconfigured dynamically as one sees fit. While expressing a desired reconfiguration is relatively simple, actually evolving a running system, without shutting it down, is complex. This is even more complex when considering failures that may happen during the reconfiguration process.

At the heart of this reconfiguration capability lies the *reconfiguration protocol*, a protocol that is responsible for incrementally and correctly evolving a running system. This evolution happens incrementally, invoking individual reconfiguration operations on components. Therefore, a key challenge of this protocol is to compute and order the set of individual reconfiguration operations that are necessary to evolve one assembly of components into another. This is complex

M. Butler and W. Schulte (Eds.): FM 2011, LNCS 6664, pp. 103–117, 2011.

because the ordering of reconfiguration operations must never violate several invariants regarding the overall structure of the evolving assembly, and must also respect a reconfiguration grammar per component. Respecting this grammar is crucial as it underlies the programming model given to component developers. In addition, failures may happen during a reconfiguration and must be handled in a way that continuously respects both the invariants and the reconfiguration grammar.

Reconfigurable component-based software has been the subject of quite some work during the last decade [3,8,6,7], and has made its way into most modern middleware platforms such as Eclipse, Web application servers, Web browsers, and even main-stream operating systems such as Windows or Linux. However, tolerating failures that occur during such reconfigurations remains a crucial challenge [16]. The protocol presented in this paper is the first protocol, to the best of our knowledge, to tolerate multiple failures occuring at reconfiguration time.

We designed and implemented such a protocol in the SYNERGY virtual machine, an experimental Java virtual machine that is fully component-aware and strives to guarantee robust software reconfigurations. Soon after a first version was partially running, it became obvious that the complexity of the protocol required a more formal approach, relying on specifying and verifying the protocol to help not only the design and implementation efforts but also increase the confidence of the overall robustness of the protocol.

We specified the reconfiguration protocol using LOTOS NT [4] and verified it with the CADP toolbox [9]. LOTOS NT is a simplified variant of the E-LOTOS standard [10] that combines the best features of imperative programming languages and value-passing process algebras. LOTOS NT has a user-friendly syntax, and supports the description of complex data types written using a functional specification language. This makes specifications easy to understand and write by system designers. In our case, this greatly simplified the design and analysis process. This reduced gap between the specification and the real implementation of the system drastically improved the confidence of system experts in the relevance of the verification process. Moreover, the late introduction of formal techniques and the establishment of a virtuous circle between the design, the specification, the verification, and the implementation efforts, were a success. It lowered the entry costs for specification specialists because the specification could be approached incrementally, in parallel with the design and implementation of the real system. It also helped us understand the finer points of the protocol earlier, thereby significantly reducing the implementation and testing efforts.

The rest of this paper is organized as follows. Section 2 and 3 introduce the concept of a component assembly and the reconfiguration protocol, respectively. We present the LOTOS NT specification language and the specification of the reconfiguration protocol in Section 4. Section 5 details the different checks we have done and presents some experimental results. After comparing our experience with related work in Section 6, we conclude this paper in Section 7 with the lessons we have learned.

2   Component Assembly

In the component paradigm, complex systems are designed and built as a component assembly, depicted in Figure 1. Components are independent fragments of software, assembled together by wiring imports to exports. For each component, its exports describe services that the component is willing to provide and imports describe service requirements, that is, services that the component needs to function properly. A wire from an import to an export indicates that the service requirement described by the import is to be satisfied by the provided service described by the export.

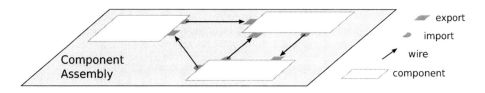

Fig. 1. A Component Assembly

To be correct, a component assembly must respect certain invariants that correlate the lifecycle of components, the different semantics of imports, and the wiring of imports to exports. There are three semantics for an import: vital, mandatory, and optional. Vital imports represent services that are needed to construct and initialize a component. Mandatory imports represent references to services that are needed by a component to be functional. Finally, optional imports express that the component may function without the corresponding services. There are four states to the component lifecycle: *registered, constructed, resolved,* and *failed.* An import is said to be *satisfied* if it is wired to an export and the component of that export is resolved. Due to space limitations, we only give below the four main invariants:

INV.1 A component is constructed if all its vital imports are satisfied.
INV.2 A component is resolved, if all its mandatory and vital imports are satisfied.
INV.3 There can be no wire from a resolved component to either a constructed, registered, or failed component.
INV.4 If a component is failed or registered, none of its exports are wired.

A component starts its life when it is registered in the assembly. It is constructed when its vital imports are satisfied. When constructed, a component has created the services it exports, but they are not yet available to use by other components. When a component is resolved, all its mandatory requirements are satisfied; it is therefore fully functional and the services it exports are available to use.

3   The Reconfiguration Protocol

The rôle of the reconfiguration protocol is to reconfigure the running system, called the *concrete assembly*. As depicted in Figure 2, the reconfiguration to apply to the concrete assembly is given to the protocol as two abstract assemblies: the *current assembly* and the *target assembly*. The *current assembly* is an abstract description of the current state of the running system. The *target assembly* is an abstract description of the desired assembly for the running system. Comparing the current and target assemblies, the protocol computes the ordered set of reconfiguration operations that must be invoked on the concrete assembly in order to reconfigure it to conform to the target assembly definition.

While computing the set of necessary operations is relatively straightforward, ordering these operations correctly is a real challenge. Correctness is defined here as (i) invariants must be respected before and after each operation, (ii) per component, the sequence of reconfiguration operations must respect the grammar corresponding to the automaton depicted in Figure 3. This correctness is crucial because it is the cornerstone of the programming model exposed to component developers. Firstly, invariants control the lifecycle of components that governs when a component is operational and when wired services may be used. Secondly, the grammar is the behavioural contract given to component developers regarding reconfigurations.

Embracing this correctness all at once is complex, so we will discuss it in three incremental steps. First, we will only consider the optional and mandatory semantics on imports, ignoring the vital semantics. Second, we will focus on the vital semantics, and third we will consider reconfiguration failures. Interestingly enough, these three steps correspond to the actual steps we followed when cooperatively designing and specifying the protocol.

Without considering the vital semantics (INV.1), the V-shape order depicted in Figure 4 is correct. During the *down phase*, it starts with *down operations* (unresolve, unwire, and destruct) applied to all components in the depicted order. During the *up phase*, it finishes with *up operations* (construct, wire, and resolve) in the depicted order. This precise order ensures that all our invariants (but INV.1) are never violated.

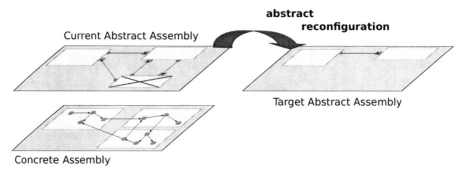

Fig. 2. Concrete and Abstract Assemblies

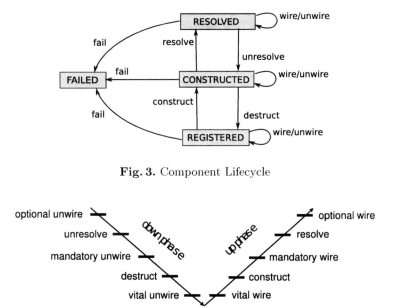

Fig. 3. Component Lifecycle

Fig. 4. Our V-shaped Protocol

When considering INV.1, this V-shape ordering is no longer sufficient. INV.1 states that the vital imports of a component must be *satisfied* before that component can be constructed. To be satisfied, a vital import must be wired to a component that is already resolved. This implies that some components be resolved before some others can be constructed, however, our V-shape protocol always constructs before it resolves. To ensure that INV.1 is never violated, we must group components in different sets that we process in the correct order.

To compute these sets and order their processing, we leverage the fact that vital imports define a Direct Acyclic Graph (DAG) over an assembly of components. This DAG is useful because it splits components into layers that can be processed in distinct up and down phases of the V-shape protocol, as depicted in Figure 5. Thus, we no longer apply the down phase to all components and then the up phase to all components. We selectively apply the down phase per layer, going down in the DAG from leaf components down to the root. We then selectively apply the up phase per layer, going up in the DAG from the root up to leaf components. At each layer, we go through the complete down phase (resp. up phase) on all components belonging to that layer.

We now consider *reconfiguration failures*: any reconfiguration operation invoked on the concrete assembly by the reconfiguration protocol may fail. Modeling such failures is important because they happen in running systems, either because of exceptional situations or bugs. It is important to insist that these failures are not failures of our protocol but the failure of individual concrete

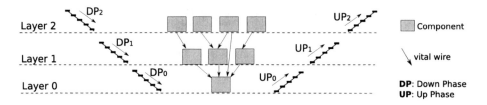

Fig. 5. Combining the V-shape Protocol with the DAG

components. Our protocol resists such failures, assists the running system to recover from them, and then continues to make progress towards the target assembly.

When a component C of the concrete assembly fails to execute a reconfiguration operation, our protocol immediately suspends its V-shape processing (Figure 5) in order to recover from the occured failure. First, it marks the component C as failed. Second, it reconfigures the concrete assembly, striving to re-establish its consistency regarding INV.3 and INV.4. In other words, the impact of the failure is propagated throughout the concrete assembly, restoring all invariants. Obviously, since reconfiguration operations are invoked on the concrete assembly during this failure propagation, nested failures may occur. To cope with nested failures, the failure propagation is a fixpoint. This fixpoint terminates because the maximum number of failures is bounded by the number of components. When the fixpoint terminates, the running system has fully recovered from failures; its concrete assembly respects all our invariants.

Before our protocol can loop over on the complete V-shape protocol of Figure 5, trying to make further progress towards the target assembly, it needs to recover the consistency of both abstract assemblies. First, since the concrete assembly has been changed by the failure propagation described above, the current assembly must be changed so that it describes the concrete assembly accurately. The target abstract assembly must also be changed; the impact of component failures must be propagated throughout the target assembly, adapting it to the new reality that some components have failed. Note that failed components are not automatically repaired by this reconfiguration protocol; component repairs are managed by higher-level protocols in SYNERGY. Comparing these two modified assemblies, the protocol loops, computing a new ordered set of reconfiguration operations and resumes the reconfiguration of the concrete assembly, evolving it further towards the new desired assembly.

4   Specification in LOTOS NT

We specified the protocol in LOTOS NT [4], one of the input languages of the CADP verification toolbox [9]. We chose LOTOS NT as our specification language because (i) it provides expressive enough operators, in particular rich datatype descriptions, for modelling the reconfiguration protocol, (ii) its user-friendly notation simplifies the specification writing, and (iii) it is equipped with state-of-the-art verification tools in order to check that the protocol works correctly.

LOTOS NT in a Nutshell. LOTOS NT [4] is a simplified variant of the E-LOTOS standard [10] that attempts to combine the best features of imperative programming languages and value-passing process algebras. LOTOS NT has a user-friendly syntax and a formal operational semantics defined in terms of labeled transition systems (LTSs). LOTOS NT is supported by the LNT.OPEN tool of CADP, which enables the on-the-fly exploration of the LTSs corresponding to LOTOS NT specifications. We give in Figure 6 the behavioural fragment of LOTOS NT we use in this paper.

LOTOS NT terms (denoted by B) are built from actions, sequential composition ("$;$"), conditional ("**if**"), assignments ("$:=$"), looping behaviour ("**while**"), choice ("**select**"), and parallel composition ("**par**"). Communication is carried out by rendezvous on gates G with bidirectional transmission of multiple values (for simplicity, in Fig. 6 we consider actions with only two values being sent in both directions). Synchronizations may also contain optional guards ("**where**") expressing Boolean conditions on received values. The parallel composition operator allows multiway rendezvous on the same gate. Processes are parameterized by gates and input/output data variables.

LOTOS NT specifications can be analysed using CADP [9], a verification toolbox that has been in continuous development since the late 80s. CADP is dedicated to the design, analysis, and verification of asynchronous systems consisting of concurrent processes interacting via message passing. The toolbox contains 42 tools that can be used to make different analyses such as simulation, model-checking, equivalence-checking, compositional verification, test case generation, or performance evaluation. CADP is widely used (760 licenses granted in 2009) and was successfully applied to real-world and industrial cases studies in many different fields such as telecommunication protocols, hardware design, embedded systems, or avionics.

The Reconfiguration Protocol in LOTOS NT. The specification in LOTOS NT consists of three parts: data types (300 lines), functions (2500 lines), and processes (900 lines). The protocol is quite small in number of lines of specification. However, it is highly complex (*e.g.*, several nested loops, see Sections 2 and 3), and its formal analysis induced numerous revisions and improvements of the protocol.

Data types describe mainly the assembly (components, imports/exports, wires, etc). Functions define first all the reconfigurations we need in the reconfiguration protocol to make the current assembly evolve towards the target assembly

$$
\begin{aligned}
B ::=\ & G(!E, ?x)\ \textbf{where}\ E'\ |\ B_1; B_2\ |\ \textbf{if}\ E\ \textbf{then}\ B\ \textbf{end if} \\
|\ & \textbf{var}\ x{:}T\ \textbf{in}\ x := E;\, B\ \textbf{end var}\ |\ \textbf{while}\ E\ \textbf{loop}\ B\ \textbf{end loop} \\
|\ & \textbf{select}\ [\textbf{var}\ x_1{:}T_1, ..., x_n{:}T_n\ \textbf{in}]\ B_1\ []\ ...\ []\ B_n\ \textbf{end select} \\
|\ & \textbf{par}\ G\ \textbf{in}\ B_1||...||B_n\ \textbf{end par}\ |\ P[g_1, ..., g_m](E_1, ..., E_n)
\end{aligned}
$$

Fig. 6. Syntax of the LOTOS NT Fragment

e.g., adding/removing a wire, changing a component state, adding/removing a port, etc). Some functions also apply the failure propagation on both assemblies, and others check structural invariants that assemblies must preserve throughout the whole protocol (these functions are used for verification purposes – see Section 5). Let us show an example: the type defining the set of wires and the function disconnect_wires traversing these wires (wires) and disconnecting those connected to a given component (cid). We can see with this example that LOTOS NT uses the basis ingredients of the functional programming style, namely pattern matching (case) and recursion.

```
type TWires is set of TWire end type
type TWire is
  twire (id:TID, cexport:TID, cimport:TID, idimport:TID, idexport:TID)
end type
function disconnect_wires (cid: TID, wires: TWires): TWires is
  case wires in
  var w:TWire, l: TWires in
      nil -> return nil
    | cons(w,l) -> if (w.cimport==cid) or (w.cexport==cid) then
                     return disconnect_wires(cid,l)
                   else
                     return cons(w,disconnect_wires(cid,l))
                   end if
  end case
end function
```

Processes are used to specify the behaviour of each step in the V-shape, the failure occurrence, and the main behaviour (down and up phases applied *wrt.* the layered structure plus failure handling). Each step is specified as a LOTOS NT process which handles a specific task (*e.g.*, removing some optional wires from the current assembly, first step of the V-shape). To fulfill its task, the process calls functions to access and modify the current assembly. For verification purposes, the process body also contains some *actions* to tag some specific moments of the protocol execution such as the reconfiguration operations, a failure arrival, or the beginning of the V-shape. We show below the process pdestruct which takes as input two assemblies, a list of components which need to be destructed, a Boolean indicating whether a failure occured during this step, the identifier of the component that failed, and the layer being processed (list of component identifiers). These two last parameters are output parameters. The process destructs each component of the list. For each component, the function destruct is called, and is in charge of updating the component state in the current assembly (current). We can see that for each reconfiguration, here destruction of a component, a possible failure is generated as well. One can observe some examples of actions (DESTRUCT and FAILURE) which will appear in the corresponding LTS and that will be used for the forthcoming verification of the protocol.

```
process pdestruct [DESTRUCT:any, FAILURE:any]
    ( inout current:TAssembly, target:TAssembly, lcompo:STID,
      out fail:Bool, out cfailed:TID, cl:STID ) is
  var h: TID, modif: Bool, currenttmp: TAssembly in
    while not(is_empty_stid(lcompo)) and not(fail) loop
      h:=head_stid(lcompo); lcompo:=tail_stid(lcompo); modif:=false;
      if is_in_set(h,cl) then
        eval currenttmp:=destruct(h,current,target,!?modif);
        if modif then
          select
            current:=currenttmp; DESTRUCT (!h)
            []
            FAILURE (!fdestruct of TFail,!h of TID);
            fail:=true; cfailed:=h
  end select end if end if end loop end var
end process
```

Another process is used to invoke the whole protocol (p10). For each step the corresponding process is called to apply the different required reconfigurations. The down and up phases are preceded by the computation of the DAG (see Section 3) which guides the order of application of the different reconfigurations. When a failure occurs, the protocol executes a LOTOS NT function which propagates the effects of this failure on both assemblies, and restarts the V-shape. The main process consists of the parallel composition between the process pfailure and the process p10 implementing the protocol. Processes in p10 (*e.g.*, pdestruct) may fail, and the process pfailure controls these failures through synchronizations on action FAILURE. We can see in the process alphabet various actions used to tag some specific moments of the protocol (*e.g.*, START, PROPAGATE, FINISH) or to retrieve some information from the assemblies being reconfigured (*e.g.*, CHECKINVARIANTS, VERIFWIRE). These actions are used to analyse the protocol, see Section 5.

```
process MAIN [UNRESOLVE:any, UNWIRE:any, REMOVEIMPORT:any,
    REMOVEEXPORT:any, FAILURE:any, START:any, PROPAGATE:any,
    FINISH:any, CHECKINVARIANTS:any, VERIFWIRE:any, ...] is
  var source, target: TAssembly in
    source:=archi_source(); target:=archi_target();
    par FAILURE in
        p10[UNRESOLVE,UNWIRE,...](source,target) || pfailure[FAILURE]
    end par
  end var
end process
```

From this specification and two assemblies (current and target), CADP exploration tools generate an LTS describing all the possible executions of the protocol. In this LTS, transitions are labelled with the actions introduced previously. Suppose a simple assembly with two components C1 and C2 where C1 is resolved and C2 is registered (current assembly). We want to add a wire between

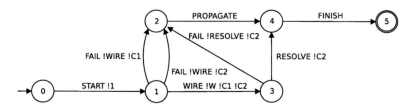

Fig. 7. LTS Resulting from the Protocol Application on a Simple System

both components (we assume that available ports already exist) and resolve C2 (target assembly). Figure 7 shows a simplified version of the LTS the protocol specification produces. We can see that **START** !1 corresponds to the beginning of the protocol application and 1 indicates that this is the first time we enter the V-shape. **FINISH** is used to tag the termination of the reconfiguration protocol. In between, the assembly is reconfigured: **WIRE** !W !C1 !C2 indicates that a wire identified by W is added between components C1 and C2, **RESOLVE** !C2 indicates that C2 is resolved. Components can also fail, *e.g.*, **FAIL**! **RESOLVE** !C2 meaning that component C2 has failed during the resolution phase. Every failure is followed by a propagation on both assemblies (**PROPAGATE**), and in this case both assemblies become the same since the protocol finishes (**FINISH**) right after this step.

Verification techniques presented in the next section take as input such LTSs. Depending on the input assembly, the resulting LTS may completely differ and sometimes consists of hundreds of thousands of states and transitions. For these reasons, we need some automated techniques to check that the protocol works as expected.

5   Verification Using CADP

We verified the following three facets of the protocol: structural invariants, reconfiguration grammar, and temporal properties. Firstly, invariants focus on assembly structures, and we checked that all invariants are preserved throughout the whole protocol application, *e.g.,* if a component is constructed, all its vital imports are satisfied (INV.1 in Section 2). These invariants are checked using functions which traverse the data terms storing the assemblies being reconfigured, and return Boolean values. The resulting Boolean is returned as parameter of a specific action **CHECKINVARIANTS**, and we use a simple liveness property to check that all these actions appearing in the state space never come with a *false* value. Temporal properties are verified by formalising them into μ-calculus which is the temporal logic used in CADP. We then used the Evaluator model-checker [18] that automatically says whether those properties are verified or not throughout the execution of the protocol.

Secondly, reconfiguration grammars ensure that components respect the correct ordering of actions (see Section 3) throughout the protocol. We verify for each component involved in a system under reconfiguration that its grammar is never violated. This is checked using first hiding and reduction techniques on the whole state space to keep only operations corresponding to that component. Then, we check that the resulting LTS is branching equivalent to the grammar using the Bisimulator equivalence checker [2].

These checks are important but they do not detect subtle errors that can occur in the specification such as forbidden sequences of actions. Temporal properties complement these two kinds of check by analysing the application order of operations during the protocol execution. We identified 14 temporal properties that the protocol must satisfy. Examples of such temporal properties are the following: *"if a component is constructed it is illegal to unwire vital imports"*, or *"there is no sequence where the V-shape is started twice without a failure in-between"*. Temporal properties are specified in μ-calculus and verified with Evaluator. As an illustration, the second property mentioned above in natural language is written as follows in μ-calculus:

```
[ true* . "START !*" . (not "FAILURE !* !*")* . "START !*" ] false
```

Experiments. Experiments were conducted on more than 200 hand-crafted examples, ranging from simple assemblies to the most pathological ones. Table 1 summarizes some of the numbers obtained on illustrative examples of our dataset. The current and target assemblies used as input to the protocol are characterized using the number of components, the maximum number of wires, and the number of reconfigurations necessary to evolve the current assembly into the target assembly. For each example, the corresponding LTS is generated using CADP by enumerating all the possible executions of the system. Verification is a time-consuming process because checking each invariant and property presented above requires traversal of the whole LTS. To reduce this verification time, we first minimize the raw LTS (using CADP reduction techniques respecting strong equivalence) to obtain an equivalent LTS where all duplicated states and paths have been removed. Hence, all verifications are performed on the reduced LTS only.

The last column gives the time to execute the whole process (LTS generation and reduction as well as checking invariants, equivalences, and properties).

Table 1. Experimental Results

	Size			LTS (states/transitions)		Time
	components	wires	reconfigurations	raw	reduced	m:s
0010	4	5	8	115/134	44/58	1:12
0018	6	9	6	94/107	52/65	1:27
0066	9	15	13	335/401	110/157	1:54
0086	11	19	27	10,353/12,598	915/1,304	2:24
0137	16	17	11	41,386/46,758	553/671	3:37
0204	17	26	48	473,935/586,330	6,696/9,257	44:15
0207	17	28	52	875,762/1,081,136	9,964/13,873	198:22

Experiments have been carried out on a Pentium 4 (2.2GHz, 1GB RAM) running Linux. These times grow exponentially as the number of reconfigurations increases. Thus, by adding only a few more reconfigurations (examples 0204 and 0207 in Table 1), the LTS is almost twice as large, and the time required for generation and verification purposes is multiplied by almost five. Fortunately, such state explosion is not a real problem in our case. Indeed, growing the reconfiguration size is much less important than covering pathological reconfiguration cases.

All the LTSs presented in this table have been obtained assuming that any reconfiguration operation on any component may fail. Furthermore, we do not consider only one failure, but all possible sequences of failures. This explains why, although our test-case assemblies are quite small, the corresponding LTSs contain up to hundreds of thousands of states and transitions. The size of these LTSs depends on the number of reconfiguration operations that need to be invoked: the more operations, the larger the resulting LTS. This also means that each failure is propagated throughout both the current and target assemblies, generating two new assemblies on which the protocol is applied again. In other words, each failure simulation generates a new test case for the protocol. Starting with 200 examples that were manually crafted, the protocol has been applied and verified over more than 2000 pairs of assemblies[1].

6   Related Work

In this section, we focus on approaches proposing formal techniques for describing and analysing dynamically reconfigurable systems. The approach proposed in our paper shares common principles with others related works that address the safety of dynamic reconfigurations through formal approaches. In particular, our V-shape ordering provides a notion of incremental consistency that is linked to the concept of a *transitional invariant* proposed in [15]. Transitional invariants are used to verify the correctness of programs during and after reconfigurations. However, in [15], such invariants are only verified on abstract specifications of programs and reconfigurations.

Our approach is also close to [20], which generates adaptive programs from formal models. Nevertheless, while our approach considers structural invariants that are application-independent, the solutions proposed in [20] focus on high-level behavioural constraints that are application-specific. Such constraints shall be individually modeled (for example using Petri nets) as well as the different reconfigurations that can be applied on the system. For each specific application, the designer can also define some properties using LTL formulas and check them on the aforementioned models using model-checking techniques.

Another set of works [12,17,1,19] aims at proposing various formal models (Darwin, Wright, etc.) to specify component-based systems whose architectures can evolve (addition/removal of components/wires) at run-time. Our approach

---

[1] This number has been computed experimentally by keeping track of all new assemblies generated while applying the protocol.

differs in at least two points: (i) we started and focused on a real implementation in Java and did not follow the classic V-shaped software lifecycle[2], and (ii) our goal in this work was mostly to verify and debug the reconfiguration protocol at hand, and not only to formalise it.

Graph grammars, in particular Reo, have been used in [14] for modeling dynamic reconfigurations of systems evolving in changing environments, and verifying properties (safety, consistency) on them. In [13], the authors also advocate the use of analysis tools to check that these changes do not affect the integrity or consistency of the system. More precisely, they show how dynamic software architectures can be specified using FSP, and some reachability and safety properties checked using LTSA. Our approach follows the same line of work, but the reconfiguration protocol is much more complex (*e.g.*, import semantics, failure tolerance, or component configuration) and therefore deserved more expressive specification languages and more powerful verification tools.

Another related work is [5], where the authors verify some temporal properties using model-checking techniques on a dynamic reconfiguration protocol used in agent-based applications. There is also a reference implementation in Java. However, analysis techniques were applied *a posteriori* on a protocol which was already working as expected, whereas we use formal verification *a priori* during the protocol design and development.

In [11], the authors present the formal verification of an operating system microkernel. They proved the functional correctness of the microkernel using the Isabelle theorem prover. The formal specification was generated automatically from an Haskell prototype, and the final implementation was manually encoded in C. This formal process helped to detect and correct many bugs in the system algorithms. Here, we focused on an alternative approach which requires much less effort in the verification process (automated versus semi-automated verification). Nevertheless, although model-checking techniques are very suitable to detect bugs in any kind of application, they do not ensure correctness of the system as it may be achieved using theorem proving techniques.

7   Concluding Remarks

We have presented in this paper a robust reconfiguration protocol which is part of the SYNERGY virtual machine. This protocol applies a number of architectural changes to a current assembly to reach a target assembly. This protocol preserves over its application some structural invariants and is resistant to failures that may occur during the reconfiguration process. Its specification and verification helped to detect several issues which enabled us to revise several parts of the protocol, for instance: introduction of two additional (un)wire phases (a single wire/unwire was originally present in the V-shaped protocol), several corrections of the failure propagation algorithm, and several corrections in the reconfiguration grammar and structural invariants.

---

[2] This software lifecycle is completely different from the V-shaped protocol we propose in this paper.

We think that this experience was successful due to the late introduction of specification and verification techniques in the design process (a Java implementation was already available, but was still under development). Therefore, we had several iterations between designing, specifying, and verifying the protocol on the one hand, and completing its implementation on the other hand. Through these iterations, the specification and verification refined our understanding of the finer points of the procotol, ultimately fixing bugs in the most pathological cases that would have been impossible to identify manually. In addition, this work shows that formal techniques and tools are not only of interest for criticial systems but are also necessary for the design and development of complex system protocols existing in dynamically reconfigurable systems.

Finally, we would like to emphasize that this was one of the first real-world applications of the LOTOS NT specification language. LOTOS NT, thanks to its user-friendly and programming-like notation, makes specification languages much more accessible to software engineers, and is expected to become mainstream for specifying concurrent and distributed systems.

Acknowledgements. The authors would like to thank Frédéric Lang and the anonymous reviewers for their comments on a former version of this paper.

References

1. Allen, R., Douence, R., Garlan, D.: Specifying and Analyzing Dynamic Software Architectures. In: Astesiano, E. (ed.) ETAPS 1998 and FASE 1998. LNCS, vol. 1382, pp. 21–37. Springer, Heidelberg (1998)
2. Bergamini, D., Descoubes, N., Joubert, C., Mateescu, R.: BISIMULATOR: A Modular Tool for On-the-Fly Equivalence Checking. In: Halbwachs, N., Zuck, L.D. (eds.) TACAS 2005. LNCS, vol. 3440, pp. 581–585. Springer, Heidelberg (2005)
3. Bruneton, É., Coupaye, T., Leclercq, M., Quéma, V., Stefani, J.B.: The Fractal Component Model and its Support in Java. Software – Practice and Experience 36(11-12), 1257–1284 (2006)
4. Champelovier, D., Clerc, X., Garavel, H., Guerte, Y., Powazny, V., Lang, F., Serwe, W., Smeding, G.: Reference Manual of the LOTOS NT to LOTOS Translator (Version 5.1). INRIA/VASY, 109 pages (2010)
5. Cornejo, M.A., Garavel, H., Mateescu, R., De Palma, N.: Specification and Verification of a Dynamic Reconfiguration Protocol for Agent-Based Applications. In: Proc. of DAIS 2001. IFIP Conference Proceedings, vol. 198, pp. 229–244. Kluwer, Dordrecht (2001)
6. Coulson, G., Blair, G., Clarke, M., Parlavantzas, N.: The Design of a Configurable and Reconfigurable Middleware Platform. Distributed Computing 15(2), 109–126 (2002)
7. Coulson, G., Blair, G., Grace, P., Taiani, F., Joolia, A., Lee, K., Ueyama, J., Sivaharan, T.: A Generic Component Model for Building Systems Software. ACM Trans. Comput. Syst. 26(1), 1–42 (2008)
8. David, P.-C., Ledoux, T.: An Aspect-Oriented Approach for Developing Self-Adaptive Fractal Components. In: Löwe, W., Südholt, M. (eds.) SC 2006. LNCS, vol. 4089, pp. 82–97. Springer, Heidelberg (2006)

9. Garavel, H., Mateescu, R., Lang, F., Serwe, W.: CADP 2006: A Toolbox for the Construction and Analysis of Distributed Processes. In: Damm, W., Hermanns, H. (eds.) CAV 2007. LNCS, vol. 4590, pp. 158–163. Springer, Heidelberg (2007)

10. ISO/IEC. Enhancements to LOTOS (E-LOTOS). International Standard 15437:2001. International Organization for Standardization — Information Technology (2001)

11. Klein, G., Elphinstone, K., Heiser, G., Andronick, J., Cock, D., Derrin, P., Elkaduwe, D., Engelhardt, K., Kolanski, R., Norrish, M., Sewell, T., Tuch, H., Winwood, S.: seL4: Formal Verification of an OS Kernel. In: Proc. of SOSP 2009, pp. 207–220. ACM, New York (2009)

12. Kramer, J., Magee, J.: The Evolving Philosophers Problem: Dynamic Change Management. IEEE TSE 16(11), 1293–1306 (1990)

13. Kramer, J., Magee, J.: Analysing Dynamic Change in Distributed Software Architectures. IEE Proceedings - Software 145(5), 146–154 (1998)

14. Krause, C., Maraikar, Z., Lazovik, A., Arbab, F.: Modeling Dynamic Reconfigurations in Reo using High-level Replacement Systems. Science of Computer Programming 76(1), 23–36 (2011)

15. Kulkarni, S.S., Biyani, K.N.: Correctness of Component-Based Adaptation. In: Crnković, I., Stafford, J.A., Schmidt, H.W., Wallnau, K. (eds.) CBSE 2004. LNCS, vol. 3054, pp. 48–58. Springer, Heidelberg (2004)

16. Léger, M., Ledoux, T., Coupaye, T.: Reliable Dynamic Reconfigurations in a Reflective Component Model. In: Grunske, L., Reussner, R., Plasil, F. (eds.) CBSE 2010. LNCS, vol. 6092, pp. 74–92. Springer, Heidelberg (2010)

17. Magee, J., Kramer, J.: Dynamic Structure in Software Architectures. In: SIGSOFT FSE 1996, pp. 3–14. ACM, New York (1996)

18. Mateescu, R., Sighireanu, M.: Efficient On-the-Fly Model-Checking for Regular Alternation-Free Mu-Calculus. Science of Computer Programming 46(3), 255–281 (2003)

19. Wermelinger, M., Lopes, A., Fiadeiro, J.L.: A Graph Based Architectural (Re)configuration Language. In: Proc. of ESEC / SIGSOFT FSE 2001, pp. 21–32. ACM, New York (2001)

20. Zhang, J., Cheng, B.H.C.: Model-based Development of Dynamically Adaptive Software. In: Proc. of ICSE 2006, pp. 371–380. ACM, New York (2006)

Formal Development of a Tool for Automated Modelling and Verification of Relay Interlocking Systems

Anne E. Haxthausen, Andreas A. Kjær, and Marie Le Bliguet

DTU Informatics, Technical University of Denmark, DK-2800 Lyngby, Denmark
ah@imm.dtu.dk

Abstract. This paper describes a tool for formal modelling relay interlocking systems and explains how it has been stepwise, formally developed using the RAISE method. The developed tool takes the circuit diagrams of a relay interlocking system as input and gives as result a state transition system modelling the dynamic behaviour of the interlocking system, i.e. the dynamic behaviour of the circuits depicted in the diagrams. The resulting state transition system (model) is expressed in the SAL language such that the SAL model checker can be used to model check required properties of this model of the interlocking system. The tool has been applied to the circuit diagrams of Stenstrup station in Denmark and the resulting formal model has then been model checked to satisfy a number of required safety properties.

1   Introduction

The task of a railway interlocking system is to control signals and points of a railway network such that the railway traffic is safe, i.e. collisions and derailing of trains are avoided. In Denmark many interlocking systems are still implemented by electrical relay circuits and these are verified by manual inspection of the associated circuit diagrams. Such a manual inspection is very difficult and time consuming and may as a result of that be insufficient and error prone. That is not satisfactory for such a safety-critical application. For that reason Railnet Denmark (Banedanmark) asked us to research a better verification method.

Our solution has been to develop a set of tools [9] supporting *automated* analysis and verification of relay interlocking systems. To make the tool set user friendly for railway engineers we decided to centre the tools around a *domain-specific language* for expressing documentation such as relay circuit diagrams that are usually made for relay interlocking systems. The tools comprise editors for creating the documentation as well as analysis and verification tools that take the documentation as input. Hence, to analyse or verify an interlocking system, the railway engineer should just create the documentation of the relay interlocking system to be investigated and then apply to this documentation relevant tools from the tool set. In [5] is described how a *graphical editor* for creating circuit diagrams and a *simulator* that can visualize the dynamic behaviour of

M. Butler and W. Schulte (Eds.): FM 2011, LNCS 6664, pp. 118–132, 2011.

the circuits were developed. In the present paper we will describe how we have developed a tool supporting the *formal verification* of relay interlocking systems. Details of this work can be found in [2,10].

We choose to develop a tool for *formal* (mathematical based) verification as this is the most rigorous and effective way to completely verify a system. Formal methods are now increasingly being used for safety-critical systems and many standards for the development of safety-critical systems strongly recommend or even require the use of formal methods. This is for instance the case for the European CENELEC standards for railway applications. We have chosen the *model checking* [3] approach to verification as this allows for full automation. Many tools for model checking exist and we choose as a first experiment to use the SAL symbolic model checker [1]. In order to use the model checker to verify an interlocking system the following must be provided: (1) a state transition model of the dynamic behaviour of the implemented interlocking system, (2) a state transition model of the dynamic behaviour of the environment giving inputs (from operators and track side equipment) to the system, and (3) a specification of the required system behaviour (e.g. safety requirements). The model checker can then automatically check that the system model satisfies the required properties. A model of the dynamic behaviour of an interlocking system can be derived from the circuit diagrams documenting the implementation of the interlocking system. However, to make such a derivation manually is very time consuming and there is the risk of making bugs. Therefore we decided to make a tool for *automated generation* of such a model from the circuit diagrams. For similar reasons tools for automated generation of a model of the behaviour of the environment and automated generation of a formal specification of the required system properties should be developed. So far we have implemented a generator for system models and a generator for one class of required system properties called confidence conditions. In the future we plan also to implement generators for safety conditions and behavioural environment models.

We did not only decide to develop the above mentioned tools for generating formal models and formal properties that can be formally verified using existing automated model checking tools, we also decided to use formal methods for the development of these generator tools. We choose the RAISE formal method [15,16] as the authors had previous good experience in using that method. Other methods such as VDM [7] and Z [18], that are also well suited for specifying data types and functions manipulating data, could alternatively have been used.

Paper overview. This paper primarily concerns the development of the model generator tool and its use. The confidence condition generator was developed in a similar way. First, in Section 2, we give an informal introduction to the railway domain, and in Section 3, we informally describe the model generator tool. Then, in Section 4, we give an overview of the formal development of the model generator tool, and in Sections 5–6 we describe some of the details of this development. In Section 7, we report on how we have applied the tool to verify the interlocking system for Stenstrup station in Denmark. Finally, in Section 8 some conclusions are drawn and some related work is mentioned.

2   The Railway Application Domain

This section introduces concepts of the railway domain relevant for this paper.

2.1   Track-Side Equipment

The considered interlocking systems use track-side equipment to monitor and control trains:

Track circuits: The railway tracks are divided into sections each having a track circuit for train detection. The interlocking system uses this for monitoring the occupancy status of the individual track sections.

Points: Tracks are joined at points which can guide trains into different directions depending on the position of the points. An operator can switch the points. The interlocking system monitors and controls the positions of points.

Signals: Signals are placed at the entrance of some track sections. They can show GO and STOP aspects. The interlocking system sets the signals to inform the train drivers whether they are allowed to enter these sections.

2.2   Route Based Interlocking

The interlocking systems we are considering in this paper use a *route based* approach to interlocking. The basic ideas of this approach are:

- Trains should drive on *routes* through the network.
- Each route is covered by an entrance signal that informs whether it is allowed for a train to enter the route or not. Trains are assumed to respect this.
- Two trains must never be allowed to drive on conflicting (i.e. overlapping) routes at the same time. *(To prevent collisions.)*
- Before a train is allowed to enter a route, the points in the route must be locked in positions making the route connected (i.e. it is physically possible to go from one end of the route to the other end without derailing), and the route must be empty (i.e. there are no trains on the route). *(To prevent derailing and collisions, respectively.)*
- The points of a route must not be switched while a train is driving on the route. *(To prevent derailing.)*

2.3   Relay Circuits

The interlocking systems we are considering are implemented by electrical relay circuits. The circuits are made up of components such as power supplies (each having a positive and a negative pole), relays, contacts, lamps inside signals,

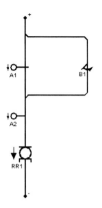

Fig. 1. Diagram for circuit controlling relay $RR1$

and buttons, connected by wires. A *relay* is an electrical switch operated by an electromagnet to connect or disconnect a number of contacts in a circuit. When current flows through the relay, the magnet is *drawn* and some of the associated contacts are connected (these contacts are said to be *upper contacts*) while others (the *lower contacts*) are disconnected. When no current flows through the relay, the magnet is *dropped* and the associated upper and lower contacts will be disconnected and connected, respectively. When contacts are connected/disconnected this may imply that sub-circuits containing these contacts become live/dead. This again may imply that relays of these sub-circuits are drawn or dropped, and so on. The system can get input from the environment:

- buttons can be pushed (and later released) by an operator,
- for each track section there is a (track) relay that is dropped/drawn when a train enters/leaves that track section, and,
- for each point there is a (point) relay that is dropped/drawn when that point is moved into a new position.

The track relays and point relays are said to be *external*, while the relays controlled by the interlocking system are said to be *internal*.

2.4   Relay Circuit Diagrams

The Danish railways use diagrams to document the electrical circuits of a relay system. For each internal relay one of the diagrams shows the sub-circuit that controls that relay. An example of such a diagram is shown in Figure 1. This diagram shows the sub-circuit controlling a relay named $RR1$. The circuit consists of a number of components connected by wires. The wires are depicted as black lines. At the top is the positive pole and at the bottom is the negative pole of the power supply. Relay $RR1$ is shown using this signature:

The downwards arrow informs that in the initial state this relay is dropped. (If it had been drawn the arrow would have been upwards.) A number of contacts belonging to other relays occur in this circuit. E.g. a contact belonging to a relay named $A1$ is shown using this signature:

The downwards arrow informs that in the initial state relay $A1$ is dropped. The horizontal bar breaks the wire – this indicates that the contact is disconnected in the initial state. If it had not been breaking the wire it would have indicated that the contact had been connected in the initial state, as it is the case for $A2$. Also a button $B1$ is shown in the diagram using this signature:

A pushed button is shown by this signature:

2.5   Dynamic Behaviour of Relay Circuits

In this section we present an example of the dynamics of a circuit. The example shows a scenario where a button of a circuit is pushed. In Figure 2 the first four states of the circuit in this scenario are visualised in a diagram of the circuit. Wires that are current carrying are shown by a grey colour. State 0 is the initial state. In the initial state, no wires are current carrying. When the button is pushed, current flows from plus to minus through relay 37, see state 1. As a consequence of this, relay 37 is drawn and its associated upper contact becomes connected, opening a second path of current from plus to minus through relay 33, see state 2. As current flows through relay 33, this will be drawn, see state 3. In state 3 no more internal events can happen.

2.6   Required System Properties

We have identified three kinds of required properties for a relay interlocking system:

- *Confidence conditions* expressing that the circuits are well-designed in the sense that (1) there are no cycles where the same sequence of internal relay events is repeated over and over again as the reaction to an input, and, (2) there are no critical races (hence the system always reacts in the same way to the same input).
- *Low level safety conditions* expressing that the rules for train route based interlocking (see Section 2.2) are satisfied.
- *High level safety conditions* expressing that there are no potential train collisions and no potential derailing of trains. These conditions are independent of the chosen approach to interlocking.

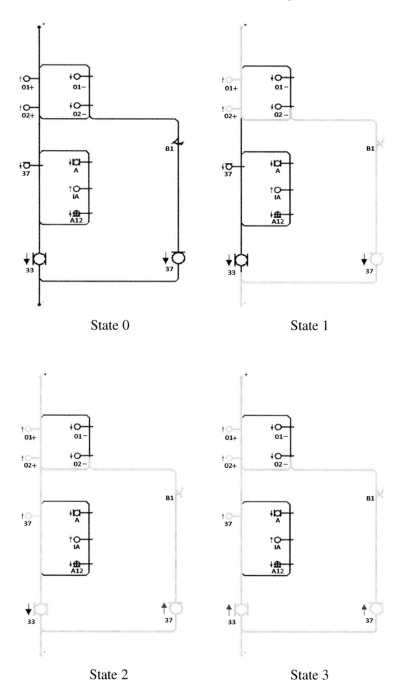

Fig. 2. A state sequence for a circuit. State 0: Initial state; State 1: Button is pushed; State 2: Relay 37 is drawn and its associated contact is connected; State 3: Relay 33 is drawn.

3   Informal Description of the Model Generator Tool

In this section we informally explain the model generator tool. Given (an XML representation of) the circuit diagrams of a relay interlocking system, the tool will generate a state transition system model expressed in RSL-SAL[1] as described below.

State space and initial state: Relays and other components change state over time. We are in particular interested in the states of the relays as it is possible to express all the required system properties as LTL formulas over their states. The states of relays depend on the states of buttons and contacts, however, the state of a contact can be derived from the state of the relay to which it belongs. Therefore we have chosen the state space to consist of:

- a Boolean variable b for each button b in the given diagrams
- a Boolean variable r for each relay r in the given diagrams

When a variable is **true** it means pushed and drawn, respectively. The initial state of the buttons is **false**, and for internal relays it is derived from the information in the diagrams.

Transition rules: For each internal relay r there are two rules, one for drawing it and one for dropping it:

$$[\,\text{draw\_r}\,] \sim r \wedge \text{isConducting\_r} \rightarrow r' = \textbf{true},$$
$$[\,\text{drop\_r}\,]\ r \wedge \sim \text{isConducting\_r} \rightarrow r' = \textbf{false}$$

The first rule expresses that r may[2] be set to true (meaning that r becomes drawn) when r is dropped and conducting current, while the second rule expresses that r may be set to false (meaning that r becomes dropped) when r is drawn and not conducting current. The condition *isConducting_r* for current to flow through a relay r is a logical formula determined as follows from the circuit diagram that shows the circuit controlling r. Current will flow through the relay if there is a path from the positive pole to the negative pole that goes through the relay and all contacts within this path are connected and all buttons are pushed. Now for a given relay there are several potential paths, $p_1, ..., p_n$, for current to flow through it. For each potential path p_i we express the condition *isConducting_p_i* for that path to be conductive. Then the condition for the relay to be conducting is the disjunction of these conditions:

$$\text{isConducting\_r} = \text{isConducting\_p}_1 \vee ... \vee \text{isConducting\_p}_n$$

---

[1] RSL-SAL [14] is an extension of the RAISE Specification Language [15] with constructs for defining state transition systems and assertions in the temporal logic LTL. RSL-SAL specifications can be translated into a representation in the SAL language [4] upon which the SAL model checker can be applied.

[2] This transition *will* be taken in any execution if there are no race conditions.

The condition for a potential path to be conductive is a conjunction of conditions for its contacts to be connected and its buttons to be pushed. The condition for a button b to be pushed is b. The condition for an upper contact and a lower contact belonging to relay r to be connected is r and $\neg r$, respectively.

As an example, the tool will from the diagram in Figure 1 generate the following two rules for relay $RR1$:

$$[\,\text{draw\_RR1}\,] \sim\!RR1 \wedge ((A1 \wedge \sim\!A2) \vee (B1 \wedge \sim\!A2)) \rightarrow RR1' = \textbf{true},$$
$$[\,\text{drop\_RR1}\,] \;\; RR1 \wedge \sim\!((A1 \wedge \sim\!A2) \vee (B1 \wedge \sim\!A2)) \rightarrow RR1' = \textbf{false}$$

Note that transition rules for external relays and buttons belong to the model of the *environment* and should be generated by another generator. For a description of these rules, see [2,10]. As in [13], we do not model all details of the environment, but only record the needed assumptions about this. However, while we record the assumptions in the form of an abstract transitions system model, [13] uses a more property-oriented specification in an interval logic.

4   Development Overview

In this section we give an overview of how we used the RAISE [15,16] formal method to develop the tool for automated generation of models of relay interlocking systems. The tool was informally described in Section 3.

RAISE allows for *stepwise refinement* as described in [8]. Refinement is a verifiable transformation of an abstract (high-level) formal specification into a concrete (low-level/translatable) specification or a program. Stepwise refinement allows this process to be done in stages. One of the advantages of using stepwise refinement is abstraction: One can start specifying the essential, generic properties of a system without being implementation biased. Design decisions (such as choice of algorithms and data structures) can be deferred to later refinement steps. For the present development we started with an abstract specification in the RAISE Specification Language, RSL [15], refined this into a concrete RSL specification, and finally translated that into a Java implementation. The two first steps are sketched in Sections 5–6.

The main component of the developed model generator tool is a function that maps a Java representation of circuit diagrams into a Java representation of the state transition system that models the behaviour of the interlocking system. It is this function that we have formally developed. Other components of the tool are used to create the Java representation of the diagrams from an XML

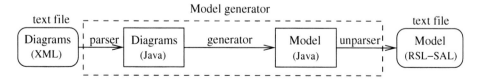

Fig. 3. Input, output, and Java components of the model generator

representation of these (to be obtained from the circuit diagram editor [5]), and to convert the Java representation of the state transition system model into an RSL-SAL representation of this, see Figure 3.

5   Abstract Specification

The main components of the initial RSL specification are an abstract data type for circuit diagrams, a data type for paths of current in a circuit (diagram), a data type for models, and a function for generation of models from diagrams.

5.1   Circuit Diagrams

A circuit diagram consists of components that are connected by wires. There are several potential ways of choosing a data representation for such diagrams. At this early phase of development we want to defer a decision on which representation to use. Therefore we just introduce an abstract type (a sort) *Diagram* for diagrams:

   type Diagram

and declare signatures (see below) for a number of *Diagram* observer functions.

Components: The components of a diagram are identified by identifiers. We introduce a sort type *Id* for such identifiers:

   type Id

There exists different kinds of components in a diagram, e.g. a positive pole, a negative pole, relays, contacts, and buttons. Observer functions are introduced in order to identify which kind of component an identifier *Id* represents in a *Diagram*:

   value
      isPlus : Id × Diagram → **Bool**,
      isMinus : Id × Diagram → **Bool**,
      isRelay : Id × Diagram → **Bool**,
      isContact : Id × Diagram → **Bool**,
      isButton : Id × Diagram → **Bool**

For each kind of component additional observer functions are introduced to provide additional information that can be found in a diagram for that kind of component. For instance, for relays identified by an *Id* in a *Diagram*, we introduce a function that returns the initial state that it is given in the *Diagram*:

   value relayState : Id × Diagram $\xrightarrow{\sim}$ State

Here *State* is an enumeration type having two values *up* and *down*, representing the possible initial states of a relay:

   type State == up | down

Wires/connections: We introduce an observer function *areNeighbours* that can be used to determine whether two components represented by two *Ids* are neighbours (i.e. are connected by a wire) in a *Diagram*:

> **value** areNeighbours : Id × Id × Diagram → **Bool**

Well-formedness: Not all values of type *Diagram* represent legal diagrams. Therefore we introduce a function, *isWfDiagram*, that can be used to decide whether a diagram is legal:

> **value**
>   isWfDiagram : Diagram → **Bool**
>   isWfDiagram(d) ≡ ...

This function is explicitly defined in terms of the *Diagram* observer functions introduced above. It checks for instance that the *areNeighbours* function is symmetric and anti reflexive, that no *Id* in the *Diagram* represents more than one component, and that the *Diagram* contains one positive and one negative pole.

5.2   Paths in a Diagram

We specify the notion of *paths of current* for a diagram (informally explained in Section 3). A path can be represented by a list of component *Ids*:

> **type** Path = Id*

The following function can be used to test whether a list of identifiers constitute a *legal* path in a diagram, i.e. is a list of connected components without repetitions, the first is the positive pole and the last is the negative pole:

> **value**
>   isWfPath : Path × Diagram $\xrightarrow{\sim}$ **Bool**
>   isWfPath(p, d) ≡ ...

We introduce a function that for a legal diagram and a component identifier of that diagram returns all legal paths that go though the identified component:

> **value**
>   allPathsFor : Id × Diagram $\xrightarrow{\sim}$ Path-**set**
>   allPathsFor(id, d) ≡ {p | p : Path • isWfPath(p,d) ∧ id ∈ **elems** p }
>   **pre** isWfDiagram(d) ∧ id ∈ allIds(d)

Here *allIds* is a function that gives the set of all identifiers of a diagram.

5.3   Models

We introduce RSL types for representing state transition systems (as those explained in Section 3):

type
  TransitionSystem ::
    initialisation : Assignment-**set**
    transitionRules : TransitionRule-**set**

A transition system consists of (1) an initialisation that is a set of assignments defining the initial state and (2) a set of transition rules. The types of *Assignment* and *TransitionRule* are straight forward and not shown here to save space.

5.4   Generator Function

The generator function that from a set of legal circuit diagrams can derive a state transition system model of a relay system (as informally described in Section 3) is now explicitly defined:

value
  generateModel : Diagram-**set** $\overset{\sim}{\to}$ TransitionSystem
  generateModel(ds) ≡ ...
  pre isWfDiagrams(ds)

This function uses a number of auxiliary functions. One of these is the *allPaths-For* function. *allPathsFor(r, d)* is used to find the set of potential paths of current through a relay r in a diagram d when formulating the transition rules for r. Other auxiliary functions are used to find abstract representations of the following conditions from Section 3: *isConducting_r* for a relay r and *isConducting_p_i* for a path p_i.

6   Refinement into a Concrete Specification

In this section we refine the RSL specification into a concrete RSL specification that is translatable into Java.

6.1   Refinement of Sorts

Abstract types (sorts) such as *Diagram* and *Id* are not translatable, so these are now refined into concrete types. For component identifiers *Id* we choose text strings as representation:

type Id = **Text**

Diagrams are chosen to be represented by short records having two fields, one field that map component *Id*s into *Component*s, and one field that contains a set of *Wires*:

type
  Diagram ::
    getComponentMap : Id $\overrightarrow{m}$ Component
    getWires : Wire-**set**

For each kind of component a record type is introduced containing a field for each kind of attribute. For instance, for relays we introduce the following type:

type Relay :: getInitState : State

The *Component* type is the union of all the component types (*Relay* etc):

type Component = Pole | Relay | Button | Contact | ...

A *Wire* is represented by the *Id*s of the two components that it connects:

type Wire = Id × Id

6.2   Refinement of Functions

The *Diagram* observer functions that were only given a function signature should be given an explicit definition in order to become executable. For instance, the definition of the *areNeighbours* function is refined into:

value
    areNeighbours : Id × Id × Diagram → **Bool**
    areNeighbours(id1, id2, d) ≡
      (id1, id2) ∈ getWires(d) ∨ (id2, id1) ∈ getWires(d)

The *allPathsFor* function (see Section 5.2) was completely specified by a set comprehension, but this is not translatable as it does not give an algorithm for finding the legal paths through a component in a diagram. The explicit definition is therefore refined as follows:

value
    allPathsFor : Id × Diagram $\overset{\sim}{\to}$ Path-**set**
    allPathsFor(id, d) ≡
      { p | p : Path • p ∈ makePathsBetweenPoles(d) ∧ id ∈ **elems** p}
      pre isWfDiagram(d) ∧ id ∈ allIds(d)

where *makePathsBetweenPoles : Diagram $\overset{\sim}{\to}$ Path*-**set** is an explicitly defined function that finds all legal paths from the positive pole to the negative pole. It is based on the backtracking algorithm in [17] and a detailed explanation of this can be found in [2].

While the other presented refinement steps have been correct by default, the refinement of *allPathsFor* requires a proof that the old and new definitions are equivalent. We have made a proof of this by informally proving:

∀ d : Diagram, p : Path •
    p ∈ makePathsBetweenPoles(d) ≡ isWfPath(p, d) **pre** isWfDiagram(d)

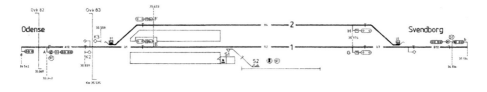

Fig. 4. Stenstrup station

7   Experiments

We applied the developed model generator to the diagrams for the interlocking system for Stenstrup station in Denmark. The station layout for Stenstrup is shown in Figure 4. The diagrams involved 4 buttons, 46 internal relays and 10 external relays. The generated transition system model contained > 61 Boolean variables and 92 transition rules for internal relays. Transition rules for the environment were added by hand. The confidence condition generator mentioned in the introduction generated 102 confidence conditions. Further 40 safety conditions were formulated by hand. We translated the model and the conditions into SAL using the RAISE tools, and then we used the SAL model checker to verify that the resulting model satisfied all the conditions.

The advantage of using our model generator is two-fold: It would not only have been very time consuming to derive the 92 rules manually from the diagrams, there would also have been the risk of making bugs.

8   Conclusions

Summary. This paper has two contributions: (1) a tool that supports formal verification of relay interlocking systems and (2) a description of how this tool was formally developed using the RAISE method.

Given the circuit diagrams of a relay interlocking system, the tool can be used to automatically generate a formal model of the relay interlocking system, and then a model checker can be used to verify that required properties always hold for the generated model. To use such an automated, formal verification approach is a great improvement compared to manual inspections of diagrams: It is faster and less error prone, it is much more complete wrt. what is being checked, and the checking it-self is exhaustive considering all possible scenarios. The approach has successfully been applied to the relay interlocking system for Stenstrup station.

The tool was formally developed starting with an abstract (property-oriented) specification that was refined into a concrete specification that could directly be transformed into Java code. Some of the advantages we experienced with this approach were:

- It was easier first to make an abstract specification in which some types were declared without a data representation and some functions were not given

an algorithm, and then later make a concrete specification in which data representations for types and algorithms for the functions were invented.
- It was easier to define data types and algorithms in a concrete RSL specification and translate these into Java, than coding them directly in Java.

In a similar way we have developed a tool that can generate confidence conditions from circuit diagrams.

Future work. In future work we plan to develop tools that from track layouts and other railway data can generate transition rules for the dynamic behaviour of the environment and safety conditions, respectively. We have already informally described a procedure for such generations, so it should be straight forward to implement. We also plan to apply the tools to larger stations to test to which extent the method is scalable without state space explosion problems. In case of state space explosion, techniques such as compositional reasoning and induction to avoid that should be investigated. One idea could be to combine bounded model checking with inductive reasoning, as done in [11].

Related work. The first author of this paper and other authors have also made research into model checking of railway control systems, see e.g. [12,11], but these systems have been computer based and not implemented by relay circuits, and therefore they have not made models of relay circuits. Eriksson [6] has formally verified an interlocking system containing relay circuits, but he used theorem proving and not model checking, and his proof obligations do not include our circuit confidence conditions. Furthermore, the other authors have to our knowledge not been using formal methods for the development of their tools.

Acknowledgements. The authors would like to thank Kirsten Mark Hansen, Railnet Denmark, for providing the initial idea for this project and for many valuable discussions and suggestions.

References

1. Symbolic Analysis Laboratory, SAL, home page (2001), `http://sal.csl.sri.com`
2. Le Bliguet, M., Kjær, A.A.: Modelling Interlocking Systems for Railway Stations. Technical Report IMM-M.Sc.-2008-68, Informatics and Mathematical Modelling, Technical University of Denmark, Richard Petersens Plads, Building 321, DK-2800 Kgs. Lyngby, Master thesis supervised by Anne Haxthausen (2008), `http://orbit.dtu.dk` (under department records)
3. Clarke, E.M., Grumberg, O., Peled, D.: Model Checking. MIT Press, Cambridge (1999)
4. de Moura, L., Owre, S., Shankar, N.: The SAL Language Manual. Technical Report SRI-CSL-01-02, SRI International (2003), `http://sal.csl.sri.com`
5. Eriksen, L.E., Pedersen, B.: Simulation of Relay Interlocking Systems. Technical Report IMM-B.Sc.-2007-04, Informatics and Mathematical Modelling, Technical University of Denmark, Richard Petersens Plads, Building 321, DK-2800 Kgs. Lyngby (2007), Bachelor thesis supervised by Anne Haxthausen and Hubert Baumeister, `http://www2.imm.dtu.dk/pubdb/p.php?5306`

6. Eriksson, L.-H.: Using Formal Methods in a Retrospective Safety Case. In: Heisel, M., Liggesmeyer, P., Wittmann, S. (eds.) SAFECOMP 2004. LNCS, vol. 3219, pp. 31–44. Springer, Heidelberg (2004)

7. Fitzgerald, J., Larsen, P.G.: Modelling Systems – Practical Tools and Techniques in Software Development, 2nd edn. Cambridge University Press, Cambridge (2009)

8. Haxthausen, A.E.: Developing a Domain Model for Relay Circuits. International Journal of Software and Informatics 3(2–3), 241–272 (2009)

9. Haxthausen, A.E.: Towards a Framework for Modelling and Verification of Relay Interlocking Systems. In: Kordon, F. (ed.) Monterey Workshops 2010. LNCS, vol. 6662, pp. 176–192. Springer, Heidelberg (2011)

10. Haxthausen, A.E., Le Bliguet, M., Kjær, A.A.: Modelling and Verification of Relay Interlocking Systems. In: Choppy, C., Sokolsky, O. (eds.) Monterey Workshop 2008. LNCS, vol. 6028, pp. 141–153. Springer, Heidelberg (2010)

11. Haxthausen, A.E., Peleska, J., Kinder, S.: A Formal Approach for the Construction and Verification of Railway Control Systems. Formal Aspects of Computing 23(2), 191–219 (2011); The article is also available electronically on SpringerLink, http://www.springerlink.com/openurl.aspgenre=article&id=doi:10.1007/s00165-009-0143-6

12. Huber, M., King, S.: Towards an integrated model checker for railway signalling data. In: Eriksson, L.-H., Lindsay, P.A. (eds.) FME 2002. LNCS, vol. 2391, pp. 204–223. Springer, Heidelberg (2002)

13. Jones, C.B., Hayes, I.J., Jackson, M.A.: Deriving specifications for systems that are connected to the physical world. In: Jones, C.B., Liu, Z., Woodcock, J. (eds.) Formal Methods and Hybrid Real-Time Systems. LNCS, vol. 4700, pp. 364–390. Springer, Heidelberg (2007)

14. Perna, J.I., George, C.: Model Checking RAISE Applicative Specifications. In: Proceedings of the Fifth IEEE International Conference on Software Engineering and Formal Methods, pp. 257–268. IEEE Computer Society Press, Los Alamitos (2007)

15. The RAISE Language Group. The RAISE Specification Language. The BCS Practitioners Series. Prentice Hall Int. (1992)

16. The RAISE Method Group. The RAISE Development Method. The BCS Practitioners Series. Prentice Hall Int. (1995)

17. Skiena, S.S.: Combinatorial Search and Heuristic Methods. In: The Algorithm Design Manual. Springer, Heidelberg (1998)

18. Woodcock, J.C.P., Davies, J.: Using Z: Specification, Proof and Refinement. Prentice Hall International Series in Computer Science. Prentice-Hall, Englewood Cliffs (1996)

Relational Reasoning via SMT Solving

Aboubakr Achraf El Ghazi and Mana Taghdiri

Karlsruhe Institute of Technology, Germany
{elghazi,mana.taghdiri}@kit.edu
http://asa.iti.kit.edu/

Abstract. This paper explores the idea of using a SAT Modulo Theories (SMT) solver for proving properties of relational specifications. The goal is to automatically establish or refute consistency of a set of constraints expressed in a first-order relational logic, namely Alloy, without limiting the analysis to a bounded scope. Existing analysis of relational constraints – as performed by the Alloy Analyzer – is based on SAT solving and thus requires finitizing the set of values that each relation can take. Our technique complements this approach by axiomatizing all relational operators in a first-order SMT logic, and taking advantage of the background theories supported by SMT solvers. Consequently, it can potentially prove that a formula is a tautology – a capability completely missing from the Alloy Analyzer – and generate a counterexample when the proof fails. We also report on our experiments of applying this technique to various systems specified in Alloy.

Keywords: First-order relational logic, SAT Modulo Theories, Z3, Alloy, Relational specification, Constraint solving.

1 Introduction

Many computational problems can be specified declaratively as a set of constraints expressed in a first-order relational logic. Safety properties of structure-rich systems, in particular, have been successfully expressed in Alloy [14], a typed, first-order relational logic with a built-in transitive closure operator. Due to its expressiveness and yet simplicity, Alloy has become a popular choice for describing high-level designs of various systems such as network configurations [24], naming architectures [17], and file-systems [15,20]. It has also been used as an intermediate logic in many program checking tools such as Jalloy [27], JForge [7], Karun [25], and TestEra [16].

Besides its expressiveness and intuitive syntax, Alloy's fully automatic constraint solver – the Alloy Analyzer – is an important reason for its popularity. The Analyzer checks a collection of Alloy constraints, looking for an instance that satisfies all the constraints, but violates a property of interest. This analysis, however, is always performed with respect to a *bounded scope* in which only a finite number of values is considered for each type. This is because Alloy constraints are translated to a propositional logic and solved using a SAT solver. Therefore, although the Alloy Analyzer can produce counterexamples efficiently,

M. Butler and W. Schulte (Eds.): FM 2011, LNCS 6664, pp. 133–148, 2011.
© Springer-Verlag Berlin Heidelberg 2011

it can never *prove* the correctness of a property – not even for the simplest constraints. Furthermore, since arithmetic expressions in Alloy are directly translated to SAT via bit blasting, they can be analyzed with respect to only a few bits. Consequently, Alloy offers limited support for numerical constraints.

In order to overcome these limitations, we introduce a new approach in which Alloy constraints are analyzed using an SMT solver rather than a SAT solver. SMT solvers are particularly attractive because they can efficiently prove a rich combination of decidable background theories without sacrificing completeness or full automation. Furthermore, their increasing capability of handling quantifiers [5,11,12] supports an intuitive, non-finitized translation of first-order relational logic. Similar to SAT solvers, many SMT solvers can produce satisfying instances as well as unsatisfiable cores that improve their usability.

Our previous work [13] described how a subset of Alloy could be analyzed using the Yices SMT solver [8]. That analysis could prove properties of certain Alloy models, but it required type finitization for handling the transitive closure operator. Therefore, a complete proof was impossible in the presence of transitive closure. Our current technique, however, handles the whole Alloy language without requiring any type finitization and thus is potentially capable of proving properties of any Alloy model. Furthermore, it produces SMT formulas in the standard SMT-LIB language, so they can be analyzed by various SMT solvers.

We mitigate the bounded-analysis problem of Alloy by specifying all relational operators as first-order axioms in SMT2 – SMT-LIB, version 2.0 [4] – exploiting the increasing power of SMT solvers in handling quantifiers. However, since the Alloy logic is undecidable, axiomatizing certain Alloy constructs such as its hierarchical type system, transitive closure, set cardinality, and multiplicity keywords is particularly challenging; a naive translation can generate undecidable formulas that cannot be proven by SMT solvers. Therefore, we have carefully developed our translation rules to ensure that (1) the translation is always sound, and (2) it performs well in practice, i.e. the SMT formulas resulting from commonly-used Alloy idioms and patterns can be proven by the solver.

Due to our arbitrary use of quantifiers, our target logic is undecidable, and thus the instance returned by the SMT solver may be marked as "unknown". This indicates that the instance may be spurious, and must be double-checked. However, if the SMT solver outputs "unsat", it is guaranteed that the set of formulas is unsatisfiable. Consequently, our approach is a complement to the Alloy Analyzer: when the Alloy Analyzer fails to find a counterexample, our technique will translate the constraints to SMT2, aiming at proving the correctness of the property of interest. Therefore, the user can benefit from both the Alloy Analyzer's sound counterexamples, and the SMT solvers' sound proofs.

We report on the theoretical foundations of analyzing the Alloy relational logic using an SMT solver. We describe the translation rules in detail and report on our experiments of applying those rules to 8 systems already specified in Alloy. We checked a total of 20 assertions using the Z3 SMT solver [6] and the results are encouraging: out of the 15 valid assertions, 12 were successfully proven correct, and sound counterexamples were generated for 4 out of the 5 invalid assertions.

$$
\begin{aligned}
problem &::= typeDcl^* relDcl^* fact^* [assertion] \\
typeDcl &::= \textbf{sig}\ identifier\ [\textbf{in}\ type] \\
relDcl &::= rel : type\ [[mult] \rightarrow [mult]\ type]^* \\
mult &::= \textbf{lone} \mid \textbf{some} \mid \textbf{one} \mid \textbf{set} \\
fact &::= formula \\
assertion &::= formula \\
exp &::= type \mid var \mid rel \mid \textbf{none} \mid exp + exp \\
&\mid exp\ \&\ exp \mid exp - exp \mid exp.exp \\
&\mid exp \rightarrow exp \mid \tilde{}exp \mid \hat{}exp \mid \textbf{Int}\ intExp \\
intExp &::= number \mid \#exp \mid \textbf{int}\ var \\
&\mid intExp\ intOp\ intExp \mid (\textbf{sum}\ [var : exp]^+ \mid intExp)
\end{aligned}
$$

$$
\begin{aligned}
formula &::= exp\ \textbf{in}\ exp \\
&\mid intExp\ intComp\ intExp \\
&\mid \textbf{not}\ formula \mid formula\ \textbf{and}\ formula \\
&\mid formula\ \textbf{or}\ formula \\
&\mid \textbf{all}\ var : exp \mid formula \\
&\mid \textbf{some}\ var : exp \mid formula \\
intOp &::= + \mid - \\
intComp &::= < \mid > \mid = \\
type &::= identifier \mid \textbf{Int} \\
rel &::= identifier \\
var &::= identifier
\end{aligned}
$$

Fig. 1. Abstract syntax for the core Alloy logic

This suggests that although our motivation was to prove valid assertions, our technique can be useful for invalid assertions too. The analysis time in most cases was close to zero seconds, witnessing the efficiency of using SMT solvers.

2 Background

2.1 The Alloy Language

Alloy [14] is a typed, first order relational logic with an object-oriented-like syntax. As shown in Figure 1, a problem expressed in Alloy is a collection of type declarations, relation declarations, formulas marked as fact, and possibly an assertion to check. The Alloy Analyzer looks for an instance that satisfies all the facts, but violates the assertion. This analysis is performed with respect to a *finite scope*, an upper bound on the number of elements of each type, and thus absence of an instance does not constitute proof of correctness.

Type Declarations. Alloy types represent sets of atoms. The signature *sig A{}* declares a top-level type named *A* whereas *sig B in A{}* declares a type *B* as a subtype (subset) of the type *A*.

Relation Declarations. Relations are declared as fields of signatures. That is, *sig A {r : B → C}* declares *r* as a relation of type $A \rightarrow B \rightarrow C$. A relation can be constrained by the multiplicity keywords *lone* (at most one), *some* (at least one), *one* (exactly one), and *set* (any number). A declaration $r : A\ m \rightarrow n\ B$ constrains *r* to associate each element of *A* with *n* elements of *B*, and each element of *B* with *m* elements of *A* where *m* and *n* are multiplicity keywords.

Expressions. Basic Alloy expressions are relations. Sets are unary relations, and scalars are singleton unary relations. The built-in relation *none* denotes the empty set. Set operators union, intersection, and difference are denoted by "+", "&", and "-" respectively. The "." operator denotes relational join: for two relations *p* and *q* with arities *m* and *n*, the expression *p.q* is defined as $\{(p_1, .., p_{m-1}, q_2, .., q_n) \mid (p_1, .., p_m) \in p\ \wedge\ (q_1, .., q_n) \in q\ \wedge\ p_m = q_1\}$. The expression $p \rightarrow q$ denotes Cartesian product of *p* and *q*, and $\tilde{}$ represents the transpose of a binary relation, i.e. $\tilde{}r = \{(r_2, r_1) \mid (r_1, r_2) \in r\}$. The operator $\hat{}$ denotes transitive closure, and is defined only on homogeneous binary relations.

Integer expressions denote primitive integers. The built-in type *Int* represents the set of all atoms carrying primitive integers. The expression *Int ie* denotes the atom carrying the integer denoted by the integer expression *ie*, whereas *int v* denotes the integer value of the atom represented by the variable *v*. Integer expressions are obtained from constant numbers and set cardinality #, and combined using arithmetic operators. These operators are distinguished from set operators using the type information. The expression $(sum\ x : A \mid ie)$ computes the sum of the values that the integer expression *ie* can take for all distinct bindings of the variable *x* in *A*.

Formulas. Basic Alloy formulas are formed using the subset operator *in* and the integer comparison operators, and combined using logical operators. In a quantified formula $(Q\ x : e \mid F)$, the formula *F* is based on *x*, the expression *e* bounds the values of *x*, and *Q* is either a universal or existential quantifier.

2.2   The SMT2 Language

We translate Alloy problems to SMT2 – the SMT-LIB standard, version 2.0 [4] as supported by the Z3 SMT solver[1] [6]. SMT-LIB supports various theories and defines a common language for SMT problems. Our generated formulas use the quantified theories of free sorts, linear integer arithmetic, and uninterpreted functions with equality, and thus fit in the AUFLIA logic [4].

Declarations. The logic underlying SMT2 is a many-sorted first-order logic with equality. It supports `Int`, `Real`, and `Bool`, and allows users to declare new sorts (types) using the `declare-sort` command.

Functions are the basic building blocks of SMT formulas. The command $(\texttt{declare-fun}\ f\ (A_1, \cdots, A_{n-1})\ A_n)$ declares $f : A_1 \times \cdots \times A_{n-1} \rightarrow A_n$. All functions are *total*, i.e. they are defined for all elements of their domain. Constants are functions that take no arguments, i.e. a constant *v* of type *A* is declared as $(\texttt{declare-fun}\ v\ ()\ A)$.

Assertions. The command $(\texttt{assert}\ f)$ asserts a formula *f* in the current logical context. Basic formulas are function applications and can be combined using the boolean operators `and`, `or`, `not`, and `=>` (implies). Universal and existential quantifiers are denoted by $(\texttt{forall}\ (a_1\ A_1)..(a_n\ A_n)\ f)$ and $(\texttt{exists}\ (a_1\ A_1)..(a_n\ A_n)\ f)$ respectively.

Analysis. We use the $(\texttt{set-logic}\ l)$ command to tell the solver what combination of theories is being used, and $(\texttt{check-sat})$ to instruct the solver to check whether the conjunction of the given assertions is satisfiable or not.

3   Approach

We translate well-typed Alloy problems to SMT2 by specifying the semantics of Alloy constructs as first-order axioms. Therefore, Alloy problems can be analyzed

---

[1] The syntax of Z3 is slightly different from SMT-LIB in the use of parentheses.

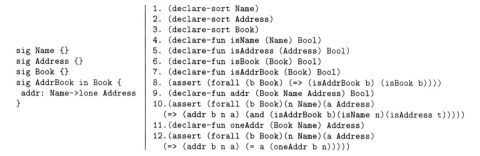

```
sig Name {}                    1. (declare-sort Name)
sig Address {}                 2. (declare-sort Address)
sig Book {}                    3. (declare-sort Book)
sig AddrBook in Book {         4. (declare-fun isName (Name) Bool)
 addr: Name->lone Address      5. (declare-fun isAddress (Address) Bool)
}                              6. (declare-fun isBook (Book) Bool)
                               7. (declare-fun isAddrBook (Book) Bool)
                               8. (assert (forall (b Book) (=> (isAddrBook b) (isBook b))))
                               9. (declare-fun addr (Book Name Address) Bool)
                              10. (assert (forall (b Book)(n Name)(a Address)
                                   (=> (addr b n a) (and (isAddrBook b)(isName n)(isAddress t)))))
                              11. (declare-fun oneAddr (Book Name) Address)
                              12. (assert (forall (b Book)(n Name)(a Address)
                                   (=> (addr b n a) (= a (oneAddr b n)))))
```

Fig. 2. An example of translating Alloy declarations

without type finitization or sacrificing full automation. However, due to Alloy's undecidability and our extensive use of quantifiers, the resulting SMT formulas can be undecidable. Thus the SMT solver may fail to establish or refute an assertion and can generate an "unknown" instance that may be invalid. We try to minimize the chances of producing invalid instances in practice by choosing an axiomatization that performs best for commonly-used Alloy patterns and idioms according to our experiments.

3.1   Type and Relation Declarations

Since SMT2 does not support subtype declarations, we translate Alloy's hierarchical type system implicitly. Top-level Alloy types are translated to uninterpreted SMT2 sorts, but subtypes are specified only through axioms. Extra axioms are needed for specifying those relations that are defined over subtypes.

Figure 2 provides an example. On the left, an address book is represented by an Alloy relation addr: AddrBook -> Name -> lone Address where AddrBook is a subtype of Book. On the right, our SMT2 translation is shown. The top-level types Name, Address, and Book are declared as uninterpreted sorts in Lines 1-3. Lines 4-7 declare an uninterpreted membership function for each Alloy type. A membership function isT is defined over the top-level, supertype T' of a type T to denote which elements of T' belong to T. Membership functions are necessary for specifying the semantics of subtypes[2]. Line 8 specifies the subtype semantics, i.e. all elements of AddrBook should belong to Book.

Since all SMT2 functions are total, arbitrary relations are specified using a function with an additional boolean column whose value is true for the tuples that are included in that relation, and false for all others. Line 9 declares addr as a boolean-valued function over its top-level types. Line 10 constrains addr to be defined only for the intended type of AddrBook × Name × Address. The multiplicity keyword lone is specified by Lines 11-12. Line 11 declares an uninterpreted function oneAddr that maps each element of Book × Name to exactly one element of Address. Line 12 constrains addr to be a subset of oneAddr, and thus to map every element of Book × Name to at most one address.

---

[2] Membership functions of top-level types are often avoidable. They are included in this example for uniformity.

$D : AlloyPar \rightarrow SMTCommand^*$ $S : Alloy\ type$

$T_i : AlloyExpr \rightarrow SMTSort$ $r : Alloy\ relation$

$E : AlloyExpr \times \overrightarrow{SMTVar} \rightarrow SMTFormula$ $v : SMT\ variable$

$E[S, v] = (isName[S]\ v)$

$E[r, \langle v_1, .., v_n \rangle] = (name[r]\ v_1\ ..\ v_n)$

$D[\textbf{sig}\ S] = \{(\textbf{declare-sort}\ name[S]),$ If S is top-level

$\quad (\textbf{declare-fun}\ isName[S]\ (T_1[S])\ \textbf{Bool})\}$

$D[\textbf{sig}\ S_1\ \textbf{in}\ S_2] = \{D[\textbf{sig}\ S_1], (\textbf{assert}\ (\textbf{forall}\ (v\ T_1[S_1])\ (\Rightarrow E[S_1, v]\ E[S_2, v])))\}$

$D[r : S_1 \text{->}\ ..\ \text{->} S_n] = \{(\textbf{declare-fun}\ name[r]\ (T_1[S_1]\ ..\ T_1[S_n])\ \textbf{Bool}),$

$\quad (\textbf{assert}\ (\textbf{forall}\ (v_1\ T_1[S_1])\ ..\ (v_n\ T_1[S_n])(\Rightarrow E[r, \langle v_1, .., v_n \rangle]\ (\textbf{and}\ E[S_1,\ v_1]\ ..\ E[S_n,\ v_n]))))\}$

$D[r : S_1 \text{->}\ ..\ \text{-> set}\ S_n] = D[r : S_1 \text{->}\ ..\ \text{->} S_n]$

$D[r : S_1 \text{->}\ ..\ \text{-> lone}\ S_n] = \{D[r : S_1 \text{->}\ ..\ \text{->} S_n],$

$\quad (\textbf{declare-fun}\ oneName[r]\ (T_1[S_1]\ ..\ T_1[S_{n-1}])\ T_1[S_n]),$

$\quad (\textbf{assert}\ (\textbf{forall}\ (v_1\ T_1[S_1])\ ..\ (v_n\ T_1[S_n])(\Rightarrow E[r, \langle v_1, .., v_n \rangle]\ (= v_n\ (oneName[r]\ v_1..v_{n-1}))))\}$

$D[r : S_1 \text{->}\ ..\ \text{-> some}\ S_n] = \{D[r : S_1 \text{->}\ ..\ \text{->} S_n],$

$\quad (\textbf{declare-fun}\ oneName[r]\ (T_1[S_1]\ ..\ T_1[S_{n-1}])\ T_1[S_n]),$

$\quad (\textbf{assert}\ (\textbf{forall}\ (v_1\ T_1[S_1])\ ..\ (v_{n-1}\ T_1[S_{n-1}])$

$\quad\quad (\Rightarrow (\textbf{and}\ E[S_1, v_1]\ ..\ E[S_{n-1}, v_{n-1}])\ E[r,\ \langle v_1, .., v_{n-1}, (oneName[r]\ v_1\ ..\ v_{n-1}) \rangle])))\}$

$D[r : S_1 \text{->}\ ..\ \text{-> one}\ S_n] = \{D[r : S_1 \text{->}\ ..\ \text{-> lone}\ S_n], D[r : S_1 \text{->}\ ..\ \text{-> some}\ S_n]\}$

Fig. 3. Translation rules for Alloy type and relation declarations

Figure 3 gives the translation rules for Alloy type and relation declarations. The main translation function D generates a collection of SMT commands for an Alloy paragraph. This figure defines D only for Alloy declarations; facts and assertions are covered in Sec. 3.2. For an Alloy expression e of type $S_1 \times .. \times S_n$, the auxiliary function $T_i[e]$ returns the SMT sort that corresponds to the top-level, supertype of S_i. Function E translates intermediate Alloy expressions. $E[e, \overrightarrow{v}]$ returns an SMT formula that encodes that a list of SMT variables $\overrightarrow{v}$ is included in the relation resulting from evaluating e. Figure 3 defines E as needed by this set of rules. Other cases are covered in the next sections. Sorts and functions declared in SMT2 are named using the functions $name$, $isName$, and $oneName$. The function $name$ returns a unique name for each Alloy type and relation. $isName$ denotes the type membership function, and $oneName$ denotes the helper function used for encoding multiplicity constraints.

As shown in Figure 3, an Alloy top-level type is translated to a sort in SMT2. A membership function is declared for each Alloy type to represent the elements that are included in that type. Subtypes are further constrained to be subsets of their immediate supertypes. An Alloy relation is translated to a boolean-valued SMT2 function. Since only top-level types are declared as sorts, this function is declared over top-level types. An extra constraint ensures that the relation is defined only for its intended types (and not their supertypes). Multiplicity keywords can be desugared to basic Alloy constraints. For example, $r : S_1 \rightarrow$ **lone** S_2 is equivalent to $r : S_1 \rightarrow S_2$ with the additional constraint **all** $x :$ $S_1, y, z : S_2 \mid ((y$ **in** $x.r)$ **and** $(z$ **in** $x.r)) \Rightarrow (y = z)$. However, since multiplicity applied to the last column is widely-used in Alloy, we optimize this case. For a relation $r : S_1 \rightarrow .. \rightarrow$ **mult** S_n with a multiplicity keyword **mult**, we declare a function $oneName[r]$ that maps every tuple of $(T_1[S_1] \times .. \times T_1[S_{n-1}])$ to exactly

$F : AlloyFormula \rightarrow SMTFormula$ $fact, assertion, f : Alloy\ formula$
$D[fact] = (\textbf{assert}\ F[fact])$ $e : Alloy\ expression$
$D[assertion] = (\textbf{assert}\ F[\textbf{not}\ assertion])$ $x : Alloy\ variable$
$F[\textbf{not}\ f] = (\textbf{not}\ F[f])$ $v, w : SMT\ variable$
$F[f_1\ \textbf{and}\ f_2] = (\textbf{and}\ F[f_1]\ F[f_2])$
$F[f_1\ \textbf{or}\ f_2] = (\textbf{or}\ F[f_1]\ F[f_2])$
$F[\textbf{all}\ x : e\,|\,f] = (\textbf{forall}\ (v\ T_1[e])\ (\texttt{=>}\ E[e, v]\ F[f][v/x]))$
$F[\textbf{some}\ x : e\,|\,f] = (\textbf{exists}\ (v\ T_1[e])\ (\textbf{and}\ E[e, v]\ F[f][v/x]))$
$F[e_1\ \textbf{in}\ e_2] = (\textbf{forall}\ (v_1\ T_1[e_1])\ ..\ (v_n\ T_n[e_1])(\texttt{=>}\ E[e_1, <v_1, .., v_n>]\ E[e_2, <v_1, .., v_n>]))$
$E[\tilde{}\,e, <v_1, v_2>] = E[e, <v_2, v_1>]$
$E[e_1\ \texttt{+}\ e_2, <v_1, .., v_n>] = (\textbf{or}\ E[e_1, <v_1, .., v_n>]\ E[e_2, <v_1, .., v_n>])$
$E[e_1\ \texttt{\&}\ e_2, <v_1, .., v_n>] = (\textbf{and}\ E[e_1, <v_1, .., v_n>]\ E[e_2, <v_1, .., v_n>])$
$E[e_1\ \texttt{-}\ e_2, <v_1, .., v_n>] = (\textbf{and}\ E[e_1, <v_1, .., v_n>]\ (\textbf{not}\ E[e_2, <v_1, .., v_n>]))$
$E[e_1\ \texttt{->}\ e_2, <v_1, .., v_n, .., v_{n+m}>] = (\textbf{and}\ E[e_1, <v_1, .., v_n>]\ E[e_2, <v_{n+1}, .., v_{n+m}>])$
$E[e_1.e_2, <v_1, .., v_{n-1}, v_{n+2}.., v_{n+m}>] = (\textbf{exists}\ (w\ T_n[e_1])$
                       $(\textbf{and}\ E[e_1, <v_1, .., v_{n-1}, w>]\ E[e_2, <w, v_{n+2}, .., v_{n+m}>]))$

$E[\textbf{none}, v] = \textbf{false}$
$E[x, v] = (\texttt{=}\ x\ v)$

Fig. 4. Translation rules for Alloy formulas

one element of $T_1[S_n]$. For `lone`, elements of r must be included in $oneName[r]$, for `some`, r must include all elements of $oneName[r]$ that belong to the intended type of $S_1 \times .. \times S_n$, and for `one`, both conditions must hold.

3.2 Formulas

Figure 4 gives the translation rules for Alloy facts (that are assumed to be true) and assertions (that are intended to be checked). We negate an assertion so that any instance found by the SMT solver will be a counterexample to the assertion. If the solver finds no instances, the assertion is proven correct.

In addition to the translation functions defined in Figure 3, Figure 4 uses the function F to translate Alloy formulas. Negation, conjunction, and disjunction in Alloy are mapped to those in SMT2. A quantified Alloy formula ($\textbf{Q}\ x : e\,|\,f$) is translated to an SMT formula that bounds x to $T_1[e]$, and uses either an implication (for universal quantifiers) or a conjunction (for existential quantifiers) of e to constrain the values of x. The notation $[v/x]$ substitutes v for all occurrences of x^3. The Alloy formula (e_1 `in` e_2) is well-formed only when $arity[e_1] = arity[e_2]$ and is translated by specifying that every element of e_1 is included in e_2.

$E[e, <v_1, .., v_n>]$ produces an SMT formula that encodes that $<v_1, .., v_n>$ is included in the relation corresponding to e. Since the original Alloy constraints are well-typed, $n = arity[e]$. Defining E for relational transpose, union, intersection, and difference is straightforward. An expression e_1`->`e_2 contains a tuple $<v_1, .., v_n, .., v_{n+m}>$ iff e_1 contains $<v_1, .., v_n>$ and e_2 contains $<v_{n+1}, .., v_{n+m}>$ where $n = arity[e_1]$ and $m = arity[e_2]$. Relational join is similar except that it requires an existentially quantified variable for the merged column of the two relations. $E[\textbf{none}, v] = false$ because $none$ denotes the empty set, and the scalar case of $E[x, v]$ is defined as equality. Since in the expression $E[x, v]$, the variable x is declared in Alloy and v in SMT2, the formula ($\texttt{=}\ x\ v$) is not well-formed by itself. However, the translation rules will substitute an SMT variable for x after this formula is plugged in its enclosing formula.

---

[3] Alloy's universal quantifiers cannot be applied to non-unary relations, and existential quantifies over non-unary relations can be desugared using multiple unary relations.

1. (**declare-fun** $trName[r]$ (**Int** $T_1[r]$ $T_2[r]$) **Bool**)
2. (**assert** (**forall** (i **Int**) (v_1 $T_1[r]$) (v_2 $T_2[r]$)) (=> (< i 1) (**not** ($trName[r]$ i v_1 v_2)))))
3. (**assert** (**forall** (v_1 $T_1[r]$) (v_2 $T_2[r]$)) (= ($trName[r]$ 1 v_1 v_2) $E[r,$ <v_1, v_2>])))
4. (**assert** (**forall** (i **Int**) (v_1 $T_1[r]$) (v_2 $T_2[r]$)) (=> (> i 1)
    (= ($trName[r]$ i v_1 v_2) (**or** ($trName[r]$ (- i 1) v_1 v_2)
                (**exists** (w $T_1[r]$) (**and** ($trName[r]$ (- i 1) v_1 w)$E[r,$ <w, v_2>]))))))))
$E[\hat{\ }r,$ <v_1, v_2>] = (**exists** (i **Int**) ($trName[r]$ i v_1 v_2))

Fig. 5. Translation rules for the transitive closure of a relation r

3.3 Transitive Closure

The Alloy expression $\hat{\ }r$ computes the smallest symmetric and transitive relation that contains r where $r : S \rightarrow S$ is a binary homogeneous relation. Since the Alloy Analyzer checks Alloy problems with respect to finite scopes, it soundly unrolls $\hat{\ }r$ to $r+r.r+..+r^{(n)}$ where n is the upper bound on the size of S. In our analysis, however, types are infinite and so any finite unrolling of transitive closure will be unsound. Figure 5 gives our axioms using an integer-based inductive definition. In the interest of space, here we only describe the translation of $\hat{\ }r$ where r is a relation explicitly declared in Alloy. The general case of $\hat{\ }e$ requires normalizing the expression e and applying a generalized version of these rules.

Line 1 of Figure 5 declares a helper SMT function $trName[r]$ to compute transitive closure. For any integer i, ($trName[r]$ i) denotes the expression $r + r.r + .. + r^{(i)}$. This is specified inductively (on the value of i) using axioms 2-4. Line 2 specifies that ($trName[r]$ i) does not contain any elements if $i < 1$. Line 3 constrains the base case of ($trName[r]$ 1) to be equal to r, and Line 4 specifies ($trName[r]$ i) in terms of ($trName[r]$ ($i - 1$)) for $i > 1$. Finally, the definition of E specifies that a pair <v_1, v_2> is included in the relation resulting from evaluating $\hat{\ }r$ iff <v_1, v_2> is included in ($trName[r]$ i) for some integer i.

3.4 Integer Expressions

Arithmetic expressions in Alloy are handled by bit blasting, using a fixed, user-defined bitwidth (usually less than 7 [1]). Overflows are truncated silently. Better handling of arithmetic expressions was needed in many applications [26]. Thus we deviate from the Alloy's behavior and translate integer expressions using the SMT2 theory of linear integer arithmetic that supports infinite integers.

Figure 6 gives the rules. Function I translates an Alloy integer expression to an SMT2 expression of type integer. Alloy's built-in type Int is mapped to the SMT2's built-in sort Int. Unlike Alloy that distinguishes between integer atoms and primitive integers, the SMT logic allows a single integer type. Comparison and arithmetic operators in Alloy are translated to those in SMT2. $E[Int\ ie, v]$ specifies that a variable v corresponds to the atom carrying ie iff the (integer) values of v and $I[ie]$ are equal. The int operator becomes the identity function.

In the interest of space, we discuss the translation of #r where r is a unary relation explicitly declared in Alloy. The general case of #e requires normalizing the expression e and applying a generalized version of the rules. Our approach allows the cardinality of a (possibly cyclic) relation to be arbitrarily large (but finite). To compute #r, we define a mapping $ordName[r]$ from every element of

$I : AlloyIntExpr \rightarrow SMTExpr$ $ie : Alloy\ integer\ expression$

$T_1[\textbf{Int}] = \textbf{Int}$ $n : Number$

$F[ie_1\ intComp\ ie_2] = (intComp\ I[ie_1]\ I[ie_2])$

$E[\textbf{Int}\ ie, v] = (=\ I[ie]\ v)$

$E[\textbf{Int}, v] = true$ if v is of type Int, $false$ otherwise

$I[n] = n$

$I[\textbf{int}\ x] = x$

$I[ie_1\ intOp\ ie_2] = (intOp\ I[ie_1]\ I[ie_2])$

$I[\#r] = crdName[r]$

$I[(\textbf{sum}\ x : r\ |\ ie)] = (sumName[r]\ 1\ crdName[r])$

1.(**declare-fun** $crdName[r]$ () **Int**)

2.(**declare-fun** $ordName[r]$ ($T_1[r]$) **Int**)

3.(**declare-fun** $invName[r]$ (**Int**) $T_1[r]$)

4.(**declare-fun** $trgName[r]$ (**Int**) **Bool**)

5.(**assert** (**and** (>= $crdName[r]$ 0) (=> (= $crdName[r]$ 0)(**forall** (v $T_1[r]$) (**not** $E[r, v]$))))))

6.(**assert** (**forall** (v $T_1[r]$)(=> $E[r, v]$ (**and** (<= 1 ($ordName[r]$ v)) (<= ($ordName[r]$ v) $crdName[r]$))))))

7.(**assert** (**forall** (v $T_1[r]$)(=> $E[r, v]$(= v ($invName[r]$ ($ordName[r]$ v))))))

8.(**assert** (**forall** (i **Int**)(=> (**and** (<= 1 i)(<= i $crdName[r]$))(= i ($ordName[r]$ ($invName[r]$ i))))))

9.(**assert** (**forall** (i **Int**)(=> (**and** (<= 1 i)(<=i $crdName[r]$)) $E[r, (invName[r]i)]$):**pat** {($trgName[r]$ i)}))

10.(**assert** (=> (< 0 $crdName[r]$) ($trgName[r]$ 1)))

11.(**assert** (**forall** (i **Int**)(=> (**and** (<= 1 i)(< i $crdName[r]$))($trgName[r]$(+ i 1))) :**pat** {($trgName[r]$ i)}))

12.(**declare-fun** $sumName[r]$ (**Int Int**) **Int**)

Fig. 6. Translation rules for Alloy integer expressions

1. $(name[r]\ v_1\ ..\ v_n) = (=\ v_n(oneName[r]\ v_1\ ..\ v_{n-1}))$ if r is a function

2. $cardName[none] = 0$, $cardName[e] = 1$ if e is a singleton relation

3. (**forall** (v $Sort[w]$) (=> (= v w) f)) = $f[w/v]$

4. (**exists** (v $Sort[w]$) (**and** (= v w) f)) = $f[w/v]$

5. (**and** (**forall** (v T)(=> f_1 f_2)) (**forall** (w T)(=> f_2 f_1))) = (**forall** (v T)(= f_1 f_2))

Fig. 7. Simplification rules

r to one distinct integer $i \geq 1$. We constrain the integers to be consecutive so that $\#r$ is the largest integer used in the mapping. Lines 1-4 of Figure 6 define the helper functions. Line 5 specifies that $crdName[r] \geq 0$ and if it is 0, then r must be empty. Lines 6-9 specify that $invName[r]$ is the inverse of $ordName[r]$ and that there is a one-to-one correspondence between the elements of r and the integers $1 \leq i \leq crdName[r]$. Thus $crdName[r] = |r|$. (The existence of $crdName[r]$ ensures that $|r|$ is finite.) Since the Z3 SMT solver instantiates universal quantifiers based on the ground terms syntactically used in the formulas, we introduce the helper function $trgName[r]$ to ensure that the numeric axioms are sufficiently instantiated. Lines 10 and 11 constrain ($trgName[r]$ i) to be $true$ for $1 \leq i \leq |r|$ which triggers the instantiation of Axiom 9, which in turn triggers the instantiation of the other axioms.

Leino et.al. [18] introduced efficient first-order axioms for comprehensions of the form $Q\{L \leq i < H, T\}$ where Q is a function (e.g. sum, min), L and H are the lower and upper bounds on the integer i, and T is an integer term based on i. Alloy's *sum* expressions are computed over integer-carrying relations. Thus no integer bounds are explicitly available. However, using our cardinality axioms, we have $(sum\ x : r\ |\ ie) = sum\{1 \leq i \leq |r|,\ I[ie][invName[i]/x]\}$ which makes Leino's axioms and patterns directly applicable. Figure 6 declares $sumName[r]$ to compute this sum expression for the required integer bounds. Definition of $sumName[r]$ is based on Leino's axioms and is skipped in the interest of space.

3.5   Simplifications

The SMT formulas generated by previous rules can be substantially simplified while their semantics is preserved. Out of the 12 Alloy assertions proven successfully in our experiments (see Sec. 4), only 3 can be proven before simplification.

   The simplification rules are given in Figure 7. Rule 1 simplifies the expressions involving functional relations. For any Alloy relation $r : S_1 \rightarrow .. \rightarrow$ **one** S_n, a tuple $<v_1, .., v_n>$ is included in the corresponding function $name[r]$ iff $v_n = (oneName[r]\ v_1, .., v_{n-1})$. Rule 2 simplifies cardinality for the obvious cases of empty and singleton relations. This is determined syntactically based on the type information. Rules 3 and 4 eliminate quantifiers based on the semantics of scalar values. They substitute the free variable w for the quantified variable v used in a formula f. These rules are valid because w represents a single value in $Sort[w]$. Rule 3 holds since in any logical context, $(\forall v : Sort[w]\ |\ ((v = w) \implies f)) \equiv (\forall v \in \{w\}\ |\ f) \equiv f[w/v]$, and Rule 4 holds because $(\exists v : Sort[w]\ |\ ((v = w) \wedge f)) \equiv (\exists v \in \{w\}\ |\ f) \equiv f[w/v]$. Rule 5 converts the equality hidden in bidirectional implications to an explicit equality. It is applied when f_1 and f_2 are syntactically identical except possibly for the names of the bound variables; no decision procedure calls are involved.

   Simplification is done in multiple passes. The first pass applies Rules 1 and 2 to all formulas. Consecutive passes apply Rules 3-5 iteratively until no more rules are applicable. Since these rules strictly reduce the number of quantifiers, this process terminates.

3.6   Correctness

An Alloy problem is a structure $AP = <T_{top}, T_{sub}, R, F>$ where T_{top}, T_{sub}, R, and F respectively denote the set of top-level types, subtypes, relations, and formulas[4] declared in AP. An Alloy instance $I_a = (U_a, v_a)$ defines a universe of atoms U_a and a valuation v_a that maps every type and relation of AP to a set of elements and tuples derived from U_a, respectively. I_a satisfies AP iff

 - Types are well-formed. That is, (1) for $t \in T_{sub}$ that is a subtype of $t' \in T_{top} \cup T_{sub}$, we have $v_a(t) \subseteq v_a(t')$, and (2) for $t, t' \in T_{top}$, we have $v_a(t) \cap v_a(t') = \emptyset$.
 - Relations are well-formed. That is, for $r \in R$ of type $t_1 \rightarrow .. \rightarrow [m]\ t_n$, we have $v_a(r) \subseteq v_a(t_1) \times .. \times v_a(t_n)$ and the multiplicity constraint of m holds.
 - Any $f \in F$ evaluates to true under I_a. That is, $[\![f]\!]^{I_a} = true$ where $[\![]\!]^{I_a}$ is defined inductively on the grammar of Figure 1 (see [14]).

Similarly, an SMT2 problem is a structure $SP = <S, G, A>$ where S, G, and A respectively denote the set of sorts, functions, and assertions declared in SP.

---

[4] We assume that the assertion is negated and conjoined with the formula F.

An SMT instance $I_s = (U_s, v_s)$ defines a universe of elements U_s and a valuation v_s that defines the values of sorts and functions. An instance I_s satisfies SP iff

- Sorts are well-formed. That is, for $s, s' \in S$, we have $v_s(s) \cap v_s(s') = \emptyset$.
- Functions are well-formed. That is, for $g \in G$ of type $(s_1 \,..\, s_n \; s)$, $v_s(g)$ gives a total function from $v_s(s_1) \times .. \times v_s(s_n)$ to $v_s(s)$.
- Any $a \in A$ evaluates to true under I_s. That is, $[\![a]\!]^{I_s} = true$ where $[\![\,]\!]^{I_s}$ is defined inductively for SMT2 formulas (see [4]).

Our analysis complements that of the Alloy Analyzer by providing proof capability. Thus to show its soundness, it is sufficient to show that for any Alloy problem AP, if our SMT2 translation $D[AP]$ is unsatisfiable, implying that the assertion in AP is a tautology, then AP is unsatisfiable too. But since Alloy computes arithmetic with respect to a fixed bitwidth, mathematically valid numeric formulas (based on infinite integers) may be invalid in Alloy due to overflows[5]. Thus unsatisfiability of $D[AP]$ implies unsatisfiability of AP only in the absence of integer overflows, or equivalently, the following theorem holds:

Theorem 1. *If an Alloy problem $AP =< T_{top}, T_{sub}, R, F >$ has a satisfying instance for which none of the arithmetic computations overflow, its translation $D[AP] =< S, G, A >$ has a satisfying instance too.*

Proof. For any instance $I_a = (U_a, v_a)$ that satisfies AP, we construct an instance $I_s = (U_s, v_s)$ that satisfies $D[AP]$. Without loss of generality, we define $U_s = U_a$, and define v_s as follows. For $s \in S$ corresponding to $t \in T_{top}$, define $v_s(s) = v_a(t)$. For $g \in G$, (1) if g is a membership function for $t \in T_{top} \cup T_{sub}$, then $(v_s(g)[u] = true) \leftrightarrow (u \in v_a(t))$ for all $u \in U_a$, (2) if g is a boolean-valued function for $r \in R$, then $(v_s(g)[u_1, .., u_n] = true) \leftrightarrow (<u_1, .., u_n> \in v_a(r))$, (3) if g is a multiplicity function for $r \in R$, then $(v_s(g)[u_1, .., u_{n-1}] = u_n) \Rightarrow (<u_1, .., u_n> \in v_a(r))$ for multiplicities "some" and "one", and $(<u_1, .., u_n> \in v_a(r)) \Rightarrow (v_s(g)[u_1, .., u_{n-1}] = u_n)$ for "lone", (4) if g corresponds to $\hat{}\,r$, then for $1 \leq i \leq |U_a|$, define $v_s(g)[i, u_1, u_2] = true \Leftrightarrow <u_1, u_2> \in v_a(r) \cup v_a(r).v_a(r) \cup .. \cup v_a(r)^{(i)}$. For $i > |U_a|$, define $v_s(g)[i, u_1, u_2] = v_s(g)[|U_a|, u_1, u_2]$, and (5) for cardinality-related g, let $v_s(g) = |v_a(r)|$ if g is $crdName[r]$, $(v_s(g)[u_i] = i) \Leftrightarrow (v_a(r) = \{u_1, .., u_n\})$ if g is $ordName[r]$, $(v_s(g)[i] = u_i) \Leftrightarrow (v_a(r) = \{u_1, .., u_n\})$ if g is $invName[r]$, and $(v_s(g)[i] = true) \Leftrightarrow (1 \leq i \leq |v_a(r)|)$ if g is $trgName[r]$. Sorts and functions are well-formed under I_s because types and relations are well-formed under I_a. The property $[\![a]\!]^{I_s} = true$ is proved by cases: it holds for the assertions produced by each translation rule based on the semantics of Alloy and SMT2. Absence of integer overflows ensures that any arithmetic computation yields the same result in both logics. Details are skipped in the interest of space.

4   Experiments

We have evaluated our technique by checking 20 assertions in 8 Alloy problems[6]: the address book of an email client where aliases and groups are allowed, the

---

[5] For example, $2 + 2 > 2$ does not hold in Alloy with a bitwidth of 3.
[6] Available at http://www.rz.uni-karlsruhe.de/~ kh133/alloyToSMT/

query interface and aggregation mechanism of Microsoft COM, the operations of a memory accessed by abstract addresses, a system for managing media files, the mark and sweep garbage collection algorithm, the own-grandpa puzzle, and a hand shaking protocol among spouses. The Alloy models of these problems are included in the Alloy 4 distribution, and represent various combinations of hierarchical types, nested relational joins, transitive closure, nested quantifiers, set cardinality, and arithmetic operations[7]. To further check our arithmetic rules, we also translated the queens' arrangement puzzle for an $n \times n$ chessboard [1].

We applied our translation and simplification rules to these models and used Z3 2.16 to solve the resulting SMT formulas. Table 1 gives the results. It also reports on the performance of the Alloy Analyzer 4 (AA). The time (in second) is measured on an Intel Core2Quad, 2.8GHz, 8GB memory. The Alloy analysis time is the total of the time spent on generating CNF and solving it using the SAT4J solver. The Z3 analysis time is what it reports using the *-st* option.

The assertions in the top part of the table are expected to be valid, i.e. their Alloy models contain developers' comments that no counterexamples are expected. The scope column in this case denotes the maximum scope for which AA can check the assertion before reaching the time-out of 180 seconds. The result column gives the outcome of running Z3: *proved* if it returns "unsat" when looking for a counterexample, implying that the assertion is successfully proven, and *false CE* if it returns a spurious counterexample. Out of the 15 valid assertions, 12 were proven correct by our analysis. However, none of the assertions of *mark sweep* could be proven. As the scope column suggests, this problem is structurally more complex than the other problems; AA cannot check those assertions even for a scope of 10 before reaching time-out. This problem is particularly difficult because it simulates the recursion involved in the mark and sweep algorithm by applying transitive closure to union and join of multiple relations. These expressions occur within nested quantifiers or in both sides of the subset or intersection operators. Since such structures create deeply-nested quantifiers in our translation, Z3 cannot readily prove those assertions. We are investigating other translation possibilities to reduce the complexity of such cases.

The assertions in the bottom part of the table are invalid, i.e. AA generates sound counterexamples for them. The scope column in this case gives the smallest scope required by AA to find a counterexample. Although the main goal of our approach is to prove valid assertions, we analyzed these invalid assertions to evaluate our technique in case of a counterexample. For the first 4 assertions, Z3 is capable of producing an instance that although marked as "unknown", it demonstrates a true counterexample (denoted by *sound CE*).

Since our approach requires no type finitization, its performance is always independent of scope. Exceptions are the *15Queens* and *puzzle* assertions that hard-code the scope using set cardinality. We have chosen our translation rules so that the generated SMT formulas are easy to solve, witnessed by the fact that the Z3 analysis time in most cases is close to zero. However, when producing a satisfying instance for formulas containing cardinality, Z3 has to deeply

---

[7] Currently we do not support models that use Alloy's utility library.

Table 1. Evaluation results

		Alloy Analyzer		Our Analysis by Z3	
Problem	Assertion	Scope	Time (sec)	Time (sec)	Result
address book	delUndoesAdd	31	80.91	0.00	proved
	addIdempotent	31	112.66	0.01	proved
COM	theorem1	14	175.46	0.00	proved
	theorem2	14	177.97	0.00	proved
	theorem3	14	168.51	0.00	proved
	theorem4a	14	174.89	0.00	proved
	theorem4b	14	166.68	0.00	proved
abstract memory	writeRead	44	179.44	0.00	proved
	writeIdempotent	29	98.67	0.03	proved
media assets	hidePreservesInv	87	86.03	0.00	proved
	pasteAffectsHidden	29	138.34	0.00	proved
mark sweep	soundness1	9	81.52	0.12	false CE
	soundness2	8	28.84	0.11	false CE
	completeness	7	32.52	0.14	false CE
nQueen	solCondition	73	173.51	0.05	proved
address book	addLocal	3	0.05	0.10	sound CE
media assets	cutPaste	3	0.19	0.06	sount CE
own grandpa	ownGrandpa	4	0.01	0.12	sound CE
nQueen	15Queens	15	4.95	13.53	sound CE
handshake	puzzle	10	2.47	time out	N/A

instantiate all the cardinality helper functions. Therefore, its runtime for $15Queen$ is worse than AA, and it times out for *puzzle*. This is not necessarily true for provable assertions as witnessed by *solCondition* which also involves cardinality constraints. Since AA performs well in finding small counterexamples, we suggest that the user checks his intended assertion using AA first, and then runs our analysis to prove potentially valid assertions.

5   Related Work

Previous attempts to prove Alloy properties used interactive theorem provers. Dynamite [10] proves properties of Alloy specifications using the PVS theorem prover [21], via a translation to fork algebra. It introduces a PVS pretty-printer that shows proof steps in Alloy, reducing the burden of guiding the prover. Prioni [3] integrates the Alloy Analyzer with the Athena theorem prover. To overcome the challenge of finding proofs, Prioni provides a lemma library that captures commonly-used Alloy patterns.

Compared to theorem provers that perform a complete analysis but are not fully automatic, SMT solvers are fully automatic, but may fail to prove quantified formulas. Recent SMT solvers, however, have shown significant advances in handling quantifiers. Z3 integrates the superposition calculus in the DPLL framework [5,12], and CVC3 uses improved E-matching instantiation strategies [11]. SMT solvers have been used to increase the automation level of many theorem provers. The PVS [21] and Isabelle/HOL [9] logics, e.g., have been translated to Yices input language [8]. Although such translations address higher-order logics with a rich combination of types predicates, recursive data types, records, etc., they do not support constructs such as transitive closure and set cardinality.

Abadi, et. al. [2] verified some Alloy problems while identifying decidable fragments of many-sorted first-order logic. However, they only support a restricted form of transitive closure, and no integer arithmetic or cardinality. Lev-Ami, et. al. [19] introduced a method for simulating reachability properties that arise in program verification. Similar to our technique, they specify the semantics of transitive closure using first-order axioms. However, they use additional (coloring) axioms to aid the underlying prover (SPASS [22]). The coloring axioms are either provided by users or generated by heuristics. Although not immediately clear, a similar approach may be applicable to translating Alloy's transitive closure. Automated theorem provers (ATP) such as SPASS provide an unbounded analysis based on superposition calculus, but their lack of support for linear arithmetic makes them less attractive for reasoning about a rich logic like Alloy.

Suter, et. al. [23] presented a decision procedure for the quantifier-free Boolean Algebra with Presburger Arithmetic (QFBAPA) capable of handling sets and their cardinalities. They reduce QFBAPA to integer linear arithmetic (QFPA) which is solved by the decision procedures of Z3. Set cardinality is computed using the integers that represent the cardinality of Venn regions – the regions built by the maximal overlapping degree of a finite collection of sets. Since Alloy cardinality can be applied to arbitrary expressions (possibly containing variables) with arbitrary arities, this technique is not readily applicable to our translation.

6   Conclusions

We presented a new approach for analyzing problems expressed in Alloy, a first-order relational logic. Its main advantage is the ability to prove an assertion correct, a capability totally missing from the Alloy Analyzer (AA). We suggest our analysis be used to complement AA: when AA fails to find a counterexample, our tool can be used to prove the assertion correct. We avoid type finitization altogether and use the theories supported by SMT solvers instead.

Due to Alloy's undecidability and our arbitrary use of quantifiers, resulting SMT formulas can be undecidable. However, among different ways of axiomatizing an Alloy construct, we have carefully chosen the one that performs best in practice. While more experiments on larger Alloy models are needed to fully evaluate our technique, current results show that Z3 can correctly handle most of the valid and invalid properties, witnessing the effectiveness of the approach. Improving the cases that Z3 failed to handle is left for future work.

Although we focused on Alloy, our translation rules demonstrate a general approach that can be applied in various contexts. In particular, we described how to specify multiplicity constraints using uninterpreted functions, transitive closure using the theory of linear integer arithmetic, and cardinality of (possibly cyclic) relations using bijective integer functions.

AA provides some predefined library functions (e.g. ordering) that trigger special optimizations in AA. Investigating an efficient translation of widely-used Alloy libraries (e.g. ordering, graph, and relation) is left for future work. We will also investigate how to use SMT solvers' unsatisfiable cores and next satisfying solution to improve the usability of our technique. Our current translation deviates from Alloy semantics in handling arithmetic using infinite integers. While we believe that this is more suitable for most system descriptions, we will also provide an alternative fixed bitwidth arithmetic using bit-vectors in the future.

References

1. The Alloy community, http://alloy.mit.edu/community/
2. Abadi, A., Rabinovich, A., Sagiv, M.: Decidable fragments of many-sorted logic. Preprint submitted to Elsevier (2009)
3. Arkoudas, K., Khurshid, S., Marinov, D., Rinard, M.: Integrating model checking and theorem proving for relational reasoning. In: RELMICS, pp. 21–33 (2003)
4. The satisfiability modulo theories library, http://goedel.cs.uiowa.edu/smtib
5. Bonacina, M.P., Lynch, C., de Moura, L.: On deciding satisfiability by dPLL($\Gamma+\mathcal{T}$) and unsound theorem proving. In: Schmidt, R.A. (ed.) CADE-22. LNCS, vol. 5663, pp. 35–50. Springer, Heidelberg (2009)
6. de Moura, L., Bjorner, N.: Z3: An efficient SMT solver. In: Ramakrishnan, C.R., Rehof, J. (eds.) TACAS 2008. LNCS, vol. 4963, pp. 337–340. Springer, Heidelberg (2008)
7. Dennis, G., Chang, F., Jackson, D.: Modular verification of code with SAT. In: ISSTA, pp. 109–120 (2006)
8. Dutertre, B., de Moura, L.: The Yices SMT Solver. Tool Document (2006)
9. Erkök, L., Matthews, J.: Using Yices as an automated solver in Isabelle/HOL. In: AFM (2008)
10. Frias, M.F., Pombo, C.G.L., Moscato, M.M.: Alloy analyzer+PVS in the analysis and verification of alloy specifications. In: Grumberg, O., Huth, M. (eds.) TACAS 2007. LNCS, vol. 4424, pp. 587–601. Springer, Heidelberg (2007)
11. Ge, Y., Barrett, C., Tinelli, C.: Solving quantified verification conditions using satisfiability modulo theories. AMAI 55(1), 101–122 (2009)
12. Ge, Y., Moura, L.: Complete instantiation for quantified formulas in satisfiabiliby modulo theories. In: Bouajjani, A., Maler, O. (eds.) CAV 2009. LNCS, vol. 5643, pp. 306–320. Springer, Heidelberg (2009)
13. El Ghazi, A.A., Taghdiri, M.: Analyzing Alloy constraints using an SMT solver: A case study. In: AFM, Edinburgh, United Kingdom (2010)
14. Jackson, D.: Software Abstractions: Logic, Lang. and Analysis. MIT Press, Cambridge (2006)
15. Kang, E., Jackson, D.: Formal modeling and analysis of a flash filesystem in Alloy. In: Börger, E., Butler, M., Bowen, J.P., Boca, P. (eds.) ABZ 2008. LNCS, vol. 5238, pp. 294–308. Springer, Heidelberg (2008)
16. Khurshid, S.: Generating Structurally Complex Tests from Declarative Constraints. PhD thesis, MIT (2003)
17. Khurshid, S., Jackson, D.: Exploring the design of an intentional naming scheme with an automatic constraint analyzer. In: ASE (2000)
18. Leino, R., Monahan, R.: Reasoning about comprehensions with first-order SMT solvers. In: SAC, pp. 615–622 (2009)

19. Lev-ami, T., Immerman, N., Reps, T., Sagiv, M., et al.: Simulating reachability using first-order logic. In: Nieuwenhuis, R. (ed.) CADE 2005. LNCS (LNAI), vol. 3632, pp. 99–115. Springer, Heidelberg (2005)
20. Nolte, T.: Exploring filesystem synchronization with lightweight modeling and analysis. Master's thesis, MIT (2002)
21. Owre, S., Shankar, N., Rushby, J.: PVS: A prototype verification system. In: CADE-11 (1992)
22. Spass: Automated prover for FOL with equality, http://www.spass-prover.org/
23. Suter, P., Steiger, R., Kuncak, V.: Sets with cardinality constraints in satisfiability modulo theories. In: Jhala, R., Schmidt, D. (eds.) VMCAI 2011. LNCS, vol. 6538, pp. 403–418. Springer, Heidelberg (2011)
24. Taghdiri, M., Jackson, D.: A lightweight formal analysis of a multicast key management scheme. In: König, H., Heiner, M., Wolisz, A. (eds.) FORTE 2003. LNCS, vol. 2767, pp. 240–256. Springer, Heidelberg (2003)
25. Taghdiri, M., Jackson, D.: Inferring specifications to detect errors in code. JASE 14(1), 87–121 (2007)
26. Torlak, E.: A Constraint Solver for Software Engineering. PhD thesis, MIT (2009)
27. Vaziri, M.: Finding Bugs in Software with Constraint Solver. PhD thesis (2004)

Building VCL Models and Automatically Generating Z Specifications from Them

Nuno Amálio, Christian Glodt, and Pierre Kelsen

University of Luxembourg, 6, r. Coudenhove-Kalergi, L-1359 Luxembourg
{nuno.amalio,christian.glodt,pierre.kelsen}@uni.lu

Abstract. VCL is a visual and formal language for abstract specification of software systems. Its novelty lies in its capacity to describe predicates visually. This paper presents work-in-progress on a tool for VCL; the tool version presented here supports the VCL notations of structural and assertion diagrams (a subset of the whole VCL suite), enabling the generation of Z specifications from them.

Keywords: formal methods, visual languages, Z, model-driven development.

1 Introduction

Diagrams are widely used in modern day software engineering. There are, however, several issues with existing visual languages (VLs) such as UML. Diagrams are effective provided they make use of certain properties of visual descriptions that benefit cognition [1,2]. One problem is that most VLs, like UML, have not been designed to be *cognitive-effective* and to make use of such properties [2]. Another problem is that mainstream VLs have not been designed with a formal semantics [3]; they are mostly used without formal semantics, which precludes formal model analysis. Furthermore, most VLs cannot describe all properties visually; UML, for instance, uses the textual OCL to describe invariants and operations.

This paper presents our first results on a tool to support the visual contract language (VCL) [4,5]. VCL is formal, designed with usability in mind and to express predicates visually. It aims at making formal methods usage more practical; in particular: (a) to be usable by a variety of engineers, not necessarily formal methods experts; (b) to enable engineers to focus on software design; and (c) to use formal methods, but hiding them from the lay user. This enables the formation of teams with a good combination of skills; some individuals may be experts in the domain, others in the formal method.

2 VCL Tool

The *visual contract builder* (VCB)[1], VCL's tool presented here, is an Eclipse plug-in built using the GMF framework[2]. VCB's version presented here supports

---

[1] http://vcl.gforge.uni.lu
[2] http://www.eclipse.org/modeling/gmf/

M. Butler and W. Schulte (Eds.): FM 2011, LNCS 6664, pp. 149–153, 2011.

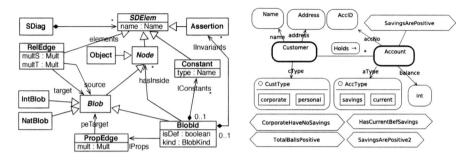

(a) Metamodel of VCL structural diagrams   (b) A VCL Structural Diagram

Fig. 1. Metamodel of VCL structural diagrams and sample instance

the construction of VCL structural and assertion (or constraint) diagrams (a subset of the whole VCL suite, see [4]).

VCB provides editors to construct VCL diagrams. These editors are built from metamodels that describe the abstract syntax of the VCL notations. VCL's metamodels are described in terms of object-oriented (OO) class *metamodels* specified in Alloy, which were refined to build diagram editors using GMF. All Alloy metamodels can be found in `http://vcl.gforge.uni.lu/metamodels`.

Figure 1(a) gives a UML class diagram that partially describes the metamodel of VCL structural diagrams (SDs). An instance of this metamodel is given in Fig. 1(b). The rounded contours in Fig. 1(b) are blobs. Blob `Int` is an instance of metaclass `IntBlob`; all other blobs are instances of `BlobId`. `Customer` and `Account`, drawn with a bold line, are domain blobs (`kind` meta-attribute has value `domain`); all others are value blobs (`kind` meta-attribute has value `value`). `CustType` and `AccType`, represented with symbol ◯, are definition blobs (`isDef` meta-attribute has value `true`); the objects inside these blobs (meta-association `hasInside`) are instances of metaclass `Object`. Property edges (instances of metaclass `PropEgde`), such as `name` and `address`, define state properties of blobs. `Holds` is a relation edge (metaclass `RelEdge`) connected to `Customer` (meta-association `source`) and `Account` (meta-association `target`) with multiplicity `one` (meta-attribute `multS`) to `many` (meta-attribute `multT`). Elements of Fig. 1(b) depicted as elongated hexagons are instances of metaclass `Assertion`; `SavingsArePositive` is a local assertion of blob `Account` (meta-association `lInvariants`); all others are global assertions.

VCB uses type-checking to check well-formedness. This helps to find subtle errors in an efficient way. VCB type-checks diagrams based on VCL's type system, and generates Z from type-correct diagrams only. Currently, VCB maps diagrams to Z specifications expressed in the ZOO style of object-orientation [3,6]. The generated Z is type-checked using Community Z Tools (CZT)[3]; in most cases, this is a mere sanity check: all type errors in diagrams are captured using VCL type-checking.

---

[3] `http://czt.sourceforge.net/`

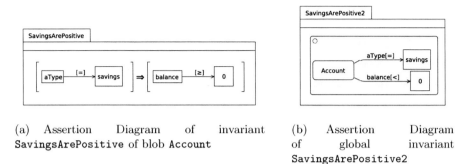

(a) Assertion   Diagram   of   invariant
SavingsArePositive of blob Account

(b) Assertion   Diagram
of   global   invariant
SavingsArePositive2

Fig. 2. VCL diagrams of *Simple Bank* [6,4] constructed using the VCL tool

3   Illustration

Figures 1(b) and 2 present VCL structural and assertion diagrams of the *Simple Bank* case study [6,4] drawn using VCB (see [4] for details). The Z generated by VCB for this case study's VCL model, along with a demo of VCB, can be found at http://vcl.gforge.uni.lu/SBDemo.

Assertion diagram (AD) of Fig. 2(a) describes the local invariant **Savings-ArePositive**, identified in the SD of Fig. 1(b); in VCB, double-clicking the invariant on the SD takes the user to the AD. This AD says that savings accounts must have positive balances using a logical implication formula. The Z predicate that is generated for this AD is: $aType = savings \Rightarrow balance \geq 0$.

The same constraint is expressed in the AD of Fig. 2(b), using a set formula. It defines the set of **Accounts** that are savings and have negative balances using a definition blob, which is shaded to say that the set must be empty. The Z predicate resulting from the diagram is:

$$\{o : sAccount \mid (stAccount\ o).aType = savings \wedge (stAccount\ o).balance < 0\} = \varnothing$$

The blob definition results in a Z set comprehension. Here, *sAccount* is set of *Account* objects; *stAccount* is a function mapping account objects to their state.

4   Discussion

We believe that we achieve usability gains by hiding the formal method from the lay user[4]. Four people developed the large VCL model of [5], only one is a Z expert. The VCL approach may be relevant for the critical systems industry that uses formal methods, such as Z [7]. Users writing specifications do not necessarily need to be trained in a formal method, they could use a VL, such as VCL, that abstracts away from the underlying formal method(s); based on [5], VCL appears to be easier to learn than Z.

VCL has been designed to exploit many target formal languages, not just Z. We intend to map VCL to other languages in the future to produce partial or total specifications from VCL diagrams; this enables use of the verification capabilities of the target language.

---

[4] We intend to assess this claim empirically in the future.

5 Related Work

The AutoZ tool [8] generates Z specifications, expressed in the ZOO style, from UML class (similar to VCL SDs) and state diagrams, following the *UML + Z* approach of [3]. Predicates of invariants are expressed textually in Z. VCL describes predicates visually and generates Z from them. AutoZ uses Z type-cheking to check well-formedness of diagrams, which complicates error-reporting. VCB type-checks diagrams directly based on VCL's type-system.

Constraint diagrams [9] is a VL that describes predicates visually. Its semantic basis is similar to VCL (set theory). To our knowledge, there are no visual diagram editors to support this VL. VL of [9] emphasises reasoning with diagrams; VCL generates Z to enable formal reasoning at the Z level.

Visual OCL (VOCL) [10], a VL based on OCL, expresses predicates visually and has a semantics based on graph transformations. There is a tool with a visual editor (http://tfs.cs.tu-berlin.de/vocl/) for VOCL. This tool, however, does not support UML class diagrams (similar to VCL SDs). Unlike VCB, VOCL tool only supports basic types and only generates simple OCL expressions. VCB supports both ADs and SDs, checks consistency of ADs (predicates) against SDs (structures), and generates complete Z Specifications.

6 Conclusions and Future Work

This paper presents work-in-progress on VCL's tool: the *Visual Contract Builder* (VCB)[5]. VCB version presented here supports the construction of VCL structural and assertion (or constraint) diagrams (a subset of the whole VCL suite), enabling the generation of Z specifications from them. It is the first step towards tool support for VCL. The most relevant contribution of the work presented here is a tool supporting a software engineering visual language that has a formal basis, expresses predicates visually, and enables the generation of formal specifications that can be processed independently on their own. To our knowledge, no other tool supports a language that describes predicates visually, and generates complete formal specifications. This is also a contribution to VCL's development: (a) it demonstrates VCL's formal semantics, and (b) it supports the novel notation of assertion diagrams (ADs).

Future work will complete the tool support for ADs (modular mechanisms of VCL ADs [4] are currently not supported), the type system for structural and assertion diagrams, and will extend the tool to support VCL's descriptions of behaviour using the VCL notations of behaviour and contract diagrams (see [4]).

References

1. Larkin, J.H., Simon, H.A.: Why a diagram is (sometimes) worth ten thousand words. Cognitive Science 11, 65–99 (1987)
2. Moody, D.L.: The "physics" of notations: Toward a scientific basis for constructing visual notations in software engineering. IEEE TSE 6(35), 756–779 (2009)

---

[5] http://vcl.gforge.uni.lu/

3. Amálio, N.: Generative frameworks for rigorous model-driven development. Ph.D. thesis, Dept. Computer Science, Univ. of York (2007)
4. Amálio, N., Kelsen, P.: Modular design by contract visually and formally using VCL. In: VL/HCC 2010 (2010)
5. Amálio, N., Kelsen, P., Ma, Q., Glodt, C.: Using VCL as an aspect-oriented approach to requirements modelling. TAOSD VII, 151–199 (2010)
6. Amálio, N., Polack, F., Stepney, S.: An object-oriented structuring for Z based on views. In: Treharne, H., King, S., Henson, M., Schneider, S. (eds.) ZB 2005. LNCS, vol. 3455, pp. 262–278. Springer, Heidelberg (2005)
7. Hall, A.: Correctness by construction: Integrating formality into a commercial development process. In: Eriksson, L.-H., Lindsay, P.A. (eds.) FME 2002. LNCS, vol. 2391, pp. 139–157. Springer, Heidelberg (2002)
8. Williams, J., Polack, F.: Automated formalisation for verification of diagrammatic models. ENTCS 263, 211–226 (2010)
9. Fish, A., Flowe, J., Howse, J.: The semantics of augmented constraint diagrams. Journal of Visual Languages and Computing 16, 541–573 (2005)
10. Bottoni, P., Koch, M., Parisi-Presicce, F., Taentzer, G.: A visualization of OCL using collaborations. In: Gogolla, M., Kobryn, C. (eds.) UML 2001. LNCS, vol. 2185, pp. 257–271. Springer, Heidelberg (2001)

The 1st Verified Software Competition: Experience Report

Vladimir Klebanov, Peter Müller, Natarajan Shankar, Gary T. Leavens,
Valentin Wüstholz, Eyad Alkassar, Rob Arthan, Derek Bronish,
Rod Chapman, Ernie Cohen, Mark Hillebrand, Bart Jacobs,
K. Rustan M. Leino, Rosemary Monahan, Frank Piessens, Nadia Polikarpova,
Tom Ridge, Jan Smans, Stephan Tobies, Thomas Tuerk, Mattias Ulbrich,
and Benjamin Weiß

www.vscomp.org

Abstract. We, the organizers and participants, report our experiences
from the 1st Verified Software Competition, held in August 2010 in Edinburgh at the VSTTE 2010 conference.

1 Introduction

Research on SAT solving and automatic theorem proving has been boosted by
the competitions held in connections with conferences such as SAT, CADE, and
CAV. The regular comparisons of tools help the community by exhibiting the
practical impact of algorithms and implementation strategies, and help its clients
by providing an assessment of the performance of individual tools as well as of
the research field overall.

Inspired by this success, participants of the Verified Software Initiative [8]
decided to start a program verification competition, which was first organized
by Peter Müller and Natarajan Shankar and held at the VSTTE 2010 conference.
While the long-term objective is to provide similar benefits to the community
like the ATP, SAT, and SMT competitions, the goals for the initial event were
much more modest—to create interest among researchers and tool builders, to
get an impression of how such an event is received by the community, and to
gain experience in designing and carrying out a verification competition.

The competition was explicitly held as a forum where researchers could demonstrate the strengths of their tools rather than be punished for their shortcomings.
There were no deliberate attempts to expose weaknesses such as unsoundness or
incompleteness of the verification tools, or missing support for certain language
features. The organizers presented five small programs and suggestions what to
prove about them (such as the absence of run-time errors, functional behavior, or
termination). After the presentation followed a four-hour thinking period where
no tool use was allowed. After that, the participants had two hours to develop their
solutions. The participants could work in teams of up to three people, provided
that all of them were physically present on site. The physical presence allowed the
organizers to interact with the participants and to get immediate feedback about
the challenge problems and the organization of the competition.

M. Butler and W. Schulte (Eds.): FM 2011, LNCS 6664, pp. 154–168, 2011.

Table 1. Solutions overview

Team	Tool	Problems solved										Implementation / specification language	Tool web site
		at competition					in the aftermath						
		Sum&Max	Invert	LinkedList	N Queens	Queue	Sum&Max	Invert	LinkedList	N Queens	Queue		
A.Tsyban 1	Isabelle	▨	☐	☐	☐	☐	▨ᵃ	☐	▨ᵃ	☐	☐	C / Hoare logic	
anonHolHacker 1	HOL4	☐	☐	☐	☐	▨	☐	☐	☐	☐	▨ᵃ	HOL	hol.sourceforge.net
Holfoot 1	Holfoot	▨	☐	☐	☐	☐	▨	▨	▨	▨	▨	C-like / sep. logic	holfoot.heap-of-problems.org
KeY 3	KeY	▨	▨	☐	☐	☐	▨ᵃ	▨ᵃ	▨	▨	▨	Java / JML(+)	key-project.org/VSComp2010
Leino 1	Dafny	▨	☐	▨	☐	☐	▨ᵃ	☐	▨ᵃ	▨	▨ᵃ	Dafny	research.microsoft.com/dafny/
SparkULike 1	SPARK	▨	☐	☐	☐	☐	▨ᵃ	☐	▨	☐	☐	SPARK	libre.adacore.com
MonaPoli 2	Boogie	▨	☐	▨	☐	☐	▨ᵃ	☐	▨	☐	▨	Boogie	research.microsoft.com/boogie/
Resolve 1	Resolve	☐	☐	☐	▨ᵇ	☐	▨	▨	▨	▨	▨ᵃ	Resolve	resolve.cse.ohio-state.edu:8080/ResolveVCWeb/
RobArthan 1	ProofPower	▨	☐	▨	☐	☐	▨ᵃ	☐	▨ᵃ	☐	☐	HOL	www.lemma-one.com/ProofPower/index/
VC Crushers 3	VCC	▨	☐	▨	☐	☐	▨	▨	▨	▨	▨	C / VCC annotat.	vcc.codeplex.com
VeriFast 1	VeriFast	▨	☐	▨	☐	☐	▨	▨	▨ᵃ	▨	▨	C, Java / sep. logic	www.cs.kuleuven.be/~bartj/verifast/

Numeral = number of persons at competition

ᵃ solution unchanged since competition
ᵇ solved before the competition

Single entry = language integrating implementation and specification

▨ solved   ☐ not solved   ▨ substantial partial solution

There was no ranking of solutions or winner announcement. The evaluation committee (Gary Leavens, Peter Müller, and Natarajan Shankar) manually inspected the solutions and pointed out strengths and weaknesses according to the criteria of completeness, elegance, and (reported) automation; these subjective results were presented at the conference to foster discussions among the participants. Not ranking the results allowed in particular a comparison of different verification approaches, whereas a fair ranking would have required standardization and grouping by disciplines (such as automatic vs. interactive or modular vs. whole-program verification).

This setup proved to be successful. Eleven teams participated in the competition and submitted in total 19 (partial) solutions to the five challenge problems (reproduced in Section 2). For this paper, the participants also had the chance to revise or complete their solutions (see Table 1 for an overview). Ten out of 11 original teams report their experiences in Section 3. A number of challenges, common issues, and conclusions are presented in Section 4.

The original problem statements, all team solutions, as well as an extended version of this report are available on the competition web site.

2   The Challenge Problems

This section presents short versions of the competition problems, which were prepared by the organizers together with Valentin Wüstholz. The original problem descriptions included reference implementations in pseudocode and test cases.

Problem 1: SUM&MAX. Given an N-element array of natural numbers, write a program to compute the sum and the maximum of the elements in the array. Prove the postcondition that $\mathtt{sum} \leqslant N \cdot \mathtt{max}$.

Problem 2: INVERTing an Injection. Invert an injective (and thus surjective) array A of N elements in the subrange from 0 to $N - 1$. Prove that the output array B is injective and that $\mathtt{B[A}[i]\mathtt{]} = i$ for $0 \leqslant i < N$.

Problem 3: Searching a LINKEDLIST. Given a linked-list representation of a list of integers, find the index of the first element that is equal to zero. Show that the program returns a number i equal to the length of the list if there is no such element. Otherwise, the element at index i must be equal to zero, and all the preceding elements must be non-zero.

Problem 4: N QUEENS. Write and verify a program to place N queens on an $N \times N$ chess board so that no queen can capture another one with a legal move. If there is no solution, the algorithm should indicate that.

Problem 5: Amortized QUEUE. An applicative queue with a good amortized complexity can be implemented using a pair of linked lists, such that the front list joined to the *reverse* of the rear list gives the abstract queue. The queue offers the operations Enqueue(item: T) to place an element at the rear of the queue, Tail() to return the queue without the first element, and Front() to return the first element of the queue. The implementation must maintain the invariant `queue.rear.length` $\leqslant$ `queue.front.length` (prove this). Also, show that a client invoking the above operations observes an abstract queue given by a sequence.

3   The Team Reports

3.1   Team anonymousHolHacker (Tom Ridge)

HOL4 [14] is an interactive theorem prover for higher-order logic, broadly similar to systems such as Isabelle/HOL, HOL Light, and ProofPower. HOL4 has good automated proof support, including powerful equality reasoning (simplification, i.e., rewriting with directed equalities), complete first-order proof search, and decision procedures for decidable fragments of arithmetic. Extensive libraries of theorems covering many common data types and functions are also provided.

Competition. Only QUEUE was attempted during the competition.

The HOL statement uses an abstraction function `abstr` to construct the queue by joining (`++`) the two underlying implementation lists (represented as the pair `impl`):

```
abstr impl = (front impl) ++ (REVERSE (rear impl))
```

All the data types, functions, and required properties given in the problem statement are fairly directly transcribed in HOL. Three very simple arithmetic facts are established, and proof of the required properties then proceeds essentially by case analysis on lists, and simplification, with a few trivial instances of first-order proof (first-order proof with appropriate case splitting and other library lemmas would automatically prove all the required properties outright). Induction is not explicitly needed in the proofs, so that QUEUE is in some ways simpler than the other problems. However, the arithmetic facts and various HOL4 library lemmas about lists essentially are inductive: the simplicity of our proofs (the lack of induction) derives from the maturity of the HOL4 system, especially the automation for arithmetic lemmas, and the extensive libraries of theorems about lists.

The HOL4 solution is given at a relatively abstract level, and no attempt is made to address imperative features such as linked lists and pointer manipulation.

3.2   Team Holfoot (Thomas Tuerk)

Holfoot is an instantiation of a general separation logic framework inside the HOL4 [14] theorem prover. It is able to reason about the partial correctness of programs written in a simple, low-level imperative language, which is designed to resemble C. This language contains pointers, local and global variables, dynamic memory allocation/deallocation, conditional execution, while loops, and recursive procedures with call-by-value and call-by-reference arguments. Moreover, concurrency is supported by conditional critical regions and a parallel composition operator.

Holfoot follows in the footsteps of the separation logic tool Smallfoot [4]. It uses the same programming language and a similar specification language but gives them a rigorous formal semantics in HOL. As all inferences pass through the HOL4 kernel, the Holfoot proofs are highly trustworthy with respect to the defined formal semantics. Also, while Smallfoot is concerned only with the shape of data structures, Holfoot can reason about their content as well, supporting full functional verification. Holfoot can handle arrays and pointer arithmetic.

Simple specifications, like the Smallfoot examples or a fully functional specification of reversing a singly linked list can be verified automatically in Holfoot. More complicated ones like fully functional specifications of quicksort or insertion into a red-black tree require interactive proofs. These interactive proofs can use all the infrastructure of HOL4.

Competition. The Holfoot team consists only of Thomas Tuerk, the developer of Holfoot. Unluckily, only the first example was solved during the competition due to time limitations. This is mainly due to Thomas Tuerk not being familiar with HOL4's arithmetic reasoning infrastructure. INVERT was tried, but not finished during the competition.

Aftermath. Since the competition, all problems have been solved using Holfoot. As a separation logic tool, Holfoot is aimed at reasoning about dynamic data structures. Therefore, Holfoot is especially good at reasoning about QUEUE. For other examples, HOL4's infrastructure for defining new predicates and functions was beneficial. INVERT for example uses a newly defined function to translate the original problem into a functional one inside HOL4.

3.3 Team KeY (Vladimir Klebanov, Mattias Ulbrich, Benjamin Weiß)

The KeY system [3] is a verification tool for Java programs. At the core of the system is a deductive prover working in first-order Dynamic Logic for Java (JavaDL). Properties of programs can be specified in JML or OCL, which KeY translates into proof obligations in JavaDL. Specifying directly in JavaDL is also possible.

The KeY system is not strictly a verification condition generator (VCG), but a theorem prover for program logic interleaving symbolic execution of programs, first-order reasoning, arithmetic, and symbolic state simplification, etc. Via its SMT export interface, the system can also use external solvers (such as Z3) to discharge goals.

For programs annotated with requirements and sufficient loop invariants, the system can often find verification proofs automatically. On the other hand, the system does expose an explicit proof object of (relatively) good understandability. The user can provide guidance to the prover by manipulating the proof manually at key points—for instance adding lemmas or instantiating quantifiers.

Competition. At the competition, the KeY team consisted of three developers with in-depth knowledge of the system. We used a pre-release of KeY 1.6. By the end of the allotted time, we had solved SUM&MAX and INVERT, which fall into the class where KeY is strongest (functional-arithmetical properties).

Both problems could be specified without difficulties in standard JML. The specifications were complete regarding the problem formulation. For SUM&MAX, we have also specified and proven that the program indeed computes the sum and the maximum of the array. KeY found the proof automatically (with one goal discharged by a tweaked strategy setting), and the pure prover running time was about six seconds. Quite some time was wasted on INVERT in search of the loop invariant, which turned out to be simpler than expected. In the proof, it was necessary to invoke Z3 *and* manually instantiate two quantifiers (in the surjectivity precondition). Attempts to solve LINKEDLIST were not successful within the given time limit. We did not attempt N QUEENS or QUEUE.

Aftermath. After the competition, complete solutions to the three outstanding problems have been produced, using a development branch of the KeY system [12], which is stronger in handling recursive data structures. An extended variant of JML was used for specification. The solutions to LINKEDLIST and QUEUE are inspired by those of Leino (Section 3.4): dynamic frames in the form of ghost fields are used for framing, and mathematical sequences for specifying functional behavior. The total effort spent was two person-weeks, which included some extensions to the verification system.

3.4   Team Leino (Rustan Leino)

Dafny is an object-based language with built-in specification constructs [9]. To a first approximation, it is like Java (but without subclasses) with Eiffel- or JML-like specifications. Language features that are especially useful when writing specifications include sets and sequences, ghost variables, and user-defined recursive functions. Dafny uses mathematical integers (implemented by big-nums), which avoids overflow errors.

The Dafny verifier statically checks all specifications, language rules (e.g., array index bounds), termination, and other conditions (e.g., well-foundedness of functions). To help it along, a user supplies assertions like method pre- and post-conditions, loop invariants, and termination metrics. The compiler then omits specifications and other ghost constructs from the compiled code. Like VCC, the Dafny verifier is built using Boogie [2,11], which in turn uses the SMT-solver Z3 [7] as its reasoning engine. The preferable way to develop Dafny programs is in the Microsoft Visual Studio IDE, where the Dafny verifier runs in the background and verification errors are reported as the program is being designed.

Competition. Solving SUM&MAX came down to adding a one-line loop invariant.

To solve LINKEDLIST, I associated with every linked-list node a ghost variable whose value is the sequence of list elements from that point onward in the list. To state the appropriate invariant about that ghost variable, one must account for which linked-list nodes contribute to the value, which is done using a common "dynamic frames" specification idiom in Dafny.

The linked list in QUEUE is similar to the one in LINKEDLIST, but stores in every node the length of the remaining list and provides additional operations like `Concat` and `Reverse`. To build an amortized queue from two linked lists, one reversed, is then straightforward using a user-defined function that returns the reverse of a given sequence.

The competition was an adrenalin rush and a race against the clock. I had gone into it hoping to finish all five problems, but ended up with incomplete attempts at INVERT and N QUEENS. In retrospect, I may have finished INVERT had I ignored N QUEENS.

As the author of the tool, I may not be a good judge of its user-friendliness. But for me, I found the immediate feedback from the verifier running in the background useful throughout.

Aftermath. The difficulty with INVERT lies in getting the SMT solver to make use of the given surjectivity property. The general trick is state a lemma, an assert statement whose condition supplies the reasoning engine with a stepping stone in the proof. In particular, the lemma will mention terms that trigger reasoning about quantifiers that also mention those terms. In INVERT, the surjectivity property does not contain any terms that can be used in a lemma, so I introduced a dummy function for that purpose.

I found N QUEENS to be the most difficult problem, because it involves verifying the absence of a solution in those cases where the given search strategy does not find one. After some more verbose attempts, I was able to get this down to two lemmas.

3.5   Team SPARKuLike (Rod Chapman)

SPARK is a contractualized subset of the Ada language, specifically designed for the construction of high-assurance software. It has an industrial track record spanning some twenty years, including use in projects such as the EuroFighter Typhoon, the Lockheed-Martin C130J, and the NSA's Tokeneer demonstrator system. The overriding design goal of the language is the provision of a sound verification system, which is based on information-flow analysis, Hoare logic, and theorem proving.

Rather than tackling all the problems in this challenge, I decided to take on the first (SUM&MAX), but aiming at a complete implementation and proof to the standard that we would expect for industrial safety-critical code. In particular, the solution offers a complete proof of partial correctness, type safety, and termination. Test cases were also developed that offer a respectable coverage of boundary conditions and structural coverage. The proof of type safety also covers the absence of arithmetic overflow. This was not required by the competition rules, but was felt to be achievable in SPARK through the judicious selection of well-defined ranges for the basic numeric types—a common practice in SPARK. Indeed, failure to specify numeric ranges is normally considered an outright design error in SPARK.

The solution took 107 minutes total, broken down as follows: Planning 5, Design 40, Coding and Proof 50, Compile 1, Test 1, Review and Write-up 10. The very low times for Compile and Test are encouraging—essentially no defects were discovered at this stage. The SPARK Verification Condition Generator produces 18 VCs, of which 14 are proved automatically. The remaining 4 VCs require some additional Lemmas and are completed with the interactive prover.

3.6   Team MonaPoli (Rosemary Monahan, Nadia Polikarpova)

Boogie 2 [11] is an intermediate verification language designed to accommodate the encoding of verification conditions for imperative, object-oriented programs. Boogie [2] is a static verifier that accepts Boogie 2 programs as input and generates verification conditions, which are then submitted to one of the supported theorem provers (the default being the SMT solver Z3 [7]). In this competition, we chose to write our solutions directly in Boogie 2, using the Boogie tool and Z3 (version 2.11 during the competition, version 2.15 for the final version) to verify our solutions.

Competition. At the competition the MonaPoli team consisted of Nadia Polikarpova and Rosemary Monahan, two people who had just met at VSTTE 2010. Both had used the Boogie tool but primarily as an underlying component of verifiers for other languages. The team worked together and submitted solutions to SUM&MAX and LINKEDLIST.

We attempted LINKEDLIST first. Specifying heap-manipulating programs in Boogie 2 requires explicitly defining the heap, so we defined the linked list by mapping a list cell to its stored value and to the next list cell. Our specification included auxiliary functions which calculated the length of the list, determined if a value was in the list, and returned the value at a particular position in the list. Our main observation from this solution was that while the need to specify the heap is an overhead, it ensures that the specifier has a complete understanding of the program semantics. The solution we submitted at the competition was incomplete as we used two unproved lemmas. Our solution for the paper is complete and proves automatically in about 2 seconds.

Our solution to SUM&MAX was easily specified and automatically verified in less than 2 seconds. Our main observation here was that specifications for small, integer- and array-manipulating programs in Boogie 2 are simple and concise.

We did not prove termination for any of the problems as Boogie 2 does not directly support termination measures.

Aftermath. After the competition, solutions to INVERT and QUEUE were completed.

In INVERT, proving that one array is an inversion of another simply requires the addition of an obvious loop invariant. Proving that an array is injective is more complicated. The main difficulty was making Boogie instantiate the surjectivity precondition. Instead, we introduced a ghost set mirroring all seen values of A and loop invariants stating that the set cardinality is exactly k (k being the loop counter) and that all elements are in $[0; N)$. To this end, we formalized a small theory of sets.

QUEUE delivered a more interesting experience as theories of sequences and heap allocation were required. These were not difficult to specify but were quite labor-intensive. However, once these theories have been written, it is possible to solve a whole range of similar problems, so the effort is not wasted.

When dealing with linked data structures, one typically needs to define inductive properties. We noticed that in order for Z3 to handle them effectively it is important to use induction on structure instead of induction on integers. Verification of the list and queue implementations was also greatly simplified by the fact that both classes are immutable: no advanced techniques for specifying footprints of the methods (such as dynamic frames) were required.

3.7   Team Resolve (Derek Bronish)

Resolve is a tool-supported programming and specification language for full-functional verification of imperative component-based programs [13]. The language emphasizes strict separation of client- and implementer-views of components, providing full modularity both in terms of human comprehensibility and the proof process. The key to this approach is the maintenance of value semantics for all types, so references cannot "leak" across component boundaries.

Verification conditions generated automatically from Resolve code may be discharged either by interfaces with third-party provers such as Isabelle and Z3, or by SplitDecision, an internally-developed tool that applies theorems of the mathematical theories that pervade the specification language (e.g., strings, finite sets, tuples, etc.).

Competition. The Resolve group representative did not originally intend to participate in the competition and has only submitted QUEUE, for which we already had a solution posted to the web.

Most notably, the Resolve solution to this problem (the `StackRealization` of the `QueueTemplate`, viewable online at `http://resolve.cse.ohio-state.edu:8080/ResolveVCWeb`) uses an abstraction to separate the queue from extraneous implementation details such as the nodes and pointers that may comprise the lists' concrete realizations. In other words, the amortized queue is represented as two stacks, which themselves may use a linked-list representation, but the implementation details of the stacks are separated from the proof of the queue implementation. An important tenet of Resolve is that such modularity is required for verification efforts to scale upwards to more complex software systems.

Aftermath. Since the competition proper, solutions to all five problems have been composed in Resolve. An important attribute of the solutions, allowing all of the VCs to be discharged either mechanically or simply by hand, is the use of specifier-supplied mathematical definitions to hide quantifiers. For example, the postcondition for INVERT can be expressed as:

```
a.lb = #a.lb and a.ub = #a.ub and
IS_INVERTED_UP_TO(a.ub + 1, #a, a)
```

This states that the bounds of the array are not changed, and the outgoing value of the array is completely inverted with respect to its incoming value. The definition of `IS_INVERTED_UP_TO` is rather complicated and involves a universal quantifier, but this definition never needs to be expanded in order to verify the code. Instead, one simply applies universal algebraic lemmas such as:

$$i = \texttt{a.lb} \implies \texttt{IS\_INVERTED\_UP\_TO}(i, \texttt{a}, \texttt{b})$$

How best to design a verification system that allows specifiers to provide such definitions and lemmas, demonstrate the validity of the lemmas as a one-time cost, and then incorporate proven lemmas into its automated reasoning engine is an ongoing research question, which experience in this competition has revealed is important and promising for the future of Resolve.

3.8   Team RobArthan (Rob Arthan)

ProofPower [1] is a tool supporting specification and proof in HOL (Mike Gordon's polymorphic formulation of Church's simple type theory) and other languages, most notably the Z notation, via semantic embeddings in HOL. Proof-Power is the basis for an Ada verification system called the Ada Compliance Tool developed for QinetiQ, who use it for verifying safety-critical control software, using Z specifications derived from Simulink diagrams.

Competition. For the competition, as I felt that functional programming was rather under-represented at VSTTE, I decided to write recursive definitions in HOL of functional programs and verify those. The resulting "programs" are executable in ProofPower using the rewriting engine, although this is not really a general purpose execution environment.

The conservative extension mechanism used to make the definitions imposes a consistency proof obligation. This proof obligation is discharged automatically for all the examples in the solutions and the syntactic form of the definitions then guarantees termination.

The solutions are modular in the sense that the new functions are defined by combining existing functions, and theorems about those new functions are derived from theorems about their constituent functions. The list searching solution first defines a polymorphic search function with a higher-order parameter giving the search criteria and instantiates it to search for zeroes in a list of integers.

This means that one can do particular calculations in the theorem prover with the results as theorems. I just did this for testing purposes in the competition, but it is an important technique in the application of systems like ProofPower to mathematical and engineering problems requiring highly-assured calculations, e.g., Tom Hales's Flyspeck project uses this kind of technique in HOL Light and Isabelle/HOL.

I was the only ProofPower user at VSTTE at the time of the competition, so I formed a team of one. I am one of the main authors of the system. Given the time available, I chose SUM&MAX and LINKEDLIST as the problems most amenable to the techniques I was using. The other problems could easily be handled in much the same way, but a few more hours would be required.

3.9   Team VC Crushers (Eyad Alkassar, Ernie Cohen, Mark Hillebrand, Stephan Tobies)

VCC is an assertional, first-order deductive verifier for industrial-strength concurrent C (and assembly) code. VCC verification is based on modular two-state invariants, which allow the encoding of a variety of verification disciplines. (There is explicit syntactic support for Spec#-style ownership.) To overcome the restrictions of first-order reasoning, ghost state/code are typically used to maintain inductively defined information (e.g., the reachable nodes of a recursive data structure), with ghost code substituting for prover guidance. (For example, simulation is encoded by maintaining the abstract state as ghost state, with explicit updates to this state witnessing the simulation.) Verification conditions are discharged by an automatic prover (currently, Z3), but there is also a backend connection to Isabelle/HOL. VCC currently verifies only partial correctness (but termination is coming soon).

The VC Crushers team consisted of three persons during competition time, who were joined by a fourth person (Ernie Cohen) afterwards.

Competition. SUM&MAX was solved modulo two assumptions related to C's use of bounded (machine) integers. The first assumption was that the sum maintained in the loop did not overflow. This has to either be assumed in the loop, provided as a precondition, or taken into account in the postcondition. The second assumption was of a nonlinear arithmetic property that Z3 could not handle effectively for bounded integers. In addition to the required postcondition, we also proved that the result for the maximum is a bound for the individual elements and that the function result is the summation of the array elements. LINKEDLIST was also fully solved during the contest, but using an overly complex list specification with many superfluous invariants in the list data structure. INVERT was attempted during the competition, and was partially but not completely finished.

Aftermath. The remaining problems were solved after the competition.

For SUM&MAX, we discovered that the nonlinear arithmetic assumption could be proven by Z3 for unbounded integers (which helps explain why other Z3-based verifiers did not run into the same problem). The work-around in our solution is to "guide" Z3 by asserting the unbounded property (essentially making it available as a lemma). We also removed the no-overflow assumption by weakening the postcondition to say that either the result is correct or the (unbounded) sum overflows.

In INVERT, we use a ghost map parameter *inverse* to the function to encode surjectivity of the input array A. The central hint to the prover to show the postconditions on the output array B is to rewrite B[j] to B[A[*inverse*[j]]]; getting Z3 to do this automatically required using a custom trigger. Alternatively, we could have explicitly provided a hint (by mentioning a term of the form B[A[*inverse*[j]]]) where needed.

In our contest solution for LINKEDLIST, we used an overly complex list implementation (one that maintains the reachability relation through arbitrary first-order surgery on lists). However, this complexity is not needed for the contest problems, so we re-did the verification using a much simpler list implementation (used also for QUEUE).

The main difficulty in N QUEENS is how to express the non-existence of the solution when the search procedure returns false. Our C implementation uses arrays (and destructive updates) to work on the board. VCC does not allow assertions to quantify over heaps (for reasons related to logical consistency), so we instead used maps (a mathematical abstraction) to reason about the solution space (with the same encoding as for boards). To express that there is no solution in a certain search state, we state that all solutions sharing the same prefix as the current board are inconsistent (i.e., have a queen i capturing a queen j).

In VCC, reading an object requires evidence that it still exists. In most cases (including typical sequential code), this is done by owning the object. When the object has to be shared, this is usually done by owning a ghost object (called a claim) whose invariant guarantees the existence of the object in question. Manipulating these claims increases the annotation burden, but allows the data to eventually be destroyed. On the other hand, this problem tacitly assumes garbage collection, since the code creates shared data with no way to reclaim it. We verified a version of the problem that does its own memory management (essentially consuming data passed into functions); the solution verifies quite conveniently using ownership, but does not allow reuse. As expected, the solution had to make additional assumptions (or preconditions) to make sure that memory allocations do not fail and that the queues do not grow too large.

3.10 Team VeriFast (Bart Jacobs, Frank Piessens, Jan Smans)

VeriFast is a verifier for single- and multithreaded C and Java programs. It takes as input C or Java source files, annotated with pre- and postconditions, loop invariants, definitions of inductive data types, fixpoint functions, recursive separation logic predicates, lemma functions, as well as some proof steps in specially marked comments. It outputs either "0 errors found" or both the source location of a potential error, and a symbolic execution trace leading up to the error, with the symbolic heap, the symbolic store, and the path condition at each execution step. These can be browsed conveniently in the VeriFast IDE.

When designing VeriFast, we put a very strong premium on predictable performance. To deal with heap effect framing, we copycat Smallfoot [4] and perform symbolic execution with memory represented as a separating conjunction of "heap chunks", i.e., separation logic predicate applications. The SMT solver is used only to reason about the arguments of the heap chunks, i.e., the data values. Furthermore, we avoid general quantification in specifications—in fact, it is currently not supported. The only quantifiers that are made available to the SMT solver are those that axiomatize the inductive data types and fixpoint functions (primitive recursive functions over inductive data types); these behave very predictably. The approach pays off: VeriFast's typical sub-second verification times enable a comfortable interactive annotation-insertion experience.

Competition. One member of our team, Bart Jacobs, participated at VSTTE and the competition. The first problem he tackled was SUM&MAX. He first tried a Java version, since we have some automation for dealing with arrays in Java. Unfortunately, however, our automation proved quite incomplete. Bart had so much trouble dealing with the complex terms involving `take`, `drop`, `append`, etc. that described the inductive list representing the contents of the array, that he decided the automation was working against him, so he switched to C where VeriFast has no special support for arrays. A C array can be described using a simple recursive predicate. This allowed him to complete SUM&MAX, but by then the competition was more than halfway through. Along the way, however, he also struggled with an incompleteness in the theory of multiplication and inequalities in the version of Z3 that he was using.

He then moved to LINKEDLIST, which, since based on a nice recursive data structure, was a piece of cake for VeriFast.

Finally, he started on QUEUE, which, it seemed, should have been easy for the same reason. However, again, VeriFast's automation started acting up. Sharing of immutable data structures can be expressed in VeriFast using fractional permissions [5]. VeriFast automatically splits and merges fractional chunks as necessary—usually. In this case, it did not, so some time-consuming contortions were necessary to get the sharable linked list implementation finished, not leaving time to complete other problems.

The main conclusion that we took away from the competition is that automation is evil :-). Nonetheless, we will of course continue to work on more and better automation.

Aftermath. We have now completed all problems. QUEUE was fairly easy, once the right encoding of sharability was found. (Quantify over the list's fraction, or over each field's fraction separately? Quantifying over each field's fraction works better.) Completing INVERT and N QUEENS required developing quite a bit of theory, which was labor-intensive but possible in VeriFast. For example, for INVERT we proved surjectivity of A from injectivity and boundedness.

4   Conclusions

Results of the competition. SUM&MAX was the easiest problem, solved by everybody attempting it. INVERT—while not very difficult—challenged the systems' quantifier handling in presence of linear arithmetic. LINKEDLIST provided differentiation in reasoning about heap data structures. N QUEENS and QUEUE were perceived by most as outside the achievable in the competition time frame. Altogether, N QUEENS was probably the most difficult problem, combining complex reasoning and a difficulty to express when there is no legal solution.

The issue of theory reasoning. A common issue in the competition was the battle to solve the arising SMT problems. In the majority of cases, the solvers were successful. When they were not (this was most notable in INVERT), the stress for the users was high. In the aftermath, we have seen a wide range of more or less elaborate workarounds for such cases. Better ways for the user to guide the proof search (and for the system to give feedback) are needed. The inference speed, on the other hand, was generally deemed adequate in this competition.

The issues of ADTs and modularity. For LINKEDLIST and QUEUE, participants have produced solutions of different flavors of modularity. An interesting solution class were behavioral specifications, i.e., the ones completely separating interface and implementation. In LINKEDLIST, such separation required introducing additional methods for constructing lists, even though they did not contribute to the computation required in the problem. A desirable property of specifications is a clear syntactic separation of interface and implementation (at best, keeping them in separate files), as it makes understanding modularity concepts easier.

Concerning the use of abstract data types (ADTs), there is still a gap between different reasoning traditions. Foundational systems like HOL have elaborate and well-established ADT theories, while verification systems for imperative and OO code mainly use ADTs in an ad hoc manner. A systematic connection between the two realms remains a challenge.

Judging solutions and competition organization. The competition made apparent that even a qualitative evaluation of solutions, with an informal setup and no ranking, is not an easy task. Solutions varied greatly in their requirement formalization and proof methods. Understanding the details of a solution (let alone validating it with a tool) requires a significant effort from an evaluation committee. Helpful in this regard could be holding a dialogue with the developers, or using a structured questionnaire such as [6]. Certain merits of a solution can be effectively measured [10] (the web version of this report contains statistics on solution verbosity), while others (e.g., elegance) remain subjective. Discussing verification solutions is not as standardized or automated as judging other reasoning tool competitions, but it is extremely instructive.

Other suggestions concerning organization were to include more advanced programming concepts (e.g., concurrency), to allow remote participation thus opening the competition to a wider public, or to assign a separate time slot to each individual problem to achieve a clearer differentiation.

Relevance of the competition. The competition (and its aftermath) has shown that all systems are—in the hands of an experienced user—capable of solving any problem. At the same time, already the very "simple" problems posed have exposed many practical issues with current verification tools. These issues are typically not thematized by the way we judge progress in program verification today, i.e., by how big a project can be verified with essentially unlimited resources. The competition with its limited time slot offers a very useful complementary perspective on verification's way to wide practical use.

An afterword from the organizers. The first Verified Software Competition exceeded the expectations of its organizers. We were impressed by the interest the competition received and by the enthusiasm of the participants, which is also demonstrated by the effort spent in the aftermath of the competition to solve the remaining problems. There was a strong encouragement to continue organizing such events. We hope the competition becomes a recurring part of the VSTTE conference and contributes to the Verified Software Initiative.

References

1. Arthan, R., Jones, R.: Z in HOL in ProofPower. BCS FACS FACTS, 2005-1
2. Barnett, M., Chang, B.-Y.E., DeLine, R., Jacobs, B., Leino, K.R.M.: Boogie: A modular reusable verifier for object-oriented programs. In: de Boer, F.S., Bonsangue, M.M., Graf, S., de Roever, W.-P. (eds.) FMCO 2005. LNCS, vol. 4111, pp. 364–387. Springer, Heidelberg (2006)
3. Beckert, B., Hähnle, R., Schmitt, P.H. (eds.): Verification of Object-Oriented Software: The KeY Approach. LNCS, vol. 4334. Springer, Heidelberg (2007)
4. Berdine, J., Calcagno, C., O'Hearn, P.W.: Smallfoot: Modular automatic assertion checking with separation logic. In: de Boer, F.S., Bonsangue, M.M., Graf, S., de Roever, W.-P. (eds.) FMCO 2005. LNCS, vol. 4111, pp. 115–137. Springer, Heidelberg (2006)
5. Bornat, R., Calcagno, C., O'Hearn, P., Parkinson, M.: Permission accounting in separation logic. In: POPL (2005)
6. COST Action IC0701. Verification problem repository, www.verifythis.org
7. de Moura, L., Bjørner, N.: Z3: An efficient SMT solver. In: Ramakrishnan, C.R., Rehof, J. (eds.) TACAS 2008. LNCS, vol. 4963, pp. 337–340. Springer, Heidelberg (2008)
8. Hoare, C., Misra, J., Leavens, G.T., Shankar, N.: The verified software initiative: A manifesto. ACM Comput. Surv. 41, 1–22 (2009)
9. Leino, K.R.M.: Dafny: An automatic program verifier for functional correctness. In: Clarke, E.M., Voronkov, A. (eds.) LPAR-16 2010. LNCS, vol. 6355, pp. 348–370. Springer, Heidelberg (2010)
10. Leino, K.R.M., Moskal, M.: VACID-0: Verification of ample correctness of invariants of data-structures, edition 0. In: Proceedings of Tools and Experiments Workshop at VSTTE (2010)
11. Leino, K.R.M., Rümmer, P.: A polymorphic intermediate verification language: Design and logical encoding. In: Esparza, J., Majumdar, R. (eds.) TACAS 2010. LNCS, vol. 6015, pp. 312–327. Springer, Heidelberg (2010)
12. Schmitt, P.H., Ulbrich, M., Weiß, B.: Dynamic frames in Java dynamic logic. In: Beckert, B., Marché, C. (eds.) FoVeOOS 2010. LNCS, vol. 6528, pp. 138–152. Springer, Heidelberg (2011)
13. Sitaraman, M., Adcock, B., Avigad, J., Bronish, D., Bucci, P., Frazier, D., Friedman, H., Harton, H., Heym, W., Kirschenbaum, J., Krone, J., Smith, H., Weide, B.: Building a push-button RESOLVE verifier: Progress and challenges. In: Formal Aspects of Computing, pp. 1–20 (2010)
14. Slind, K., Norrish, M.: A brief overview of HOL4. In: Mohamed, O.A., Muñoz, C., Tahar, S. (eds.) TPHOLs 2008. LNCS, vol. 5170, pp. 28–32. Springer, Heidelberg (2008)

Validated Compilation through Logic

Guodong Li*

Fujitsu Labs of America, CA

Abstract. To reason about programs written in a language, one needs to define its formal semantics, derive a reasoning mechanism (e.g. a program logic), and maximize the proof automation. Unfortunately, a compiler may involve multiple languages and phases; it is tedious and error prone to do so for each language and each phase.

We present an approach based on the use of higher order logic to ease this burden. All the Intermediate Representations (IRs) are special forms of the logic of a prover such that IR programs can be reasoned about directly in the logic. We use this technique to construct and validate an optimizing compiler. New techniques are used to compile-with-proof all the programs into the logic, *e.g.* a logic specification is derived automatically from the monad interpretation of a piece of assembly code.

1 Introduction

Giving realistic programming languages like C a correct semantics is difficult. It is even more so to make such semantics tractable so that we can reason about non-trivial programs in a formal setting. Some widely used functional languages have been given a formal semantics, *e.g.* ML has a formal operational semantics [13]. However, these semantics do not as yet provide a practical basis for formal reasoning about programs, although they are extremely valuable as reference documents and for proving meta-theorems (like type preservation).

We may use logic to model practically useful systems, and then manipulate the programs at the logic level. This method allows formal reasoning to the maximum extent since applications are modeled directly in logic. In addition, to connect the logic to realistic languages, we may translate programs written in (a subset of) a realistic high level language such as ML or C to equivalent logic specifications, then prove properties on them. This procedure is much easier than working directly on source programs.

Furthermore, the properties proved on a high level program may not hold on the binary form since compilers may introduce bugs and users often make over-simplifying assumptions on the machine model. This requires the implementation and validation of an extensible compiler, which is extremely tedious when it involves multiple Intermediate Representations (IRs) and compilation phases.

In this paper we use higher order logic to represent IRs and use term rewriting to perform program transformations. A typical application is a validated compiler from high level languages like ML or C to assembly code. All the IRs are special forms of the term language dwelling within the logic of a theorem prover

---

* The presented work is done at the University of Utah.

M. Butler and W. Schulte (Eds.): FM 2011, LNCS 6664, pp. 169–183, 2011.
© Springer-Verlag Berlin Heidelberg 2011

such that IR programs can be reasoned about using the ordinary mathematics provided by the prover. Program transformations can be cleanly isolated and specified as term rewrites. One of the keys is to compile-with-proof all the programs into the logic. For example, a logic specification is derived automatically from the monad representation of a piece of assembly code.

The presented work is inspired by our software compiler [10,11,12] which produces assembly code for a subset of the specification language of the HOL theorem prover — Total Functional Language (TFL) [20] — a pure, total functional programming layer built on top of higher order logic and implemented in both the HOL-4 [8] and Isabelle [17] systems. Its front-end [12] translates a source function into a simpler intermediate format by compiling away many advanced features, *e.g.* it performs monomorphisation and defunctionalization to eliminate polymorphism and higher order functions. Its back-end [10] generates from this intermediate format an equivalent *imperative* program, which will be translated to other imperative IRs and finally to the machine code. In particular, the imperative IRs (with explicit syntax and semantics) include HSL, CFL and SAL.

This back-end turned out to be the bottleneck of the entire compiler due mainly to the difficulty in reasoning about these IRs. For example, the verification of programs manipulating heaps and stacks is very tedious. It is also inflexible, failing to accommodate extensions and modifications smoothly. For instance, since the incorporation of some traditional optimizations requires the formalization of relevant control flow and data flow analysis, almost all such optimizations are opted out in the back-end.

The first goal of this paper is to present a new back-end based on *target code decompilation* to solve these problems. Given a piece of target code (possibly with tricky control flow and non-terminating), this back-end generates HOL functions modeling the semantics of this code. These functions are then automatically proved to be equivalent to the front-end outputs. The back-end also supports the decompilation of unstructured code produced by third-party code generators such as GCC. One big advantage is that we do not need any rule system or ad-hoc reasoning framework. Instead the decompilation is basically a functional interpretation of the imperative machine code. Such interpretation reveals the intrinsic control flow of a flat program. We show that this method works for *arbitrary* control flow while the reasoning mechanism is intuitive and natural.

The second goal is to extend the front-end to accept more realistic source languages. Particularly, we present an approach to compile a small subset of C to TFL by deductively synthesizing functions from imperative programs. This allows a safe source translation from a simple C program to one accepted by our compiler so that the big burden of implementing a validated C compiler is gone. This tiny (but first) step allows us to reason about a C program (of the allowed syntax) directly in the prover's logic rather than using ad-hoc mechanisms.

The third goal is to use only a small number of succinct transformations to bridge the gap introduced by the the new back-end and front-end, yet is able to produce code of the same quality as modern compilers like GCC do. In sum, this paper demonstrates the first attempt to unite all phases of an optimizing compiler together in a logic: both high level and low level programs are compiled into the logic; all transformations are performed and validated in the logic. Using the logic as the universal IR makes easier the compilation and its validation.

Motivating Example. We show below the ML (or TFL) and C versions of a program involving the calculation of the factorial of input x.

ML$_{ex}$

C_{ex}

ML$_{ex}$	C_{ex}
$f_{ex}\ (x,y) \doteq$	
$\quad$ let $f_{fact}\ (x,a) =$	f_{ex} (unsigned x, unsigned y) {
$\quad\quad$ (if $x = 0$ then (x,a)	$\quad$ unsigned $a = 1$;
$\quad\quad\quad$ else $f_{fact}\ (x-1, x*a))$	$\quad$ while $(x \neq 0)$
$\quad$ in	$\quad\quad \{a = x*a;\ x = x-1;\ \}$
$\quad$ let $(v_0, v_1) = f_{fact}\ (x,1)$ in	$\quad$ if $(a \geq y)$ return $a - y$;
$\quad$ if $v_1 \geq y$ then $v_1 - y$	$\quad$ else return $a + 2 * y$;
$\quad$ else $v_1 + 2 * y$	}

We may ask two questions: (1) do they terminate? and (2) are they equivalent (with respect to their semantics)? Before answering these questions we have to give them formal semantics and reasoning mechanisms. Our front-end is able to translate the C version C_{ex} to the ML version ML$_{ex}$, which is written in the term language of the HOL logic. This leads immediately to the proof of their equivalence. Moreover, HOL's TFL package is able to automatically prove that they terminate when $x \geq 0$.

A compiler may generate the following ARM-style assembly code cs_{ex}. This code first sets register r_1's value to 1. It then checks whether r_0 is 0; if yes then jumps to label l_{+5} by increasing the program pointer by 4; and so forth.

$l:$ mov r_1 1	$l_{+4}:$ b (-3)	$l_{+8}:$ mul r_2 2 r_2
$l_{+1}:$ beq r_0 0 $(+4)$	$l_{+5}:$ blt r_1 r_2 $(+3)$	$l_{+9}:$ add r_1 r_1 r_2
$l_{+2}:$ mul r_1 r_1 r_0	$l_{+6}:$ sub r_1 r_1 r_2	$l_{+10}:$
$l_{+3}:$ sub r_0 r_0 1	$l_{+7}:$ b $(+3)$	

Our goal is to not only produce the assembly code, but also prove the compilation correct. Specifically, the relation between the input in (r_0, r_2) before the execution and the output in r_1 after the execution shall be represented by f_{ex}. Our compiler transforms f_{ex} into a lower level format shown below.

$f_{ex_1}\ (r_0, r_2) \doteq$
let $f(r_0, r_1) =$
$\quad$ if $r_0 = 0$ then (r_0, r_1) else let $r_1 = r_1 * r_0$ in let $r_0 = r_0 - 1$ in $f\ (r_0, r_1)$ in
let $r_1 = 1$ in let $(r_0, r_1) = f(r_0, r_1)$ in
if $r_1 < r_2$ then let $r_2 = 2 * r_2$ in let $r_1 = r_1 + r_2$ in r_1 else let $r_1 = r_1 - r_2$ in r_1

It is not difficult to produce code cs_{ex} from function f_{ex_1} (our compiler applies straight-forward translation to do this). The main challenge is to prove their semantics equivalence. For this we might take another look at the relation between the code and the function. Suppose we are given the code cs_{ex}, can we "decompile" it to a function like f_{ex_1}? If yes then we obtain a logic function of cs_{ex} which is equivalent to f_{ex_1} as well as f_{ex}. We may do this for the code produced by third-party generators such as GCC.

2 Extended Front-End

TFL is a subset of the higher order logic built in HOL, thus their syntax and the semantics have already been defined in the logic. So do all the IRs. That is, programs written in TFL or IRs are simply mathematical functions defined in the HOL logic. It is this feature that enables us to use standard mathematics to reason about these languages. This supports much flexibility and allows the meaning of a program to be transparent. Mimicking the ML language, TFL is a polymorphic, higher order and terminating functional language supporting algebraic datatypes and pattern matching.

Compiling Imperative Programs. Importing terminating ML programs into TFL is easy due to the high similarity in their syntaxes and semantics. It is also possible to import programs written in an imperative language such as a small subset of C. As a demonstration, we develop a method for such a subset (denoted here as C0) with the following structures, where e represents C expressions.

$$s ::= v := e \mid \textbf{return } v \mid s; s \mid \textbf{IF } e \textbf{ THEN } s \textbf{ ELSE } s \mid \textbf{WHILE } e \ s \mid v := p_{id} \ s$$

In order to connect the semantics of a C0 structure S to a TFL function f, we introduce the following judgment to characterize S's axiomatic semantics as a predicate, where $\sigma[x]$ returns the value of variable x in state σ; and eval S σ returns the new state after S's execution. Notation (i, f, o) specifies that: if the initial value of input i is v, then in the state after the execution of S, the value left in output o is equal to applying the function f to the initial value v. Basically, a judgment can be obtained by instantiating the P and Q in a Hoare triple $\{P\}$ s $\{Q\}$ to $\lambda\sigma.\,\sigma[i] = v$ and $\lambda\sigma.\,\sigma[o] = f\ v$ respectively. If a judgment synthesizes f with respect to the input i and output o, then we claim that structure S correctly implements function f.

$$S \vdash (i, f, o) \doteq \forall\sigma\forall v.\,(\sigma[i] = v) \Rightarrow ((\text{eval } S\ \sigma)[o] = f\ v)$$

In Figure 1 we show a couple of rules for synthesizing a function by composing the judgments. A judgment may contain an extra field ex (explained later). Notation $\hat{v}$ generates a TFL variable for a C0 variable v; and $\hat{e}$ returns the TFL expression corresponding to a C0 expression e. Notation fv returns the free variables in an expression. We use $\doteq$ to introduce abbreviations. To mitigate the burden on termination proof we axiomatize some of these rules.

Rule assgn builds a judgment for a C0 assignment $v := e$. The input consists of all the free variables in e and the output is v; the synthesized function calculates the expression e. Rule return synthesizes an identity function for the same input and output v. Rules seq, cond, while and call are used to synthesize functions for sequential structures, conditional structures, loops and procedure calls respectively. The "while" in rule while is defined by while $c\ f \doteq \lambda x.\ \text{if } \neg\ c\ x$ then x else while $c\ f\ (f\ x)$.

An important rule, frame, is used to match the inputs and outputs of different judgments. For instance, suppose we want to use the seq rule to compose

$$\frac{i \doteq \mathtt{fv}\ e}{v := e \ \vdash\ \langle i,\ \lambda \hat{i}.\hat{e},\ v\rangle}\ \text{assgn} \qquad \frac{}{\mathtt{return}\ v \ \vdash\ \langle v,\ \lambda \hat{v}.\hat{v},\ v\rangle}\ \text{return}$$

$$\frac{S_1 \ \vdash\ \langle i_1,\ f_1,\ o_1\rangle \downarrow ex_1 \quad S_2 \ \vdash\ \langle o_1,\ f_2,\ o_2\rangle \downarrow ex_2}{S_1;\ S_2 \ \vdash\ \langle i_1,\ f_2 \circ f_1,\ o_2\rangle \downarrow (ex_1 \cup ex_2)}\ \text{seq}$$

$$\frac{S_1 \ \vdash\ \langle i,\ f_1,\ o\rangle \downarrow ex_1 \quad S_2 \ \vdash\ \langle i,\ f_2,\ o\rangle \downarrow ex_2}{\mathtt{IF}\ e\ \mathtt{THEN}\ S_1\ \mathtt{ELSE}\ S_2 \ \vdash\ \langle i,\ (\lambda \hat{i}.\ \mathtt{if}\ \hat{e}\ \mathtt{then}\ f_1\ \hat{i}\ \mathtt{else}\ f_2\ \hat{i}),\ o\rangle \downarrow (ex_1 \cup ex_2)}\ \text{cond}$$

$$\frac{S \ \vdash\ \langle i,\ f,\ i\rangle \downarrow ex}{\mathtt{WHILE}\ e\ S \ \vdash\ \langle i,\ \mathtt{while}\ (\lambda \hat{i}.\hat{e})\ f,\ i\rangle \downarrow ex}\ \text{while}$$

$$\frac{p_{id}\ i := S \quad S \ \vdash\ \langle i,\ f,\ o\rangle \downarrow ex}{w := p_{id}\ v \ \vdash\ \langle v,\ f,\ w\rangle \downarrow \{v \in ex \mid v\ \text{is global}\}}\ \text{call}$$

$$\frac{S \ \vdash\ \langle i,\ f,\ o\rangle \downarrow ex}{S \ \vdash\ \langle i,\ \lambda \hat{i}.\ \mathtt{let}\ (\hat{o}_1, \hat{o}_2) = f\ \hat{i}\ \mathtt{in}\ \hat{o}_1,\ o_1\rangle \downarrow (ex \cup \{o_2\})}\ \text{shrink}$$

$$\frac{S \ \vdash\ \langle i,\ f,\ o\rangle \downarrow ex \quad v \notin ex \quad v \notin o}{S \ \vdash\ \langle (i, v),\ (\lambda(\hat{i}, \hat{v}).(f\ \hat{i}, \hat{v})),\ (o, v)\rangle \downarrow ex}\ \text{frame}$$

Fig. 1. Compositional rules for converting C0 to TFL

judgments $S_1 \vdash \langle i_1, f_1, o_1\rangle$ and $S_2 \vdash \langle i_2, f_2, o_2\rangle$. If $o_1 \neq i_2$, we must adjust the judgments to make $o_1 = i_2$. This is accomplished by the frame rule which allows adding extra variables into the input and output.

Since all the variables updated in a structure will appear in the output, we might safely assume that those not in the output are unchanged. As in separation logic [18], we can add these unchanged variables into the input/output using the frame rule if needed. On the other hand, as in the shrink rule, we may remove from the output those variables which will not be referenced anymore. The *exception* set ex records the updated variables, the application of frame should rule out them. When the exception set is empty we do not present it.

The application of the composition rules is syntax directed, and proceeds in a bottom-up manner. For illustration, consider the C version of the running example. The judgments for the two statements within the loop are as follows.

$$a := x * a \ \vdash\ \langle (x, a),\ \lambda(x, a).\ x * a,\ a\rangle \qquad x := x - 1 \ \vdash\ \langle x,\ \lambda x.\ x - 1,\ x\rangle$$

Since the output of the first judgment is not the same as the input of the second judgment, we apply the frame rule to adjust and then compose them.

$$a := x * a \ \vdash\ \langle (x, a),\ \lambda(x, a).\ (x, x * a),\ (x, a)\rangle$$
$$x := x - 1 \ \vdash\ \langle (x, a),\ \lambda(x, a).\ (x - 1, a),\ (x, a)\rangle$$
$$a := x * a;\ x := x - 1 \ \vdash\ \langle (x, a),\ \lambda(x, a).\ (x - 1, x * a),\ (x, a)\rangle$$

Let g_1 be an abbreviation of $\lambda(x, a).\ (x - 1, x * a)$. Next we apply the while rule to get a judgment for the loop. The composition of this judgment and the one for a := 1 yields a new judgment, where $g_2 \doteq (\mathtt{while}\ (\lambda(x, a).x \neq 0)\ g) \circ (\lambda x.(x, 1))$.

$$\mathtt{WHILE}\ (x \neq 0)\ \{a := x * a;\ x := x - 1;\} \ \vdash\ \langle (x, a),\ \mathtt{while}\ (\lambda(x, a).x \neq 0)\ g,\ (x, a)\rangle$$
$$a := 1;\ \mathtt{WHILE}\ (x \neq 0)\ \{a := x * a;\ x := x - 1;\} \ \vdash\ \langle x,\ g_2,\ (x, a)\rangle$$

Similarly we obtain the judgment for the conditional statement.

if $(a \geq y)$ return $a - y$; else $a + 2 * y$; $\vdash$
$\langle (a, y),\ \lambda(a, y).$ if $a \geq y$ then $a - y$ else $a + 2 * y,\ (a, y) \rangle$

We can eliminate the unused variable x (through rule shrink) from the judgment. Then we add the y into the input and output through the frame rule.

$a := 1$; WHILE $(x \neq 0)$ $\{a := x * a;\ x := x - 1;\}$
$\vdash \langle x,\ \lambda(x, a).\,\text{let } (x, a) = g_2\ (x, a)\ \text{in } a,\ a \rangle \downarrow \{x\}$
$\vdash \langle (x, y),\ (\lambda((x, a), y).\,(\text{let } (x, a) = g_2\ (x, a)\ \text{in } a,\ a),\ (a, y)) \rangle \downarrow \{x\}$

Finally we synthesize a function for the entire program which can be rewritten and simplified to ML_{ex} by applying some rewrite rules about "while" and "let".

$$(\lambda(a, y).\text{ if } a \geq y \text{ then } a - y \text{ else } a + 2 * y) \circ (\lambda((x, a), y).\,(\text{let } (x, a) = g_2\ (x, a)\ \text{in } a,\ y))$$

3   De-compiling Assembly Code

The back-end decompiles an assembly program to equivalent HOL functions. The "decompilation with proof" trick is first used by us in [10] to synthesize a function from an intermediate program. Magnus et al [16] extended this method to decompile ARM code. Unfortunately, these methods are based on rule composition — as we show in the previous section — the function is constructed by composing rules in a bottom-up manner. The code must be well structured since these methods need to discover the control flow structures to guide the composition. What is worse, such methods require substantial effort on soundness proof, as demonstrated in [19,15] where most of the space of a paper is used to explain the rule system and its proof. They are also difficult to extend; and a minor modification may demand redoing the entire proof of the rule system.

For example, it is difficult to identify the control flow (*e.g.* loops) of the following Ackerman program, let alone coming up with rules to reason about it.

```
unsigned Ack (unsigned m, unsigned n)
{ if (m == 0) return n + 1;
   if (n == 0) return Ack(m - 1, 1);
   return Ack(m - 1, Ack(m, n - 1)); }
```

We present here a new way to model and decompile low level programs. The operational semantics of machine instructions are modeled as state monads, and the control flow is represented by monad binding. We use automatic deduction and pure rewriting to translate monad representations to HOL functions. Our method makes the soundness proof trivial and is able to handle unstructured and non-terminating code that will fail the attempts made in [10,16].

Machine Language. We use a small subset of the ARM instructions and a simplified machine model to illustrate the method. A code fragment consists of a union (or list) of labeled instruction $l : instr$. The union of code fragments cs_0 and cs_1 is denoted as $cs_0 \cup cs_1$ where $\cup$ is the usual set union operator which is commutative and associative. Sometimes we write $\{l : [instr_1, \ldots, instr_n]\}$ for $\{l : instr_1\} \cup \{l_{+1} : instr_2\} \cup \ldots \cup \{l_{+n-1} : instr_n\}$.

The program semantics is described by an evaluation relation $\sigma \succ cs \rightarrow \sigma'$, which relates state σ at the moment of entry to a piece of code cs to the possible states at the corresponding possible moments of exit σ'. A state σ consists of a label l modeling the pc and a data state s. For a single instruction $instr$, notation $\sigma \succ instr \rightarrow \sigma'$ specifies that the execution of $instr$ leads pre-state σ to post-state σ'. We give below some examples, where $s[x]$ returns x's value in data state s, $s \uplus (x, v)$ denotes the update of s by setting x's value to v.

$$(l, s) \succ \{l : \text{sub } r_0 \ r_1 \ n\} \rightarrow (l + 1, s \uplus (r_0, s[r_1] - n)))$$
$$(l, s) \succ \{l : \text{blt } r_1 \ 5 \ (+n)\} \rightarrow \begin{cases} (l + n, s) & \text{if } s[r_1] < 5 \\ (l + 1, s) & \text{otherwise} \end{cases}$$

The relation summerizes the operational semantics of a single instruction is $(l, s) \succ \{l : instr\} \rightarrow (\textbf{next } instr \ s \ l, \textbf{decode } instr \ s)$, where **next** models label undates, and **decode** models the transitions of the data state s.

Decompilation. We use monads to model side-effect computations. Essentially, our monad is a state monad where the state is the data state $s : state$.

```
datatype MONAD = Monad of state → ('α # state)
exec (Monad f) ≐ f
```

The monad operations >>=, >> and **return** are defined as expected

```
f >>= g ≐ Monad (λs. let (v,s') = exec f s in exec (g v) s')
f >> g  ≐ f >>= λ(). g
return x ≐ Monad (λ s. (x, s)) .
```

We record the program counter (pc) in the value of a monad by instantiating type α to type MVALUE. Specifically, TO f_l models how the pc is updated : suppose the pc's old value is l, then its new value becomes $f_l \ l$. Constructor END is for the case where the pc is out of the program domain.

```
datatype MVALUE = TO of (n → n) | END
```

The operational semantics of an instruction is modeled by a state monad. Recall that next and decode return the next pc and the next state respectively.

$[\![inst]\!]$ = Monad (λs. (TO (λl. next inst s l), decode inst s))

We show below some examples. The dummy monad $[\![\epsilon]\!]$ satisfies exec $[\![\epsilon]\!]$ s = (END, s).

```
[[sub r2 r1 r0]] = Monad (λs. (TO (λl.l+1), s ⊎ (r2, s[r1]-s[r0])))
[[b (+n)]] = Monad (λs. (TO (λl.n+1), s))
[[ε]] = return END
```

Code Specification. Our decompiler derives functions from a code fragment in a top down manner. The key is to associate each labeled instruction $l : inst$ with a monad f so as to generate an *instruction specification* of format $(l, f, inst)$ such that f models the computation (of the entire code) starting from label l. The union of instruction specifications constitutes a *code specification*. For example, in the following code specification, monads f_1 and f_2 are associated with the first two instructions such that f_1 and f_2 model the code's computation from l and l_{+1} respectively. The trick here is we do not have to know what exactly f_1 and f_2 are; instead, it suffices to know the relation between them: $f_1 = [\![\text{mov } r_1 \ r_0]\!] \gg f_2$.

$$\{(l, f_1, \text{mov } r_1 \ r_0), \ (l_{+1}, f_2, \text{add } r_2 \ r_1 \ r_0), \ldots\}$$

The relation between all monads represents the *well formedness* of a code fragment: it is well formed iff for any instruction specification $(l, f, instr)$, the monad f equals to the binding of the monad corresponding to $instr$ and the one at the the place to which the pc will go. In the following definition, function f_of returns the function in the monad value, *i.e.* $f\_of \ (\text{TO } l_f) = l_f$. Notation $get\_f \ code\_spec \ l$ returns the instruction specification at label l; if l is not in the domain of the code, then the dummy monad $[\![\epsilon]\!]$ is returned.

$$\begin{aligned}
&\text{code\_wf } code\_spec = \\
&\quad \forall l \forall f \forall instr. \ (l, f, instr) \in code\_spec \Rightarrow \\
&\quad f = [\![instr]\!] \gg= (\lambda f_l. \ get\_f \ code\_spec \ ((f\_of \ f_l) \ l))
\end{aligned}$$

Rewriting a *code_spec* with code_wf's definition and the semantics of jump instructions will give us a first order predicate depicting the relations between the monads in *code_spec*. We call this predicate *monad representation (MR)*. For example, the MR of the loop in the running example contains four monads, where eq_branch $x \ y \ f_1 \ f_2 \doteq \text{Monad } (\lambda s. \text{ if } s[x] = s[y] \text{ then exec } f_1 \ s \text{ else exec } f_2 \ s)$.

$$\begin{aligned}
loop\_spec &= \left\{ \begin{array}{l} (l_{+1}, f_1, \text{beq } r_0 \ 0 \ (+4)), \ (l_{+2}, f_2, \text{mul } r_1 \ r_1 \ r_0), \\ (l_{+3}, f_3, \text{sub } r_0 \ r_0 \ 1), \quad (l_{+4}, f_4, \text{b } (-3)) \end{array} \right\} \\
&\text{code\_wf } loop\_spec = \\
&(f_1 = \text{eq\_branch } r_0 \ 0 \ [\![\epsilon]\!] \ f_2) \wedge (f_2 = [\![\text{mul } r_1 \ r_1 \ r_0]\!] \gg f_3) \wedge \\
&(f_3 = [\![\text{sub } r_0 \ r_0 \ 1]\!] \gg f_4) \wedge (f_4 = f_1)
\end{aligned}$$

Not all monads in an MR are important. In the *loop_spec* example, monad f_1 is the most important one since it models the computation of the entire loop. We call such monads *anchor* monads since they mark the important control flow points in the code. Other monads (*e.g.* f_2, f_3 and f_4 in *loop_spec*) can be absorbed into anchor monads. We are free to pick any subset as anchor monads; different pickings will lead to derived functions of different formats (and the same semantics). Our compiler's picking is based on the IR's control flow.

$$f_1 = \text{eq\_branch } r_0 \ 0 \ [\![\epsilon]\!] \ ([\![\text{mul } r_1 \ r_1 \ r_0]\!] \gg [\![\text{sub } r_0 \ r_0 \ 1]\!] \gg f_1) \qquad (1)$$

The next step is to eliminate the instruction monads within an anchor monad to obtain the *normal form* of this anchor monad. This norm uses "let" and "if then else" expressions to depict the control flow of the original code. In order to distinguish a resource from the variable representing it, from now on we use

R_i to denote the the ith register, and $M[i]$ the memory slot at i. We write $\hat{x}$ for the variable corresponding to resource x, e.g. $\hat{R}_0 = r_0$ and $\hat{R}_1 = r_1$. The rewrite rules for converting an MR to its normal form include

$$[\![\text{mov } x \ y]\!] = \text{Monad } (\lambda s.(\text{TO } (l.l + 1), \text{let } \hat{x} = s[y] \text{ in } s \uplus (x, \hat{x})))$$
$$[\![\text{sub } x \ y \ z]\!] = \text{Monad } (\lambda s.(\text{TO } (l.l + 1), \text{let } \hat{x} = s[y] - s[z] \text{ in } s \uplus (x, \hat{x}))) .$$

Function Derivation. This phase derives HOL functions from the normal forms of anchor monads. Definition **read_monad** read the value from the state after the execution; **de_comp** decompiles-with-proof monad f to function g.

```
read_monad f s x = let (_,s') = exec f s in s'[x]
de_comp f (in,g,out) = ∀x. g x = read_monad f (s ⊎ (in,x)) out
```

The decompilation of monads not referring to other monads is straight-forward. The monad f_1 in loop_spec refers to itself; this reference will be converted to the call of the derived function associated with f_1. The decompiler generates the following theorem for the *loop_spec*.

$$loop\_spec \ \wedge \ \textbf{de\_comp } f_1 \ ((R_0, R_1), g, (R_0, R_1)) \Rightarrow$$
$$g \ (r_0, r_1) = \text{if } r_0 = 0 \text{ then } r_1 \text{ else let } r_1 = r_1 * r_0 \text{ in let } r_0 = r_0 - 1 \text{ in } g \ (r_0, r_1)$$

A stronger theorem as below may be derived by inducting on g's first argument. However the above theorem (which requires no induction) is sufficient since it warrants that only correct code will produce the expected function.

$$loop\_spec \Rightarrow \textbf{de\_comp } f_1 \ ((R_0, R_1), g, (R_0, R_1))$$

The MR of a piece of code (especially unstructured code) may contain multiple anchor monads connected with respect to the control flow. The derived functions should be connected in a similar way. Consider the following example.

$$(f_1 = \text{if } \dots \text{ then } \cdots \gg [\![\epsilon]\!] \text{ else } \cdots \gg f_2) \wedge$$
$$(f_2 = \text{if } \dots \text{ then } \cdots \gg f_3 \text{ else } \cdots \gg f_1) \wedge$$
$$(f_3 = \text{if } \dots \text{ then } \cdots \gg f_2 \text{ else } \cdots \gg f_3) .$$

The derived functions would look like the following, where i and o represent the input and output respectively, e_1 and e_2 are *input patterns* connecting the derived functions. Input patterns can is obtained through a simple fix-point calculation similar to the use-def analysis. That is, the input expression corresponding to monad f contains all the resources which will be used later.

$$(g_1 \ i = \text{if } \dots \text{ then } \dots \ o \text{ else let } \dots \text{ in } g_2 \ e_1) \wedge$$
$$(g_2 \ e_1 = \text{if } \dots \text{ then let } \dots \text{ in } g_3 \ e_2 \text{ else let } \dots \text{ in } g_1 \ i) \wedge$$
$$(g_3 \ e_2 = \text{if } \dots \text{ then let } \dots \text{ in } g_2 \ e_1 \text{ else let } \dots \text{ in } g_3 \ e_2)$$

Projective Functions. In essence, the process of function derivation is to project monad functions onto specific inputs and outputs. The derived functions maintain the same (control-flow) structures as the monad ones. We can further extend the well-formedness definition to accommodating these functions. The

(f, sig) in the following definition indicates that g is a projective function of monad f over input/output signatures sig. The decompilation constructs such functions automatically with respect to their signatures.

$$\begin{aligned}
&\text{code\_proj\_wf } code\_spec = \\
&\quad \forall l \forall f \forall pj \forall instr. \, (l, f, pj, instr) \in code\_spec \Rightarrow \\
&\quad f = [\![instr]\!] \gg= (\lambda f_l.\, \text{get\_f } code\_spec \, ((f\_of \, f_l) \, l)) \wedge \\
&\quad \forall (g, sig) \in pj. \forall s. \, \text{read\_monad } f \, s \, sig = g \, (s[sig])
\end{aligned}$$

This extension helps derive more readable functions by considering data separation [18]. Considering the following pseudo-code, where the first instruction invokes a recursive function rf which does not modify r_1's value. The decompilation derives $g_{1,1} = rf$, $g_{1,2} = \lambda x.x$, and $g_{2,1}(r_0, r_1) = \text{let } (r_0, r_1) = (rf \, r_0, (\lambda x.x) \, r_1) \text{ in } r_0 + r_1$, i.e. $g_{2,1}(r_0, r_1) = \text{let } r_0 = rf \, r_0 \text{ in } (r_0 + r_1, r_1)$. The recursive function $g_{1,1}$ is succinct since it does not take r_1 as an extra argument. The fact that r_1 is not changed is recorded by the identity function $g_{1,2}$. This technique performs the task of the "separation logic" in [15,16,14], but again needs no ad-hoc and intractable program logic.

$$\begin{aligned}
&(l, \quad f_1, \{(g_{1,1}, r_0), (g_{1,2}, r_1)\}, \, r_0 = rf \, r_0) \\
&(l_{+1}, f_2, \{(g_{2,1}, (r_0, r_1))\}, \qquad \text{add } r_0 \, r_0 \, r_1)
\end{aligned}$$

Procedure Call. The relation between monads represents the control flow. Procedure call poses a challenge when the return address is not given statically.

In ARM, the caller stores the return address (*i.e.* the label of the next instruction after the call) into the link register lr, which will be fetched by the callee upon exit. In the following code the procedure at $l' - l'_{+3}$ are called twice. Instruction bl stores the returns address (l_{+1} or l_{+4}) into the link register lr.

$$\begin{aligned}
&(l, \quad f_1, \text{bl } l') \qquad\quad (l_{+3}, \quad , \text{bl } l') \qquad\quad\quad (l'_{+1}, \quad , \text{sub } r_0 \, r_0 \, r_1) \\
&(l_{+1}, f_2, \text{mul } r_2 \, r_0 \, r_1) \, (l_{+4}, f_3, \text{mov } r_1 \, r_0) \qquad (l'_{+2}, \quad , \text{b } (-2)) \\
&(l_{+2}, \quad , \text{mov } r_0 \, r_2) \qquad (l', \quad f_c, \text{beq } r_0 \, r_1 \, (+3)) \, (l'_{+3}, f'_c, \text{b } lr)
\end{aligned}$$

In the MR below, monads f_c and f'_c model the computation starting from the entry and the exit point of the procedure respectively. Monad f'_c picks the next monad according to the return address stored in lr, *e.g.* f_2 is chosen when the return address is l_{+1}. The last case, which will never be encountered, handles the situation where the return address is unknown.

$$\begin{aligned}
&(f_1 = [\![\text{mov } lr \, l_{+1}]\!] \gg f_c) \wedge (f_c = \text{eq\_branch } r_0 \, r_1 \, f'_c \, ([\![\text{sub } r_0 \, r_0 \, r_1]\!] \gg f_c)) \\
&(f'_c = \text{Monad}(\lambda s. \, \text{case } s[lr] \, \text{of} \\
&\qquad\qquad\qquad\qquad l_{+1} \rightarrow \text{exec } f_2 \, s \\
&\qquad\qquad\qquad | \quad l_{+4} \rightarrow \text{exec } f_3 \, s \\
&\qquad\qquad\qquad | \quad k \rightarrow \text{exec } (\text{get\_f } code\_spec \, k) \, s)) \wedge \\
&(f_2 = [\![\text{mov } r_2 \, r_0 \, r_1]\!] \gg [\![\text{mov } r_0 \, r_2]\!] \gg [\![\text{mov } lr \, l_{+4}]\!] \gg f_c) \wedge (f_3 = [\![\text{mov } r_1 \, r_0]\!] \gg \ldots)
\end{aligned}$$

The decompilation of this MR is straightforward. Some derived functions are curried and take lr as an extra argument (an alternative is to use a projective function described above to model how lr is updated). We introduce function g'_c

to model the recursive procedure. Note that $\forall l \in \{l_{+1}, l_{+4}\}. g_c\, l = g_c'$. The derived function g_c is converted to a form in the procedure call style.

$(g_1\ (r_0, r_1) = \text{let } lr = l_{+1} \text{ in } g_c\ lr\ (r_0, r_1)) \wedge$
$(g_2\ (r_0, r_1) = \text{let } r_2 = r_0 + r_1 \text{ in let } r_0 = r_2 \text{ in let } lr = l_{+4} \text{ in } g_c\ lr\ (r_0, r_1)) \wedge$
$(g_c'\ (r_0, r_1) = \text{if } r_0 = r_1 \text{ then } (r_0, r_1) \text{ else let } r_0 = r_0 - r_1 \text{ in } g_c'\ (r_0, r_1))$
$g_c\ l_{+1}\ (r_0, r_1) = \text{if } r_0 = r_1 \text{ then } g_2\ (r_0, r_1) \text{ else let } r_0 = r_0 - r_1 \text{ in } g_c\ l_{+1}\ (r_0, r_1)$
$\qquad\qquad\quad = \text{let } (r_0, r_1) = g_c'\ (r_0, r_1) \text{ in } g_2\ (r_0, r_1)$
$g_c\ l_{+4}\ (r_0, r_1) = \text{let } (r_0, r_1) = g_c'\ (r_0, r_1) \text{ in } g_3\ r_0\ .$

Then function g_1 can be simplified to a format where function g_c' is called twice, which is consistent with the control flow structure of the source code.

$g_1\ (r_0, r_1) = g_c\ l_{+1}\ (r_0, r_1) = \text{let } (r_0, r_1) = g_c'\ (r_0, r_1) \text{ in } g_2\ (r_0, r_1)$
$\qquad\qquad = \text{let } (r_0, r_1) = g_c'\ (r_0, r_1) \text{ in let } r_2 = r_0 + r_1 \text{ in}$
$\qquad\qquad\quad \text{let } r_0 = r_2 \text{ in let } (r_0, r_1) = g_c'\ (r_0, r_1) \text{ in } g_3\ r_0$

4   Example Program Transformations

In this section we show some examples of performing program transformations in the logic which extend our previous work [10,11,12].

Lightweight Closure Conversion. This conversion captures the free variables for nested functions in an environment as passed to the function as an extra argument. The function body is modified so that references to free variables are now references to the environment parameter. When a function is referenced, the function is paired with the environment as a closure.

The clos_init rule creates a closure for closing the first free variable v in the body of function f. Administrative term clos is used to record the transformed function and the environment. By definition $\forall c.\, \text{clos}\ (f, c) = f$. We uses tactics (at the meta-level) to control the application of this rule such that it will not be applied to functions without free variables. Rule clos_one handles extra free variables and builds the environment as a tuple. It is applied repeatedly until no free variable remains in the function body.

[clos_init] $\text{let } f = g\ v \text{ in } e\ f \iff \text{let } f = \text{clos}\ (g,\ v) \text{ in } e\ (f\ v)$
[clos_one] $\text{let } f = \text{clos}\ ((\lambda c.\, g\ v\ c),\ c) \text{ in } e\ (f\ c) \iff$
$\qquad\qquad \text{let } f = \text{clos}\ ((\lambda(c, v).\, g\ v\ c), (c, v)) \text{ in } e\ (f\ (c, v))$

We show below a simple example, where f' is an abbreviation of $\lambda x.\, x + y + z$. The final step performs explicit tuple allocation, where #1 and #2 take the first and second components of a tuple respectively.

$\text{let } f = \lambda x.\, x + y + z \text{ in } f\ 1 \qquad =$
$\text{let } f = (\lambda y.\, f')\ y \text{ in } (\lambda f.\, f\ 1)\ f \iff$
$\text{let } f = \text{clos}\ ((\lambda y.\, f'),\ y) \text{ in } (\lambda f.\, f\ 1)\ (f\ y) \qquad =$
$\text{let } f = \text{clos}\ ((\lambda y.\, (\lambda z.\, \lambda y.\, f')\ z\ y),\ y) \text{ in } (\lambda f.\, f\ 1)\ (f\ y) \iff$
$\text{let } f = \text{clos}\ ((\lambda(y, z).\, f'),\ (y, z)) \text{ in } (\lambda f.\, f\ 1)\ (f\ (y, z)) \qquad =$
$\text{let } f = \lambda(y, z).\, \lambda x.\, x + y + z \text{ in } f\ (y, z)\ 1 \qquad =$
$\text{let } f\ c\ x = \text{let } y = \#1\ c \text{ in let } z = \#2\ c \text{ in } x + y + z \text{ in } f\ (y, z)\ 1$

Example Optimization: Common Subexpression Elimination. Working on the normalized IR form, this optimization avoids redundant evaluation of the same expression by reusing the result of the first evaluation.

$$[\mathsf{cse}]\ \mathsf{let}\ x = e\ \mathsf{in}\ f\ e\ \longleftrightarrow\ \mathsf{let}\ x = e\ \mathsf{in}\ f\ x$$

Exposing Heap and Stack. This phase places heap objects and stack objects in the memory. To model the memory, we introduce a function m mapping addresses to values. Heap variables and stack variables are indexed indirectly through the heap register hp and frame register fp respectively. A stack variable t_i is represented by $m[fp - i - 1]$; and a heap variable $a[r_i]$ is by $m[hp + \hat{a} + r_i]$ where $\hat{a}$ is the starting address of heap object a.

The rewrite rules for heap allocation include the following, where p_h marks the starting address of the available heap space, and new is used to allocate memory for n elements of type τ. An administrative term let_m has the same semantics as let does. It is used to mark the "let" expressions involving memory accesses. To validate the transformation, it suffices to eliminate all the "let_m"s.

[heap_alloc]
$$\mathsf{let}_m\ a = \mathsf{new}\ (\tau, n)\ \mathsf{in}\ e\ (a[i])\ \longleftrightarrow$$
$$\mathsf{let}_m\ p_h = p_h + n * (\mathsf{size}\ \tau)\ \mathsf{in}\ \mathsf{let}_m\ a = p_h\ \mathsf{in}\ e\ (m[hp + a + i * (\mathsf{size}\ \tau)])$$

5   Results

Our development contains around 12,000 lines of code (with 5,000 are legacy code from the previous version of the compiler [10,11,12]) including the definitions, proof and automation scripts. Most of the new theorems are for the formalization of C0 and the target language together with reasoning mechanisms.

We compare our compiler with GCC. Each program is written in a TFL version and a C version. TFL functions obtained from C versions are compared and shown to be equivalent to the manually defined ones. Currently the conversion succeeds in most cases but needs manual effort when the program is less TFL like due to insufficient compositional rules or automaton scripts. The other phases (*e.g.* de-compilation) are fully automated.

We tested several small programs including two block ciphers TEA and RC6. Although these programs are not big, they exhibit non-trivial control flows and tricky recursions. Essentially, our method goes in a per-function manner, thus is able to scale to larger programs which are usually composed of small functions.

To compare the two compilers, we measure the size of the generated assembly code in terms of executable instructions and the code's execution time. The time is normalized with respect to our compiler (regarded as 100%). We write drivers iterating over various inputs and link the generated code to the drivers. The time information may be inaccurate because (1) we run the programs on an ARM emulator (*i.e.* use arm-elf-run provided by the GNU ARM Toolchain) rather than a real processor; and (2) we pick only a fixed set of test cases.

Program	Code Size		Code Performance		=?
	Our Compiler	GCC4	Our Compiler	GCC4	
Factorial	7	7	100%	90%	*
Ackerman	17	21	100%	90%	*
Fibonacci	15	14	100%	95%	*
TEA	77	66	100%	80%	*
RC6	92	104	100%	90%	*

GCC 4.1.1 is given the option -O2 (thus function inlining and inter-procedure optimizations are disabled). These programs barely exhibit such advanced features as polymorphism and higher order functions. Our compiler tends to be slower than GCC because GCC applies better flow analysis and instruction selection/scheduling than our compiler does. However, since our compiler also applies many optimizations, $e.g.$ convert tail recursive function calls into loops, it can rival with GCC in performance for these programs. Note that our compiler can beat GCC with less optimizations ($e.g.$ no instruction merging).

An interesting point is to compare the functions derived from the codes generated by these compilers. These functions should be equal if the compilers are correct. As indicated in column "=?", we have proved that the compilers generate equivalent codes for all test programs by comparing the derived functions. We notice that the code generated by our compiler and GCC are often similar in terms of control flow structures; the main difference lies in the use of different instruction selection and scheduling schemes for basic blocks. Currently this equivalent proof is done manually (especially when two functions have different control flows, which fails simple tactics that check only the equivalence of basic blocks) and can be automated in the future. Note that, for our compiler, the decompiled function g_1 is alpha-equivalent to the IR function g_2 produced by the front-end since cs_{g_2}, the code from which g_1 derives, inherits the control flow structure from g_2. Our compiler can serve as the canonical one when checking the correctness of third-party compilers.

6   Related Work and Conclusions

There has been much work on translating functional languages; one of the most influential has been the paper of Tolmach and Oliva [21] which developed a translation from SML-like functional language to Ada. Hickey and Nogin [7] worked in MetaPRL to construct a compiler from a full higher order, untyped, functional language to Intel x86 code, based entirely on higher-order rewrite rules. They use higher-order abstract syntax to represent programs and do not define any semantics. These works do not prove the compilers correct.

Hannan and Pfenning [6] constructed a verified compiler in LF for the untyped λ-calculus. The target machine is a variant of the CAM runtime and differs a lot from real machines. Chlipala [4] considered compiling a simply-typed λ-calculus to assembly language. He proved semantics preservation based on denotational semantics assigned to the intermediate languages. These source languages are the bare lambda calculus and is thus much simpler than TFL.

Chlipala [5] further considered translating a simple impure functional language to an idealized assembly language. One of main points is to avoid binder manipulation by using a parametric higher-order abstract syntax to represent programs; while in our case this is automatically taken care of by the prover. Its representative optimization, common subexpression elimination, is accomplished in our compiler by a one-line rewrite rule.

Benton and Hur [1] interprets types as binary relations to connect the denotational semantics of a simply typed functional language and the operational behavior of low-level programs in a SECD machine. This allows, as we did, the modeling of low-level code using a mathematical, domain-theoretic functions, as well as the proof of a simple compiler. But we need not to define the semantics in terms of tricky and customized interpretations.

Leroy [2,9] verified a compiler from a subset of C, *i.e.* Clight, to PowerPC assembly code in the Coq system. The semantics of Clight is completely deterministic and specified as big-step operational semantics. The proof of semantics preservation for the translation proceeds by induction over the Clight evaluation derivation; while our proofs proceed by verifying the rewriting steps. As demonstrated in [22], his compiler needs extensive manual effort to verify new optimizations; while our rewriting based approach is very flexible and easy to accommodate non-trivial optimizations. In fact our modeling of IRs directly in the logic is intended to mitigate the burden of manual proof.

The decompiler from ARM presented in this paper has same purpose as [16,14] does, but uses a totally different reasoning method. We do not rely on a Hoare Logic built for ARM, and overcome many limitations brought by composing reasoning rules in a bottom-up style (*e.g.* unable to handle unstructured code).

Charguéraud [3] proposed a method to decompile pure Caml programs into logical formulas that implies the programs' post-conditions. Similar to our C0 front-end, this method supports performing the correctness proof of a source program in the higher-order logic of a theorem prover. Such technique can also be used to compile-with-proof Caml programs into TFL functions.

Conclusions and Future Work. We have presented an approach to compile both high level and low level languages into a logic, and perform validated program transformations to construct an optimizing compiler. We plan to augment the front-end to accept larger subsets of C, *e.g.* with support for structs and pointers; and incorporate more aggressive optimization techniques into the compiler. We also plan to generate code for other platforms such as X86, and bytecode languages such as LLVM.

References

1. Benton, N., Hur, C.-K.: Biorthogonality, step-indexing and compiler correctness. In: ACM International Conference on Functional programming, ICFP (2009)
2. Blazy, S., Dargaye, Z., Leroy, X.: Formal verification of a C compiler front-end. In: Misra, J., Nipkow, T., Karakostas, G. (eds.) FM 2006. LNCS, vol. 4085, pp. 460–475. Springer, Heidelberg (2006)

3. Charguéraud, A.: Program verification through characteristic formulae. In: ACM International Conference on Functional Programming, ICFP (2010)
4. Chlipala, A.: A certified type-preserving compiler from lambda calculus to assembly language. In: Programming Language Design and Implementation, PLDI (2007)
5. Chlipala, A.: A verified compiler for an impure functional language. In: ACM Symposium on the Principles of Programming Languages, POPL (2010)
6. Hannan, J., Pfenning, F.: Compiler verification in LF. In: 7th Symposium on Logic in Computer Science, LICS (1992)
7. Hickey, J., Nogin, A.: Formal compiler construction in a logical framework. Journal of Higher-Order and Symbolic Computation 19(2-3), 197–230 (2006)
8. The HOL-4 Theorem Prover, http://hol.sourceforge.net/
9. Leroy, X.: Formal certification of a compiler backend, or: programming a compiler with a proof assistant. In: ACM Symposium on the Principles of Programming Languages, POPL (2006)
10. Li, G., Owens, S., Slind, K.: Structure of a proof-producing compiler for a subset of higher order logic. In: 16th European Symposium on Programming, ESOP (2007)
11. Li, G., Slind, K.: Compilation as rewriting in higher order logic. In: 21th Conference on Automated Deduction, CADE-21 (2007)
12. Li, G., Slind, K.: Trusted source translation of a total function language. In: Ramakrishnan, C.R., Rehof, J. (eds.) TACAS 2008. LNCS, vol. 4963, pp. 471–485. Springer, Heidelberg (2008)
13. Milner, R., Tofte, M., Harper, R., MacQueen, D.: The Definition of Standard ML, Revised Edition. MIT Press, Cambridge (1997)
14. Myreen, M.O.: Verified just-in-time compiler on x86. In: ACM Symposium on the Principles of Programming Languages, POPL (2010)
15. Myreen, M.O., Gordon, M.J.C.: Hoare logic for realistically modelled machine code. In: Grumberg, O., Huth, M. (eds.) TACAS 2007. LNCS, vol. 4424, pp. 568–582. Springer, Heidelberg (2007)
16. Myreen, M.O., Gordon, M.J.C., Slind, K.: Machine-code verification for multiple architectures: An application of decompilation into logic. In: Formal Methods in Computer Aided Design, FMCAD (2008)
17. Nipkow, T., Paulson, L.C., Wenzel, M.: Isabelle/HOL— A Proof Assistant for Higher-Order Logic. LNCS, vol. 2283. Springer, Heidelberg (2002)
18. Reynolds, J.C.: Separation logic: A logic for shared mutable data structures. In: IEEE Symposium on Logic in Computer Science, LICS (2002)
19. Saabas, A., Uustalu, T.: A compositional natural semantics and hoare logic for low-level languages. Theoretical Computer Science 373(3), 273–302 (2007)
20. Slind, K.: Reasoning about Terminating Functional Programs. PhD thesis, Institut für Informatik, Technische Universität München (1999)
21. Tolmach, A., Oliva, D.P.: From ML to Ada: Strongly-typed language interoperability via source translation. Journal of Functional Programming 8(4), 367–412 (1998)
22. Tristan, J.-B., Leroy, X.: Formal verification of translation validators: A case study on instruction scheduling optimizations. In: ACM Symposium on the Principles of Programming Languages, POPL (2008)

Certification of Safe Polynomial Memory Bounds⋆

Javier de Dios and Ricardo Peña

Departamento de Sistemas Informáticos y Computación
Universidad Complutense de Madrid, Spain
jdcastro@aventia.com, ricardo@sip.ucm.es

Abstract. In previous works, we have developed several algorithms for inferring upper bounds to heap and stack consumption for a simple functional language called *Safe*. The bounds inferred for a particular recursive function with n arguments takes the form of symbolic n-ary functions from $(\mathbb{R}^+)^n$ to $\mathbb{R}^+$ relating the input argument sizes to the number of cells or words respectively consumed in the heap and in the stack. Most frequently, these functions are multivariate polynomials of any degree, although exponential and other functions can be inferred in some cases.

Certifying memory bounds is important because the analyses could be unsound, or have been wrongly implemented. But the certifying process should not be necessarily tied to the method used to infer those bounds. Although the motivation for the work presented here is certifying the bounds inferred by our compiler, we have developed a certifying method which could equally be applied to bounds computed by hand.

The certification process is divided into two parts: (a) an off-line part consisting of proving the soundness of a set of proof rules. This part is independent of the program being certified, and its correctness is established once forever by using the proof assistant Isabelle/HOL; and (b) a compile-time program-specific part in which the proof rules are applied to a particular program and their premises proved correct.

The key idea for the first part is proving an Isabelle/HOL theorem for each syntactic construction of the language, relating the symbolic information asserted by the proof-rule to the dynamic properties about the heap and stack consumption satisfied at runtime. For the second part, we use a mathematical tool for proving instances of Tarski's decision problem on quantified formulas in real closed fields.

Keywords: Memory bounds, formal certificates, proof assistants, Tarski's decision problem.

1 Introduction

Certifying program properties consists of providing mathematical evidence about them. In a Proof Carrying Code (PCC) environment [17], these proofs should

---

⋆ Work supported by the Spanish projects TIN2008-06622-C03-01/TIN (STAMP) and S2009/TIC-1465 (PROMETIDOS).

M. Butler and W. Schulte (Eds.): FM 2011, LNCS 6664, pp. 184–199, 2011.
© Springer-Verlag Berlin Heidelberg 2011

be checked by an appropriate tool. The certified properties may be obtained either manually, interactively, or automatically, but whatever is the effort needed for generating them, the PCC paradigm insists on their checking to be fully automatic.

In our setting, the certified property (safe memory bounds) is automatically inferred as the product of several static analyses, so that the certificate can be generated by the compiler without any human intervention. Certifying the inferred property is needed to convince a potential consumer that the static analyses are sound and that they have been correctly implemented in the compiler.

Inferring safe memory bounds in an automatic way is a complex task, involving in our case several static analyses:

- A region inference analysis [15] decides in which regions different data structures should be allocated, so that they could be safely destroyed when the region is deallocated. At the same time, the live memory is kept to a minimum (in other words, the analysis detects the maximum possible garbage).
- A size analysis infers upper bounds to the size of certain variables.
- A termination analysis [14] is used to infer upper bounds to the number of internal calls of recursive functions.
- A space inference analysis [16], uses the results of the above analyses to infer upper bounds to the heap and stack consumption.

Memory bounds could also be manually obtained, but in this case the computation must determine all the additive and multiplicative constants. This is usually a tedious and error-prone task.

But, once the memory bounds have been obtained, certifying them should be a simpler task. It is common folklore in the PCC framework that to find a proof is always more complex than to check it. A good example of this is ranking function synthesis in termination proofs of recursive and iterative programs. A ranking function is a kind of certificate or *witness* of termination. To find them is a rather complex task. Sometimes, linear methods [20] or sophisticated polyhedra libraries are used [10,1]. Others, more powerful methods such as SAT solvers [3] or non-linear constraint solvers [11] are needed. But, once the ranking function has been obtained, certifying termination consists of 'simply'[1] proving that it strictly decreases at each program transition in some well-founded order. This shows that the certifying and the inference processes are not necessarily tied.

In this paper we propose a simple way of certifying upper memory bounds whatever complex the method to obtain them has been. In the first part, we develop a set of syntax-driven proof-rules allowing to infer safe upper memory bounds to the execution of any expression, provided we have already upper bounds for its sub-expressions. Then we prove their soundness by relating the symbolic information inferred by a rule to the dynamic properties about the heap and stack consumption satisfied at runtime. In order to get complete confidence on the rules, we have used the Isabelle/HOL proof assistant [19] for this task.

---

[1] If the ranking function is not linear, proving that it decreases may be not so simple, and even it might be undecidable.

In the second part we explain how, given a candidate upper bound for a recursive function, the compiler can apply the proof-rules and infer a new upper bound, which will be correct provided the candidate upper bound is correct. Our main proof-rule states that if the derived bound *is smaller than or equal to the candidate one*, then both are correct. In order to certify this latter inequality, we propose to use a computer algebra tool for proving instances of Tarski's decision problem on quantified formulas involving polynomials over the real numbers [21]. To our knowledge, this is the first time that the described method is used to certify memory upper bounds.

The plan of the paper is as follows: after this introduction, in Sec. 2 we briefly summarize the characteristics and semantics of our functional language *Safe*; sections 3, 4, and 5 are devoted to presenting the proof-rules and to proving their soundness; Sec. 6 explains the certification process and how a symbolic algebra tool is used as a certificate checker; Sec. 7 presents a small case study illustrating the certificate generation and checking; finally, Sec. 8 presents some related work and draws the paper conclusions.

2   The Language

Safe is a first-order eager language with a syntax similar to Haskell's. Fig. 1 shows a mergesort algorithm written in *Full-Safe*. Its runtime system uses *regions*, i.e. disjoint parts of the heap where the program allocates data structures. They are automatically inferred [15] and made explicit in the intermediate language, called *Core-Safe*, and in the internal types. For instance, the types inferred for the functions of Fig. 1 are (the ρ's are region types):

$$
\begin{aligned}
&\textit{unshuffle} :: [a]@\rho \rightarrow \rho_1 \rightarrow \rho_2 \rightarrow ([a]@\rho_1, [a]@\rho_1)@\rho_2 \\
&\textit{merge} \quad :: [a]@\rho \rightarrow [a]@\rho \rightarrow \rho \rightarrow [a]@\rho \\
&\textit{msort} \quad :: [a]@\rho' \rightarrow \rho \rightarrow [a]@\rho
\end{aligned}
$$

The meaning for e.g. *unshuffle* is that it receives a list in region ρ and two region arguments of types ρ_1, ρ_2. The first one is used to return the two result lists, and the second one for storing the tuple containing them. It is important to note that the number of regions a function may deal with can be statically determined. The *Core-Safe* versions of *merge* and *msort* can be seen in Sec. 7.

```
unshuffle []     = ([],[])
unshuffle (x:xs) = (x:ys2, ys1)
                   where (ys1,ys2) = unshuffle xs

merge []      ys = ys
merge (x:xs) []  = x:xs
merge (x:xs) (y:ys) | x <= y    = x : merge xs     (y:ys)
                    | otherwise = y : merge (x:xs) ys

msort []  = []
msort [x] = [x]
msort xs  = merge (msort xs1) (msort xs2)
            where (xs1, xs2) = unshuffle xs
```

Fig. 1. *mergesort* algorithm in *Full-Safe*

$$E \vdash (h,k), td, c \Downarrow (h,k), c, ([\,]_k, 0, 1) \quad [Lit]$$

$$E[x \mapsto v] \vdash (h,k), td, x \Downarrow (h,k), v, ([\,]_k, 0, 1) \quad [Var]$$

$$\frac{j \le k \quad fresh(p)}{E[\overline{a_i \mapsto v_i}^n, r \mapsto j] \vdash (h,k), td, C\,\overline{a_i}^n\, @\, r \Downarrow (h \uplus [p \mapsto (j, C\,\overline{v_i}^n)], k), p, ([j \mapsto 1]_k, 1, 1)} \quad [Cons]$$

$$\frac{(f\,\overline{x_i}^n\, @\, \overline{r_j}^l = e) \in \Sigma_D \quad [\overline{x_i \mapsto E(a_i)}^n, \overline{r_j \mapsto E(r'_j)}^l, self \mapsto k+1] \vdash (h, k+1), n+l, e \Downarrow (h', k+1), v, (\delta, m, s)}{E \vdash (h,k), td, f\,\overline{a_i}^n\, @\, \overline{r'_j}^l \Downarrow (h'|_k, k), v, (\delta|_k, m, \max\{n+l, s+n+l-td\})} \quad [App]$$

$$\frac{E \vdash (h,k), td, a_1 \Downarrow (h,k), v_1, ([\,]_k, 0, 1) \quad E \vdash (h,k), td, a_2 \Downarrow (h,k), v_2, ([\,]_k, 0, 1)}{E \vdash (h,k), td, a_1 \oplus a_2 \Downarrow (h,k), v_1 \oplus v_2, ([\,]_k, 0, 2)} \quad [Primop]$$

$$\frac{E \vdash (h,k), 0, e_1 \Downarrow (h',k), v_1, (\delta_1, m_1, s_1) \quad E \cup [x_1 \mapsto v_1] \vdash (h',k), td+1, e_2 \Downarrow (h'',k), v, (\delta_2, m_2, s_2)}{E \vdash (h,k), td, \mathbf{let}\, x_1 = e_1\, \mathbf{in}\, e_2 \Downarrow (h'',k), v, (\delta_1 + \delta_2, \max\{m_1, |\delta_1| + m_2\}, \max\{2 + s_1, 1 + s_2\})} \quad [Let]$$

$$\frac{C = C_r \quad E \cup [\overline{x_{r_i} \mapsto v_i}^{n_r}] \vdash (h,k), td + n_r, e_r \Downarrow (h',k), v, (\delta, m, s)}{E[x \mapsto p] \vdash (h[p \mapsto (j, C\,\overline{v_i}^n)], k), td, \mathbf{case}\, x\, \mathbf{of}\, \overline{C_i\,\overline{x_{ij}}^{n_i} \to e_i} \Downarrow (h',k), v, (\delta, m, s + n_r)} \quad [Case]$$

Fig. 2. Resource-Aware Operational semantics of *Core-Safe* expressions

The smallest memory unit is the *cell*, a contiguous memory space big enough to hold a data construction. A cell contains the constructor identity and a representation of the free variables to which the constructor is applied. These may consist either of basic values, or of pointers to other constructions. Each cell is allocated at constructor application time. A *region* is a collection of cells. It is created empty and it may grow up while it is active. Region deallocation frees all its cells. The allocation and deallocation of regions are associated with function calls: a *working region*, denoted by the reserved identifier *self*, is allocated when entering the call, and deallocated upon exiting it. Inside the function, data structures not belonging to the output may be built there.

Fig. 2 shows the *Core-Safe* big-step semantic rules, with extra annotations added in order to obtain the resources used by evaluating an expression. The expressions are self-explained and typical of most first-order functional languages. A judgement of the form $E \vdash (h,k), td, e \Downarrow (h',k), v, (\delta, m, s)$ means that expression e is evaluated in an environment E mapping variables to values, and in a heap (h,k) with $0 \ldots k$ active regions. As a result, a heap (h',k) and a value v are obtained, and a resource vector (δ, m, s), explained below, is consumed. Argument td refers to the number of positions used by E in the abstract machine stack, and it plays a role in rule *App*.

We denote data constructors by C, constants by c, variables by x, and atoms —an atom is either a constant or a variable— by a. Σ_D is a global environment containing all the function definitions. By $h|_k$ we denote the heap h with all regions above k deleted. A heap (h,k) contains a mapping h between pointers p and constructor cells $(j, C\,\overline{v_i}^n)$, where j, $0 \le j \le k$, is the cell region. The allocation and deallocation of regions is apparent in rule *App*.

The first component of the resource vector is a partial function $\delta : \mathbb{N} \to \mathbb{N}$ giving for each active region i the difference between the cells in the final and initial heaps. By $dom\ \delta$ we denote the subset $\{0 \ldots k\}$ in which δ is defined. By $[\,]_k$ we denote the function $\lambda i \in \{0 \ldots k\}.0$. By $|\delta|$ we mean the sum $\sum_{i \in dom\ \delta} \delta\ i$ giving the total balance of cells. The remaining components m and s respectively give the *minimum* number of fresh cells in the heap and of words in the stack needed to successfully evaluate e, i.e. the peak memory used during e's evaluation. When e is the main expression, these figures give us the total memory needs of a particular run of the *Safe* program.

3   Function Signatures

A *Core-Safe* function f is defined as an $n + m$ argument expression:

$$f :: t_1 \to \ldots \to t_n \to \rho_1 \to \ldots \to \rho_m \to t$$
$$f\ x_1 \cdots x_n\ @\ r_1\ \cdots r_m = e_f$$

where $r_1 \cdots r_m$ are the region arguments. A function may charge space costs to heap regions and to the stack. In general, these costs depend on the *sizes* of the function arguments. We define the size of an algebraic type term to be the number of cells of its recursive spine. This is always at least 1. We define the size of a Boolean value to be zero. However, for an integer argument we choose its size to be its value because frequently space costs depend on the value of a numeric argument. As a consequence, all the costs and sizes of a function f can be expressed as functions on f's argument sizes:

$$\mathbb{F}_f = \{\xi : (\mathbb{R}^+ \cup \{+\infty\})^n \to \mathbb{R}^+ \cup \{+\infty, -\infty\} \ | \ \xi \text{ is monotonic}\}$$

Cost or size $+\infty$ are used to represent that the analysis is not able to infer a bound, while $-\infty$ is used to express that the cost or size is not defined. For instance, the following function, where xs is assumed to be a list size,

$$\lambda xs. \begin{cases} xs - 3 & \text{if } xs \geq 4 \\ -\infty & \text{otherwise} \end{cases}$$

is undefined for sizes xs smaller than 4 (i.e. for lists with less than 3 elements).

They are ordered as expected, $-\infty \leq 0$, and $\forall x \in \mathbb{R}^+.x \leq +\infty$, so $-\infty \sqcup x = x$ and $+\infty \sqcup x = +\infty$. Arithmetic monotonic operations with $\pm\infty$ are defined as follows, where $x \in \mathbb{R}^+$ while $y \in \mathbb{R}^+ \cup \{+\infty, -\infty\}$:

$$-\infty + y = -\infty \qquad -\infty * y = -\infty \qquad +\infty + x = +\infty \qquad +\infty * x = +\infty$$

The domain of cost functions $(\mathbb{F}_f, \sqsubseteq, \bot, \top, \sqcup, \sqcap)$ is a complete lattice with the usual order $\sqsubseteq$ between functions. The rest of the components are standard. Notice that it is closed under the operations $\{+, \sqcup, *\}$.

Function f above may charge space costs to a maximum of $m + 1$ regions: it may create cells in any output region $r_1 \ldots r_m$, and additionally in its *self* region. Each region r has a region type. We denote by R_f the set $\{\rho_1 \ldots \rho_m\}$ of argument region types, and by ρ_{self}^f the type of region *self* of function f.

Looked at from outside, the charges to the *self* region are not visible, so we define $\mathbb{D}_f = \{\Delta \ | \ \Delta : R_f \to \mathbb{F}_f\}$ as the complete lattice of functions describing the space costs charged by f to visible regions. We will call *abstract heaps* to these functions.

Definition 1. *A* function *signature for f is a triple $(\Delta_f, \mu_f, \sigma_f)$, where Δ_f belongs to $\mathbb{D}_f$, and μ_f, σ_f belong to $\mathbb{F}_f$.*

The aim is that Δ_f is an upper bound to the cost charged by f to visible regions, (i.e. to the increment in *live memory* due to a call to f), and μ_f, σ_f respectively are upper bounds to the heap and stack *peaks* contributed by f's evaluation.

4   Proof-Rules

When dealing with an expression e, we assume it belongs to the body e_f of a function definition $f\ \overline{x_i}^n\ @\ \overline{r_j}^m\ =\ e_f$, that we will call the *context function*, assumed to be well-typed.

We consider available a local type environment θ giving the types of all (free and bound) variables in e_f. It allows to type e_f and all its sub-expressions. Also a local environment ϕ giving for every (free and bound) variable its size as a symbolic function of the sizes of f's formal arguments $\overline{x_i}^n$. Finally, a *global type environment* Σ_T giving for every function and data constructor of the program their most general types.

Let Σ be a *global signature environment* giving, for each *Safe* function g in scope, its signature $(\Delta_g, \mu_g, \sigma_g)$, and let td (abbreviation of *top-depth*) be a natural number. This is a quantity used by the compiler to control the size of the runtime environment stored in the stack (it is the same argument used in the operational semantics, see Sec. 2). It has an impact on the stack consumption and so it will be needed in our judgements.

We inductively define a *derivation* relation as a set of proof-rules. The intended meaning of a judgement of the form $\theta, \phi, td \vartriangleright_f e, \Sigma \vdash (\Delta, \mu, \sigma)$ is that Δ, μ, σ are safe upper bounds for respectively the live heap contributed by evaluating the expression e, the additional peak heap needed by e, and its additional peak stack. The context information needed is: a valid global signature environment Σ, two valid local environments θ (for types) and ϕ (for sizes), a runtime environment top depth td, and the name f of the context function.

In Figure 3 we show the proof-rules for the most relevant *Core-Safe* expressions. Predicate $def(\xi)$ expresses that the size ξ is defined according to its type: if ξ has an algebraic type, $def(\xi) \equiv \xi \geq 1$; if it is an integer, $def(\xi) \equiv \xi \geq 0$; otherwise $def(\xi) \equiv True$. We use the guarded notation $[G \rightarrow \xi]$, as equivalent to ξ if G holds, and to $-\infty$ otherwise. By $[\ ]_f$ we denote the constant function $\lambda\rho \in R_f \cup \{\rho_{self}^f\} \cdot \lambda\overline{x_i}^n \cdot [\wedge_{i=1}^n def(x_i) \rightarrow 0]$, and by $[\rho' \rightarrow \xi]_f$ we denote:

$$\lambda\rho \in R_f \cup \{\rho_{self}^f\} \cdot \lambda\overline{x_i}^n \cdot \begin{cases} [\wedge_{i=1}^n def(x_i) \rightarrow 0] & \text{if } \rho \neq \rho' \\ [\wedge_{i=1}^n def(x_i) \rightarrow \xi] & \text{if } \rho = \rho' \end{cases}$$

We abbreviate $\lambda\overline{x_i}^n \cdot [\wedge_{i=1}^n def(x_i) \rightarrow c]$ by c, when $c \in \mathbb{R}^+$. By $|\Delta|$ we mean $\sum_{\rho \in dom\ \Delta} \Delta\ \rho$.

Rules $[Lit]$, $[Var]$, $[Primop]$ and $[Cons]$ exactly reflect the corresponding resource-aware semantic rules shown in Fig. 2.

When a function application $g \; \overline{a_i}^l \; @ \; \overline{r_j}^q$ is found, its signature $\Sigma \, g$ is applied to the sizes of the actual arguments, $\overline{\phi \; a_i \; \overline{x_j}}^{n^l}$. Some different region types of g may instantiate to the same actual region type of f. This type instantiation mapping $\psi : R_g \rightarrow R_f \cup \{\rho^f_{self}\}$ is provided by the compiler, and we will require it to be consistent with the typing environment θ and with the actual region arguments of the application. We call this property *argument preserving* and denote it as $argP(\psi, \overline{\rho_j}^q, \theta, \overline{r_j}^q)$. In essence it says that the types of the actual region arguments $\overline{r_j}^q$ given by θ coincide with the formal region types $\overline{\rho_j}^q$ of g after being instantiated by ψ.

The memory consumed by g in the formal regions mapped by ψ to the same f's actual region must be accumulated in order to get the charge to this region of f. In the $[App]$ rule of Figure 3, function $instance_f$ converts an abstract heap for g into an abstract heap for f. We define $instance_f(\Delta_g, \psi, \overline{a_i}^l)$ as the abstract heap Δ with domain $R_f \cup \{\rho^f_{self}\}$ such that:

$$\forall \rho \in dom \; \Delta \, . \, \Delta \, \rho = \lambda \, \overline{x_i}^n \, . \, [G \, (\overline{a_i}^n) \rightarrow \sum_{\rho' \in R_g \wedge \psi \; \rho' = \rho} \Delta_g \, \rho' \, (\overline{\phi \; a_i \; \overline{x_i}}^{n^l})]$$

where $G \, (\overline{a_i}^n) \equiv \bigwedge_{i=1}^{l} def(\phi \; a_i \; \overline{x}^n)$. Notice that if any of the sizes $\phi \; a_i \; \overline{x_i}^n$ is not defined, then Δ_g applied to it is neither defined. It is easy to see that Δ, μ and σ defined in rule $[App]$ are monotonic. If $\exists i \in \{1 \ldots l\} \, . \, \neg def(\phi \; a_i \; \overline{x_i}^n)$, then Δ, μ and σ return $-\infty$, which guarantees monotonicity since $-\infty$ is the smallest value in the domain. For the rest of the arguments, monotonicity is guaranteed by the monotonicity of Δ_g, μ_g and σ_g.

Rule $[Let]$ reflects the corresponding resource-aware semantic rule, while rule $[Case]$ uses the least upper bound operator $\bigsqcup$ in order to obtain an upper bound to the cost of any of the branches.

In Fig. 4 we show the proof rule for recursive functions. In fact, it could also be applied to non-recursive ones. By $\lfloor \Delta \rfloor$ we denote the projection of Δ over R_f, obtained by removing the region ρ^f_{self} from Δ. This rule is the most relevant

$$\theta, \phi, td \triangleright_f c, \Sigma \vdash ([\,]_f, 0, 1) \quad [Lit]$$

$$\theta, \phi, td \triangleright_f x, \Sigma \vdash ([\,]_f, 0, 1) \quad [Var]$$

$$\theta, \phi, td \triangleright_f a_1 \oplus a_2, \Sigma \vdash ([\,]_f, 0, 2) \quad [Primop]$$

$$\theta, \phi, td \triangleright_f C \; \overline{a_i}^n \; @ \; r, \Sigma \vdash ([\theta \; r \mapsto 1]_f, 1, 1) \quad [Cons]$$

$$\frac{\Sigma \, g = (\Delta_g, \mu_g, \sigma_g) \qquad G \, (\overline{a_i}^n) \equiv \bigwedge_{i=1}^{l} def(\phi \; a_i \; \overline{x}^n) \qquad argP(\psi, \overline{\rho_j}^q, \theta, \overline{r_j}^q)}{\theta, \phi, td \triangleright_f g \; \overline{a_i}^l \; @ \; \overline{r_j}^q, \Sigma \vdash (\Delta, \mu, \sqcup\{l + q, \sigma + l + q - td\})} \quad [App]$$

with $\mu = \lambda \overline{x}^n . [G \, (\overline{a_i}^n) \rightarrow \mu_g \, (\overline{\phi \; a_i \; \overline{x}}^{n^l})] \qquad \sigma = \lambda \overline{x}^n . [G \, (\overline{a_i}^n) \rightarrow \sigma_g \, (\overline{\phi \; a_i \; \overline{x}}^{n^l})] \qquad \Delta = instance_f(\Delta_g, \psi, \overline{a_i}^l)$

$$\frac{\theta, \phi, 0 \triangleright_f e_1, \Sigma \vdash (\Delta_1, \mu_1, \sigma_1) \qquad \theta, \phi, td + 1 \triangleright_f e_2, \Sigma \vdash (\Delta_2, \mu_2, \sigma_2)}{\theta, \phi, td \triangleright_f \, \text{let} \; x_1 = e_1 \; \text{in} \; e_2, \Sigma \vdash (\Delta_1 + \Delta_2, \sqcup\{\mu_1, \lfloor\Delta_1\rfloor + \mu_2\}, \sqcup\{2 + \sigma_1, 1 + \sigma_2\})} \quad [Let]$$

$$\frac{(\forall i) \; \theta, \phi, td + n_i \triangleright_f e_i, \Sigma \vdash (\Delta_i, \mu_i, \sigma_i)}{\theta, \phi, td \triangleright_f \, \text{case} \; x \; \text{of} \; \overline{C_i \; \overline{x_{ij}}^{n_i} \rightarrow e_i}^n, \Sigma \vdash (\bigsqcup_{i=1}^n \Delta_i, \bigsqcup_{i=1}^n \mu_i, \bigsqcup_{i=1}^n (\sigma_i + n_i))} \quad [Case]$$

Fig. 3. Proof-rules for *Core-Safe* expressions

$$\dfrac{(f\ \overline{x_i}^{\,l}\text{@}\,\overline{r_j}^{\,q} = e_f)\in \Sigma_D\quad \theta.\phi.l+q\rhd_f e_f.\Sigma \uplus \{f\mapsto(\Delta.\mu.\sigma)\}\vdash (\Delta'.\mu'.\sigma')\quad (\lfloor\Delta'\rfloor.\mu'.\sigma')\sqsubseteq(\Delta.\mu.\sigma)}{\theta.\phi.l+q\rhd_f e_f.\Sigma\vdash(\Delta'.\mu'.\sigma')}\ \ [Rec]$$

Fig. 4. Proof-rule for a (possibly) recursive *Core-Safe* function definition

contribution of the paper, since it reduces proving upper memory bounds to checking inequalities between functions over the real numbers. In words, its says that if a triple (Δ,μ,σ) (obtained by whatever means) is to be proved a safe upper bound for the recursive function f, a sufficient condition is:

1. Introduce (Δ,μ,σ) in the environment Σ as a candidate signature for f.
2. By using the remaining proof-rules, derive a triple (Δ',μ',σ') as a new upper bound for f's body.
3. Prove $(\lfloor\Delta'\rfloor,\mu',\sigma')\sqsubseteq(\Delta,\mu,\sigma)$.

The rule asserts that (Δ',μ',σ') is a correct bound for e_f without any assumption for f in Σ. By deleting the *self* region, then $(\lfloor\Delta'\rfloor,\mu',\sigma')$ is a correct signature for f, and so will it be (Δ,μ,σ), which is greater than or equal to it.

The first two steps are routine tasks. The only difficulty remaining is proving the third. As we will see in Sec. 6, for polynomial functions this can be done by converting it into a decision problem of Tarski's theory of closed real fields.

5   Soundness Theorems

Let $f\ \overline{x_i}^{\,n}\text{@}\,\overline{r_j}^{\,m}=e_f$, be the context function and θ,ϕ the local type and size environments for f. The steps we shall follow in this section are: (1) we shall introduce a notion of semantic satisfaction of a memory bound by an expression; (2) we shall define what a valid signature and a valid signature environment are; (3) we shall refine the semantic satisfaction to a conditional one subject to the validity of a global signature environment; and (4) we shall prove that the proof-rules of figures 3 and 4 are sound with respect to the given semantic notions.

Definition 2. *Given a pointer p belonging to a heap h, the following function returns the number of cells in h of the data structure starting at p:*

$$size(h[p\mapsto(j,C\ \overline{v_i}^{\,l})],p)=1+\sum_{i\in RecPos\ C} size(h,v_i)$$

where $RecPos\ C$ denotes the recursive positions of constructor C, given by the global type environment Σ_T. We agree that $size(h,c)=0$ for any constant c, except if c is an integer argument of f. In that case, $size(h,c)=c$.

For example, if p points to the first cons cell of the list $[1,2,3]$ in the heap h then $size(h,p)=4$.

At runtime, a region type ρ becomes mapped to an active region $i\in\{0\ldots k\}$. Let us call $\eta::R_f\cup\{\rho^f_{self}\}\rightarrow\{0\ldots k\}$ to this mapping. Our type system guarantees that the following property holds across any evaluation:

Definition 3. *Assuming that k denotes the topmost region of a given heap, we say that the mapping η is* admissible, *denoted* admissible $\eta\,k$, *if:*

$$\rho^f_{self} \in dom\ \eta \wedge \eta\ \rho^f_{self} = k \wedge \forall \rho \in (dom\ \eta) - \{\rho^f_{self}\} \cdot \eta\ \rho\ < k$$

The type system also guarantees a consistency property between types and values that we will not define formally here[2]. By *consistent $\theta\,\eta\,E\,h$* we mean that the types given by θ to the free variables, the values of these variables in the runtime environment E and heap h, and the mapping η, do not contradict each other.

Finally, by *valid$_f$ $\theta\,\phi$* we intuitively mean that each variable of the body e_f has a type in θ, and a symbolic size in ϕ as a function of the domain $\mathbb{F}_f$. Moreover, in any evaluation of e_f, the types are consistent with the values and the region mapping η, this one is admissible, and the symbolic sizes are upper bounds of the corresponding runtime sizes.

The semantic satisfaction of a memory bound by an expression is defined as follows: whenever θ, ϕ are valid environments, and some minor static and dynamic properties hold, then (Δ, μ, σ) is a correct bound for the memory consumption of expression e in any of its possible evaluations.

Definition 4. *Let $f\ \overline{x_i}^n\ @\ \overline{r_j}^m = e_f$ be the context function, and e a sub-expression of e_f. We say that e satisfies the bound (Δ, μ, σ) in the context of $\theta, \phi,$ and td, denoted $\theta, \phi, td \rhd_f e \models \llbracket (\Delta, \mu, \sigma) \rrbracket$, if:*

$$valid_f\ \theta\ \phi \rightarrow P_{dom} \wedge (\forall E\ h\ k\ h'\ v\ \eta\ \delta\ m\ s\ \overline{s_i}^n\ .\ P_{\Downarrow} \wedge P_{dyn} \wedge P_{size} \wedge P_{\eta} \rightarrow P_{\Delta} \wedge P_{\mu} \wedge P_{\sigma})$$

$$P_{dom} \stackrel{def}{=} dom\ \Delta = R_f \cup \{\rho^f_{self}\}$$

$$P_{\Downarrow} \stackrel{def}{=} E \vdash (h, k), td, e \Downarrow (h', k), v, (\delta, m, s)$$

$$P_{dyn} \stackrel{def}{=} (\overline{x_i}^n \cup fv\ e \cup \overline{r_j}^m \cup self) \subseteq dom\ E \wedge dom\ \eta = dom\ \Delta$$

$$P_{size} \stackrel{def}{=} \forall i \in \{1..n\}\ .\ s_i = size(h, E\ x_i)$$

$$P_{\eta} \stackrel{def}{=} admissible(\eta, k)$$

$$P_{\Delta} \stackrel{def}{=} \forall j \in \{0 \ldots k\}\ .\ \textstyle\sum_{\eta\ \rho = j} \Delta\ \rho\ \overline{s_i}^n \geq \delta\ j$$

$$P_{\mu} \stackrel{def}{=} \mu\ \overline{s_i}^n \geq m$$

$$P_{\sigma} \stackrel{def}{=} \sigma\ \overline{s_i}^n \geq s$$

Definition 5. *A global bound environment Σ is* valid, *denoted $\models \Sigma$, if it belongs to the following inductively defined set:*

1. $\models \emptyset$, *i.e. the empty environment is always valid.*
2. *If $\models \Sigma$, and $(f\ \overline{x_i}^l\ @\ \overline{r_j}^m = e_f) \in \Sigma_D$, and there exist Δ, μ, σ such that for any valid local environments θ and ϕ, property $\theta, \phi, (l + m) \rhd_f e_f \models \llbracket (\Delta, \mu, \sigma) \rrbracket$ holds, then $\models \Sigma \uplus \{f \mapsto (\lfloor \Delta \rfloor, \mu, \sigma)\}$.*

---

[2] http://dalila.sip.ucm.es/safe provides an extended version of this paper with all the formal definitions and hand-written proofs; http://dalila.sip.ucm.es/safe/ bounds provides the Isabelle/HOL proof-scripts of the lemmas of this section.

When proving a memory bound for an expression, we will usually need a valid global environment in order to get from it correct signatures for the functions called by the expression. We will then say that the satisfaction of the bound is *conditional* to the validity of the environment.

Definition 6. *An expression e conditionally satisfies a bound (Δ, μ, σ) with respect to a signature environment Σ, in the context of θ, ϕ, and td, denoted $\theta, \phi, td \rhd_f e, \Sigma \models [\![(\Delta, \mu, \sigma)]\!]$, if $\models \Sigma \to \theta, \phi, td \rhd_f e \models [\![(\Delta, \mu, \sigma)]\!]$.*

We are now in a position to state and prove the main theorem establishing that the proof-rules of figures 3 and 4 are sound.

Theorem 1 (Soundness)

$$\text{If } \theta, \phi, td \rhd_f e, \Sigma \vdash (\Delta, \mu, \sigma), \text{ then } \theta, \phi, td \rhd_f e, \Sigma \models [\![(\Delta, \mu, \sigma)]\!]$$

The proof of the theorem is rather involved (around 4500 Isabelle/HOL lines). We sketch here the main steps:

1. We define a restricted big-step semantics with an upper bound n to the longest chain of f's recursive calls: $E \vdash (h, k), td, e \Downarrow_{f,n} (h', k), v, (\delta, m, s)$.
2. We prove that $E \vdash (h, k), td, e \Downarrow (h', k), v, (\delta, m, s)$ if and only if $\exists n \,.\, E \vdash (h, k), td, e \Downarrow_{f,n} (h', k), v, (\delta, m, s)$.
3. We define appropriate notions of satisfaction $\theta, \phi, td \rhd_f e \models_{f,n} [\![(\Delta, \mu, \sigma)]\!]$, validity $\models_{f,n} \Sigma$, and conditional validity $\theta, \phi, td \rhd_f e, \Sigma \models_{f,n} [\![(\Delta, \mu, \sigma)]\!]$ in which the longest chain of f's recursive calls is bounded by n.
4. We prove:

$$
\begin{aligned}
\forall n \,.\, \theta, \phi, td \rhd_f e \models_{f,n} [\![(\Delta, \mu, \sigma)]\!] &\equiv \theta, \phi, td \rhd_f e \models [\![(\Delta, \mu, \sigma)]\!] \\
\forall n \,.\, \models_{f,n} \Sigma &\equiv \models \Sigma \\
\forall n \,.\, \theta, \phi, td \rhd_f e, \Sigma \models_{f,n} [\![(\Delta, \mu, \sigma)]\!] &\Rightarrow \theta, \phi, td \rhd_f e, \Sigma \models [\![(\Delta, \mu, \sigma)]\!]
\end{aligned}
$$

5. By induction on the $\vdash$ derivation, and by cases on the last rule applied, we prove: $\theta, \phi, td \rhd_f e, \Sigma \vdash (\Delta, \mu, \sigma) \Rightarrow \forall n \,.\, \theta, \phi, td \rhd_f e, \Sigma \models_{f,n} [\![(\Delta, \mu, \sigma)]\!]$.

6   Certification

The proof-rules presented in Sec. 4 are valid whatever are the monotonic functions considered for describing sizes and costs. However, for certification purposes we restrict ourselves to the smaller class of monotonic **Max-Poly** functions:

Definition 7. *The class **Max-Poly** over $\bar{x}^n$ is the smallest set of expressions containing constants in $\mathbb{R}^+$, variables $y \in \bar{x}^n$, and closed under the operations $\{+, *, \sqcup\}$. We will call any element of **Max-Poly** a max-poly.*

We will call a max-poly function to a function of the form $\lambda \bar{x}^n.p$ in $(\mathbb{R}^+)^n \to \mathbb{R}^+$, where p is a max-poly over $\bar{x}^n$.

Notice that all the three operations are commutative and associative, and that $+$ and $*$ distribute over $\sqcup$ in $\mathbb{R}^+$. The latter makes that any max-poly can be normalized to a form $p_1 \sqcup \ldots \sqcup p_n$, where all the p_i are ordinary polynomials. This property extends also to max-poly functions.

In our case and disregarding $+\infty$ (which in fact means absence of a bound), the size and cost functions return a value in $\mathbb{R}^+ \cup \{-\infty\}$. As they are monotonic, in each dimension i they return $-\infty$ in some (possibly empty) interval $[0..k_i)$, and when $(\forall i \, . \, x_i \geq k_i)$ they return a value greater than or equal to 0. This property can be expressed by a Boolean guard on the x_i. Inspired by this, we restrict our elementary functions to have the form $[G \rightarrow f]$, where G is a guard of the form $\bigwedge_{i=1}^{n}(p_i \geq k_i)$, $k_i \in \mathbb{R}^+$, and all the $p_i(\overline{x}^n)$ and $f(\overline{x}^n)$ are multivariate max-polys over the set $\overline{x}^n$ of variables. The meaning of this notation, which we will call *atomic guarded function* (AGF in what follows), is:

$$[G \rightarrow f] \stackrel{\text{def}}{=} \lambda \overline{x}^n \, . \begin{cases} -\infty & \text{if } \neg G(\overline{x}^n) \\ f(\overline{x}^n) & \text{if } G(\overline{x}^n) \end{cases}$$

Operating with AGFs satisfies the following properties (a, b, c denote AGFs):

1. $[G_1 \rightarrow f_1] + [G_2 \rightarrow f_2] = [G_1 \wedge G_2 \rightarrow f_1 + f_2]$
2. $[G_1 \rightarrow f_1] * [G_2 \rightarrow f_2] = [G_1 \wedge G_2 \rightarrow f_1 * f_2]$
3. $[G_1 \rightarrow [G_2 \rightarrow f]] = [G_1 \wedge G_2 \rightarrow f]$
4. $(a \sqcup b) + c = (a + c) \sqcup (b + c)$
5. $(a \sqcup b) * c = (a * c) \sqcup (b * c)$

As a consequence, any function obtained by combining AGFs with $\{+, *, \sqcup\}$ can be normalized to:

$$[G_1 \rightarrow f_1] \sqcup \ldots \sqcup [G_l \rightarrow f_l]$$

We will call it a *normalized AGF set*. Now, coming back to the proof-rules of figures 3 and 4, if we introduce in the environment Σ of the *Rec* rule a triple (Δ, μ, σ) consisting of normalized AGF sets, and then derive a triple (Δ', μ', σ'), the latter can be expressed also as normalized AGF sets. This is because the operations involved in the remaining proof-rules are $\{+, *, \sqcup\}$, and the instantiations of the *App* rule. The latter consists of substituting max-polys for variables inside a max-poly. The result will also be a max-poly.

So, the check $(\lfloor \Delta' \rfloor, \mu', \sigma') \sqsubseteq (\Delta, \mu, \sigma)$ of the *Rec* rule reduces to checking inequalities of the form:

$$[G_1 \rightarrow f_1] \sqcup \ldots \sqcup [G_l \rightarrow f_l] \sqsubseteq [G'_1 \rightarrow f'_1] \sqcup \ldots \sqcup [G'_m \rightarrow f'_m]$$

Assuming that all the AGFs are functions over $\overline{x}^n$, this is in turn equivalent to:

$$\forall \overline{x}^n \, . \, \bigwedge_{i=1}^{l} \bigvee_{j=1}^{m} [G_i \rightarrow f_i] \sqsubseteq [G'_j \rightarrow f'_j]$$

Then, the elementary operation is comparing two AGFs. This can be expressed as follows:

$$[G \rightarrow f] \sqsubseteq [G' \rightarrow f'] = G \rightarrow (G' \wedge f \leq f')$$

The comparison $f \leq f'$ consists of comparing two max-polys of the form $p_1 \sqcup \ldots \sqcup p_r$ and $q_1 \sqcup \ldots \sqcup q_s$, which we can decide by applying again the same idea:

$$f \leq f' = \bigwedge_{i=1}^{r} \bigvee_{j=1}^{s} p_i \leq q_j$$

Summarizing, to decide $(\lfloor \Delta' \rfloor, \mu', \sigma') \sqsubseteq (\Delta, \mu, \sigma)$ we generate first-order formulas in Tarski's theory of real closed fields [21]. It is well known that this theory is decidable, although the existent algorithms are not efficient at all. For instance, Collins' quantifier elimination algorithm [9], which is recognized to be a great improvement over the original Tarski's procedure, has still a worst case complexity polynomial in the maximum degree of the involved polynomials and doubly exponential in the number of quantified variables. It is implemented in several symbolic algebra tools such as Mathematica. We have used the QEPCAD system built by Collins' group [7] which contains an improved version of original Collins' algorithm.

Fortunately, the number of quantified variables in our case is the number of arguments of the *Safe* function being certified, and this is usually very small, typically from one to three. So for practical purposes the QEPCAD system, or a similar tool, can be used as a certificate checker. The *Safe* compiler is used, not only to generate the initial triple (Δ, μ, σ) for every *Safe* function, but also to derive the triple (Δ', μ', σ'), to normalize both, and eventually to generate the proof obligations in the form of Tarski's formulas. For the moment, the compiler and the QEPCAD system have not been directly connected and some manual intervention is required.

7   Case Study

In Fig. 5 we show the *Core-Safe* versions of the algorithms `merge` and `msort`, in which regions are explicit. We will explain in detail how the proof-rules are

```
merge x y @ r = case x of
               []     -> y
               ex:x' -> case y of
                         []     -> x
                         ey:y' -> let c = ex <= ey in
                                  case c of
                                    True  -> let z1 = merge x' y @ r in
                                               ex:z1 @ r
                                    False -> let z2 = merge x y' @ r in
                                               ey:z2 @ r

msort x @ r = case x of
              []     -> x
              ex:x' -> case x' of
                        []  -> x
                        _:_ -> let (x1,x2) = unshuffle x @ self self in
                               let z1      = msort x1 @ r          in
                               let z2      = msort x2 @ r          in
                               merge z1 z2 @ r
```

Fig. 5. functions *merge* and *msort* in *Core-Safe*

applied to `merge` (a simple example which produces an uninteresting linear Tarski problem), and then we will show in less detail the process for `msort` (which produces a more interesting quadratic one). Let us assume that the candidate memory bound obtained by the *Safe* compiler for *merge* live heap, assuming $\theta\, r = \rho$, is:

$$\Delta_{merge}\,\rho = [x \geq 2 \wedge y \geq 1 \rightarrow x + y - 2] \qquad \text{-- } A$$
$$\sqcup\, [x \geq 1 \wedge y \geq 2 \rightarrow x + y - 2] \qquad \text{-- } B$$
$$\sqcup\, [x \geq 1 \wedge y \geq 1 \rightarrow 0] \qquad \text{-- } C$$

This signature gives 0 cells when both lists are empty, i.e. $x = 1 \wedge y = 1$, and $x + y - 2$ cells otherwise.

Now, we introduce this signature in the environment Σ and apply the proof rules of Fig. 3. Remember that the *Cons* proof-rule gets $[x \geq 1 \wedge y \geq 1 \rightarrow 1]$ charged to region ρ. This is because, for a list l, $def(l) \equiv l \geq 1$. The *Let* rule asks for the addition of the involved Δ's, and the *Case* one for $\sqcup$ of the branches. Also, the sizes of the internal call arguments are $x' = x - 1$ and $y' = y - 1$, because of the pattern matching. All in all, we obtain as derived bound the following function:

$$\Delta'_{merge}\,\rho = [x \geq 1 \wedge y \geq 1 \rightarrow 0]$$
$$\sqcup\, [x \geq 1 \wedge y \geq 1 \rightarrow 0]$$
$$\sqcup\, (([x - 1 \geq 2 \wedge y \geq 1 \rightarrow x - 1 + y - 2] \sqcup [x - 1 \geq 1 \wedge y \geq 2 \rightarrow x - 1 + y - 2]$$
$$\sqcup\, [x - 1 \geq 1 \wedge y \geq 1 \rightarrow 0]) + [x \geq 1 \wedge y \geq 1 \rightarrow 1])$$
$$\sqcup\, (([x \geq 2 \wedge y - 1 \geq 1 \rightarrow x + y - 1 - 2] \sqcup [x \geq 1 \wedge y - 1 \geq 2 \rightarrow x + y - 1 - 2]$$
$$\sqcup\, [x \geq 1 \wedge y - 1 \geq 1 \rightarrow 0]) + [x \geq 1 \wedge y \geq 1 \rightarrow 1])$$

The first two terms correspond to the branches ending in a variable, so the *Var* rule applies. The other two correspond to the branches having internal calls, by applying the rules *App*, *Cons*, and *Let*. The primitive operator $\leq$ adds a trivial term not shown. After normalization and simplification, we get:

$$\Delta'_{merge}\,\rho = [x \geq 1 \wedge y \geq 1 \rightarrow 0] \qquad \text{-- } C'$$
$$\sqcup\, [x \geq 3 \wedge y \geq 1 \rightarrow x + y - 2] \sqcup [x \geq 2 \wedge y \geq 1 \rightarrow 1] \qquad \text{-- } A' \sqcup A''$$
$$\sqcup\, [x \geq 2 \wedge y \geq 2 \rightarrow x + y - 2] \qquad \text{-- } D'$$
$$\sqcup\, [x \geq 1 \wedge y \geq 3 \rightarrow x + y - 2] \sqcup [x \geq 1 \wedge y \geq 2 \rightarrow 1] \qquad \text{-- } B' \sqcup B''$$

Obviously, for all x, y we get $C' \sqsubseteq C$, $A' \sqsubseteq A$, $B' \sqsubseteq B$, and both $D' \sqsubseteq A$ and $D' \sqsubseteq B$. It is also easy to convince ourselves that A'' is dominated by A and B'' is dominated by B. Then, the inequality $\lfloor \Delta'_{merge} \rfloor \sqsubseteq \Delta_{merge}$ holds.

The candidate `msort` live memory bound inferred by our compiler, assuming Δ_{merge} as above, and the following bound obtained for *unshuffle*:

$$\Delta_{unshuffle} = \begin{bmatrix} \rho_1 \mapsto [x \geq 2 \rightarrow x + 1] \sqcup [x \geq 1 \rightarrow 2] \\ \rho_2 \mapsto [x \geq 2 \rightarrow x] \sqcup [x \geq 1 \rightarrow 1] \end{bmatrix}$$

is

$$\Delta_{msort}\,\rho = [x \geq 2 \rightarrow \frac{4}{3}x^2 - 3x] \sqcup [x \geq 1 \rightarrow 0]$$

Introducing this candidate bound in the environment, applying the proof-rules, normalizing, and simplifying lead to:

$$\Delta'_{msort} = \begin{bmatrix} \rho \mapsto [x \geq 3 \rightarrow \frac{2}{3}x^2 - \frac{3}{2}x - \frac{17}{6}] \sqcup [x \geq 1 \rightarrow 0] \\ \rho_{self} \mapsto [x \geq 2 \rightarrow 2x + 1] \sqcup [x \geq 1 \rightarrow 3] \end{bmatrix}$$

Notice that the charges to the *self* region are not needed in the comparison $\lfloor \Delta'_{msort} \rfloor \sqsubseteq \Delta_{msort}$. The relevant inequality is then:

$$\forall x . \quad \ldots \left(x \geq 3 \rightarrow x \geq 2 \wedge (\frac{2}{3}x^2 - \frac{3}{2}x - \frac{17}{6} \leq \frac{4}{3}x^2 - 3x) \right) \ldots$$

When this formula is given to QEPCAD, it answers *True* in about 100 msec. Then, $\lfloor \Delta'_{msort} \rfloor \sqsubseteq \Delta_{msort}$ holds.

8   Related Work and Conclusion

A seminal paper on static inference of memory bounds is [13]. A special type inference algorithm generates a set of linear constraints which, if satisfiable, they build a safe linear bound on the heap consumption. Afterwards, the authors extended this work to certificate generation [4], the certificate being an Isabelle/HOL proof-script which in essence was a proof of correctness of the type system, specialized for the types of the program being certified.

One of the authors extended in [12] the type system of [13] in order to infer polynomial bounds. Although not every polynomial could be inferred by this system, the work was a remarkable step forward in the area. They do not pay attention to certificates in this paper but there is an occasional comment on that the same ideas of [4] could be applied here.

In [8] an abstract interpretation based algorithm for controlling that memory is not allocated inside loops in Java programs is verified by using the Coq proof-assistant [5]. Here there is no program-specific certificate, but a general proof of correctness of the analysis algorithm.

With respect to our proof-rules, they clearly have an abstract interpretation flavour, and that is the reason why the lattice points above or equal to the fix-point of the interpretation are correct solutions. For recursive functions, we have adapted to our framework the technique first explained in [18]. This technique has also been used in other works (see e.g. [2]) where procedure global environments occur, and recursive procedures must be verified. The main idea is to explicitly introduce the depth of recursive call chains in the environment, and then doing some form of induction on this depth.

We have found inspiration on some work on quasi-interpretations for characterizing the complexity classes of rewriting systems [6], where **Max-Poly** plays a role. The existence of a quasi-interpretation belonging to **Max-Poly** is used to decide that some systems are in the classes PTIME or PSPACE. They show that the problem is decidable by generating formulas in first-order Tarski's theory. The formulas are existentially quantified and they assert the existence of a quasi-interpretation, although no attempt to synthesize one is done.

Our work finds for the first time a way of separating the bound inference problem from the certification one. We have shown that certification need not be a kind of proof of correctness of the inference algorithm. The *Rec* proof-rule and the idea of certifying bounds by checking an inequality $P \sqsubseteq Q$ between polynomial-like functions should work as well for other languages admitting syntax-driven proof-rules monotonic in a complete lattice. It could then be applied to languages, such as the functional one used in [13,12], where other algorithms are used to compute the candidate bounds. Additionally, our language deals with the memory deallocation due to the region mechanism. Most of other approaches infer and/or certify bounds to the *total* allocated memory, as opposed to the *live* and *peak* memory, respectively reached after and during program evaluation.

Acknowledgements. We are grateful to our colleague Maria Emilia Alonso for putting us on the tracks of the QEPCAD system.

References

1. Alias, C., Darte, A., Feautrier, P., Gonnord, L.: Multi-dimensional Rankings, Program Termination, and Complexity Bounds of Flowchart Programs. In: Cousot, R., Martel, M. (eds.) SAS 2010. LNCS, vol. 6337, pp. 117–133. Springer, Heidelberg (2010)
2. Aspinall, D., Beringer, L., Hofmann, M., Loidl, H.-W., Momigliano, A.: A program logic for resources. Theoretical Computer Science 389, 411–445 (2007)
3. Ben-Amram, A.M., Codish, M.: A SAT-Based Approach to Size Change Termination with Global Ranking Functions. In: Ramakrishnan, C.R., Rehof, J. (eds.) TACAS 2008. LNCS, vol. 4963, pp. 218–232. Springer, Heidelberg (2008)
4. Beringer, L., Hofmann, M., Momigliano, A., Shkaravska, O.: Automatic Certification of Heap Consumption. In: Baader, F., Voronkov, A. (eds.) LPAR 2004. LNCS (LNAI), vol. 3452, pp. 347–362. Springer, Heidelberg (2005)
5. Bertot, Y., Casteran, P.: Interactive Theorem Proving and Program Development Coq'Art: The Calculus of Inductive Constructions. In: Texts in Theoretical Computer Science. An EATCS Series. Springer, Heidelberg (2004)
6. Bonfante, G., Marion, J.-Y., Moyen, J.-Y.: Quasi-interpretations. Technical Report, Loria (2004), http://www.loria.fr/~moyen
7. Brown, C. W.: QEPCAD: Quantifier Elimination by Partial Cylindrical Algebraic Decomposition (2004), http://www.cs.usna.edu/qepcad/B/QEPCAD.html
8. Cachera, D., Jensen, T., Pichardie, D., Schneider, G.: Certified Memory Usage Analysis. In: Fitzgerald, J.S., Hayes, I.J., Tarlecki, A. (eds.) FM 2005. LNCS, vol. 3582, pp. 91–106. Springer, Heidelberg (2005)
9. Collins, G.E.: Quantifier Elimination for Real Closed Fields by Cylindrical Algebraic Decomposition. In: Brakhage, H. (ed.) GI-Fachtagung 1975. LNCS, vol. 33, pp. 134–183. Springer, Heidelberg (1975)
10. Colón, M., Sipma, H.: Practical Methods for Proving Program Termination. In: Brinksma, E., Larsen, K.G. (eds.) CAV 2002. LNCS, vol. 2404, pp. 442–454. Springer, Heidelberg (2002)
11. Contejean, E., Marché, C., Tomás, A.-P., Urbain, X.: Mechanically proving termination using polynomial interpretations. Journal of Automated Reasoning 34(4), 315–355 (2006)

12. Hoffmann, J., Hofmann, M.: Amortized Resource Analysis with Polynomial Potential. A Static Inference of Polynomial Bounds for Functional Programs. In: Gordon, A.D. (ed.) ESOP 2010. LNCS, vol. 6012, pp. 287–306. Springer, Heidelberg (2010)

13. Hofmann, M., Jost, S.: Static prediction of heap space usage for first-order functional programs. In: Proc. 30th ACM Symp. on Principles of Programming Languages, POPL 2003, pp. 185–197. ACM Press, New York (2003)

14. Lucas, S., Peña, R.: Rewriting Techniques for Analysing Termination and Complexity Bounds of SAFE Programs. In: LOPSTR 2008, Valencia, Spain, pp. 43–57 (2008)

15. Montenegro, M., Peña, R., Segura, C.: A Simple Region Inference Algorithm for a First-Order Functional Language. In: Escobar, S. (ed.) WFLP 2009. LNCS, vol. 5979, pp. 145–161. Springer, Heidelberg (2010)

16. Montenegro, M., Peña, R., Segura, C.: A space consumption analysis by abstract interpretation. In: van Eekelen, M., Shkaravska, O. (eds.) FOPARA 2009. LNCS, vol. 6324, pp. 34–50. Springer, Heidelberg (2010)

17. Necula, G.C.: Proof-Carrying Code. In: ACM SIGPLAN-SIGACT Principles of Programming Languages, POPL1997, pp. 106–119. ACM Press, New York (1997)

18. Nipkow, T.: Hoare Logics for Recursive Procedures and Unbounded Nondeterminism. In: Bradfield, J.C. (ed.) CSL 2002 and EACSL 2002. LNCS, vol. 2471, pp. 103–119. Springer, Heidelberg (2002)

19. Nipkow, T., Paulson, L., Wenzel, M.: Isabelle/HOL. A Proof Assistant for Higher-Order Logic LNCS, vol. 2283. Springer, Heidelberg (2002)

20. Podelski, A., Rybalchenko, A.: A Complete Method for the Synthesis of Linear Ranking Functions. In: Steffen, B., Levi, G. (eds.) VMCAI 2004. LNCS, vol. 2937, pp. 239–251. Springer, Heidelberg (2004)

21. Tarski, A.: A Decision Method for Elementary Algebra and Geometry. University of California Press, Berkeley (1948)

Relational Verification Using Product Programs[*]

Gilles Barthe[1], Juan Manuel Crespo[1], and César Kunz[1,2]

[1] IMDEA Software Institute
[2] Universidad Politécnica de Madrid

Abstract. Relational program logics are formalisms for specifying and verifying properties about two programs or two runs of the same program. These properties range from correctness of compiler optimizations or equivalence between two implementations of an abstract data type, to properties like non-interference or determinism. Yet the current technology for relational verification remains underdeveloped. We provide a general notion of product program that supports a direct reduction of relational verification to standard verification. We illustrate the benefits of our method with selected examples, including non-interference, standard loop optimizations, and a state-of-the-art optimization for incremental computation. All examples have been verified using the Why tool.

1 Introduction

Relational reasoning provides an effective mean to understand program behavior: in particular, it allows to establish that the same program behaves similarly on two different runs, or that two programs execute in a related fashion. Prime examples of relational properties include notions of simulation and observational equivalence, and 2-properties, such as non-interference and continuity. In the former, the property considers two programs, possibly written in different languages and having different notions of states, and establishes a relationship between their execution traces, whereas in the latter only one program is considered, and the relationship considers two executions of that program.

In spite of its important role, and of the wide range of properties it covers, there is a lack of applicable program logics and tools for relational reasoning. Indeed, existing logics [4,20] are confined to reasoning about structurally equal programs, and are not implemented. This is in sharp contrast with the more traditional program logics for which robust tool support is available. Thus, one natural approach to bring relational verification to a status similar to standard verification is to devise methods that soundly transform relational verification tasks into standard ones. More specifically for specifications expressed using pre and post-conditions, one would aim at developing methods to transform Hoare quadruples of the form $\{\varphi\}\, c_1 \sim c_2 \,\{\psi\}$, where φ and ψ are relations on the states

---

[*] Partially funded by European Projects FP7-231620 HATS and FP7-256980 NESSoS, Spanish project TIN2009-14599 DESAFIOS 10, Madrid Regional project S2009TIC-1465 PROMETIDOS. C. Kunz is funded by a Juan de la Cierva Fellowship, MICINN, Spain.

M. Butler and W. Schulte (Eds.): FM 2011, LNCS 6664, pp. 200–214, 2011.

of the command c_1 and the states of the command c_2, into Hoare triples of the form $\{\bar{\varphi}\} c \{\bar{\psi}\}$, where $\bar{\varphi}$ and $\bar{\psi}$ are predicates on the states of the command c, and such that the validity of the Hoare triple entails the validity of the original Hoare quadruple; using $\models$ to denote validity, the goal is to find c, $\bar{\varphi}$ and $\bar{\psi}$ s.t.

$$\models \{\bar{\varphi}\} c \{\bar{\psi}\} \quad \Rightarrow \quad \models \{\varphi\} c_1 \sim c_2 \{\psi\}$$

Consider two simple imperative programs c_1 and c_2 and assume that they are separable, i.e. operate on disjoint variables. Then we can let assertions be first-order formulae over the variables of the two programs, and achieve the desired effect by setting $c \equiv c_1; c_2$, $\bar{\varphi} \equiv \varphi$ and $\bar{\psi} \equiv \psi$. This method, coined self-composition by Barthe, D'Argenio and Rezk [2], is sound and relatively complete, but it is also impractical [19]. In a recent article, Zaks and Pnueli [21] develop another construction, called cross-product, that performs execution of c_1 and c_2 in lock-step and use it for translation validation [22], a general method for proving the correctness of compiler optimizations. Cross-products, when they exist, meet the required property; however their existence is confined to structurally equivalent programs and hence they cannot be used to validate loop optimizations that modify the control flow of programs, nor to reason about 2-properties such as non-interference and continuity, because such properties consider runs of the program that do not follow the same control flow.

The challenge addressed in this paper is to provide a general notion of product programs which allows transforming relational verification tasks into standard ones, without the setbacks of cross-products or self-composition. In our setting, a product between two programs c_1 and c_2 is a program c which combines synchronous steps, in which instructions from c_1 and c_2 are executed in lockstep, with asynchronous steps, in which instructions from c_1 or c_2 are executed separately. Products combine the best of cross-products and self-composition: the ability of performing asynchronous steps recovers the flexibility and generality of self-composition, and make them applicable to programs with different control structures, whereas the ability of performing synchronous steps is the key to make the verification of c as effective as the verification of cross-products and significantly easier than the verification of the programs obtained by self-composition. Concretely, we demonstrate how product programs can be combined with off-the-shelf verification tools to carry relational reasoning on a wide range of examples, including: various forms of loop optimizations, static caching for incremental computation, SSE transformations for increasing performance on multi-core platforms, information flow and continuity analyses. All examples have been formally verified using the Why framework with its SMT back-end; in one case, involving complex summations on arrays, we used a combination of the SMT back-end and the Coq proof assistant back-end—however it is conceivable that the proof obligations could be discharged automatically by declaring suitable axioms in the SMT solver.

Contents. The paper is organized as follows: Section 2 introduces the product construction and shows the need for a generalization of cross-product and self-composition. Section 3 defines product programs and shows how they enable reducing relational verification to existing standard logics. Section 4 illustrates the usefulness of our method through examples drawn from several settings including non-interference and translation validation of loop optimizations [1]. In particular, we provide a formal proof of Static Caching [14], a challenging optimization used for incremental computation e.g. in image processing or computational geometry.

2   Motivating Examples

Continuity is a relational property that measures the robustness of programs under changes: informally, a program is continuous if small variations on its inputs only causes small variations on its output. While program continuity is formalized by a formula of the form $\forall \epsilon > 0. \exists \delta > 0. \; P$, see e.g. [6], continuity can be often derived from the stronger notion of 1-sensitivity, see e.g. [18]. Informally, a program is 1-sensitive if it does not make the distance grow, i.e. the variation of the outputs of two different runs is upper bounded by the variation of the corresponding inputs.

Consider the standard bubble-sort algorithm shown at the left of Figure 1. Suppose that instead of the expected array a the algorithm is fed with an array a' satisfying the following relation: $|a[i] - a'[i]| < \epsilon$ for all i in the range of a and a' and for an infinitesimally small positive value ϵ. Clearly, the permutations performed by the sorting algorithm over a and a' can differ, as the variation ϵ may affect the validity of the guard $a[j-1] > a[j]$ that triggers the permutations. Fortunately, this small variation on the input data can at most cause a small variation in the final result. Indeed, one can verify the validity of the relational judgment $\models \{\forall i. |a[i] - a'[i]| < \epsilon\} \, c \sim c' \, \{\forall i. |a[i] - a'[i]| < \epsilon\}$, where c stands for the sorting algorithm in Figure 1 and c' for the result of substituting every variable v in c by its primed version v'. Instead of relying on a special purpose logic to reason about program continuity, we suggest to construct a product program that performs the execution steps of c and c' synchronously. Since c and c' have the same structure, it is immediate to build the program d, shown at the left of Figure 1, that weaves the instructions of c and c'[1]. The algorithm d simulates every pair of executions of c and c' synchronously, capturing all executions of c and c'. Notice that the program product synchronizes the loops iterations of its components, as their loop guards are equivalent and thus perform the same number of iterations. This is not the case with the conditional statements inside the loop body, as the small variations on the contents of the array a w.r.t. a' may break the equivalence of the guards $a[j-1] > a[j]$ and $a'[j'-1] > a'[j']$.

One can use a standard program logic to verify the validity of the non relational judgment $\models \{\forall i. |a[i] - a'[i]| < \epsilon\} \, d \, \{\forall i. |a[i] - a'[i]| < \epsilon\}$. Since the program product is a correct representation of its components, the validity of this judgment over d is enough to establish the validity of the relational judgment over c and c'.

---

[1] This introductory section omits the insertion of **assert** statements described in Section 3.

Source code:

```
i := 0;
while (i < N) do
    j := N − 1;
    while (j > i) do
        if (a[j − 1] > a[j]) then
            x := a[j];
            a[j] := a[j − 1];
            a[j − 1] := x;
        j − −
    i++
```

Program product:

```
i := 0;  i' := 0;
while (i < N) do
    j := N − 1;  j' := N − 1;
    while (j > i) do
        if (a[j − 1] > a[j]) then
            x := a[j];  a[j] := a[j − 1];  a[j − 1] := x;
        if (a'[j' − 1] > a'[j']) then
            x' := a'[j'];  a'[j'] := a'[j' − 1];  a'[j' − 1] := x';
        j − −;  j' − −
    i++;  i' ++
```

Fig. 1. Continuity of bubble-sort algorithm

As appears from the example above, it is possible to build a program product from structurally equivalent programs by a total synchronization of the loops, as in the example above. Structural equivalence is, however, a significant constraint as it rules out many interesting cases of relational reasoning, including the translation validation examples in Section 4. Consider the case of the loop pipelining optimization shown in Figure 6. The source and transformed programs have a similar structure: a loop statement plus some initialization and clean-up code. However, both programs cannot be synchronized a priori, since the number of loop iterations in the source and transformed program do not coincide. A more difficult situation arises when verifying the correctness of static-caching, shown in Figure 7, since it involves synchronizing two nested loops with different depths.

A first intuition on the construction of products from structurally dissimilar components is shown in the following basic example (assume $0 \leq N$):

Source code:

```
i := 0;
while (i ≤ N) do
    x += i;
    i++
```

Transformed code:

```
j := 1;
while (j ≤ N) do
    y += j;
    j++
```

Program product (simplified):

```
i := 0;  x += i;  i++;  j := 1;
while (i ≤ N) do
    y += j;  j++;
    x += i;  i++;
```

To build the product program, the first loop iteration of the source code is unrolled before synchronizing the loop statements. This simple idea maximizes synchronization instead of relying plainly on self-composition, which requires a greater specification and verification effort. Indeed, the sequential composition of the source and transformed program requires providing invariants of the form $x = X + \frac{i(i−1)}{2}$ and $y = Y + \frac{j(j−1)}{2}$, respectively (under the preconditions $x = X$ and $y = Y$). In contrast, by the construction of the product, the trivial loop invariant $i = j \wedge x = y$ is sufficient to verify that the two programs above satisfy the pre and post-relation $x = y$.

In the rest of the paper, we develop a more flexible notion of program products, extending the construction of products from components that are not structurally equal or with a different number of loop iterations.

3   Program Products

Our reduction of relational verification into standard verification relies on the ability of constructing, for any pair of programs c_1 and c_2, a product program c that simulates the execution steps of its constituents. We first introduce a basic program setting that will serve to formalize the ideas exposed in this article, and then provide a formalization of product program.

3.1   Programming Model

Commands are defined by the following grammar rule:

$$c \quad ::= \quad x := e \mid a[e] := e \mid \mathsf{skip} \mid \mathsf{assert}(b) \mid c; c \mid \mathsf{if}\ b\ \mathsf{then}\ c_1\ \mathsf{else}\ c_2 \mid \mathsf{while}\ b\ \mathsf{do}\ c$$

in which x ranges over a set of integer variables $\mathcal{V}_i$, a ranges over a set of array variables $\mathcal{V}_a$ (we assume $\mathcal{V}_i \cap \mathcal{V}_a = \emptyset$ and let $\mathcal{V}$ denote $\mathcal{V}_i \cup \mathcal{V}_a$), and $e \in \mathsf{AExp}$ and $b \in \mathsf{BExp}$ range over integer and boolean expressions. Execution states are represented as $\mathcal{S} = (\mathcal{V}_i + (\mathcal{V}_a \times \mathbb{Z})) \rightarrow \mathbb{Z}$, and we let σ be a state in $\mathcal{S}$. The semantics of integer and boolean expressions are given by $(\llbracket e \rrbracket)_{e \in \mathsf{AExp}} : \mathcal{S} \rightarrow \mathbb{Z}$ and $(\llbracket b \rrbracket)_{b \in \mathsf{BExp}} : \mathcal{S} \rightarrow \mathbb{B}$, respectively. The semantics of commands is standard, deterministic, and defined by a relation $\langle c, \sigma \rangle \leadsto \langle c', \sigma' \rangle$ in Figure 2, with $\langle \mathsf{skip}, \sigma \rangle$ denoting final configurations. Notice that the execution of a statement $\mathsf{assert}(b)$ blocks if b is not satisfied. We let $\langle c, \sigma \rangle \Downarrow \sigma'$ denote $\langle c, \sigma \rangle \leadsto^\star \langle \mathsf{skip}, \sigma' \rangle$.

An assertion ϕ is a first-order formula with variables in $\mathcal{V}$. We let $\llbracket \phi \rrbracket$ denote the set of states satisfying ϕ. Finally, we let $\mathsf{var}(c) \subseteq \mathcal{V}$ and $\mathsf{var}(\phi) \subseteq \mathcal{V}$ denote the set of (free) variables of a command c and assertion ϕ, respectively.

In order to simplify the definition of valid relational judgment, we introduce a notion of separable commands: two commands c_1 and c_2 are separable if they have disjoint set of variables: $\mathsf{var}(c_1) \cap \mathsf{var}(c_2) = \emptyset$. Two states are separable if they have disjoint domains. For all separable states σ_1 and σ_2, we define $\sigma_1 \uplus \sigma_2$ as the union of finite maps: $(\sigma_1 \uplus \sigma_2)\, x$ is equal to $\sigma_1\, x$ if $x \in \mathsf{dom}(\sigma_1)$ and equal to $\sigma_2\, x$ if $x \in \mathsf{dom}(\sigma_2)$. Under this separability assumption, one can identify assertions as relations on states: $(\sigma_1, \sigma_2) \in \llbracket \phi \rrbracket$ iff $\sigma_1 \uplus \sigma_2 \in \llbracket \phi \rrbracket$. The formal statement of valid relational specifications is then given by the following definition.

Definition 1. *Two commands c_1 and c_2 satisfy the pre and post-relation φ and ψ, denoted by the judgment $\models \{\varphi\}\, c_1 \sim c_2\, \{\psi\}$ if for all states $\sigma_1, \sigma_2, \sigma_1', \sigma_2'$ s.t. $\sigma_1 \uplus \sigma_2 \in \llbracket \varphi \rrbracket$ and $\langle c_1, \sigma_1 \rangle \Downarrow \sigma_1'$ and $\langle c_2, \sigma_2 \rangle \Downarrow \sigma_2'$, we have $\sigma_1' \uplus \sigma_2' \in \llbracket \psi \rrbracket$.*

Our goal is to reduce validity of relational judgments to validity of Hoare triples, hence we also define the notion of valid Hoare triple. For technical reasons,

$$\frac{}{\langle \mathsf{assert}(b), \sigma \rangle \leadsto \langle \mathsf{skip}, \sigma \rangle}\, \llbracket b \rrbracket \sigma \qquad \frac{\langle c_1, \sigma \rangle \leadsto \langle c_1', \sigma' \rangle}{\langle c_1; c_2, \sigma \rangle \leadsto \langle c_1'; c_2, \sigma' \rangle} \qquad \frac{\langle c_1, \sigma \rangle \leadsto \langle \mathsf{skip}, \sigma' \rangle}{\langle c_1; c_2, \sigma \rangle \leadsto \langle c_2, \sigma' \rangle}$$

$$\frac{}{\langle \mathsf{while}\ b\ \mathsf{do}\ c, \sigma \rangle \leadsto \langle c; \mathsf{while}\ b\ \mathsf{do}\ c, \sigma \rangle}\, \llbracket b \rrbracket \sigma \qquad \frac{}{\langle \mathsf{while}\ b\ \mathsf{do}\ c, \sigma \rangle \leadsto \langle \mathsf{skip}, \sigma \rangle}\, \llbracket \neg b \rrbracket \sigma$$

Fig. 2. Program semantics (excerpt)

we adopt a stronger definition of validity, which requires that the command is non-blocking w.r.t. the precondition of the triple, where a command c is φ-nonblocking if its execution can always progress under the precondition φ. That is, for all states σ, σ' and command $c' \neq \mathsf{skip}$ such that $\sigma \in [\![\varphi]\!]$ and $\langle c, \sigma \rangle \rightsquigarrow^* \langle c', \sigma' \rangle$, there exists c'' and σ'' such that $\langle c', \sigma' \rangle \rightsquigarrow \langle c'', \sigma'' \rangle$.

Definition 2. *A triple $\{\varphi\}c\{\psi\}$ is valid, denoted by the judgment $\vDash \{\varphi\} c \{\psi\}$, if c is φ-nonblocking and for all $\sigma, \sigma' \in \mathcal{S}$, $\sigma \in [\![\varphi]\!]$ and $\langle c, \sigma \rangle \Downarrow \sigma'$ imply $\sigma' \in [\![\psi]\!]$.*

Such a notion of validity can be established using an extension of Hoare logic with the following rule to deal with assert statements:

$$\vdash \{b \wedge \phi\} \, \mathsf{assert}(b) \, \{\phi\}$$

3.2 Product Construction

We start in this section with a set of rules appropriate for structurally equivalent programs. Then, we extend the set of rules with a structural transformation to deal with structurally dissimilar programs.

Figure 3 provides a set of rules to derive a product construction judgment $c_1 \times c_2 \to c$. The construction of products introduces assert statements to verify that the resulting program simulates precisely the behavior of its components. These validation constraints are interpreted as local assertions, which are discharged during the program verification phase. For instance, in the rule that synchronizes two loop statements, the insertion of the statement $\mathsf{assert}(b_1 \Leftrightarrow b_2)$ just before the evaluation the loop guards b_1 and b_2 enforces that the number of loop iterations coincide. The resulting product containing assert statements can thus be verified with a standard logic. If a command c is the product of c_1 and c_2, then the validity of a relational judgment between c_1 and c_2 can be deduced from the validity of a standard judgment on c.

Proposition 1. *For all statements c_1 and c_2 and pre and post-relations φ and ψ, if $c_1 \times c_2 \to c$ and $\vDash \{\varphi\} c \{\psi\}$ then $\vDash \{\varphi\} c_1 \sim c_2 \{\psi\}$.*

A constraint of the product construction rules in Fig. 3 is that two loops with non-equivalent guards must be sequentially composed. In the rest of this section we propose a structural transformation that extends relational verification by product construction to non-structurally equivalent programs.

We characterize the structural transformations extending the construction of products as a refinement relation, denoted with a judgment of the form $c \succcurlyeq c'$. It is a refinement relation in the sense that every execution of c is an execution of c' except when c' blocks:

Definition 3. *A command c' is a refinement of c, if for all states σ, σ':*

1. *if $\langle c', \sigma \rangle \Downarrow \sigma'$ then $\langle c, \sigma \rangle \Downarrow \sigma'$, and*
2. *if $\langle c, \sigma \rangle \Downarrow \sigma'$ then either the execution of c' with initial state σ blocks, or $\langle c', \sigma \rangle \Downarrow \sigma'$.*

$$\frac{}{c_1 \times c_2 \to c_1; c_2} \qquad \frac{c_1 \times c_2 \to c \qquad c_1' \times c_2' \to c'}{(c_1; c_1') \times (c_2; c_2') \to c; c'}$$

$$\frac{c_1 \times c_2 \to c}{(\text{while } b_1 \text{ do } c_1) \times (\text{while } b_2 \text{ do } c_2) \to \text{assert}(b_1 \Leftrightarrow b_2); \text{while } b_1 \text{ do } (c; \text{assert}(b_1 \Leftrightarrow b_2))}$$

$$\frac{c_1 \times c_2 \to c \qquad c_1' \times c_2' \to c'}{(\text{if } b_1 \text{ then } c_1 \text{ else } c_1') \times (\text{if } b_2 \text{ then } c_2 \text{ else } c_2') \to \text{assert}(b_1 \Leftrightarrow b_2); \text{if } b_1 \text{ then } c \text{ else } c'}$$

$$\frac{c_1 \times c \to c_1' \qquad c_2 \times c \to c_2'}{(\text{if } b \text{ then } c_1 \text{ else } c_2) \times c \to \text{if } b \text{ then } c_1' \text{ else } c_2'}$$

Fig. 3. Product construction rules

$$\frac{}{\vdash \text{if } b \text{ then } c_1 \text{ else } c_2 \succcurlyeq \text{assert}(b); c_1} \qquad \frac{}{\vdash \text{if } b \text{ then } c_1 \text{ else } c_2 \succcurlyeq \text{assert}(\neg b); c_2}$$

$$\frac{}{\vdash \text{while } b \text{ do } c \succcurlyeq \text{assert}(b); c; \text{while } b \text{ do } c}$$

$$\frac{}{\vdash \text{while } b \text{ do } c \succcurlyeq \text{while } b \wedge b' \text{ do } c; \text{while } b \text{ do } c} \qquad \frac{}{\vdash \text{while } b \text{ do } c \succcurlyeq \text{assert}(b); c; \text{assert}(\neg b)}$$

$$\frac{\vdash c \succcurlyeq c'}{\vdash \text{while } b \text{ do } c \succcurlyeq \text{while } b \text{ do } c'} \qquad \frac{\vdash c_1 \succcurlyeq c_1' \qquad \vdash c_2 \succcurlyeq c_2'}{\vdash \text{if } b \text{ then } c_1 \text{ else } c_2 \succcurlyeq \text{if } b \text{ then } c_1' \text{ else } c_2'}$$

$$\frac{\vdash c \succcurlyeq c' \qquad \vdash c' \succcurlyeq c''}{\vdash c \succcurlyeq c''} \qquad \frac{}{\vdash c \succcurlyeq c} \qquad \frac{\vdash c_1 \succcurlyeq c_1' \qquad \vdash c_2 \succcurlyeq c_2'}{\vdash c_1; c_2 \succcurlyeq c_1'; c_2'}$$

Fig. 4. Syntactic reduction rules

We provide in Figure 4 a particular set of structural rules defining judgments of the form $\vdash c \succcurlyeq c'$. From the rules given in the figure, one can see that the executions of c and c' coincide for every initial state that makes the introduced assert statements valid. One can prove that the judgment $\vdash c \succcurlyeq c'$ establishes a refinement relation by showing that for every assertion φ, if c' is φ-nonblocking then for all $\sigma \in [\![\varphi]\!]$ such that $\langle c, \sigma \rangle \Downarrow \sigma'$ we have $\langle c', \sigma \rangle \Downarrow \sigma'$.

We enrich the set of rules defining the construction of products by adding an extra rule that introduces a preliminary refinement transformation over the product components:

$$\frac{c_1 \succcurlyeq c_1' \qquad c_2 \succcurlyeq c_2' \qquad c_1' \times c_2' \to c}{c_1 \times c_2 \to c}$$

Proposition 1 remains valid for the extended proof system. The following proposition reduces the problem of proving the validity of a relational judgment into two steps: the construction of the corresponding program product plus a standard verification over the program product.

Proposition 2. *For all statements c_1 and c_2 and pre and post-relations φ and ψ, if $c_1 \times c_2 \to c$ and $\vdash \{\varphi\} c \{\psi\}$ then $\models \{\varphi\} c_1 \sim c_2 \{\psi\}$.*

4   Case Studies

This section illustrates the application of product construction for the verification of relational properties, such as non-interference and the correctness of program transformations. These program transformations include loop optimizations, and static-caching, a complex optimization described later in this section. For each of the examples in this section, a product construction has been verified with the Why tool (and the Frama-C tool with the Jessie plugin). Building a product program from a pair of components is undecidable in general, but feasible in the scenarios we are considering. Products can be constructed in an automatic manner for structure-preserving optimizations, as well as for the verification of non-interference properties, for which a type-system based approach has already been suggested by Terauchi and Aiken. Some complex loop optimizations require involved products, in which case templates can be provided.

As shown in Table 1, most of the examples could be automatically verified: the column P.O. indicates the number of proof obligations generated, and the column SMT those that have been automatically discharged by SMT solvers. For the static-caching and loop interchange examples, the remaining proof obligations have been discharged in the Coq proof assistant.

Logical Verification of Non-interference

Non-interference is a confidentiality policy defined in terms of two executions of the same program. Given a program c and a set of public variables $x_1, \ldots, x_k$, the property ensures that two terminating runs of c starting in states with equal public variables, end in states with equal public variables:

$$\bigwedge_{x \in \{x_1, \ldots, x_k\}} \sigma_1 \, x = \sigma'_1 \, x \; \wedge \; \langle c, \sigma_1 \rangle \rightsquigarrow \sigma_2 \; \wedge \; \langle c, \sigma'_1 \rangle \rightsquigarrow \sigma'_2 \implies \bigwedge_{x \in \{x_1, \ldots, x_k\}} \sigma_2 \, x = \sigma'_2 \, x.$$

(For simplicity, we express non-interference w.r.t. scalar variables, the extension to array variables being immediate.) Non-interference can thus be formulated as a relational judgment:

$$\vDash \{x_1 = x'_1 \wedge .. \wedge x_k = x'_k\} \, c \sim c' \, \{x_1 = x'_1 \wedge .. \wedge x_k = x'_k\}$$

where c' is the result of replacing every variable v in c by v'.

Table 1. Automatic validation of case studies

Example	SMT/P.O.	Example	SMT/P.O.'s
Non-interference	42/42	Loop reversal	13/13
Loop alignment	49/49	Strength reduction	5/5
Loop pipelining	73/73	Loop interchange	36/37
Loop unswitching	123/123	Loop fission	15/15
Code sinking	435/435	Cyclic hashing	13/13
Static caching	162/176	Bubble sort continuity	62/62

$\{Pre : es = es' \wedge \forall i : 0 \leq i < N : ps[i].PID = ps'[i].PID \wedge$
$\quad ps[i].JoinInd = ps'[i].JoinInd \wedge (ps[i].JoinInd \Rightarrow ps[i].salary = ps'[i].salary)\}$
$\quad i := 0; \ i' := 0; \ \text{assert}(i < N \Leftrightarrow i' < N);$
$\quad \text{while } (i < N) \text{ do}$
$\quad\quad \text{assert}(ps[i].JoinInd \Leftrightarrow ps'[i'].JoinInd);$
$\quad\quad \text{if } (ps[i].JoinInd) \text{ then}$
$\quad\quad\quad j := 0; \ j' := 0; \ \text{assert}(j < M \Leftrightarrow j' < M);$
$\quad\quad\quad \text{while } (j < M) \text{ do}$
$\quad\quad\quad\quad \text{assert}(ps[i].PID = es[j].EID \Leftrightarrow ps'[i'].PID = es'[j'].EID);$
$\quad\quad\quad\quad \text{if } (ps[i].PID = es[j].EID) \text{ then}$
$\quad\quad\quad\quad\quad tab[i].employee := es[j]; \ tab'[i'].employee := es'[j];$
$\quad\quad\quad\quad\quad tab[i].payroll := ps[i]; \ tab'[i'].payroll := ps'[i];$
$\quad\quad\quad\quad j\texttt{++}; \ j'\texttt{++}; \ \text{assert}(i < N \Leftrightarrow i' < N);$
$\quad\quad i\texttt{++}; \ i'\texttt{++}; \ \text{assert}(i < N \Leftrightarrow i' < N);$
$\{Post : \forall i : 0 \leq i < N : ps[i].JoinInd \Rightarrow tab[i] = tab'[i]\}$

Fig. 5. Non-interference product

We illustrate the application of relational verification by product construction for the verification of an example drawn from [9]. Figure 5 shows the construction of the program product (the original program can be obtained by slicing out the statements containing primed variables). This simple algorithm merges a table containing personal information with a table containing salary information. A special field $JoinInd$ indicates whether the personal information is private and should not be included as the result of the join operation.

The pre and postcondition provided in Figure 5 establish that the input data marked as private does not interfere with the final result: if the values stored in the input arrays coincide for the public indices (i.e., for i s.t. $ps[i].JoindInd$ is true), then the return data coincides at the public indices (we let a formula of the form $a = \bar{a}$ stand for $\forall i \in [0, N-1]. \ a[i] = \bar{a}[i]$.)

Self-composition is another method that embeds the verification of non-interference in standard program logics, by reducing it to the verification of sequential compositions of the form $\models \{x_1 = x'_1 \wedge .. \wedge x_k = x'_k\} c; c' \{x_1 = x'_1 \wedge .. \wedge x_k = x'_k\}$. This method based on sequential composition is not amenable for automatic tools, as it requires providing and verifying an intermediate assertion ϕ such that the judgments

$$\models \{x_1 = x'_1 \wedge \ldots \wedge x_k = x'_k\} c \{\phi\} \quad \text{and} \quad \models \{\phi\} c' \{x_1 = x'_1 \wedge \ldots \wedge x_k = x'_k\}$$

hold. In practice, this is a significant obstacle, as it may require understanding and verifying a functional specification for the program c. Terauchi and Aiken propose an alternative program composition [19], that can be seen as a particular instance of our product construction, defined in terms of an information-flow type system.

Translation Validation of Loop Pipelining

Loop pipelining is a non-trivial optimization that reduces the proximity of memory references inside a loop, in order to introduce parallelization opportunities.

Source program:

$i := 0;$
while $(i < N)$ do
    $a[i]$++; $b[i]$ += $a[i];$
    $c[i]$ += $b[i];$ i++

Transformed program:

$j := 0;$
$\bar{a}[0]$++; $\bar{b}[0]$ += $\bar{a}[0];$
$\bar{a}[1]$++;
while $(j < N-2)$ do
    $\bar{a}[j+2]$++;
    $\bar{b}[j+1]$ += $\bar{a}[j+1];$
    $\bar{c}[j]$ += $\bar{b}[j];$ j++
$\bar{c}[j]$ += $\bar{b}[j];$
$\bar{b}[j+1]$ += $\bar{a}[j+1];$
$\bar{c}[j+1]$ += $\bar{b}[j+1]$

Product program:

$\{a = \bar{a} \wedge b = \bar{b} \wedge c = \bar{c}\}$
  $i := 0;$ $j := 0;$ assert$(i < N);$
  $a[i]$++; $b[i]$ += $a[i];$
  $c[i]$ += $b[i];$ i++;
  $\bar{a}[0]$++; $\bar{b}[0]$ += $\bar{a}[0];$
  assert$(i < N);$
  $a[i]$++; $b[i]$ += $a[i];$
  $c[i]$ += $b[i];$ i++; $\bar{a}[1]$++;
  assert$(i < N \Leftrightarrow j < N-2);$
  while $(i < N)$ do
    $a[i]$++; $b[i]$ += $a[i];$ $c[i]$ += $b[i];$ i++
    $\bar{a}[j+2]$++; $\bar{b}[j+1]$ += $\bar{a}[j+1];$
    $\bar{c}[j]$ += $\bar{b}[j];$ j++
    assert$(i < N \Leftrightarrow j < N-2);$
  $\bar{c}[j]$ += $\bar{b}[j];$ $\bar{b}[j+1]$ += $\bar{a}[j+1];$ $\bar{c}[j+1]$ += $\bar{b}[j+1]$
$\{a = \bar{a} \wedge b = \bar{b} \wedge c = \bar{c}\}$

Fig. 6. Loop pipelining

Consider the simple example shown in Fig. 6 (drawn from [13].) Assume a, b, and c are arrays of size N, with $2 \leq N$.

The program product shown in Fig. 6 pairs the initialization statements over $\bar{a}[0]$, $\bar{b}[0]$, and $\bar{a}[1]$ with the first and second loop iterations of the original program. Similarly, the final assignments to $\bar{b}[N-2]$, $\bar{c}[N-2]$ and $\bar{c}[N-1]$ are executed synchronously with the final loop iteration of the original loop. The remaining $N-2$ loop iterations are synchronized together. In order to verify that $a = \bar{a} \wedge b = \bar{b} \wedge c = \bar{c}$ is a valid pre and post condition, we require a specification that establishes the equalities in b and $\bar{b}$ and c and $\bar{c}$, except for the indices j and $j+1$. In particular, the loop invariant must state that $b[j+1] = \bar{b}[j+1] + a[j+1]$, $c[j] = \bar{c}[j] + b[j]$, and $c[j+1] = \bar{c}[j+1] + b[j+1]$, and $b[i'] = \bar{b}[i']$ and $c[i'] = \bar{c}[i']$ for any other index i'.

Static Caching

In this section we turn our attention to static caching [14], an optimization that has not been considered from the perspective of translation validation. To the best of our knowledge, we provide the first formal validation of such optimization.

Static caching removes redundant computations by exploiting memoized intermediate results. One of its applications is the row summation algorithm in Fig. 7. The algorithm takes as input an $N \times L$ matrix a and returns an array s of length $N-M+1$ (assume $M \leq N$) such that $s[i] = \sum_{i',j'=i,0}^{M,L} a[i',j']$, for all $i \in [0, N-M]$. The original program performs a significant amount of redundant computation. Let $b[i]$ stand for $\sum_{j=0}^{N} a[i,j]$. One can see that for all i, $s[i]$ differs from $s[i+1]$ on the value $b[i+M] - b[i]$. The computations of the summations $b[i']$ for $i' \in [i+1, i+M-1]$ are thus redundant and can be removed. In the optimized version of the algorithm, the array b of size N is used to store the intermediate

Source program:

$i_1 := 0;$
while $(i_1 \leq N - M)$ do
$\quad s[i_1] := 0; \ k_1 := 0;$
$\quad$ while $(k_1 \leq M - 1)$ do
$\quad \quad l_1 := 0;$
$\quad \quad$ while $(l_1 \leq L - 1)$ do
$\quad \quad \quad s[i_1] += a[i_1 + k_1, l_1]; \ l_1 ++;$
$\quad \quad k_1 ++;$
$\quad i_1 ++$

Transformed program:

$t[0] := 0; \ k_2 := 0;$
while $(k_2 \leq M - 1)$ do
$\quad b[k_2] := 0; \ l_2 := 0;$
$\quad$ while $(l_2 \leq L - 1)$ do
$\quad \quad b[k_2] += a[k_2, l_2]; \ l_2 ++;$
$\quad t[0] += b[k_2]; \ k_2 ++;$
$i_2 := 1;$
while $(i_2 \leq N - M)$ do
$\quad b[i_2 + M - 1] := 0; \ l_2 := 0;$
$\quad$ while $(l_2 \leq L - 1)$ do
$\quad \quad b[i_2 + M - 1] += a[i_2 + M - 1, l_2]; \ l_2 ++;$
$\quad z := b[i_2 + M - 1] - b[i_2 - 1];$
$\quad t[i_2] := t[i_2 - 1] + z; \ i_2 ++$

Fig. 7. Static caching: source and optimized code

computation of row summations. The matrix summations are computed using the computations saved in the array b, and then stored in the array t. As a result, the transformed algorithm has a quadratic complexity, whereas the complexity of the original algorithm is cubic.

Figure 8 shows the product of the original row-summation algorithm and of its optimized version. The specification states that the output arrays s and t coincide in the range $[0, N-M]$ after the synchronous execution of the original and optimized program. The correctness of the product w.r.t. its specification can be verified by simple arithmetic reasoning.

5   Related Work

Relational logics provide a syntactical counterpart to semantic relational methods, and can be used for similar purposes. To date, relational logics have been applied to prove compiler correctness, program equivalence [3], and non-interference:

Program equivalence. Relational Hoare Logics [4] (RHL), and its cousin Relational Separation Logic [20], provide a set of elegant and intuitive judgment rules to reason about program equivalence. The main drawback of RHL's core rules is that they can only account for structurally equal programs. This restriction can be lifted by introducing one-sided rules to deal with each particular case; such one-sided rules play a role similar to simulation in our setting. There is a tight connection between relational Hoare logics and products: one can isolate a core fragment cRHL of RHL such that derivability in this fragment coincides with derivability of the product in Hoare logic: i.e. $\vdash_{\mathrm{cRHL}} \{\varphi\} c_1 \sim c_2 \{\psi\}$ iff $c_1 \times c_2 \to c$ and $\vdash \{\varphi\} c \{\psi\}$. Moreover, one can define for every refinement relation $\succcurlyeq$ an extension $\mathrm{cRHL}_{\succcurlyeq}$ of the core logic such that $\vdash_{\mathrm{cRHL}_{\succcurlyeq}} \{\varphi\} c_1 \sim c_2 \{\psi\}$ iff $c_1 \times c_2 \to c$ and $\vdash \{\varphi\} c \{\psi\}$.

Product program:

{true}

$i_1 := 0$; assert$(i_1 \leq N-M)$; $s[i_1] := 0$; $k_1 := 0$; $t[0] := 0$; $k_2 := 0$;
assert$(k_1 \leq M-1 \Leftrightarrow k_2 \leq M-1)$;
while $(k_1 \leq M-1)$ $\{Inv_1\}$ do
    $l_1 := 0$; $b[k_2] := 0$; $l_2 := 0$; assert$(l_1 \leq L-1 \Leftrightarrow l_2 \leq L-1)$;
    while $(l_1 \leq L-1)$ $\{Inv_2\}$ do
        $s[i_1]$+=$a[i_1+k_1, l_1]$; l_1++; $b[k_2]$ += $a[k_2, l_2]$; l_2++;
        assert$(l_1 \leq L-1 \Leftrightarrow l_2 \leq L-1)$;
    k_1++; $t[0]$ += $b[k_2]$; k_2++; assert$(k_1 \leq M-1 \Leftrightarrow k_2 \leq M-1)$;
i_1++; $i_2 := 1$; assert$(i_1 \leq N-M \Leftrightarrow i_2 \leq N-M)$;
while $(i_1 \leq N-M)$ $\{Inv_3\}$ do
    $b[i_2+M-1] := 0$; $l_2 := 0$;
    while $(l_2 \leq L-1)$ $\{Inv_4\}$ do
        $b[i_2+M-1]$+=$a[i_2+M-1, l_2]$; l_2++;
    $z := b[i_2+M-1] - b[i_2-1]$; $t[i_2] := t[i_2-1] + z$; i_2++;
    $s[i_1] := 0$; $k_1 := 0$;
    while $(k_1 \leq M-1)$ $\{Inv_5\}$ do
        $l_1 := 0$;
        while $(l_1 \leq L-1)$ $\{Inv_6\}$ do
            $s[i_1]$+=$a[i_1+k_1, l_1]$; l_1++;
        k_1++;
    i_1++
assert$(i_1 \leq N-M \Leftrightarrow i_2 \leq N-M)$;

$\{\forall i \in [0, N-M].\ s[i] - t[i]\}$

Fig. 8. Static caching: Program product

$Inv_2 \doteq i_1 = 0 \wedge k_1 = k_2 \wedge l_1 = l_2 \wedge k_1 \leq M \wedge l_1 \leq L \wedge$
$$s[i_1] = t[0] + b[k_1] = \sum_{k'=0}^{k_1-1} b[k'] + b[k_1] \wedge$$
$$\forall k' \in [0, k_1).\ b[k'] = \sum_{l'=0}^{L-1} a[k', l'] \wedge b[k_1] = \sum_{l'=0}^{l_1-1} a[k_1, l']$$

$Inv_3 \doteq i_1 = i_2 \wedge i_1 \leq N-M+1 \wedge \forall i' \in [0, i_1) \Rightarrow s[i'] = t[i'] = \sum_{k'=0}^{M-1} b[k'+i'] \wedge$
$$\forall i' \in [0, i_1+M-1).\ b[i'] = \sum_{l'=0}^{L-1} a[i', l']$$

$Inv_4 \doteq Inv_3 \wedge k_1 \leq M \wedge l_2 \leq L \wedge b[i_2+M-1] = \sum_{l'=0}^{l_2-1} a[i_2+M-1, l'] \wedge$
$$s[i_1] = \sum_{k'=0}^{k_1-1} b[k'+i_1]$$

$Inv_6 \doteq Inv_3 \wedge k_1 \leq M \wedge l_1 \leq L \wedge b[i_2+M-1] = \sum_{l'=0}^{L-1} a[i_2+M-1, l'] \wedge$
$$s[i_1] = \sum_{k'=0}^{k_1-1} b[k'+i_1] + \sum_{l'=0}^{l_1-1} a[i_1+k_1, l']$$

Fig. 9. Static caching: Loop invariants (excerpt)

Compiler correctness. Translation validation [17,22,1] is a general method for ensuring the correctness of optimizing compilation by means of a validator which checks after each run of the compiler that the source and target programs are semantically equivalent. Pnueli et al. define Translation Validation for optimizations defined in terms of instruction replacement, reordering of loop iterations, and elimination of loop iterations, handled by the proof rules (VALIDATE),

(PERMUTE), and (REDUCE), respectively. A drawback of the (PERMUTE) rule is that it can only deal with reordering optimizations, i.e., relating loops with the same number of iterations, disabling the verification of non-consonant loop transformations, such as loop fusion and distribution. In a later work [11], the permute rule is generalized to account for such optimizations.

In an independent line of work, Necula [16] develops a translation validation prototype based on GCC, in terms of a simulation relation between source and transformed program points, and constrained to the validation of structure preserving optimizations. Parametrized equivalence checking [13] lifts the limitations of Necula's relational validation approach to consonant optimizations by combining it with Pnueli et al.'s PERMUTE rule. However, they use a simplified permute rule that restricts reasoning to loops in which every pair of iterations is pair-wise independent, and thus can only account for basic transformations.

A combination of the work in [16] with the PERMUTE rule is provided by Kundu et al. [13]. A current deficiency of the correlation inference is the inability to account for asynchronous steps as presented in our work.

Program products. The notion of program product has been previously exploited for the verification of non-interference properties and compiler correctness.

Self-composition [2,8] provides a sound and complete means to capture non-interference, by traditional verification of the sequential composition of a program with a slightly modified version of itself. Terauchi and Aiken [19] suggested to improve self-composition by a type directed transformation, a special case of our product construction. Naumann [15] builds on Terauchi and Aiken results to encompass the verification of programs with dynamic allocation.

A notion of program products is present in the work of Pnueli and Zack, i.e. *cross-products* [21], for establishing compiler correctness by reducing the relational verification of the original and transformed programs to the analysis of a single program. The restriction of cross-products to structurally equal programs limits the application of the framework to structure preserving transformations.

Beyond properties Other applications of relational methods include regression verification [10], verification of 2-safety properties [19,7], including determinism [5]. Furthermore, quantitative properties such as continuity [6] or indistinguishability [12] appear as a natural generalization of 2-safety properties.

Clarkson and Schneider [7] provide a general theory of hyperproperties, i.e. set of properties such as non-interference or average response time, which cannot be described as properties, i.e., set of traces. This theory establishes a general classification of policies, but does not (intend to) provide a verification method.

6   Further Work and Conclusions

Relational reasoning provides a mean to enforce a wide range of correctness and security properties, but have lacked methods and tools that are available for traditional program logics. This paper develops a notion of product between programs and reduces verification of relational properties between two programs to verification of functional properties of their product. The notion of product program is general and flexible, and overcomes the limitations of previous approaches.

In this paper, we have concentrated on product programs in the setting of a simple imperative language. However, our constructions extend to products across programs written in two different languages, and also accommodate nondeterminism and dynamic allocation. Moreover, we have achieved greater generality by relying on alternative representations of programs, such as flow graphs or their generalizations.

An important goal for further work is to develop methods and tools for building products, and to connect them with off-the-shelf tools to provide a complete framework for relational verification. In a separate line of work, we are investigating applications of products to probabilistic programs, and intend to apply the resulting formalism to provable security [3] and privacy [18].

References

1. Barrett, C.W., Fang, Y., Goldberg, B., Hu, Y., Pnueli, A., Zuck, L.D.: TVOC: A translation validator for optimizing compilers. In: Etessami, K., Rajamani, S.K. (eds.) CAV 2005. LNCS, vol. 3576, pp. 291–295. Springer, Heidelberg (2005)
2. Barthe, G., D'Argenio, P., Rezk, T.: Secure Information Flow by Self-Composition. In: Foccardi, R. (ed.) Computer Security Foundations Workshop, pp. 100–114. IEEE Press, Los Alamitos (2004)
3. Barthe, G., Grégoire, B., Zanella Béguelin, S.: Formal certification of code-based cryptographic proofs. In: Shao, Z., Pierce, B.C. (eds.) Principles of Programming Languages, pp. 90–101. ACM Press, New York (2009)
4. Benton, N.: Simple relational correctness proofs for static analyses and program transformations. In: Jones, N.D., Leroy, X. (eds.) Principles of Programming Languages, pp. 14–25. ACM Press, New York (2004)
5. Burnim, J., Sen, K.: Asserting and checking determinism for multithreaded programs. Communications of the ACM 53(6), 97–105 (2010)
6. Chaudhuri, S., Gulwani, S., Lublinerman, R.: Continuity analysis of programs. In: Principles of Programming Languages, pp. 57–70 (2010)
7. Clarkson, M.R., Schneider, F.B.: Hyperproperties. In: Computer Security Foundations Symposium, pp. 51–65 (2008)
8. Darvas, A., Hähnle, R., Sands, D.: A theorem proving approach to analysis of secure information flow. In: Hutter, D., Ullmann, M. (eds.) SPC 2005. LNCS, vol. 3450, pp. 193–209. Springer, Heidelberg (2005)
9. Dufay, G., Felty, A.P., Matwin, S.: Privacy-sensitive information flow with JML. In: Nieuwenhuis, R. (ed.) CADE 2005. LNCS (LNAI), vol. 3632, pp. 116–130. Springer, Heidelberg (2005)
10. Godlin, B., Strichman, O.: Regression verification. In: Design Meets Automation, pp. 466–471. ACM Press, New York (2009)
11. Goldberg, B., Zuck, L.D., Barrett, C.W.: Into the loops: Practical issues in translation validation for optimizing compilers. Electr. Notes Theor. Comput. Sci. 132(1), 53–71 (2005)
12. Goldreich, O.: Foundations of Cryptography. Cambridge University Press, Cambridge (2004)

13. Kundu, S., Tatlock, Z., Lerner, S.: Proving optimizations correct using parameterized program equivalence. In: Programming Languages Design and Implementation, pp. 327–337 (2009)
14. Liu, Y.A., Stoller, S.D., Teitelbaum, T.: Static caching for incremental computation. ACM Transactions on Programming Languages and Systems 20(3), 546–585 (1998)
15. Naumann, D.A.: From coupling relations to mated invariants for checking information flow. In: Gollmann, D., Meier, J., Sabelfeld, A. (eds.) ESORICS 2006. LNCS, vol. 4189, pp. 279–296. Springer, Heidelberg (2006)
16. Necula, G.C.: Translation validation for an optimizing compiler. ACM SIGPLAN Notices 35(5), 83–94 (2000)
17. Pnueli, A., Singerman, E., Siegel, M.: Translation validation. In: Steffen, B. (ed.) TACAS 1998. LNCS, vol. 1384, pp. 151–166. Springer, Heidelberg (1998)
18. Reed, J., Pierce, B.C.: Distance makes the types grow stronger: a calculus for differential privacy. In: Hudak, P., Weirich, S. (eds.) ICFP, pp. 157–168. ACM, New York (2010)
19. Terauchi, T., Aiken, A.: Secure information flow as a safety problem. In: Hankin, C., Siveroni, I. (eds.) SAS 2005. LNCS, vol. 3672, pp. 352–367. Springer, Heidelberg (2005)
20. Yang, H.: Relational separation logic. Theoretical Computer Science 375(1-3), 308–334 (2007)
21. Zaks, A., Pnueli, A.: CoVaC: Compiler validation by program analysis of the cross-product. In: Cuellar, J., Sere, K. (eds.) FM 2008. LNCS, vol. 5014, pp. 35–51. Springer, Heidelberg (2008)
22. Zuck, L.D., Pnueli, A., Goldberg, B.: Voc: A methodology for the translation validation of optimizing compilers. J. UCS 9(3), 223–247 (2003)

Specifying Confidentiality in *Circus*

Michael J. Banks and Jeremy L. Jacob

Department of Computer Science, University of York, UK
{Michael.Banks,Jeremy.Jacob}@cs.york.ac.uk

Abstract. This paper presents an approach for extending the *Circus* formalism to accommodate information flow security concerns. Working with the semantics of *Circus*, we introduce a notation for specifying which aspects of *Circus* processes are confidential and should not be revealed to low-level users. We also describe a novel procedure for verifying that a process satisfies its confidentiality properties.

Keywords: *Circus*, information flow security, confidentiality properties, unifying theories of programming, verifying security.

1 Introduction

How can software engineers obtain robust assurances that a system does not leak secret data to its users (and other entities) who lack an appropriate security clearance? We say that information flows from a system to a user if that user can analyse its interactions with the system to deduce details about the system's behaviour. The study of techniques for measuring and regulating information flow is a central topic in theoretical studies of computer security [1,2].

When building a system that handles secret data — such as cryptographic keys or classified documents — it is vital to ensure the system's design does not induce undesirable information flows about that data to low-level (untrusted or unprivileged) users. A *confidentiality property* prescribes an upper bound on information flow from a system to a low-level user, to prevent that user from deducing secret information from its interactions with the system. These properties are inherently non-functional, and so they cannot be specified using the facilities provided by conventional formal methods.

The rationale for combining functionality and confidentiality requirements within a formal framework is to simplify the task of building systems that are "secure by construction". Without systematic support for modelling confidentiality properties alongside functional specifications, we can argue that a system satisfies a given confidentiality property only by resorting to *ad hoc* reasoning. In this paper, we outline how the *Circus* formalism [3,4,5] can be extended with facilities for specifying the confidentiality properties that a system should satisfy, in addition to a specification of the system's desired behaviour.

The contributions of this paper are as follows. First, in Section 3, we present a syntax for specifying confidentiality properties over *Circus* processes and define its semantics in Section 4. Second, in Section 5, we describe a method for

M. Butler and W. Schulte (Eds.): FM 2011, LNCS 6664, pp. 215–230, 2011.

verifying that a *Circus* process satisfies the confidentiality properties encoded in its specification. Third, in Section 6, we identify how *Circus* processes can be refined while preserving confidentiality properties. In Section 7, we compare our approach with existing frameworks for integrating confidentiality properties into formal software development. We summarise our work in Section 8.

2   *Circus*

Circus is a formal specification language which integrates the CSP process algebra with the state-based specification facilities of Z to achieve a cohesive framework for modelling state-rich concurrent and reactive systems.

A *Circus* process specifies an internal (private) state, a state invariant and a collection of named *actions*, which can be grouped into Z schema expressions and guarded commands (representing operations on the state), invocations of other actions (by name) and CSP constructs (modelling interaction with the environment). The behaviour of a *Circus* process is defined by a distinguished nameless main action, which follows the declarations of the other actions.

Example 1. The following *Circus* process, *Cell*, represents a memory cell that stores an integer value from the *hin* channel and broadcasts it on the *hout* channel. The cell can be switched between two modes. In public mode, the value currently stored in the cell is also broadcast on the *lout* channel; whereas in private mode, an arbitrary value is broadcast on *lout*.

$$MODE == \{PUB, PRV\}$$
channel on, off
channel $hin, hout : \mathbb{N}$
channel $lout : MODE \times \mathbb{N}$
process $Cell \triangleq$ **begin**
$\quad$ **state** $Mem \triangleq [\, val : \mathbb{N}, m : MODE \,]$
$\quad Init \triangleq [\, Mem' \mid val' = 0 \wedge m' = PUB \,]$
$\quad Read \triangleq \left(\begin{array}{l} m = PUB \ \& \ lout!(PUB, val) \rightarrow Skip \\ \Box \ m = PRV \ \& \ \bigsqcap_{n \in \mathbb{N}} lout!(PRV, n) \rightarrow Skip \\ \Box \ hout!val \rightarrow Skip \end{array} \right)$
$\quad Write \triangleq hin?n \rightarrow val := n?$
$\quad Switch \triangleq (on \rightarrow m := PRV) \Box (off \rightarrow m := PUB)$
$\quad \bullet\ Init\, ;\, \mu X \bullet (Read \ \Box \ Write \ \Box \ Switch)\, ;\, X$
end

The denotational semantics of *Circus* is defined using Hoare and He's *Unifying Theories of Programming* (UTP) [6]. We describe this semantics here briefly, but we encourage the reader to consult the definitive account by Oliveira et al. [5].

Each *Circus* action A is defined as a *reactive design* of the form $\mathbf{R}(Pre \vdash Post)$, where *Pre* is a condition over the state variables that must hold for A to commence proper execution; and *Post* describes a relation between initial states of A (satisfying *Pre*) and all later states that A may reach at a stable intermediate or final point in its execution.

In addition to the state variables of A, *Circus* features eight distinguished observational variables to model the behaviour of A as visible to the environment: ok records that A has been properly started; ok' records that A has reached a stable (observable) intermediate or final state; $wait$ records that A is waiting to commence its execution; $wait'$ indicates that A is awaiting interaction with the environment, while $\neg\, wait'$ indicates that A has terminated; tr records the process trace up to the point when A is started; tr' records the trace up to the intermediate or final state reached by A; ref' gives the set of events refused by A at the state it has reached; and ref is included for consistency.

3 Specifying Confidentiality Properties

In this section, we outline a lightweight notation for specifying confidentiality properties over *Circus* processes; we formalise its semantics in the next section.

Consider a *Circus* process P which interacts with a low-level user Low. We assume that Low may possess two sources of information about the behaviour of P: namely, (i) its own interactions with P (constituting partial observations of P's behaviour); and (ii) its *a priori* knowledge of P's design.

We model Low's interface to P in terms of the observational variables of P. We expect that Low can perceive whether the process is running normally (the ok and ok' variables) and whether the process is waiting for interaction with the environment (the $wait$ and $wait'$ variables). However, Low cannot observe P's state variables, because they are hidden from the environment [4].

We define Low's *window*, $\mathcal{L}$, to be the set of events communicated by P to the environment that are visible to Low through its interface. We model each event in $\mathcal{L}$ as a pair (c, i), where c is the channel name and i is the value transmitted on the channel [5]. The portion of the process trace $tr' - tr$ that is visible to Low is given by $(tr' - tr) \restriction \mathcal{L}$. Moreover, the set of events refused by P that Low may perceive is given by $ref' \cap \mathcal{L}$.

We say that two behaviours of a process P are *Low-indistinguishable* if their valuations of ok, ok' and $wait, wait'$ are equal, the projections of their respective traces through $\mathcal{L}$ are identical and, if these behaviours are non-terminating, the projections of their refusal sets through $\mathcal{L}$ are identical.

Definition 1 (Indistinguishability). *The UTP predicate $I(\mathcal{L})$ captures the indistinguishability of two behaviours $\varPhi$ and $\widetilde{\varPhi}$ of P — where $\widetilde{\varPhi}$ is expressed over a renaming of P's observational variables — as viewed through window $\mathcal{L}$:*

$$I(\mathcal{L}) \triangleq \left(\begin{array}{cc} ok = \widetilde{ok} \wedge ok' = \widetilde{ok'} & \wedge\ (tr' - tr) \restriction \mathcal{L} = (\widetilde{tr'} - \widetilde{tr}) \restriction \mathcal{L} \\ \wedge\ wait = \widetilde{wait} \wedge wait' = \widetilde{wait'} \wedge (wait' \Rightarrow ref' \cap \mathcal{L} = \widetilde{ref'} \cap \mathcal{L}) \end{array} \right) \quad (1)$$

The notion of Low-indistinguishable behaviours is central to our formulation of confidentiality. A confidentiality property stipulates that, for each behaviour $\varPhi$

of P involving a confidential activity ψ, it must be possible for P to exhibit alternative "cover story" behaviours that are Low-indistinguishable to Φ but do not involve ψ. The purpose of these non-confidential cover stories is to conceal occurrences of ψ from Low. If P may exhibit these cover story behaviours, then Low cannot deduce from its interaction with P that ψ has occurred, because Low is unable to rule out the possibility that any of the cover story behaviours associated with Φ may have occurred instead.

We introduce a confidentiality annotation, or κ-*annotation* for short, as our template for specifying confidentiality properties over *Circus* processes.

Definition 2 (κ-annotation). *A κ-annotation is a tuple $\langle C, O, \mathcal{L}, D \rangle$, where $\mathcal{L}$ denotes the window of Low, C and D are Circus actions and O is a set of Z schemata known[1] as obligations.*

The C action represents activities of the process over which a confidentiality property applies. Each obligation $\theta \in O$ is used in combination with C to specify — in terms of the initial and final states of C — which C activities of a process are classed as confidential and which C activities serve as cover stories for those confidential activities. θ is composed of two parts:

- The declaration part of θ specifies a *frame* of initial and final state variables of C (and their types), together with any input or output variables associated with events performed by C. These variables are partitioned into two classes: the confidential variables are denoted by v and v'; while the cover story variables are denoted using a renaming $(\widetilde{v}, \widetilde{v}')$ of v and v'.
- The predicate part of θ describes a relation between activities of C: for each confidential C activity expressed in terms of v and v', a range of cover story C activities are expressed using the $\widetilde{v}$ and $\widetilde{v}'$ variables.

An obligation expresses a closure condition over the behaviours of P. For each behaviour Φ of P featuring a C activity ψ that θ marks as confidential, θ demands that P exhibits *at least one* alternative Low-indistinguishable behaviour $\widetilde{\Phi}$ featuring a C activity $\widetilde{\psi}$ that is marked as a cover story for ψ by θ. Since θ may offer multiple cover stories, the designer of P has the flexibility to choose which of those cover story activities are exhibited by P.

Given two obligations θ_1 and θ_2 with the same frame, we say θ_2 is *at least as strong* as θ_1 if and only if (i) every activity ψ marked as confidential by θ_1 is also marked as confidential in θ_2; and (ii) every cover story activity for ψ required by θ_2 is also required by θ_1. Formally:

$$\theta_1 \leq \theta_2 \triangleq [\, \mathsf{conf}(\theta_1) \Rightarrow \mathsf{conf}(\theta_2) \,] \wedge [\, (\mathsf{conf}(\theta_1) \wedge \theta_2) \Rightarrow \theta_1 \,] \qquad (2)$$

where $\mathsf{conf}(\theta)$ is defined to be $(\exists \, \widetilde{v}, \widetilde{v}' \bullet \theta)$ and $[\, X \,]$ denotes the universal closure of X over all variables [6].

The D parameter of a κ-annotation is a *Circus* action specifying activities of P that serve to declassify any confidential C activities that took place previously

---

[1] The term "obligation" is borrowed from Seehusen and Stølen [7].

in P's execution. Hence, a κ-annotation becomes active when a C activity is performed and then persists until it expires when a D activity is completed. To specify that declassification does not takes place, we can write $D = Stop$, since the *Stop* action (representing deadlock) never completes [5].

Example 2. Suppose we insist that whenever the *Cell* process (from Example 1) is operating in private mode, no information about the value written to the cell may be revealed to Low, until the cell reverts to public mode. We can specify a κ-annotation $\kappa_{pr} = \langle C_{pr}, O_{pr}, \mathcal{L}, D_{pr} \rangle$ to capture this requirement, where:

$$C_{pr} = hin?n \rightarrow Skip \qquad O_{pr} = \bigcup_{x \in \mathbb{N}} \left\{ [\, m, \widetilde{m} : \{PRV\}, \widetilde{n?} : \mathbb{N} \mid \widetilde{n?} = x \,] \right\}$$
$$D_{pr} = off \rightarrow Skip \qquad \mathcal{L} = (\{on, off\} \times \{Sync\}) \cup (\{lout\} \times (Mode \times \mathbb{N}))$$

By selecting the parameters of a κ-annotation carefully, we can encode a wide range of security requirements over the state and behaviour of *Circus* processes.

We can compare the strength of κ-annotations by lifting the $\leq$ ordering over their sets of obligations. Given two κ-annotations $\kappa_1 = \langle C, O_1, \mathcal{L}, D \rangle$ and $\kappa_2 = \langle C, O_2, \mathcal{L}, D \rangle$ over the same window, we write $\kappa_1 \preceq \kappa_2$ if and only if each obligation $\theta_1 \in O_1$ can be matched by an obligation $\theta_2 \in O_2$ such that $\theta_1 \leq \theta_2$.

Definition 3 (κ-ordering). *κ_2 is at least as strong as κ_1 if and only if:*

$$\kappa_1 \preceq \kappa_2 \triangleq \forall \theta_1 \in O_1 \bullet \exists \theta_2 \in O_2 \bullet \theta_1 \leq \theta_2 \tag{3}$$

4   The Semantics of κ-Annotations

In previous work, we have described a generic framework for expressing confidentiality properties over models of systems in the UTP [8]. We now adapt this framework to define the semantics of κ-annotations over *Circus* processes.

The observational variables of a *Circus* process model the process's behaviour in terms of all interactions that it may make with its environment. However, these variables do not record the multiple intermediate states that the process may pass through during its execution. We need to extend the semantics of *Circus* actions to capture these details.

A *snapshot* of an action A records the values of the observational variables of a process (abbreviated to x) immediately prior to an invocation of A at some point in the process's execution, together with the values of the observational variables of the process (abbreviated to x') at the intermediate or final state reached by A. We record each snapshot $i \geq 1$ by extending the alphabet of A with new lists of (fresh) observational variables x_i and x'_i that are isomorphic to x and x' respectively. We define a UTP healthiness condition $\mathbf{S}_i$ to extend *Circus* actions with the semantics of snapshots:

$$\mathbf{S}_i(A) \triangleq \left(\begin{array}{c} A \wedge (s_i \Rightarrow s'_i) \wedge (x'_i = x_i \lhd s'_i = s_i \rhd x'_i = x' \wedge x_i = x) \\ \wedge (s'_i \wedge i > 1 \Rightarrow s'_{i-1}) \wedge (s'_i \wedge wait \Rightarrow s_i) \end{array} \right) \tag{4}$$

The Boolean variables s_i and s'_i are used to record whether snapshot i is triggered by the action. Each $\mathbf{S}_i$-healthy action triggers snapshot i only if s_i is unset and s'_i is set. Otherwise, the x_i and x'_i variables are kept constant by the action.

The order in which snapshots are triggered is monotonically increasing: for each $i > 1$, a $\mathbf{S}_i$-healthy action does not trigger snapshot i before snapshot $i-1$ is triggered. Finally, the $(s'_i \wedge \textit{wait} \Rightarrow s_i)$ condition ensures that an action does not trigger a snapshot if the action is waiting to commence execution.

At the level of *Circus* processes, we write P_k to denote the process P, where each action of P is made $\mathbf{S}_i$-healthy for each $i \in 1..k$. We restrict P_k to exactly k snapshots by specifying $\neg s_i \wedge s'_i$ for each $i \in 1..k$ and hiding those variables from the environment:

$$P_k^+ \triangleq \exists s_1, s'_1, \ldots, s_k, s'_k \bullet P_k \wedge ok \wedge (\forall i \in 1..k \bullet \neg s_i \wedge s'_i) \qquad (5)$$

In addition, the ok variable ensures that P_k^+ is properly started.

Given a κ-annotation $\langle C, O, \mathcal{L}, D \rangle$, let θ denote an obligation in O and ψ denote an activity of C marked as confidential by $\mathsf{conf}(\theta)$. Suppose that Low makes an interaction ϕ with P that is consistent with a behaviour Φ of P featuring an instance of ψ. The predicate encoding all such behaviours of P is:

$$\mathsf{Sec}(P, C, \theta) \triangleq P_2^+ \wedge (C \wedge \neg C_f^f \wedge \neg \textit{wait}' \wedge \mathsf{conf}(\theta))[x_1, x'_2/x, x'] \qquad (6)$$

where $C \wedge \neg C_f^f \wedge \neg \textit{wait}' \wedge \mathsf{conf}(\theta)$ denotes all non-diverging[2] and terminating activities of C that involve an activity described by $\mathsf{conf}(\theta)$. The x_1 and x'_2 variables of P_2^+ record the state of P before and after such activities.

We say that Φ *fulfils* θ if ψ also corresponds to at least one alternative Low-indistinguishable behaviour $\widetilde{\Phi}$ of P featuring a cover story $\widetilde{\psi}$ given by θ that is related to ψ by θ. In other words, Φ fulfils θ if Low cannot establish that ψ *must* have occurred from its observation of Φ, because Low cannot distinguish Φ from $\widetilde{\Phi}$ and so cannot rule out that $\widetilde{\psi}$ may have occurred instead. For this to be the case, each confidential behaviour of P encoded by Sec must also satisfy the predicate $\exists \widetilde{x}, \widetilde{x}' \bullet \mathsf{Cov}(P, \mathcal{L}, C, \theta)$:

$$\mathsf{Cov}(P, \mathcal{L}, C, \theta) \triangleq \left(\begin{array}{l} \exists \widetilde{x_1}, \widetilde{x'_1}, \widetilde{x_2}, \widetilde{x'_2} \bullet \widetilde{P_2^+} \wedge I(\mathcal{L}) \wedge J(\mathcal{L}) \\ \wedge \, (\widetilde{C} \wedge \neg \widetilde{C_f^f} \wedge \neg \widetilde{\textit{wait}'} \wedge \theta)[x_1, x'_2, \widetilde{x_1}, \widetilde{x'_2}/x, x', \widetilde{x}, \widetilde{x}'] \end{array} \right) \qquad (7)$$

where $\widetilde{A} = A[\widetilde{x}, \widetilde{x}', \widetilde{x_1}, \widetilde{x_2}/x, x', x_1, x_2]$ and $J(\mathcal{L})$ is a predicate over the tr_1, tr'_2 and $\widetilde{tr_1}, \widetilde{tr'_2}$ snapshot trace variables that is satisfied only if the confidential and cover story activities of C take place at the same point of P's execution, as observed through the $\mathcal{L}$ window. $J(\mathcal{L})$ is defined as:

$$J(\mathcal{L}) \triangleq (tr_1 - tr) \restriction \mathcal{L} = (\widetilde{tr_1} - \widetilde{tr}) \restriction \mathcal{L} \wedge (tr_2 - tr_1) \restriction \mathcal{L} = (\widetilde{tr_2} - \widetilde{tr_1}) \restriction \mathcal{L} \qquad (8)$$

---

[2] A_c^b denotes $A[b, c/ok', \textit{wait}]$ [5]. For each *Circus* action A we have $A = \mathbf{R}(\neg A_f^f \vdash A_f^t)$ [5,6], so $A \wedge \neg A_f^f$ denotes all behaviours of A where A's precondition is met.

Alternatively, Φ fulfils θ if Φ also features a declassification activity encoded by D that takes place in Φ after ψ is performed:

$$\mathsf{Dec}(P, D) \triangleq \forall x_3, x_4' \bullet (D \wedge \neg D_f^f \wedge \neg \mathit{wait}')[x_3, x_4'/x, x'] \Rightarrow \exists x_3', x_4' \bullet P_4^+ \quad (9)$$

A process P *satisfies* a κ-annotation $\kappa = \langle C, O, \mathcal{L}, D \rangle$ if and only if, for each obligation $\theta \in O$, each behaviour of P conforming to $\mathsf{Sec}(P, C, \theta)$ fulfils θ.

Definition 4 (Satisfaction). *P satisfies* κ *if and only if* $P \models \kappa$ *holds:*

$$P \models \langle C, O, \mathcal{L}, D \rangle \triangleq \forall \theta \in O \bullet \left[\begin{array}{c} \mathsf{Sec}(P, C, \theta) \wedge \neg\, \mathsf{Dec}(P, D) \\ \Rightarrow \exists \widetilde{x}, \widetilde{x}' \bullet \mathsf{Cov}(P, \mathcal{L}, C, \theta) \end{array} \right] \quad (10)$$

Example 3. The *Cell* process satisfies the κ_{pr} property. Informally, each behaviour of *Cell* featuring a *hin* event when $m = PRV$ cannot be distinguished by Low from every other *hin* event, so Low cannot rule out any of the cover stories specified by κ_{pr} until after the declassification event *off* takes place.

Lemma 1 states that the condition for verifying that P satisfies a κ-annotation is monotonic with respect to the κ-ordering; that is, if P satisfies κ, then it also satisfies all κ-annotations weaker than κ.

Lemma 1 (Monotonicity of $\models$). *If* $P \models \kappa_2$ *holds, then* $P \models \kappa_1$ *also holds for all* κ_1 *such that* $\kappa_1 \preceq \kappa_2$.

5   Propagation: Divide and Conquer!

Since the $\models$ condition is defined over the whole space of a process's behaviours, applying it to any non-trivial process could be extremely difficult in practice. In this section, we describe a procedure for verifying κ-annotations against a restricted, but useful, class of *Circus* processes.

This procedure requires a process's main action to consist of an initialisation action followed by a recursive loop over a generalised external choice of labelled guarded compound actions that we call *blocks*. Henceforth, we say that a process following this form is a *block-structured process* (BSP). We can divide a BSP into its component blocks and then identify proof obligations over individual blocks that imply the $\models$ condition.

Definition 5 (Block-structured process). *The main action of a Circus BSP with label set L is structured as follows:*

$$\mathit{Init}\,; \left(\mu X \bullet \Box_{l \in L}(g.l \,\&\, A.l)\,; X \right) \quad (11)$$

where the Init action initialises the process state and, for each $l \in L$, $g.l$ is a guard (on the v variables) and $A.l$ is a divergence-free (compound) Circus action. Each block $B.l$ behaves as $(g.l \wedge A.l)$ if $g.l$ holds and as Stop otherwise [5].

If process P is block-structured, we can safely assume (by Definition 5) that each block $B.l$ of P may only be started in states satisfying $g.l$.

Let $\delta \subseteq L \times L$ denote a relation between block labels that maps i to j if and only if P may perform $B.j$ immediately following $B.i$; that is, P may invoke $B.i$ in a state such that $B.i$ terminates in a state that satisfies $B.j$'s guard:

$$\delta \triangleq \left\{ i \mapsto j \; \middle| \; \exists x, x' \bullet \left(Init \, ; \, \mu X \bullet \left(\begin{array}{c} \square_{l \in L} \, B.l \, ; \, X \\ \square \, (B.i \wedge \neg wait') \end{array} \right) \right) \wedge g.j[v'/v] \right\} \quad (12)$$

In addition, let $\mathsf{AllDec}(B.l, D)$ denote a predicate that holds only if every terminating behaviour of $B.l$ started from a state satisfying $g.l$ involves a declassification activity specified by D:

$$\mathsf{AllDec}(B, D) \triangleq \left(\begin{array}{l} \forall x, x' \bullet B \wedge \neg B_f^f \wedge \neg wait' \\ \quad \Rightarrow \exists x_1, x_1', x_2, x_2' \bullet B_2^+ \wedge (D \wedge \neg D_f^f)[x_1, x_2'/x, x'] \end{array} \right) \quad (13)$$

5.1 Block-Level Verification

Given a BSP P and a κ-annotation κ, we analyse each block of P individually to verify that no sequence of blocks that P may perform can leak confidential information to Low. In effect, this analysis assumes that Low is able to observe the block sequence performed by P. This assumption is pessimistic but it is sound — as it over-approximates Low's observational abilities — and it enables us to reason about information flow to Low on a block-by-block basis.

Throughout this section, we assume that C and D actions specified by κ are *enclosed* by the blocks of P.

Definition 6 (Enclosure). *An action A is enclosed by a BSP P if and only if, whenever P can perform an activity described by $A \wedge \neg A_f^f \wedge \neg wait'$, that activity is performed within a single block of P.*

For each block $B.l$ of P, we need to identify all behaviours of $B.l$ featuring confidential activities that are *not* subsequently declassified (as specified by D) within $B.l$. These behaviours are given by the predicate $\mathsf{R}(\kappa, \theta, B.l)$:

$$\mathsf{R}(\kappa, \theta, B) \triangleq \exists x_1, x_1', x_2, x_2' \bullet \mathsf{Sec}(B, C, \theta) \wedge \neg \, \mathsf{Dec}(B, D) \quad (14)$$

For each of these behaviours of $B.l$ featuring a confidential activity ψ, the predicate $\mathsf{Q}(\kappa, \theta, B.l)$ relates that behaviour to all Low-indistinguishable behaviours of $B.l$ featuring cover story activities related to ψ by θ:

$$\mathsf{Q}(\kappa, \theta, B) \triangleq \forall x_1, x_1', x_2, x_2' \bullet \left(\begin{array}{c} \mathsf{Sec}(B, C, \theta) \wedge \neg \, \mathsf{Dec}(B, D) \\ \Rightarrow \mathsf{Cov}(B, \mathcal{L}, C, \theta) \end{array} \right) \quad (15)$$

Observe that, if no C activity conforming to $\mathsf{conf}(\theta)$ can take place within $B.l$, then $\mathsf{R}(\kappa, \theta, B.l)$ will yield false.

It follows from the semantics of $\models$ that, in order for each behaviour Φ of $B.l$ given by $\mathsf{R}(\kappa, \theta, B.l)$ to fulfil θ within the context of $B.l$, there must exist at least one behaviour $\widetilde{\Phi}$ of $\widetilde{B.l}$ that $\mathsf{Q}(\kappa, \theta, B.l)$ associates with Φ. We define a proof obligation po to capture this requirement:

$$\mathsf{po}(B, (R, Q)) \triangleq \left[B \wedge R \Rightarrow \exists \widetilde{x}, \widetilde{x}' \bullet \widetilde{B} \wedge Q \right] \tag{16}$$

$\mathsf{po}(B.l, (\mathsf{R}(\kappa, \theta, B.l), \mathsf{Q}(\kappa, \theta, B.l)))$ treats $B.l$ in isolation from the other blocks of P. Hence, discharging this proof obligation does not guarantee that all behaviours of P fulfil θ, because Low may analyse its full interaction with P to obtain knowledge about the state of P before and after an invocation of $B.l$.

To ascertain that each P behaviour as a whole fulfils θ, we also need to verify that all sequences of blocks that P can perform do not reveal confidential information to Low about the behaviour of $B.l$. Hence, we introduce a procedure for *propagating* the R and Q predicates across the blocks of P, to enable us to verify in a piece-wise fashion that no possible execution of P can violate θ.

5.2 Forwards Propagation

Given a block $B.i$ where $R.i = \mathsf{R}(\kappa, \theta, B.i)$ and $Q.i = \mathsf{Q}(\kappa, \theta, B.i)$, we can calculate a pair of predicates $(R', Q') = \mathsf{fw}(B.i, (R.i, Q.i))$ encoding all final states of $B.i$ that can be reached by all terminating behaviours of $B.i$ classed as confidential by $R.i$, together with the final states of all Low-indistinguishable (and terminating) behaviours of $B.i$ classed as cover stories by $Q.i$:

$$\mathsf{fw}(B, (R, Q)) \triangleq \left(\begin{array}{l} (\exists x \bullet B \wedge R \wedge \neg wait')[x/x'], \\ (\exists x, \widetilde{x} \bullet B \wedge \widetilde{B} \wedge Q \wedge I^*(\mathcal{L}) \wedge \neg wait')[x, \widetilde{x}/x', \widetilde{x}'] \end{array} \right) \tag{17}$$

The $I^*(\mathcal{L})$ predicate denotes $I(\mathcal{L})$ extended with Low's ability to perceive deadlock of P when $B.i$ terminates, which arises only if $B.i$ reaches a final state in which none of the guards of the blocks of P are enabled. Hence, if a behaviour of $B.i$ involving a confidential activity terminates in a deadlocking state, then the associated cover story behaviours of $B.i$ should also terminate in a deadlocking state, to preserve Low-indistinguishability:

$$I^*(\mathcal{L}) \triangleq I(\mathcal{L}) \wedge (\neg wait' \wedge \forall l \in L \bullet \neg g.l[v'/v] \Rightarrow \neg \forall l \in L \bullet \neg \widetilde{g.l}[\widetilde{v}'/\widetilde{v}]) \tag{18}$$

We have $I^*(\mathcal{L}) = I(\mathcal{L})$ if every final state that a block of P may reach enables one or more guards of P.

For each block $B.j$ where $i \mapsto j \in \delta$, we need to verify that Low's interactions with $B.j$ do not provide Low with information about the behaviour of $B.i$ that allows Low to retrospectively rule out all cover stories given by $Q.i$. This is guaranteed by $\mathsf{po}(B.j, \mathsf{fw}(B.i, (R.i, Q.i)))$, which implies that if $B.j$ is started from any final state of $B.i$ marked as confidential, then each interaction with $B.j$ that Low may make could have instead been generated by $B.j$ started from any final state of $B.i$ marked as a cover story.

Moreover, we need to prove that each sequence of blocks that P can perform following $B.i$ does not leak confidential information to Low. This can be done by verifying the last block in the sequence against the (R, Q) pair obtained by recursively propagating $(R.i, Q.i)$ forwards through each block in the sequence.

We can incorporate declassification into forwards propagation by altering the δ relation. For each block $B.t$ where $\mathsf{AllDec}(B.t, D)$ holds, we need not propagate a confidentiality requirement further than $B.t$, because it is relaxed when $B.t$ terminates. Thus, we can remove from δ all transitions leading from $B.t$:

$$\delta_D \triangleq \delta \setminus \{t \mapsto j \mid t, j \in L \wedge \mathsf{AllDec}(B.t, D)\} \tag{19}$$

We now formulate a verification condition for the forwards propagations of κ over all blocks of a process. For each block $B.l$, the set of all forwards propagations of the obligations contained within κ of all blocks of P that may lead to an invocation of $B.l$ is given by $\overrightarrow{\rho}(\kappa, l)$:

$$\overrightarrow{\rho}(\kappa, l) \triangleq \{\rho \mid i \in L \wedge \theta \in O \wedge (l, \rho) \in \mathsf{fwds}(\{(i, \mathsf{RQ}(\kappa, \theta, B.i))\})\} \tag{20}$$

$$\mathsf{fwds}(K) \triangleq K \cup \mathsf{fwds}(\{(j, \mathsf{fw}\,(B.i, \rho)) \mid i \mapsto j \in \delta_D \wedge (i, \rho) \in K\}) \tag{21}$$

where ρ denotes (R, Q) and $\mathsf{RQ}(\kappa, \theta, B)$ is shorthand for $(\mathsf{R}(\kappa, \theta, B), \mathsf{Q}(\kappa, \theta, B))$. We calculate $\mathsf{fwds}(K)$ by iterating until a fixed point is reached.

The set $\overrightarrow{\rho}(\kappa, l)$ contains all forwards propagations of κ through all sequences of blocks from $B.i$ up to $B.l$. This set represents a sound approximation of κ through the blocks of the process up to $B.l$. Hence, it is sufficient to discharge $\mathsf{po}(B.l, \rho)$ for each $\rho \in \overrightarrow{\rho}(\kappa, l)$ in order to verify that $B.l$ does not reveal information about the state of P to Low that could violate any instance of κ applicable to the blocks that may take place prior to $B.l$.

5.3   Backwards Propagation

Forwards propagation is capable of verifying that confidential information about the behaviour of each block $B.i$ is not disclosed by any sequence of blocks that may follow $B.i$. However, this procedure leaves open the possibility that a process may have performed a sequence of blocks leading up to a state in which $B.i$ may perform a confidential activity but cannot instead perform the requisite cover story activities required by κ. Again, it may be possible for Low to infer confidential information about the behaviour of $B.i$ by analysing its interaction with the process to identify information about the initial state of $B.i$.

To ensure that Low cannot rule out cover stories for $B.i$ based on its knowledge about the behaviour of the previous blocks executed by a process, it suffices to propagate each $\mathsf{RQ}(\kappa, \theta, B.i)$ pair backwards to all blocks that may precede $B.i$. The confidentiality requirement on the process state immediately prior to an invocation of $B.i$ is given by $\mathsf{bw}\,(B.i, \mathsf{RQ}(\kappa, \theta, B.i))$:

$$\mathsf{bw}\,(B, (R, Q)) \triangleq \begin{pmatrix} (\exists\, x' \bullet B \wedge R \wedge \neg\, wait)[x'/x], \\ (\exists\, x', \widetilde{x} \bullet B \wedge \widetilde{B} \wedge Q \wedge I(\mathcal{L})) \wedge \neg\, wait)[x', \widetilde{x}'/x, \widetilde{x}] \end{pmatrix} \tag{22}$$

$$\overleftarrow{\rho}(\kappa, l) \triangleq \{\rho \mid j \in L \wedge \theta \in O \wedge (l, \rho) \in \mathsf{bwds}(\{(j, \mathsf{RQ}(\kappa, \theta, B.j))\})\} \tag{23}$$

$$\mathsf{bwds}(K) \triangleq K \cup \mathsf{bwds}(\{(i, \mathsf{bw}\,(B.j, \rho)) \mid i \mapsto j \in \delta \wedge (j, \rho) \in K\}) \tag{24}$$

$\overleftarrow{\rho}(\kappa, l)$ gives the set of all backwards propagations of κ from the blocks of the process to $B.l$. Again, discharging $\mathsf{po}(B.l, \rho)$ for each $\rho \in \overleftarrow{\rho}(\kappa, l)$ suffices to establish that $B.l$ does not reveal information about the state of P to Low that may violate the κ-annotations of the blocks following $B.l$.

It is also necessary to verify that all initial states of P satisfy the backwards-propagated κ-annotations of the blocks that may be performed immediately after *Init*. This is assured by discharging $\mathsf{po}(Init, \overleftarrow{\rho}(\kappa, Init))$, where:

$$\overleftarrow{\rho}(\kappa, Init) \triangleq \bigcup_{l \in L} \{\mathsf{bw}(B.l, \rho) \mid \rho \in \overleftarrow{\rho}(\kappa, l) \wedge (\exists x, x' \bullet Init \wedge g.l[v'/v])\} \quad (25)$$

5.4   Verifying Confidentiality

Forwards and backwards propagation can be applied together to a BSP P to verify each block of P against κ. We now sketch a proof that this procedure — with one important caveat — is sufficient to demonstrate that P satisfies κ.

First, we relate the po proof obligation to the $\models$ condition. Given a κ-annotation $\langle C, O, \mathcal{L}, D \rangle$ and an individual block B, if we can demonstrate that each behaviour of B conforming to $\mathsf{Sec}(B, C, \theta)$ fulfils θ for each $\theta \in O$, then we can conclude that B satisfies κ in isolation. This is formalised in Lemma 2.

Lemma 2 (po entails $\models$). *For any block B and κ-annotation $\kappa = \langle C, O, \mathcal{L}, D \rangle$:*

$$\forall \theta \in O \bullet \mathsf{po}(B, \mathsf{RQ}(\kappa, \theta, B)) \quad implies \quad B \models \kappa \quad (26)$$

We now extend the scope of Lemma 2 to enclose multiple blocks. Consider any two blocks $B.i$ and $B.j$ of P where $i \mapsto j \in \delta$ and $B.i$ or $B.j$ may exhibit an activity marked as confidential by κ. To justify that $(B.i \, ; B.j) \models \kappa$ holds, we need to discharge four proof obligations over $B.i$ and $B.j$ for each $\theta \in O$:

$$\mathsf{po}(B.i, \mathsf{RQ}(\kappa, \theta, B.i)) \qquad \mathsf{po}(B.j, \mathsf{RQ}(\kappa, \theta, B.j))$$
$$\mathsf{po}(B.j, \mathsf{fw}\,(B.i, \mathsf{RQ}(\kappa, \theta, B.i))) \qquad \mathsf{po}(B.i, \mathsf{bw}\,(B.j, \mathsf{RQ}(\kappa, \theta, B.j)))$$

Together, these four proof obligations imply that each behaviour of $(B.i \, ; B.j)$ marked as confidential by C and θ is concealed by at least one alternative Low-indistinguishable behaviour of $(B.i \, ; B.j)$ marked as a cover story.

In order to generalise this result to arbitrary sequences of blocks, we need to restrict our attention to κ-annotations where each obligation features *exactly one* cover story activity for each confidential activity. (This restriction ensures the same cover story is propagated forwards and backwards through the process.)

Definition 7 ($\widehat{\kappa}$-annotation). *A $\widehat{\kappa}$-annotation $\langle C, O, \mathcal{L}, D \rangle$ is a κ-annotation where the condition $\forall\, v, v' \bullet \mathsf{conf}(\theta) \Rightarrow \exists_1 \widetilde{v}, \widetilde{v}' \bullet \theta$ holds for each $\theta \in O$.*

Naturally, a $\widehat{\kappa}$-annotation can always be obtained from a κ-annotation κ by strengthening each obligation of κ.

We say that P is $\widehat{\kappa}$-*safe* if we can prove the blocks of P uphold the respective forwards and backwards propagations of $\widehat{\kappa}$ through P.

Definition 8 ($\widehat{\kappa}$-safety). *A BSP P is safe w.r.t. $\widehat{\kappa} = \langle C, O, \mathcal{L}, D \rangle$ if and only if P encloses C and D; po($Init$, $\overleftarrow{\rho}(\widehat{\kappa}, Init)$) holds and, for each $l \in L$, we have:*

$$\mathsf{po}(B.l, \mathsf{RQ}(\widehat{\kappa}, \theta, B.l)) \quad and \quad \forall \rho \in \overrightarrow{\rho}(\widehat{\kappa}, l) \cup \overleftarrow{\rho}(\widehat{\kappa}, l) \bullet \mathsf{po}(B.l, \rho) \quad (27)$$

If process P is $\widehat{\kappa}$-safe, then no sequence of blocks that P may perform may leak confidential information to Low. It follows that, if P is $\widehat{\kappa}$-safe, then P must satisfy κ. This result is encapsulated by Theorem 1.

Theorem 1. *If a BSP P is $\widehat{\kappa}$-safe, then $P \models \widehat{\kappa}$ holds.*

A trivial consequence of Theorem 1 and Lemma 1 that, if P is $\widehat{\kappa}$-safe and $\kappa \preceq \widehat{\kappa}$ holds, then P must satisfy κ as well as $\widehat{\kappa}$.

6 Confidentiality-Preserving Refinement

Behavioural refinement maintains the functionality of *Circus* processes, but may not preserve confidentiality properties [9]. This so-called "refinement paradox" arises because naïvely refining away non-determinism within a process P may remove behaviours from P that are required as cover stories by the κ-annotations of P, without also removing the associated confidential behaviours. Such refinement steps violate the $\models$ condition.

Example 4. Consider the following refinement of the *Read* block of *Cell*:

$$Read \triangleq \left(\begin{array}{l} m = PUB \ \& \ lout!(PUB, val) \rightarrow Skip \\ \Box \ m = PRV \ \& \ lout!(PRV, val \ \mathsf{mod} \ 2) \rightarrow Skip \\ \Box \ hout!val \rightarrow Skip \end{array} \right)$$

This refinement is manifestly insecure with respect to κ_{pr} specified in Example 2, because if Low observes a *lout* event when $m = PRV$, it can deduce one bit of information about the value of val, in violation of half of the obligations of κ_{pr}.

When developing a process by stepwise refinement, it would be wasteful to reach a concrete process design that violates its κ-annotations. This problem can be overcome by strengthening process refinement in *Circus* to uphold κ-annotations.

Definition 9 (Secure process refinement). *For processes P_1 and P_2 we say that P_2 is a secure refinement of P_1 w.r.t. a κ-annotation κ — written $P_1 \sqsubseteq_{\mathcal{P}}^{\kappa} P_2$ — if P_2 is a process refinement of P_1 and P_2 satisfies κ.*

Observe that $P_1 \sqsubseteq_{\mathcal{P}}^{\kappa} P_2$ requires only that P_2 satisfies κ, whereas P_1 itself need not be secure. However, an insecure refinement may result in a process that cannot be refined securely, so we propose that a BSP should be verified to satisfy its κ-annotations by applying propagation at an early stage of its development. Thereafter, each refinement step should maintain those κ-annotations. This can be achieved by retaining the $\overrightarrow{\rho}$ and $\overleftarrow{\rho}$ sets generated by propagation and re-using them at each refinement step to verify that it preserves $\widehat{\kappa}$-safety.

Consider a BSP P that has been proved to be $\widehat{\kappa}$-safe. By Definition 8, we know that each block $B.l$ of P upholds each member of $\overrightarrow{\rho}(\widehat{\kappa}, l)$ and $\overleftarrow{\rho}(\widehat{\kappa}, l)$, as well as $RQ(\kappa, \theta, B.l)$. Suppose we refine P to obtain a BSP P' by replacing $B.l$ in P with $B.l'$, where $B.l \sqsubseteq B.l'$. If we have $g.l = g.l'$, then P' can only feature transitions between blocks that are possible for P (i.e. $\delta_{P'} \subseteq \delta_P$). In Theorem 2, we present conditions on $B.l'$ that are sufficient to establish that P' is $\widehat{\kappa}$-safe.

Theorem 2. *If P is $\widehat{\kappa}$-safe and P' equals P except with $B.l'$ in place of $B.l$ (where $g.l = g.l'$ and $B.l \sqsubseteq B.l'$), then P' is $\widehat{\kappa}$-safe if for every cover story behaviour of $B.l$ specified by $RQ(\widehat{\kappa}, \theta, B.l)$ and each member of $\overrightarrow{\rho}(\widehat{\kappa}, l) \cup \overleftarrow{\rho}(\widehat{\kappa}, l)$ where $B.l'$ features an associated confidential behaviour, the same cover story behaviour is present in $B.l'$. These conditions are formalised as follows:*

$$\forall (R, Q) \in \{RQ(\widehat{\kappa}, \theta, B.l)\} \cup \overrightarrow{\rho}(\widehat{\kappa}, l) \cup \overleftarrow{\rho}(\widehat{\kappa}, l) \bullet \mathsf{saferef}(B.l, B.l', (R, Q))$$

$$where \quad \mathsf{saferef}(B, B', (R, Q)) \triangleq \left[B' \wedge R \wedge \widetilde{B} \wedge Q \Rightarrow \widetilde{B'} \right]$$

7 Related Work

In software engineering, it is conventional to implement security policies by building access control into the system design. However, the notion of information flow security is more generally applicable than access control: while confidentiality properties specify *what* information should not be disclosed to low-level users, access control mechanisms describe *how* that information should be protected. Furthermore, access control does not account for Low inferring secret information indirectly from its interaction with a system [1].

Our κ-annotations share the spirit of Jacob's *security specifications* [9,10], which are functions from low-level observations of a system to the minimal set of system behaviours that a low-level user must be unable to distinguish from those observations. The same idea underlies our earlier work on encoding confidentiality properties in the UTP [8], where we define an abstract formulation of confidentiality properties across the spectrum of UTP theories. By specialising this formulation to the semantics of *Circus*, we have achieved a framework where these properties can be integrated directly into formal software developments.

In many of the existing frameworks for expressing confidentiality properties, such as Mantel's MAKS [11], the occurrence (or non-occurrence) of particular high-level events is taken to be confidential. We abstract from this event-centric style by taking *Circus* actions over the state of processes as the basis of our confidentiality encoding. In addition, our model of Low's observational abilities is based on the failures-divergences semantics of CSP — as encoded in the UTP semantics of *Circus* — and is therefore richer than the trace-based models of Low's observations frequently employed in these frameworks.

The confidentiality properties encoded by our κ-annotations are (in general) weaker than the *noninterference* property, which stipulates that no input from a high-level user can influence any output to a low-level user [12]. We contend that a more fine-grained approach to specify limits on information flow to low-level users is beneficial to software engineers, because it affords greater flexibility in designing systems to meet their functionality and security requirements.

Unlike noninterference, our notion of confidentiality does not stop a trusted (yet treacherous) high-level user from actively leaking secrets to low-level users by influencing their interactions with the system using a pre-arranged signalling protocol. While deliberate disclosure of secret data by malicious high-level users is troublesome in security-critical environments, we contend that no technical measures can prevent such users from leaking data outside the system domain.

Our propagation procedure is related to the *unwinding* technique [12], which aims to simplify the task of verifying a system against a confidentiality property. Unwinding transforms a global confidentiality property (typically expressed in terms of trace sets) over a system into conditions over its individual state transitions, which can then be discharged using traditional proof methods [11].

Our work shares some ideas with Morgan's recent *shadow semantics* [13,14], which extends the refinement calculus for sequential programs to ensure that refinement does not introduce new information flows about secret data to Low. The shadow semantics assumes that Low can observe a program's control flow; likewise, we assume that Low can deduce the sequence of blocks performed by a process. However, the shadow semantics goes a step further, by distinguishing between *atomic* and *composite* non-determinism and allowing Low to monitor how composite non-determinism is resolved in a program's execution. This means that refinement of composite non-determinism is security-preserving. We do not grant Low that ability, because κ-annotations do not cleanly partition the whole process state into secret and non-secret variables. Moreover, applying the shadow semantics for refinement in our framework would require *Circus* to be extended with an alternative semantics for non-determinism.

We have covered many of the topics discussed here in greater depth in earlier work [8]. A fuller survey of the various approaches for formalising and reasoning about information flow security can be found elsewhere [1,2].

8   Conclusions

In this paper, we have presented a framework for specifying confidentiality properties over *Circus* processes and a procedure for verifying that a *Circus* process satisfies those properties. The close integration of our framework with the specification facilities of *Circus* is original and is supported by the UTP foundations of *Circus*. While we have taken *Circus* as the formal foundation of our framework, the underlying principles are general and could be translated to other formalisms besides *Circus* (especially those with a UTP semantics).

Our ongoing research aims to elevate confidentiality properties to the status of "first-class citizens" in *Circus* developments, with suitable techniques and automated tools to support the verification of process designs against confidentiality properties and for checking the correctness of refinement steps. We hypothesise that the work presented in this paper, together with the underlying *Circus* platform, may provide the foundations of a viable engineering approach for developing software in tandem with information flow security concerns. We are currently working on a case study project to evaluate this hypothesis.

We have left several pertinent topics unexplored in this paper, such as the consequences of concurrency and probabilistic behaviour for information flow and confidentiality. We leave the investigation of these topics to future work.

Finally, taking a formal approach to security engineering can increase confidence that a system does not leak secrets to low-level users, but it is unwise to assume that any system implementation is secure in all circumstances. In particular, our framework does not address sources of information leakage that arise at the hardware level, such as its responsiveness or power consumption [15]. The task of extending formal methods to address these factors is likely to be challenging, but would be a significant step towards engineering secure systems.

Acknowledgements. Michael Banks is supported by a UK EPSRC DTA studentship. We are grateful to the anonymous referees for their helpful comments and to Matthew Naylor for proofreading.

References

1. McLean, J.: Security models. In: Marciniak, J. (ed.) Encyclopedia of Software Engineering, vol. 2, pp. 1136–1145. John Wiley & Sons, Inc., Chichester (1994)
2. Ryan, P.: Mathematical models of computer security. In: Focardi, R., Gorrieri, R. (eds.) FOSAD 2000. LNCS, vol. 2171, pp. 1–62. Springer, Heidelberg (2001)
3. Cavalcanti, A., Sampaio, A., Woodcock, J.: A refinement strategy for Circus. Formal Aspects of Computing 15(2-3), 146–181 (2003)
4. Oliveira, M.V.: Formal Derivation of State-Rich Reactive Programs using Circus. PhD thesis, Department of Computer Science, University of York (2005)
5. Oliveira, M., Cavalcanti, A., Woodcock, J.: A UTP semantics for Circus. Formal Aspects of Computing 21(1), 3–32 (2009)
6. Hoare, C.A.R., He, J.: Unifying Theories of Programming. International Series in Computer Science. Prentice Hall Inc., Englewood Cliffs (1998)
7. Seehusen, F., Stølen, K.: Information flow security, abstraction and composition. IET Information Security 3(1), 9–33 (2009)
8. Banks, M.J., Jacob, J.L.: Unifying theories of confidentiality. In: Qin, S. (ed.) UTP 2010. LNCS, vol. 6445, pp. 120–136. Springer, Heidelberg (2010)
9. Jacob, J.L.: On the derivation of secure components. In: Proceedings of the 1989 IEEE Symposium on Security and Privacy, pp. 242–247. IEEE Computer Society, Los Alamitos (1989)
10. Jacob, J.L.: Security specifications. In: Proceedings of the 1988 IEEE Symposium on Security and Privacy, pp. 14–23 (1988)
11. Mantel, H.: A Uniform Framework for the Formal Specification and Verification of Information Flow Security. PhD thesis, Universität Saarbrücken (July 2003)
12. Goguen, J.A., Meseguer, J.: Unwinding and inference control. In: Proceedings of the 1984 IEEE Symposium on Security and Privacy, pp. 75–86. IEEE Computer Society, Los Alamitos (1984)
13. Morgan, C.: The shadow knows: Refinement and security in sequential programs. Science of Computer Programming 74(8), 629–653 (2009)

14. Morgan, C.: Compositional noninterference from first principles. Formal Aspects of Computing (to appear)
15. Clark, J.A., Stepney, S., Chivers, H.: Breaking the model: Finalisation and a taxonomy of security attacks. Electronic Notes in Theoretical Computer Science 137(2), 225–242 (2005)

A   Proofs

Formal proofs of the theorems and lemmas presented in this paper are available from `http://www-users.cs.york.ac.uk/~mbanks/`.

Formally Verifying Isolation and Availability in an Idealized Model of Virtualization*

Gilles Barthe[1], Gustavo Betarte[2], Juan Diego Campo[2], and Carlos Luna[2]

[1] IMDEA Software, Madrid, Spain
[2] InCo, Facultad de Ingeniería, Universidad de la República, Uruguay

Abstract. Hypervisors allow multiple guest operating systems to run on shared hardware, and offer a compelling means of improving the security and the flexibility of software systems. We formalize in the Coq proof assistant an idealized model of a hypervisor, and formally establish that the hypervisor ensures strong isolation properties between the different operating systems, and guarantees that requests from guest operating systems are eventually attended.

1 Introduction

Hypervisors allow several operating systems to coexist on commodity hardware, and provide support for multiple applications to run seamlessly on the guest operating systems they manage. Moreover, hypervisors provide a means to guarantee that applications with different security policies can execute securely in parallel, by ensuring isolation between their guest operating systems. In effect, hypervisors are increasingly used as a means to improve system flexibility and security, and authors such as [10] predict that their use will become ubiquitous in enterprise data centers and cloud computing.

The increasingly important role of hypervisors in software systems makes them a prime target for formal verification. Indeed, several projects have set out to formally verify the correctness of hypervisor implementations. One of the most prominent initiatives is the Microsoft Hyper-V verification project [8,16], which has made a number of impressive achievements towards the functional verification of the legacy implementation of the Hyper-V hypervisor, a large software component that combines C and assembly code (about 100 kLOC of C and 5kLOC of assembly). The overarching objective of the formal verification is to establish that a guest operating system cannot observe any difference between executing through the hypervisor or directly on the hardware. The other prominent initiative is the L4.verified project [14], which recently completed the formal verification of the seL4 microkernel, a general purpose operating system

---

* Partially funded by European Project FP7 256980 NESSoS, Spanish project TIN2009-14599 DESAFIOS 10, Madrid Regional project S2009TIC-1465 PROMETIDOS and project ANII-Clemente Estable PR-FCE-2009-1-2568 Virtual-Cert.

M. Butler and W. Schulte (Eds.): FM 2011, LNCS 6664, pp. 231–245, 2011.

of the L4 family. The main thrust of the formal verification is to show that an implementation of the microkernel correctly refines an abstract specification.

Reasoning about implementations provides the ultimate guarantee that deployed hypervisors provide the expected properties. There are however significant hurdles with this approach, especially if one focuses on proving security properties rather than functional correctness. First, the complexity of formally proving non-trivial properties of implementations might be overwhelming in terms of the effort it requires; worse, the technology for verifying some classes of security properties may be underdeveloped: specifically, liveness properties are notoriously hard to prove, and there is currently no established method for verifying security properties involving two system executions, a.k.a. 2-properties [7], for implementations. Second, many implementation details are orthogonal to the security properties to be established, and may complicate reasoning without improving the understanding of the essential features for guaranteeing isolation among guest operating systems. Thus, there is a need for complementary approaches where verification is performed on idealized models that abstract away from the specifics of any particular hypervisor, and yet provide a realistic setting in which to explore the security issues that pertain to the realm of hypervisors.

This article initiates such an approach by developing a minimalistic model of a hypervisor, and by formally proving that the hypervisor correctly enforces isolation between guest operating systems, and under mild hypotheses guarantees basic availability properties to guest operating systems. In order to achieve some reasonable level of tractability, our model is significantly simpler than the setting considered in the Microsoft Hyper-V verification project, it abstracts away many specifics of memory management such as translation lookaside buffers (TLBs) and shadow page tables (SPTs) and of the underlying hardware and runtime environment such as I/O devices. Instead, our model focuses on the aspects that are most relevant for isolation properties, namely read and write resources on machine addresses, and is sufficiently complete to allow us to reason about isolation properties. Specifically, we show that an operating system can only read and modify memory it owns, and a non-influence property [18] stating that the behavior of an operating system is not influenced by other operating systems. In addition, our model allows reasoning about availability; we prove, under reasonable conditions, that all requests of a guest operating system to the hypervisor are eventually attended, so that no guest operating system waits indefinitely for a pending request. Overall, our verification effort shows that the model is adequate to reason about safety properties (read and write isolation), 2-safety properties (OS isolation), and liveness properties (availability).

Contents of the paper. Section 2 provides a primer on virtualization, focusing on the elements that are most relevant for our formal model, which we develop in Section 3. Isolation properties are considered in Section 4, whereas availability is discussed in Section 5. Section 6 considers related work; further work and conclusions are presented in Section 7. The formal development is available at http://www.fing.edu.uy/inco/grupos/gsi/proyectos/virtualcert.php, and can be verified using the Coq proof assistant (version 8.2) [21].

Notation. We use standard notation for equality and logical connectives. We extensively use record types, enumerated types, and (parametric) sum types. Record types are of the form $\{l_1 : T_1, \ldots, l_n : T_n\}$, whereas their elements are of the form $\langle t_1, \ldots, t_n \rangle$. Field selection is abbreviated using dot notation. Enumerated types and parametric sum types are defined using Haskell-like notation; for example, we define for every type T the type $option\ T \stackrel{\text{def}}{=} None \mid Some\ (t : T)$. We also make an extensive use of partial maps: the type of partial maps from objects of type A into objects of type B is written $A \mapsto B$. Application of a map m on an object of type a is denoted $m[a]$ and map update is written $m[a] := b$, where b overwrites the value, if any, associated to a. Finally, runs are modeled co-inductively, using streams. The type of streams of type A is written $[A]_\infty$. Objects of type $[A]_\infty$ are constructed with the (infix) operator ::, hence $x :: xs$ is of type $[A]_\infty$ whenever x is of type A and xs is of type $[A]_\infty$. Given $s : [A]_\infty$ we let $s[i]$ denote the i-th element of s.

2   A Primer on Virtualization

Virtualization is a technique used to run on the same physical machine multiple operating systems, called *guest operating systems*. The hypervisor, or Virtual Machine Monitor [11], is a thin layer of software that manages the shared resources (e.g. CPU, system memory, I/O devices). It allows guest operating systems to access these resources by providing them an abstraction of the physical machine on which they run. One of the most important features of a virtualization platform is that its OSs run isolated from one another. In order to guarantee isolation and to keep control of the platform, a hypervisor makes use of the different execution modes of a modern CPU: the hypervisor itself and trusted guest OSs run in supervisor mode, in which all CPU instructions are available; while untrusted guest operating systems will run in user mode in which privileged instructions cannot be executed.

Historically there have been two different styles of virtualization: *full virtualization* and *paravirtualization*. In the first one, each virtual machine is an exact duplicate of the underlying hardware, making it possible to run unmodified operating systems on top of it. When an attempt to execute a privileged instruction by the OS is detected the hardware raises a trap that is captured by the hypervisor and then it emulates the instruction behavior. In the paravirtualization approach, each virtual machine is a simplified version of the physical architecture. The guest (untrusted) operating systems must then be modified to run in user CPU mode, changing privileged instructions to hypercalls, i.e. calls to the hypervisor. A hypercall interface allows OSs to perform a synchronous software trap into the hypervisor to perform a privileged operation, analogous to the use of system calls in conventional operating systems. An example use of a hypercall is to request a set of page table updates, in which the hypervisor validates and applies a list of updates, returning control to the calling OS when this is completed.

In this work, we focus on the memory management policy of a paravirtualization style hypervisor, based on the Xen virtualization platform [6]. Several features of the platform are not yet modeled (e.g. I/O devices, interruption system, or the possibility to execute on multi-cores), and are left as future work.

3 The Model

In this section we present and discuss the formal specification of the idealized model. We first introduce the set of states, and the set of actions; the latter include both operations of the hypervisor and of the guest operating systems. The semantics of each action is specified by a precondition and a postcondition. Then, we introduce a notion of valid state and show that state validity is preserved by execution. Finally, we define execution traces.

3.1   Informal Overview of the Memory Model

The most important component of the state is the memory model, which we proceed to describe. As illustrated in Figure 1, the memory model involves three types of addressing modes and two address mappings: the machine address is the real machine memory; the physical memory is used by the guest OS, and the virtual memory is used by the applications running on an operating system.

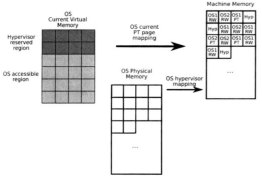

Fig. 1. Memory model of the platform

The *virtual memory* is the one used by applications running on OSs. Each OS stores a partial mapping of virtual addresses to machine addresses. This will allow us to represent the translation of the virtual addresses of the applications executing in the OS into real hardware addresses. Moreover, each OS has a designated portion of its virtual address space (usually abbreviated VAS) that is reserved for the hypervisor to attend hypercalls. We say that a virtual address *va* is accessible by the OS if it belongs to the virtual address space of the OS which is not reserved for the hypervisor. We denote the type of virtual addresses by *vadd*.

The *physical memory* is the one addressed by the kernel of the guest OS. In the Xen [6] platform, this is the type of addresses that the hypervisor exposes to the domains (the untrusted guest OSs in our model). The type of physical addresses is written *padd*.

The *machine memory* is the real machine memory. A mechanism of page classification was introduced in order to cover concepts from certain virtualization platforms, in particular Xen. The model considers that each machine address that appears in a memory mapping corresponds to a memory page. Each page has at most one unique owner, a particular OS or the hypervisor, and is classified either as a data page with read/write access or as a page table, where the mappings between virtual and machine addresses reside. It is required to register (and classify) a page before being able to use or map it. The type of machine addresses is written $madd$.

As to the mappings, each OS has an associated collection of page tables (one for each application executing on the OS) that map virtual addresses into machine addresses. When executed, the applications use virtual addresses, therefore on context switch the current page table of the OS must change so that the currently executing application may be able to refer to its own address space. Neither applications nor untrusted OSs have permission to read or write page tables, because these actions can only be performed in supervisor mode. Every memory address accessed by an OS needs to be associated to a virtual address. The model must guarantee the correctness of those mappings, namely, that every machine address mapped in a page table of an OS is owned by it.

The mapping that associates, for each OS, machine addresses to physical ones is, in our model, maintained by the hypervisor. This mapping might be treated differently by each specific virtualization platform. There are platforms in which this mapping is public and the OS is allowed to manage machine addresses. The physical-to-machine address mapping is modified by the actions `page_pin` and `page_unpin`, as shall be described in Section 3.3.

3.2   Formalizing States

The platform state consists of a collection of components that we now proceed to describe.

Operating systems. We start from a type os_ident of identifiers for guest operating systems, and a predicate $trusted\_os$ indicating whether a guest operating system is trusted. The state contains information about each guest OS current page table, which is a physical address, and information on whether it has a hypercall pending to be resolved. Formally the information is captured by a mapping oss_map that associates OS identifiers with objects of type os, where $os \overset{\text{def}}{=} \{curr\_page : padd, hcall : option\ Hyper\_call\}$, and $oss\_map \overset{\text{def}}{=} os\_ident \mapsto os$.

Execution modes. Most hardware architectures distinguish at least two execution modes, namely $user\ mode$ (usr) and $supervisor\ mode$ (svc). These modes are used as a protection mechanism, where $privileged$ instructions are only allowed to be executed in supervisor mode. In our model, untrusted OSs execute in user mode while trusted ones and the hypervisor execute in supervisor mode. When an untrusted OS needs to execute a privileged operation, it requests the hypervisor to do it on its behalf. Execution modes are formalized by the enumerated type $exec\_mode$, where $exec\_mode \overset{\text{def}}{=} usr \mid svc$.

Moreover, there is a single active OS in each state. After requesting the hypervisor to execute some service, the active guest OS will turn in processor execution mode $waiting$ until the service is completed and the execution control returned, switching then its execution mode to *running*. Active OS execution mode is formalized by the type $os\_activity \stackrel{\text{def}}{=} running \mid waiting$.

Memory mappings. The mapping that, given an OS returns the corresponding mapping from physical to machine addresses, is formalized as an object of the type $hypervisor\_map$, where $hypervisor\_map \stackrel{\text{def}}{=} os\_ident \mapsto (padd \mapsto madd)$. The real platform memory is formalized as a mapping that associates to a machine address a page, thus $system\_memory \stackrel{\text{def}}{=} madd \mapsto page$. A page consists of a page content and a reference to the page owner. Page contents can be either (readable/writable) values, an OS page table or nothing; note that a page might have been created without having been initialized, hence the use of option types. Page owners can be the hypervisor, a guest OS or none. Formally:

$$content \stackrel{\text{def}}{=} RW\ (v : option\ Value) \mid PT\ (va\_to\_ma : vadd \mapsto madd) \mid Other$$

$$page\_owner \stackrel{\text{def}}{=} Hyp \mid Os\ (osi : os\_ident) \mid No\_Owner$$

$$page \stackrel{\text{def}}{=} \{page\_content : content, page\_owned\_by : page\_owner\}$$

States. The states of the platform are modeled by a record with six components:

$$State \stackrel{\text{def}}{=} \{ \begin{array}{ll} active\_os & : os\_ident, \\ aos\_exec\_mode & : exec\_mode, \\ aos\_activity & : os\_activity, \\ oss & : oss\_map, \\ hypervisor & : hypervisor\_map, \\ memory & : system\_memory\} \end{array}$$

The component $active\_os$ indicates which is the active operating system and aos_exec_mode and $aos\_activity$ the corresponding execution and processor mode. The component oss stores the information of the guest operating systems of the platform. $hypervisor$ and $memory$ are the mappings used to formalize the memory model described in the previous section.

In the sequel, we use the following notation. Given states s and s', we define $s \sim_{map,idx} s'$ to be the relation that establishes that s and s' differ at most in the value associated to the index idx of the component map in the state s', and $s \sim_{c_1,\ldots,c_n = v_1,\ldots,v_n} s'$ the relation that establishes that s and s' differ at most in the values $v_1, \ldots, v_n$ of the components $c_1, \ldots, c_n$ in state s'. Moreover, we define the predicate $os\_accessible(va)$, that holds if va belongs to the set of virtual addresses accessible by any OS.

Valid state. We define a notion of valid state that captures essential properties of the platform. Formally, the predicate $valid\_state$ holds on state s if s satisfies the following properties: i) a trusted OS has no pending hypercalls; ii) if the active OS is in running mode then no hypercall requested by it is pending; iii) if the hypervisor or a trusted OS is running the processor must be in supervisor mode; iv) if an untrusted OS is running the processor must be in user mode; v) the hypervisor maps an OS physical address to a machine address owned by that same OS. This mapping is also injective; vi) all page tables of an OS o

map accessible virtual addresses to pages owned by o and not accessible ones to pages owned by the hypervisor; vii) the current page table of any OS is owned by that OS; viii) any machine address ma which is associated to a virtual address in a page table has a corresponding pre-image, which is a physical address, in the hypervisor mapping. All properties have a straightforward interpretation in our model. For example, the first property is captured by the proposition: $\forall \, osi : os\_ident, \; trusted\_os(osi) \rightarrow (s.oss[osi]).hcall \; = \; None$. Valid states are invariant under execution, as shall be shown later.

3.3   Actions

Table 1 summarises a subset of the actions specified in the model, and their effects. Actions can be classified as follows: i) hypervisor calls new, delete, pin, unpin and lswitch; ii) change of the active OS by the hypervisor (switch); iii) access, from an OS or the hypervisor, to memory pages (read and write); iv) update of page tables by the hypervisor on demand of an untrusted OS or

$Pre \; s \; (\textbf{read} \; va) \overset{\text{def}}{=} os\_accessible(va) \; \wedge \; s.aos\_activity \; = \; running \; \wedge$
$\quad \exists \; ma : madd, \; va\_mapped\_to\_ma(s, va, ma) \; \wedge$
$\quad is\_RW((s.memory[ma]).page\_content)$
$Post \; s \; (\textbf{read} \; va) \; s' \overset{\text{def}}{=} s \; = \; s'$

$Pre \; s \; (\textbf{write} \; va \; val) \overset{\text{def}}{=} os\_accessible(va) \; \wedge \; s.aos\_activity \; = \; running \; \wedge$
$\quad \exists \; ma : madd, \; va\_mapped\_to\_ma(s, va, ma) \; \wedge$
$\quad is\_RW((s.memory[ma]).page\_content)$
$Post \; s \; (\textbf{write} \; va \; val) \; s' \overset{\text{def}}{=} \exists \; ma : madd, \; va\_mapped\_to\_ma(s, va, ma) \; \wedge$
$\quad s'.memory \; = \; (s.memory[ma] := \langle RW(Some \; val), s.active\_os \rangle) \; \wedge$
$\quad s \sim_{memory, ma} s'$

$Pre \; s \; (\textbf{chmod}) \overset{\text{def}}{=} s.aos\_activity \; = \; waiting \; \wedge \; (s.oss[s.active\_os]).hcall \; = \; None$
$Post \; s \; (\textbf{chmod}) \; s' \overset{\text{def}}{=}$
$\quad (trusted\_os(s.active\_os) \; \wedge \; s \sim_{aos\_exec\_mode, aos\_activity \; = \; svc, running} s') \; \vee$
$\quad (\neg \; trusted\_os(s.active\_os) \; \wedge \; s \sim_{aos\_exec\_mode, aos\_activity \; = \; usr, running} s')$

$Pre \; s \; (\textbf{page\_pin\_untrusted} \; o \; pa \; t) \overset{\text{def}}{=}$
$\quad \neg \; trusted\_os(o) \; \wedge \; s.aos\_activity \; = \; waiting \; \wedge$
$\quad (s.oss[o]).hcall \; = \; Some \; (Hyperv\_call\_pin(pa, t)) \; \wedge$
$\quad physical\_address\_not\_allocated(s.hypervisor[o], pa) \; \wedge$
$\quad \exists \; ma : madd, \; memory\_available(s.memory, ma)$
$Post \; s \; (\textbf{page\_pin\_untrusted} \; o \; pa \; t) \; s' \overset{\text{def}}{=}$
$\quad \exists \; ma : madd, memory\_available(s.memory, ma) \; \wedge$
$\quad newmem \; = \; (s.memory[ma] := newpage(t, o)) \; \wedge$
$\quad newoss \; = \; (s.oss[o] := \langle None, (s.oss[o]).curr\_page \rangle) \; \wedge$
$\quad newhyperv \; = \; (s.hypervisor[o, pa] := ma) \; \wedge$
$\quad s \sim_{oss, hypervisor, memory \; = \; newoss, newhyperv, newmem} s'$

Fig. 2. Formal specification of actions semantics

Table 1. Actions

read *va*	A guest OS reads virtual address *va*.
write *va val*	A guest OS writes value *val* in virtual address *va*.
new_untrusted *o va pa*	The hypervisor adds (on behalf of the OS *o*) a new ordered pair (mapping virtual address *va* to the machine address *ma*) to the current memory mapping of the untrusted OS *o*, where *pa* translates to *ma* for *o*.
del_untrusted *o va*	The hypervisor deletes (on behalf of the *o* OS) the ordered pair that maps virtual address *va* from the current memory mapping of *o*.
switch *o*	The hypervisor sets *o* to be the active OS.
hcall *c*	An untrusted OS requires privileged service *c* to be executed by the hypervisor.
ret_ctrl	Returns the execution control to the hypervisor.
chmod	The hypervisor changes the execution mode from supervisor to user mode, if the active OS is untrusted, and gives to it the execution control.
page_pin_untrusted *o pa t*	The memory page that corresponds to physical address *pa* (for untrusted OS *o*) is registered and classified with type *t*.
page_unpin_untrusted *o pa*	The memory page that corresponds to physical address *pa* (for the untrusted OS *o*) is un-registered.

by a trusted OS directly (new and delete); v) changes of the execution mode (chmod, ret_ctrl); and vi) changes in the hypervisor memory mapping (pin and unpin), which are performed by the hypervisor on demand of an untrusted OS or by a trusted OS directly. These actions model (de)allocation of resources.

Actions Semantics. The behaviour of actions is specified by a precondition *Pre* and by a postcondition *Post* of respective types: $Pre : State \rightarrow Action \rightarrow Prop$, and $Post : State \rightarrow Action \rightarrow State \rightarrow Prop$. Figure 2 provides the axiomatic semantics of some relevant actions, namely, read, write, chmod and page_pin_untrusted (the names of the auxiliary predicates used should be self-explanatory). Notice that what is specified is the effect the execution of an action has on the state of the platform. In particular, the action read does not return the accessed value.

The precondition of the action read *va* requires that *va* is accessible by the active OS, that there exists a machine address *ma* to which *va* is mapped, that the active OS is running and that the page indexed by the machine address *ma* is readable/writable. The postcondition requires the execution of this action to keep the state unchanged. The precondition of the action write is identical to that of the action read. The postcondition establishes that the state after the execution of the action only differs in the value (*val*) of the page associated to *ma*, which is owned by the active OS. The precondition of the action chmod requires that there must not be a pending hypercall for the active OS. The postcondition establishes that after the execution of the action, if the active OS is a trusted one, then the effect on the state is to change its execution mode to supervisor mode. Otherwise, the execution mode is set to user mode. In both cases, the processor mode is set to *running*.

The execution of the action `page_pin_untrusted` requires, in the first place, that the hypervisor is running and that the active OS is untrusted. In addition to that, the OS o must be waiting for an hypercall to *pin* the physical address pa of type t, pa must not be already allocated and there must be machine memory available. The effect of the action is to create and allocate at machine address ma a new page of type t whose owner is the OS o and bind, in the hypervisor mapping, the physical address pa to ma. The rest of the state remains unchanged.

One-step execution. The execution of an action is specified by the $\hookrightarrow$ relation:

$$\frac{valid\_state(s) \quad Pre\ s\ a \quad Post\ s\ a\ s'}{s \overset{a}{\hookrightarrow} s'}$$

Whenever an action occurs for which the precondition holds, the (valid) state may change in such a way that the action postcondition is established. The notation $s \overset{a}{\hookrightarrow} s'$ may be read as *the execution of the action a in a valid state s results in a new state s'*. Note that this definition of execution does not consider the cases where the preconditions of the actions are not fulfilled.

Invariance of valid state. One-step execution preserves valid states, that is to say, the state resulting from the execution of an action is also a valid one.

Lemma 1. $\forall\ (s\ s' : State)\ (a : Action),\ s \overset{a}{\hookrightarrow} s' \rightarrow valid\_state(s')$

3.4   Traces

Isolation properties are eventually expressed on execution traces, rather than execution steps; likewise, availability properties are formalized as fairness properties stating that something good will eventually happen in an execution traces. Thus, our formalization includes a definition of execution traces and proof principles to reason about them.

Informally, an execution trace is defined as a stream (an infinite list) of states that are related by the transition relation $\hookrightarrow$, i.e. an object of the form $s_0 \overset{a_0}{\hookrightarrow} s_1 \overset{a_1}{\hookrightarrow} s_2 \overset{a_2}{\hookrightarrow} s_3 \dots$ such that every execution step $s_i \overset{a_i}{\hookrightarrow} s_{i+1}$ is valid. Formally, an execution trace is defined as a stream ss of pairs of states and actions, such that for every $i \geq 0$, $s[i] \overset{a[i]}{\hookrightarrow} s[i+1]$, where $ss[i] = \langle s[i], a[i] \rangle$ and $ss[i+1] = \langle s[i+1], a[i+1] \rangle$. We let *Trace* define the type of traces.

State properties are lifted to properties on pairs of states and actions in the obvious way. Moreover, state properties can be lifted to properties on traces; formally, each predicate P on states can be lifted to predicates $\square\ P$ (read always P) and $\Diamond\ P$ (read eventually P). The former $\square\ P$ is defined co-inductively defined by the clause $\square(P, s :: ss)$ iff $P(s)$ and $\square(P, ss)$, whereas the latter $\Diamond\ P$ is defined inductively by the clauses $\Diamond(P, s :: ss)$ iff $P(s)$ or $\Diamond(P, ss)$; each modality has an associated reasoning principle attached to its definition. Similar modalities can be defined for relations, and can be used to express isolation properties. In particular, given a relation R on states, and two traces ss_1 and ss_2, we have $\square(R, ss_1, ss_2)$ iff $R(ss_1[i], ss_2[i])$ for all i.

4   Isolation Properties

We formally establish that the hypervisor enforces strong isolation properties: an operating system can only read and modify memory that it owns, and its behavior is independent of the state of other operating systems. The properties are established for a single step of execution, and then extended to traces.

Read isolation. Read isolation captures the intuition that no OS can read memory that does not belong to it. Formally, read isolation states that the execution of a **read** va action requires that va is mapped to a machine address ma that belongs to the active OS current memory mapping, and that is owned by the active OS.

Lemma 2. $\forall\ (s\ s' : State)\ (va : vadd),$
$s \xrightarrow{read\ va} s'\ \rightarrow\ \exists\ ma : madd,\ va\_mapped\_to\_ma(s, va, ma)\ \wedge$
$\exists\ pg : page,\ pg = s.memory[ma]\ \wedge\ pg.page\_owned\_by = s.active\_os$

The property is proved by inspection of the pre and postcondition for the **read** action, using the definition of valid state.

Write Isolation. Write isolation captures the intuition that an OS cannot modify memory that it does not own. Formally, write isolation states that, unless the hypervisor is running, the execution of any action will at most modify memory pages owned by the active OS or it will allocate a new page for that OS.

Lemma 3. $\forall\ (s\ s' : State)\ (a : Action)\ (ma : madd),$
$s \xrightarrow{a} s'\ \rightarrow\ \neg hyper\_running(s)\ \rightarrow$
$s'.memory[ma] = s.memory[ma] \vee owner\_or\_free(s.memory, ma, s.active\_os)$

where $hyper\_running$ and $owner\_or\_free$ respectively denote that the hypervisor is running, and that the owner of the given machine address is either the given OS or it is free.

The property is proved by case analysis on the action executed. The relevant cases are the actions that are performed by the active OS and that modify the memory; for each such action, the property follows from its pre and postconditions, and from the definition of valid state.

OS Isolation. OS isolation captures the intuition that the behavior of any OS does not depend on other OSs states, and is expressed using the notion of *equivalence* w.r.t. an operating system osi. Formally, two states s and s' are osi-equivalent, denoted $s \equiv_{osi} s'$, if the following conditions are satisfied: i) osi has the same hypercall in both states, or no hypercall in both states; ii) the current page tables of osi are the same in both states; iii) all page table mappings of osi that maps a virtual address to a RW page in one state, must map that address to a page with the same content in the other; iv) the hypervisor mappings of osi in both states are such that if a given physical address maps to some RW page, it must map to a page with the same content on the other state. Note that we cannot require that memory contents be the same in both states for them to be *osi*-equivalent, because on a `page_pin` action, the hypervisor can assign an arbitrary (free) machine address to the OS, so we consider *osi*-equivalence without taking into account the actual value of the machine addresses assigned. In particular, two *osi*-equivalent states can have different page table memory pages, which contain mappings from virtual to arbitrary machine addresses, but such that the contents of such an arbitrary machine address be the same on both states, if it corresponds to a RW page. This definition bears some similarity with notions of indistinguishable states used for reasoning about non-interference in object-oriented languages [5].

OS isolation states that *osi*-equivalence is preserved under execution of any action, and is formalized as a "step-consistent" unwinding lemma, see [20].

Lemma 4. $\forall\ (s_1\ s_1'\ s_2\ s_2' : State)\ (a : Action)\ (osi : os\_ident),$
$$s_1 \equiv_{osi} s_2\ \rightarrow s_1 \overset{a}{\hookrightarrow} s_1'\ \rightarrow\ s_2 \overset{a}{\hookrightarrow} s_2'\ \rightarrow\ s_1' \equiv_{osi} s_2'$$

The proof of OS isolation relies on write isolation, on Lemma 5, and on an isolation lemma for the case where *osi* is the active OS of both states s_1 and s_2.

The next lemma formalizes a "locally preserves" unwinding lemma in the style of [20], stating that the *osi*-component of a state is not modified when another operating system is executing.

Lemma 5. $\forall\ (s\ s' : State)\ (a : Action)\ (osi : os\_ident),$
$$\neg\ os\_action(s, a, osi)\ \rightarrow\ s \overset{a}{\hookrightarrow} s'\ \rightarrow\ s \equiv_{osi} s'$$

where $os\_action(s, a, osi)$ holds if, in the state s, *osi* is the active and running OS and therefore is executing action a, or otherwise the hypervisor is executing the action a on behalf of *osi*.

Extensions to traces. All isolation properties extend to traces, using coinductive reasoning principles. In particular, the extension of OS isolation to traces establishes a non-influence property [18]. Formally, we define for each operating system *osi* a predicate *same_os_actions* stating that two steps have the same set of actions w.r.t. *osi*: concretely, $same\_os\_actions(osi, ss_1, ss_2)$ holds provided for all i the actions in $ss_1[i]$ and $ss_2[i]$ are the same *os_action* for *osi*, or both are arbitrary actions not related to *osi*.

Lemma 6. $\forall\ (ss_1\ ss_2 : Trace)\ (osi : os\_ident),$
$$same\_os\_actions(osi, ss_1, ss_2)\ \rightarrow (ss_1[0] \equiv_{osi} ss_2[0])\ \rightarrow \Box(\equiv_{osi}, ss_1, ss_2)$$

For technical reasons related to the treatment of coinductive definitions in Coq (specifically the need for corecursive definitions to be productive), our formalization of non-influence departs from common definitions of non-interference and non-influence, which rely on a purge function that eliminates the actions that are not related to *osi*. One can however define an erasure function *erase* that replaces actions that are not related to *osi* by `silent` actions, and prove for all traces ss that $\Box(\equiv_{osi}, ss, erase(osi, ss))$.

5 Availability

An essential property of virtualization platforms is that all guest operating systems are given access to the resources they need to proceed with their execution.

In this section, we establish a strong fairness property, showing that if the hypervisor only performs chmod actions whenever no hypercall is pending, then no OS blocks indefinitely waiting for its hypercalls to be attended. The assumption on the hypervisor is satisfied by all reasonable implementations of the hypervisor; one possible implementation that would satisfy this restriction is an eager hypervisor which attends hypercalls as soon as it receives them and then chooses an operating system to run next. If this is the case, then when the chmod action is executed, no hypercalls are pending on the whole platform.

Formally, the assumption on the hypervisor is modelled by considering a restricted set of execution traces in which the initial state has no hypercall pending, and in chmod actions can only be performed whenever no hypercall is pending. Then, the strong fairness property states that: if the hypervisor returns control to guest operating systems infinitely often, then infinitely often there is no pending hypervisor call.

Lemma 7. $\forall\ (ss : Trace), \neg\ hcall(ss[0]) \rightarrow \Box(chmod\_nohcall, ss) \rightarrow$
$$\Box(\Diamond \neg\ hyper\_running, ss) \rightarrow \Box(\Diamond \neg\ hcall, ss)$$

where $hcall$ and $chmod\_nohcall$ respectively denote that there is an hypercall pending and that chmod actions only arise when no hypercall is pending.

The proof of the strong fairness property proceeds by co-induction and relies on showing that $\neg\ hyper\_running(s) \rightarrow \neg\ hcall(s)$ is an invariant of all traces that satisfy the hypothesis of the lemma.

Note that our strong fairness property is independent of the scheduler: in particular, the hypothesis $\Box(\Diamond \neg\ hyper\_running, ss)$ does not guarantee that each operating system will be able to execute infinitely often. Further restricting the implementation of the hypervisor so as to guarantee that the hypervisor is fair to each guest operating system is left for future work.

6   Related Work

There have been many efforts to formally verify (parts of) operating systems, see [15] for a survey. The Microsoft Hyper-V verification project focuses on proving the functional correctness of the deployed implementation of the Hyper-V hypervisor [8,16] or of a simplified, baby, implementation [2]. Using VCC, an automated verifier for annotated C code, these works aim to prove that the hypervisor correctly simulates the execution of the guest operating systems, in the sense that the latter cannot observe any difference from executing on their own on a standard platform. At a more specific level, these works provide a detailed account of many components that are not considered in our work, including page tables [1], devices [3] and cache [8]. The cache is of particular interest from the point of view of security, and Cohen [8] reports on finding cache attacks in the Microsoft Hyper-V verification project. Indeed, the cache constitutes a shared resource which might leak information if not flushed when changing of active operating system. Formalizing the cache and giving sufficient conditions for proving isolation in its presence is a prime goal for future work.

The L4.verified project [14] focuses on proving that the functional correctness of an implementation of seL4, a microkernel whose main application is as an hypervisor running paravirtualized Linux. The implementation consists of approximately 9kLOC of C and 600 lines of assembler, and has been shown to be a valid refinement of a very detailed abstract model that considers for example page tables and I/O devices. Their current work focuses on showing isolation properties; one difference is that in our model the access to a page is restricted to a unique owner, whereas they rely on more flexible capability systems [9].

More recently, the Verve project [23] has initiated the development of a new operating system whose type safety and memory safety has been verified using a combination of type systems and Hoare logic. Outside these projects, several projects have implemented small hypervisors, to reduce the Trusted Computing Base, or with formal verification in mind [22], but we are not aware of any completed proof of functional correctness or security.

Our work is also related to formal verification of isolation properties for separation kernels. Earlier works on separation kernels [13,12,17] formalize a simpler model where memory is partitioned a priori. In contrast, our model allows the partition to evolve and comprises three types of addressing modes and is close to those of virtualization platforms, where memory requested by the OSs is dynamicaly allocated from a common memory pool. Dealing with this kind of memory management adds significant complications in isolation proofs.

Our work is also inspired by earlier efforts to prove isolation for smartcard platforms. Andronick, Chetali and Ly [4] use the Coq proof assistant to establish that the JavaCard firewall mechanism ensures isolation properties between contexts—sets of applications that trust each other. Oheimb and coworkers [18,19] independently verify isolation properties for Infineon SLE 88 using the Isabelle proof assistant. In particular, their work formalizes a notion of non-influence that is closely related to our isolation properties.

7   Conclusion and Future Work

We have developed an idealized model of a hypervisor and established within this model isolation and availability properties that are expected from virtualization platforms. The formal development is about 20kLOC of Coq (see Figure 3), including proofs, and forms a suitable basis for reasoning about hypervisors.

Model and basic lemmas	4.8k
Valid state invariance	8.0k
Read and write isolation	0.6k
OS Isolation and lemmas	6.0k
Traces, safety and availability	1.0k
Total	20.4k

Fig. 3. LOC of Coq development

There are several directions for future work: one immediate direction is to complete our formalization with a proof of correctness of the hypervisor, as in the Hyper-V verification project. Indeed, there are strong connections between OS isolation and We also intend to enrich our model with shared resources; concretely, we intend to concentrate on the cache and to provide sufficient conditions for isolation properties to hold in its presence. Another immediate direction is to prove isolation and availability properties on an implementation of the hypervisor, using recent work by the authors. Finally, it is of interest to understand how to adapt our models to other virtualization paradigms such as full virtualization and microvisors.

Acknowledgments. Thanks to Andres Krapf, Anne Pacalet, Francois Armand and Christian Jacquemot for their involvement at early stages of the project, Julio Pérez for his contribution on proof checking and June Andronick, Gerwin Klein, Toby Murray, and FM reviewers for feedback on the paper.

References

1. Alkassar, E., Cohen, E., Hillebrand, M., Kovalev, M., Paul, W.: Verifying shadow page table algorithms. In: Bloem, R., Sharygina, N. (eds.) 10th International Conference on Formal Methods in Computer-Aided Design, FMCAD 2010. IEEE CS, Switzerland (2010)
2. Alkassar, E., Hillebrand, M., Paul, W., Petrova, E.: Automated Verification of a Small Hypervisor. In: Leavens, G.T., O'Hearn, P., Rajamani, S.K. (eds.) VSTTE 2010. LNCS, vol. 6217, pp. 40–54. Springer, Heidelberg (2010)
3. Alkassar, E., Paul, W., Starostin, A., Tsyban, A.: Pervasive verification of an os microkernel: Inline assembly, memory consumption, concurrent devices. In: Leavens, G.T., O'Hearn, P., Rajamani, S.K. (eds.) VSTTE 2010. LNCS, vol. 6217, pp. 71–85. Springer, Heidelberg (2010)
4. Andronick, J., Chetali, B., Ly, O.: Using Coq to Verify Java Card Applet Isolation Properties. In: Basin, D., Wolff, B. (eds.) TPHOLs 2003. LNCS, vol. 2758, pp. 335–351. Springer, Heidelberg (2003)
5. Banerjee, A., Naumann, D.: Stack-based access control for secure information flow. Journal of Functional Programming 15, 131–177 (2005); Special Issue on Language-Based Security
6. Barham, P., Dragovic, B., Fraser, K., Hand, S., Harris, T., Ho, A., Neugebauer, R., Pratt, I., Warfield, A.: Xen and the art of virtualization. In: SOSP 2003: Proceedings of the Nineteenth ACM Symposium on Operating Systems Principles, pp. 164–177. ACM Press, New York (2003)
7. Clarkson, M.R., Schneider, F.B.: Hyperproperties. Journal of Computer Security 18(6), 1157–1210 (2010)
8. Cohen, E.: Validating the microsoft hypervisor. In: Misra, J., Nipkow, T., Sekerinski, E. (eds.) FM 2006. LNCS, vol. 4085, p. 81. Springer, Heidelberg (2006)
9. Elkaduwe, D., Klein, G., Elphinstone, K.: Verified protection model of the seL4 microkernel. In: Shankar, N., Woodcock, J. (eds.) VSTTE 2008. LNCS, vol. 5295, pp. 99–114. Springer, Heidelberg (2008)
10. Garfinkel, T., Warfield, A.: What virtualization can do for security. login: The USENIX Magazine 32 (December 2007)
11. Goldberg, R.P.: Survey of virtual machine research. IEEE Computer Magazine 7, 34–45 (1974)
12. Greve, D., Wilding, M., Mark Van Eet, W.: A separation kernel formal security policy. In: Proc. Fourth International Workshop on the ACL2 Theorem Prover and Its Applications (2003)

13. Heitmeyer, C.L., Archer, M., Leonard, E.I., McLean, J.: Formal specification and verification of data separation in a separation kernel for an embedded system. In: Proceedings of the 13th ACM Conference on Computer and Communications Security, CCS 2006, pp. 346–355. ACM, New York (2006)
14. Klein, G., Andronick, J., Elphinstone, K., Heiser, G., Cock, D., Derrin, P., Elkaduwe, D., Engelhardt, K., Kolanski, R., Norrish, M., Sewell, T., Tuch, H., Winwood, S.: seL4: Formal verification of an OS kernel. Communications of the ACM (CACM) 53(6), 107–115 (2010)
15. Klein, G.: Operating system verification – an overview. Sādhanā 34(1), 27–69 (2009)
16. Leinenbach, D., Santen, T.: Verifying the microsoft hyper-V hypervisor with VCC. In: Cavalcanti, A., Dams, D. (eds.) FM 2009. LNCS, vol. 5850, pp. 806–809. Springer, Heidelberg (2009)
17. Martin, W., White, P., Taylor, F.S., Goldberg, A.: Formal construction of the mathematically analyzed separation kernel. In: The Fifteenth IEEE International Conference on Automated Software Engineering (2000)
18. von Oheimb, D.: Information Flow Control Revisited: Noninfluence = Noninterference + Nonleakage. In: Samarati, P., Ryan, P., Gollmann, D., Molva, R. (eds.) ESORICS 2004. LNCS, vol. 3193, pp. 225–243. Springer, Heidelberg (2004)
19. von Oheimb, D., Lotz, V., Walter, G.: Analyzing SLE 88 memory management security using Interacting State Machines. International Journal of Information Security 4(3), 155–171 (2005)
20. Rushby, J.M.: Noninterference, Transitivity, and Channel-Control Security Policies. Technical Report CSL-92-02, SRI International (1992)
21. The Coq Development Team. The Coq Proof Assistant Reference Manual – Version V8.2 (2008)
22. Tews, H., Weber, T., Poll, E., van Eekelen, M.C.J.D.: Formal Nova interface specification. Technical Report ICIS–R08011, Radboud University Nijmegen, Robin deliverable D12 (May 2008)
23. Yang, J., Hawblitzel, C.: Safe to the last instruction: automated verification of a type-safe operating system. In: Proceedings of PLDI 2010, pp. 99–110. ACM, New York (2010)

The Safety-Critical Java Memory Model: A Formal Account

Ana Cavalcanti, Andy Wellings, and Jim Woodcock

University of York, Department of Computer Science, York, UK

Abstract. Safety-Critical Java (SCJ) is a version of Java for real-time programming that facilitates certification of implementations of safety-critical systems. It is the result of an international effort involving industry and academia. What we provide here is, as far as we know, the first formalisation of the SCJ model of memory regions. We use the Unifying Theories of Programming (UTP) to enable the integration of our theory with refinement models for object-orientation and concurrency. In developing the SCJ theory, we also make a contribution to the UTP by providing a general theory of invariants (of which the SCJ theory is an instance). Our results are a first essential ingredient to formalise the novel programming paradigm embedded in SCJ, and enable the justification and development of reasoning techniques based on refinement.

Keywords: semantics, UTP, integration, refinement.

1 Introduction

Two language (subsets) have dominated high-integrity real-time engineering. Ada [2], which provides good support through its Spark [1] and Ravenscar subsets [4] and the Spark Examiner Toolset, has a limited community. Safe(r) subsets of C/C++ are often the choice, but lack support for formal development. In both cases, various modern programming features found useful in other sectors of the software industry are left out on the grounds of safety.

An international effort has produced a high-integrity real-time version of Java: Safety-Critical Java (SCJ) [13]. It achieves a compromise between the safety of Ada and the popularity of C/C++, and provides an ambitious novel take on the combined safe use of object orientation and real-time programming. SCJ lacks, however, a formal underpinning for its programming models. In this paper, we provide a formalisation for its memory management model.

SCJ is based on a subset of Java augmented by the Real-Time Specification for Java (RTSJ) [19]. To understand the full implications of the SCJ memory model, it is necessary to appreciate the run-time data structures maintained by a Java Virtual Machine. The main concern is the heap and the stacks. All objects are placed on the heap, which is scanned by a garbage collector to remove any that are unreachable. Variables that are local to methods are stored in a stack; each thread of control has an associated stack. Variables and object fields can

M. Butler and W. Schulte (Eds.): FM 2011, LNCS 6664, pp. 246–261, 2011.

be of a primitive type (int, short, and so on) or of a reference type. We ignore here all issues associated with native methods.

The RTSJ supplements Java's garbage-collected heap memory model with support for memory regions [18] called *memory areas*. As with the Java heap, these regions are used to store dynamically created objects.

SCJ restricts the RTSJ memory model to prohibit use of the heap. The RTSJ and SCJ introduce two new memory areas: scoped and immortal memory. Objects allocated in a scoped memory have a lifetime that is determined by the number of threads that are currently using that scoped memory area. When there are no such threads, all the objects are collected. In contrast, objects created in immortal memory have a lifetime equal to that of the program. A program can have many scoped memory areas, but only a single instance of immortal memory. To avoid dangling references, there are rules that must be obeyed by reference assignments. Violation of these rules results in runtime exceptions. SCJ defines a fixed structure for the use of scoped memories.

In Java, programmers need not be concerned with memory management. In contrast, in SCJ (and the RTSJ), a programmer must consider in which area to create objects according to their anticipated lifetime. Tools and techniques are needed to ensure efficient use of memory and absence of run-time errors.

SCJ includes annotations that can be used to document programs, and enable static verification of properties including memory safety. The work in [17] presents rules for use of the annotations, and a tool that checks statically that these rules are followed. It is not trivial to convince ourselves that the rules proposed achieve the level of memory safety claimed. While we do not necessarily expect to find any problems, the formalisation of the memory model is essential for the justification of the soundness of such techniques.

Our first contribution is an informal description of the SCJ memory model that explains the rationale for its design. (For a discussion of the design of the concurrency model, we refer to [20].) As a second contribution, we provide a relational semantics for this model; it is based on Hoare and He's Unifying Theories of Programming (UTP) [10]. Finally, we present a general UTP theory for operation and state invariants, which we instantiate to capture in an elegant and concise way the properties of the SCJ structure of memory areas.

The UTP is a relational framework that supports refinement-based reasoning about a variety of paradigms. It covers models for concurrent, functional and logic programming, for instance. It has also been used to define constructs related to object-orientation [15] and time [16]. By casting the SCJ memory model in the UTP, we pave the way for its integration with these theories, that cater for other, also very important, aspects of an SCJ program.

Next, we present informally the SCJ memory model; an introduction to the UTP is provided in Section 3. Section 4 presents a UTP theory for program invariants. In Section 5, we use those results to formalise the SCJ memory model. We draw our conclusions, and discuss related and future work in Section 6.

2   Safety-Critical Java Memory Model

SCJ recognises that safety-critical software varies considerably in complexity. At one end of the spectrum, the application consists of a single thread executing a single function on a single processor with a simple timing constraint. At the other end, it is multithreaded executing in multiple modes on multiple processors. Consequently, there are three compliance levels for SCJ programs and implementations. In this work, we are concerned with Level 1, which, roughly, corresponds in complexity to the Ravenscar profile for Ada.

The SCJ programming model is based on the notion of missions, which are managed by a mission sequencer (see Figure 1). At Level 1, missions may be composed into sequences, but nested missions are prohibited. A Level 1 mission consists of a bounded set of asynchronous event handlers (ASEH). Here, these can be considered as being equivalent to real-time threads. Both periodic and aperiodic threads are supported. Each thread executes a sequence of releases that are either time triggered (periodic) or event triggered (aperiodic). Consequently, an SCJ program is a concurrent program with threads of control for the main program, the mission sequencer, and one for each of the ASEHs.

The main goal of the SCJ memory model is to support dynamic memory management. Traditionally, safety-critical systems do not allocate memory during the execution of a mission due to (a) the error-prone nature of manual allocation and deallocation schemes (typified by `malloc` and `free` in C), and (b) the complexity of automatic deallocation schemes based on garbage collection.

The region-based approach of the RTSJ provides safer and more predictable support for dynamic memory management, but the overall model is still complex. SCJ, consequently, constrains the use of its features: garbage collection is not supported, and only a restricted version of the scoped memory model is provided.

Basically, the structure of the memory areas is fixed as shown in Figure 2. Every thread of control in an SCJ program has a default memory allocation context. This is the area in which created objects are placed. The main program's thread of control has immortal memory as its default allocation context. It is this thread that, for instance, creates the mission sequencer and any objects that should exist throughout the lifetime of the program.

The mission sequencer's thread of control is started with immortal memory as its default allocation context. It creates the mission memory, a scoped area that becomes the default allocation context for a mission. There is no thread of control associated with a mission. Instead, the mission sequencer's thread

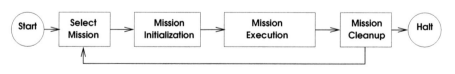

Fig. 1. Safety Critical Mission Phases (taken from [13])

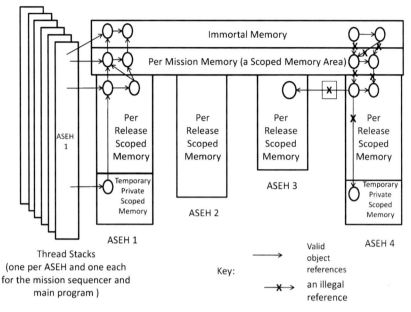

Fig. 2. SCJ memory model

performs the mission initialisation, during which the ASEHs are created. The mission memory is cleared at the end of each mission. Any objects that must remain across missions must be stored in immortal memory.

Each ASEH has an associated per-release memory area: the default memory allocation context for its releases. It is cleared at the end of each release, for reuse in the next release. Any object that is required to live across releases must be placed in mission memory. An ASEH can create a temporary private scoped memory area and change its default allocation context to the newly created area. More than one of these can be created and they are used in a LIFO manner. The stack of private temporary memory areas arises from nested calls to a `create` method. As the inner calls are finished, memory areas are popped off.

In the example shown in Figure 2 there are, therefore, six thread-of-control stacks: one for the main program, one for the mission sequencer, and one for each ASEH; a single immortal memory – accessible by all threads of control; a single mission memory – accessible by the ASEHs and the mission sequencer; one private per-release memory area for each ASEH – accessible only by the associated ASEH; and a stack of temporary private scoped memory area for each ASEH – accessible only by the associated ASEH.

The aim of this restricted model is to ensure that dangling references cannot occur, and that programs are amenable to static analysis techniques that can determine the absence of run-time errors, such as illegal-assignment errors. A tool is provided in [17]. Section 5 formalises this model in the UTP.

3   Unifying Theories of Programming

In the UTP, relations are defined by predicates over an alphabet (set) of observational variables that record information about the behaviour of a program. In
the theory of general relations, these include the programming variables v, and
their dashed counterparts v', with v used to refer to an initial observation of
the value of v, and v' to a later observation. The set of undecorated (unprimed)
variables in the alphabet αP of a predicate P is called its input alphabet $in\alpha P$,
and the set of dashed variables is its output alphabet $out\alpha P$. A condition is a
predicate whose alphabet includes only input variables.

Theories are characterised by an alphabet and by healthiness conditions defined by monotonic idempotent functions from predicates to predicates. The
predicates of a theory with an alphabet A are all the predicates on A which are
fixed points of the healthiness conditions. As an example, we consider designs.

The general theory of relations does not distinguish between terminating and
nonterminating programs. This is achieved in the theory of designs, which includes two extra boolean observational variables to record the start and the
termination of a program: ok and ok'. The monotonic idempotents used to specify the healthiness conditions for designs can be defined as follows.

H1 $P = ok \Rightarrow P$

H2 $P = P \; ; J, \text{ where } J \;\widehat{=}\; (ok \Rightarrow ok') \land v' = v$

If P is **H1**-healthy, then it makes no restrictions on the final value of variables
before it starts. If P is **H2**-healthy, then termination must be a possible outcome
from every initial state. The functional composition of **H1** and **H2** is named **H**.

Every design D can be written in the form $P \vdash Q$, where P is its precondition,
and Q its postcondition; $P \vdash Q$ is defined as $ok \land P \Rightarrow ok' \land Q$. Precisely, every
design D can be written as $\neg\, D^f \vdash D^t$, where f is the boolean false, t is true,
and D^b is the predicate $D[b/ok']$ obtained by substituting b for ok' in D.

Typically, a theory defines a number of programming operators of interest.
Common operators like assignment, sequence, and conditional, are defined for
general relations. A conditional is written as $P \triangleleft b \triangleright Q$; its behaviour is (described
by) P if the condition b holds, else it is defined by Q.

$$P \triangleleft b \triangleright Q \;\widehat{=}\; (b \land P) \lor (\neg b \land Q), \text{ where } \alpha(b) \subseteq \alpha(P) = \alpha(Q).$$

Sequence is relational composition.

$$P;\; Q \;\widehat{=}\; \exists\, w_0 \bullet P[w_0/w'] \land Q[w_0/w], \text{ where } out\alpha(P) = in\alpha(Q)' = w'$$

The relation $P;\; Q$ is defined by a quantification that relates the intermediate
values of the variables. It is required that $out\alpha(P)$ is equal to $in\alpha(Q)'$, which is
named w'. The sets w, w', and w_0 are used as lists that enumerate the variables
of w and the corresponding decorated variables in the same order.

A central concern of the UTP is refinement. A program P is refined by a
program Q, written $P \sqsubseteq Q$, if, and only if, $P \Leftarrow Q$, for all possible values of the

variables of the alphabet. The set of alphabetised predicates form a complete lattice with this ordering. Recursion is modelled by weakest fixed points.

The design that models skip, the program that terminates without changing any variable, is $\mathbb{I} \; \widehat{=} \; (true \vdash v' = v)$, where v is the list of programming variables in the alphabet. Interestingly, $\mathbb{I}$ is the left identity of sequential composition, but not necessarily the right identity. This requires that the precondition does not contain dashed variables, a property not adequate, for instance, in the theory of reactive designs used as a concurrency model (for CSP).

A theory needs to be closed with respect to the programming operators: they need to take healthy predicates to healthy predicates, so that they can be used to define models compositionally. In the next section, we provide some general results for the healthiness conditions of a theory of designs with invariants.

4   Invariants in the UTP

In [10], designs are used to construct more general relations to model, for example, reactive programs. For these, even in the presence of divergence, some properties hold. In [9], we take this approach in a theory for objects and sharing as available in Java. Our theory, in that case, captures physical properties of sharing; for instance, variables that share a location have the same value.

On the other hand, when an SCJ program aborts, there is no guarantee that its restrictions on memory areas are maintained. We, therefore, present our theory as a subset of the theory of designs. Other examples of subtheories of designs are presented in the line of work established in [12], which provides UTP theories for BPEL-like languages, with new forms of nontermination to handle exceptions. Here, we provide a general account of design subtheories characterised by invariants and with the standard notion of termination.

It is in the spirit of the UTP to define theories for particular programming features, and combine them to capture more complex paradigms. In this line, it could be conceivable to treat the memory structure of SCJ programs and termination separately. We would characterise a subtheory of relations using a healthiness condition **HSCJ**, for instance, and then use **H** to embed it in the theory of designs. For an **HSCJ**-healthy predicate P whose alphabet does not include ok and ok', however, the design $\mathbf{H}(P)$ is $\neg \, P \vdash false$. Its precondition considers the possibility of **HSCJ** not holding (even in an non-abortive state), and, in this case, it is miraculous. What we need instead is a theory that allows for the memory restrictions to be violated just in the case of nontermination.

In what follows, subtheories of designs are defined by healthiness conditions that either capture operation invariants or invariants of a single state observation. In both cases, invariants are only broken by nontermination.

4.1   Operation Invariants

For an operation invariant defined by a predicate Ψ, the subtheory of designs that satisfy this invariant is characterised by the healthiness condition **OIH**.

OIH(Ψ) $D = D \wedge (ok \wedge \neg \, D^f \Rightarrow \Psi)$

An **OIH**(Ψ)-healthy design ensures that, when its precondition holds, so does Ψ.

Theorem 1. OIH(Ψ) *is a monotonic idempotent function on designs.*

Proof. First, we show that **OIH**(Ψ)(D) is a design.

$\quad$ **OIH**(Ψ)(D)

$\quad = (\neg\, D^f \vdash D^t) \wedge (ok \wedge \neg\, D^f \Rightarrow \Psi)$

$\qquad\qquad\qquad\qquad$ [property of designs and definition of **OIH**(Ψ)]

$\quad = (ok \wedge \neg\, D^f \Rightarrow ok' \wedge D^t) \wedge (ok \wedge \neg\, D^f \Rightarrow \Psi) \qquad$ [definition]

$\quad = \neg\, D^f \vdash D^t \wedge \Psi \qquad$ [propositional calculus and definition of designs]

Since $ok \wedge \neg\, (\neg\, D^f \vdash D^t \wedge \Psi)^f = ok \wedge \neg\, D^f$, then **OIH**($\Psi$) is idempotent. Finally, to establish monotonicity, we consider designs D_1 and D_2 such that $D_1 \Rightarrow D_2$. That **OIH**(Ψ)(D_1) $\Rightarrow$ **OIH**(Ψ)(D_2), follows from $\neg\, D_2^f \Rightarrow \neg\, D_1^f$. $\qquad\square$

We define the healthy identity $\mathrm{II}_{OI}(\Psi) \;\widehat{=}\; \textbf{OIH}(\Psi)(\mathrm{II})$. For reflexive Ψ, that is, for those such that $\Psi[v/v']$, we have that $\mathrm{II}_{OI}(\Psi)$ is the sequence left unit.

Theorem 2. *If Ψ is reflexive, $\mathrm{II}_{OI}(\Psi); D = D$, for every* **OIH**($\Psi$)*-healthy D.*

Proof

$\quad \mathrm{II}_{OI}(\Psi); D$

$\quad = \textbf{OIH}(\Psi)(\mathrm{II}); \textbf{OIH}(\Psi)(D) \quad$ [definition of II_{OI} and D is **OIH**(Ψ)-healthy]

$\quad = (true \vdash v' = v \wedge \Psi); (\neg\, D^f \vdash D^t \wedge \Psi) \qquad\qquad$ [Theorem 1]

$\quad = ok \wedge \neg\, (\Psi[v/v'] \wedge D^f) \Rightarrow ok' \wedge \Psi[v/v'] \wedge D^t \wedge \Psi$

$\qquad\qquad$ [definition of sequence and design, and predicate calculus]

$\quad = ok \wedge \neg\, D^f \Rightarrow ok' \wedge D^t \wedge \Psi \qquad\qquad\qquad$ [Ψ is reflexive]

$\quad = D \qquad$ [definition of design, Theorem 1, and D is **OIH**(Ψ)-healthy]

$\hfill\square$

$\mathrm{II}_{OI}(\Psi)$ is not necessarily the right unit. Like in the theory of general designs, this requires that the precondition refers to no dashed variables. Proofs of this and other results mentioned below can be found in [6].

$\quad$ **OIH**(Ψ) is closed with respect to conjunction, disjunction (which models non-determinism) and conditional. For closedness with respect to sequence, we need Ψ to be transitive, that is, (Ψ; Ψ) $\Rightarrow \Psi$. The set of **OIH**(Ψ)-healthy designs is a complete lattice, since it is the image of a monotonic idempotent healthiness condition [10]. So, recursion can still be defined using weakest fixed points. The bottom and top of the lattice are the same as that for the lattice of designs: abort, that is, the design (*false* $\vdash$ *true*), and magic, (*true* $\vdash$ *false*).

4.2   State Invariants

For a state invariant defined by a condition ψ, the subtheory of designs whose input variables satisfy ψ is characterised by the following healthiness condition.

ISH(ψ) $D = D \vee (ok \wedge \neg D^f \wedge \psi \Rightarrow ok' \wedge D^t)$

The invariant ψ is part of the precondition of **ISH**(ψ)-healthy D.

Theorem 3. ISH(ψ) *is an idempotent function on designs.*

Proof. First, we show that **ISH**$(\psi)(D)$ is a design.

$\quad$ **ISH**$(\psi)(D)$

$\quad = (\neg D^f \vdash D^t) \vee (ok \wedge \neg D^f \wedge \psi \Rightarrow ok' \wedge D^t)$

$\qquad\qquad\qquad\qquad$ [property of designs and definition of **ISH**(Ψ)]

$\quad = (ok \wedge \neg D^f \Rightarrow ok' \wedge D^t) \vee (ok \wedge \neg D^f \wedge \psi \Rightarrow ok' \wedge D^t)$ $\qquad$ [definition]

$\quad = \neg\, ok \vee D^f \vee \neg\, \psi \vee ok' \wedge D^t$ $\qquad\qquad\qquad$ [propositional calculus]

$\quad = \neg\, D^f \wedge \psi \vdash D^t$ $\qquad\qquad$ [propositional calculus and definition of designs]

The arguments for idempotence and monotonicity are similar to those used in Theorem 1. $\qquad\qquad\qquad\qquad\qquad\qquad\qquad\qquad\qquad\qquad\qquad\qquad$ □

We define the healthy identity $\mathit{II}_{IS}(\psi) \,\hat{=}\, \mathbf{ISH}(\psi)(\mathit{II})$. It is indeed the left-unit of sequence; this is a simple consequence of the definitions of $\mathit{II}_{IS}(\psi)$ and sequence, and Theorem 3 above. Again, right unit does not hold in all cases.

$\quad$ **ISH**(ψ) is closed with respect to conjunction, disjunction, conditional, and sequence. The bottom of the lattice that it defines is abort, but the top is $(\psi \vdash \mathit{false})$. This is miraculous only when ψ holds.

$\quad$ The subtheory of designs whose output variables satisfy ψ' is characterised by the following healthiness condition. The predicate ψ' is that obtained by substituting all output alphabet variables for their input counterparts in ψ.

OSH(ψ) $D = D \wedge (ok \wedge \neg D^f \wedge \psi \Rightarrow \psi')$

We observe that **OSH**(ψ) can be defined as **OIH**$(\psi \Rightarrow \psi')$, and that $\psi \Rightarrow \psi'$ is reflexive and transitive. So, it satisfies all the properties discussed in the previous section. Most importantly, as shown below, **ISH**(ψ) and **OSH**(ψ) commute.

Theorem 4. ISH(ψ) *and* **OSH**(ψ) *commute.*

Proof

$\quad$ **OSH**$(\psi) \circ$ **ISH**$(\psi)(D)$

$\quad = $ **OSH**$(\psi)(\neg\, ok \vee D^f \vee \neg\, \psi \vee ok' \wedge D^t)$

$\qquad\qquad\qquad$ [function composition, Theorem 3, and propositional calculus]

$$= \neg\,(\neg\,ok \vee D^f \vee \neg\,\psi) \vdash (\neg\,ok \vee D^f \vee \neg\,\psi \vee D^t) \wedge (\psi \Rightarrow \psi')$$
$$\text{[Theorem 1 and propositional calculus]}$$

$$= \neg\,D^f \wedge \psi \vdash ok \wedge \neg\,D^f \Rightarrow (D^t \wedge (\psi \Rightarrow \psi'))$$
$$\text{[propositional calculus and definition of designs]}$$

$$= \neg\,(\neg\,ok \vee D^f) \wedge \psi \vdash \neg\,ok \vee D^f \vee D^t \wedge (\psi \Rightarrow \psi')$$
$$\text{[propositional calculus and definition of designs]}$$

$$= \mathbf{ISH}(\neg\,ok \vee D^f \vee ok' \wedge D^t \wedge (\psi \Rightarrow \psi'))$$
$$\text{[propositional calculus, definition of designs, and Theorem 3]}$$

$$= \mathbf{ISH}(\neg\,D^f \vdash D^t \wedge (\psi \Rightarrow \psi')) \qquad\qquad \text{[definition of designs]}$$
$$= \mathbf{ISH}(\psi) \circ \mathbf{OSH}(\psi)(D) \qquad \text{[Theorem 1 and function composition]}$$

$$\square$$

As shown above, an $\mathbf{ISH}(\psi)$ and $\mathbf{OSH}(\psi)$-healthy design D can be written as $(\neg\,D^f \wedge \psi \vdash D^t \wedge \psi')$, so that ψ is assumed and established. Since $\mathbf{ISH}(\psi)$ and $\mathbf{OSH}(\psi)$ are idempotent, by Theorem 4, so is $\mathbf{SIH}(\psi) \mathrel{\widehat{=}} \mathbf{ISH}(\psi) \circ \mathbf{OSH}(\psi)$ [10]; this is our healthiness condition for a theory with state invariant ψ.

When healthiness functions $\mathbf{C1}$ and $\mathbf{C2}$ commute, then every predicate that is $(\mathbf{C1} \circ \mathbf{C2})$-healthy is also $\mathbf{C1}$ and $\mathbf{C2}$-healthy. From this and the theorems above and in Section 4.1, we can conclude that $\mathbf{SIH}(\psi)$ distributes through conjunction, disjunction, conditional, and sequence.

Finally, for operation and state invariants Ψ_1 and ψ_2, $\mathbf{OIH}(\Psi_1)$ and $\mathbf{SIH}(\psi_2)$ commute. So, using an argument similar to that above, we can conclude that a theory characterised by $\mathbf{IH}(\Psi_1, \psi_2) \mathrel{\widehat{=}} \mathbf{OIH}(\Psi_1) \circ \mathbf{SIH}(\psi_2)$ is closed with respect to conjunction, disjunction, conditional, and sequence. The same applies to theories characterised by two operation invariants Ψ_1 and Ψ_2; $\mathbf{OIH}(\Psi_1)$ and $\mathbf{OIH}(\Psi_2)$ commute, and define a theory with invariant $\Psi_1 \wedge \Psi_2$. A similar result holds for state invariants ψ_1 and ψ_1. The UTP theory for the SCJ memory model presented in the next section combines several operation and state invariants.

5   A Theory for the Safety-Critical Java Memory Model

In this section, we consider first a theory that captures the structure of memory areas in SCJ. Afterwards, we extend it to take into account the values of the variables stored in the memory areas.

Type definitions. The elements of the stacks (for the program, mission sequencer, and handlers) are frames, which define a context of execution for a method. To provide a model for a frame, we introduce the notion of a variable name as an element of the unspecified set *VName*, and of a reference: from a set *Ref*. We also define the set of values as *Value* = *PValue* $\cup$ *Ref*, where *PValue* is the unspecified set of primitive values and the special value *null*. With these, we can define *Frame* = *VName* $\nrightarrow$ *Value*, so that a frame is a partial function associating the names of the variables in scope to their values.

A function *refsIn* : *Frame* → $\mathbb{F}\,Ref$ defines the finite set of references (to objects in a memory area) in the stack. It is defined as *refsIn* f = ran($f \vartriangleright Ref$), using the range restriction operator $\vartriangleright$.

We identify a memory area with its contents; we do not capture issues related to size. Concretely, we define the set $MAreaC = Ref \nrightarrow OValue$ of memory contents, where *OValue* is the set of record (object) values: functions that associate fields to their values, that is, $OValue = VName \nrightarrow Value$.

We also define two functions *refsRes*, *refsIn* : $MAreaC \rightarrow \mathbb{F}\,Ref$. For a memory area *ma*, the set *refsRes ma* contains the references that identify objects that reside in *ma*. The references used in these objects (to refer to other objects in the same or in other memory areas) are those in *refsIn ma*. Precisely, *refsRes ma* = dom *ma*, and *refsIn ma* = $\bigcup$(ran$($ (_ $\vartriangleright Ref)($ ran *ma* $))$). For a memory area *ma* (or more precisely, for the contents *ma* of a memory area), ran *ma* gives its objects. By using relational image _$($ _ $)$ to apply the operator (_ $\vartriangleright Ref$) to all of them, we project out all their fields with a primitive or *null* value. The ranges of these objects are the references used in *ma*; distributed union provides a single set containing all of them.

In order to identify the handlers of a mission, we consider the set *HName*. It contains valid handler identifiers, or names.

The alphabet of our theory includes eight extra observational variables defined below, and their dashed counterparts, in addition to *ok*, *ok'*, and the programming variables (and their dashed counterparts). We have nine healthiness conditions, which are also specified and discussed in the sequel.

Alphabet. First, we have the stacks *pStack*, *msStack* : stack *Frame* for the program and the mission sequencer. The set *handlers* : $\mathbb{F}\,HName$ records the handlers of the current mission, and the variable *hStack* : *handlers* → stack *Frame* groups their stacks as a total function associating each handler to its stack.

To record the memory areas, we have first *immortal*, *mission* : *MAreaC*. The per-release memory areas are grouped in *perR* : *handlers* → *MAreaC*. The temporary private memory areas are organised in a stack as recorded in the alphabet variable *tPriv* : *handlers* → stack *MAreaC*. A simple model for a stack is, of course, a sequence, whose last element is the top of the stack.

A stacked temporary private memory area is called a parent in relation to all those areas of the same handler that are stacked afterwards. More generally, the immortal memory area is the parent of the mission memory area, which is a parent of all per-release memory areas. Additionally, the per-release memory area of a handler is a parent of all its stacked temporary private memory areas.

Healthiness conditions. We can only add object values to the immortal area. This is an operation invariant, and gives rise to our first healthiness condition **HSCJ1**. To define it, we introduce a function *profile* : $MAreaC \rightarrow (Ref \nrightarrow \mathbb{F}\,VName)$. For a memory area *ma*, the function *profile ma* associates each reference residing in *ma* with the set of fields of the object that it identifies in *ma*. This is the domain of the function (in *OValue*) that defines that object. Formally, we have *profile ma* = $\{r : \text{dom } ma \bullet r \mapsto \text{dom}(ma\ r)\}$. Our healthiness condition **HSCJ1** requires that the immortal memory is changed only by adding new references to its profile. Existing references remain, and the structure of the objects to which they point (as captured by their sets of field names) is preserved.

HSCJ1 $\;\widehat{=}\;$ **OIH**(*profile immortal* $\subseteq$ *profile immortal'*)

The operation invariant for **HSCJ1** is reflexive and transitive, because $\subseteq$ is.

The references in the program stack can only target objects in the immortal memory. This is specified by the healthiness condition **HSCJ2**, which uses a lifted version of *refsIn* : stack *Frame* $\rightarrow$ $\mathbb{F}$ *Ref* that applies to stacks of frames *sf* (instead of frames or memory areas). We can define it in terms of the version of *refsIn* for frames as *refsIn sf* $= \bigcup(refsIn(\!|$ ran *sf* $|\!))$. The range of *sf* is a set of frames; we use relational image to apply *refsIn* to all of them. The distributed union collects together all references occurring in all frames of *sf*.

HSCJ2 $\;\widehat{=}\;$ **SIH**(*refsIn pStack* $\subseteq$ *refsRes immortal*)

Analogously, the references in the immortal memory can only target objects in the immortal memory itself. This is the state invariant specified below.

HSCJ3 $\;\widehat{=}\;$ **SIH**(*refsIn immortal* $\subseteq$ *refsRes immortal*)

Similarly, the references in the mission-sequencer stack and in the mission memory area are for objects either in the immortal or in the mission memory areas. To capture this healthiness condition, we define *refsRes* : $\mathbb{F}$ *MAreaC* $\rightarrow$ $\mathbb{F}$ *Ref*, for a set of memory areas *mas* as *refsRes mas* $= \bigcup(refsRes(\!|$ *mas* $|\!))$. It collects the references in each of the memory areas in *mas*.

HSCJ4 $\;\widehat{=}\;$ **SIH**(*refsIn msStack* $\subseteq$ *refsRes* {*immortal, mission*})
HSCJ5 $\;\widehat{=}\;$ **SIH**(*refsIn mission* $\subseteq$ *refsRes* {*immortal, mission*})

For each handler, the references in its stack are for objects in its own temporary private areas, in its own per-release area, or in the mission or immortal memory.

HSCJ6 $\;\widehat{=}\;$ **SIH** $\left(\begin{array}{l} \forall\, h : handlers \bullet \\ \quad refsIn\,(hStack\,h) \subseteq \\ \qquad refsRes\,(\{immortal, mission, perR\,h\} \cup \mathrm{ran}(tPriv\,h)) \end{array} \right)$

For each handler, the references in its per-release memory area are for objects in that same area, or in the mission or immortal memory areas.

HSCJ7 $\;\widehat{=}\;$ **SIH** $\left(\begin{array}{l} \forall\, h : handlers \bullet \\ \quad refsIn\,(perR\,h) \subseteq refsRes\{immortal, mission, perR\,h\} \end{array} \right)$

Finally, in a temporary private memory area of any handler, the references target objects that can be in the immortal memory, in the mission memory, in the associated per-release memory for the same handler, in a parent stacked area, or in that same temporary private memory area.

HSCJ8 $\;\widehat{=}\;$
$\quad$ **SIH** $\left(\begin{array}{l} \forall\, h : handlers;\; i : 1\mathinner{\ldotp\ldotp}\#(tPriv\,h) \bullet \\ \quad refsIn\,(tPriv\,h\,i) \subseteq \\ \qquad refsRes(\{immortal, mission, perR\,h\} \cup \{j : 1\mathinner{\ldotp\ldotp} i \bullet tPriv\,h\,j\}) \end{array} \right)$

We use $\#s$ to denote the size of the sequence (or stack) s.

Finally, the memory areas are disjoint in their use of the reference space.

HSCJ9 $\widehat{=}$
  SIH(disjoint $\langle refsRes\ immortal,\ refsRes\ mission \rangle \frown$ seqPR $perR \frown$ seqTP $tPriv$)

We use seqPR $perR$ and seqTP $tPriv$ to denote the sequences of sets of references residing in the per-release and temporary private memory areas in $perR$ and $tPriv$. We omit the formal definition of these functions.

Our theory contains the fixed points of the healthiness conditions above. They are the fixed points of **HSCJ**, which we define as the composition of all the healthiness functions. With the results in Section 4, we conclude that **HSCJ** is closed with respect to conjunction, disjunction, conditional, and sequence.

The healthiness conditions **HSCJ2** to **HSCJ8** are enough to ensure that every SCJ program makes a safe use of memory, in the sense that, at no point, it has a variable in a stack whose value is a dangling reference or can be used to reach a dangling reference. **HSCJ10** justifies the treatment of the separate memory areas as a single global memory. We take advantage of that in the sequel, when we consider the value of the variables in the stacks.

What we have not captured is the fact that during the lifetime of a mission, we can only add objects to the mission memory. Similarly, objects can only be added to each of the per-release and temporary private memory areas until they are cleared. For the immortal memory, we have **HSCJ1**. It is not the case, however, that *profile mission* $\subseteq$ *profile mission'*, for example, is an invariant of our theory. Since the mission area can be cleared, and later reused when a new mission is started, then there is no guarantee that *mission'* is at all related to *mission* in every pair of observations of an SCJ program. The same comments apply to the per-release and private temporary memory areas in *perR* and *tPriv* in relation to the handler releases and the calls to the `create` method.

To establish the required properties, we need to keep a record of the sequence of missions that have been executed. Additionally, to restrict the use of the per-release and temporary private memory areas, during the execution of a mission, we need to keep the history of releases and calls to the `create` method for each ASEH. Details of how history can be added to our theory can be found in [6]. For instance, we keep a sequence of identifiers for the missions that have been executed, with a special identifier used to indicate that there is no mission currently executing. This approach is similar to that adopted in [16,5] to cater for passage of time in the UTP theories for timed and synchronous processes.

Programming variables and their values. Programming variables in the alphabet can be specification or allocated variables. Specification variables are used to write abstract definitions of the behaviour of programs; they model, for instance, inputs and outputs. Allocated variables are included in one of the stacks.

Our next three healthiness conditions require that the value of every allocated variable in the alphabet is in accordance with what is recorded in the stacks. To define them, we use a function $vars :$ stack $Frame \to \mathbb{F}\ VName$ that characterises the set of active variables in a given stack: those in the domains of the frames;

formally, $vars\ sf = \bigcup \mathrm{dom}(\ \mathrm{ran}\ sf\ )$, provided there are no redeclarations, that is, disjoint $\{i : 1 .. \#sf \bullet i \mapsto \mathrm{dom}(sf\ i)\}$. (As usual, we assume that variable names are not reused to avoid handling stacks of values for alphabet variables.)

The value of a variable vn (according to a stack sf and its associated memory areas mas) is characterised by a set A of sequences of variable names, and a function V that associates some of these sequences to primitive values. If the value associated with vn in sf is primitive or *null*, then $\langle vn \rangle$ is the only sequence in A. If, on the other hand, the value of vn is a reference (to an object), then we also have all the (possibly infinite) extensions of $\langle vn \rangle$ that identify a field of that object, or a field of one of its fields, and so on. The function V associates the sequences of variable names that identify a variable or an object field with a primitive or null value to this value. This characterisation of values is the same used in [9], where we have defined a UTP theory for the Java memory model that captures the structure of objects and sharing.

Formally, we define the value $!(vn, sf, mas)$ using a dereferencing function $!\_ : VName \times \mathrm{stack}\ Frame \times \mathbb{F}\ MAreaC \rightarrow \mathbb{P}\ SName \times (SName \nrightarrow PValue)$, specified as $!(vn, sf, mas) = (A(vn, sf, mas), V(vn, sf, mas))$. Here, $SName$ is the set of possibly infinite sequences of variable names (from $VName$). The set $SName \nrightarrow PValue$ is that of the finite partial functions from $SName$ to $PValue$.

The set $A(vn, sf, mas)$ is defined as shown below.

$$A(vn, sf, mas) = \left\{ \begin{array}{l} sn : SName\ | \\ \left(\begin{array}{l} \mathrm{head}\ sn = vn\ \wedge \\ \mathbf{let}\ u == sval(vn, sf) \bullet \\ \quad u \in PValue \wedge tail\ sn = \langle \rangle \vee path(tail\ sn, \bigcup mas, u) \end{array} \right) \end{array} \right\}$$

Here $sval(vn, sf) = (\bigcup(\mathrm{ran}\ sf))\ vn$ is the value of vn as recorded in sf. The fact that there are no variable redeclarations guarantees that $(\bigcup(\mathrm{ran}\ sf))$ is a function. The condition $path(sn, ma, r)$ requires that the sequence of variable names sn identifies a path in the memory area ma starting from the reference r. We use it above to make sure that the extensions of $\langle vn \rangle$ are in accordance with the information in the memory areas mas. With the assumption that they are disjoint, we consider $\bigcup mas$. The starting reference is the value u of vn in sf.

The formal definition of $path(sn, ma, r)$ is as follows. We require the existence of a (possibly infinite) sequence sr of references that can be traversed using the sequence of names sn. The last value of sn, if any, might be a primitive value, rather than a reference, so the type of sr is $SVal$, the set of sequences of values.

$$path(sn, ma, r) \Leftrightarrow \left(\exists sr : SVal \bullet \left(\left(\begin{array}{l} \mathrm{head}\ sr = r\ \wedge \\ \left(\begin{array}{l} \forall\ i : \mathrm{dom}\ sn \bullet \\ \left(\begin{array}{l} (sr\ i) \in \mathrm{dom}\ ma \wedge (sn\ i) \in \mathrm{dom}(ma\ (sr\ i)) \wedge \\ sr(i+1) = ma\ (sr\ i)\ (sn\ i) \end{array} \right) \end{array} \right) \end{array} \right) \right) \right)$$

For each name $sn\ i$ in sn, the corresponding value $sr\ i$ in sr must be a reference in ma to an object $ma\ (sr\ i)$ with a field named $sn\ i$. Additionally, the next value $sr\ (i + 1)$ in sr must be the value $ma\ (sr\ i)\ (sn\ i)$ of that field.

The definition of $V(vn, sf, mas)$ is in many ways similar, and we omit it here.

The condition **HV1** requires that the value of every variable v in the program stack is given by *pStack* itself and its associated *immortal* area.

$$\textbf{HV1} \; \hat{=} \; \textbf{SIH}(\bigwedge v : vars(pStack) \bullet v =!(v, pStack, \{immortal\}))$$

The healthiness conditions **HV2** and **HV3** are similar. The former considers the mission-sequencer stack, and the latter the handlers stacks.

$$\textbf{HV2} \; \hat{=} \; \textbf{SIH}(\bigwedge v : vars(msStack) \bullet v =!(v, msStack, \{immortal, mission\}))$$

$$\textbf{HV3} \; \hat{=}$$
$$\textbf{SIH} \left(\begin{array}{l} \forall h : handlers \bullet (\bigwedge v : vars(hStack\ h) \bullet \\ v =!(v, hStack\ h, \{immortal, mission, perR\ h\} \cup ran\,(tPriv\ h))) \end{array} \right)$$

Implicitly, these conditions require that all variables v in the stacks are in the alphabet, since they are in the alphabet of the conjunctions.

We define **HV** as the composition of the functions **HV1-HV3**.

6   Conclusions

To the best of our knowledge, we have presented here the only formal characterisation of the SCJ memory model available so far. This is an essential ingredient to justify the soundness of assertion-based static checking techniques (like that in [17]). As a UTP theory, our model is also adequate for unification with existing models of concurrency, object orientation, and timing.

We reuse the ideas of an existing UTP model for objects and sharing [9] to address the relationship between the structure established by the references in the memory areas and the values of the programming variables and attribute accesses. What we do not cover are features of models like [11,7]; these do not consider the issue of variable values, but provide support for reasoning about the memory graph structure. For SCJ, we will need to build on such techniques to take advantage of the separation enforced by the memory areas.

Another assertion-based technique proposed for SCJ is SafeJML [8]. It extends the well-established JML [3] to cover functionality and timing properties. The focus is on annotations that allow the use of existing technology for worst-case execution-time analysis to reason about SCJ programs.

Another contribution of this paper is a general characterisation of subset theories of designs. With this, we have given an elegant definition for the SCJ theory. Our general results are useful for all theories for programs that do not exhibit special forms of termination, and do not provide guarantees on abortion.

Our model does not capture the flow of control of an SCJ program, as partially depicted in Figure 1. This is the subject of ongoing work, which formalises the SCJ programming model in *Circus* [14], a refinement language based on Z and CSP. The semantic model of *Circus* is based on the UTP, and it is our plan to use the theory presented here as basis for the design of an extension of *Circus* that is appropriate to reason about SCJ programs. The intended model of a complete SCJ program will a predicate of the stateless CSP theory, just like that of a complete *Circus* program. So, it will have the form shown below, where the alphabet variables representing the memory structure are local.

var *immortal, mission* . . . ; *P*; **end** *immortal, mission* . . .

In this case, *P* will be a predicate in the theory resulting from the embedding of the SCJ model presented here in the *Circus* theory of reactive designs. In the long run, we plan to provide a reasoning framework for SCJ programs that can cater for concurrency, object-orientation, time, and sharing.

Acknowledgements. This work is funded by EPSRC (grant EP/H017461/1) and UKIERI (grant SAO8-047).

References

1. Barnes, J.: High Integrity Software: The SPARK Approach to Safety and Security. Addison-Wesley, Reading (2003)
2. Barnes, J.: Programming in Ada 95. Addison-Wesley, Reading (2005)
3. Burdy, L., et al.: An overview of JML tools and applications. Software Tools for Technology Transfer 7(3), 212–232 (2005)
4. Burns, A.: The Ravenscar Profile. Ada Letters XIX, 49–52 (1999)
5. Butterfield, A., Sherif, A., Woodcock, J.C.P.: Slotted-circus. In: Davies, J., Gibbons, J. (eds.) IFM 2007. LNCS, vol. 4591, pp. 75–97. Springer, Heidelberg (2007)
6. Cavalcanti, A.L.C., Wellings, A., Woodcock, J.C.P.: The Safety-Critical Java Mission Model: a formal account – Extended Version. Technical report (2011), http://www-users.cs.york.ac.uk/ alcc/CWW11b.pdf
7. Chen, Y., Sanders, J.: Compositional Reasoning for Pointer Structures. In: Yu, H.-J. (ed.) MPC 2006. LNCS, vol. 4014, pp. 115–139. Springer, Heidelberg (2006)
8. Haddad, G., Hussain, F., Leavens, G.T.: The Design of SafeJML, A Specification Language for SCJ with Support for WCET Specification. In: JTRES. ACM, New York (2010)
9. Harwood, W., Cavalcanti, A.L.C., Woodcock, J.C.P.: A Theory of Pointers for the UTP. In: Fitzgerald, J.S., Haxthausen, A.E., Yenigun, H. (eds.) ICTAC 2008. LNCS, vol. 5160, pp. 141–155. Springer, Heidelberg (2008)
10. Hoare, C.A.R., Jifeng, H.: Unifying Theories of Programming. Prentice-Hall, Englewood Cliffs (1998)
11. Hoare, C.A.R., Jifeng, H.: A trace model for pointers and objects. Programming methodology, pp. 223–245 (2003)
12. Jifeng, H.: UTP semantics for web services. In: Davies, J., Gibbons, J. (eds.) IFM 2007. LNCS, vol. 4591, pp. 353–372. Springer, Heidelberg (2007)
13. Locke, D., et al.: Safety Critical Java Specification. The Open Group, UK (2010), jcp.org/aboutJava/communityprocess/edr/jsr302/index.html
14. Oliveira, M.V.M., Cavalcanti, A.L.C., Woodcock, J.C.P.: A UTP Semantics for *Circus*. Formal Aspects of Computing 21(1-2), 3–32 (2009)
15. Santos, T.L.V.L., Cavalcanti, A.L.C., Sampaio, A.C.A.: Object-Orientation in the UTP. In: Dunne, S., Stoddart, B. (eds.) UTP 2006. LNCS, vol. 4010, pp. 18–37. Springer, Heidelberg (2006)

16. Sherif, A., et al.: A process algebraic framework for specification and validation of real-time systems. Formal Aspects of Computing 22(2), 153–191 (2010)
17. Tang, D., Plsek, A., Vitek, J.: Static Checking of Safety Critical Java Annotations. In: JTRES.ACM, New York (2010)
18. Tofte, M., Talpin, J.-P.: Region-based memory management. Information and Computation 132(2), 109–176 (1997)
19. Wellings, A.: Concurrent and Real-Time Programming in Java. Wiley, Chichester (2004)
20. Wellings, A., Kim, M.: Asynchronous event handling and safety critical Java. In: JTRES. ACM, New York

Failure-Divergence Refinement of Compensating Communicating Processes*

Zhenbang Chen[1], Zhiming Liu[2], and Ji Wang[1]

[1] National Laboratory for Parallel and Distributed Processing, Changsha, China
[2] International Institute for Software Technology, The United Nations University, Macao

Abstract. Compensating CSP (cCSP) extends CSP for specification and verification of long running transactions. The original cCSP is a modest extension to a subset of CSP that does not consider non-deterministic choice, synchronized composition, and recursion. There are a few further extensions. However, it remains a challenge to develop a fixed-point theory of process refinement in cCSP. This paper provides a complete solution to this problem and develops a theory of cCSP, corresponding to the theory of CSP, so that the verification techniques and their tools, such as FDR, can be extended for compensating processes.

1 Introduction

Service-oriented architecture (SOA) is a critical enabling technology for programming business processes composed of disparate services available on the web. These processes are required to have the "transactional characteristic": if a failure occurs in the execution, the changes made before the failure must be *undone* or *compensated*. The transactional property of business processes is different from the ACID properties of *atomic transactions* (or *short-life transactions*). A general business process is usually a long running transaction (LRT) [13] that takes a substantial amount of time to complete, involving interactions across many systems and possibly requiring human interventions [14]. The mechanism to ensure ACID by the holding of locks and tight coordination of the participating systems cannot be applied to LRTs. Furthermore, it is not required for such a business process to undo the entire change committed in case of an occurrence of a failure. Instead, a weakened or partial recovery is often required by the application. For example, when a flight booking is canceled, a cancelation fee is charged and only part of the payment can be recovered. For this reason, models of LRTs, such as Sagas [12] and BizTalk [15], allow programmer-specified undoing and recovery actions that are called *compensation*.

Compensation supports flexible treatment of different exceptional scenarios, but the flexibility makes the handling of failures complicated and ad-hoc. To help programmers master the complexity, Web Service languages, such as WS-BPEL and XLANG, provide mechanisms for exception handling. A common design principle of these languages is a combination of exception handling and failure recovery. In some situations, an exception is raised when a LRT is aborted and caught by a programmed handler.

---

* Supported in parts by projects NSFC 60725206, National 973 project 2011CB302603, NSFC 60970031, NSFC 61073022, and the MSTDF project GAVES.

M. Butler and W. Schulte (Eds.): FM 2011, LNCS 6664, pp. 262–277, 2011.

In some other cases, actions of a LRT are programmed with the corresponding compensatory actions so that when a failure occurs, the recovery actions of the committed actions are activated and executed in their reverse order. This is the model of the backward recovery in Sagas [12] implemented in BizTalk.

The need for better understanding of complex LRTs and their mission-critical applications motivate the research on formal theories of compensation programming, *e.g.* [1,4,3,11]. They differ mostly in the features that they support. For examples, non-deterministic choice and limited recursion are supported by the process calculus in [11], but not by cCSP in [6]. However, little discussion is given by the designers of the languages about the decisions they made. This indicates an insufficient understanding on what common features of LRTs should and can be formalized.

Contribution. We extend the version of cCSP in [6], with non-deterministic choices, synchronization among parallel processes, and recursion (cf. Section 2). The main contribution is a semantic theory of *failures* and *divergences* of LRTs (cf. Sections 3&4). The theory includes a *complete partial order* (CPO) of the failure-divergences of processes that allows the calculation of a unique fixed-point of any recursive compensable process. The CPO also characterizes programming of LRTs (cf. Section 5). It is a well-known challenge to establish, or even to show the existence of, such a fixed-point theory for a language like CSP with internal-choice and synchronization [18]. Literature, *e.g.* [8], also shows that if the internal choice is added to CCS, it is difficult to define a partial order to characterize the notion of refinement. This problem is even harder for the extended cCSP, due to the abstract mechanisms for exception handling and compensation behavior. The technical details in Section 3&4 and the proofs of the theorems and laws in the technical report [10] show the inventive thinking needed. Because the application potential of cCSP, the extension and its well established failure-divergence semantic theory are important. Similar to the unification role that the failure-divergence semantics of CSP plays, the failure-divergence semantic theory integrates as its sub-theories the operational semantics, trace semantics, stable failures semantics [9] of cCSP. It completes the semantic theory of cCSP for specification of LRTs and can be used to underpin the extension to FDR of CSP [17] and the cCSP theorem proving tool [16] for verification of LRTs.

Related work. cCSP in [6] is an extension to CSP [17] for LRTs. The recovery mechanism in cCSP is the same as the backward recovery in Sagas [12]. There are two types of processes in cCSP, the *standard processes* and *compensable processes*. The standard processes are only a subset of CSP processes, but with additional processes for exception handling and transaction block. A compensable process specifies the behavior of the recovery when an exception occurs. Non-deterministic choices and synchronization are not allowed in cCSP and thus it only has a trace semantics [4] and an operational semantics [7]. The consistency between these two semantics is studied in [16].

Our early work in [9] extends cCSP with the operators of non-deterministic choice, synchronized parallel composition, hiding and renaming, and defines a stable failures semantics. But that semantic model does not allows us to establish a fixed-point theory for recursion with a meaningful CPO. Thus, a new semantic domain has to be defined, instead of simple extension of the stable failures semantic domain with a divergence set, so as to define refinement and calculate fixed-points.

The main reason why we develop a semantic theory of LRTs by extending the original cCSP is because that cCSP shares most of the common features of other formal models [2,11]. Also, CSP-like process calculi are used to give formal semantics of protocol description languages and orchestration languages, *e.g.* [5].

2   Syntax of the Extended cCSP

Assume a *finite* set Σ of names representing the *normal events* that the cCSP processes can perform, called the *alphabet* of processes. The syntax of the extended cCSP is defined in Fig. 1, where $a \in \Sigma$ represents an event, $X \subseteq \Sigma$ is a finite subset, and $R \subseteq \Sigma \times \Sigma$ is a *renaming relation*. cCSP defines two kinds of processes, the *standard processes* ranged over by P, and the *compensable processes* ranged over by PP.

$$P ::= a \mid P;P \mid P \sqcap P \mid P \Box P \mid P \parallel_X P \mid P \setminus X \mid P[\![R]\!] \mid P \rhd P \mid [PP] \mid \mathbf{skip} \mid \mathbf{stop} \mid$$
$$\mathbf{throw} \mid \mathbf{yield} \mid \mu\, p.F(p)$$
$$PP ::= P \div P \mid PP;PP \mid PP \sqcap PP \mid PP \Box PP \mid PP \parallel_X PP \mid PP \boxtimes PP \mid PP \setminus X \mid$$
$$PP[\![R]\!] \mid \mathbf{skipp} \mid \mathbf{throww} \mid \mathbf{yieldd} \mid \mu\, pp.FF(pp)$$

Fig. 1. The standard processes add four additional kinds of processes to CSP: **throw** throws an exception and interrupts the execution of the process, **yield** either terminates successfully or yields to an interruption from environment to interrupt the execution, $P \rhd Q$ behaves like P and it executes Q if there is an exception thrown by P, the transaction block $[PP]$ represents a long-running transaction specified by the compensable process PP

The standard processes extend those of the classical CSP processes with exception handling, interruption and transaction block specified by a compensable process. A compensable process is constructed from *compensation pairs* of the form $P \div Q$, in which the execution of the process Q can compensate the effect of the execution of P. P is called the *forward (sub-) process* and Q the *compensation (sub-) process*. The internal and external choices in the compensable processes are made according to the forward sub-processes. PP and QQ in $PP \parallel_X QQ$ synchronize on the events in X occurring in the behaviors of both forward and compensation sub-processes of PP and QQ. It is written $PP\|QQ$ when X is empty. $PP \boxtimes QQ$ is the speculative choice between two compensable processes, in which PP and QQ run in parallel until one of them succeeds, and after that the other is compensated. Process **skipp** immediately terminates successfully without the need to be compensated, and **throww** throws an exception and **yieldd** either terminates successfully or yields to an interruption.

3   Failure-Divergence Semantics of Standard Processes

3.1   Basic Notations

Let A^* denote the set of finite sequences of the elements in a set A of symbols. In particular, Σ^* is the set of *interaction traces* of the cCSP processes. Let $\Omega = \{\checkmark, !, ?\}$ be disjoint with Σ. Events in Ω are called *terminals* and they indicate different terminating scenarios: "$\checkmark$" represents that the execution terminates successfully, "!" indicates that the execution terminates with an occurrence of an exception, and "?" represents that the execution terminates by yielding to an interruption from environment. The traces of cCSP processes are thus formed from symbols in $\Gamma = \Sigma \cup \Omega$. Let $s \cdot t$ denote the *concatenation* of traces s and t, and $T_1 \cdot T_2$ the set of concatenated traces of the trace sets T_1 and T_2. In particular, for a non-empty subset A of Ω, let $\Sigma_A^\star = \Sigma^* \cdot A$ denote the set of traces terminated with events in A, and let $\Sigma_A^\circledcirc = \Sigma^* \cup \Sigma_A^\star$. Thus, $\Sigma_{\{\checkmark\}}^\star$ is the set of *successfully terminated traces*. We use $\Sigma^\star$ and $\Sigma^\circledcirc$ as the shorthands of $\Sigma_\Omega^\star$ and $\Sigma_\Omega^\circledcirc$.

Processes need to follow different rules to synchronize on different terminals. We order the three terminals such that ! $\prec$? $\prec$ $\checkmark$ and define $\omega_1 \| \omega_2 = \omega_1$ if $\omega_1 \preceq \omega_2$, and $\omega_1 \| \omega_2 = \omega_2 \| \omega_1$. Therefore, the synchronization of any terminal with an exception will result in an exception, and composition terminates successfully iff both parties do.

For two traces $s, t \in \Sigma^\circledcirc$ and a subset $X \subseteq \Sigma$, the set of synchronized traces $s \underset{X}{\|} t$, $s \| t$ when $X = \{\}$, is defined in the same way as in CSP [17] when $s, t \in \Sigma^*$, otherwise terminals of s and t synchronize in the following two patterns, where $s_1, t_1 \in \Sigma^*$.

$$s_1 \cdot \langle \omega \rangle \underset{X}{\|} t_1 = \{\}, \quad s_1 \cdot \langle \omega_1 \rangle \underset{X}{\|} t \cdot \langle \omega_2 \rangle = \{u \cdot \langle \omega_1 \| \omega_2 \rangle \mid u \in s_1 \underset{X}{\|} t_1\}$$

3.2 Semantics of Standard Processes

The FD semantics $[\![P]\!]$ of a process P is a pair $(\mathcal{F}(P), \mathcal{D}(P))$, where $\mathcal{F}(P) \subseteq \Sigma^\circledcirc \times \mathbb{P}(\Gamma)$ is the *failure set* and $\mathcal{D}(P) \subseteq \Sigma^\circledcirc$ the *divergence set*. The sets of *traces* and *terminated traces* of P are defined from the failures $\mathcal{F}(P)$ below.

$$traces(P) \;\hat{=}\; \{s \mid (s, \{\}) \in \mathcal{F}(P)\}, \;\; trace_t(P) \;\hat{=}\; traces(P) \cap \Sigma^\star$$

We require that the FD semantics of P satisfies the axioms of the FD semantics of the classical CSP processes given in [17], for example, the divergence set $\mathcal{D}(P)$ is suffix closed and the trace set $traces(P)$ is prefix closed. However, the axioms about terminated traces need to be modified as follows.

$$s \cdot \langle \omega \rangle \in traces(P) \Rightarrow (s, \Gamma \setminus \{\omega\}) \in \mathcal{F}(P), \; where \; \omega \in \Omega \tag{1}$$

$$s \in \mathcal{D}(P) \cap \Sigma^* \wedge t \in \Sigma^\circledcirc \Rightarrow s \cdot t \in \mathcal{D}(P) \tag{2}$$

$$s \cdot \langle \omega \rangle \in \mathcal{D}(P) \Rightarrow s \in \mathcal{D}(P), \; where \; \omega \in \Omega \tag{3}$$

In what follows we define the *failure function* $\mathcal{F} : \mathcal{P} \to \mathbb{P}(\Sigma^\circledcirc \times \mathbb{P}(\Gamma))$ and the *divergence function* $\mathcal{D} : \mathcal{P} \to \mathbb{P}(\Sigma^\circledcirc)$, where $\mathcal{P}$ denotes the set of all standard processes.

Atomic and basic processes. The semantics of the processes a, **skip** and **stop** are the same as their semantics in CSP. The divergence sets of processes **throw** and **yield** are both empty, and their failure sets are defined below.

$$\mathcal{F}(\mathbf{throw}) = \{(\langle\rangle, X) \mid X \subseteq \Gamma \wedge\; ! \notin X\} \cup \{(\langle!\rangle, X) \mid X \subseteq \Gamma\}$$
$$\mathcal{F}(\mathbf{yield}) = \{(\langle\rangle, X) \mid X \subseteq \Gamma \wedge\; ? \notin X\} \cup \{(\langle?\rangle, X) \mid X \subseteq \Gamma\}$$
$$\cup \{(\langle\rangle, X) \mid X \subseteq \Gamma \wedge \checkmark \notin X\} \cup \{(\langle\checkmark\rangle, X) \mid X \subseteq \Gamma\}$$

We use **div** to represent the process diverging immediately, *i.e.* $\langle\rangle \in \mathcal{D}(\mathbf{div})$.

Choices. The semantics of the internal choice is the same as defined in CSP, but note that **yield** $\sqcap$ **skip** $=$ **yield** holds. External choice is different from internal choice on the empty trace $\langle \rangle$, at which $P \square Q$ can refuse an event only if both P and Q can refuse it. Also, care should be taken about the terminals "?" and "!" when defining the failures to ensure the axiom (1).

$$\begin{aligned}
\mathcal{D}(P \square Q) = {} & \mathcal{D}(P) \cup \mathcal{D}(Q) \\
\mathcal{F}(P \square Q) = {} & \{(\langle \rangle, X) \mid (\langle \rangle, X) \in \mathcal{F}(P) \cap \mathcal{F}(Q)\} \\
& \cup \{(s, X) \mid (s, X) \in \mathcal{F}(P) \cup \mathcal{F}(Q) \wedge s \neq \langle \rangle\} \\
& \cup \{(\langle \rangle, X) \mid X \subseteq \Gamma \setminus \{\omega\} \wedge \langle \omega \rangle \in \mathit{traces}(P) \cup \mathit{traces}(Q) \wedge \omega \in \Omega\} \\
& \cup \{(s, X) \mid s \in \mathcal{D}(P \square Q) \wedge X \subseteq \Gamma\}
\end{aligned}$$

Sequential composition. The sequential composition here is also different from the classic CSP [17] because of the terminals "!" and "?".

$$\begin{aligned}
\mathcal{D}(P; Q) = {} & \mathcal{D}(P) \cup \{s \cdot t \mid s \cdot \langle \checkmark \rangle \in \mathit{traces}(P) \wedge t \in \mathcal{D}(Q)\} \\
\mathcal{F}(P; Q) = {} & \{(s, X) \mid s \in \Sigma_{\{?,!\}}^{\circledast} \wedge (s, X \cup \{\checkmark\}) \in \mathcal{F}(P)\} \\
& \cup \{(s \cdot t, X) \mid s \cdot \langle \checkmark \rangle \in \mathit{traces}(P) \wedge (t, X) \in \mathcal{F}(Q)\} \\
& \cup \{(s, X) \mid s \in \mathcal{D}(P; Q) \wedge X \subseteq \Gamma\}
\end{aligned}$$

Parallel composition. We first define the divergence set of $P \parallel_X Q$, and then its failure set. The composition diverges if either P or Q diverges, which is

$$\begin{aligned}
\mathcal{D}(P \parallel_X Q) = {} & \{u \cdot v \mid v \in \Sigma^{\circledast}, \exists s \in \mathit{traces}(P), t \in \mathit{traces}(Q) \bullet \\
& u \in (s \parallel_X t) \cap \Sigma^* \wedge (s \in \mathcal{D}(P) \vee t \in \mathcal{D}(Q))\}
\end{aligned}$$

To define the failure set of the composition, we understand that $P \parallel_X Q$ can refuse an event in $X \cup \Omega$ if either P or Q can, and it can refuse an event outside $X \cup \Omega$ only if both P and Q can refuse it. For a failure (s, Y) of P and a failure (t, Z) of Q, recall classical definition in CSP of the synchronized failure set:

$$(s, Y) \parallel_X (t, Z) = \{(u, Y \cup Z) \mid Y \setminus (X \cup \Omega) = Z \setminus (X \cup \Omega) \wedge u \in s \parallel_X t\} \qquad (4)$$

We need to adjust this definition for cCSP to take into account the following two different cases of synchronization on terminals.

1. If P or Q cannot perform a terminal after executing s or t, the composition cannot terminate. In this case Definition (4) applies. For example, let $\Sigma = \{a, b\}$, P be the process a and Q the process b; **throw**. As $(\langle \rangle, \{b, \checkmark, !, ?\})$ is a failure of P and $(\langle b \rangle, \{b, \checkmark, ?\})$ a failure of Q, $P \| Q$ has the failure $(\langle b \rangle, \{b, \checkmark, !, ?\})$. This case is reflected in the upper case in the definition Equation 5.
2. If both P and Q can terminate, the synchronized terminal, represented by $\ominus$ in the definition Equation 5, should be excluded from the refusal set. For example, let $\Sigma = \{a\}$, P be the process a and Q the process a; **throw**. As $(\langle a \rangle, \{a, !, ?\})$ is a failure of P and $(\langle a \rangle, \{a, \checkmark, ?\})$ a failure of Q, P can perform $\checkmark$ and Q can perform ! to terminate, respectively. Their synchronization result is !, which does not appear in the refusal set $(\langle a \rangle, \{a, \checkmark, ?\})$ of $P \parallel_{\{a\}} Q$. If Definition (4) were applied, the refusal set would be $(\langle a \rangle, \{a, \checkmark, ?, !\})$ and $P \parallel_{\{a\}} Q$ would deadlock after executing $\langle a \rangle$.

The synchronized failure set of two failures is thus defined as

$$
(s, Y) \underset{X}{\parallel} (t, Z) =
\begin{cases}
\{(u, Y \cup Z) \mid Y \setminus (X \cup \Omega) = Z \setminus (X \cup \Omega) \wedge u \in s \underset{X}{\parallel} t\} \\
\qquad \text{if } (s, Y \cup \Omega) \in \mathcal{F}(P) \vee (t, Z \cup \Omega) \in \mathcal{F}(Q) \\
\\
\{(u, (Y \cup Z) \setminus \Theta(\omega_1, \omega_2)) \mid Y \setminus (X \cup \Omega) = Z \setminus (X \cup \Omega) \wedge \\
\qquad\qquad u \in s \underset{X}{\parallel} t\} \quad \textbf{otherwise}
\end{cases}
\tag{5}
$$

Two variables ω_1 and ω_2 are used in Equation (5). For the failure (s, Y) of P, ω_1 is the terminal event that P *must* perform after s, which is when the following condition holds

$$
\forall (s, Y_1) \in \mathcal{F}(P) \bullet Y \subseteq Y_1 \Rightarrow (\omega_1 \in \Omega \wedge \omega_1 \notin Y_1)
\tag{6}
$$

The value of ω_1 is not defined, represented by $\perp$, if there is no terminal event that P must perform after s. The value of ω_2 is determined in the same way for the failure (t, Z) of Q. The function Θ that synchronizes ω_1 and ω_2 is defined as follows.

$$
\Theta(\omega_1, \omega_2) = \Theta(\omega_2, \omega_1) =
\begin{cases}
\{\omega_1 \| \omega_2\} & \omega_1 \in \Omega \wedge \omega_2 \in \Omega \\
\{\omega_1\} & \omega_1 \in \Omega \wedge \omega_2 = \perp \\
\{\} & \omega_1 = \perp \wedge \omega_2 = \perp
\end{cases}
$$

For example, consider P as the process **skip** $\sqcap$ **throw**. P has the failures $(\langle\rangle, \{\checkmark, ?\})$ and $(\langle\rangle, \{?, !\})$. There is no ω_1 satisfying the Equation (6) for the failure $(\langle\rangle, \{?\})$ of P.
Now the failure set of $P \underset{X}{\parallel} Q$ is defined below.

$$
\begin{aligned}
\mathcal{F}(P \underset{X}{\parallel} Q) = \quad & \{(u, E) \mid \exists (s, Y) \in \mathcal{F}(P), (t, Z) \in \mathcal{F}(Q) \bullet (u, E) \in (s, Y) \underset{X}{\parallel} (t, Z)\} \\
& \cup \{(u, Y) \mid u \in \mathcal{D}(P \underset{X}{\parallel} Q) \wedge Y \subseteq \Gamma\}
\end{aligned}
$$

Consider $a \underset{\{a\}}{\parallel} (a; \textbf{throw})$ as an example, and $\Sigma = \{a\}$. Its divergence set is $\{\}$, and its failure set is $\{(\langle\rangle, X) \mid X \subseteq \Omega\} \cup \{(\langle a \rangle, X) \mid X \subseteq \{a, \checkmark, ?\}\} \cup \{(\langle a, ! \rangle, X) \mid X \subseteq \Gamma\}$. Parallel composition is *commutative*, *associative* and *distributive* over internal choice.

Exception handling. $P \rhd Q$ behaves similarly to $P; Q$, but Q starts to execute only after an exception is thrown in P.

$$
\begin{aligned}
\mathcal{D}(P \rhd Q) = \quad & \mathcal{D}(P) \cup \{s \cdot t \mid s \cdot \langle ! \rangle \in traces(P) \wedge t \in \mathcal{D}(Q)\} \\
\mathcal{F}(P \rhd Q) = \quad & \{(s, X) \mid s \in \Sigma^{\circledast}_{\{\checkmark, ?\}} \wedge (s, X \cup \{!\}) \in \mathcal{F}(P)\} \\
& \cup \{(s \cdot t, X) \mid s \cdot \langle ! \rangle \in traces(P) \wedge (t, X) \in \mathcal{F}(Q)\} \cup \{(s, X) \mid s \in \mathcal{D}(P \rhd Q) \wedge X \subseteq \Gamma\}
\end{aligned}
$$

The exception handling is *associative* and *distributive* over internal choices to both left and right sides of $\rhd$. The hiding and renaming operators are not affected by the new terminals, and their definitions remain the same as those in the classical CSP.

4   Failure-Divergence Semantics of Compensable Processes

The semantics $[\![PP]\!]$ of a compensable process PP consists of its forward behavior and compensation behavior. It is thus defined as a tuple (F, D, F^c, D^c) of four sets. (F, D) are the *forward failures* and *forward divergences* (or forward FD sets), and (F^c, D^c)

the *compensation FD sets* of PP, where $F^c \subseteq \Sigma^\star \times \Sigma^\circledast \times \mathbb{P}(\Gamma)$ and $D^c \subseteq \Sigma^\star \times \Sigma^\circledast$ are called the *compensation failures* and *compensation divergences* of PP, respectively. The forward FD sets satisfy the axioms of the semantics of the standard processes given in Section 3.2. A compensation failure (s, s_1, X) and a compensation divergence (s, s_1) record a failure and a divergence of the compensation behavior for the forward execution trace s, respectively. We define the set of *the forward terminated traces* $trace_f(PP)=\{s \mid (s, s_1, X) \in F^c\}$ in F^c (also denoted by $trace_f(F^c)$), and the set $trace_n(PP) = trace_f(PP)\backslash D$ of the *non-divergent* forward terminated traces. The compensation behavior (F^c, D^c) is required to satisfy the following axioms.

$$trace_f(F^c) = \{s \mid (s, s_1) \in D^c\}, \quad trace_f(F^c) \subseteq \Sigma^\star \cap \{s \mid (s, \{\}) \in F\} \tag{7}$$

For an s in $trace_f(F^c)$, let $(F^c, D^c)|s = (\{(s_1, X) \mid (s, s_1, X) \in F^c\}, \{s_1 \mid (s, s_1) \in D^c\})$, which is a FD pair and required to satisfy the axioms of standard processes. For the semantics (F, D, F^c, D^c) of a PP, let $fp(PP)$ denote the *forward process behavior* (F, D), and $cp(PP, s)$ the *compensation behavior* $(F^c, D^c)|s$ for s. We will overload the semantic functions $\mathcal{F}$ and $\mathcal{D}$ and the process operators of standard processes and apply them to $fp(PP)$ and $cp(PP, s)$. For example, $\mathcal{F}(fp(PP)) = F$ and $\mathcal{D}(fp(PP)) = D$.

We are now to define the semantic function $\llbracket \cdot \rrbracket$ on the set $\mathcal{PP}$ of all the compensable processes in terms of four semantics functions $(\mathcal{F}_f, \mathcal{D}_f, \mathcal{F}_c, \mathcal{D}_c)$:

- the *forward failure* (FF) function $\mathcal{F}_f : \mathcal{PP} \to \mathbb{P}(\Sigma^\circledast \times \mathbb{P}(\Gamma))$,
- the *forward divergence* (DF) function $\mathcal{D}_f : \mathcal{PP} \to \mathbb{P}(\Sigma^\circledast)$,
- the *compensation failure* (FC) function $\mathcal{F}_c : \mathcal{PP} \to \mathbb{P}(\Sigma^\star \times \Sigma^\circledast \times \mathbb{P}(\Gamma))$, and
- the *compensation divergence* (DC) function $\mathcal{D}_c : \mathcal{PP} \to \mathbb{P}(\Sigma^\star \times \Sigma^\circledast)$.

Compensation pair $P \div Q$. If the forward behavior specified by P terminates successfully, the recovery behavior specified by Q is recorded so that it can be executed to compensate the effect of P when triggered by an exception later. Otherwise, Q will not be executed. In the semantics $P \div Q$, the successfully terminated forward behavior defined by the traces in $trace_t(P) \cap \Sigma^\star_{\{\checkmark\}}$ is to be compensated by the execution of Q, and the non-successful terminated traces in $\Sigma^\star_{\{!,?\}}$ by "nothing", *i.e.* skip, respectively.

$$\mathcal{F}_f(P \div Q) = \mathcal{F}(P), \quad \mathcal{D}_f(P \div Q) = \mathcal{D}(P)$$
$$\mathcal{F}_c(P \div Q) = ((trace_t(P) \cap \Sigma^\star_{\{\checkmark\}}) \times \mathcal{F}(Q)) \cup ((trace_t(P) \cap \Sigma^\star_{\{!,?\}}) \times \mathcal{F}(\text{skip}))$$
$$\mathcal{D}_c(P \div Q) = ((trace_t(P) \cap \Sigma^\star_{\{\checkmark\}}) \times \mathcal{D}(Q)) \cup ((trace_t(P) \cap \Sigma^\star_{\{!,?\}}) \times \mathcal{D}(\text{skip}))$$

The forward sub-processes of **skipp**, **throww** and **yieldd** are **skip**, **throw** and **yield**, respectively. Their compensation sub-processes are all **skip**. Because $trace_t(\text{stop})$ is empty, $\mathcal{F}_c(\text{stop} \div P)$ and $\mathcal{D}_c(\text{stop} \div P)$ are both empty for any P, we use **stopp** to denote any of these **stop** $\div P$ whose forward behavior is **stop**.

Transaction block. A transaction block $[PP]$ is a standard process, and its semantics is derived from the semantics of the compensable process PP in the block.

$$\mathcal{D}([PP]) = \quad \mathcal{D}_f(PP) \cup \{s_1 \cdot s_2 \mid (s, s_2) \in \mathcal{D}_c(PP) \wedge s = s_1 \cdot \langle ! \rangle\}$$
$$\mathcal{F}([PP]) = \quad \{(s, X) \mid s \in \Sigma^\circledast_{\{\checkmark, ?\}} \wedge (s, X \cup \{!\}) \in \mathcal{F}_f(PP)\}$$
$$\cup \{(s_1 \cdot s_2, X) \mid (s, s_2, X) \in \mathcal{F}_c(PP) \wedge s = s_1 \cdot \langle ! \rangle\} \cup \{(s, X) \mid s \in \mathcal{D}([PP]) \wedge X \subseteq \Gamma\}$$

The compensation of PP is executed to recover from an exception occurred in the forward behavior. The divergences of $[PP]$ contain the DF and DC sets of PP. The failures $\mathcal{F}([PP])$ contain (a). the failures in the FF set that do not terminate with the exception terminal, (b). the failures in the FF set that terminate with the exception terminal extended with their corresponding compensation failures, and (c). the failures caused by the divergences. In general $[P \div Q] = P \triangleright \mathbf{skip}$ holds and in particular, $[\mathbf{throw} \div P] = \mathbf{skip}$ and $[\mathbf{stopp}] = \mathbf{stop}$.

Internal choice. The semantics of internal choice $PP \sqcap QQ$ is as follows.

$$\mathcal{D}_f(PP \sqcap QQ) = \mathcal{D}_f(PP) \cup \mathcal{D}_f(QQ), \quad \mathcal{F}_f(PP \sqcap QQ) = \mathcal{F}_f(PP) \cup \mathcal{F}_f(QQ)$$
$$\mathcal{F}_c(PP \sqcap QQ) = \mathcal{F}_c(PP) \cup \mathcal{F}_c(QQ), \quad \mathcal{D}_c(PP \sqcap QQ) = \mathcal{D}_c(PP) \cup \mathcal{D}_c(QQ)$$

For example, $(a \div b_1 \sqcap a \div b_2) = (a \div (b_1 \sqcap b_2))$, whose FC set is $\{\langle b, \checkmark \rangle\} \times (\mathcal{F}(b_1) \cup \mathcal{F}(b_2))$, and the DC set is $\{\langle a, \checkmark \rangle\} \times (\mathcal{D}(b_1) \cup \mathcal{D}(b_2))$, i.e. $\{\}$. Internal choice is *idempotent, commutative* and *associative*.

External choice. The external choice is also made during the forward behavior, but by the environment.

$$\mathcal{D}_f(PP \square QQ) = \mathcal{D}(fp(PP) \square fp(QQ)), \quad \mathcal{F}_f(PP \square QQ) = \mathcal{F}(fp(PP) \square fp(QQ))$$
$$\mathcal{F}_c(PP \square QQ) = \mathcal{F}_c(PP) \cup \mathcal{F}_c(QQ), \quad \mathcal{D}_c(PP \square QQ) = \mathcal{D}_c(PP) \cup \mathcal{D}_c(QQ)$$

For example, $\mathcal{D}_c(\mathbf{stopp} \square a \div b) = \mathcal{D}_c(\mathbf{stopp} \sqcap a \div b) = \{\}$, and the equality still holds if $\mathcal{D}_c$ is replaced by $\mathcal{F}_c$. For the corresponding FF sets however, $\mathcal{F}_f(\mathbf{stopp} \square a \div b) = \mathcal{F}(a)$ but $\mathcal{F}_f(\mathbf{stopp} \sqcap a \div b) = \mathcal{F}(a) \cup \mathcal{F}(\mathbf{stop})$. $\square$ is *idempotent, commutative* and *associative*.

Sequential composition. In a sequential composition $PP;QQ$, the forward behaviors of PP and QQ are composed first, and the corresponding compensation behaviors $cp(PP, s_1)$ and $cp(QQ, s_2)$ are composed in the reverse direction, just like the model of Sagas [12]. The forward behavior of $PP;QQ$ is the sequential composition of the forward behaviors of PP and QQ.

$$\mathcal{D}_f(PP;QQ) = \mathcal{D}(fp(PP);fp(QQ)), \quad \mathcal{F}_f(PP;QQ) = \mathcal{F}(fp(PP);fp(QQ))$$

Let $\mathbb{T}_n$ be the set $trace_n(PP) \times trace_f(QQ)$. The compensation behavior of $PP;QQ$ is defined by the two cases below.

1. The forward execution of PP terminates successfully and the compensation behaviors of PP and QQ will be sequentially composed in the reverse order.

$$\mathcal{D}_c^1 = \{(s \cdot t, s_c) \mid \exists (s \cdot \langle \checkmark \rangle, t) \in \mathbb{T}_n \bullet s_c \in \mathcal{D}(cp(QQ, t); cp(PP, s \cdot \langle \checkmark \rangle))\}$$
$$\mathcal{F}_c^1 = \{(s \cdot t, s_c, X_c) \mid \exists (s \cdot \langle \checkmark \rangle, t) \in \mathbb{T}_n \bullet (s_c, X_c) \in \mathcal{F}(cp(QQ, t); cp(PP, s \cdot \langle \checkmark \rangle))\}$$

2. PP fails or diverges in the forward behavior, process cannot reach QQ, and only the compensation behavior of PP would be recorded.

$$\mathcal{D}_c^2 = \{(s, s_c) \mid (s, s_c) \in \mathcal{D}_c(PP) \wedge (s \neq t \cdot \langle \checkmark \rangle \vee s \notin trace_n(PP))\}$$
$$\mathcal{F}_c^2 = \{(s, s_c, X_c) \mid (s, s_c, X_c) \in \mathcal{F}_c(PP) \wedge (s \neq t \cdot \langle \checkmark \rangle \vee s \notin trace_n(PP))\}$$

Hence, the DC and FC sets of $PP;QQ$ are $\mathcal{D}_c(PP;QQ) = \mathcal{D}_c^1 \cup \mathcal{D}_c^2$ and $\mathcal{F}_c(PP;Qq) = \mathcal{F}_c^1 \cup \mathcal{F}_c^2$. Sequential composition is *associative* and *distributive* over internal choice.

Parallel composition. In a composition $PP \parallel_X QQ$, the forward behaviors of PP and QQ synchronize on X, so do their compensation behaviors.

$$\mathcal{D}_f(PP \parallel_X QQ) = \mathcal{D}(fp(PP) \parallel_X fp(QQ)), \quad \mathcal{F}_f(PP \parallel_X QQ) = \mathcal{F}(fp(PP) \parallel_X fp(QQ))$$
$$\mathcal{D}_c(PP \parallel_X QQ) = \{(s, s_c) \mid \exists s_1 \in trace_f(PP), s_2 \in trace_f(QQ)\bullet$$
$$s \in (s_1 \parallel_X s_2) \wedge s_c \in \mathcal{D}(cp(PP, s_1) \parallel_X cp(QQ, s_2))\}$$
$$\mathcal{F}_c(PP \parallel_X QQ) = \{(s, s_c, X) \mid \exists s_1 \in trace_f(PP), s_2 \in trace_f(QQ)\bullet$$
$$s \in (s_1 \parallel_X s_2) \wedge (s_c, X) \in \mathcal{F}(cp(PP, s_1) \parallel_X cp(QQ, s_2))\}$$

Consider two examples. First, the equation $[(a\div b_1 \parallel_{\{a\}} b\div b_2);\mathbf{throww}] = a;b_1 \parallel b_2$ shows the synchronization between the forward behaviors. Then, $a_1\div b_1 \parallel_{\{a_1, a_2\}} a_2\div b_2 = \mathbf{stopp}$ demonstrates a deadlock in the forward behavior.

Speculative Choice. In a speculative choice $PP \boxtimes QQ$, the forward behaviors of PP and QQ will run in parallel first without synchronization. If one succeeds, the compensation of the other will be invoked. The forward execution of $PP \boxtimes QQ$ fails if both parties fail, and the compensation behaviors of PP and QQ will run in parallel to recover. Let $\mathbb{T}$ be the set $trace_f(PP) \times trace_f(QQ)$, $\mathcal{D}_f^1$ (or $\mathcal{D}_f^2$) be the divergences in the case when the first party (or the second party, resp.) succeeds and the second party (or the first party, resp.) has to recover, where $\omega \in \Omega$:

$$\mathcal{D}_f^1 = \{s \mid \exists(t_1\cdot\langle\checkmark\rangle, t_2\cdot\langle\omega\rangle) \in \mathbb{T} \bullet s \in (t_1\|t_2)\cdot\mathcal{D}(cp(QQ, t_2\cdot\langle\omega\rangle))\}$$
$$\mathcal{D}_f^2 = \{s \mid \exists(t_1\cdot\langle\omega\rangle, t_2\cdot\langle\checkmark\rangle) \in \mathbb{T} \bullet s \in (t_1\|t_2)\cdot\mathcal{D}(cp(PP, t_1\cdot\langle\omega\rangle))\}$$

The DF set of $PP \boxtimes QQ$ is thus defined as $\mathcal{D}_f(PP \boxtimes QQ) = \mathcal{D}(PP_f \parallel QQ_f) \cup \mathcal{D}_f^1 \cup \mathcal{D}_f^2$.

Similarly, we define $\mathcal{F}_f^1$ (or $\mathcal{F}_f^2$) to be the failures when the second (or the first) party succeeds and the first (or the second) party has to recover:

$$\mathcal{F}_f^1 = \{(s\cdot t, X) \mid \exists(t_1\cdot\langle\checkmark\rangle, t_2\cdot\langle\omega\rangle) \in \mathbb{T} \bullet s \in (t_1\|t_2) \wedge (t, X) \in \mathcal{F}(cp(QQ, t_2\cdot\langle\omega\rangle))\}$$
$$\mathcal{F}_f^2 = \{(s\cdot t, X) \mid \exists(t_1\cdot\langle\omega\rangle, t_2\cdot\langle\checkmark\rangle) \in \mathbb{T} \bullet s \in (t_1\|t_2) \wedge (t, X) \in \mathcal{F}(cp(PP, t_1\cdot\langle\omega\rangle))\}$$

The FF set of $PP \boxtimes QQ$ is thus the union of the following five sets, where $\omega_1, \omega_2 \in \Omega \setminus \{\checkmark\}$.

$$\mathcal{F}_f(PP \boxtimes QQ) = \quad \{(s, X) \mid s \in \Sigma^* \wedge (s, X \cup \Omega) \in \mathcal{F}(PP_f \parallel QQ_f)\} \cup \mathcal{F}_f^1 \cup \mathcal{F}_f^2$$
$$\cup \{(s, X) \mid \exists(t_1\cdot\langle\omega_1\rangle, t_2\cdot\langle\omega_2\rangle) \in \mathbb{T}\bullet s \in (t_1\|t_2) \wedge X \subseteq \Gamma \setminus \{\omega_1\|\omega_2\}\}$$
$$\cup \{(s\cdot\langle\omega_1\|\omega_2\rangle, X) \mid \exists(t_1\cdot\langle\omega_1\rangle, t_2\cdot\langle\omega_2\rangle) \in \mathbb{T}\bullet s \in (t_1\|t_2) \wedge X \subseteq \Gamma\}$$

The first set includes the failures of the interleaving forward execution of PP and QQ, and the last two sets handle the synchronization of the terminals if both parties fail.

There are the following three cases when compensation of $PP \boxtimes QQ$ diverges.

1. PP succeeds in the forward parallel execution of PP and QQ, and the compensation to the effect of PP diverges.

$$\mathcal{D}_c^1 = \{(s, s_c) \mid \exists(t_1\cdot\langle\checkmark\rangle, t_2\cdot\langle\omega\rangle) \in \mathbb{T}\bullet s \in T_1 \wedge s_c \in \mathcal{D}(cp(PP, t_1\cdot\langle\checkmark\rangle))\}$$

where $T_1 = (t_1\|t_2)\cdot trace_t(cp(QQ, t_2\cdot\langle\omega\rangle))$. Notice that the overall compensation of PP by $PP \boxtimes QQ$ can only start after the effect of QQ is compensated.

2. Symmetrically, QQ succeeds in the forward parallel execution of PP and QQ, and the compensation to the effect of QQ diverges, where $T_2=(t_1\|t_2)\cdot trace_t(cp(PP,t_1\cdot\langle\omega\rangle))$.
$$\mathcal{D}_c^2 = \{(s,s_c)|\exists(t_1\cdot\langle\omega\rangle,t_2\cdot\langle\checkmark\rangle) \in \mathbb{T}\bullet s{\in}T_2{\wedge}s_c \in \mathcal{D}(cp(QQ,t_2\cdot\langle\checkmark\rangle))\}$$

3. Both parties of the parallel forward execution of PP and QQ fail to terminate successfully, and the parallel compensation of the parties diverges, where $\omega_1,\omega_2{\in}\Omega\backslash\{\checkmark\}$.
$$\mathcal{D}_c^3= \{(s,s_c)|\exists(t_1\cdot\langle\omega_1\rangle,t_2\cdot\langle\omega_2\rangle){\in}\mathbb{T}\bullet s{\in}(t_1\cdot\langle\omega_1\rangle\|t_2\cdot\langle\omega_2\rangle){\wedge}$$
$$s_c{\in}\mathcal{D}(cp(PP,t_1\cdot\langle\omega_1\rangle)\|cp(QQ,t_2\cdot\langle\omega_2\rangle)))\}$$

Therefore, the DC set of $PP \boxtimes QQ$ is defined as $\mathcal{D}_c(PP{\boxtimes}QQ){=}\mathcal{D}_c^1{\cup}\mathcal{D}_c^2{\cup}\mathcal{D}_c^3$. Similarly, $\mathcal{F}_c(PP{\boxtimes}QQ)$ is $\mathcal{F}_c^1{\cup}\mathcal{F}_c^2{\cup}\mathcal{F}_c^3$, where

$$\mathcal{F}_c^1 = \{(s,s_c,X)|\exists(t_1\cdot\langle\checkmark\rangle,t_2\cdot\langle\omega\rangle){\in}\mathbb{T}\bullet s{\in}T_1{\wedge}(s_c,X){\in}\mathcal{F}(cp(PP,t_1\cdot\langle\checkmark\rangle))\}$$
$$\mathcal{F}_c^2 = \{(s,s_c,X) \mid \exists(t_1\cdot\langle\omega\rangle,t_2\cdot\langle\checkmark\rangle) \in \mathbb{T} \bullet s \in T_2 \wedge (s_c,X) \in \mathcal{F}(cp(QQ,t_2\cdot\langle\checkmark\rangle))\}$$
$$\mathcal{F}_c^3 = \{(s,s_c,X) \mid \exists(t_1\cdot\langle\omega_1\rangle,t_2\cdot\langle\omega_2\rangle) \in \mathbb{T} \bullet s \in (t_1\cdot\langle\omega_1\rangle\|t_2\cdot\langle\omega_2\rangle){\wedge}$$
$$(s_c,X) \in \mathcal{F}(cp(PP,t_1\cdot\langle\omega_1\rangle) \| cp(QQ,t_2\cdot\langle\omega_2\rangle)))\}$$

Hiding and renaming. Hiding and renaming are defined in the standard way on the forward behavior and the compensation behavior, respectively.

$$\mathcal{D}_f(PP\backslash X) = \mathcal{D}(fp(PP)\backslash X), \quad \mathcal{F}_f(PP\backslash X) = \mathcal{F}(fp(PP)\backslash X)$$
$$\mathcal{D}_c(PP\backslash X) = \{(s,s_c)|\exists s_1{\in}trace_f(PP)\bullet s{=}s_1\backslash X{\wedge}s_c{\in}\mathcal{D}(cp(PP,s_1)\backslash X)\}$$
$$\mathcal{F}_c(PP\backslash X) = \{(s,s_c,X)|\exists s_1{\in}trace_f(PP)\bullet s{=}s_1\backslash X{\wedge}(s_c,X) \in \mathcal{F}(cp(PP,s_1)\backslash X)\}$$

Similarly, the semantics of renaming is as follows.

$$\mathcal{D}_f(PP[\![R]\!]) = \mathcal{D}(fp(PP)[\![R]\!]), \quad \mathcal{F}_f(PP[\![R]\!]){=}\mathcal{F}(fp(PP)[\![R]\!])$$
$$\mathcal{D}_c(PP[\![R]\!]) = \{(s,s_c)|\exists s_1{\in}trace_f(PP)\bullet s_1 \; R \; s{\wedge}s_c{\in}\mathcal{D}(cp(PP,s_1)[\![R]\!])\}$$
$$\mathcal{F}_c(PP[\![R]\!]) = \{(s,s_c,X)|\exists s_1{\in}trace_f(PP)\bullet s_1 \; R \; s{\wedge}(s_c,X){\in}\mathcal{F}(cp(PP,s_1)[\![R]\!])\}$$

Both hiding and renaming are distributive among internal choice. Not like renaming, hiding is not distributive among external choice. For example, the compensable process $((a;a_1){\div}b\Box(a;a_2){\div}b) \setminus \{a\}$ equals $a_1 \div b \sqcap a_2 \div b$.

5   Refinement Theory and Recursion Semantics

We define an order $\sqsubseteq$ on the semantic domain of the standard processes, and a partial order $\sqsubseteq_c$ on that of the compensable processes. Each of the domains with the respective order forms a CPO, and their corresponding process operators are monotonic and continuous. The two orders are linked by the transaction block constructor $[PP]$. These form the theoretical foundation for the fixed-point theories of recursive standard and compensable processes, and for the refinement calculus of cCSP. We refer the reader to the technical report [10] for the proofs of theorems and laws.

5.1   Refinement of Standard Processes

The order $(F_1, D_1) \sqsubseteq (F_2, D_2)$ holds for the two FD pairs if $F_1 \supseteq F_2$ and $D_1 \supseteq D_2$. The FD refinement of a standard process P_1 by a standard process P_2 is defined as

$$P_1 \sqsubseteq P_2 \; \widehat{=} \; \mathcal{F}(P_1) \supseteq \mathcal{F}(P_2) \wedge \mathcal{D}(P_1) \supseteq \mathcal{D}(P_2) \tag{8}$$

It means the refinement P_2 is neither more likely to refuse an interaction from the environment nor more likely to diverge than P_1.

Theorem 1. *The semantic domain of standard processes is a CPO under the refinement order $\sqsubseteq$, and **div** is the bottom (least) element. And the operators of standard processes are continuous w.r.t. $\sqsubseteq$.*

Recursive standard processes. If $\mu\,p.F(p)$ is a constructive standard process, its semantics is the *least fixed point* of the semantic function $[\![F]\!]$ of F. The semantics can be calculated, according to Theorem 1, as $\bigsqcup\{F^n(\mathbf{div}) \mid n \in \mathbb{N}\}$, where $F^0(\mathbf{div}) = \mathbf{div}$ and $F^{(n+1)}(\mathbf{div}) = F(F^n(\mathbf{div}))$, and $\bigsqcup S$ represents the least upper bound of the set S. For example, assume Σ is $\{a\}$, the failures $\mathcal{F}(\mu\,p.\,(a;p)) = \{(a^i, X) \mid i \in \mathbb{N} \wedge X \subseteq \Omega\}$, where $a^0 = \langle\rangle$ and $a^{i+1} = \langle a\rangle\cdot a^i$, and the divergences $\mathcal{D}(\mu\,p.\,(a;p)) = \{\}$.

5.2 Refinement Order of Compensable Processes

Given two tuples $PP_i = (F_i, D_i, F_i^c, D_i^c)$, $i \in \{1, 2\}$, of the semantic domain of compensable processes, we define the order

$$(F_1, D_1, F_1^c, D_1^c) \sqsubseteq_c (F_2, D_2, F_2^c, D_2^c) \stackrel{\wedge}{=} F_1 \supseteq F_2 \wedge D_1 \supseteq D_2 \wedge F_1^c \supseteq F_2^c \wedge D_1^c \supseteq D_2^c \qquad (9)$$

A compensable process PP_2 is a *FD-refinement* of PP_1, also denoted by $PP_1 \sqsubseteq_c PP_2$, if their semantics are related by the order $\sqsubseteq_c$.

Theorem 2. *The semantic domain of compensable processes is a CPO w.r.t. $\sqsubseteq_c$ and **div $\div$ div** is the bottom element. And the operators of compensable processes are continuous w.r.t. $\sqsubseteq_c$.*

Theorem 3. *The two refinement relations $\sqsubseteq_c$ and $\sqsubseteq$ are consistently related.*

1. *If $PP_1 \sqsubseteq_c PP_2$ then $[PP_1] \sqsubseteq [PP_2]$.*
2. *Refinement of compensable processes can be constructed from the refinement of forward or compensation processes.*

$$Q_1 \sqsubseteq Q_2 \Rightarrow P \div Q_1 \sqsubseteq_c P \div Q_2, \quad P_1 \sqsubseteq P_2 \Rightarrow P_1 \div Q \sqsubseteq_c P_2 \div Q$$

We thus can reduce refinement of compensable processes to that of standard processes.

Recursive compensable processes. Theorem 2 ensures the existence of the least fixed point of a recursive compensable process $\mu\,pp.FF(pp)$, which is calculated as follows: $\bigsqcup\{FF^n(\mathbf{div} \div \mathbf{div}) \mid n \in \mathbb{N}\}$. Consider $\mu\,pp.(a \div b\,;\,pp)$ for example. Its forward semantics is equal to the semantics of $\mu p.(a\,;\,p)$, and both the FC and DC sets are empty.

5.3 Laws of Long Running Transactions

The semantic theory provides the basis for proving fundamental laws of programming of long running transactions. Figure 2 gives some basic laws.

Compensation. The Saga nature of the backward recovery is reflected by the two laws below, where P, P_1 and P_2 are assumed not to terminate with an exception terminal.

$$[P \div Q;\mathbf{throww}] = P;Q, \quad [P_1 \div Q_1; P_2 \div Q_2;\mathbf{throww}] = P_1;P_2;Q_2;Q_1$$

Units and zeros

$\mathbf{skip};P = P,$ $P;\mathbf{skip} = P,$ $P \rhd \mathbf{throw} = P,$ $\mathbf{throw} \rhd P = P$

$\mathbf{skipp};PP = PP,$ $PP;\mathbf{skipp} = PP,$ $\mathbf{throw};P = \mathbf{throw},$ $\mathbf{throww};PP = \mathbf{throww}$

$\mathbf{skip} \rhd P = \mathbf{skip},$ $\mathbf{yield} \rhd P = \mathbf{yield},$ $\mathbf{stop} \rhd P = \mathbf{stop}$

Basic terminal processes

$\mathbf{skip} \square \mathbf{yield} = \mathbf{yield},$ $\mathbf{skip} \square \mathbf{throw} = \mathbf{skip} \sqcap \mathbf{throw},$ $\mathbf{yield} \square \mathbf{throw} = \mathbf{yield} \sqcap \mathbf{throw}$

$\mathbf{yield} \parallel_X \mathbf{skip} = \mathbf{yield},$ $\mathbf{throw} \parallel_X \mathbf{skip} = \mathbf{throw},$ $\mathbf{throw} \parallel_X \mathbf{yield} = \mathbf{throw}$

Distribution laws

$[PP \sqcap QQ]=[PP] \sqcap [QQ],$ $[PP \square QQ]=[PP] \square [QQ],$ $P \div (Q \sqcap R)=P \div Q \sqcap P \div R$

$(P \sqcap Q) \div R=(P \div R) \sqcap (Q \div R),$ $(P \div Q) \backslash X=(P \backslash X \div Q \backslash X),$ $[PP \backslash X]=[PP] \backslash X$

Fig. 2. Basic laws of long running transactions

Furthermore, the parallel composition enjoys the following laws.

$$[(P \div Q) \| \mathbf{throww}] = P;Q, \quad P_1 \div Q_1 \parallel_X P_2 \div Q_2 = (P_1 \parallel_X P_2) \div (Q_1 \parallel_X Q_2)$$

where $P, Q, P_i, Q_i, i \in \{1,2\}$, do not diverge and terminate successfully, and with the same assumption, the following two laws hold.

$$[(P_1 \div Q_1;P_2 \div Q_2) \| \mathbf{throww}] = P_1;P_2;Q_2;Q_1$$
$$[(P_1 \div Q_1 \parallel_X P_2 \div Q_2);\mathbf{throww}] = (P_1 \parallel_X P_2);(Q_1 \parallel_X Q_2)$$

For P_1, P_2, Q_1, Q_2 that do not diverge and terminate successfully, the speculative choice non-deterministically chooses one side to compensate if both succeed, which is

$$[(P_1 \div Q_1 \boxtimes P_2 \div Q_2);\mathbf{throww}] = (P_1 \| P_2);((Q_1;Q_2) \sqcap (Q_2;Q_1))$$

Interruption. In a composition of standard processes, the interruption of one process by the other does not have priority over other events. That is, if P does not non-divergently terminate in an yield terminal, *i.e.* $trace_t(P) \cap \Sigma^{\star}_{\{?\}}=\{\}$, we have

$$\mathbf{throw} \| (\mathbf{yield};P) = \mathbf{throw} \sqcap (P;\mathbf{throw})$$

A compensable process can be interrupted by **yieldd** to yield to an interruption from the environment, but a compensable process will not be interrupted if no **yieldd** is used (cf. the laws of **Compensation**). We thus have the following two laws, in which all the standard processes will not diverge and are assumed to terminate successfully.

$$[(\mathbf{yieldd};P_1 \div Q_1;\mathbf{yieldd};P_2 \div Q_2) \| \mathbf{throww}] = \mathbf{skip} \sqcap (P_1;Q_1) \sqcap (P_1;P_2;Q_2;Q_1)$$
$$[(\mathbf{yieldd};P_1 \div Q_1) \| (\mathbf{yieldd};P_2 \div Q_2) \| \mathbf{throww}] = \mathbf{skip} \sqcap (P_1;Q_1) \sqcap (P_2;Q_2) \sqcap$$
$$((P_1 \| P_2);(Q_1 \| Q_2))$$

6 Case study

An Online Travel Agency provides Web Services for booking air tickets, reserving hotel rooms and renting cars. It interacts with business partners including Travelers, Airlines, Hotels, Car Rental Centers and Banks. The business processes are described below.

A traveler makes a request to the Agency for arranging a travel. After receiving the request, the Agency processes it and then starts the air ticket booking, hotel reservation and car rental processes in parallel. Assume the Agency interacts with two airlines to get air tickets. If tickets are available from both airlines, the Agency non-deterministically chooses one. However, it is often that the Agency has to repeatedly request for the car rental service from the center at the destination before a car is available. If all the three processes succeed the Agency sends the booking information to the traveler and waits for her confirmation. After receiving the confirmation, the Agency makes a request to the bank, according to the information given by the traveler, for the payment service. If this is successful, the Agency sends the completed booking to the traveler, including the reservation details. If an exception occurs in any of the above steps, the whole business process will be recovered by compensating the steps that have been carried successfully, *e.g.* canceling the air tickets, room reservations or car rentals, and the Agency sends a letter to the traveler for an apology. The alphabet Σ of the processes is

$$
\begin{aligned}
\Sigma = \{ & \text{reqTravel, letter, reqHotel, okRoom, noRoom,} \\
& \text{cancelHotel, bookAir1, okAir1, noAir1, cancelAir1,} \\
& \text{bookAir2, okAir2, noAir2, cancelAir2, reqCar, noCar,} \\
& \text{hasCar, cancelCar, confirm, agree, disAgree, checkCredit,} \\
& \text{valid, inValid, payment, refund, pValid, pInValid, result} \}
\end{aligned}
$$

The processes Agency, Air1, Air2, Car, Hotel and Bank are as follows.

```
Agency = (reqTravel ÷ letter);Res;
           (confirm;(agree □ (disAgree;throw))) ÷ skip;
           (checkCredit;(valid □ (inValid;throw))) ÷ skip;
           (payment ÷ refund);(pValid □ (pInValid;throw)) ÷ skip;
           result ÷ skip
Res     = (reqHotel;(okRoom□(noRoom;throw)))÷cancelHotel‖
           ((yieldd;(bookAir1;(okAir1□(noAir1;throw)))÷cancelAir1)⊠
           (yieldd;(bookAir2;(okAir2□(noAir2;throw)))÷cancelAir2))‖
           μ pp.(reqCar÷skip;((noCar÷skip);pp)□(hasCar÷cancelCar)))
Hotel   = reqHotel÷skip;(okRoom÷cancelHotel⊓(noRoom÷skip;throww))
Air1    = bookAir1÷skip;(okAir1÷cancelAir1⊓(noAir1÷skip;throww))
Air2    = bookAir2÷skip;(okAir2÷cancelAir2⊓(noAir2÷skip;throww))
Car     = μ pp.(reqCar ÷ skip;((noCar÷skip);pp)⊓(hasCar÷cancelCar)))
Bank    = (checkCredit;(valid ⊓ (inValid;throw))) ÷ skip ;
           (payment÷refund);(pValid⊓(pInValid;throw))÷skip
```

The global business process (GBP) is the transaction block of the synchronized parallel composition of the above five processes.

$$
\text{GBP} = [(((((\text{Agency} \parallel_{X_1} \text{Hotel}) \parallel_{X_2} \text{Air1}) \parallel_{X_3} \text{Air2}) \parallel_{X_4} \text{Car}) \parallel_{X_5} \text{Bank})], \quad \text{where}
$$

$$
\begin{aligned}
X_1 &= \{\text{reqHotel, okRoom, noRoom, cancelHotel}\} \\
X_2 &= \{\text{bookAir1, okAir1, noAir1, cancelAir1}\} \\
X_3 &= \{\text{bookAir2, okAir2, noAir2, cancelAir2}\} \\
X_4 &= \{\text{reqCar, noCar, hasCar, cancelCar}\} \\
X_5 &= \{\text{checkCredit, valid, inValid, payment, refund, pValid, pInValid}\}
\end{aligned}
$$

Use of laws. GBP is a complex process. We thus hide some events in the forward behavior to get an abstract view, denoted by ABP $\hat{=}$ GBP $\setminus X$, where

$X = (X_1 \cup X_2 \cup X_3 \cup X_4 \cup X_5 \cup Y) \setminus Z$, where
$Y = \{\texttt{confirm}, \texttt{agree}, \texttt{disAgree}, \texttt{result}\}$
$Z = \{\texttt{noCar}, \texttt{payment}, \texttt{refund}, \texttt{cancelHotel}, \texttt{cancelAir1},$
      $\texttt{cancelAir2}, \texttt{cancelCar}\}$

By the laws, we can transform the process ABP to the equivalent process ABP1 below.

```
ABP1      = reqTravel ÷ letter;Cancel;PayRefund
Cancel    = CH ‖ CA ‖ CC
CH        = (throw ⊓ skip) ÷ cancelHotel
CA        = CA1 ⊠ CA2
CA1       = yieldd;((throw ⊓ skip) ÷ cancelAir1)
CA2       = yieldd;((throw ⊓ skip) ÷ cancelAir2)
CC        = μ pp. ((noCar ÷ skip;pp) ⊓ (skip ÷ cancelCar))
PayRefund = (throww ⊓ skipp);payment ÷ refund;(throww ⊓ skipp)
```

Analysis. The formal theory, including the formal semantics and laws, can be used for rigorous analysis of progress GBP. For example, we can show the following results.

- GBP does not deadlock, may diverge if the car rental service cannot provide a car for the Agency. In that case events reqCar and noCar will be performed for an infinite number of times and they are in set X_4 of synchronized events.
- There are *five* different cases when an exception is raised: 1). no ticket from the airlines, 2). no room in the hotel, 3). the traveler refuses the offer, 4). credit card checking fails, and 5). authorization of payment fails. In any case, there are different cases for recovery because of the parallel composition in the reservation process.
- When there is no divergence but an exception, the compensation in GBP is
  ```
  refund ⊓ skip;
  (cancelAir1⊓cancelAir2⊓skip)‖(cancelHotel⊓skip)‖cancelCar;
  letter
  ```
  Therefore, event letter is the last action to be performed in the compensation when an exception occurs. When an exception is raised after the air ticket booking, *e.g.* when the traveler sends her disagreement, either cancelAir1 or cancelAir2 may be performed. The ticket booking can also be interrupted by an exception outside the airlines, Air1 and Air2, *e.g.* when no room is available in the hotel.

7   Conclusion

The full theory of CSP [17] is extended for specification and verification of LRTs. The extended theory of compensating CSP supports non-deterministic choice, parallel composition with synchronization and recursion. It allows us to handle problems of deadlock, livelock and nested LRTs. Its FD semantic theory also supports LRT program design by refinement, and transformations of specifications through algebraic laws.

The theory contributes to improving fundamental understanding of LRTs, and to underpinning the development of valid tool support to design and verification of LRTs.

From the way that the theory is developed, it is feasible to extend FDR to support our extended theory of cCSP. In addition, automated reasoning about LRTs can be developed based on our theory by following the ideas in the prototype theorem prover in [16]. Tool development along these two directions is part of our future research agenda.

Acknowledgement. We thank the referees for their valuable comments; our colleagues C. Bertolini, L. Chen, A.P. Ravn and H. Wang for the discussions and comments. The 2nd author acknowledges the support of NSFC 61073022 to his visit to Miaomiao Zhang at Tongji University in November 2010 when part of the research was done.

References

1. Bocchi, L., Laneve, C., Zavattaro, G.: A calculus for long-running transactions. In: Najm, E., Nestmann, U., Stevens, P. (eds.) FMOODS 2003. LNCS, vol. 2884, pp. 124–138. Springer, Heidelberg (2003)
2. Bruni, R., Butler, M.J., Ferreira, C., Hoare, C.A.R., Melgratti, H.C., Montanari, U.: Comparing two approaches to compensable flow composition. In: Abadi, M., de Alfaro, L. (eds.) CONCUR 2005. LNCS, vol. 3653, pp. 383–397. Springer, Heidelberg (2005)
3. Bruni, R., Melgratti, H.C., Montanari, U.: Theoretical foundations for compensations in flow composition languages. In: Proc. POPL 2005, pp. 209–220. ACM Press, New York (2005)
4. Butler, M.J., Ferreira, C.: An operational semantics for StAC, a language for modelling long-running business transactions. In: De Nicola, R., Ferrari, G.-L., Meredith, G. (eds.) COORDINATION 2004. LNCS, vol. 2949, pp. 87–104. Springer, Heidelberg (2004)
5. Butler, M.J., Ferreira, C., Ng, M.Y.: Precise modelling of compensating business transactions and its application to BPEL. J. UCS 11(5), 712–743 (2005)
6. Butler, M.J., Hoare, C.A.R., Ferreira, C.: A trace semantics for long-running transactions. In: Abdallah, A.E., Jones, C.B., Sanders, J.W. (eds.) Communicating Sequential Processes. LNCS, vol. 3525, pp. 133–150. Springer, Heidelberg (2005)
7. Butler, M., Ripon, S.: Executable semantics for compensating CSP. In: Bravetti, M., Kloul, L., Tennenholtz, M. (eds.) EPEW/WS-EM 2005. LNCS, vol. 3670, pp. 243–256. Springer, Heidelberg (2005)
8. Castagna, G., Gesbert, N., Padovani, L.: A theory of contracts for web services. In: Necula, G.C., Wadler, P. (eds.) POPL, pp. 261–272. ACM, New York (2008)
9. Chen, Z., Liu, Z.: An Extended cCSP with Stable Failures Semantics. In: Cavalcanti, A., Deharbe, D., Gaudel, M.-C., Woodcock, J. (eds.) ICTAC 2010. LNCS, vol. 6255, pp. 121–136. Springer, Heidelberg (2010)
10. Chen, Z., Liu, Z., Wang, J.: A theory of failure-divergence refinement for long running transactions. Technical Report 447, UNU-IIST (2011), http://www.iist.unu.edu/www/docs/techreports/reports/report447.pdf
11. Fischer, J., Majumdar, R.: Ensuring consistency in long running transactions. In: Proc. ASE 2007, pp. 54–63. ACM, New York (2007)
12. Garcia-Molina, H., Salem, K.: SAGAS. In: Proc. SIGMOD 1987, pp. 249–259. ACM Press, New York (1987)
13. Gray, J., Reuter, A.: Transaction Processing: Concepts and Techniques. Morgan Kaufmann, San Francisco (1993)
14. Little, M.C.: Transactions and web services. Commun. ACM 46(10), 49–54 (2003)

15. Microsoft. Biztalk server, http://www.microsoft.com/biztalk/default.asp
16. Ripon, S., Butler, M.J.: PVS embedding of cCSP semantic models and their relationship. Electr. Notes Theor. Comput. Sci. 250(2), 103–118 (2009)
17. Roscoe, A.W.: The Theory and Practice of Concurrency. Prentice Hall PTR, Upper Saddle River (1997)
18. Roscoe, A.W.: The three platonic models of divergence-strict CSP. In: Fitzgerald, J.S., Haxthausen, A.E., Yenigun, H. (eds.) ICTAC 2008. LNCS, vol. 5160, pp. 23–49. Springer, Heidelberg (2008)

Termination without ✓ in CSP

Steve Dunne

School of Computing
University of Teesside, Middlesbrough, TS1 3BA, UK
s.e.dunne@tees.ac.uk

Abstract. We recast each of the three standard denotational models of
CSP, namely Traces, Stable Failures and Failures-Divergences, by replacing the ✓ pseudo-event in each of them by an explicit representation of
the termination traces of a process. The resulting recast models have
simpler axiomatisations than their respective original counterparts and
admit formulations of the compositional semantics of the basic processes
and operators of CSP which are arguably clearer and therefore more intuitively appealing than those in the original models. Furthermore, the
recast models facilitate the resolution of certain longstanding problematic issues, such as the offering of termination in an external choice alongside other behaviours, without resort to any incongruous special-casing
which might compromise their regularity.

1   Introduction

Communicating Sequential Processes or CSP [5,11] is a well-known process algebra typifying the *event-based* approach to concurrency, in which a process is
characterised entirely by its externally observable possible patterns of interaction with its environment via shared primitive events drawn from a specified
alphabet of possible such events. The concurrent and reactive aspects of CSP
are by now surely widely appreciated, and yet –ironically, despite its name– the
sequential aspect of CSP is probably still less generally understood. Perhaps this
isn't surprising given that introductory presentations of CSP tend to defer any
consideration of successful process termination and the sequential composition
of processes to a point where when these topics are finally touched on they come
across as something of an afterthought.

In this paper we attempt to redress the balance somewhat by focusing almost
entirely on the subject of termination of CSP processes. Our aim is to dispense altogether with the problematic pseudo-event ✓ (pronounced "tick" or "success")
which has traditionally been incorporated into the semantics of CSP to signify
the termination of processes and define their sequentially composed behaviour.
To this end we will recast each of the three standard denotational models of
CSP, namely the Traces, Stable Failures and Failures-Divergences models, by replacing the ✓ pseudo-event in each of them by an explicit representation of the
termination traces of a process. We will show how the resulting recast models
all have simpler axiomatisations than their respective original counterparts and

M. Butler and W. Schulte (Eds.): FM 2011, LNCS 6664, pp. 278–292, 2011.

admit formulations of the compositional semantics of the basic processes and operators of CSP which are arguably clearer and therefore more intuitively appealing than their corresponding formulations in the original models. Furthermore the recast models provide an appropriate context in which certain longstanding problematic issues, such as the offering of termination in an external choice alongside other behaviours, are naturally resolved without the need to resort to incongruous special-casing which compromises the regularity of the model.

At the same time we will construct isomorphisms –that is, order-preserving bijections– between each new model and its standard counterpart. These ensure that the new models have precisely the same interpretive power as their standard counterparts in giving meanings to the valid process expressions of the CSP language.

The event alphabet.   To simplify our presentation we will assume that all the CSP processses we encounter share the same event alphabet Σ unless explicitly stated otherwise. We denote the set of all finite traces of events in Σ by Σ^* and infinite traces by Σ^ω. We will use $\Sigma^\checkmark$ as an abbreviation for $\Sigma \cup \{\checkmark\}$. Likewise, we will use $\Sigma^{*\checkmark}$ as an abbreviation for $\Sigma^* \cup \{s \frown \langle\checkmark\rangle \mid s \in \Sigma^*\}$: that is, the set of finite traces Σ^* of regular events together with the further traces obtained by appending $\checkmark$ to each of them.

Compositions of traces.   If s and t are traces in Σ^* then $s \mathbin{|||} t$ denotes the set of all interleavings of s and t. Also, given a subset $X \subseteq \Sigma$ of regular events then $s \mathbin{\underset{X}{\|}} t$ is the *interface parallel composition* of s and t over X: that is, the set of modified interleavings of s and t after synchronisation on the (shared) events of X. Indeed $s \mathbin{|||} t$ is equivalent to the empty-interface parallel composition $s \mathbin{\underset{\{\}}{\|}} t$. Formal definitions of these trace operators can be found in [11, chap. 2].[1]

2   A Selective Overview of CSP

We assume that the reader is already acquainted with CSP as a specification language for concurrent communicating processes, so in this section we will merely air some of our operational intuitions about CSP processes and briefly review the standard denotational models of CSP. We hope this may be helpful in giving some intuitive insight into the effectiveness of the recast denotational models that we shall later present.

2.1   Deadlock, Divergence and Termination

From an operational perspective it is quite possible for a CSP process to be immortal in the sense that it carries on interacting with its environment for ever by successively engaging in and/or refusing the communication events which

---

[1] Note that for us these trace operators need no modification as given in [11, chap. 6] to accommodate $\checkmark$, since the traces we will compose are always $\checkmark$-free.

that environment offers, albeit that such everlasting interactions of a process might well dwindle in some cases to the living death of *deadlock* in which the process thereafter consistently refuses to engage in any event whatsoever. The significant point here, though, is that even a deadlocked process continues to exist despite its moribund condition.

On the other hand, it is also quite possible for a CSP process to suffer a genuine demise and thereby altogether cease to exist. This can occur in two ways: a process may *diverge* or it may *successfully terminate*. Divergence is irrecoverable in the sense that if it occurs it will fatally infect any larger system of which the divergent process is part. In contrast, successful termination is benign in that a terminating process thereby passes the processing baton to its sequential successor within the larger system of which both processes form part.

2.2   The Standard CSP Semantic Models $\mathcal{T}$, $\mathcal{F}$ and $\mathcal{N}$

The three most prominent semantic models in the CSP literature are the Traces model $\mathcal{T}$, the Stable-Failures model $\mathcal{F}$ and the Failures-Divergences model $\mathcal{N}$ [11]. Each of these induces its own particular congruence over process terms of the CSP language, a congruence being an equivalence relation which is compositional with respect to the language operators. Each of these congruences is fully abstract with respect to some characteristic simple but significant operational test which usefully distinguishes processes in some way.

– **Traces** ($\mathcal{T}$). In this model each process P is denoted simply by its set traces(P) of finite traces of events in which it may engage. This model completely ignores divergence, so much so that it equates the immediately divergent process DIV with the immediately deadlocking process STOP. It is adequate for reasoning about safety, *i.e.* whether any given event *can* occur, but not liveness, *i.e.* in what circumstances any given event *must* occur.

– **Stable Failures** ($\mathcal{F}$). In this model each process P is characterised by its finite traces traces(P) and its stable failures, failures(P). It is theoretically and practically significant as the weakest congruence which preserves deadlock [13]. This model also largely ignores divergence, although the presence of the latter can sometimes be inferred from the lack of any stable failure associated with a particular trace of the process. For example, in this model we can distinguish between STOP and DIV since although these have the same traces, they have different stable-failure relations.

– **Failures-Divergences** ($\mathcal{N}$). In this model each finitely nondeterministic process P is characterised by its divergences-augmented failures relation failures$_\perp$(P), and its extension-closed set of divergences divergences(P). $\mathcal{N}$ is the *de facto* standard semantic model for finitely nondeterministic CSP. It takes a drastic view of divergence which regards a process as utterly unpredictable, and therefore capable of any other behaviour whatsoever, once divergence becomes a possibility. Thus $\mathcal{N}$ interprets DIV as the least deterministic of all processes, immediately capable of any behaviour whatsoever.

2.3 Infinite Traces

As has just been noted, the model $\mathcal{N}$ can only satisfactorily distinguish between (at most)-finitely nondeterministic CSP processes. If unboundedly nondeterministic processes are admitted into consideration then in order to satisfactorily distinguish between these $\mathcal{N}$ has to be extended by introducing a further component comprising the infinite traces of each process. Of course, a CSP process doesn't have to be unboundedly nondeterministic in order to possess infinite traces, but the infinite traces of an at-most finitely nondeterministic CSP process can always be inferred from its finite ones, so don't have to be explicitly represented in a model which confines its attention to such processes. Since the infinite traces of a process are *ipso facto* irrelevant in regard to its terminating behaviour, we do not consider them any further in this paper.

2.4 Process Refinement

In each of the models $\mathcal{T}$, $\mathcal{F}$ and $\mathcal{N}$ the refinement relation between processes is modelled by reverse containment of the corresponding components of their denotations in that model. For example, a process P is refined in $\mathcal{F}$ by a process Q, written formally as $P \sqsubseteq_{\mathcal{F}} Q$, if and only if $\mathsf{traces}(Q) \subseteq \mathsf{traces}(P)$ and $\mathsf{failures}(Q) \subseteq \mathsf{failures}(P)$.

The refinement relations of $\mathcal{T}$ and $\mathcal{F}$ make these models complete lattices, which allows us to give a recursive CSP process expression a greatest-fixed-point semantics in each of them. On the other hand $\mathcal{N}$'s refinement relation only induces a complete partial order (cpo) on processes, which obliges us to interpret a recursive CSP process expression in $\mathcal{N}$ as a least fixed point.

2.5 Denoting Termination

In all three models $\mathcal{T}$, $\mathcal{F}$ and $\mathcal{N}$ the successful termination of a process is represented by the special signal event ✓, pronounced "tick" or "success", by which the process communicates to its environment that it has just terminated, the ✓ being duly appended to the trace of events in which the process has engaged. The problem here is that ✓ is quite different from all the other events in the alphabet of a process.

For example, unlike those other events it is not really a mutual interaction between the process and its environment since it doesn't require the active co-operation of the environment for it to occur. Nor does it seem to be meaningful for a process to offer its environment a choice between ✓ and any given ordinary event of its alphabet, or for ✓ to occur other than as the last event in a trace. This has the unfortunate effect of considerably complicating the axiomatisations of the three models with the need for special axioms constraining the role of ✓ in those models. It similarly complicates the semantics in each of the models of many of the CSP operators. A number of the problems associated with the existing treatment of termination in the **Failures-Divergences** semantic model of CSP are identified in detail by Howells and d'Inverno [7].

Intriguingly, Roscoe does mention in a footnote in [11, p144] the possibility of including the termination traces as a separate component of the representation of a process in $\mathcal{N}$, although he seems to suggest this not as an alternative to the use of $\checkmark$ in the model, but rather as a way of augmenting $\checkmark$ so as to avoid the need to record refusals once a process has communicated a $\checkmark$. Roscoe's remark is nevertheless noted by Josephs [8], who incorporates "success traces" in his Traces/Successes model for dataflow sequential processes in order to facilitate his definition of sequential composition of such processes. He is obliged to do so because, as he explains, the standard CSP approach of modelling termination by the special event $\checkmark$ would not work for his Data-Flow Sequential Processes.

3   Recasting the Denotational Models of CSP

In this section and the two succeeding ones we take the three standard denotational models of CSP and recast each of them in turn by eliminating the problematic special signal event $\checkmark$ in favour of an explicit representation of the terminating traces of each process. Our aim in doing so is not to enhance the expressive power of any of these three models, but rather simply to clarify their respective existing expressive capabilities. To distinguish them from their standard counterparts $\mathcal{T}$, $\mathcal{F}$ and $\mathcal{N}$ we will refer to the recast models respectively as $\mathcal{T}_m$, $\mathcal{F}_m$ and $\mathcal{N}_m$, the subscript m in each case signifying that termination traces are denoted explicitly therein.

3.1   The Model $\mathcal{T}_m$

In the recast Traces model $\mathcal{T}_m$ each process P is represented by the pair

$$(\text{trs}\,(P), \text{tms}\,(P))$$

where $\text{trs}\,(P) \subseteq \Sigma^*$ and $\text{tms}\,(P) \subseteq \Sigma^*$. Here $\text{trs}\,(P)$ is the set of all possible traces of regular events in which P may engage, while $\text{tms}\,(P)$ is the set of termination traces of P: that is, the (possibly empty) subset of $\text{trs}\,(P)$ comprising just those traces after engaging in any of which P may then immediately terminate.

The components $\text{trs}\,(P)$ and $\text{tms}\,(P)$ must satisfy the following two axioms:

- T1. $\text{trs}\,(P)$ is non-empty and prefix-closed.
- T2. $\text{tms}\,(P) \subseteq \text{trs}\,(P)$.

Since our next semantic model $\mathcal{F}_m$ is a refinement of $\mathcal{T}_m$, we postpone consideration of how to calculate the $\mathcal{T}_m$ semantics of individual CSP process expressions until section 4.2.

3.2   The Isomorphism between $\mathcal{T}_m$ and $\mathcal{T}$

Given the denotation of a process P in $\mathcal{T}_m$ we can extract its denotation in $\mathcal{T}$ as follows:

$$\text{traces}(P) \quad = \quad \text{trs}\,(P) \,\cup\, \{\, s \,^\frown \langle \checkmark \rangle \mid s \in \text{tms}\,(P) \}.$$

Conversely, given its denotation in $\mathcal{T}$ we can extract the denotation of P in $\mathcal{T}_m$ as follows:

$$\mathsf{trs}(P) \;=\; \mathsf{traces}(P) \cap \Sigma^*$$

$$\mathsf{tms}(P) \;=\; \{\, s \mid s ^\frown \langle\checkmark\rangle \in \mathsf{traces}(P)\,\}.$$

3.3 Persistent Failures *versus* Stable Failures

In order to obtain apropriate intuitive operational insights into our next recast models $\mathcal{F}_m$ and $\mathcal{N}_m$, it is first necessary to introduce the concept of a *persistent failure* which we will now describe.

From the operational viewpoint, an internal transition can cause a CSP process unilaterally to withdraw an offer to engage in some specific event. A CSP process is said to be *stable* if it is in a state where it can make no internal progress via any internal transition. [12, p174]. Thus, there is no danger of a stable process withdrawing an offer previously made to engage in an event owing to an internal transition. By extension, a stable failure of a CSP process is an observation of the form $s \mapsto X$, where $s \in \Sigma^{*\checkmark}$ and $X \subseteq \Sigma^\checkmark$, denoting that the process has been observed to engage in the trace of events s and thereby reach a stable state in which it refused all the events in X. Unfortunately, this intuitively reassuring notion of stability is compromised by the possibility of termination, which is associated in the standard CSP semantic models $\mathcal{T}$, $\mathcal{F}$ and $\mathcal{N}$ with the occurrence of the pseudo-event $\checkmark$ rather than an internal transition. This means that a nominally stable process which can terminate immediately may effectively withdraw an offer to engage in some specified event simply by unilaterally electing to terminate instead.

The problem is addressed in both $\mathcal{F}$ and $\mathcal{N}$ by the rather heavy-handed resort of allowing a process to refuse any set of regular events of its alphabet whenever it is immediately capable of terminating. Unfortunately, this really only exchanges one problem for another, since such artificially contrived refusals are not actually detectable by the process's environment, in the sense that the environment cannot thereby inhibit the process's further progress as it can with a normal refusal.

We provide a surer solution to the problem by replacing the notion of a stable state by the stronger one of a *persistent* state. A CSP process is said to be in a *persistent* state if it can neither make internal progress via any internal transition nor terminate. The only way, therefore, that a process can escape from a persistent state is by engaging in one of the regular events of its alphabet, which of course requires the co-operation of its environment. The notion of a persistent state leads on naturally to that of a persistent failure. A *persistent failure* of a CSP process is an observation of the form $s \mapsto X$, where $s \in \Sigma^*$ and $X \subseteq \Sigma$, denoting that the process has been observed to engage in the trace of events s and thereby reach a persistent state in which it is refusing all the events in X offered by the environment. The significant point here is that once such a state is reached it must persist as long as the environment dictates, because the process cannot extricate itself unilaterally by terminating.

4   The Model $\mathcal{F}_m$

In the recast Stable Failures model $\mathcal{F}_m{}^2$ each CSP process P is represented by the triple

$$(\mathsf{trs}\,(P), \mathsf{tms}\,(P), \mathsf{fails}\,(P))$$

where $\mathsf{trs}\,(P) \subseteq \Sigma^*$, $\mathsf{tms}\,(P) \subseteq \Sigma^*$ and $\mathsf{fails}\,(P) \subseteq \Sigma^* \times \mathbb{P}\,\Sigma$. Here $\mathsf{trs}\,(P)$ and $\mathsf{tms}\,(P)$ are the same as in $\mathcal{T}_m$, while $\mathsf{fails}\,(P)$ is P's persistent-failures relation.

The components $\mathsf{trs}\,(P)$, $\mathsf{tms}\,(P)$ and $\mathsf{fails}\,(P)$ must satisfy axioms T1 and T2 as for $\mathcal{T}_m$, plus the following three axioms:

- PF1. $\mathrm{dom}(\mathsf{fails}\,(P)) \subseteq \mathsf{trs}\,(P)$.
- PF2. $s \mapsto X \in \mathsf{fails}\,(P) \ \wedge\ Y \subseteq X \ \Rightarrow\ s \mapsto Y \in \mathsf{fails}\,(P)$.
- PF3. $s \mapsto X \in \mathsf{fails}\,(P) \ \wedge\ Y \subseteq \Sigma \ \wedge\ (\forall\, a \mid a \in Y \,.\, s ^\frown \langle a \rangle \notin \mathsf{trs}\,(P))$
$$\Rightarrow\ s \mapsto X \cup Y \in \mathsf{fails}\,(P).$$

4.1   The Isomorphism between $\mathcal{F}_m$ and $\mathcal{F}$

Given the denotation of a process P in $\mathcal{F}_m$, we can extract its denotation in $\mathcal{F}$ as follows:

$$
\begin{aligned}
\mathsf{traces}(P) \ &= \ \ \mathsf{trs}\,(P) \ \cup\ \{\, s ^\frown \langle \checkmark \rangle \mid s \in \mathsf{tms}\,(P) \,\} \\[4pt]
\mathsf{failures}\,(P) \ &= \ \ \mathsf{fails}\,(P) \ \cup\ \{\, s \mapsto X \cup \{\checkmark\} \mid s \mapsto X \in \mathsf{fails}\,(P) \,\} \\
&\quad\ \cup\ \{\, s \mapsto X \mid s \in \mathsf{tms}\,(P) \ \wedge\ X \subseteq \Sigma \,\} \\
&\quad\ \cup\ \{\, s ^\frown \langle \checkmark \rangle \mapsto X \mid s \in \mathsf{tms}\,(P) \ \wedge\ X \subseteq \Sigma^{\checkmark} \,\}.
\end{aligned}
$$

Conversely, given P's denotation in $\mathcal{F}$, we can extract that of it in $\mathcal{F}_m$ thus:

$$
\begin{aligned}
\mathsf{trs}\,(P) \ &= \ \ \mathsf{traces}(P) \ \cap\ \Sigma^* \\[4pt]
\mathsf{tms}\,(P) \ &= \ \ \{\, s \mid s ^\frown \langle \checkmark \rangle \in \mathsf{traces}(P) \,\} \\[4pt]
\mathsf{fails}\,(P) \ &= \ \ \{\, s \mapsto X \mid s \in \mathsf{trs}\,(P) \ \wedge\ s \mapsto X \cup \{\checkmark\} \in \mathsf{failures}\,(P) \,\}.
\end{aligned}
$$

4.2   Calculating the $\mathcal{F}_m$ Semantics of Processes

Here we show how to calculate the $\mathcal{F}_m$ semantics of basic CSP processes and operators. Since the semantics is compositional, this permits us in principle to calculate the $\mathcal{F}_m$ semantics of an arbitrarily complicated CSP process expression. Note that since the first two components $\mathsf{trs}\,(P)$ and $\mathsf{tms}\,(P)$ of the denotation of a process P here in $\mathcal{F}_m$ also comprise its denotation in $\mathcal{T}_m$, this also shows how to calculate the $\mathcal{T}_m$ semantics of any CSP process expression.

---

[2] Since $\mathcal{F}$'s stable failures are superseded in $\mathcal{F}_m$ by persistent failures, perhaps we could more accurately call $\mathcal{F}_m$ our Persistent Failures model.

Primitive processes.   We note that of the three primitive CSP processes STOP, SKIP and DIV, only STOP has any persistent failures at all. We also note that STOP and DIV are only distinguished by their persistent failures, and hence are identified in the $\mathcal{T}$ model, exactly as we would expect.

$$\begin{array}{lll}
\mathsf{trs}(\mathsf{STOP}) = \{\langle\rangle\} & \mathsf{trs}(\mathsf{SKIP}) = \{\langle\rangle\} & \mathsf{trs}(\mathsf{DIV}) = \{\langle\rangle\} \\
\mathsf{tms}(\mathsf{STOP}) = \{\} & \mathsf{tms}(\mathsf{SKIP}) = \{\langle\rangle\} & \mathsf{tms}(\mathsf{DIV}) = \{\} \\
\mathsf{fails}(\mathsf{STOP}) = \{\langle\rangle\} \times \mathbb{P}\,\Sigma & \mathsf{fails}(\mathsf{SKIP}) = \{\} & \mathsf{fails}(\mathsf{DIV}) = \{\}
\end{array}$$

Sequential composition.   Since the termination traces of processes are explicitly recorded in $\mathcal{F}_m$, this yields a pleasingly simple semantics of the sequential composition $(P \,;\, Q)$ of processes P and Q without the need to hide an intermediate ✓ occurring between P and Q as is necessary in $\mathcal{F}$:

$$\begin{array}{lll}
\mathsf{trs}(P \,;\, Q) & = & \mathsf{trs}(P) \;\cup\; \{s \,\frown\, t \mid s \in \mathsf{tms}(P) \wedge t \in \mathsf{trs}(Q)\} \\
\mathsf{tms}(P \,;\, Q) & = & \{s \,\frown\, t \mid s \in \mathsf{tms}(P) \wedge t \in \mathsf{tms}(Q)\} \\
\mathsf{fails}(P \,;\, Q) & = & \mathsf{fails}(P) \;\cup\; \{s \,\frown\, t \mapsto X \mid s \in \mathsf{tms}(P) \wedge t \mapsto X \in \mathsf{fails}(Q)\}
\end{array}$$

Internal and external choice.   Both these operators have straightforward semantics in $\mathcal{F}_m$. It can be seen that they differ only the calculation of their initial persistent failures, *i.e.* those associated with the empty trace $\langle\rangle$:

$$\begin{array}{lll}
\mathsf{trs}(P \sqcap Q) & = & \mathsf{trs}(P) \;\cup\; \mathsf{trs}(Q) \\
\mathsf{tms}(P \sqcap Q) & = & \mathsf{tms}(P) \;\cup\; \mathsf{tms}(Q) \\
\mathsf{fails}(P \sqcap Q) & = & \mathsf{fails}(P) \;\cup\; \mathsf{fails}(Q)
\end{array}$$

$$\begin{array}{lll}
\mathsf{trs}(P \,\square\, Q) & = & \mathsf{trs}(P) \;\cup\; \mathsf{trs}(Q) \\
\mathsf{tms}(P \,\square\, Q) & = & \mathsf{tms}(P) \;\cup\; \mathsf{tms}(Q) \\
\mathsf{fails}(P \,\square\, Q) & = & (\mathsf{fails}(P) \cap \mathsf{fails}(Q)) \\
& & \cup \; \{s \mapsto X \mid s \neq \langle\rangle \,\wedge\, s \mapsto X \in \mathsf{fails}(P) \cup \mathsf{fails}(Q)\}
\end{array}$$

Interleaving.   The traces of the interleaved composition $(P \,|||\, Q)$ of processes P and Q are simply the interleaved traces of P and Q :

$$\mathsf{trs}(P \,|||\, Q) \;\; = \;\; \{u \mid s \in \mathsf{trs}(P) \wedge t \in \mathsf{trs}(Q) \wedge u \in s \,|||\, t\}.$$

Modelling so-called *distributed* termination, the termination traces of $(P \,|||\, Q)$ are simply the interleaved termination traces of P and Q :

$$\mathsf{tms}(P \,|||\, Q) \;\; = \;\; \{u \mid s \in \mathsf{tms}(P) \wedge t \in \mathsf{tms}(Q) \wedge u \in s \,|||\, t\}.$$

The persistent failures of $(P \,|||\, Q)$ comprise those interleaved pairs of persistent failures of P and Q which share a common refusal set, plus the persistent failures of either process interleaved with the termination traces of the other:

$$\begin{array}{lll}
\mathsf{fails}(P \,|||\, Q) & = & \{u \mapsto X \mid s \mapsto X \in \mathsf{fails}(P) \wedge t \mapsto X \in \mathsf{fails}(Q) \wedge u \in s \,|||\, t\} \\
& & \cup \;\; \{u \mapsto X \mid s \mapsto X \in \mathsf{fails}(P) \wedge t \in \mathsf{tms}(Q) \wedge u \in s \,|||\, t\} \\
& & \cup \;\; \{u \mapsto X \mid s \in \mathsf{tms}(P) \wedge t \mapsto X \in \mathsf{fails}(Q) \wedge u \in s \,|||\, t\}.
\end{array}$$

Interface parallel composition. The traces and termination traces of the interface parallel composition $(P \parallel_X Q)$ of processes P and Q are defined similarly to their pure interleaving counterparts above, except of course that the pairs of traces involved are now interface-parallel-composed rather than just interleaved:

$$\mathsf{trs}(P \parallel_X Q) \;=\; \{u \mid s \in \mathsf{trs}(P) \wedge t \in \mathsf{trs}(Q) \wedge u \in s \parallel_X t\}$$

$$\mathsf{tms}(P \parallel_X Q) \;=\; \{u \mid s \in \mathsf{tms}(P) \wedge t \in \mathsf{tms}(Q) \wedge u \in s \parallel_X t\}.$$

The persistent failures of $(P \parallel_X Q)$ are defined similarly to those of $(P \mathbin{|||} Q)$, except that the refusal sets of interface-parallel-composed pairs of failures of P and Q now only have to coincide in their portions outside the interface set X:

$$\mathsf{fails}(P \parallel_X Q) \;=\;$$

$$\{u \mapsto Y \cup Z \mid Y \setminus X = Z \setminus X \ \wedge \ s \mapsto Y \in \mathsf{fails}(P) \wedge t \mapsto Z \in \mathsf{fails}(Q) \ \wedge \ u \in s \parallel_X t\}$$

$$\cup \ \{u \mapsto Y \mid s \mapsto Y \in \mathsf{fails}(P) \ \wedge \ t \in \mathsf{tms}(Q) \ \wedge \ u \in s \parallel_X t\}$$

$$\cup \ \{u \mapsto Y \mid s \in \mathsf{tms}(P) \ \wedge \ t \mapsto Y \in \mathsf{fails}(Q) \ \wedge \ u \in s \parallel_X t\}.$$

In fact, pure interleaving is really just interface parallel composition with an empty interface: that is to say, $(P \mathbin{|||} Q) \;=\; (P \parallel_{\{\}} Q)$.

5   The Model $\mathcal{N}_{\mathsf{m}}$

In the recast Failures-Divergences model $\mathcal{N}_{\mathsf{m}}$ each CSP process P is represented by the triple

$$(\mathsf{fails}_\perp(P), \ \mathsf{tms}_\perp(P), \ \mathsf{divs}(P))$$

where $\mathsf{fails}_\perp(P) \subseteq \Sigma^* \times \mathbb{P}\,\Sigma$, $\mathsf{tms}_\perp(P) \subseteq \Sigma^*$ and $\mathsf{divs}(P) \subseteq \Sigma^*$. Here $\mathsf{divs}(P)$ is the set of extension-closed divergences of P: that is, the extension-closure of the set of traces of regular events after engaging in which P may then immediately diverge; $\mathsf{tms}_\perp(P)$ is the set of terminating traces of P augmented by $\mathsf{divs}(P)$; and $\mathsf{fails}_\perp(P)$ is the divergence-augmented persistent-failures relation of P: it thus comprises all the persistent failures of P together with all of $\mathsf{divs}(P) \times \mathbb{P}\,\Sigma$. We define the convenient abbreviation $\mathsf{trs}_\perp(P)$[3], where

$$\mathsf{trs}_\perp(P) \quad =_{df} \quad \mathsf{dom}(\mathsf{fails}_\perp(P)) \ \cup \ \mathsf{tms}_\perp(P).$$

The axioms for $\mathcal{N}_{\mathsf{m}}$ are as follows:

- F1. $\mathsf{trs}_\perp(P)$ is non-empty and prefix-closed.
- F2. $s \mapsto X \in \mathsf{fails}_\perp(P) \wedge Y \subseteq X \ \Rightarrow \ s \mapsto Y \in \mathsf{fails}_\perp(P)$.
- F3. $s \mapsto X \in \mathsf{fails}_\perp(P) \wedge Y \subseteq \Sigma \wedge (\forall a \mid a \in Y . \ s \,^\frown \langle a \rangle \notin \mathsf{trs}_\perp(P))$
  $$\Rightarrow \ s \mapsto X \cup Y \in \mathsf{fails}_\perp(P).$$

- D1. $\mathsf{divs}(P)$ is extension-closed.
- D2. $s \in \mathsf{divs}(P) \wedge X \subseteq \Sigma \ \Rightarrow \ s \in \mathsf{tms}_\perp(P) \wedge s \mapsto X \in \mathsf{fails}_\perp(P)$.

---

[3] But note that $\mathsf{trs}_\perp(P)$ is not a primary component of the $\mathcal{N}_{\mathsf{m}}$ semantics of P.

5.1   The Isomorphism between $\mathcal{N}_m$ and $\mathcal{N}$

Given the denotation of a process P in $\mathcal{N}_m$ we can extract its denotation in $\mathcal{N}$ as follows:

$$
\begin{aligned}
\text{divergences}(P) \;&=\; \text{divs}(P) \;\cup\; \{\, s \cap \langle \checkmark \rangle \mid s \in \text{divs}(P) \,\} \\
\text{failures}_\perp(P) \;&=\; \text{fails}_\perp(P) \;\cup\; \{\, s \mapsto X \cup \{\checkmark\} \mid s \mapsto X \in \text{fails}_\perp(P) \,\} \\
&\qquad \cup\; \{\, s \mapsto X \mid s \in \text{tms}_\perp(P) \,\wedge\, X \subseteq \Sigma \,\} \\
&\qquad \cup\; \{\, s \cap \langle \checkmark \rangle \mapsto X \mid s \in \text{tms}_\perp(P) \,\wedge\, X \subseteq \Sigma^\checkmark \,\}.
\end{aligned}
$$

Conversely, we can extract P's denotation in $\mathcal{N}_m$ from that of it in $\mathcal{N}$ thus:

$$
\begin{aligned}
\text{divs}(P) \;&=\; \text{divergences}(P) \,\cap\, \Sigma^* \\
\text{tms}_\perp(P) \;&=\; \{\, s \mid s \cap \langle \checkmark \rangle \in \text{dom}(\text{failures}_\perp(P)) \,\} \\
\text{fails}_\perp(P) \;&=\; \{\, s \mapsto X \mid s \in \Sigma^* \,\wedge\, s \mapsto X \cup \{\checkmark\} \in \text{failures}_\perp(P) \,\}.
\end{aligned}
$$

5.2   Calculating the $\mathcal{N}_m$ Semantics of Processes

The $\mathcal{N}_m$ semantics of CSP process expressions are complicated by the need to incorporate the effect of a process's divergences, but otherwise their construction follows similar principles to those we have already seen for $\mathcal{F}_m$ in Section 4.2. We therefore give the following semantic formulations in $\mathcal{N}_m$ without further comment:

Primitive processes

$$
\begin{aligned}
\text{divs}(\text{STOP}) &= \{\} & \text{divs}(\text{SKIP}) &= \{\} & \text{divs}(\text{DIV}) &= \Sigma^* \\
\text{tms}_\perp(\text{STOP}) &= \{\} & \text{tms}_\perp(\text{SKIP}) &= \{\langle\rangle\} & \text{tms}_\perp(\text{DIV}) &= \Sigma^* \\
\text{fails}_\perp(\text{STOP}) &= \{\langle\rangle\} \times \mathbb{P}\,\Sigma & \text{fails}_\perp(\text{SKIP}) &= \{\} & \text{fails}_\perp(\text{DIV}) &= \Sigma^* \times \mathbb{P}\,\Sigma
\end{aligned}
$$

Sequential composition

$$
\begin{aligned}
\text{divs}(P\,;\,Q) \;&=\; \text{divs}(P) \;\cup\; \{\, s \cap t \mid s \in \text{tms}_\perp(P) \wedge t \in \text{divs}(Q) \,\} \\
\text{tms}_\perp(P\,;\,Q) \;&=\; \{\, s \cap t \mid s \in \text{tms}_\perp(P) \wedge t \in \text{tms}_\perp(Q) \,\} \;\cup\; \text{divs}(P) \\
\text{fails}_\perp(P\,;\,Q) \;&=\; \text{fails}_\perp(P) \;\cup\; \{\, s \cap t \mapsto X \mid s \in \text{tms}_\perp(P) \wedge t \mapsto X \in \text{fails}_\perp(Q) \,\}
\end{aligned}
$$

Internal and external choice

$$
\begin{aligned}
\text{divs}(P \sqcap Q) \;&=\; \text{divs}(P) \;\cup\; \text{divs}(Q) \\
\text{tms}_\perp(P \sqcap Q) \;&=\; \text{tms}_\perp(P) \;\cup\; \text{tms}_\perp(Q) \\
\text{fails}_\perp(P \sqcap Q) \;&=\; \text{fails}_\perp(P) \;\cup\; \text{fails}_\perp(Q)
\end{aligned}
$$

$$
\begin{aligned}
\text{divs}(P \,\square\, Q) \;&=\; \text{divs}(P) \;\cup\; \text{divs}(Q) \\
\text{tms}_\perp(P \,\square\, Q) \;&=\; \text{tms}_\perp(P) \;\cup\; \text{tms}_\perp(Q) \\
\text{fails}_\perp(P \,\square\, Q) \;&=\; (\text{fails}_\perp(P) \cap \text{fails}_\perp(Q)) \\
&\qquad \cup\; \{\, s \mapsto X \mid s \neq \langle\rangle \,\wedge\, s \mapsto X \in \text{fails}_\perp(P) \cup \text{fails}_\perp(Q) \,\} \\
&\qquad \cup\; \{\, \langle\rangle \mapsto X \mid \langle\rangle \in \text{divs}(P) \cup \text{divs}(Q) \,\wedge\, X \subseteq \Sigma \,\}
\end{aligned}
$$

Interleaving

$$\mathsf{divs}\,(P \ ||| \ Q) \ =$$
$$\{u \,\widehat{\ }\, v \mid s \in \mathsf{trs}_\perp(P) \wedge t \in \mathsf{trs}_\perp(Q) \ \wedge \ (s \in \mathsf{divs}\,(P) \vee t \in \mathsf{divs}\,(Q)) \ \wedge \ u \in s \ ||| \ t \ \wedge \ v \in \Sigma^* \}$$

$$\mathsf{tms}_\perp(P \ ||| \ Q) \ = \ \{u \mid s \in \mathsf{tms}_\perp(P) \wedge t \in \mathsf{tms}_\perp(Q) \wedge u \in s \ ||| \ t\} \ \cup \ \mathsf{divs}\,(P \ ||| \ Q)$$

$$\mathsf{fails}_\perp(P \ ||| \ Q) \ = \ \{u \mapsto X \mid s \mapsto X \in \mathsf{fails}_\perp(P) \wedge t \mapsto X \in \mathsf{fails}_\perp(Q) \wedge u \in s \ ||| \ t\}$$
$$\cup \ \{\{u \mapsto X \mid s \mapsto X \in \mathsf{fails}_\perp(P) \wedge t \in \mathsf{tms}_\perp(Q) \wedge u \in s \ ||| \ t\}$$
$$\cup \ \{\{u \mapsto X \mid s \in \mathsf{tms}_\perp(P) \wedge t \mapsto X \in \mathsf{fails}_\perp(Q) \wedge u \in s \ ||| \ t\}$$
$$\cup \ (\mathsf{divs}\,(P \ ||| \ Q) \times \mathbb{P}\,\Sigma)$$

Interface parallel composition

$$\mathsf{divs}\,(P \parallel_X Q) \ =$$
$$\{u \,\widehat{\ }\, v \mid s \in \mathsf{trs}_\perp(P) \wedge t \in \mathsf{trs}_\perp(Q) \ \wedge \ (s \in \mathsf{divs}\,(P) \vee t \in \mathsf{divs}\,(Q)) \ \wedge \ u \in s \parallel_X t \ \wedge \ v \in \Sigma^* \}$$

$$\mathsf{tms}_\perp(P \parallel_X Q) \ = \ \{u \mid s \in \mathsf{tms}_\perp(P) \wedge t \in \mathsf{tms}_\perp(Q) \wedge u \in s \parallel_X t\} \ \cup \ \mathsf{divs}\,(P \parallel_X Q)$$

$$\mathsf{fails}_\perp(P \parallel_X Q) \ =$$
$$\{u \mapsto Y \cup Z \mid Y \setminus X = Z \setminus X \ \wedge \ s \mapsto Y \in \mathsf{fails}_\perp(P) \ \wedge \ t \mapsto Z \in \mathsf{fails}_\perp(Q) \ \wedge \ u \in s \parallel_X t\}$$
$$\cup \ \{u \mapsto Y \mid s \mapsto Y \in \mathsf{fails}_\perp(P) \wedge t \in \mathsf{tms}_\perp(Q) \wedge u \in s \parallel_X t\}$$
$$\cup \ \{u \mapsto Y \mid s \in \mathsf{tms}_\perp(P) \wedge t \mapsto Y \in \mathsf{fails}_\perp(Q) \wedge u \in s \parallel_X t\}$$
$$\cup \ (\mathsf{divs}\,(P \parallel_X Q) \times \mathbb{P}\,\Sigma)$$

6   Termination and External Choice

An external choice of the form $P \ \square \ \mathsf{SKIP}$ has always been regarded in the CSP literature as problematic because, as Roscoe [11, p140] says,

> .....the concept of offering the environment the choice of the process terminating or not is both strange in iself, and fits most uneasily with the principle that $\checkmark$ is something a process signals to say it *has* terminated.

Hoare [5] originally banned such choices altogether, while Roscoe introduces his special $\square$-SKIP resolve rule [11, p141] to accommodate them:

$$P \ \square \ \mathsf{SKIP} \ = \ (P \ \square \ \mathsf{SKIP}) \ \sqcap \ \mathsf{SKIP}.$$

This is reflected in Roscoe's denotational semantics of $\mathcal{F}$ by the incorporation of the *ad hoc* component

$$\{\langle\rangle \mapsto X \mid X \subseteq \Sigma \wedge \langle\checkmark\rangle \in \mathsf{traces}(P) \cup \mathsf{traces}(Q)\}$$

in his definition of $\mathsf{failures}\,(P \ \square \ Q)$ [11, p210], and in his denotational semantics of $\mathcal{N}$ by the incorporation of the corresponding component

$$\{\langle\rangle \mapsto X \mid X \subseteq \Sigma \wedge \langle\checkmark\rangle \in \mathsf{traces}_\perp(P) \cup \mathsf{traces}_\perp(Q)\}$$

in his definition of $\mathsf{failures}_\perp(P \,\square\, Q)$ [11, p198]. Schneider [12], on the other hand, elects not to special-case external choices such as $P \,\square\, \mathsf{SKIP}$, but has to sacrifice the right-unit law $P \,;\, \mathsf{SKIP} = P$ in consequence.

In contrast, the definitions of the external-choice operator $\square$ in our recast models $\mathcal{F}_\mathsf{m}$ and $\mathcal{N}_\mathsf{m}$ contain no special provision for an immediately terminating operand such as SKIP, and yet in each of them we can still easily infer Roscoe's above $\square$-SKIP resolve rule. We demonstrate this for $\mathcal{F}_\mathsf{m}$ as follows. First we note from 5.2 that for any pair of CSP processes P and Q

$$\mathsf{trs}(P \,\square\, Q) \;=\; \mathsf{trs}(P \,\sqcap\, Q) \;=\; \mathsf{trs}(P) \cup \mathsf{trs}(Q)$$

and

$$\mathsf{tms}(P \,\square\, Q) \;=\; \mathsf{tms}(P \,\sqcap\, Q) \;=\; \mathsf{tms}(P) \cup \mathsf{tms}(Q),$$

and hence that

$$\begin{aligned}
\mathsf{trs}((P \,\square\, Q) \,\sqcap\, Q) &= (\mathsf{trs}(P) \cup \mathsf{trs}(Q)) \cup \mathsf{trs}(Q) \\
&= \mathsf{trs}(P) \cup \mathsf{trs}(Q) \;=\; \mathsf{trs}(P \,\square\, Q)
\end{aligned}$$

and

$$\begin{aligned}
\mathsf{tms}((P \,\square\, Q) \,\sqcap\, Q) &= (\mathsf{tms}(P) \cup \mathsf{tms}(Q)) \cup \mathsf{tms}(Q) \\
&= \mathsf{tms}(P) \cup \mathsf{tms}(Q) \;=\; \mathsf{tms}(P \,\square\, Q).
\end{aligned}$$

Taking Q as SKIP then gives us that

$$\mathsf{trs}((P \,\square\, \mathsf{SKIP}) \,\sqcap\, \mathsf{SKIP}) \;=\; \mathsf{trs}(P \,\square\, \mathsf{SKIP})$$

and

$$\mathsf{tms}((P \,\square\, \mathsf{SKIP}) \,\sqcap\, \mathsf{SKIP}) \;=\; \mathsf{tms}(P \,\square\, \mathsf{SKIP}).$$

We also note from 5.2 that

$$\mathsf{fails}(\mathsf{SKIP}) \;=\; \{\} \quad \text{and} \quad \mathsf{fails}(R \,\sqcap\, S) \;=\; \mathsf{fails}(R) \cup \mathsf{fails}(S).$$

Hence by taking R as $(P \,\square\, \mathsf{SKIP})$ and S as SKIP we have that

$$\begin{aligned}
\mathsf{fails}((P \,\square\, \mathsf{SKIP}) \,\sqcap\, \mathsf{SKIP}) &= \mathsf{fails}(P \,\square\, \mathsf{SKIP}) \cup \mathsf{fails}(\mathsf{SKIP}) \\
&= \mathsf{fails}(P \,\square\, \mathsf{SKIP}) \cup \{\} \;=\; \mathsf{fails}(P \,\square\, \mathsf{SKIP}).
\end{aligned}$$

$\square$

7   CSP in the Unifying Theories of Programming

In Hoare and He's Unifying Theories of Programming (UTP) [6] CSP processes over an event alphabet Σ are encoded as alphabetised binary relations over a variable alphabet which includes (in addition to regular state variables v, v' encoding the internal parameterised state of a process and the fundamental UTP boolean auxiliary variables ok', ok denoting the non-divergence of the current process and its sequential predecessors) the following auxiliary variables:

- the trace variables tr, tr' of type Σ^* denote the trace of events engaged in by the current process's sequential predecessors (tr), and also that trace extended by the events in which the current process itself has engaged (tr');

- the waiting status variables $wait, wait'$ of type $\mathsf{Boolean}$ denote whether the current process's immediate sequential predecessor had really terminated $(wait = \text{false})$, and whether the current process itself has terminated $(wait' = \text{false})$ or is merely awaiting interaction with its environment $(wait' = \text{true})$;

- the refusal-set variables ref, ref' of type $\mathbb{P}\,\Sigma$ denote a set of events (ref) which the current process's immediate sequential predecessor was observed to refuse, assuming it was in a waiting state, and a set of events (ref') which the current process itself is observed to refuse, assuming it is awaiting interaction with its environment.

Any CSP process P can be encoded as a reactive design $\mathsf{R}(p \vdash q)$ where R is the idempotent "reactive healthifier" for UTP reactive processes [6, ch 8], and $p \vdash q$ is a standard UTP design with an *assumption* p, which can refer to v, tr and tr', and a *commitment* q which can refer to v, tr, v', tr', $wait'$ and ref'. A reactive design A can always be re-expressed in the *normalised* form

$$\mathsf{R}(\neg\ A[\text{true}, \text{false}, \text{false}/ok, wait, ok'] \ \vdash\ A[\text{true}, \text{false}, \text{true}/ok, wait, ok']),$$

which ensures that its commitment and assumption incorporate certain fundamental reactive properties –for example $tr \leq tr'$, which insists that the initial trace tr is a prefix of the final trace tr'.

Extracting the $\mathcal{N}$ semantics of a UTP reactive design. Cavalcanti and Woodcock [3] show how to extract $\mathcal{N}$'s standard failures-divergences denotational semantics of a UTP reactive design. If a CSP process A is represented by a UTP reactive design $\mathsf{R}(p \vdash q)$ in normalised form, then[4]

$$
\begin{aligned}
\mathsf{failures}_\perp(A) \quad = \quad & \\
& \{(tr' - tr) \mapsto ref' \mid (p \Rightarrow q)\} \\
\cup\ & \{(tr' - tr) \mapsto (ref' \cup \{\checkmark\}) \mid (p \Rightarrow q) \wedge wait'\} \\
\cup\ & \{((tr' - tr) ^\frown \langle\checkmark\rangle) \mapsto ref' \mid (p \Rightarrow q) \wedge \neg\ wait'\} \\
\cup\ & \{((tr' - tr) ^\frown \langle\checkmark\rangle) \mapsto (ref' \cup \{\checkmark\}) \mid (p \Rightarrow q) \wedge \neg\ wait'\}
\end{aligned}
$$

and

$$\mathsf{divergences}(A) \quad = \quad \{tr' - tr \mid \neg\ p\} \ \cup\ \{(tr' - tr) ^\frown \langle\checkmark\rangle \mid \neg\ p\}\ .$$

It can be seen that these extractions of $\mathsf{failures}_\perp(A)$ and $\mathsf{divergences}(A)$ are significantly complicated by the need to account for the $\checkmark$ pseudo-event in the $\mathcal{N}$ semantics of A. Such complications reveal the underlying misalignment between the UTP representation of a CSP process as a reactive design and its denotation in $\mathcal{N}$ owing to the use of $\checkmark$ in the latter.

Extracting the $\mathcal{N}_\mathsf{m}$ semantics of a UTP reactive design. In contrast the extraction of A's semantics in $\mathcal{N}_\mathsf{m}$ is much more straightforward:

$$\mathsf{divs}(A) \quad = \quad \{tr' - tr \mid \neg\ p\}\ .$$

$$\mathsf{tms}_\perp(A) \quad = \quad \{tr' - tr \mid (p \Rightarrow q) \wedge \neg\ wait'\}\ .$$

$$\mathsf{fails}_\perp(A) \quad = \quad \{(tr' - tr) \mapsto ref' \mid (p \Rightarrow q) \wedge wait'\}\ .$$

---

[4] The accidental omission of one of the terms here in the extraction of $\mathsf{failures}_\perp(A)$ originally given in [3] was subsequently rectified in [2].

This indicates how much more closely the UTP representation of a CSP process as a reactive design is aligned to its $\mathcal{N}_m$ semantics than to its $\mathcal{N}$ semantics.

7.1 Correctness Perspectives

It may have occurred to the reader to wonder why we didn't also seek to extract the $\mathcal{T}_m$ and $\mathcal{F}_m$ semantics of the process A from its UTP reactive-design representation. In fact this is because neither of those extractions is fundamentally possible. A UTP reactive design only captures the total-correctness semantics of the CSP process it represents, and a total-correctness semantics is characterised by its strictness with respect to divergence. This means that divergence always completely masks any specific non-divergent behaviour the artifact concerned might otherwise have exhibited, by admitting all behaviours whatsoever in any circumstance which potentially leads to divergence. This is exactly the case with $\mathcal{N}/\mathcal{N}_m$, but not with the other models.

Indeed, by ignoring divergence altogether $\mathcal{T}/\mathcal{T}_m$ in particular reveals itself as being based on partial correctness rather than total correctness. On the other hand the case of $\mathcal{F}/\mathcal{F}_m$ is more complex since, as explained in [4], it turns out to be based on a notion of correctness intermediate between partial and general correctness.

8   Conclusion

Our recasting of the three CSP standard semantic models has revealed an implicit termination-traces component which each of these has always tacitly possessed yet concealed by embedding it within the other denotational components by means of the ✓-pseudo-event encoding trick. Our recast semantic models should therefore be significant for developers of tools such as FDR [10], ProB [1,9] and CSP-related theorem provers, since by making the termination traces explicit they offer a cleaner denotational basis for exploring and reasoning about CSP-formulated systems than do the standard semantic models with their more problematic encoding of termination behaviour by means of ✓.

Acknowledgements.   I wish to thank the anonymous referees for their comments on the original draft of this paper, and also Phil Brooke and Bill Stoddart for helpful discussions about this work.

References

1. Butler, M., Leuschel, M.: Combining CSP and B for specification and property verification. In: Fitzgerald, J., Hayes, I.J., Tarlecki, A. (eds.) FM 2005. LNCS, vol. 3582, pp. 221–236. Springer, Heidelberg (2005)
2. Cavalcanti, A.L.C., Gaudel, M.-C.: A note on traces refinement and the *conf* relation in the unifying theories of programming. In: Butterfield, A. (ed.) UTP 2008. LNCS, vol. 5713, pp. 42–61. Springer, Heidelberg (2010)

3. Cavalcanti, A.L.C., Woodcock, J.C.P.: A tutorial introduction to CSP in *unifying theories of programming*. In: Cavalcanti, A., Sampaio, A., Woodcock, J. (eds.) PSSE 2004. LNCS, vol. 3167, pp. 220–268. Springer, Heidelberg (2006)
4. Dunne, S.E.: Of wlp and CSP. Electron. Notes Theor. Comput. Sci. 259, 35–45 (2009)
5. Hoare, C.A.R.: Communicating Sequential Processes. Prentice-Hall, Englewood Cliffs (1985)
6. Hoare, C.A.R., Jifeng, H.: Unifying Theories of Programming. Prentice-Hall, Englewood Cliffs (1998)
7. Howells, P., d'Inverno, M.: A CSP model with flexible parallel termination semantics. Formal Aspects of Computing 21(5), 421–449 (2009)
8. Josephs, M.B.: Models for data-flow sequential processes. In: Abdallah, A.E., Jones, C.B., Sanders, J.W. (eds.) Communicating Sequential Processes. LNCS, vol. 3525, pp. 85–97. Springer, Heidelberg (2005)
9. Leuschel, M., Fontaine, M.: Probing the depths of CSP-M: A new FDR-compliant validation tool. In: Liu, S., Maibaum, T., Araki, K. (eds.) ICFEM 2008. LNCS, vol. 5256, pp. 278–297. Springer, Heidelberg (2008)
10. Formal Systems (Europe) Ltd. Failures-divergence refinement: FDR2 user manual (2010), `http://www.fsel.com/fdr2_manual.html`
11. Roscoe, A.W.: The Theory and Practice of Concurrency. Prentice-Hall, Englewood Cliffs (1998)
12. Schneider, S.: Concurrent and Real-time Systems: The CSP Approach. Wiley, Chichester (2000)
13. Valmari, A.: The weakest deadlock-preserving congruence. Information Processing Letters 53, 341–346 (1995)

Timed Migration and Interaction with Access Permissions

Gabriel Ciobanu[1] and Maciej Koutny[2]

[1] Institute of Computer Science, Romanian Academy
and A.I.Cuza University of Iasi
700506 Iasi, Romania
`gabriel@iit.tuiasi.ro`

[2] School of Computing Science
Newcastle University
Newcastle upon Tyne, NE1 7RU, United Kingdom
`maciej.koutny@newcastle.ac.uk`

Abstract. We introduce and study a process algebra able to model the systems composed of processes (agents) which may migrate within a distributed environment comprising a number of distinct locations. Two processes may communicate if they are present in the same location and, in addition, they have appropriate access permissions to communicate over a channel. Access permissions are dynamic, and processes can acquire new access permissions or lose some existing permissions while migrating from one location to another. Timing constraints coordinate and control both the communication between processes and migration between locations. We completely characterise those situations when a process is always guaranteed to possess safe access permissions. The consequences of such a result are twofold. First, we are able to validate systems where one does not need to check (at least partially) access permissions as they are guaranteed not to be violated, improving efficiency of implementation. Second, one can design systems in which processes are not blocked (deadlocked) because of the lack of dynamically changing access permissions.

Keywords: distributed systems, mobile agents, communication, access permissions, operational semantics, specification, static analysis.

1 Introduction

The increasing complexity of mobile applications in which the timing aspects are important to the system operation means that the need for their effective analysis and verification is becoming critical. In this paper we explore formal modelling of mobile systems where one can also specify time-related aspects of migrating processes and, crucially, security aspects expressed by access permissions to communication channels. Building on our previous work on TiMo presented in [8], we introduce PerTiMo (**Per**missions, **Ti**mers and **Mo**bility)

M. Butler and W. Schulte (Eds.): FM 2011, LNCS 6664, pp. 293–307, 2011.

which is a process algebra supporting process migration (strong mobility), local interprocess communication over shared channels controlled by access permissions that processes must possess, and timers (driven by local clocks) controlling the execution of actions. An important feature of the proposed model is that access permissions are dynamic. More precisely, processes can acquire new access permissions, or lose some of their current access permissions while moving from one location to another, modelling a key security related feature. Processes are equipped with input and output capabilities which are active up to pre-defined time deadlines and, if these communications are not taken, alternative continuations for the process behaviour are followed. Another timing constraint allows one to specify the latest time for moving a process from one location to another. These two kinds of timing constraints help in the control and coordination of both migration and communication in distributed systems. We provide the syntax and operational semantics of PerTiMo which is a discrete time semantics incorporating maximally parallel executions of actions using local clocks.

To introduce the basic components of PerTiMo, we use a *TravelShop* running example in which a client process attempts to pay as little as possible for a ticket to a pre-defined destination. The scenario involves five locations and six processes. The role of each of the locations is as follows: (i) *home* is a location where the client process starts and ends its journey; (ii) *travelshop* is a main location of the service which is initially visible to the client; (iii) *standard* and *special* are two internal locations of the service where clients can find out about the ticket prices; and (iv) *bank* is a location where the payment is made. The role of each of the processes is as follows:

- *client* is a process which initially resides in the *home* location, and is determined to pay for a flight after comparing two offers (standard and special) provided by the travel shop. Upon entering the travel shop, *client* receives the location of the standard offer and, after moving there and obtaining this offer, the client is given the location where a special offer can be obtained. After that *client* moves to the bank and pays for the cheaper of the two offers, and then returns back to *home*.
- *agent* first informs *client* where to look for the standard offer and then moves to *bank* in order to collect the money from the till. After that *agent* returns back to *travelshop*.
- *flightinfo* communicates the standard offer to clients as well as the location of the special offer.
- *saleinfo* communicates the special offer to clients together with the location of the bank. *saleinfo* can also accept an update by the travel shop of the special offer.
- *update* initially resides at the *travelshop* location and then migrates to *special* in order to update the special offer.
- *till* resides at the *bank* location and can either receive e-money paid in by clients, or transfer the e-money accumulated so far to *agent*.

PerTiMo uses *timers* in order to impose deadlines on the execution of communications and migrations. Moreover, processes need to possess appropriate

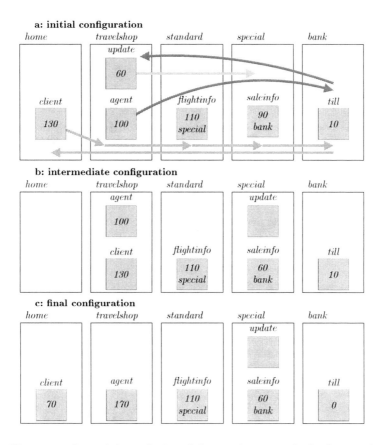

Fig. 1. Three snapshots of the evolution of the running example. In the initial configuration we indicated the intended migration paths of three processes. The intermediate configuration illustrates the phase of the evolution after some initial movements of the client and after updating the second flight price. The final configuration shows the state of the system after a successful payment has been made; the total sum of e-money owned by the client (*70*), agent (*170*) and till (*0*) is exactly the same as the sum at the beginning of the evolution when the client has *130*, agent *100* and till *10*. Note that the channels used by processes to communicate information are not shown.

access permissions in order to send and receive information. Figure 1 portrays three possible stages of the evolution of the *TravelShop* system.

Each location has its local clock which determines the timing of actions executed at that location. The timeout of a migration action indicates the network time limit for that action (similar to TTL in TCP/IP).

We use x to denote a finite tuple $(x_1, \ldots, x_k)$ whenever it does not lead to a confusion, and if X is a tuple of sets $(X_1, \ldots, X_k)$ then $\prod X$ denotes $X_1 \times \ldots \times X_k$. We assume that the reader is familiar with the basic concepts of process algebras [14]. All proofs of our results can be found in [9].

2   Syntax and Semantics of PERTIMO

Timing constraints for migration allow one to specify what is the time window for a process to move from one location to another. E.g., a timer (such as $\Delta 5$) of a migration action $\mathsf{go}^{\Delta 5}\,home$ indicates that the process will move to *home* within 5 time units. It is also possible to constrain the waiting for a communication on a channel; if a communication action does not happen before a deadline, the waiting process gives up and switches its operation to an alternative. E.g., a timer (such as $\Delta 4$) of an output action $a^{\Delta 4}\,!\,\langle 13\rangle$ makes the channel available for communication only for the period of 4 time units. We assume suitable data sets including a set *Loc* of *locations* and a set *Chan* of *communication channels*. We use a set *Id* of process identifiers, and each $id \in Id$ has arity m_{id}.

To communicate over a channel at a given network location, the sender process should have a '*put*' access permission, and the receiving process a '*get*' access permission. The set Γ of access permissions of a process is a subset of *AccPerm* $\stackrel{\text{df}}{=} \{put, get\} \times Chan \times Loc$. We use the notation $get\langle a@l\rangle$ to denote an access permission $(get, a, l) \in AccPerm$, and $put\langle a@l\rangle$ to denote $(put, a, l) \in AccPerm$. Intuitively, we work with access permissions to sockets where l represents an IP address, and a represents a communication port.

We allow access permissions of a process to change while moving from one location to another. To model this, we use the following four basic access permission modification operations: $put^+_{a@l}$, $get^+_{a@l}$, $put^-_{a@l}$ and $get^-_{a@l}$, where l is a location and a is a communication channel. The first two ($put^+_{a@l}$ and $get^+_{a@l}$) add access permissions, while the latter two ($put^-_{a@l}$ and $get^-_{a@l}$) remove access permissions. For instance, $put^+_{a@l}(\Gamma) = \Gamma \cup \{put\langle a@l\rangle\}$. Then an *access permission modification* operation is either the identity on *AccPerm*, or a composition of some basic access permission modification operations such that if $put^+_{a@l}$ is used in the composition then $put^-_{a@l}$ is not used (giving and removing an access permission at the same time do not make sense). For a given network, we then specify what are the changes to the access permission sets of processes migrating from one location to another. This is specified as a mapping *apm* which, for each pair (l, l') of locations, returns a permission modification operation; if a process with the current access permissions Γ moves from location l to location l', its new set of access permissions becomes $apm(l, l')(\Gamma)$.

The syntax of PERTIMO is given in Table 1, where P are *processes*, PP *processes with (access) permissions*, and N *networks*. Moreover, for each $id \in Id$, there is a unique process definition of the form:

$$id(u_1, \ldots, u_{m_{id}} : X_1^{id}, \ldots, X_{m_{id}}^{id}) \stackrel{\text{df}}{=} P_{id} , \tag{1}$$

where the u_i's are distinct variables playing the role of parameters, and the X_i^{id}'s are data sets. Processes of the form stop and $id(\boldsymbol{v})$ are called *primitive*. In Table 1, it is assumed that:

- $a \in Chan$ is a channel, and $t \in \mathbb{N} \cup \{\infty\}$ is a time deadline;
- each v_i is an expression built from values, variables and allowed operations;
- each u_i is a variable, and each X_i is a data set;

Table 1. PERTIMO syntax. The length of $\boldsymbol{u}$ is the same as that of $\boldsymbol{X}$, and the length of $\boldsymbol{v}$ in $id(\boldsymbol{v})$ is m_{id}.

Processes	$P ::= a^{\Delta t}\,!\,\langle \boldsymbol{v}\rangle$ **then** P **else** P'	(output)
	$a^{\Delta t}\,?\,(\boldsymbol{u}{:}\boldsymbol{X})$ **then** P **else** P'	(input)
	$\mathbf{go}^{\Delta t}\,l$ **then** P	(move)
	$P\,\vert\,P'$	(parallel)
	$\mathbf{stop}$	(termination)
	$id(\boldsymbol{v})$	(recursion)
	$\text{\textcircled{s}}\,P$	(stalling)
Typed Processes	$PP ::= P:\varGamma \;\vert\; PP\,\vert\,PP'$	
Networks	$N ::= l\,[\![\,PP\,]\!] \;\vert\; N\,\vert\,N'$	

Shorthand notation:

$a\,!\,\langle \boldsymbol{v}\rangle \;\rightarrow\; P$ will be used to denote $a^{\Delta\infty}\,!\,\langle \boldsymbol{v}\rangle$ **then** P **else stop**

$a\,?\,(\boldsymbol{u}{:}\boldsymbol{X}) \;\rightarrow\; P$ will be used to denote $a^{\Delta\infty}\,?\,(\boldsymbol{u}{:}\boldsymbol{X})$ **then** P **else stop** .

- l is a location or a variable, and $\varGamma$ a set of action permissions; and
- $\text{\textcircled{s}}$ is a special symbol used to express that a process is temporarily stalled.

The only variable binding construct is $a^{\Delta t}\,?\,(\boldsymbol{u}{:}\boldsymbol{X})$ **then** P **else** P' which binds the variables $\boldsymbol{u}$ within P (but *not* within P'). We use $fv(P)$ to denote the free variables of a process P (and similarly for processes with access permissions and networks). For a process definition as in (1), we assume that $fv(P_{id}) \subseteq \{u_1, \ldots, u_{m_{id}}\}$ and so the free variables of P_{id} are parameter bound. Processes are defined up to the alpha-conversion, and $\{v/u, \ldots\}P$ is obtained from P by replacing all free occurrences of a variable u by v, possibly after alpha-converting P in order to avoid clashes. Moreover, if $\boldsymbol{v}$ and $\boldsymbol{u}$ are tuples of the same length then $\{\boldsymbol{v}/\boldsymbol{u}\}P = \{v_1/u_1, v_2/u_2, \ldots, v_k/u_k\}P$.

A network N is *well-formed* if the following hold:

- there are no free variables in N;
- there are no occurrences of the special symbol $\text{\textcircled{s}}$ in N;
- assuming that id is as in the recursive equation (1), for every $id(\boldsymbol{v})$ occurring in N or on the right hand side of any recursive equation, the expression v_i is of type corresponding to X_i^{id} (where we use the standard rules of determining the type of an expression).

Intuitively, a process $a^{\Delta t}\,!\,\langle \boldsymbol{v}\rangle$ **then** P **else** P' attempts to send a tuple of values $\boldsymbol{v}$ over the channel a for t time units. If successful, it then continues as process P; otherwise it continues as the alternative process P'. Similarly, $a^{\Delta t}\,?\,(\boldsymbol{u}{:}\boldsymbol{X})$ **then** P **else** P' is a process that attempts for t time units to input a tuple of values from data set $\boldsymbol{X}$, and substitute them for the variables $\boldsymbol{u}$. Mobility is implemented by a process $\mathbf{go}^{\Delta t}\,l$ **then** P which moves from the current location to the location given by l within t time units. Note that since l can be a variable, and so its value is assigned dynamically through communication

Table 2. PERTIMO network modelling the running example together with the relevant access permission modification operations (those omitted are all equal to the identity mapping on *AccPerm*).

$TravelShop \overset{\text{df}}{=}$
  $home \, [\![\, client(130):\varnothing \,]\!] \mid$
  $travelshop \, [\![\, agent(100):\{put\langle flight@travelshop\rangle\} \mid update(60):\varnothing \,]\!] \mid$
  $standard \, [\![\, flightinfo(110,special):\{put\langle info@standard\rangle, get\langle info@standard\rangle\} \,]\!] \mid$
  $special \, [\![\, saleinfo(90,bank):\{put\langle info@special\rangle, get\langle info@special\rangle\} \,]\!] \mid$
  $bank \, [\![\, till(10):\{put\langle pay@bank\rangle, get\langle pay@bank\rangle\} \,]\!]$

$apm(home, travelshop)$	$\overset{\text{df}}{=}$	$get^+_{flight@travelshop}$
$apm(travelshop, standard)$	$\overset{\text{df}}{=}$	$get^+_{info@standard}$
$apm(travelshop, special)$	$\overset{\text{df}}{=}$	$put^+_{info@special}$
$apm(standard, special)$	$\overset{\text{df}}{=}$	$get^+_{info@special} \circ get^-_{info@standard}$
$apm(special, bank)$	$\overset{\text{df}}{=}$	$put^+_{pay@bank} \circ get^-_{info@special} \circ get^-_{pay@bank}$
$apm(travelshop, bank)$	$\overset{\text{df}}{=}$	$get^+_{pay@bank}$

$client(init:eMoney) \overset{\text{df}}{=}$
  $\mathbf{go}^{\Delta 5} \; travelshop \rightarrow flight \,?\,(standardoffer:Loc) \rightarrow$
  $\mathbf{go}^{\Delta 4} \; standardoffer \rightarrow info \,?\,(p1:eMoney, specialoffer:Loc) \rightarrow$
  $\mathbf{go}^{\Delta 3} \; specialoffer \rightarrow info \,?\,(p2:eMoney, paying:Loc) \rightarrow$
  $\mathbf{go}^{\Delta 6} \; paying \rightarrow pay \,!\,\langle \min\{p1,p2\}\rangle \rightarrow$
  $\mathbf{go}^{\Delta 4} \; home \rightarrow client(init - \min\{p1,p2\})$

$agent(balance:eMoney) \overset{\text{df}}{=}$
  $flight \,!\,\langle standard\rangle \rightarrow \mathbf{go}^{\Delta 10} \; bank \rightarrow$
  $pay \,?\,(profit:eMoney) \rightarrow \mathbf{go}^{\Delta 12} \; travelshop \rightarrow$
  $agent(balance + profit)$

$update(saleprice:eMoney) \overset{\text{df}}{=}$
  $\mathbf{go}^{\Delta 0} \; special \rightarrow info \,!\,\langle saleprice\rangle \rightarrow \mathbf{stop}$

$flightinfo(price:eMoney, next:Loc) \overset{\text{df}}{=}$
  $info \,!\,\langle price, next\rangle \rightarrow flightinfo(price, next)$

$saleinfo(price:eMoney, next:Loc) \overset{\text{df}}{=}$
  $info^{\Delta 10} \,?\,(newprice:eMoney)$
  $\mathbf{then} \; saleinfo(newprice, next)$
  $\mathbf{else} \; info \,!\,\langle price, next\rangle \rightarrow saleinfo(price, next)$

$till(cash:eMoney) \overset{\text{df}}{=}$
  $pay^{\Delta 1} \,?\,(newpayment:eMoney)$
  $\mathbf{then} \; till(cash + newpayment)$
  $\mathbf{else} \; pay^{\Delta 2} \,!\,\langle cash\rangle \; \mathbf{then} \; till(0) \; \mathbf{else} \; till(cash)$

with other processes, migration actions support a *flexible* scheme for movement of processes from one location to another.

A network $l\,[\![\, P : \Gamma \,]\!]$ specifies a process P with the access permissions Γ running at a location l. Finally, process expressions of the form $\circledS P$ represent a purely technical device which is used in our formalisation of structural operational semantics of PERTIMO; intuitively, it specifies a process P which is temporarily *stalled* and cannot execute any action.

One might wonder why a process can delay migration to another location. The point is that by allowing this we can model in a simple way the non-determinism in the movement of processes which is, in general, outside the control of a system designer. Thus the timer in this case indicates the upper bound of the migration time.

The specification of the running example which captures the essential features of the scenario described in the introduction is given in Table 2. We assume that $Loc = \{home, travelshop, standard, special, bank\}$ and $Chan = \{info, flight, pay\}$. Table 2 shows the process network *TravelShop* modelling the scenario, as well as the access permission modification operations which are applied to the process expressions when they move around the five locations of the network.

The first component of the operational semantics of PERTIMO is the structural equivalence $\equiv$ on networks, similar to that used in [4]; it is the smallest congruence such that the equalities (EQ1–EQ4) in Table 3 hold. Its role is to rearrange a network in order to apply the action rules which are also given in Table 3. Using (EQ1–EQ4), one can always transform a given network N into a finite parallel composition of networks of the form:

$$l_1 \llbracket P_1{:}\Gamma_1 \rrbracket \mid \ldots \mid l_n \llbracket P_n{:}\Gamma_n \rrbracket \tag{2}$$

such that no process P_i has the parallel composition operator at its topmost level. Each subnetwork $l_i \llbracket P_i{:}\Gamma_i \rrbracket$ is called a *component* of N, the set of all components is denoted by $comp(N)$, and the parallel composition (2) is called a *component decomposition* of the network N. Note that these notions are well-defined since component decomposition is unique up to the permutation of the components (see Remark 1 below).

Table 3 introduces two kinds of action rules, $N \xrightarrow{\lambda} N'$ and $N \xrightarrow{\sqrt{l}} N'$. The former is an execution of an action λ, and the latter a time step at location l. In the rule (TIME), $N \nrightarrow_l$ means that no l-action λ (i.e., an action of the form $id@l$ or $l \triangleright l'$ or $@l$ or $a\langle v\rangle @l$) can be applied to N. Moreover, $\phi_l(N)$ is obtained by taking the component decomposition of N and simultaneously replacing all components of the form $l \llbracket a^{\Delta t}\omega \text{ then } P \text{ else } Q : \Gamma \rrbracket$ by $l \llbracket Q : \Gamma \rrbracket$ if $t = 0$, and otherwise by $l \llbracket a^{\Delta t-1}\omega \text{ then } P \text{ else } Q : \Gamma \rrbracket$, where ω stands for $!\langle v\rangle$ or $?(u{:}X)$. After that, the occurrences in N of the special symbol $\circledS$ are erased.

So far we defined located executions of actions. An entire computational step is captured by a derivation $N \xRightarrow{\Lambda} N'$, where $\Lambda = \{\lambda_1, \ldots, \lambda_n\}$ is a finite multiset of l-actions for some location l such that

$$N \xrightarrow{\lambda_1} \cdots \xrightarrow{\lambda_n} \xrightarrow{\sqrt{l}} N' \ .$$

We also call N' *directly reachable* from N. In other words, we can capture the cumulative effect of the concurrent execution of the multiset of actions Λ at location l. Intuitively, networks evolution conforms to the locally maximally

Table 3. Four rules of the structural equivalence (Eq1-Eq4), and seven action rules (CALL, MOVE, WAIT, COM, PAR, EQUIV, TIME) of the operational semantics.

(Eq1) $$N \,|\, N' \;\equiv\; N' \,|\, N$$

(Eq2) $$(N \,|\, N') \,|\, N'' \;\equiv\; N \,|\, (N' \,|\, N'')$$

(Eq3) $$l \,[\![\, PP \,|\, PP' \,]\!] \;\equiv\; l \,[\![\, PP \,]\!] \,|\, l \,[\![\, PP' \,]\!]$$

(Eq4) $$l \,[\![\, P \,|\, Q : \varGamma \,]\!] \;\equiv\; l \,[\![\, P : \varGamma \,|\, Q : \varGamma \,]\!]$$

(CALL) $$l \,[\![\, id(\boldsymbol{v}) : \varGamma \,]\!] \;\xrightarrow{id@l}\; l \,[\![\, \text{\textcircled{S}} \,\{\boldsymbol{v}/\boldsymbol{u}\} P_{id} : \varGamma \,]\!]$$

(MOVE) $$l \,[\![\, \mathbf{go}^{\Delta t} \; l' \; \mathbf{then} \; P : \varGamma \,]\!] \;\xrightarrow{l \triangleright l'}\; l' \,[\![\, \text{\textcircled{S}} P : apm(l, l')(\varGamma) \,]\!]$$

(WAIT)
$$\frac{t > 0}{l \,[\![\, \mathbf{go}^{\Delta t} \; l' \; \mathbf{then} \; P : \varGamma \,]\!] \;\xrightarrow{@l}\; l \,[\![\, \text{\textcircled{S}} \, \mathbf{go}^{\Delta t-1} \; l' \; \mathbf{then} \; P : \varGamma \,]\!]}$$

(COM)
$$\frac{put\langle a@l\rangle \in \varGamma \qquad get\langle a@l\rangle \in \varGamma' \qquad \boldsymbol{v} \in \prod \boldsymbol{X}}{l \,[\![\, a^{\Delta t} \,! \, \langle \boldsymbol{v}\rangle \; \mathbf{then} \; P \; \mathbf{else} \; Q : \varGamma \;|\; a^{\Delta t'} \,? \, (\boldsymbol{u}{:}\boldsymbol{X}) \; \mathbf{then} \; P' \; \mathbf{else} \; Q' : \varGamma' \,]\!]}$$
$$\xrightarrow{a\langle \boldsymbol{v}\rangle @l} \quad l \,[\![\, \text{\textcircled{S}} P : \varGamma \;|\; \text{\textcircled{S}} \, \{\boldsymbol{v}/\boldsymbol{u}\} P' : \varGamma' \,]\!]$$

(PAR)
$$\frac{N \xrightarrow{\lambda} N'}{N \,|\, N'' \xrightarrow{\lambda} N' \,|\, N''}$$

(EQUIV)
$$\frac{N \equiv N' \qquad N' \xrightarrow{\lambda} N'' \qquad N'' \equiv N'''}{N \xrightarrow{\lambda} N'''}$$

(TIME)
$$\frac{N \not\xrightarrow{}_l}{N \xrightarrow{\sqrt{}_l} \phi_l(N)}$$

parallelism paradigm since one executes in a single location l as many as possible concurrent action before applying a local time rule which signifies the passage of a unit of time at location l.

The two results below ensure that derivations are well defined. First, one cannot execute an unbounded sequence of action moves without time progress.

Proposition 1. *If N is a network and $N \xrightarrow{\lambda_1} \cdots \xrightarrow{\lambda_k} N'$, then $k \leq |comp(N)|$.*

Second, if we start with a well-formed network, execution proceeds through alternating executions of time steps and contiguous sequences of local actions making up what can be regarded as a maximally concurrent step (note the role of the special symbols \text{\textcircled{S}}). This intuition is reinforced by the following result.

Proposition 2. *Let N be a well-formed network. If $N \xrightarrow{\lambda_1} \cdots \xrightarrow{\lambda_n} N'$, then we have $N \xrightarrow{\lambda_{i_1}} \cdots \xrightarrow{\lambda_{i_n}} N'$, for every permutation $i_1, \ldots, i_n$ of $1, \ldots, n$.*

It is worth noting that the semantical treatment of PERTIMO — itself a continuation of the idea developed for TIMO — goes beyond interleaving semantics by introducing an explicit representation of local maximal parallelism and local time progress in the network evolution.

Our last result in this section is that the rules of Table 3 preserve well-formedness of networks.

Proposition 3. *Networks reachable from a well-formed network are well-formed.*

Table 4 illustrates execution steps based on the scenario illustrated in Figure 1 (note that Λ_2 represents a parallel execution of two actions). We indicate only the main rules used in the derivation of steps. Each execution step takes a single unit of time in the location at which it has been executed and some timers are decremented by one (e.g., the timer $\Delta 3$ of channel *info* in U_0 is changed to $\Delta 2$ in U_1). Other timers which have expired cause an immediate migration or the selection of the alternative part of a communication action (see W_1 which is evolving to W_2).

Note that the last network expression derived from *TravelShop* in Table 4 corresponds to the intermediate configuration shown in Figure 1(b). Note also that in the representation of Figure 1(b) we show the *home* location, even though it is not present in the last network expression in Table 4. The reason is that the *client* process has moved to *travelshop*, and there is at present no process residing at *home*. This situation changes in the final configuration of Figure 1(c) where *client* has completed its migration and came back to its initial location.

Remark 1. Component decomposition is unique since the rule (CALL) treats recursive definitions as function calls which take a unit of time. Another consequence of such a treatment is that it is impossible to execute an infinite sequence of action steps without executing any time steps. Both these properties would not hold if, instead of an action rule (CALL), we would have a structural rule of the form $l [\![id(\boldsymbol{v}) : \Gamma]\!] \equiv l [\![\{\boldsymbol{v}/\boldsymbol{u}\} P_{id} : \Gamma]\!]$. $\qquad\qquad \square$

3   Safe Access Permissions

In this section we attempt to verify that a migrating process possesses a sufficiently rich set of initial access permissions such that, whenever later on it attempts to communicate over a channel, it has the required safe access permission. While doing so we need to take into account that migrating processes have their access permission sets modified according to the mapping *apm*. If we succeed, then an important security problem related to migration and access permissions is solved in the sense that never an unauthorised attempt to communicate over a channel happens during network evolutions.

Throughout this section we assume that all the data sets are finite (see Remark 2), and that the right hand side P_{id} of each recursive definition (1) is either a primitive process (i.e., $P_{id} = \mathtt{stop}$ or $P_{id} = id'(\boldsymbol{w})$) or P_{id} uses exactly one application of one of the process operators to some primitive process(es). This does not diminish the generality of the proposed method since we can always transform all recursive definition into the simple form using additional process

Table 4. Execution steps for the running example where $\Lambda_1 = \{client@home\}$, $\Lambda_2 = \{agent@travelshop, update@travelshop\}$, $\Lambda_3 = \{flightinfo@standard\}$, $\Lambda_4 = \{saleinfo@special\}$ and $\Lambda_5 = \{till@bank\}$

TravelShop

$$\xrightarrow{\;\;\Lambda_1\;\;\Lambda_2\;\;\Lambda_3\;\;\Lambda_4\;\;\Lambda_5\;\;} \qquad\qquad 6 \times \text{(Call)}$$

$home\,[\![\,\mathbf{go}^{\Delta^5}\ travelshop \to P_0 : \varnothing\,]\!]\ |$
$travelshop\,[\![\,Q_0 : \{put\langle flight@travelshop\rangle\}\ |\ \mathbf{go}^{\Delta^0}\ special \to R_0 : \varnothing\,]\!]\ |$
$standard\,[\![\,U_0 : \{put\langle info@standard\rangle, get\langle info@standard\rangle\}\,]\!]\ |$
$special\,[\![\,V_0 : \{put\langle info@special\rangle, get\langle info@special\rangle\}\,]\!]\ |$
$bank\,[\![\,W_0 : \{put\langle pay@bank\rangle, get\langle pay@bank\rangle\}\,]\!]$

$$\xrightarrow{\;\;\{home\,\triangleright\,travelshop\}\;\;\{travelshop\,\triangleright\,special\}\;\;} \qquad\qquad 2 \times \text{(Move)}$$

$travelshop\,[\![\,flight\,\mathbf{?}\,(standardoffer{:}Loc) \to P_1{:}\{get\langle flight@travelshop\rangle\}\ |$
$\qquad\qquad flight\,\mathbf{!}\,\langle standard\rangle \to Q_1{:}\{put\langle flight@travelshop\rangle\}\,]\!]\ |$
$standard\,[\![\,U_1 : \{put\langle info@standard\rangle, get\langle info@standard\rangle\}\,]\!]\ |$
$special\,[\![\,info^{\Delta^9}\,\mathbf{?}\,(newprice : eMoney)$
$\qquad\qquad \to V_1 : \{put\langle info@special\rangle, get\langle info@special\rangle\}\ |$
$\qquad info\,\mathbf{!}\,\langle 60\rangle \to \mathbf{stop} : \{put\langle info@special\rangle\}\,]\!]\ |$
$bank\,[\![\,W_1 : \{put\langle pay@bank\rangle, get\langle pay@bank\rangle\}\,]\!]$

$$\xrightarrow{\;\;\{flight\langle standard\rangle@travelshop\}\;\;\{info\langle 60\rangle@special\}\;\;} \qquad\qquad 2 \times \text{(Com)}$$

$travelshop\,[\![\,P_2{:}\{get\langle flight@travelshop\rangle\}\ |\ Q_1{:}\{put\langle flight@travelshop\rangle\}\,]\!]\ |$
$standard\,[\![\,U_2 : \{put\langle info@standard\rangle, get\langle info@standard\rangle\}\,]\!]\ |$
$special\,[\![\,V_2 : \{put\langle info@special\rangle, get\langle info@special\rangle\}\ |\ \mathbf{stop} : \{put\langle info@special\rangle\}\,]\!]\ |$
$bank\,[\![\,W_2 : \{put\langle pay@bank\rangle, get\langle pay@bank\rangle\}\,]\!]$

$P_0 = flight\,\mathbf{?}\,(standardoffer{:}Loc) \to P_1$
$P_1 = \mathbf{go}^{\Delta^4}\ standardoffer \to info\,\mathbf{?}\,(p1{:}eMoney, specialoffer{:}Loc) \to$
$\qquad \mathbf{go}^{\Delta^3}\ specialoffer \to info\,\mathbf{?}\,(p2{:}eMoney, paying{:}Loc) \to$
$\qquad \mathbf{go}^{\Delta^6}\ paying \to pay\,\mathbf{!}\,\langle\min\{p1,p2\}\rangle \to$
$\qquad \mathbf{go}^{\Delta^4}\ home \to client(130 - \min\{p1,p2\})$
$P_2 = \{standard/standardoffer\}P_1$
$Q_0 = flight\,\mathbf{!}\,\langle standard\rangle \to Q_1$
$Q_1 = \mathbf{go}^{\Delta^{10}}\ bank \to$
$\qquad pay\,\mathbf{?}\,(profit{:}eMoney) \to \mathbf{go}^{\Delta^{12}}\ travelshop \to agent(100 + profit)$
$R_0 = info\,\mathbf{!}\,\langle 60\rangle \to \mathbf{stop}$
$U_0 = info^{\Delta^3}\,\mathbf{!}\,\langle 110, special\rangle \to flightinfo(110, special)$
$U_1 = info^{\Delta^2}\,\mathbf{!}\,\langle 110, special\rangle \to flightinfo(110, special)$
$U_2 = flightinfo(110, special)$
$V_0 = info^{\Delta^{10}}\,\mathbf{?}\,(newprice{:}eMoney)\ \mathbf{then}\ saleinfo(newprice, bank)$
$\qquad\qquad\qquad\qquad \mathbf{else}\ info\,\mathbf{!}\,\langle 90, bank\rangle \to saleinfo(90, bank)$
$V_1 = info^{\Delta^9}\,\mathbf{?}\,(newprice{:}eMoney)\ \mathbf{then}\ saleinfo(newprice, bank)$
$\qquad\qquad\qquad\qquad \mathbf{else}\ info\,\mathbf{!}\,\langle 90, bank\rangle \to saleinfo(90, bank)$
$V_2 = saleinfo(60, bank)$
$W_0 = pay^{\Delta^1}\,\mathbf{?}\,(newpayment{:}eMoney)\ \mathbf{then}\ till(10 + newpayment)$
$\qquad\qquad\qquad\qquad \mathbf{else}\ pay^{\Delta^2}\,\mathbf{!}\,\langle 10\rangle\ \mathbf{then}\ till(0)\ \mathbf{else}\ till(10)$
$W_1 = pay^{\Delta^0}\,\mathbf{?}\,(newpayment{:}eMoney)\ \mathbf{then}\ till(10 + newpayment)$
$\qquad\qquad\qquad\qquad \mathbf{else}\ pay^{\Delta^2}\,\mathbf{!}\,\langle 10\rangle\ \mathbf{then}\ till(0)\ \mathbf{else}\ till(10)$
$W_2 = pay^{\Delta^2}\,\mathbf{!}\,\langle 10\rangle\ \mathbf{then}\ till(0)\ \mathbf{else}\ till(10)$

Table 5. Derivation rules for processes with safe access permissions

$$(\text{TSUB}) \qquad \frac{\Gamma' \subseteq \Gamma \quad \Gamma' \vdash_l P}{\Gamma \vdash_l P}$$

$$(\text{TSTOP}) \qquad \varnothing \vdash_l \texttt{stop}$$

$$(\text{TMOVE}) \qquad \frac{apm(l,l')(\Gamma) \vdash_{l'} P}{\Gamma \vdash_l \texttt{go}^{\Delta t} \, l' \texttt{ then } P}$$

$$(\text{TOUT}) \qquad \frac{put\langle a@l\rangle \in \Gamma \quad \Gamma \vdash_l P \quad \Gamma \vdash_l Q}{\Gamma \vdash_l a^{\Delta t} ! \langle v\rangle \texttt{ then } P \texttt{ else } Q}$$

$$(\text{TIN}) \qquad \frac{get\langle a@l\rangle \in \Gamma \quad \forall v \in \prod \boldsymbol{X} : \Gamma \vdash_l \{v/u\}P \quad \Gamma \vdash_l Q}{\Gamma \vdash_l a^{\Delta t} ? (u{:}\boldsymbol{X}) \texttt{ then } P \texttt{ else } Q}$$

$$(\text{TREC}) \qquad \frac{\Gamma \vdash_l id(v)^{\uparrow H}}{\Gamma \vdash_l id(v)}$$

$$(\text{TPAR}) \qquad \frac{\Gamma \vdash_l P \quad \Gamma \vdash_l Q}{\Gamma \cup \Gamma \vdash_l P \mid Q}$$

identifiers and recursive definitions without affecting the results that follow (e.g., $P \stackrel{\text{df}}{=} a \to b \to P$ is replaced by $P \stackrel{\text{df}}{=} a \to P'$ and $P' \stackrel{\text{df}}{=} b \to P$).

We use judgements of the form $\Gamma \vdash_l P$ to mean that a single-component network $l \llbracket P{:}\Gamma \rrbracket$ has *safe access permissions*. We assume the *open system* context which means that we cannot know precisely the migration patterns of a process and its communication channels which can be acquired through interaction with (unknown) processes. We plan to deal with *close systems* in future, and then take into account the time aspects (here we use time for process coordination).

Given a set *Loc* of locations together with the *apm* mapping as well a process P and location l, we want to devise rules for checking that a set of access permissions Γ satisfies $\Gamma \vdash_l P$. For instance, if $P = \texttt{go}^{\Delta 0} \, l' \texttt{ then } a^{\Delta 1} ! \langle 1\rangle \to \texttt{stop}$ and $apm(l,l') = put^-_{a@l'}$ then there is no Γ such that $\Gamma \vdash_l P$.

If P does not involve recursive definitions, the task is straightforward. One just needs to follow the syntactic structure of the process and incrementally derive Γ. Dealing with recursion is more complicated, and the solution we propose consists in unfolding a recursive process expression sufficiently many times to cover all possibilities resulting from migration. For all $id \in Id$, $n \geq 0$ and $v \in \prod \boldsymbol{X}^{id}$, the n-th *unfolding* of $id(v)$ is given by $id(v)^{\uparrow 0} \stackrel{\text{df}}{=} \texttt{stop}$ and, for $n > 0$, $id(v)^{\uparrow n} \stackrel{\text{df}}{=} P$ where P is obtained from $\{v/u\}P_{id}$ by replacing each subexpression of the form $id'(w)$ with $id'(w)^{\uparrow n-1}$.

The derivation rules for $\Gamma \vdash_l P$ are given in Table 5. The (TMOVE) rule concerns a migration from location l to l'. In order to have $l \llbracket \texttt{go}^{\Delta t} \, l' \texttt{ then } P : \Gamma \rrbracket$ with safe access permissions, it is necessary to have $l' \llbracket P : \Gamma' \rrbracket$ with safe access permissions after applying the access permission modification to Γ when moving from l to l' (note that $\Gamma' = apm(l,l')(\Gamma)$). The rule (TOUT) simply requires that a process attempting to send a message along a channel a should possess the access permission $put\langle a@l\rangle$. Similarly, the rule (TIN) requires that a process attempting to receive a message along a channel a should possess the access permission $get\langle a@l\rangle$; moreover, after receiving this message, it should have safe access permissions with the current Γ irrespective of the values carried by that message. The constant H in the rule (TREC) is $H \overset{\text{df}}{=} 2 \cdot |Loc| \cdot \left(1 + \sum_{id \in Id} |X_1^{id}| \cdot \ldots \cdot |X_{m_{id}}^{id}|\right)$. The value of H comes from rather technical considerations needed to prove results. We can always ensure that H is a well defined integer, and (TIN) is a finitary rule according to the following argument.

Remark 2. The judgement system in Table 5 makes important use of data through the (TOUT) rule as a received message may carry a location or channel name which may later be used by other rules. Other kinds of values carried by messages or present in process descriptions are ignored. Hence, for the purpose of safe access permissions, we can replace all non-location and non-channel values by a special value τ, and all the data types different from *Loc* and *Chan* by a singleton type $X = \{\tau\}$. In this way, all the data sets become finite. Hence, in particular, H is an integer value, and $\prod X$ in (TIN) is a finite set. $\quad\square$

We have defined what it means to have safe access permissions in the case of a single-component network. In the general case, a network N has *safe access permissions* if each of its components does. These two definitions are consistent in the sense that $\Gamma \vdash_l P$ iff $\Gamma \vdash_l P_i$ for every component network $l[\![P_i:\Gamma]\!]$ of a single-component network $l[\![P:\Gamma]\!]$; this follows from the rule (TPAR).

The first main result states that safe access permissions is preserved over the network evolutions defined by the operational semantics.

Theorem 1 (soundness). *If a well-formed network N has safe access permissions, and N' is reachable from N, then N' has also safe access permissions.*

The second main result is that in a network with safe access permissions there are no attempt to access a communication channel without an appropriate access permission. This result should be seen as a justification of our interest in the notion of safe access permissions.

Theorem 2 (safety of communications). *Let N be a well-formed network with safe access permissions.*

$$l[\![a^{\Delta t}\,!\,\langle v\rangle \text{ then } P \text{ else } Q : \Gamma]\!] \in comp(N) \quad \textit{implies} \quad put\langle a@l\rangle \in \Gamma$$
$$l[\![a^{\Delta t}\,?\,(u{:}X) \text{ then } P \text{ else } Q : \Gamma]\!] \in comp(N) \quad \textit{implies} \quad get\langle a@l\rangle \in \Gamma\,.$$

As an immediate corollary of Theorem 2, for a network with safe access permissions it is possible to simplify the operational rule for process communication by deleting $put\langle a@l\rangle \in \Gamma$ and $get\langle a@l\rangle \in \Gamma'$ in rule (COM), and so simplifying the implementation.

The third main result is that the notion of a network with safe access permissions is complete in the sense that a network which does not satisfy this property can always be placed in an environment which reveals its potential to break safety of interprocess communication.

Theorem 3 (completeness). *Let $N = l \llbracket P : \Gamma \rrbracket$ be a well-formed network such that $\Gamma \not\vdash_l P$. Then there is a well-formed network N' with safe access permissions as well as a well-formed network N'' reachable from $N \mid N'$ such that one of the following holds:*

- *there is a component $l' \llbracket a^{\Delta t} \, ! \, \langle v \rangle$ then P' else $P'' : \Gamma' \rrbracket$ of N'' such that $put \langle a @ l' \rangle \notin \Gamma'$;*
- *there is a component $l' \llbracket a^{\Delta t} \, ? \, (u{:}X)$ then P' else $P'' : \Gamma' \rrbracket$ of N'' such that $get \langle a @ l' \rangle \notin \Gamma'$.*

We developed a sound and complete system for safe communication and migration in open networks. Hence we are able now to validate systems where one does not need to check access permissions as they are guaranteed not to be violated, improving implementation. Moreover, the results can be extended by allowing systems in which processes are not blocked (deadlocked) because of the lack of dynamically changing access permissions.

4   Conclusions and Related Work

We introduced a distributed process algebra with processes able to migrate between different locations and timing constraints used to control migration and communication. We use local clocks and local maximal parallelism of actions. Processes have appropriate access rights to communicate; the access permissions are dynamic and can change. We have provided an operational semantics of this model, and investigated the safety of communication and migration in terms of access permissions. While we are not aware of any approach combining all these aspects regarding mobility with timing constraints, local clocks, and dynamic access permission mechanism, our work is related to a large body of literature using process algebra in (type-based) security. Several systems encompass various forms of access control policies in distributed systems; among them, the work on Dpi calculus in [13] uses type systems to control statically the access to the resources at the different locations of a distributed system. Other related work on access control in distributed systems is done in the context of the language KLAIM and its extensions, using type systems that enable the dynamic exchange of access rights. The paper [7] combines a weak form of information flow control with typed cryptographic operations to ensure safe static access control and secure network communications. The paper [5] use cryptographic operations and capability types to get a secure implementation of a typed pi-calculus in order to realise various policies for accessing the communication channels. None of these systems, however, uses together mobility as a first class citizen controlled by timing constraints, dynamic aspects of the access permissions, local clocks and parallelism. These advantages of the new model can allow to specify and enforce more diverse and expressive security policies based on access permissions. This could be done in the context of designing good programming language supporting migration in a distributed environment [16]. On the other hand, several prototype languages have been designed and experimental implementations derived from process calculi like KLAIM [4] and ACUTE [15]. These prototype languages did not become a practical programming language because hard questions revolving mainly around issues relating to security. PERTIMO is intended to help bridging the gap between the existing foundational process algebras and forthcoming realistic languages. It extends some previous attempts related to TDPI [10] and TIMO [8]. PERTIMO derives from TIMO model (a simplified distributed π-calculus with explicit timeouts) presented in [8] by adding a type system in order to express security aspects related to access permissions. The basic notion of a timeout in TIMO seemed useful and elegant. PERTIMO retains this notion and, in addition, it incorporates access permissions in order to provide formal foundations for security problems relating to the adequate protection of access control information in distributed environment.

As related work, we should mention distributed pi-calculus having an explicit notion of location, and dealing with static resources access [12] by using a type system. The paper [3] studies a π-calculus extension with a timer construct, and then enriches the timed π_t with locations. Other timed extensions of process algebras have been studied in [2] and [11]. In [6] the authors present a typed π-calculus with groups and group creation in which each name belongs to a group. The rules for good environments ensure that the names and groups declared in an environment are distinct, and that all the types mentioned in an environment are good. A consequence of the typing discipline is the ability to preserve secrets, namely preventing certain communications that would leak secrets. The type system is used for regulating the mobile computation, allowing to partition the processes into disjoint groups in order to specify the behaviour of both communication and mobility. Somehow related to our dynamic access permissions, [1] presents a parametric calculus for processes exchanging code which may contain free variables to be bound by the receiver's code (called open mobile code). Type safety is ensured by a combination of static and dynamic checks of such an exchange of open code. In this way it is possible to express rebinding of code in a distributed environment in a relatively simple way.

Deriving concrete implementation from PERTIMO is part of future work, and the approach presented in this paper is just a first step in this direction. In our future work we plan to extend the current model as follows:

- access permissions to locations to control migrations of processes;
- security levels for migrating processes to control access permissions to channels and locations;
- relaxing the synchronisation resulting from the maximally parallel semantics, by retaining maximal parallelism within each location, but allowing locations to proceed with different speed;
- rules for well-typing of values in exchanged messages;
- defining and analysing security policies for access and migration control; and
- introducing and analysing failures in process migration.

Acknowledgement. We would like to thank the anonymous reviewers for their constructive suggestions. This research was supported by the International Joint Project of the Royal Society of London, the EPSRC VERDAD project, and NSFC Grants 60910004 and 2010CB328102.

References

1. Ancona, D., Fagorzi, S., Zucca, E.: A Parametric Calculus for Mobile Open Code. ENTCS 192, 3–22 (2008)
2. Baeten, J., Bergstra, J.A.: Discrete Time Process Algebra: Absolute Time, Relative Time and Parametric Time. Fundamenta Informaticae 29, 51–76 (1997)
3. Berger, M.: Towards Abstractions For Distributed Systems Imperial College, Department of Computing (2002)
4. Bettini, L., Kannan, R., De Nicola, R., Ferrari, G.-L., Gorla, D., Loreti, M., Moggi, E., Pugliese, R., Tuosto, E., Venneri, B.: The klaim project: Theory and practice. In: Priami, C. (ed.) GC 2003. LNCS, vol. 2874, pp. 88–150. Springer, Heidelberg (2003)
5. Bugliesi, M., Giunti, M.: Secure Implementations of Typed Channel Abstractions. In: Proc. of POPL, pp. 251–262. ACM, New York (2007)
6. Cardelli, L., Ghelli, G., Gordon, A.: Secrecy and Group Creation. Inf. Comput. 196, 127–155 (2005)
7. Chothia, T., Duggan, D., Vitek, J.: Type-based Distributed Access Control. In: Proc. of CSFW 2003, pp. 170–184. IEEE Computer Society, Los Alamitos (2003)
8. Ciobanu, G., Koutny, M.: Modelling and verification of timed interaction and migration. In: Fiadeiro, J.L., Inverardi, P. (eds.) FASE 2008. LNCS, vol. 4961, pp. 215–229. Springer, Heidelberg (2008)
9. Ciobanu, G., Koutny, M.: TiMoTy: Timed Mobility with Types of Formal Methods Laboratory Romanian Academy, Institute of Computer Science, Iasi (2010)
10. Ciobanu, G., Prisacariu, C.: Timers for Distributed Systems. ENTCS 164, 81–99 (2006)
11. Corradini, F., Ferrari, G.L., Pistore, M.: On the Semantics of Durational Actions. Theoretical Computer Science 269, 47–82 (2001)
12. Hennessy, M.: A Distributed π-calculus. Cambridge University Press, Cambridge (2007)
13. Hennessy, M., Riely, J.: Resource Access Control in Systems of Mobile Agents. Information and Computation 173, 82–120 (2002)
14. Milner, R.: Communicating and Mobile Systems: the π-calculus. Cambridge University Press, Cambridge (1999)
15. Sewell, P., et al.: Acute: High-Level Programming Language Design for Distributed Computation. Journal of Functional Programming 17, 547–612 (2007)
16. Thorn, T.: Programming Languages for Mobile Code. ACM Computing Surveys 29, 213–239 (1997)

From a Community of Practice to a Body of Knowledge: A Case Study of the Formal Methods Community

Jonathan P. Bowen[1] and Steve Reeves[2]

[1] London South Bank University, Faculty of Business
Borough Road, London SE1 0AA, United Kingdom
jonathan.bowen@lsbu.ac.uk
http://www.jpbowen.com

[2] The University of Waikato, Department of Computer Science
Hamilton 3240, New Zealand
stever@cs.waikato.ac.nz
http://www.cs.waikato.ac.nz/~stever/

Abstract. A Body of Knowledge (BoK) is an ontology for a particular professional domain. A Community of Practice (CoP) is the collection of people developing such knowledge. In the paper we explore these concepts in the context of the formal methods community in general and the Z notation community, as has been supported by the Z User Group, in particular. The existing SWEBOK Software Engineering Body of Knowledge is considered with respect to formal methods and a high-level model for the possible structure of of a BoK is provided using the Z notation.

1 Introduction

The increase of collective knowledge has been an important part of human progress through the ages [30]. This increase has been possible with the development of communication through complex language that is able to capture and transmit thought between people. The ability to record this in written form has enabled long-lasting knowledge to be built upon through successive generations. The desire to record information is an innate part of human nature, allowing knowledge to be passed on to others. An organization or community has information recorded in a distributed manner, whether using information technology, paper, or human memory [9]. Capturing this collective memory is a challenge, even with today's modern technology.

Leading scientific institutions such as the Royal Society in London now recognize the importance of using advanced web-based technology to aid in the public understanding of scientific knowledge [6]. Web-based communities can be a very effective way to foster distributed creativity extremely quickly and without geographical constraints [22].

The success of Wikipedia (and there are critics, of course) is an example of a system for distributed creativity, and reflection on Wikipedia shows how a "living" document can defuse many of the criticisms that might be made of the idea of a Body of Knowledge (BoK) [33] being compiled for some technical area in a distributed and cooperative manner. For example, it is clearly never finished, continuously developing over time. It is also very easily extensible and adaptable. But, it does also, at any moment in time,

M. Butler and W. Schulte (Eds.): FM 2011, LNCS 6664, pp. 308–322, 2011.

represent a platform that people can refer to and work from, even if only as a starting point, thus driving the BoK forward, and subsequently adding to the record.

Wikis in general form an excellent framework for collaboratively developing information and knowledge [10]. They enable a community of people to add to, update, and correct information on a set of interlinked topics. As well as standard hyperlinks between items of information, wikis can also allow these items to be organized into categories that themselves can be organized in a lattice-like structure (not dissimilar to bigraphs [26]), allowing an alternative way of transferring the information. Links are normally added manually, although research has been undertaken on how this could be automated using a machine-learning approach [25].

Formal methods have a significant amount of knowledge associated with them. This has been developed over the last few decades, especially in the context of software engineering [1,15,16]. However, the important underpinnings of formal methods have not been formulated as a BoK, unlike IEEE's SWEBOK for software engineering [18].

In Section 2, we consider the formal methods community in the context of a Community of Practice (CoP), a social science framework for the developmental stages of a professional community. In Section 3, we consider the Body of Knowledge that could be desirable for a professional software engineer in the area of formal methods. In Section 4, we formalise some desirable properties of a Body of Knowledge using the Z notation. Finally in Section 5, we draw some conclusions on the current state of the formal methods Body of Knowledge and consider possible future directions.

2 Community of Practice

A critical part of knowledge development is learning. Increasingly it has been realised, recently, that this is largely social in character, although it often takes place in the workplace [12]. In this framework, the concept of legitimate peripheral participation (LPP) has been developed [23]. This approach considers how individuals move from being newcomers in a community, eventually becoming experienced in some collaborative project or endeavour. Often the initial tasks undertaken by participants are small-scale and low-risk. Nevertheless, the act of empowering these peripheral members to participate in a large-scale collaborative project promotes interaction between novices and experts. It has the potential to generate productive knowledge development within the community involved in the overall effort.

Such social considerations have also led to the theoretical framework of CoP, with a number of elements, principles, and developmental stages [31,32,17]. A CoP is a group of people with a shared interest or profession, engaged in the enrichment of communal knowledge. It involves situated learning, in which the people that are learning also apply this knowledge in the same context (e.g., during practical experience). In this section, the Z user community is used as an exemplar for the various elements, aspects, and stages of a CoP.

2.1 Fundamental Elements of a CoP

The following three fundamental elements form the structural model of a community of practice [32, chapter 2]:

1. *Domain:* A CoP must have a common interest to be effective. All the participants in the group must be able to contribute in some way within this domain. Otherwise it is just a collection of people with no particular purpose. For example, the Z notation has formed the nucleus of a CoP in a formal methods context.
2. *Community:* A CoP also needs a group of people who are willing to engage with at least some others in the group, so ultimately the entire group is transitively connected as a single entity, from a global viewpoint. This aspect is critical to the effective development of knowledge. The group of people interested in the Z notation started at the Oxford University Computing Laboratory through the inspiration of Jean-Raymond Abrial in the late 1970s and early 1980s. It has gradually spread around the world since then.
3. *Practice:* The CoP must explore both existing knowledge and develop new knowledge, based on existing concepts, but expanded through actual application in a practical sense. This leads to a set of common approaches and shared standards in applying them. The Z notation is based on predicate logic and set theory, both very standard concepts in mathematics that were originally formulated a long time before the development of Z. Schema boxes were added to the mathematics for the convenient structuring of realistic specifications. Initially case studies were specified. More recently, Z has been used for major industrial software engineering projects of a significant scale where system integrity is an important factor.

Developing a healthy CoP requires the interplay of these three elements within a community in a balanced manner, because they are all dynamically changing over time, rather than being unalterable. Whilst it is important to have the three elements controlled to a degree in a CoP, perseverance in one element will help ease the potential problems in another. As Wenger et al. have asserted, *"The art of community development is to use the synergy between domain, community, and practice to help a community evolve and fulfil its potential."* [32, page 47] Without the three elements above, a true CoP cannot evolve. With them, the community can develop a Body of Knowledge that can be used by practitioners within a particular area of expertise. This may be through books, courses, web resources, standards, etc.

2.2 Cultivating a CoP

The success or failure of a community of practice largely depends on the purpose and objective of the community combined with its interests and resources. Wenger et al. [32, chapter 3] have identified seven specific aspects that should be addressed to enable a CoP to flourish:

1. *Design the CoP to evolve naturally:* communities are naturally dynamic and the ability to adapt to the current needs of the CoP at different points in its development is important. In the case of Z, the initial community was largely based in Oxford. The Masters course at the Programming Research Group in Oxford included Z and intensive courses were also offered.
2. *Create opportunities for open discussion:* often an outsider can add value to the CoP by bringing in ideas that may not have evolved in the community if it was completely isolated. An annual Z User Meeting was established in 1986, initially in Oxford and later around the United Kingdom and then Europe. This aided the spread of Z nationally and then internationally.

3. *Welcome and allow different levels of participation:* some people will be able to devote large amounts of time to the CoP, but a much larger number will be able to commit to a small but nevertheless useful contribution. The core Z research was initially at Oxford, but later other research centres such as the University of York in the UK and the University of Queensland in Australia developed significant Z experience and made major research contributions. Others taught Z in formal methods courses within university degree programmes, without necessarily undertaking research.

4. *Develop both public and private CoP facilities:* public events are very useful for community building and smaller private interactive discussions are important to make the larger meetings more effective. The Z User Meeting, as previously mentioned, formed the core of public events for Z. This developed into the ZB Conference, with the related B-Method community, in 2000. These were important networking events for interaction between individuals too. It has now become the ABZ conference with the inclusion of ASM (Abstract State Machines) in 2008, Alloy in 2010, and VDM in 2012, held every two years [8].

5. *Focus on the value of the CoP:* the value of a community may not be immediately obvious, but it should be nurtured explicitly by creating suitable events, activities, and relationships where the value can develop naturally. As well as the Z User Meetings, there were also academic and industrial courses, available to this day. A formal Z User Group (ZUG, *http://zuser.org*) was established in 1992 to act as a focus for Z activities, with finance raised through the Z User Meetings. The production of an ISO standard for Z occupied most of the 1990s, initially based on Spivey's "Z Reference Manual" (ZRM) [29], finally to appear in 2002 [19]. This formed the focus for the Community Z Tools (CZT) project that has produced a number of open source tools based on the Z standard (see *http://czt.sourceforge.net*).

6. *Combine familiarity and excitement within the CoP:* participants should feel comfortable with the day-to-day environment provided by the community, but there should be additional events that provide a "buzz" to keep people involved. In addition to Z User Meetings, a ZFORUM mailing list was established in the 1980s, which was later linked to a specially created newsgroup, *comp.specification.z*, and is still available through Google Groups. A Z archive was established using FTP and email access at Oxford, later augmented by web-based information from 1994, including more general formal methods information, incorporated as part of the Virtual Library initiated by Tim Berners-Lee, the inventor of the web. The information is now accessible through a Formal Methods Wiki that can be updated online by the entire formal methods community under *http://formalmethods.wikia.com*.

7. *Find and nurture a regular rhythm for the CoP:* there should be periodic events and milestones that provide a temporal structure to the community, providing participants with a sense of progress and achievement. The Z User Meetings were held at first annually, then on an 18 month cycle, and now a two year cycle.

The above seven principles are recurrent aspects of the life of a CoP itself, rather than external rules that are to be imposed on the community, as is explained by Wenger et al.: *"The challenge of designing natural structures like communities of practice is creating an approach to design that redefines design itself"* [32, page 64]. If any of these considerations are deficient in a particular CoP, it can lead to the ultimate failure of the community.

2.3   Stages of Community Development

The community development of a CoP typically goes through the following five stages, although it varies from case to case in the ways and sequence a community experiences them [32, chapters 4–5].

1. *Potential:* an extant social and/or professional network is needed to bootstrap a CoP and form a core of the community. An important aspect is for members to sense enough commonality so that they feel connected. Initially for Z, there was a group of people already interested in formal methods in general at Oxford. The seed of Z formed when Jean-Raymond Abrial visited the Programming Research Group in Oxford and found a group receptive to his ideas.

2. *Coalescing:* the CoP needs to combine a good understanding of existing knowledge with visualization for what is possible in the future. The value of sharing information must be appreciated by those involved. The group at Oxford were already expert in the underlying mathematics used by Z. They also had the vision of applying this to the specification of computer-based systems.

3. *Maturing:* there must be a move from establishing goals to the first steps in realizing these. The role of the CoP must be understood and defined in a wider context with relation to the domain areas. The establishment of the Z User Meetings in 1986, together with the Z FORUM electronic newsletter distributed via email around the same time, was seminal in providing a focus for wider Z-based activities. Gradually others interested in formal methods, both within the United Kingdom and around the world, gravitated towards Z, especially through attendance of the early Z User Meetings and communication via the newsletter. ZFORUM was initially edited from contributions via email, but later messages could be submitted directly by subscribers. The IBM CICS project in the 1980s provided an example of a real industrial project that used Z successfully. During the maturing phase, a *Body of Knowledge* (BoK) [33] is gradually formed and implicitly agreed by the community, as least informally. In the case of Z, Spivey's *Z Reference Manual* was issued as a de facto standard in 1988, with a second edition in 1992 and finally an online version in 2001 [29].

4. *Stewardship:* once a CoP has matured, a momentum must be maintained with changes in personnel, etc. The knowledge of the CoP must remain relevant, up to date, and be of continuing benefit to the people involved. The establishment of the Z User Group in 1992 meant that Z had an organizational focus, with a constitution providing a chair, secretary, treasurer, and committee. Over the next decade, the ISO Z standard was produced [19]. This formalized the BoK related to Z developed by the community during the previous maturing phase.

5. *Transformation:* eventually a CoP will naturally transmogrify into some new form or disappear at the end of its useful lifetime. A formal institution may be established, several communities may form, it may become more social than professional, or the enthusiasm may die. After the production of the Z standard, the Community Z Tools project acted as a focus for open source Z tools based on the standard. The Z User Meeting became the ZB Conference and then the ABZ Conference, with a wider scope as research in Z contracted. The Z User Group became less active as conferences were organized and underwritten by the host institutions directly. While a Z community still exists, and significant industrial projects are still

using Z for high integrity applications, the focus of research and tool development has now moved to the B-Method and Event-B, together with Z-related languages and tools such as Alloy [20].

In general, the first two stages span the period of initiating and developing a community of practice. The later three stages deal with the phases of maintaining, progressing, making the community flourish; or it may falter, during its natural evolution. Any view of an existing CoP will be a snapshot at one of these stages in its lifecycle. The Z community has reached the final transformation stage.

3 Body of Knowledge

A Community of Practice (CoP) typically develops a Body of Knowledge (BoK) [33] as part of the development of a mature CoP during the maturing and stewardship phased mentioned in the previous section. A BoK provides a set of concepts, terms, activities, etc., that are useful or essential in a particular professional domain. A BoK is typically formulated by a relevant professional association and there are a number of examples in existence, including SWEBOK [18].

Issues for a BoK include knowledge representation, knowledge acquisition, adequate coverage of knowledge, and revisions to the BoK. Existing BoKs are typically presented in a hierarchical tree structure. Often there are a number of sections with parts referring to each other. Designers of BoKs are normally experts in the field who use their own knowledge, augmented with a literature and lecture survey as required. Ensuring completeness can be problematic as a result. A more distributed and community-oriented approach may be more successful in ensuring better completeness. It is possible that data mining and machine learning techniques could be used to extract and generate material for a BoK from online resources semi-automatically in the future [25].

A BoK is normally used for certification and education or training. The knowledge must reflect current best practice, which inevitably changes over time. However, updates cannot be undertaken in an uncontrolled manner since associated lecture and other education material needs to be maintained in line with the BoK.

There has been a certain amount of criticism of the very idea of developing and recording a BoK in an area like, for example, software engineering (where the complaints are based around the ever-changing nature of the subject, what "the subject" even signifies, and the fact that no two people agree on what constitutes software engineering). However, much of this criticism misses the point about the need to record "how things are now" in order that, firstly, knowledge is not lost, and, secondly, the current and future practitioners can build on the work of those from the past, as recorded. One really only needs to look at formal methods and software engineering to see, even in their highly specialised areas, and relatively short lifetimes, the continual repeating of prior work and reinvention of prior knowledge. This, surely, shows that an accepted record, no matter how partial, incomplete, imperfect, or contentious it may be, is sorely needed if we are not to repeatedly rediscover knowledge.

This role of collective memory is an important contribution of a BoK. A BoK should not merely be something against which to judge a particular academic course or a professional in a specific field.

There is a very pragmatic point to be made here too. Many accreditation bodies simply do not have the expertise or time to listen to and argue sensibly with people who, for "market" reasons *have to* achieve accreditation. Thus, they rely on documents like the IEEE SWEBOK [18] and, often with little understanding, insist they are followed, applying them thoughtlessly when considering accreditation. From experience, no amount of arguing with panels (backed-up by national bodies) about why their interpretation of the SWEBOK is wrong has any effect; indeed, it is seen as special pleading from an accreditation applicant who has not, according to the accreditation body, managed to achieve the necessary level of competence. This could be seen as a strong argument for not encouraging the development of BoKs: if accreditation bodies cannot find a BoK document then they cannot misuse it, or hide their poor knowledge and methods so easily. However, we believe that a BoK's ability to record knowledge in an authoritative manner is a very strong point in its favour that cannot be dismissed lightly. (At least it is *something* to argue against.) Thus, we are left with developing the best BoKs possible, formulating them clearly and encouraging their acceptance, and aiming to ensure that their misuse is minimised.

We would also support the conclusions in Boute's 2008 paper from [4]:

> *We have argued that the most effective way for making Formal Methods an evident part of everyday practice is not convincing the current practitioners but investing in the education of future generations. Formal Methods, in the sense of mathematical modeling, can be the lever to lift the entire computing curriculum to the scientific and professional level that would be considered acceptable in classical university-level engineering.*

In addition, IEEE and ACM have realised that it is useful to consider how we might recommend the content of an academic degree (or other course) that is designed to prepare professionals for software engineering work.

A report of the Joint Task Force on computing curricula formed by the IEEE Computer Society and the ACM has been produced [21]. This document (on *Software Engineering Education Knowledge* or "SEEK") specifically addresses the design and content of software engineering programmes, basing itself on the SWEBOK work. But, whereas the SWEBOK is intended to describe the knowledge and experience that a practising software engineer should have after four years of professional working, the SEEK uses that as a target and lays out, in essence, how to *educate* a software engineer so that they will be at the correct level, according to SWEBOK, in the required time.

We suggest that work on "FMEK" (Formal Methods Education Knowledge) and an "FMBOK" (Formal Methods Body of Knowledge) starts hand-in-hand, following the pattern that the wider software engineering community has successfully developed. Even through the state of the art in formal methods is steadily advancing [7,8,3], formal methods are now mature enough for such an initiative to be undertaken.

As the SEEK document states [21, section 2.6, page 12]:

> – *The SWEBOK is intended to cover knowledge after four years of practice.*
> – *The SWEBOK intentionally does not cover non-software engineering knowledge that a software engineer must have.*

The *Guide to the SWEBOK* [18, Foreword, page vii] itself states:

> *The steering committee organized task forces in the following areas:*
> 1. *Define Required Body of Knowledge and Recommended Practices.*
> 2. *Define Ethics and Professional Standards.*
> 3. *Define Educational Curricula for undergraduate, graduate and continuing education.*

This book supplies the first component: required body of knowledge and recommended practices. [...] The educational curriculum for undergraduates is being completed by a joint effort of the IEEE Computer Society and the ASM and is expected to be completed in 2004.

The last mentioned effort has SEEK as its result [21].

3.1 Characterising Formal Methods

Perhaps the first step we should take is to agree on what formal methods *are*. SEEK says of software engineering [21, section 2.2]:

A common misconception about software engineering is that it is primarily about process-oriented activities (i.e., requirements, design, quality assurance, process improvement, and project management). In this view, competency in software engineering can be achieved by acquiring a strong engineering background, a familiarity with a software development process and a minimal computing background, including experience using one or more programming languages. Such a background is, in fact, quite insufficient; the misconception that leads to such thinking is based on an incomplete view of the nature and challenges of software engineering.

The section from which the quotation above is extracted goes on to point out that software engineering is different from other engineering areas because it deals with an intangible, abstract "material", namely software, and needs to use discrete rather than continuous mathematics due to the discrete way that software interacts with the world.

It is also noted that software engineering has to be based on computing and mathematics, and when educating software engineers we need to have a curriculum that covers everything from theory and principles right up to development methods (which, as the report states, "*are the most visible* [part of what we do] *to those outside of the discipline*" [21]). This all applies to formal methods too.

Perhaps where the subjects notably diverge (though the boundary between theory and practice is very blurred, and perhaps is a red-herring) is when the word "engineering" is considered.

In [21, section 2.3], where the role of software engineering as an engineering disciple *per se* is discussed, the following is noted:

We must also point out that although there are strong similarities between software engineering and more traditional engineering [listed later in subsection 2.3.1 of the document]*, there are also some differences (not necessarily to the detriment of software engineering):*

- *Foundations are primarily in computer science, not in natural sciences.*
- *The focus is on discrete rather than continuous mathematics.*
- *The concentration is on abstract/logical entities instead of concrete/physical artefacts.*
- *There is no "manufacturing" phase in the traditional sense.*
- *Software "maintenance" primarily refers to continued development, or evolution, and not to conventional wear and tear.*

So, perhaps this is straying outside the boundaries of formal methods. However, SEEK then states [21, section 2.3.2 on Engineering Design]:

Software engineering differs from traditional engineering because of the special nature of software, which places a greater emphasis on abstraction, modeling, information organisation and representation, and the management of change. Software engineering also includes implementation and quality control activities normally considered in the manufacturing process design and manufacturing process steps of the product cycle. Furthermore, continued evolution (i.e., "maintenance") is also of more critical importance for software. Even with this broader scope, however, a central challenge of software engineering is still the kind of decision-making known as engineering design. An important aspect of this challenge is that the supporting process must be applied at multiple levels of abstraction.

Some of this again seems very relevant to formal methods.

3.2 Organizational Matters

SEEK sets out many templates for academic degree courses that, if followed, will guarantee that the students so educated will necessarily be on the path to the requirements of SWEBOK (which, recall, states what a professional engineer with four years of experience should have achieved).

One of the patterns provided for possible software engineering course accreditation is *Aus1*, a pattern suitable when the programme is based in a computer science department and is delivered over four years. The pattern (from page 64 of the SEEK document [21]) is shown in Table 1.

The following paragraph from the SEEK [21] is a reasonable starting point when considering the structure of an FMEK:

Chapter 2 discusses the nature of software engineering as a discipline, depicting some of the history of software engineering education, and explaining how these elements have influenced the recommendations in this document. Chapter 3 presents the guiding principles behind the development of this document. These principles were adapted from those originally articulated by the CC2001 Task Force as they began work on what became the CCCS volume. Chapter 3 also provides the description of what every SE graduate should know. Chapter 4 presents the body of Software Engineering Education Knowledge (the SEEK) that underlies the curriculum guidelines and educational program designs presented in Chapters 5 and 6, respectively. Chapter 7 discusses adaptation of the curriculum recommendations in Chapter 6 to alternative environments. Finally, Chapter 8 addresses various curriculum implementation challenges and also considers assessment approaches.

Table 1. From SEEK [21, page 61]. Software engineering programme based in a computer science department and taught over four years. (NB: the codes used in each entry are explained elsewhere in SEEK, but we present the template here just as an example.)

Year 1		Year 2		Year 3		Year 4	
Sem1A	Sem 1B	Sem2A	Sem2B	Sem3A	Sem 3B	Sem4A	Sem 4B
CS101	CS102	CS220	CS103	CS	Team proj	SE400	SE400
Calc1	Lin Alg	CS270T	SE	SE	Tech elect	SE323 NT291	Tech elect
NT181/NT272	Dig Log	SE201	Team proj	Tech elect	Tech elect	Tech elect	–
Intro EE	CS015 CS106	MA271	–	–	–	–	–

3.3 FMBOK Initiative

FMBOK (Formal Methods Body of Knowledge) is an initiative dedicated to the discussion on a BoK specifically concerned with formal methods [11]. This is an activity within the Formal Methods Europe Subgroup on Education (FME-SOE). More generally, SWEBOK (Software Engineering Body of Knowledge) has been initiated and is being standardized by the IEEE Computer Society [18].

Kenji Taguchi (National Institute of Advanced Industrial Science and Technology, AIST, Japan) and Jose Oliveira (University of Minho, Portugal) organized a panel at the TFM (Teaching Formal Methods) conference in Eindhoven in 2009 to discuss a BoK for formal methods, and the issues surrounding it. This followed a similar initiative at the FMET (Formal Methods Education and Training) workshop held in conjunction with ICFEM 2008. Prior to that, a survey was carried out by FME-SOE on formal methods courses in undergraduate degrees, and José Nuno Oliveira published a paper on formal methods courses in European higher education at TFM'04 [28]. A Model Checking Body of Knowledge (MCBOK) is now underway, aiming to follow the ISO standardization process [27].

4   Formal Model in Z

Currently, BoKs are specified in a variety of informal and sometimes verbose and rather opaque forms [33]. Typically there is some form of hierarchical structure. Here we suggest an abstract framework that could be used to formulate any BoK and ensure a number of desirable properties if followed. The framework is modelled using the Z notation [5,29], based on predicate logic and set theory [13], together with schema boxes for structuring the mathematics forming the specification. The choice of Z here simply reflects the experience and background of the authors, and is not intended to be a judgment on Z relative to other similar languages.

In modelling a BoK, we initially define two given sets, $NAMES$ of entities in the BoK and $REFS$, for references to external items that validate information in the BoK. The name space is split disjointly between entries and categories that provide structure for the entries.

$$[NAMES, REFS]$$

$$ENTRIES,$$
$$CATEGORIES : \mathbb{P}\, NAMES$$
$$\overline{}$$
$$ENTRIES \cap CATEGORIES = \varnothing$$

A basic BoK may be formulated as a finite set of entries, categories and references. Entries may include links to other entries, be categorized in a number of categories, and include citations to other literature verifying or augmenting the information:

$$
\begin{array}{l}
\_\,BOK_0\,\_\!\_\!\_\!\_\!\_\!\_\!\_\!\_\!\_ \\
entries : \mathbb{F}\, ENTRIES \\
categories : \mathbb{F}\, CATEGORIES \\
refs : \mathbb{F}\, REFS \\
\end{array}
$$

$$
\begin{array}{l}
\_\,BOK_1\,\_\!\_\!\_\!\_\!\_\!\_\!\_\!\_\!\_ \\
BOK_0 \\
links : ENTRIES \leftrightarrow ENTRIES \\
cats : NAMES \leftrightarrow CATEGORIES \\
citations : ENTRIES \leftrightarrow REFS \\
\hline
\mathrm{dom}\ links \subseteq entries \\
\mathrm{dom}\ cats \subseteq entries \cup categories \\
\mathrm{dom}\ citations \subseteq entries \\
\end{array}
$$

Links, categories, and citations should be valid. That is, links should be to actual entries in the BoK, all categories should exist in the BoK, and all citations should be to valid references. It is possible to specify entries that have no links, no categories, or no citations:

```
┌─ BOK₂ ─────────────────────────
│ BOK₁
│ ─────────────────────────────
│ ran links ⊆ entries
│ ran cats ⊆ categories
│ ran citations ⊆ refs
└─────────────────────────────────
```

```
┌─ BOK₂ₐ ────────────────────────
│ BOK₂
│ nolinks : 𝔽 ENTRIES
│ nocats : 𝔽 NAMES
│ nocites : 𝔽 ENTRIES
│ ─────────────────────────────
│ nolinks = entries \ dom links
│ nocats =
│     entries ∪ categories \ dom cats
│ nocites = entries \ dom citations
└─────────────────────────────────
```

It may be desirable for all entries to have links and categories and for all categories to have entries and/or subcategories (i.e., for *nolinks*, *nocats*, and *nocites* all to be empty).

Entries may be orphans (i.e., have no links to them) and references may be uncited in any entry:

```
┌─ BOK₂ᵦ ──────────────────────────────────
│ BOK₂ₐ
│ orphans : 𝔽 ENTRIES
│ uncited : 𝔽 REFS
│ ─────────────────────────────────────────
│ orphans = entries \ ran links
│ uncited = refs \ ran citations
└───────────────────────────────────────────
```

It may be a desirable property for there to be no orphans or uncited references (i.e., for *orphans* and *uncited* to be empty).

All entries have links, citations, and categories, although some categories may not have any entries (but could have subcategories). All entries are linked, all categories are used, and all references are cited somewhere.

```
┌─ BOK₃ ─────────────────────────────────
│ BOK₂ᵦ
│ ─────────────────────────────────────
│ entries = dom links = dom citations
│ entries ⊆ dom cats
└─────────────────────────────────────────
```

```
┌─ BOK₄ ──────────────────────────
│ BOK₃
│ ──────────────────────────────
│ ran links = entries
│ ran cats = categories
│ ran citations = refs
└──────────────────────────────────
```

Self-links and self-categories should be disallowed since these ate not helpful for structuring and navigation. More strongly, loops are not desirable in categories:

```
┌─ BOK₅ ──────────────────────────
│ BOK₄
│ ──────────────────────────────
│ id ENTRIES ∩ links = ∅
│ id CATEGORIES ∩ cats = ∅
└──────────────────────────────────
```

```
┌─ BOK₆ ──────────────────────────
│ BOK₅
│ ──────────────────────────────
│ id CATEGORIES ∩ cats⁺ = ∅
└──────────────────────────────────
```

There are some top-level categories that are not subcategories of any other category. These top-level categories provide one or more high-level starting points for traversing the information.

It is desirable for all categories to be used since an empty category does not serve any useful purpose and may be confusing. All entries are interlinked in one direction at least to provide convenient navigation around the information:

$$
\begin{array}{|l}
\hline BOK_7 \underline{\hspace{4cm}} \\
\quad BOK_6 \\
\quad toplevelcats : \mathbb{F}\ CATEGORIES \\
\hline
\quad toplevelcats = \\
\qquad \mathrm{ran}\ cats \setminus \mathrm{dom}\ cats \neq \varnothing \\
\hline
\end{array}
\qquad
\begin{array}{|l}
\hline BOK_8 \underline{\hspace{3cm}} \\
\quad BOK_7 \\
\hline
\quad \mathrm{ran}\ cats = categories \\
\hline
\end{array}
$$

If entries are not interlinked, it is questionable why they are needed in the overall BoK. More strongly, all entries may be linked in both directions:

$$
\begin{array}{|l}
\hline BOK_9 \underline{\hspace{3cm}} \\
\quad BOK_8 \\
\hline
\quad \mathrm{dom}\ links \cup \mathrm{ran}\ links^+ = entries \\
\hline
\end{array}
\qquad
\begin{array}{|l}
\hline BOK_{10} \underline{\hspace{3cm}} \\
\quad BOK_9 \\
\hline
\quad \mathrm{dom}\ links = \mathrm{ran}\ links^+ = entries \\
\hline
\end{array}
$$

All the categories and entries in the BoK are interconnected from the top-level categories by traversing up and down the category lattice:

$$
\begin{array}{|l}
\hline BOK \underline{\hspace{9cm}} \\
\quad BOK_{10} \\
\hline
\quad (cats \cup cats^\sim)^* (\!| \ toplevelcats\ |\!) = entries \cup categories \\
\hline
\end{array}
$$

(Note that the $(\!| \ldots |\!)$ notation indicates the relational image of a set.)

The above Z specification has gradually built up a number of desirable properties in a framework that could be used to specify a Body of Knowledge. Existing BoKs have no uniform framework for their formulation and presentation. Further restrictions such as a strict hierarchical classification of categories could be deemed desirable but have not been modelled here. It is suggested that an abstract framework such as this could be useful for BoKs in general and a formal methods BoK in particular.

5   Conclusions and Future Work

The formal methods community, especially that associated with the Z notation, has been explored using the framework of a Community of Practice (CoP). This is the first time that CoP has been applied in a formal methods context. Mature scientific and engineering disciplines have a generally accepted Body of Knowledge (BoK) associated with them for the education and use of professionals in the field. It is posited, based on the fact that Z, at least, appears to be in the last of the seven stages of development of a CoP, that the formal methods community is reaching a level of maturity when such a repository is necessary for the field to develop further.

In this paper, we have included a high-level model of a BoK using Z. Of course, there are many existing ontological approaches to modelling knowledge, for example, the General Formal Ontology (GFO), the Integrated Definition for Ontology Description Capture Method (IDEF5), the Knowledge Interchange Format (KIF) language based on first-order predicate calculus, the Protégé open source ontology editor, and many others [34]. It has been beyond the scope of this paper to explore these languages, methods, and tools.

The formal methods community is actually a set of interlinked communities of practice. Some, like the CoP associated with Z, are at the transformation stage of their development in a CoP context. Others, such as the related B community, are at the stewardship stage. Still others, such as the ASM community, are at the maturing stage. Overall, the formal methods CoP is sufficiently mature to warrant the development of an FMBOK Body of Knowledge and an associated FMEK (Formal Methods Educational Knowledge) to support the application of formal methods by professional software engineers.

As a specific example, taking the *Aus1* template in Table 1, we might suggest replacing "Dig Log" (digital logic), "Intro EE" (Introduction to Electronic Engineering) and "NT181/NT272" (Group Dynamics and Communication/Engineering Economics) with more foundational theoretical work, perhaps including further algebra (e.g., some "electronic category theory"), further logic (e.g., what Kleene would have called "metalogic") and a suitably adapted version of the NT181 paper with the addition of relevant examples. Also, the emphasis of the software engineering papers and the team projects should clearly be far more oriented towards high integrity systems than the mainstream software engineering papers.

We would also expect to see some of these papers covering the foundations, implementation, and use of tools to support formal methods projects. Overall though, the SEEK templates (of which *Aus1* is just one example) are probably already very suitable (certainly in terms of the short titles of the papers shown) for an FMEK: we simply need to restrict (or enrich?) the existing software engineering papers (and their foundational precursors) to be more oriented towards formal methods. At least the immense amount of work that has been dedicated to the SEEK should be the starting point; it is certainly not necessary to reformulate much of this material again. Given the wide acceptability of the SWEBOK and SEEK work, we would suggest an immediate effort towards adapting the SEEK templates would be a useful step along the way to an FMBOK.

It would also be useful, and interesting, to extend the Z specification for a BoK to specify templates like *Aus1* in Table 1, along with constraints on allowable or acceptable curricula, and links back to the BoK. The aim of an FMEK, recall, would be to give a plan for a (degree) course which, having been attained, will lead to attainment of the BoK after four years (say) of practice. Having this formalised in Z, for example, would allow the transition from education to practice to be more readily traced, as well as supported.

Formal methods are not used in isolation and there are a number of other software engineering approaches that could be combined with formal methods (e.g., agile software development [2] and software testing [14], which may at first seem orthogonal to and even incompatible with formal methods). A BoK or set of interlinked BoKs could consider the combination of various software engineering approaches that could be used in together. Knowledge would include the appropriateness of various combinations in different situations.

In summary, formal methods have developed over the past few decades though a number of interrelated communities. They have now reached a level of maturity when an associated Body of Knowledge would be a worthwhile part of the general effort to ensure that formal methods find their rightful place in the software engineering profession.

Acknowledgements. This paper was initiated by an academic visit by the first author in November 2010 to The University of Waikato, whose support is gratefully acknowledged. Kenji Taguchi (AIST, Japan) provided useful suggestions concerning BoKs in general and the FMBOK in particular. Alison H.-Y. Liu (National Taiwan Normal University) introduced the concept of CoP to us [24]. The referees also provided useful input. Jonathan Bowen is grateful for financial support from Museophile Limited.

References

1. Bjørner, D.: Software Engineering. In: Texts in Theoretical Computer Science. An EATCS Series, vol. 3, Springer, Heidelberg (2005–6)
2. Black, S.E., Boca, P.P., Bowen, J.P., Gorman, J., Hinchey, M.G.: Formal versus agile: Survival of the fittest. IEEE Computer 42(9), 37–45 (2009)
3. Boca, P.P., Bowen, J.P., Siddiqi, J. (eds.): Formal Methods: State of the Art and New Directions. Springer, London (2010)
4. Boute, R.: Formal Methods: Teaching and Practicing Computer Science at the University Level. In: Davies, J., et al. (eds.) Proceedings of the First International Workshop on Formal Methods Education and Training,Technical Report GRACE-TR-2008-03, GRACE Center, Japan (October 2008),
   http://www.grace-center.jp/downloads/GRACE-TR-2008-03.pdf
5. Bowen, J.P.Z.: A formal specification notation. In: Frappier, M., Habrias, H. (eds.) Software Specification Methods: An Overview Using a Case Study. FACIT series, ch. 1, pp. 3–19. Springer, London (2001)
6. Bowen, J.P., Borda, A.: Communicating the public understanding of science: The Royal Society website. International Journal of Technology Management 46(1/2), 146–164 (2009)
7. Bowen, J.P., Hinchey, M.G.: Ten commandments of formal methods . . . Ten years later. IEEE Computer 39(1), 40–48 (2006)
8. Bowen, J.P., Hinchey, M.G.: Ten Commandments Ten Years On: Lessons for ASM, B, Z and VSR-net. In: Abrial, J.-R., Glässer, U. (eds.) Rigorous Methods for Software Construction and Analysis. LNCS, vol. 5115, pp. 219–233. Springer, Heidelberg (2009)
9. Derida, J.: Mal d'Archive: Une Impression Freudienne. Éditions Galilée, 1995. Translated by E. Prenowitz, Archive Fever: A Freudian Impression (1996)
10. Ebersbach, A., Glaser, M., Heigl, M.: Wiki: Web Collaboration. Springer, Heidelberg (2006)
11. FMET. Towards Formal Methods Body of Knowledge (FMBOK). GRACE Center, Japan, http://grace-center.jp/en/prj_fmbok.html (accessed March 31, 2010)
12. Hara, N.: Communities of Practice: Fostering peer-to-peer learning and informal knowledge sharing in the work place, information science and knowledge management. Springer, Heidelberg (2009)
13. Henson, M.C., Reeves, S., Bowen, J.P.Z.: logic and its consequences. CAI: Computing and Informatics 22(4), 381–415 (2003)
14. Hierons, R.M., Bogdanov, K., Bowen, J.P., Cleaveland, R., Derrick, J., Dick, J., Gheorghe, M., Harman, M., Kapoor, K., Krause, P., Luettgen, G., Simons, A.J.H., Vilkomir, S.A., Woodward, M.R., Zedan, H.: Using formal specification to support testing. ACM Computing Surveys 41(2), 1–76 (2009), doi:10.1145/1459352.1459354

15. Hinchey, M.G., Bowen, J.P., Vassev, E.: Formal Methods. In: Laplante, P.A. (ed.) Encyclopedia of Software Engineering, pp. 308–320. Taylor & Francis, Abington (2010)
16. Hinchey, M.G., Jackson, M., Cousot, P., Cook, B., Bowen, J.P., Margaria, T.: Software engineering and formal methods. Communications of the ACM 51(9), 54–59 (2008), doi:10.1145/1378727.1378742
17. Hughes, J., Jewson, N., Unwin, L. (eds.): Communities of Practice: Critical perspectives. Routledge, New York (2007)
18. Abran, A., Moore, J.W., Bourque, P., Dupuis, R.: SWEBOK: Guide to the Software Engineering Body of Knowledge. IEEE Computer Society, Los Alamitos (2004), http://www.swebok.org
19. ISO. *Information Technology – Z Formal Specification Notation – Syntax, Type System and Semantics*. ISO/IEC 13568:2002, International Organization for Standardization (2002)
20. Jackson, D.: Software Abstractions: Logic, Language, and Analysis. The MIT Press, Cambridge (2006)
21. Joint Task Force on Computing Curricula. *Software Engineering 2004: Curriculum Guidelines for Undergraduate Degree Programs in Software Engineering*. Computing Curricula Series, IEEE Computer Society and Association for Computing Machinery (August 23, 2004), http://sites.computer.org/ccse/SE2004Volume.pdf
22. Kommers, P.: Creativity in web-based communities. International Journal of Web Based Communities 6(4), 410–418 (2010)
23. Lave, J., Wenger, E.: Situated Learning: Legitimate peripheral participation. Cambridge University Press, New York (1991)
24. Liu, A.H.-Y., McDaid, S., Bowen, J.P., Beazley, I.: Dulwich OnView: A museum blog run by the community for the community. In: Trant, J., Bearman, D. (eds.) Museums and the Web 2010: Proceedings, Archives & Museum Informatics, Toronto (2010), http://www.archimuse.com/mw2010/papers/liu/liu.html
25. Milne, D., Witten, I.H.: Learning to link with Wikipedia. In: Proc. ACM Conference on Information and Knowledge Management (CIKM 2008), pp. 509–518. ACM Publications, Napa Valley (2008), doi:10.1145/1458082.1458150
26. Milner, R.: Bigraphs and their algebra. In: Electronic Notes in Theoretical Computer Science, vol. 209, pp. 5–19 (2008); Proceedings of the LIX Colloquium on Emerging Trends in Concurrency Theory (LIX 2006), doi:10.1016/j.entcs.2008.04.002
27. Nishihara, H., Shinozaki, K., Hayamizu, K., Aoki, T., Taguchi, K., Kumeno, F.: Model checking education for software engineers in Japan. ACM SIGCSE Bulletin 41(2) (June 2009), doi:10.1145/1595453.1595461
28. Oliveira, J.N.: A Survey of Formal Methods Courses in European Higher Education. In: Dean, C.N., Boute, R.T. (eds.) TFM 2004. LNCS, vol. 3294, pp. 235–248. Springer, Heidelberg (2004)
29. Spivey, J.M.: The Z Notation: A reference manual (2001) (Originally published by Prentice Hall, 1st edn. (1989) 2nd edn. (1992), http://spivey.oriel.ox.ac.uk/~mike/zrm/
30. Van Doren, C.: A History of Knowledge: Past, present, and future. Ballantine Books, New York (1991)
31. Wenger, E.: Communities of Practice: Learning, Meaning, and Identity. Cambridge University Press, Cambridge (1998)
32. Wenger, E., McDermott, R.A., Snyder, W.: Cultivating Communities of Practice: A guide to managing knowledge. Harvard Business School Press, Boston (2002)
33. Wikipedia. Body of Knowledge, Wikimedia Foundation, http://en.wikipedia.org/wiki/BoK (accessed March 31, 2010)
34. Wikipedia. Ontology (information science), Wikimedia Foundation, http://en.wikipedia.org/wiki/Ontology_information_science (accessed March 31, 2010)

Verifying Linearisability with Potential Linearisation Points

John Derrick[1], Gerhard Schellhorn[2], and Heike Wehrheim[3]

[1] Department of Computing, University of Sheffield, Sheffield, UK
J.Derrick@dcs.shef.ac.uk
[2] Universität Augsburg, Institut für Informatik, 86135 Augsburg, Germany
schellhorn@informatik.uni-augsburg.de
[3] Universität Paderborn, Institut für Informatik, 33098 Paderborn, Germany
wehrheim@uni-paderborn.de

Abstract. Linearisability is the key correctness criterion for concurrent implementations of data structures shared by multiple processes. In this paper we present a proof of linearisability of the *lazy* implementation of a set due to Heller et al. The lazy set presents one of the most challenging issues in verifying linearisability: a linearisation point of an operation set by a process other than the one executing it. For this we develop a proof strategy based on refinement which uses *thread local* simulation conditions and the technique of *potential* linearisation points. The former allows us to prove linearisability for arbitrary numbers of processes by looking at only two processes at a time, the latter permits disposing with reasoning about the past. All proofs have been mechanically carried out using the interactive prover KIV.

1 Introduction

The setting of this work are data structures such as sets, stacks and queues that are shared by parallel processes. To increase the opportunities for concurrency (particularly relevant in a multicore context), implementations of these, so called, *concurrent objects* usually apply fine-grained synchronisation schemes for access. Fine-grained synchronisation disposes with locking the whole data structure during access, and locks only single elements (e.g., nodes in a linked list representation). The extreme to this are implementations of operations taking no locks at all.

Such highly concurrent algorithms are intrinsically difficult to prove correct, the down-side of the performance gain from permitting concurrency is the much harder verification problem: how can one verify that the implementation of a concurrent object is correct? Here, the key correctness property to be shown is *linearisability* [11]. It permits one to view operations on concurrent objects as though they occur atomically, in some sequential order [11]:

> Linearisability provides the illusion that each operation applied by concurrent processes takes effect instantaneously at some point between its invocation and its response.

M. Butler and W. Schulte (Eds.): FM 2011, LNCS 6664, pp. 323–337, 2011.

This "point" in between invocation and response of an operation is referred to as the *linearisation point* (LP).

A number of different techniques have been employed to verify linearisability, ranging from shape analysis [1], separation logic and rely-guarantee reasoning [21] to simulation-based methods. The concurrent algorithm considered in this paper (the lazy set of Heller et al. [9]) poses a particular challenge for verification: the linearisation point for one of the operations does not coincide with the execution of an instruction of the source code, but rather can be set by a process other than the one executing the operation. As a consequence, the real LP of this operation is only known when it finishes. This has lead to the development of a number of proof techniques for the lazy set looking into the *past*: the first approach in [20] argues that knowing the outcome of this operation its linearisation point can be found, later approaches use backward simulation proofs [3] or "hindsight" techniques [16].

In this paper we propose a new technique for verifying linearisability of the lazy set which avoids having to look into the past. The technique extends our previous approach [4,5] to cope with the class of algorithms like the lazy set. In general, we carry out a proof of *refinement*: the concurrent implementation is shown to be a valid refinement of the abstract data structure. Our proof principle consists of two levels: we have *local* (i.e., thread modular) *simulation conditions* which need to be verified for the concurrent implementation at hand, and a *general theory* which links the local conditions with linearisability and thus shows their soundness.

Both levels have been formally verified with KIV using standard higher-order logic. A web presentation with all details can be found at [12]. Unfortunately we are not able to describe the global part of the theory in this paper, where we focus on the local simulation conditions and their application to the lazy set.

The key idea of the local conditions is to define *potential* linearisation points, which solve the issue of LPs set by other processes. The next section gives our running example of the lazy set. In section 3 we introduce our refinement technique, and in section 4 we show how we can derive local proof obligations that can cope with the type of algorithm exemplified by our running example. In Section 5 we discuss how these proof obligations can be discharged for this implementation. Finally, Section 6 gives related work and concludes.

2   The Lazy Concurrent Set

Our running example is a concurrent implementation of a set data structure and its access operations. The abstract data type $A = (AS, ASInit, (AOp_p^i)_{i \in I, p \in P})$ uses a finite set of integers as abstract state: $AS \mathrel{\widehat{=}} [set : \mathbb{F}\,\mathbb{Z}]$. The set is initially empty ($ASInit$), and then allows for three operations, $I = \{1, 2, 3\}$ executed by processes $p \in P$: integers can be *added*, *removed*, and we have a test of containment: *contains*. Abstractly, all these operations are atomic. They all return a boolean result: *add* and *remove* return *true* if the set has been changed.

Here, we study the highly concurrent implementation proposed in [9]. The set is implemented by a sorted linked list. Its elements appear in the nodes of

```
add(e):                            remove(e):
  A1 : n1, n3 := locate(e);          R1 : n1, n2 := locate(e);
  A2 : if n3.val != e then           R2 :  if n2.val = e then
  A3 :     n2 := new Node(e);        R2b:     n2.mrk := true;
  A4 :     n2.next := n3;            R3 :     n3 := n2.next;
  A5 :     n1.next := n2;            R4 :     n1.next := n3;
  A6 :     res := true;              R5 :     res := true;
  A7 : else res := false             R6 : else res := false
       endif ;                            endif;
  A8 : n1.unlock();                  R7 : n1.unlock();
  A9 : n3.unlock();                  R8 : n2.unlock();
  A10: return res                    R9 : return res
```

Fig. 1. Operations add and remove

the list in a strictly increasing order. The list has two sentinel nodes: *head* with value $-\infty$ and *tail* with value ∞. Every node has a val field with an integer, a nxt field for the pointer to the next node and a mrk bit (used to mark nodes that as logically deleted).

In the algorithm, atomicity is given up as to allow for concurrency. Concurrency here means that several processes should be able to execute operations on the set at the same time, thus the steps of operations of the algorithm in Fig. 1 can be interleaved. To cope with this interleaving, each node in the list is associated with a lock. Operations n.lock() and n.unlock() lock and unlock a node n.

Operations *add* and *remove* rely on an additional operation *locate* (see Fig. 2) which finds the appropriate position of the element (to be added or removed) and then locks the two adjacent nodes. Operation *add* then checks whether the second locked node already contains the new element to be added, and if not, creates a new node and inserts it (by redirecting the pointer of the previous node) into the list. Operation *remove* proceeds in two steps (when *locate* has found the element to be removed): first, it will *mark* the node as deleted using the mrk bit in line R2b[1] (lazy). Then it will physically remove the node by redirecting pointers. Both *add* and *remove* unlock the nodes returned by *locate* at the end.

The locking scheme of operation *locate* (see Figure 2) is an *optimistic* one: while traversing the list in search of the element, it does not lock nodes. Only when the correct position has been found, the previous and current node is locked. Since these nodes might have been removed by other processes while the search loop was running, the *locate* always *validates* the found candidates. Validation has to check that neither of the locked nodes have already been logically deleted (mrk bit set), and that the nodes are still adjacent. If this fails, locate has to be restarted. Note that the marking bit is used to ensure that removal can be done as one atomic step.

Finally, the most interesting operation is *contains*. The implementation of contains is *wait-free* and uses no locks at all. It searches for the element itself

---

[1] Line R2b is the only modification of *remove* compared to the pessimistic version studied in [5].

```
locate(e):                          L11: then return pred, curr
   while (true) {                    L12: else { pred.unlock()
L1:   pred := Head;                  L13:        curr.unlock(); }
L2:   curr := pred.next;             } /* end of while(true) */
L3:   while (curr.val < e) {
L4:        pred := curr;
L5:        curr := curr.next; }      contains(e):
L6:   pred.lock();                   I1: curr := Head;
L7:   curr.lock();                   I2: while (curr.val < e)
/* validate */                       I3:       curr := curr.next;
L8 : if ! pred.mrk                   I4: if curr.mrk then res:= false;
L9:      and ! curr.mrk              I5: else res := (curr.val = e)
L10:     and pred.next = curr        I6: return res
```

Fig. 2. Operations *locate* and *contains*

(without use of *locate*) and also checks for the mrk bit. It is this omission of locking combined with the laziness of *remove* which makes verification of linearisability hard.

Our proof technique given in the next section relies on a proof of linearisability via *refinement* of the abstract type defined above to a concrete data type $C = (CS, CSInit, (COp_p^j)_{j \in J, p \in P})$ that we define now as a Z specification.

We start with modelling the global heap *mem*, which is a partial function from a basic type *Ref* of references (with $null \in Ref$) to memory cells: cells consist of a value of type $\mathbb{Z}$ (plus $-\infty, \infty$), can be locked by a process from a set P, can be marked and have a (potentially null) reference to the next node. To access these components of a cell with address r we write $r.val$, $r.lck$, $r.mrk$ and $r.nxt$, respectively. The heap *mem* together with the *head* reference forms the global state *GS*. Initially, the global state (*GSInit*) just consists of a list with head and tail node.

The local state of one process *LS* consists of the tuple of the local variables of the algorithms, together with a type $pc : PC$ for the program counter. Its initial state, given by *LSInit* (not shown) has $pc = 1$ to indicate that no operation is running. All other values of the initial state are unused, so they can be arbitrary.

The complete concrete state space *CS* is defined by combining *GS* with a local state function assigning a local state $lsf(p)$ to every process $p \in P$.

```
┌─ GS ─────────────────────────      ┌─ GSInit ──────────────────
│ head : Ref                          │ GS'
│ mem : Ref ↛                         ├──────────────────────────
│      (ℤ ∪ {−∞, ∞}) ×                │ n_h, n_t ∈ Ref
│      (P ∪ {none}) × 𝔹 × Ref         │ mem' = {n_h ↦ (−∞, none, false, n_t),
│                                     │         n_t ↦ (∞, none, false, null)}
│                                     │ head' = n_h
└─────────────────────────────       └──────────────────────────

┌─ LS ─────────────────────────      ┌─ CS ──────────────────────
│ n1, n2, n3 : Ref                    │ GS
│ curr, pred : Ref                    │ lsf : P → LS
│ res : 𝔹, e : ℤ, pc : PC             └──────────────────────────
└─────────────────────────────
```

To define the concrete operations, we first define operations COP_j on one local state. For this, each line of the algorithms is turned into one Z operation. The following gives the Z specification of lines I1 and I4 of $contains^2$.

$contains I1$
ΞGS
ΔLS
$pc = I1 \wedge pc' = I2$
$curr' = head$

$contains I4$
ΞGS
ΔLS
$pc = I4 \wedge curr.mrk \wedge pc' = I6$
$\neg res'$

These operations are then promoted (using the same standard schema as in [5]) to operations COp_p^j on CS for each process $p \in P$, which work on the local state $lsf(p)$. Initialisation $CSInit$ of the concrete state space is defined similarly.

3   Linearisability and Refinement

Linearisability requires that operations should appear as taking place atomically, i.e., take effect instantaneously at some point in time, even though the atomicity of operations has been given up in the implementation and an actual concrete execution might be an arbitrary interleaving of steps from the above algorithm. This "point in time" is the *linearisation point* (LP). Linearisability permits one to view operations on concurrent data structures as though they occur in some sequential order, namely the order of their linearisation points.

Our proof technique introduced in [4] and further elaborated in [5] relies on a proof of linearisability via *refinement*. Basically, we show that the concurrent implementation $C = (CS, CSInit, (COp_p^j)_{j \in J, p \in P})$ is a *non-atomic refinement* [6] of the abstract data type $A = (AS, ASInit, (AOp_p^i)_{i \in I, p \in P})$.

Here, non-atomic means that a step of the concrete data type COp_p^j that is part of the implementation of AOp_p^i can either match an empty step *skip* or an execution of AOp_p^i. Basically, the steps representing linearisation points have to match with the abstract operations, and all other steps correspond to *skip* steps. To do so, we first of all have to determine the linearisation points. For some simpler classes of algorithms (e.g., stack and non-lazy set considered in [5]), LPs can be determined from the current state of a process (basically, its program counter), and in our methodology are fixed by defining a so-called *status* function assigning values from a type $STATUS$:

$$STATUS ::= IDLE \mid IN \mid OUT$$

Therein, $IDLE$ represents an idle process, and IN and OUT describe the status of processes being before and after their linearisation points, respectively. With the help of the *status* function we define specific status-dependent proof obligations in [4,5]. The proof obligations are *local*, i.e., they do not consider all the

---

[2] We use the Object-Z approach and mention only those variables which are changed.

processes, but only two specific processes p and q. p is executing a step, and q represents an arbitrary other process, which might be affected. Such local proof obligations are possible for many linearizable algorithms, where typically it does not matter for one process *which* other process affects the global state, but only *how* the state is affected. This is true also for the lazy set, where the only relevant information a process sees from others is new cells being introduced or old cells being marked.

The proof obligations in [5] are particular instances of forward simulations. The status tells us whether an individual concrete step has to be matched with a *skip* or an operation of the abstract data type in the simulation. They prove that the concurrent implementation is a non-atomic refinement of an abstract data type (given that the LPs can be defined this way). In a second step, it has to be proven that this kind of non-atomic refinement actually shows linearisability (the *general theory*). Both the linearisability proofs for concrete data structures and the general proof of soundness of our refinement theory have been mechanically conducted using the interactive prover KIV [17]. None of the other approaches for verifying linearisability has a mechanised proof that their proof obligations imply Herlihy and Wing's original definition of linearisability [11].

For our case study, the proof obligations of [5] are sufficient to verify the *add* and *remove* operation, where the LP can be identified in the code. E.g., for *add* the LP is either A5 or A7 (for return value *true* and *false*).

However, this technique is not applicable to the *contains* operation (which represents a whole class of similar concurrent operations). The issue is that it is not possible to *statically* determine the linearisation point of *contains* as it depends on future behaviour of processes *other* than the one currently executing *contains*.

An example can make this clearer. Consider the list representation of the set $\{2, 4, 6\}$ in Figure 3 (a). Assume that *contains(4)* has been started and executed its while loop reaching I4. At this point, variable *curr* points to node 4 (see figure). If the next step executed is I4, *contains* would return *true* and the LP could have been the last I3, setting variable *curr*.

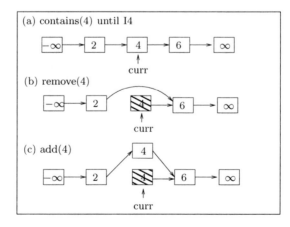

Fig. 3. Sample execution: *contains*(4) until I4 (a), then *remove*(4) (b), then *add*(4)

However, assume that we do not take I4 next, but start another process executing $remove(4)$ (completing without any interleaving of operations from other processes). At the end of $remove$ we reach situation (b) of Figure 3, leaving the node $curr$ pointing at a marked node. If we would now execute I4 next, $contains$ would return $false$. Thus taking I3 as LP is wrong (at this point the return value for contains would have been $true$). So let us assume, we choose I4 as LP. This might however still be incorrect: if the next operation is $add(4)$ which starts and completes (bringing us into situation (c)), executing I4 would still give us the wrong return value: now 4 is in the set again, so at this point in time it is not correct for $contains(4)$ to return $false$.

It turns out that for the sequence $contains(4)$ (until I4), $remove(4)$ (completely), $add(4)$ (completely), $contains(4)$ (rest), the only valid linearisation point for $contains$ is directly after the LP of $remove$. It gives the following valid sequence of abstract operations: $\langle remove(4, true), contains(4, false), add(4, true)\rangle$. However, not every $remove$ is a linearisation point for a running $contains$. It crucially depends on **where** the $contains$ currently is, and whether some more $adds$ will appear **in the future** or not.

Such a case could not be tackled by our current technique, and for the lazy set we need a proof technique which can show linearisability for (a) operations whose linearisation point is set by another process and (b) are determined by future operations. Moreover there is additional complexity in this example, and we also need a technique for situations whereby (c) one step in the implementation can linearise multiple operations (the $remove$ can potentially set the LPs of all running $contains$).

4   Local Proof Obligations

The proof obligations have to guarantee that the concrete data type is a refinement of the abstract data type. This is usually shown by defining an abstraction function $(Abs : GS \rightarrow AS)$ between concrete and abstract state space, and then showing that initialisation and operation execution of concrete and abstract data type match in a certain way ($simulation$).

Again, we aim at $local$ proof obligations, which just consider local states lsp and lsq of two representative processes p and q. Process p is executing a step of its algorithm, and process q might be affected by having to execute its linearisation point (the case in question being process p marking a cell, while process q searches for its value).

Coping with potential linearisation points: To tackle this issue we need to generalise our status function, with a new status $INOUT$ to cover the situation in which an operation has $potentially$ linearised (the types in brackets describe types of inputs and outputs). Thus for our example, a process p with status $INOUT(3, true)$ is a process which is potentially after its LP, has 3 as input and will return $true$.

$$STATUS ::= IDLE \mid IN\langle\langle\mathbb{Z}\rangle\rangle \mid OUT\langle\langle\mathbb{B}\rangle\rangle \mid INOUT\langle\langle\mathbb{Z} \times \mathbb{B}\rangle\rangle$$

For every implementation, we need to define a status function

$$status : GS \times LS \to STATUS$$

assigning a status to a process with local state $ls \in LS$ and current global state $gs \in GS$. The status of a process can change several times during execution of an operation. In particular, several status changes between $INOUT(e, true)$ and $INOUT(e, false)$ are possible if another process executes a step which affects the outcome. Every status change from IN to $INOUT$, $INOUT(e, true)$ to $INOUT(e, false)$ (and vice versa) and $INOUT$ to OUT is a potential linearisation point and has to match with the corresponding abstract operation. It may seem odd that due to the status changes several abstract *contains* appear in a thus constructed run. However, this is sound as *contains* is not modifying the set: the last operation that affects the output value of the status executed in a run is the linearisation point.

Defining the invariants: As in [5], in addition to the abstraction function our theory requires a *local invariant INV* on $GS \times LS$ to capture constraints which are always valid in our linked list implementation (e.g., that tail is always reachable from head). Last, a *disjointness* predicate D over the local states of p and q serves the purpose of keeping disjointness information about local states.

Defining the non-atomic simulation conditions: As in standard simulation conditions, our local proof obligations need to match the behaviour of the concrete and abstract operations. Since we do not have a 1-1 correspondence of abstract and concrete operation anymore, and furthermore, a concrete operation can linearise several processes, and thus match with more than one abstract operation, we have to capture different cases in our simulation conditions. The latter point requires an extension to the theory developed in [5]. Basically, four different types of matchings can occur, each being accompanied by particular status changes.

The most basic type is the classic simulation diagram: process p executes some concrete operation COp_p (bringing us from state cs to cs'), which is the linearisation point, and matches with abstract operation AOp_p (going from abstract as to as') with input in and output out. Concrete and abstract states are related via the abstraction function Abs. The left hand side of Figure 4 describes this case. When process p executes a *potential* linearisation point, both linearisation as well as a *skip* step must be possible. Therefore in this case the abstract state is not allowed to change, as shown on the right hand side. The right hand

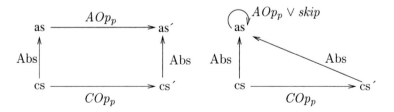

Fig. 4. Simulation types 1 and 2

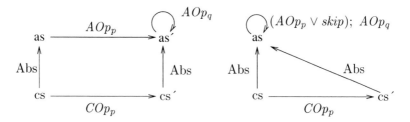

Fig. 5. Simulation types 3 and 4

diagram (with *skip*) is also used when the concrete step does not execute an LP. No processes other than *p* are affected in the two cases of Fig. 4.

The next two types (in Fig. 5) consider the case where a step of a process *p* (possibly) linearises itself as well as linearises a process *q*. The left diagram of Figure 5 shows the case where the execution of operation COp of process *p* definitely sets its own as well as the linearisation point of process *q*. Thus the simulation has to guarantee that abstractly the operation of *p* and *q* is possible. The right hand side depicts the case where the abstract operation of process *p* is either no or a potential LP for *p*, and is therefore not allowed to change the abstract state. Both cases require, that process *q* does not change the abstract state. This allows to lift the proof to a global scenario, where *p* linearises a number of operations $q_1, \ldots, q_n$, since their abstract operations can all start in the same state.

The simulation conditions have to formalise all these cases. In these, both the status of *p* and *q* are used for deciding which case applies, i.e., which kind of matching to show. Instead of writing several simulation conditions, one for each possible status change, we accumulate all cases in one condition using a so-called *exec* function. This function takes as an input the status of a process before and after executing some operation COp (*stat*, *stat'*), the corresponding abstract states *as* and *as'*, and the index *i* of the operation currently being run. From this, it determines the verification condition to be shown.

$$
\begin{aligned}
exec(&stat, i, stat', as, as') := \exists\, in, in', out, out' \bullet \\
&(stat = IN(in) \wedge stat' = OUT(out') \wedge AOp^i(in, as, as', out')) \\
\vee(&stat = IN(in) \wedge stat' = INOUT(in', out') \qquad\qquad\qquad (*)\\
&\quad \wedge\ AOp^i(in, as, as', out') \wedge in = in' \wedge as = as') \\
\vee(&stat = INOUT(in, out) \wedge stat' = OUT(out') \\
&\quad \wedge\ AOp^i(in, as, as', out') \vee (as = as' \wedge out = out')) \\
\vee(&stat = INOUT(in, out) \wedge stat' = INOUT(in', out') \\
&\quad \wedge as = as' \wedge (AOp^i(in, as, as', out') \vee out = out') \wedge in = in') \\
\vee(&stat = IN(in) \wedge stat' = IN(in') \wedge as = as' \wedge in = in') \\
\vee(&stat = INOUT(in, out) \wedge stat' = IN(in') \Rightarrow as = as' \wedge in = in') \\
\vee(&stat = OUT(out) \wedge stat' = OUT(out') \wedge as = as' \wedge out = out')
\end{aligned}
$$

As an example, consider case (*) in the definition of *exec*. If the status of a process changes from *IN* to *INOUT*, i.e., from before to potentially after the linearisation point, then a corresponding abstract operation must be executed which does not change the abstract state and gets exactly the same input and output as those in the $INOUT$ status. This ensures that e.g., a *contains* with return value *false* cannot match with an abstract *contains* returning *true*.

The case following (*) gives two possibilities for going from $INOUT(in, out)$ to $OUT(out')$. Either the potential linearisation is made permanent ($as = as' \wedge out = out'$), or the potential linearisation is discarded and a new one is established by executing AOp. In general, abstract state changes in AOp are allowed when the operation definitely linearises by setting status to $OUT(out')$.

This lets us finally define the simulation condition. Herein, we use a function *runs* which returns the (index of the) abstract operation a process in local state LS is currently executing (this can be determined from the value of the pc).

$$
\begin{aligned}
&\forall\, gs, gs' : GS, lsp, lsq, lsp', lsq' : LS \bullet \\
&\quad INV(gs, lsp) \wedge INV(gs, lsq) \wedge D(lsp, lsq) \wedge COp_p^j(gs, lsp, gs', lsp') \\
&\Rightarrow \qquad\qquad\qquad\qquad\qquad\qquad\qquad\qquad\qquad\qquad\qquad (LPO) \\
&\quad INV(gs', lsp') \wedge INV(gs', lsq) \wedge D(lsp', lsq) \\
&\qquad \wedge\, exec(status(gs, lsp), runs(lsp), status(gs', lsp'), Abs(gs), Abs(gs')) \\
&\qquad \wedge\, exec(status(gs, lsq), runs(lsq), status(gs', lsq), Abs(gs'), Abs(gs'))
\end{aligned}
$$

Basically, (LPO) requires to show that (a) the invariant and the disjointness properties are kept when a concrete operation is executed, and (b) the appropriate matching as defined by *exec* can be carried out for both p and q. Please note that lsq is left unchanged by COp_p. Since (LPO) just refers to two local states lsp and lsq , but never to the complete concrete state CS, we have obtained a *local proof obligation*.

In addition to this simulation rule, we have two simpler proof obligations considering the special cases of invocation and return steps. These disallow abstract state changes and status changes of q (no linearisation). The status of p is required to change from $IDLE$ to $IN(in)$ and from $OUT(out)$ to $IDLE$ with the correct input resp. output value of COp_p. Due to lack of space we will not give them here. We also omit the simple initialisation conditions.

5   Verification of the Case Study

Verification of the case study requires to instantiate the predicates and functions used in the proof obligation (LPO) . We start with the status function:

$$
\begin{aligned}
&ls.pc = 1 \Rightarrow status(gs, ls) = IDLE \\
&ls.pc \in \{A1, \ldots, A5, A7, R1, R2, R2b, R6\} \Rightarrow status(gs, ls) = IN(e) \\
&ls.pc \in \{A6, R3, R4, R5\} \Rightarrow status(gs, ls) = OUT(true) \\
&ls.pc \in \{A8, A9, A10, R7, R8, R9\} \Rightarrow status(gs, ls) = OUT(res) \\
&ls.pc = I1 \Rightarrow status(gs, ls) = IN(e) \\
&ls.pc \in \{I2, I3, I4\} \Rightarrow status(gs, ls) = INOUT(e, \\
&\qquad\qquad\qquad \exists\, r.reachable(curr, r, mem) \wedge r.val = e \wedge \neg\, r.mrk) \\
&ls.pc = I5 \Rightarrow status(gs, ls) = OUT(curr.val = e) \\
&ls.pc = I6 \Rightarrow status(gs, ls) = OUT(res)
\end{aligned}
$$

The definition gives the LPs of the *add* algorithm as A5 (for *res* = *true*) and A7. Before and at this point in the algorithm the status is $IN(e)$, after it $OUT(res)$. Similarly, the LPs for *remove* are the marking operation at R2b when *true* is returned, and the negative case of R2 for *false*.

The interesting clauses are the last four for the *contains* algorithm. Initially the status is $IN(e)$ for $pc = I1$, and at the end of the algorithm it has definitely linearised: at I5 the cell *curr* has been fixed, so the test $curr.val = e$ determines the output, at I6 the output is already stored in *res*.

While the algorithm executes its main loop (I2,I3,I4) we exploit that *contains* can potentially linearise at any time by using a status of the form $INOUT(e, bv)$. The correct output value bv is simple to determine: it is just the value that *contains* would return if it would now run to completion without interruption (i.e., no other process executing steps). Note that this uniform characterisation should be applicable to every algorithm with potential LPs. For the *contains* algorithm this specialises to the value bv being true iff an unmarked cell is reachable from *curr* that contains e.

By using this status definition the algorithm "changes its mind" about the linearisation point and its outcome as often as necessary. Our proof obligation just requires that every change is justified by the current set representation. In particular, a process p marking the element that is searched by process q (the step from (a) to (b) in Fig. 3) will change bv in the status of process q executing *contains* to *false*. This is justified, since it is removed from the set representation too: executing an abstract *contains* with result *false* is possible after removal, we have an instance of simulation type 3 in Fig. 5. A process q adding a cell with e behind *curr* will change bv to *true*. Again this is justified, since the element is also added to the set. Adding an element that does not become reachable (e.g., stepping from (b) to (c) in Fig. 3) will keep $bv = false$.

By using an $INOUT$ status the problem of finding the right LP is no longer a difficulty for the verification of the case study. The KIV proof of (LPO) just unfolds the definition of *exec* and checks whether the abstraction function changes correctly. All global reasoning and reasoning about the past has been moved into the generic theory.

It remains to be shown how the rest of the predicates and functions used in (LPO) are instantiated. Many of these instances are similar to the ones for verifying the pessimistic algorithm in [5]. In particular, the abstraction function just specifies that the abstract set consists of those values $r.val \neq \pm\infty$, for which a reference r is reachable from *head*. Also, the disjointness predicate D is solely used to ensure that p and q never share their newly allocated cell before adding it to the set representation (i.e., when both are at A4 or A5). The invariant consists of three parts.

$$INV(gs, ls) := (\exists\, tail \in Ref \bullet HEADTAILINV(gs, tail) \wedge$$
$$\forall\, r \in \mathrm{dom}(mem) \bullet NODEINV(gs, tail, r)) \wedge INVL(gs, ls)$$

The first part, $HEADTAILINV$ specifies the global invariant for the current data structure: a unique cell *tail* is always reachable from *head* such that $head.val = -\infty$, $tail.val = \infty$. Both *head* and *tail* are never marked.

The interesting part is the second. It gives a condition $NODEINV$ for all allocated references r. This condition is necessary, since in contrast to the pessimistic version, the lazy algorithms for *contains* and *locate* may visit arbitrary old cells that have been marked and may also have been removed from the current set representation (as shown in Fig. 3 (b)).

$NODEINV((head, mem), tail, r) :=$
$(r.nxt \neq null \Rightarrow r.nxt \in \text{dom}(mem) \wedge r.val < r.nxt.val) \wedge$
if $r.mrk$ **then** $r.val \neq -\infty \wedge reachable(r, tail, mem)$ /* class 1 */
else if $\exists r_0 \in \text{dom}(mem) \bullet r_0.nxt = r$
then $reachable(head, r, mem) \wedge reachable(r, tail, mem)$ /* class 2 */
else if $r.val = -\infty$ **then** $head = r$ /* class 3 */
else $r.val \neq \pm\infty \wedge (r.nxt = null \vee reachable(r, tail, mem))$ /* class 4 */

$NODEINV$ requires that even old cells are in strictly ascending order. It also divides the allocated cells into four classes. The first class contains all marked cells. These never contain $-\infty$, and allow to reach *tail* in a finite number of steps: the cells form a tree shape with pointers going upwards towards *tail* as the root. This ensures that *contains* never accesses dangling references. The second class are pointers that have a predecessor r_0. All these cells are part of the current set representation. Whenever *contains* or *locate* reach an *unmarked* cell by computing a successor, the cell is definitely a member of the set representation. Finally, there are cells which have no predecessor. One cell is *head* (third case). All remaining cells (fourth class) have just been allocated in *add* by some process, but have not yet been inserted into the set representation. These cells do not have a value $-\infty$ and either their *nxt* pointer is still *null* (A4) or has been set at A5, making *tail* reachable. Note that although we give the intuition, that *some* process has allocated such a cell, our *local* predicate avoids this *global* characterisation, which would have to quantify over existing processes. Figuring out a *simple*[3] classification of the allocated cells that works *locally* was the main difficulty specific to this case study.

The full invariant finally contains a local invariant $INVL$ with assertions for intermediate states of the algorithms, typically by characterising the program counter values, where they hold. The main assertion for *contains*

$(ls.pc \in \{I2, I3, I5, I6\} \Rightarrow$
$ls.curr \in \text{dom}(mem) \wedge (reachable(head, ls.curr, mem) \vee ls.curr.mrk)$

ensures, that *curr* is always an allocated reference, and is either part of the set representation or an old marked cell. A similar property is used for the local variables *pred* and *curr* of *locate*. Note that $NODEINV$ implies that this property is preserved when stepping from *curr* to *curr.nxt* in the algorithm.

---

[3] A generic, but more complex alternative is using an existentially quantified set of local cells, that must be updated where necessary. This is the preferred solution in separation logic, which hides the quantifier (and our D predicate) within the semantics of separating conjunction.

With these instances the verification of the proof obligation (LPO) in KIV is now only slightly more difficult than for the pessimistic case, and the additional complexity is solely due to the more complex invariant *NODEINV*. The technical encoding of Z schemata in KIV is the same as described in Section 7 of [5]. The proof obligation is given in KIV as three goals, one that proves invariance of $INV(gs, lsp)$, a second that proves $INV(gs, lsq)$ and $D(lsp, lsq)$, and finally one that checks the clauses about *exec*. Although an abstraction *function* is sufficient for the case study, the three goals in KIV generalise (LPO) using an abstraction *relation*, which shows that they are an instance of backward simulation. The proofs for the case study split immediately into 67 cases (one for each Z operation). Altogether the main proofs needed 276 interactions. Getting the details of the case study right took the second author about a week of work. All proofs and specifications (including the derivation from a global theory of possibilities that we could not describe here) are available on the Web [12].

6   Conclusion

The only other mechanised proof of the lazy set implementation of [9] we are aware of (except [2], which approximates a full linearizability proof by model checking executions of two fixed operations) is given in [3] using PVS. Like our approach (and [8]) it uses refinement (of IO automata) to prove linearisability.

Although the transition relation of the automaton in [3] corresponds to the disjunction of our operations in Z, the proof strategy is rather different. First, it considers the global automaton (with state CS) instead of a reduction to two processes. Second it defines an intermediate automaton specific to the case study, that splits the refinement into a forward and backward simulation, to cope with the problem that the LP of contains cannot be determined by forward simulation alone. Our approach solves the problem in the generic theory, and thus should be applicable to a wide class of algorithms. Third, the proof strategy uses a predicate *public* to distinguish locally available references from global ones, that are or have been in the set representation: a cell is not public, if it has just been allocated and is stored in the local variable $n2$ of *some* process p at A4 or A5. Such iteration over all processes is incompatible with our reduction to two processes. Finally, the proof idea follows [9]: when *contains* returns false, then there must have been a time in the past when the element was not in the set. Our theory completely avoids such reasoning about the past.

The same argument about the past is also used in [20]. In his PhD [18], Vafeiadis continues this work, giving proof obligations using separation logic and rely-guarantee reasoning. The approach has influenced our work, since Vafeiadis argues (Sect. 5.2.3), that several LPs are acceptable for read-only operations. Our mechanised proofs (that ensure that it is possible to change the *out* value when status is $INOUT$) can be viewed as a formal justification. Vafeiadis' work is not based on refinement, but adds ghost code executing abstract operations to the concrete algorithm at linearisation points. The approach is global, at the LP of *delete* the auxiliary code has to iterate over all threads running *contains*.

It has been implemented and can verify several standard algorithms automatically, though currently not the lazy set example (see [19]).

We did not have space to discuss the global theory underlying our local proof obligations: Any linearizable algorithm can be verified using backward simulation, when the abstract layer is defined using the possibilities from [11]. It is related to Theorems 13.3-5 of N. Lynch's book [14] (see also [13]) as well as to the embedding of linearizability into observational refinement given in [7]. We have mechanized the global theory in KIV and are not aware of any other approaches that have mechanically verified the soundness of their proof technique.

We conjecture that our local proof strategy is applicable to all algorithms which have potential linearisation points outside their thread and where the abstraction function does not change. The optimistic version of the set algorithm is another example of this class, as are algorithms where a potential LP exists that is determined in the future. The latter includes the "dequeue with an empty queue" case in Michael & Scott's queue [15].

Of course there remains future work. For example, two algorithms which would require further extensions include Herlihy & Wing's original queue (which requires a proof with the global theory) and the elimination stack [10], which uses a handshake to linearise a *push* and a *pop*-operation at the same time. The latter would need a reduction of the global theory to *three* processes (the two processes participating, and one representing all others), and we leave this for the future.

References

1. Amit, D., Rinetzky, N., Reps, T.W., Sagiv, M., Yahav, E.: Comparison under abstraction for verifying linearizability. In: Damm, W., Hermanns, H. (eds.) CAV 2007. LNCS, vol. 4590, pp. 477–490. Springer, Heidelberg (2007)
2. Černý, P., Radhakrishna, A., Zufferey, D., Chaudhuri, S., Alur, R.: Model checking of linearizability of concurrent list implementations. In: Touili, T., Cook, B., Jackson, P. (eds.) CAV 2010. LNCS, vol. 6174, pp. 465–479. Springer, Heidelberg (2010)
3. Colvin, R., Groves, L., Luchangco, V., Moir, M.: Formal verification of a lazy concurrent list-based set algorithm. In: Ball, T., Jones, R.B. (eds.) CAV 2006. LNCS, vol. 4144, pp. 475–488. Springer, Heidelberg (2006)
4. Derrick, J., Schellhorn, G., Wehrheim, H.: Mechanizing a correctness proof for a lock-free concurrent stack. In: Barthe, G., de Boer, F.S. (eds.) FMOODS 2008. LNCS, vol. 5051, pp. 78–95. Springer, Heidelberg (2008)
5. Derrick, J., Schellhorn, G., Wehrheim, H.: Mechanically verified proof obligations for linearizability. ACM Trans. Program. Lang. Syst. 33(1), 4 (2011)
6. Derrick, J., Wehrheim, H.: Non-atomic refinement in Z and CSP. In: Treharne, H., King, S., Henson, M., Schneider, S. (eds.) ZB 2005. LNCS, vol. 3455, pp. 24–44. Springer, Heidelberg (2005)
7. Filipovic, I., O'Hearn, P.W., Rinetzky, N., Yang, H.: Abstraction for concurrent objects. Theoretical Computer Science 411(51-52), 4379–4398 (2010)
8. Groves, L., Colvin, R.: Trace-based derivation of a scalable lock-free stack algorithm. Formal Aspects of Computing (FAC) 21(1–2), 187–223 (2009)

 9. Heller, S., Herlihy, M., Luchangco, V., Moir, M., Scherer III, W.N., Shavit, N.: A lazy concurrent list-based set algorithm. In: Anderson, J.H., Prencipe, G., Wattenhofer, R. (eds.) OPODIS 2005. LNCS, vol. 3974, pp. 305–309. Springer, Heidelberg (2006)
10. Hendler, D., Shavit, N., Yerushalmi, L.: A scalable lock-free stack algorithm. In: SPAA 2004, pp. 206–215. ACM Press, New York (2004)
11. Herlihy, M., Wing, J.M.: Linearizability: A correctness condition for concurrent objects. ACM TOPLAS 12(3), 463–492 (1990)
12. Web presentation of linearizability theory and the lazy set algorithm (2010), http://www.informatik.uniaugsburg.de/swt/projects/possibilities.html
13. Liu, Y., Chen, W., Liu, Y.A., Sun, J.: Model checking linearizability via refinement. In: Cavalcanti, A., Dams, D.R. (eds.) FM 2009. LNCS, vol. 5850, pp. 321–337. Springer, Heidelberg (2009)
14. Lynch, N.: Distributed Algorithms. Morgan Kaufmann Publishers, San Francisco (1996)
15. Michael, M.M., Scott, M.L.: Simple, fast, and practical non-blocking and blocking concurrent queue algorithms. In: Proc. 15th ACM Symp. on Principles of Distributed Computing, pp. 267–275 (1996)
16. O'Hearn, P.W., Rinetzky, N., Vechev, M.T., Yahav, E., Yorsh, G.: Verifying linearizability with hindsight. In: 29th Annual ACM SIGACT-SIGOPS Symposium on Principles of Distributed Computing (PODC), pp. 85–94 (2010)
17. Reif, W., Schellhorn, G., Stenzel, K., Balser, M.: Structured specifications and interactive proofs with KIV. In: Automated Deduction—A Basis for Applications, Interactive Theorem Proving, vol. II, ch. 1, pp. 13–39. Kluwer, Dordrecht (1998)
18. Vafeiadis, V.: Modular fine-grained concurrency verification. PhD thesis, University of Cambridge (2007)
19. Vafeiadis, V.: Automatically proving linearizability. In: Touili, T., Cook, B., Jackson, P. (eds.) CAV 2010. LNCS, vol. 6174, pp. 450–464. Springer, Heidelberg (2010)
20. Vafeiadis, V., Herlihy, M., Hoare, T., Shapiro, M.: Proving correctness of highly-concurrent linearisable objects. In: PPoPP 2006, pp. 129–136. ACM, New York (2006)
21. Vafeiadis, V., Parkinson, M.: A marriage of rely/Guarantee and separation logic. In: Caires, L., Vasconcelos, V.T. (eds.) CONCUR 2007. LNCS, vol. 4703, pp. 256–271. Springer, Heidelberg (2007)

Refinement-Based Verification of Local Synchronization Algorithms

Dominique Méry[1], Mohamed Mosbah[2], and Mohamed Tounsi[2]

[1] Loria, Université Henri Poincaré Nancy 1 France
[2] LaBRI, Université Bordeaux 1 France

Abstract. Synchronization algorithms are mandatory for simulating local computation models of distributed algorithms. Therefore, correctness of these algorithms becomes crucial, because it gives confidence that local computations are simulated as designed and do not behave harmfully. However, these algorithms are considered to be very complex to prove since they are integrating both distributed and probabilistic aspects. We derive proofs of synchronization algorithms relied upon the correct-by-construction paradigm; it is supported by a progressive and incremental process controlled by the refinement techniques. We illustrate our approach by examples like the handshake and the LC1 algorithms. These algorithms are designed for an asynchronous distributed network of anonymous processes which use the message-passing feature as a model for the communication.

Keywords: Synchronization algorithm, Probabilistic distributed algorithm, Formal method, Event-B, Visidia.

1 Introduction

A distributed system consists of a collection of computation entities that communicate together to achieve a common task. This system gives rise to a big set of distributed algorithms which are usually classified by :

1. The type of communication to apply (messages passing, shared memory..);
2. The computation entities to use (processors, mobile agents..);
3. The type of synchrony to employ (synchronous, asynchronous..).

Our work is based on asynchronous distributed network of anonymous processors, which use the messages exchange as a model for the communication. We suppose that a processor can determine the origin of each message. Formally, a distributed system can be represented by a simple, connected and undirected graph where nodes denote processors, and edges denote communication links. Distributed algorithms can be modelled using abstract entities which are simulating the distributed computation by a set of rewriting rules acting on a graph. Visidia [7] is an environment which implements this computation model and it has synchronization algorithms which are providing the choice of the next pair of adjacent nodes to modify according the set of rewriting rules. Our paper is

M. Butler and W. Schulte (Eds.): FM 2011, LNCS 6664, pp. 338–352, 2011.

focusing on these synchronization algorithms which are integrating features like probabilistic choice.

Since, as shown in [19], local computations cannot be executed on asynchronous networks without involving randomized synchronization algorithms. In other words, each node in the graph tries to synchronize with its neighbor(s) first, and if it is the case, then a local computation step can be done. Local computations are of three different types; each one of them relies upon a specific randomized synchronization algorithm. For more information about the three types of local computations, the reader should see [16]:

1. Handshake: This synchronization type implies two neighboring nodes in a local computation step.
2. LC1 (Local Computations of type 1): This synchronization type groups together nodes in a star (a star is a node with its neighbors) for executing a local computation step.
3. LC2 (Local Computations of type 2): This synchronization type is like LC1 except that local computations are more advanced.

However, the simplicity and the elegance of randomized algorithms have a heavy cost: the analysis of such systems become very complex, particularly in the context of distributed computation [23]. This arises through the interplay between probability and nondeterminism. In order to prove the correctness of these algorithms, we use an approach which is directly related to the design of correct-by-construction programs. The main idea relies upon the development of distributed algorithms following a top/down approach, which is clearly well known in earlier works of Dijkstra [10], and to use the refinement for controlling the correctness of the resulting algorithm. It relies on a more fundamental question related to the notion of problem to solve. The methodology can be based on incremental proof-based developments, which gives a real help to justify in a very progressive way the choices of design. Particularly, Event-B [2] is a formal modeling method which supports the expression of our methodological proposal suggesting proof-based guidelines. It is supported by a tool called "RODIN" [24] which provides an environment for developing correct-by-construction models for software-based systems.

However, Event-B does not handle perfectly the probability, since probabilistic Event-B is a new research trend. In fact, the first contributions in this context were proposed by C. Morgan, Thai Son Hoang and Annabelle MacIver in [21,13,17]. Annabelle MacIver et al.[17] add probability in a limited form to the classical B method[1]. In this work, authors are concentrated on "almost-certain" properties which hold with probability one. After that, C. Morgan et al. [21] spread the probability challenge to the Event-B method. Therefore, their works are still a good reflection on the probabilistic theory argued by a practical experience. Considered as the first and the most relevant work in the probabilistic Event-B study; S. Hallerstede et al. [12] have extended Event-B to allow expressing the qualitative aspect of probability. They introduce qualitative probabilistic reasoning into Event-B by means of the qualitative probabilistic choice.

More concretely, they extend Event-B by a new operator which assigns new values to variables with some positive but generally unknown probability. In fact, the probabilistic choice takes place where we already have nondeterministic choice in the assignment component. Contrary to [12], Tarasyu A. et al. [26] introduce the quantitative probabilistic choice. They add a new operator which gives some known probabilistic distribution to each particular choice should be made. In this work, author's interest was about integrating probabilistic assessment of reliability into Event-B modeling. We assert that, approaches and techniques for proving the correctness of quantitative properties is more complex than the qualitative analysis [23]. Therefore, our work diverges in its goal and its probabilistic analysis. It is mainly devoted to the synchronization algorithms for the local computation models. Also, it proposes a new approach to develop synchronization algorithms following a probabilistic refinement stepwise.

The remaining parts are organized as follows. Section 2 presents the local computations model and gives an example of a distributed algorithm described in this model. Section 3 sketches the Event-B methodology used for developing the algorithms of synchronization. In section 4, we introduce the general structure of the proof-based development and Section 5 describes the models developed for obtaining synchronization algorithms. Section 6 concludes our paper and gives future works.

2   Synchronization Algorithms for Local Computation Models

In this section, we illustrate, in an intuitive way, the notion of local computations, and particularly that of graph relabelling systems by showing how some algorithms on networks of processors may be encoded within this framework [15]. After that, we present some basic definitions of synchronization algorithms. As usual, such a network is represented by a graph whose nodes stand for processors and edges for (bidirectional) links between processors. At every time, each node and each edge are in some particular state and this state will be encoded by a node or edge label. According to its own state and to the states of its neighbours, each node may decide to perform an elementary *computation step*. After this step, the states of this node, of its neighbours and of the corresponding edges may have changed according to some specific *computation rules*. Let us recall that graph relabelling systems satisfy the following requirements:

(C1) they do not change the underlying graph but only the labelling of its components (edges and/or nodes), the final labelling being the result,
(C2) they are local, that is, each relabelling changes only a connected subgraph of a fixed size in the underlying graph,
(C3) they are locally generated, that is, the applicability condition of the relabelling only depends on the local context of the relabelled subgraph.

For such systems, the distributed aspect comes from the fact that several relabelling steps can be performed simultaneously on "far enough" subgraphs, giving the same result as a sequential realization of them, in any scheduling. A large family of classical distributed algorithms encoded by graph relabelling systems is given in [6]. In order to make the definitions easy to read, we give in the following an example of a graph relabelling system for coloring a ring. Then, the definition of local synchronization algorithms will be presented.

2.1   The 3-Coloring Problem of a Ring

Consider a ring with at least 3 nodes. The (node) 3-coloring problem consists in assigning to each node a color from a set of three colors such that two neighbours have different colors. In distributed computing, node coloring algorithms are mainly used for resource allocation. A node coloring defines a partial order on processors allowing them, for example, to execute their critical section according to the order defined by their respective colors. We provide a relabelling system to color a ring with 3 colors, starting from an arbitrary configuration. Let $\{x, y, z\}$ be the set of colors. Let S_3 be the relabelling system defined by considering the following rule R:

$$R: \overset{a}{\bullet} \xrightarrow{\quad b \quad} \overset{c}{\bullet} \longrightarrow \overset{a}{\bullet} \xrightarrow{\quad d \quad} \overset{c}{\bullet}$$
$$a,b,c,d \in \{x,y,z\};\ b \in \{a,c\}\ ;\ d \notin \{a,c\}$$

Initially, nodes are labelled at random. This relabelling system, defined by the previous rule, assigns a correct 3-coloring to the nodes of a ring.

2.2   Synchronization Algorithms

As shown in [19], local computations cannot be executed on asynchronous networks without involving randomized synchronization algorithms. In other words, each node in the graph tries to synchronize with its neighbor(s) first, and if it is the case, then a local computation step can be done. These algorithms are randomized since, deterministic algorithms cannot implement synchronous message passing in anonymous networks that passes messages asynchronously [4]. In addition, randomization offers a powerful tool for symmetry breaking and leading to faster solutions [23].

Local computations are of three different types (Handshake, LC1 and LC2); each one of them relies upon a specific randomized synchronization algorithm. In this paper, we are concerned with the first local computation type (the handshake algorithm). A handshake algorithm aims to match two neighboring nodes in the graph in order to release a computation step. Its principle is described by J. Reif et al. [25] as follows: *Suppose that each process has a special resource called channel which can be in one of two states open, closed. A handshake of two processes p, q in time t is a combination of processes states at time t so that both channels of p and q are open at the same time. Thus we are concerned by local signals so that each process indicates to at most one neighbor its readiness to send or receive data.* An informal description of the algorithm is given as follows: We suppose that each node v in the graph repeats forever the following actions:

```
The node v chooses at random one of its neighbors (we called c(v));
The node v sends 1 to c(v);
The node v receives messages from neighbors which have chosen it.
```

However, some nodes may not receive any message, as they were not chosen to be a part of a handshake. Here, two different scenarios are possible: First, there is a handshake between v and c(v), if v receives 1 from its chosen neighbor c(v). Second, if c(v) had chosen another node different from v; c(v) must respond to v by sending it a 0 message. This message is very important, since it allows the node v to realize that it was not chosen by c(v) and to restart applying the algorithm from the beginning.

The LC1 algorithm is accomplished by using 1-local election, presented as follows: Every node v selects an integer rand(v) randomly from the set $\{1..N\}$ (The constant N is an integer strictly greater than 1). The node v sends to its neighbors the value rand(v). The node v is elected in B(v,1) if for each node w of B(v, 1) different from v, rand(v)>rand(w). In this case a computation step on B(v,1) is allowed, therefore the center is able to collect labels of the leaves and to change its label.

3   Event-B Overview

The Event-B modeling language [2] defines mathematical structures into contexts and formal model of system into machines. The modeling process starts by identifying the domain of the problem expressed by means of contexts. A context states the theatrical notions required to be able to express the problem statement in a formal way[18]. It consists of the following elements: a name, a list of distinct carrier sets, a list of distinct constants and a list of named properties. Beside the context, the second component in doing formal developments in Event-B consists of the machine. It describes a reactive system characterized by a finite list of events modifying a state variable; an operational interpretation of an Event-B machine states that, traces of the current model can be generated from the initial states by applying events. A machine may encapsulate a set of mathematical items, variables, invariants and a set of events on these variables. An invariant is defined to be a predicate preserved by each event. As for an event, it is decomposed into first a guard that specifies under which circumstances it might occur and then d actions modifying the current state variables. A context associated with a given machines defines the way this machine is parameterized and can thus be instantiated [1]. Machines and context relationships are defined as follows: each machine may see a context. In other words, when a machine M sees a context C, this means that all carrier sets and constants defined in C can be used in M. A machine can be built and asserted to be a refinement of another machine. Consequently, the new machine is named a refinement or a concrete version of the first machine. The refinement [5] of a machine allows us to enrich a model in a step-by-step approach, and is the foundation of our correct-by-construction approach. Refinement provides a way to strengthen invariants and to add details to a model. It is also used to transform an abstract model into a more concrete version by modifying the state description. This is done by extending the list of state variables, by refining each abstract event into a corresponding concrete version and by adding new events. Likewise, a context can be extended to another context.

However, an Event-B model is considered as correct, when each machine, as well as the process of refinement, are proved by adequate theorems named Proof Obligations (PO); ie events preserve the invariant(s) and that each event is feasible. The management of proof obligations is a technical task supported by the RODIN tool [24], which provides an environment for developing correct-by-construction models for software-based systems.

4 The Modelling Process

As we said above, we use the proof-based development approach to gradually develop the algorithm. We start with a very abstract model and then we add details, to obtain a correct and concrete model. The development of a synchronous algorithm is done following this stepwise refinement strategy:

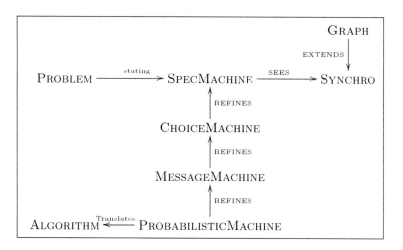

1. The first model SPECMACHINE expresses the goal of the algorithm. It represents the specification of the problem to solve by events stating a relation between initial states and the final states. It uses definitions and properties of graph in the two contexts GRAPH and SYNCHRO. For instance, a handshake is stated by an event which computes the result in one shot.
2. The second model CHOICEMACHINE refines the first model SPECMACHINE. It introduces events for expressing how nodes are making choice and refines the events of the first level.
3. The third model MESSAGEMACHINE provides further details about messages exchange. More precisely, we can observe how nodes communicate together to realize synchronization(s).

4. The fourth model PROBABILISTICMACHINE is refining the third model and it emphasizes on the introduction of a probabilistic assumption to integrate the effective probabilistic choice made by nodes.
5. An algorithm is extracted from the last model.

5   Implementing the Local Computations Model

This section presents the formal development of the handshake algorithm with some proofs.

5.1   The Handshake Algorithm Development

The GRAPH Context. The GRAPH context describes the basic properties of the network on which distributed algorithms are designed to run. Formally, a network can be straightforwardly modeled as a connected, non-oriented and simple graph where nodes denote processors and edges denote direct communication links. A graph is simple if does not have more than one edge between any two nodes and no edge starts and ends at the same node (see axm4 and axm3). An undirected graph, means that there is no distinction between two nodes associated with each edge (see axm3). A graph (oriented or not) is connected only if, for each pair of nodes, there exists a set of edges joining them (see axm5). According to Jean-Raymond Abrial et al. [9,3], a graph namely g is modeled by a set of nodes namely ND can be presented as follows:

$$
\begin{array}{l}
axm1 : g \subseteq ND \times ND \\
axm2 : dom(g) = ND \\
axm3 : g = g^{-1} \\
axm4 : id(ND) \cap g = \varnothing \\
axm5 : \forall s.s \subseteq ND \wedge s \neq \varnothing \wedge g[s] \subseteq s \Rightarrow ND \subseteq s
\end{array}
$$

The SYNCHRO Context. The SYNCHRO Context is introduced as an extension of the graph context. It defines all the correct solutions that may result from the execution of our algorithm. For this, we define *all_synchro* to be a set of all possible combinations of handshake in the graph (a possible combination is called "matching"). A matching in a graph is a subset of edges (see axm2), in which no two edges are adjacent (or, alternatively no node is adjacent to two edges in the matching (see axm5)) [11]. Like the graph, a matching is supposed to be undirected (see axm3). We add the empty set to *all_synchro* to include the case where the execution of the algorithm gives no handshake (see axm4). By means of the axm6, we state that any combination satisfying the axioms detailed above must necessarily belong to *all_synchro*.

$$
\begin{array}{l}
axm1 : all\_synchro \subseteq ND \leftrightarrow ND \\
axm2 : \forall R \cdot R \in all\_synchro \wedge R \neq \varnothing \Rightarrow R \subseteq g \\
axm3 : \forall R \cdot R \in all\_synchro \Rightarrow R = R^{-1} \\
axm4 : \varnothing \in all\_synchro \\
axm5 : \forall R \cdot R \in all\_synchro \wedge R \neq \varnothing \Rightarrow (\forall x, y \cdot x \mapsto y \in R \Rightarrow \{x\} \lhd R = \{x \mapsto y\}) \\
axm6 : \forall R \cdot R \subseteq g \wedge R = R^{-1} \wedge (\forall x, y \cdot x \mapsto y \in R \Rightarrow \{x\} \lhd R = \{x \mapsto y\}) \Rightarrow R \in all\_synchro
\end{array}
$$

The first machine: SPECMACHINE

In the first level, the machine will express only the goal of the algorithm: making a handshake between two neighboring nodes in the graph. To do this, we need to define two variables : The first called *actual_state* describes the current matching of the graph. In other words, this variable contains all the already existing handshake(s) in the graph. Formally, it is simply defined as an element belonging to *all_synchro* (see inv1). The second variable is called *result*. It is introduced in order to contain the result of running the algorithm (see inv2). Initially *result* is empty.

$$inv1 : actual\_state \in all\_synchro$$
$$inv2 : result \in ND \leftrightarrow ND$$

Beside initialization, this machine includes two events. The first, called *synchronize*, models the case where two non synchronized nodes make handshake. This event avows the result of the algorithm without giving any details about how it was found. The answer is given later in the next refinements. The second event that we can observe in this level is called *free_nodes*. It handles the case where synchronized nodes finish the handshake. The *free_nodes* updates *actual_state* and generates a new matching on the graph. It does not compute the result of the algorithm.

```
EVENT synchronise
  ANY    x, y
  WHERE
    grd1 : x ↦ y ∈ g ∧ result = ∅
    grd2 : x ∉ dom(actual_state)
    grd3 : y ∉ dom(actual_state)
    Theorem1 : (actual_state ∪
    {x ↦ y, y ↦ x}) ∈ all_synchro
  THEN
    act1 : result := {x ↦ y}
    act2 : actual_state :=
    actual_state ∪ {x ↦ y, y ↦ x}
  END
```

```
EVENT free_nodes
  ANY    x, y
  WHERE
    grd1 : x ↦ y ∈ actual_state
    grd2 : result = ∅
    Theorem2 : (actual_state \ {x ↦ y, y ↦ x})
    ∈ all_synchro
  THEN
    act1 : actual_state :=
    actual_state \ {x ↦ y, y ↦ x}
  END
```

The first, the second and the third guard of *synchronize* (grd1, grd2 and grd3) check if the two neighboring nodes x and y are not synchronized and if it is the case then the event declares the edge $x \mapsto y$ as the result of the algorithm and updates the actual_state. We prove by means of the theorem $Theorem1$ that if we add to the *actual_state* a new edge of which the end-points don't have any synchronization; then *actual_state* remains always correct and represents a new matching on the graph. As the first event, we prove by the theorem $Theorem2$ that if we remove a handshake from the *actual_state*, we preserve always the correctness on the matching of the graph. We prove by the following theorem that the deadlock cannot happen during the algorithm execution.

$$deadlock - free : result = \varnothing \Rightarrow \begin{pmatrix} (\exists x, y \cdot x \mapsto y \in g \land x \notin dom(actual\_state) \\ \land y \notin dom(actual\_state)) \\ \lor (\exists a, b \cdot a \mapsto b \in actual\_state) \end{pmatrix}$$

The second machine: CHOICEMACHINE

In this first refinement, we start introducing details of the handshake algorithm. This machine adds the choice action which is considered as the first step to realize a handshake. Also, it refines the other abstract events that are already defined in the first level. We introduce a new variable called *choice* defined as a set of nodes associated with their choice (it contains only nodes that have previously done their choice). The following invariants provide a formal definition of the new variable:

(inv1) The *choice* variable is defined as a partial function from ND to ND which means that some nodes may have no choice yet.

(inv2) A node can choose only one node from its neighbor(s).

(inv3) Synchronized nodes have made their choices before.

(inv4) If two neighboring nodes x and y are synchronized, this implies that each of them has chosen the other.

$$
\begin{array}{l}
inv1 : choice \in ND \nrightarrow ND \\
inv2 : \forall x \cdot x \in dom(choice) \Rightarrow choice[\{x\}] \subseteq g[\{x\}] \\
inv3 : actual\_state \subseteq choice \\
inv4 : \forall x, y \cdot x \mapsto y \in actual\_state \Rightarrow choice[\{x\}] = \{y\} \wedge choice[\{y\}] = \{x\}
\end{array}
$$

The following initialization establishes the invariants:

$$
\begin{array}{l}
act1 : actual\_state, choice : \mid \left(
\begin{array}{l}
actual\_state' \in all\_synchro\wedge \\
choice' \in ND \nrightarrow ND\wedge \\
(\forall x \cdot x \in dom(choice') \Rightarrow choice'[\{x\}] \subseteq g[\{x\}])\wedge \\
actual\_state' \subseteq choice'
\end{array}
\right) \\
\\
act2 : result := \varnothing
\end{array}
$$

Abstract events of the previous level still exist in this refinement, therefore they become more concrete. In fact, the guard of the *synchronise* event is reinforced by two new conditions to check if the nodes have already done the choice (x ∈ dom(choice) ∧ y ∈ dom(choice)) and if it is a mutual choice (choice[{x}]={y} ∧ choice[{y}] = {x}). For *free_node* event, we add in the assignment component a new action to precise that nodes can start again a new choice (choice:= {x,y} ◁ choice). We note that '◁' is the Event-B domain subtraction operator. It removes elements from *choice*, starting with x or y.

In this level, we introduce two new events, *make_choice* and *cannot_synchronise*, which update the *choice* set. These events refine SKIP, which is intended to model hidden actions over variables appearing in this refinement. *make_choice* event allows to a node to choose a neighbor in order to attempt synchronization. Specifically, it selects in a nondeterministic way a node y from the neighbors of x, then it adds the pair x ↦ y to the *choice* set. The second event *cannot_synchronise* specifies the case where a node fails to make a handshake. As a consequence, the node is withdrawn from the *choice* set and so a new synchronization attempt is supposed to restart. These events are given by the following specification:

$$\boxed{\begin{aligned}&\text{EVENT make\_choice}\\&\quad \text{ANY}\quad x\\&\quad \text{WHERE}\\&\qquad grd1 : result = \varnothing\\&\qquad grd2 : x \notin dom(choice)\\&\quad \text{THEN}\\&\qquad act1 :\\&\quad choice :|\ \exists y \cdot \begin{pmatrix} y \in g[\{x\}] \wedge \\ choice' = choice \cup \{x \mapsto y\}\end{pmatrix}\\&\quad \text{END}\end{aligned}}$$

$$\boxed{\begin{aligned}&\text{EVENT cannot\_synchronise}\\&\quad \text{ANY}\quad x\\&\quad \text{WHERE}\\&\qquad grd1 : x \in dom(choice) \wedge result = \varnothing\\&\qquad grd2 : x \notin dom(actual\_state)\\&\qquad grd3 : choice[\{x\}] \cap choice^{-1}[\{x\}] = \varnothing\\&\quad \text{THEN}\\&\qquad act1 : choice := \{x\} \lessdot choice\\&\quad \text{END}\end{aligned}}$$

The third machine: MESSAGESMACHINE

In the last level, we model the message exchange between nodes. In order to reach this goal, we introduce a new variable *message* representing all the sent messages over the graph (includes 0 and 1 message). This variable substitutes the abstract one *choice* which is defined in the previous model. This will give rise to a new event called *answer* which expresses when nodes should respond to a synchronization request. The invariants concerning *message* variable are specified as follows:

(inv1) The *message* variable is defined as a partial function from g to the $\{0, 1\}$ set.

(inv2) *choice* variable is replaced by the subset of 1 messages. This invariant is called gluing invariant which links together the abstract state variable and the concrete ones.

(inv3) We check through this invariant that we cannot send more than 1 message at the same time.

(inv4) A node x is able to send a 0 message to its neighbor y, if and only if y has previously sent a 1 message.

$$\boxed{\begin{aligned}&inv1 : message \in g \nrightarrow \{0, 1\}\\&inv2 : dom(message \rhd \{1\}) = choice\\&inv3 : \forall x, y \cdot x \mapsto y \mapsto 1 \in message \Rightarrow dom(message \rhd \{1\})[\{x\}] = \{y\}\\&inv4 : \forall x, y \cdot x \mapsto y \mapsto 0 \in message \Rightarrow y \mapsto x \mapsto 1 \in message\end{aligned}}$$

Initialization event is refined in order to establish the new invariants. Here, the variable *choice* is replaced with a concrete one by means of witness. In Event-B, witness is defined as a simple equality predicate involving the abstract parameters. $choice' = dom(message' \rhd \{1\})$

(grd3) in *synchronise* event allows to check if the node x had received a message from its neighbor y and vice versa. (grd4) specifies that the received message must contain 1. (grd3) in *make_choice* event guarantee that the node x has not sent a 1 message which also means that, it does not have a synchronization request in progress. In this case, a new synchronization attempt can take place only if the request has been processed (by receiving a message containing 1 or 0 from the node that was requested to do synchronization). Replying to a synchronization request is specified by the *answer* event.

```
EVENT synchronise
  ANY    x, y
  WHERE
    grd1 : x ↦ y ∈ g ∧ result = ∅
    grd2 : x ∉ dom(actual_state)
      ∧y ∉ dom(actual_state)
    grd3 : x ↦ y ∈ dom(message)
      ∧y ↦ x ∈ dom(message)
    grd4 : message(x ↦ y) = 1
      ∧message(y ↦ x) = 1
  THEN
    act1 : result := {x ↦ y}
    act2 : actual_state :=
        actual_state ∪ {x ↦ y, y ↦ x}
END
```

```
EVENT make_choice
  ANY    x
  WHERE
    grd1 : result = ∅
    grd2 : x ∉ dom(actual_state)
    grd3 : x ∉ dom(dom(message ▷ {1}))
    grd4 : ∀z·x ↦ z ∈ g ⇒
        x ↦ z ∉ dom(message)
  THEN
    act1 : choice :| ∃y·
      ( y ∈ g[{x}] ∧
        message' = message ∪ {x ↦ y ↦ 1} )
END
```

The *answer* event expresses when and how a node responds to a synchronization request from a neighbor which it did not chose. We suppose that a node x has chosen its neighbor y to establish a handshake (see grd3) and y did not answer to the request of x yet: the node x did not receive a message from y (see grd4). If there is a new message including "1" from another neighbor z different from y (see grd5); then x must send a "0" message to its neighbors z (provided that the node x has not yet responded (see grd6)). Below is the formal description of the *answer* event:

```
EVENT answer
  ANY    x, y, z
  WHERE
    grd1 : x ∉ dom(actual_state)
    grd2 : result = ∅
    grd3 : x ↦ y ∈ dom(message ▷ {1})
    grd4 : y ↦ x ∉ dom(message)
    grd5 : y ≠ z ∧ z ↦ x ↦ 1 ∈ message
    grd6 : x ↦ z ↦ 0 ∉ message
  THEN
    act1 : message := message ∪ {x ↦ z ↦ 0}
END
```

The probabilistic machine: PROBABILISTICMACHINE The refinement of the previous model introduces three kinds of choice:

- make_good_choice: the event allow to model when the choice is a good choice; it means that it corresponds to the choice of the right neighbor which is effectively handshaking. We may attach a probability to this event and this probability is equal to $1/neighbors(x)$ where $neighbors(x)$ is the number of neighbors of x.

- make_bad_choice: x is making a bad choice and does not choose a neighboor for the handshake.

- make_bad/good_choice models a choice which is either good or bad with respect to the choice of the neighbor.

EVENT make_good_choice
  ANY x
  WHERE
    $grd1 : result = \varnothing$
    $grd2 : x \notin dom(actual\_state)$
    $grd3 : x \notin dom(dom(message \rhd \{1\}))$
    $grd4 :$
    $\forall z \cdot x \mapsto z \in g \Rightarrow x \mapsto z \notin dom(message)$
    $grd5 : \exists a \cdot a \mapsto x \mapsto 1 \in message$
  THEN
    $act1 : message : |\exists y \cdot$
    $\left(\begin{array}{l} y \in g[\{x\}] \wedge y \mapsto x \mapsto 1 \in message \wedge \\ message' = message \cup \{x \mapsto y \mapsto 1\} \end{array} \right)$
  END

EVENT make_bad_choice
  ANY x
  WHERE
    $grd1 : result = \varnothing$
    $grd2 : x \notin dom(actual\_state)$
    $grd3 : x \notin dom(dom(message \rhd \{1\}))$
    $grd4 :$
    $\forall z \cdot x \mapsto z \in g \Rightarrow x \mapsto z \notin dom(message)$
    $grd5 :$
    $\exists a \cdot a \mapsto x \in dom(message \rhd \{1\})$
    $grd6 : \exists b \cdot b \in g[\{x\}]$
    $\wedge b \mapsto x \notin dom(message \rhd \{1\})$
  THEN
    $act1 : message : |\exists y \cdot$
    $\left(\begin{array}{l} y \in g[\{x\}] \wedge y \mapsto x \mapsto 1 \notin message \wedge \\ message' = message \cup \{x \mapsto y \mapsto 1\} \end{array} \right)$
  END

EVENT make_bad/good_choice
  ANY x
  WHERE
    $grd1 : result = \varnothing$
    $grd2 : x \notin dom(actual\_state)$
    $grd3 : x \notin dom(dom(message \rhd \{1\}))$
    $grd4 : \forall z \cdot x \mapsto z \in g \Rightarrow x \mapsto z \notin dom(message)$
    $grd5 : \forall c \cdot c \in g[\{x\}] \Rightarrow c \mapsto x \notin dom(message \rhd \{1\})$
  THEN
    $act1 : message : |\exists y \cdot \left(\begin{array}{l} y \in g[\{x\}], \\ \wedge message' = message \cup \{x \mapsto y \mapsto 1\} \end{array} \right)$
  END

We assert that our development is considered correct since each refinement level as well as the refinement process are proved by adequate theorems called PO (Proof Obligation). PO(s) are generated by the Rodin tool [24] and can be discharged either automatically by an integrated proof tool or through interactive proof steps. Usually, the fail of Rodin in the proof of some PO(s) is justified by the lack of appropriate automatic support in the tool for reasoning about set comprehension, disjunctions, and strict subsets [14]. However, an unproved proof obligation may indicate that a modification should be made on the current model.

Algorithm. In the following, we give an algorithm which is extracted from the last machine. To do so, we start by identifying variables which are only defined to be used in the proof processes (the variable *result* for instance). These variables will not be kept in the generated algorithm. Afterward, we translate events of the machine except the initialization event. We simplify the generated algorithm by grouping together actions which have the same conditions and by defining a number of functions to encode some elementary operations. These functions are defined as follows: *SourceOf(m)* reveals the node which has sent the message m. The function *Is1msg(m)* returns *true* if the message m is a 1 message; *false* otherwise. The function *FindNeighbors()* is used to select randomly a neighboring node.

Algorithm 1. Handshake algorithm

Input : messages// It contains the received messages
Vars: choice// It contains the choice of the node
Vars: synchro// It is true if the node is synchronized, false
        otherwise

while *synchro = false* **do**
    if *choice = ∅* **then**
        choice ← FindNeighbors();
        Send a 1 message to *choice*;
    else
        foreach *element m of messages* **do**
            if *SourceOf(m)= choice* **then**
                if *Is1msg(m)= true* **then**
                    synchro ← true;
                    // Now, the node can execute a relabeling rule;
                    break;
                else
                    choice ← ∅;
            else
                if *Is1msg(m)=true* **then**
                    Send a 0 message to *SourceOf(m)*;

---

6 Conclusion and Future Works

The paper is an exercise in developing distributed algorithms under probabilistic assumptions which are practically consistent. It aims to develop synchronization algorithms which are used in the platform VISIDIA [28] to simulate, in a safe way, rules of the local computations models. The summary of proof obligations discharged either automatically or interactively is a measure of the complexity of the development itself and we have postponed the management of probabilities as far as possible in the concretization process of the refinement relationship:

Handshake Models	Number of proof obligations	Automatically discharged	Interactively discharged
SpecMachine	10	6 (60%)	4 (40%)
ChoiceMachine	23	12 (52%)	11 (48%)
MessageMachine	43	13 (30%)	30 (70%)
ProbabilisticMachine	4	0 (0%)	4 (100%)
Total	80	31 (38.75%)	49 (61.25%)

The mechanization score in not very good and the percentage of interactively discharged Proof obligations is 61.25 %. The diagram of the refinement with machines as labels provides a general method for developing these algorithms. Now, we can use our developments to benchmark the future plugin of S. Hallerstede et al. [12] and it will be a very simple application of this technique. Other future questions are related to the management of probabilistic assumptions which may be harder to state and it is important to consider others case studies like general coloring algorithms [20,22]. We can also explore the use of the probabilistic model checking to analyze the distributed algorithms derived from Event-B models; it may appear as a validation phase of the derived algorithm.

References

1. Abrial, J.R.: The B-book: assigning programs to meanings. Cambridge University Press, New York (1996)
2. Abrial, J.R.: Modeling in Event-B: System and Software Engineering. Cambridge University Press, Cambridge (2010)
3. Abrial, J.R., Cansell, D., Méry, D.: Formal derivation of spanning trees algorithms. In: Bert, D., Bowen, J., King, S. (eds.) ZB 2003. LNCS, vol. 2651, pp. 457–476. Springer, Heidelberg (2003)
4. Angluin, D.: Local and global properties in networks of processors (extended abstract). In: Proceedings of the Twelfth Annual ACM Symposium on Theory of Computing, STOC 1980, pp. 82–93. ACM, New York (1980), http://doi.acm.org/10.1145/800141.804655, doi:10.1145/800141.804655
5. Back, R.: On correct refinement of programs. Journal of Computer and System Sciences 23(1), 49–68 (1979)
6. Bauderon, M., Métivier, Y., Mosbah, M., Sellami, A.: From local computations to asynchronous message passing systems. Tech. Rep. RR-1271-02, LaBRI (2002)
7. Bauderon, M., Mosbah, M.: A unified framework for designing, implementing and visualizing distributed algorithms. Graph Transformation and Visual Modeling Techniques (First International Conference on Graph Transformation) 72(3), 13–24 (2003)
8. Bjørner, D., Henson, M.C. (eds.): Logics of Specification Languages. EATCS Textbook in Computer Science. Springer, Heidelberg (2007)
9. Cansell, D., Méry, D.: The Event-B Modelling Method: Concepts and Case Studies, pp. 33–140. Springer, Heidelberg (2007); see [8]
10. Dijkstra, E.W.: A Discipline of Programming. Prentice-Hall, Englewood Cliffs (1976)
11. ElHibaoui, A., Métivier, Y., Robson, J.M., Saheb-Djahromi, N., Zemmari, A.: Analysis of a randomized dynamic timetable handshake algorithm. Pure Mathematics and Applications (PuMA) (0)
12. Hallerstede, S., Hoang, T.S.: Qualitative probabilistic modelling in event-B. In: Davies, J., Gibbons, J. (eds.) IFM 2007. LNCS, vol. 4591, pp. 293–312. Springer, Heidelberg (2007), http://portal.acm.org/citation.cfm?id=1770498.1770514
13. Hoang, T.S., Jin, Z., Robinson, K., McIver, A., Morgan, C.: Development via refinement in probabilistic B - foundation and case study. In: Treharne, et al. (eds.) [27], pp. 355–373
14. Hoang, T.S., Kuruma, H., Basin, D., Abrial, J.-R.: Developing topology discovery in event-B. In: Leuschel, M., Wehrheim, H. (eds.) IFM 2009. LNCS, vol. 5423, pp. 1–19. Springer, Heidelberg (2009)
15. Litovsky, I., Métivier, Y., Sopena, E.: Graph relabelling systems and distributed algorithms. In: Ehrig, H., Kreowski, H., Montanari, U., Rozenberg, G. (eds.) Handbook of Graph Grammars and Computing by Graph Transformation, vol. 3, pp. 1–56. World Scientific, Singapore (1999)
16. Litovsky, I., Métivier, Y., Sopena, É.: Different local controls for graph relabelling systems. Mathematical System Theory 28, 41–65 (1995), http://www3.labri.fr/publications/combalgo/1995/LMS95

17. McIver, A.K., Morgan, C., Hoang, T.S.: Probabilistic termination in B. In: Bert, D., Bowen, J., King, S. (eds.) ZB 2003. LNCS, vol. 2651, pp. 216–239. Springer, Heidelberg (2003)
18. Méry, D.: A simple refinement-based method for constructing algorithms. SIGCSE Bull. 41(2), 51–59 (2009)
19. Métivier, Y., Mosbah, M., Ossamy, R., Sellami, A.: Synchronizers for local computations. In: ICGT, pp. 271–286 (2004)
20. Métivier, Y., Robson, J.M., Saheb-Djahromi, N., Zemmari, A.: About randomised distributed graph colouring and graph partition algorithms. Inf. Comput. 208(11), 1296–1304 (2010)
21. Morgan, C., Hoang, T.S., Abrial, J.R.: The challenge of probabilistic Event-B - extended abstract. In: Treharne, et al. (eds.) [27], pp. 162–171
22. Yves, M., Robson, J.M., Nasser, S.-D., Zemmari, A.: An optimal bit complexity randomized distributed MIS algorithm. In: Kutten, S., Žerovnik, J. (eds.) SIROCCO 2009. LNCS, vol. 5869, pp. 323–337. Springer, Heidelberg (2010)
23. Norman, G.: Analysing randomized distributed algorithms. In: Baier, C., Haverkort, B.R., Hermanns, H., Katoen, J.-P., Siegle, M. (eds.) Validation of Stochastic Systems. LNCS, vol. 2925, pp. 384–418. Springer, Heidelberg (2004)
24. Project RODIN: Rigorous open development environment for complex systems (2004–2007), http://rodin-b-sharp.sourceforge.net/
25. Reif, J., Spirakis, P.: Real time resource allocation in distributed systems. In: PODC 1982: Proceedings of the first ACM SIGACT-SIGOPS symposium on Principles of distributed computing, pp. 84–94. ACM, New York (1982)
26. Tarasyuk, A., Troubitsyna, E., Laibinis, L.: Towards probabilistic modelling in event-B. In: Méry, D., Merz, S. (eds.) IFM 2010. LNCS, vol. 6396, pp. 275–289. Springer, Heidelberg (2010)
27. Treharne, H., King, S., Henson, M.C., Schneider, S.A. (eds.): ZB 2005. LNCS, vol. 3455, pp. 13–15. Springer, Heidelberg (2005)
28. ViSiDiA (2006), http://visidia.labri.fr

Simulating Concurrent Behaviors with Worst-Case Cost Bounds[*]

Elvira Albert[1], Samir Genaim[1], Miguel Gómez-Zamalloa[1],
Einar Broch Johnsen[2], Rudolf Schlatte[2], and S. Lizeth Tapia Tarifa[2]

[1] DSIC, Complutense University of Madrid, Spain
{elvira,samir.genaim,mzamalloa}@fdi.ucm.es
[2] Department of Informatics, University of Oslo, Norway
{einarj,rudi,sltarifa}@ifi.uio.no

Abstract. Modern software systems are increasingly being developed
for deployment on a range of architectures. For this purpose, it is interesting to capture aspects of low-level deployment concerns in high-level
modeling languages. In this paper, an executable object-oriented modeling language is extended with resource-restricted deployment components. To analyze model behavior a formal methodology is proposed
to assess resource consumption, which balances the scalability of the
method and the reliability of the obtained results. The approach applies
to a general notion of resource, including traditional cost measures (e.g.,
time, memory) as well as concurrency-related measures (e.g., requests to
a server, spawned tasks). The main idea of our approach is to combine
reliable (but expensive) worst-case cost analysis of statically predictable
parts of the model with fast (but inherently incomplete) simulations of
the concurrent aspects in order to avoid the state-space explosion. The
approach is illustrated by the analysis of memory consumption.

1 Introduction

Software systems today are increasingly being developed to be highly configurable,
not only with respect to the functionality provided by a specific instance of the
system but also with respect to the targeted deployment architecture. An example of a development method is software product line engineering [20]. In order
to capture and analyze the intended deployment variability of such software, formal models need to express and range over different *deployment scenarios*. For
this purpose, it is interesting to reflect aspects of low-level deployment in high-
level modeling languages. As our first contribution, in this paper, we propose a
notion of *resource-restricted* deployment component for an executable modeling

---

[*] This work was funded in part by the EU project FP7-231620 *HATS*
(http://www.hats-project.eu), by the Spanish Ministry of Science and Innovation (MICINN) under the TIN-2008-05624 *DOVES* project, the HI2008-0153 (Acción
Integrada) project, the UCM-BSCH-GR35/10-A-910502 Research Group and by the
Madrid Regional Government under the S2009TIC-1465 *PROMETIDOS* project.

M. Butler and W. Schulte (Eds.): FM 2011, LNCS 6664, pp. 353–368, 2011.
© Springer-Verlag Berlin Heidelberg 2011

language based on *concurrent objects* [8, 11, 14, 21, 24]. The main idea of resource-restricted deployment components is that they are parametric in the amount of resources they make available to their concurrently executing objects. This way, different deployment scenarios can be conveniently expressed at the modeling level and a model may be analyzed for a range of deployment scenarios.

As our main contribution, we develop a novel approach for estimating the *resource consumption* of this kind of resource-constrained concurrent executions which is reasonably reliable and scalable. Resource consumption is in this sense a way of understanding and debugging the model of the deployment components. Our work is based on a general notion of *resource*, which associates a cost unit to the program statements. Traditional resources are execution steps, time and memory, but one may also consider more concurrency-related resources like the number of tasks spawned, the number of requests to a server, etc.

The two main approaches to estimating resource consumption of a program execution are *static cost analysis* and *dynamic simulation* (or monitoring). Efficient simulation techniques can analyze model behavior in different deployment scenarios, but simulations are carried out for particular input data. Hence, they cannot guarantee the correctness of the model. Due to the non-determinism of concurrent execution and the choice of inputs, possible errors may go undetected in a simulation. Static cost (or resource usage) analysis aims at automatically inferring a program's resource consumption *statically*, i.e., without running the program. Such analysis must consider all possible execution paths and ensures soundness, i.e., it guarantees that the program never exceeds the inferred resource consumption for any input data. While cost analysis for sequential languages exists, the problem has not yet been studied in the concurrent setting, partly due to the inherent complexity of concurrency: the number of possible execution paths can be extremely large and the resulting outcome non-deterministic. Statically analyzing the concurrent behaviors of our resource-restricted models requires a full state space exploration and quickly becomes unrealistic.

In this paper, we propose to combine simulations with static techniques for cost analysis, which allows classes of input values to be covered by a single simulation. The main idea is to apply cost analysis to the sequential computations while simulation handles the concurrent system behavior. Our method is developed for an abstract behavioral specification language *ABS*, simplifying Creol [11, 14], which contains a functional level where computations are sequential and an concurrent object-oriented level based on concurrent objects. This separation allows a concise and clean formalization of our technique. The combination of simulation and static analysis, as proposed in this paper, suggests a middle way between full state space exploration and simulating single paths, which gives interesting insights into the behavior of concurrent systems.

Paper organization. Sec. 2 describes the ABS modeling language and the running example. Sec. 3 discusses the worst-case cost analysis of the functional parts of ABS. Sec. 4 introduces deployment components, which model resource-containing runtime entities, and in Sec. 5 we apply our techniques to the running example. Finally, Sec. 6 discusses related work and Sec. 7 concludes.

Syntactic categories.	Definitions.

Syntactic categories.

I in Interface type

D in Data type

x in Variable

e in Expression

b in Bool Expression

t in Ground Term

br in Branch

p in Pattern

Definitions.

$Dd ::= \mathbf{data}\ D = Cons;$

$Cons ::= Co[(\overline{T})] \mid (Cons \mid Cons)$

$F ::= \mathbf{def}\ T\ fn(\overline{T\ x}) = e;$

$T ::= I \mid D$

$e ::= b \mid x \mid t \mid \mathbf{this} \mid Co[(\overline{e})] \mid fn(\overline{e}) \mid \mathbf{case}\ e\ \{\overline{br}\}$

$t ::= Co[(\overline{t})] \mid \mathbf{null}$

$br ::= p \Rightarrow e;$

$p ::= \_ \mid x \mid t \mid Co[(\overline{p})]$

Fig. 1. ABS syntax for the functional level. Terms $\overline{e}$ and $\overline{x}$ denote possibly empty lists over the corresponding syntactic categories, and square brackets $[\,]$ optional elements. Boolean expressions b include comparison by equality, greater- and less-than operators.

2   A Language for Distributed Concurrent Objects

Our method is presented for *ABS*, an abstract behavioral specification language for distributed concurrent objects (simplifying Creol [11, 14] by excluding, e.g., class inheritance and dynamic class upgrades). Characteristic features of ABS are that: (1) it allows abstracting from implementation details while remaining executable; i.e., a *functional sub-language* over abstract data types is used to specify internal, sequential computations; and (2) it provides *flexible concurrency and synchronization mechanisms* by means of asynchronous method calls, release points in method definitions, and cooperative scheduling of method activations.

Intuitively, concurrent ABS objects have dedicated processors and live in a distributed environment with asynchronous and unordered communication. All communication is between named objects, typed by interfaces, by means of asynchronous method calls. (There is no remote field access.) Calls are asynchronous as the caller may decide at runtime when to synchronize with the reply from a call. Method calls may be seen as triggers of concurrent activity, spawning new activities (so-called *processes*) in the called object. Active behavior, triggered by an optional *run* method, is interleaved with passive behavior, triggered by method calls. Thus, an object has a set of processes to be executed, which stem from method activations. Among these, at most one process is *active* and the others are *suspended* in a process pool. Process scheduling is non-deterministic, but controlled by *processor release points* in a cooperative way.

An ABS *model* defines interfaces, classes, datatypes, and functions, and has a `main` method to configure the initial state. Objects are dynamically created instances of classes; their declared attributes are initialized to arbitrary type-correct values, but may be redefined in an optional method *init*. This paper assumes that models are well-typed, so method binding is guaranteed to succeed.

The functional level of ABS defines data types and functions, as shown in Fig. 1. In data type declarations Dd, a data type D has at least one constructor $Cons$, which has a name Co and a list of types T for its arguments. Function declarations F consist of a return type T, a function name fn, a list of variable declarations $\overline{x}$ of types $\overline{T}$, and an expression e. *Expressions* e include

Syntactic categories.   *Definitions.*
C, m in Names $IF ::= \textbf{interface } I \{ \overline{Sg} \}$
g in Guard $CL ::= \textbf{class } C \, [(\overline{T \; x})] \, [\textbf{implements } \overline{I}] \, \{ \overline{T \; x}; \; \overline{M} \}$
s in Statement $Sg ::= T \; m \; (\overline{T \; x})$
                             $M ::= Sg \; \{ \; \overline{T \; x}; \; s \; \}$
                             $g ::= b \mid x? \mid g \wedge g \mid g \vee g$
                             $s ::= s; s \mid x := rhs \mid \textbf{release} \mid \textbf{await } g \mid \textbf{return } e$
                             $\quad \mid \textbf{if } b \textbf{ then} \{ s \} \, [\textbf{else} \{ s \}] \mid \textbf{while } b \{ s \} \mid \textbf{skip}$
                             $rhs ::= e \mid \textbf{new } C[(\overline{e})] \mid [e]!m(\overline{e}) \mid x.\textbf{get}$

Fig. 2. ABS syntax for the concurrent object level

Boolean expressions b, variables x, (ground) terms t, the (read-only) variable **this** which refers to the object's identifier, constructor expressions $Co(\overline{e})$, function expressions $fn(\overline{e})$, and case expressions **case** $e \; \{ \overline{br} \}$. Ground terms t are constructors applied to ground terms $Co(\overline{t})$, and **null**. Case expressions have a list of branches $p \Rightarrow e$, where p is a pattern. The branches are evaluated in the listed order. Patterns include wild cards $\_$, variables x, terms t, and constructor patterns $Co(\overline{p})$. Remark that expressions may refer to object references.

Example 1. Consider a polymorphic data type for sets and a function in which checks if e is an a member of the set ss.

```
data Set<A> = EmptySet | Insert(A, Set<A>);
def Bool in<A>(Set<A> ss, A e) =
  case ss {EmptySet => False ;
           Insert(e, _) => True;
           Insert(_, xs) => in(xs, e); };
```

The concurrent object level of ABS is given in Fig. 2. Here, an interface *IF* has a name I and method signatures Sg. A class implements a list of interfaces, specifying types for its instances; a class CL has a name C, interfaces $\overline{I}$, class parameters and state variables x of type T, and methods M (The *attributes* of the class are both its parameters and state variables). A method signature Sg declares the return type T of a method with name m and formal parameters $\overline{x}$ of types $\overline{T}$. M defines a method with signature Sg, a list of local variable declarations $\overline{x}$ of types $\overline{T}$, and a statement s. Statements may access attributes of the current class, locally defined variables, and the method's formal parameters.

Right hand side expressions rhs include object creation **new** $C(\overline{e})$, method calls, and (pure) expressions e. Statements are standard for assignment $x := rhs$, sequential composition $s_1; s_2$, and **skip**, **if**, **while**, and **return** constructs. **release** unconditionally releases the processor, suspending the active process. In **await** g, the guard g controls processor release and consists of Boolean conditions b and return tests $x?$ (see below). If g evaluates to false, the processor is released and the process *suspended*. When the processor is idle, any enabled process from the object's pool of suspended processes may be scheduled. Explicit signaling is therefore redundant. Like expressions e, guards g are side-effect free.

Communication in ABS is based on asynchronous method calls, denoted $o!m(\bar{e})$. (Local calls are written $!m(\bar{e})$.) After asynchronously calling $x := o!m(\bar{e})$, the caller may proceed with its execution without blocking on the call. Here x is a future variable, o is an object (an expression typed by an interface), and $\bar{e}$ are expressions. A future variable x refers to a return value which has yet to be computed. There are two operations on future variables, which control external synchronization in ABS. First, a return test $x?$ evaluates to false unless the reply to the call can be retrieved. (Return tests are used in guards.) Second, the return value is retrieved by the expression $x.\textbf{get}$, which blocks all execution in the object until the return value is available. The statement sequence $x := o!m(\bar{e}); \; v := x.\textbf{get}$ encodes a blocking, *synchronous call*, abbreviated $v := o.m(\bar{e})$, whereas the statement sequence $x := o!m(\bar{e}); \; \textbf{await } x?; \; v := x.\textbf{get}$ encodes a non-blocking, *preemptable call*, abbreviated $\textbf{await } v := o.m(\bar{e})$.

Example 2. Consider a model of a book shop where clients can order a list of books for delivery to a country. Clients connect to the shop by calling the getSession method of an Agent object. An Agent hands out Session objects from a dynamically growing pool. Clients call the order method of their Session instance, which calls the getInfo and confirmOrder methods of a Database object shared between the different sessions. Session objects return to the agent's pool after an order is completed. (The full model is available in [5].)

```
interface Agent { Session getSession(); Unit free(Session session);}
interface Session {
           OrderResult order(List<Bname> books, Cname country);}
interface Database {
           DatabaseInfo getInfo(List<Bname> books, Cname country);
           Bool confirmOrder(List<Bname> books); }
class   DatabaseImp(Map<Bname,Binfo> bDB, Map<Cname,Cinfo> cDB)
implements Database {
 DatabaseInfo getInfo(List<=Bname> books, Cname country){
  Map<Bname,Binfo> bOrder:=EmptyMap; Pair<Cname,Cinfo> cDestiny;
  bOrder:=getBooks(bDB, books); cDestiny:=getCountry(cDB, country);
  return Info(bOrder, cDestiny);} ...
```

In the model, a DatabaseImp class stores and handles the information about the books available in the shop (in the bDB map) as well as information about the delivery countries (in the cDB map). This class has a method getInfo; given an order with a list of books and a destination country, the getInfo method extracts information about book availability from bDB and shipping information from cDB by means of function calls getBooks(bDB, books) and getCountry(cDB, country) The result from the method call has type DatabaseInfo, with a constructor of the form: Info(bOrder, cDestiny).

2.1   Operational Semantics

The operational semantics of ABS is presented as a transition system in an SOS style [19]. Rules apply to subsets of configurations (the standard context rules are not listed). For simplicity we assume that configurations can be reordered to match the left hand side of the rules (i.e., matching is modulo associativity and commutativity as in rewriting logic [18]). A run is a possibly nonterminating sequence of rule applications. When auxiliary functions are used in the semantics, these are evaluated in between the application of transition rules in a run.

Configurations cn are sets of objects, invocation messages, and futures. The associative and commutative union operator on configurations is denoted by whitespace and the empty configuration by ε. These configurations live inside curly brackets; in the term $\{cn\}$, cn captures the *entire* configuration. An *object* is a term $ob(o, C, a, p, q)$ where o is the object's identifier and C its class, a an attribute mapping representing the object's fields, p an *active process*, and q a *pool of suspended processes*. A process p consists of a mapping l of local variable bindings and a list s of statements, denoted by $\{l|s\}$ when convenient. In an *invocation message invoc*$(o, f, m, \overline{v})$, o is the callee, f the future to which the call's result is returned, m the method name, and $\overline{v}$ the call's actual parameter values. A *future fut*(f, v) has a identifier f and a reply value v (which is $\perp$ when the future's reply value has not been received). Values are object and future identifiers, Boolean expressions, and null (as well as expressions in the functional language). For simplicity, classes are not represented explicitly in the semantics, but may be seen as static tables.

Evaluating Expressions. Denote by $\sigma(x)$ the value bound to x in a mapping σ and by $\sigma_1 \circ \sigma_2$ the composition of mappings σ_1 and σ_2. Given a substitution σ and a configuration cn, denote by $[\![e]\!]^{cn}_\sigma$ a confluent and terminating reduction system which reduces expressions e to data values. Let $[\![x?]\!]^{cn}_\sigma = $ true if $[\![x]\!]^{cn}_\sigma = f$ and $fut(f, v) \in cn$ for some value $v \neq \perp$, otherwise $[\![x?]\!]^{cn}_\sigma = $ false. The remaining cases are fairly straightforward, looking up values for declared variables in σ. For brevity, we omit the reduction system for the functional level of ABS (for details, see [5]) and simply denote by $[\![e]\!]^\varepsilon_\sigma$ the evaluation of a guard or expression e in the context of a substitution σ and a state configuration cn (the state configuration is needed to evaluate future variables). The reduction of an expression always happens in the context of a given process, object state, and configuration. Thus, $\sigma = a \circ l$ (the composition of the fields a and the local variable bindings l), and cn the current configuration of the system (ignoring the object itself).

Transition Rules. Transition rules of the operational semantics transform state configurations into new configurations, and are given in Fig. 3. We assume given functions $bind(o, f, m, \overline{v}, C)$ which returns a process resulting from the method activation of m in a class C with actual parameters $\overline{v}$, callee o and associated future f; $init(C)$ which returns a process initializing instances of class C; and $atts(C, \overline{v}, o, n)$ which returns the initial state of an instance of class C with class parameters $\overline{v}$, identity o, and deployment component n. The predicate $fresh(n)$ asserts that a name n is globally unique (where n may be an identifier for an object or a future). Let *idle* denote any process $\{l|s\}$ where s is an empty statement list. Finally, we define different assignment rules for side effect free expressions (*assign1* and *assign2*), object creation (*new-object*), method calls (*async-call*), and future dereferencing (*read-fut*). Rule *skip* consumes a **skip** in the active process. Here and in the sequel, the variable s will match any (possibly empty) statement list. Rules *assign1* and *assign2* assign the value of expression e to a

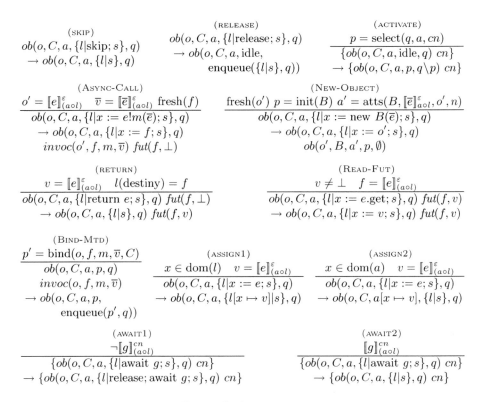

$$\frac{\text{(SKIP)}}{ob(o,C,a,\{l|\text{skip};s\},q)} \\ \to ob(o,C,a,\{l|s\},q)$$

$$\frac{\text{(RELEASE)}}{ob(o,C,a,\{l|\text{release};s\},q)} \\ \to ob(o,C,a,\text{idle}, \\ \text{enqueue}(\{l|s\},q))$$

$$\frac{p = \text{select}(q,a,cn) \quad \text{(ACTIVATE)}}{\{ob(o,C,a,\text{idle},q)\ cn\}} \\ \to \{ob(o,C,a,p,q\backslash p)\ cn\}$$

$$\frac{o' = [\![e]\!]^\varepsilon_{(a\circ l)} \quad \overline{v} = [\![\overline{e}]\!]^\varepsilon_{(a\circ l)} \ \text{fresh}(f) \quad \text{(ASYNC-CALL)}}{ob(o,C,a,\{l|x := e!m(\overline{e});s\},q)} \\ \to ob(o,C,a,\{l|x := f;s\},q) \\ invoc(o',f,m,\overline{v})\ fut(f,\bot)$$

$$\frac{\text{fresh}(o') \ p = \text{init}(B) \ a' = \text{atts}(B,[\![\overline{e}]\!]^\varepsilon_{(a\circ l)},o',n) \quad \text{(NEW-OBJECT)}}{ob(o,C,a,\{l|x := \text{new } B(\overline{e});s\},q)} \\ \to ob(o,C,a,\{l|x := o';s\},q) \\ ob(o',B,a',p,\emptyset)$$

$$\frac{v = [\![e]\!]^\varepsilon_{(a\circ l)} \quad l(\text{destiny}) = f \quad \text{(RETURN)}}{ob(o,C,a,\{l|\text{return } e;s\},q)\ fut(f,\bot)} \\ \to ob(o,C,a,\{l|s\},q)\ fut(f,v)$$

$$\frac{v \neq \bot \quad f = [\![e]\!]^\varepsilon_{(a\circ l)} \quad \text{(READ-FUT)}}{ob(o,C,a,\{l|x := e.\text{get};s\},q)\ fut(f,v)} \\ \to ob(o,C,a,\{l|x := v;s\},q)\ fut(f,v)$$

$$\frac{p' = \text{bind}(o,f,m,\overline{v},C) \quad \text{(BIND-MTD)}}{ob(o,C,a,p,q)} \\ invoc(o,f,m,\overline{v}) \\ \to ob(o,C,a,p, \\ \text{enqueue}(p',q))$$

$$\frac{x \in \text{dom}(l) \quad v = [\![e]\!]^\varepsilon_{(a\circ l)} \quad \text{(ASSIGN1)}}{ob(o,C,a,\{l|x := e;s\},q)} \\ \to ob(o,C,a,\{l[x \mapsto v]|s\},q)$$

$$\frac{x \in \text{dom}(a) \quad v = [\![e]\!]^\varepsilon_{(a\circ l)} \quad \text{(ASSIGN2)}}{ob(o,C,a,\{l|x := e;s\},q)} \\ \to ob(o,C,a[x \mapsto v],\{l|s\},q)$$

$$\frac{\neg [\![g]\!]^{cn}_{(a\circ l)} \quad \text{(AWAIT1)}}{\{ob(o,C,a,\{l|\text{await } g;s\},q)\ cn\}} \\ \to \{ob(o,C,a,\{l|\text{release};\text{await } g;s\},q)\ cn\}$$

$$\frac{[\![g]\!]^{cn}_{(a\circ l)} \quad \text{(AWAIT2)}}{\{ob(o,C,a,\{l|\text{await } g;s\},q)\ cn\}} \\ \to \{ob(o,C,a,\{l|s\},q)\ cn\}$$

Fig. 3. ABS Semantics

variable x in the local variables l or in the fields a, respectively. (We omit the standard rules for if-then-else and while).

Process Suspension and Activation. Three operations are used to manipulate a process pool q: enqueue(p,q) adds a process p to q, $q \setminus p$ removes p from q, and select(q,a,cn,t) selects a process from q (which is idle if q is empty or no process is *ready* [14]). The actual definitions are left undefined; different definitions correspond to different process scheduling policies. Let $\emptyset$ denote the empty pool. Rule *release* suspends the active process to the pool, leaving the active process idle. Rule *await1* consumes the await statement if the guard evaluates to true in the current state of the object, rule *await2* adds a release statement in order to suspend the process if the guard evaluates to false. Rule *activate* selects a process from the pool for execution if this process is *ready* to execute, i.e., if it would not directly be resuspended or block the processor [14].

Communication and Object Creation. Rule *async-call* sends an invocation message to o' with the unique identity f (by the condition fresh(f)) of a new future, the method name m, and actual parameters $\overline{v}$. Note that the return value of the new future f is undefined (i.e., $\bot$). Rule *bind-mtd* consumes an invocation method and places the process corresponding to the method activation in the process pool of the callee. Note that a reserved local variable 'destiny' is used to store the identity of the future associated with the call. Rule *return* places the return value into the call's associated future. Rule *read-fut* dereferences the future f in the case where $v \neq \bot$. Note that if this attribute is $\bot$ the reduction in this object is *blocked*. Finally, *new-object* creates a new object with a unique identifier o'. The object's fields are given default values by $\text{atts}(B, \overline{v}, o', n)$, extended with the actual values $\overline{v}$ for the class parameters and o' for this. In order to instantiate the remaining attributes, the process p is loaded (we assume that this process reduces to idle if $\text{init}(B)$ is unspecified in the class definition, and that it asynchronously calls run if the latter is specified).

3   Worst-Case Cost Bounds

The goal of this section is to infer *worst-case upper bounds* (UBs) from the (sequential) functions in our sub-language. This problem has been intensively studied since the seminal paper on cost analysis [23]. Thus, instead of a formal development, we illustrate the main steps of the analysis on the running example.

Size of terms. The cost of a function that traverses a term t usually depends on the *size* of t, and not on the concrete data structure to which t is bound. For instance, the cost of executing $dom(map)$ (which returns the domain of a map) depends on the size of map (the number of elements). Therefore, in order to infer worst-case UBs, we first need to define the meaning of *size of a term*. This is done by using *norms* [7]. A norm is a function that maps terms to their size. For instance, the *term-size* norm calculates the number of type constructors in a given term, and is defined as $|Co(t_1, \ldots, t_n)|_{ts} = 1 + \Sigma_{i=1}^{n} |t_i|_{ts}$, and, the *term-depth* norm calculates the depth of the term, and is defined as $|Co(t_1, \ldots, t_n)|_{td} = 1 + \max(|t_1|_{td}, \ldots, |t_n|_{td})$. Consider the book shop model described in Ex. 2; the database uses maps for storing information; a Map<A, B> has two constructors Ins(Pair<A, B>, Map<A, B>) and EmptyMap (to represent empty maps). For storing the information of a book sold by the shop, the model uses a constructor of the form BInfo(Bquantity, Bweight, Bbackordertime) (A more detailed description of this data type can be found in [5].). For a term:

   $t =$ Ins(Pair("b1",BInfo(5,1,2)),Ins(Pair("b2",BInfo(1,2,5)),EmptyMap))

which can represent the database of books in the shop, we have that $|t|_{ts} = 15$ and $|t|_{td} = 5$. Note that we count strings and numbers as type constructors. Norms map a given variable x to itself in order to account for the size of the term to which x is bounded. Any norm can be used in the analysis, depending on the used data structures, w.l.o.g., we will use the term-size norm.

Size relations. The getBooks function (called from method getInfo in Ex. 2) returns a sub-database (of booksDB) which contains only those books in books:

```
def Map getBooks(Map booksDB,List books) = case books {
    Nil => EmptyMap;
    Cons(b,t) => case in(dom(booksDB),b) {
        False => getBooks(booksDB,t) ;
        True => Ins(Pair(b,lookup(booksDB,b)),getBooks(booksDB,t)); };};
```

Function dom returns the set of keys of the mapping provided as argument, in is the one of Ex. 1, and, lookup returns the value that corresponds to the provided key in the provided mapping. Observe that the return value of dom is passed on to function in. Since the cost of in is part of the total cost of getBooks, we need to express its cost in terms of booksDB. This is possible only if we know which is the relation between the returned value of dom and its input value booksDB. This *input-output* relation (or a post-condition) is a conjunction of (linear) constraints that describe a relation between the sizes of the input parameters of the function and its return value, w.r.t. the selected norm. E.g., $ret \leq map$ is a possible post-condition for function dom, where map is the size of its input parameter and ret is the size of the returned term. We apply existing techniques [6] to infer such relations for our functional language. In what follows, we assume that $\mathcal{I}_P$ includes a post-conditions $\langle fn(\bar{x}), \psi \rangle$ for each function, where ψ is a conjunction of (linear) constraints over $\bar{x}$ and ret.

Cost Model. Cost analysis is typically parametric on the notion of *cost model* $\mathcal{M}$, i.e., on the resource that we want to measure [2]. Informally, a cost model is a function that maps instructions to costs. Traditional cost models are: (1) *number of instructions*, which maps all instructions to 1, i.e., $\mathcal{M}(b) = 1$ for all instructions b; and (2) *memory consumption*, which can be defined as $\mathcal{M}_h(x = t) = \mathcal{M}_h(t) = mem(t)$ where $mem(Co(t_1, \ldots, t_n)) = \mathsf{Co} + \Sigma_{i=1}^n mem(t_i)$ and $mem(x) = 0$. For any other instruction b we let $\mathcal{M}_h(b) = 0$. The symbol Co represents the amount of memory required for constructing a term of type Co. Note that we estimate only the memory required for storing terms.

Upper bounds. In order to make the presentation simpler, we assume functions are normalized such that nested expressions are flattened using **let** bindings. Using this normal form, the evaluation of an expression e consists in evaluating a sequence of sub-expressions of the form $y = fn(\bar{x})$, $y = t$, $match(y, t)$, $fn(\bar{x})$, t or x. We refer to such sequence as an execution path of e. In a static setting, since variables are not assigned concrete values, and due to the use of **case**, an expression e might have several execution paths. We denote the set of all execution paths of e by $paths(e)$. This set can be constructed from the abstract syntax tree of e. Clearly, when estimating the cost of executing an expression e we must consider all possible execution paths. In practice, we generate a set of (recursive) equations where each equation accounts for the cost of one execution path. Then, the solver of [1] is used in order to obtained a closed-form UB.

Definition 1. *Given a function* **def** T $fn(\overline{T}\ x) = e$, *its cost relation (CR) is defined as follows: for each execution path* $p \equiv b_1, \ldots, b_n \in paths(e)$, *we define an equation* $\langle fn(\bar{x}) = \Sigma_{i=1}^n \mathcal{M}(b_i) + fn_{i_1}(\bar{x}_{i_1}) + \cdots + fn_{i_k}(\bar{x}_{i_k}), \wedge_{i=1}^n \varphi_i \rangle$ *where* $fn_{i_1}(\bar{x}_{i_1}), \ldots, fn_{i_k}(\bar{x}_{i_k})$ *are all function calls in* p; *and* $\varphi_i \equiv y = |t|_{ts}$ *if* $b_i \equiv y = t$, *and* $\varphi_i \equiv \psi[ret/y]$ *if* $b_i \equiv y = f(\bar{x})$ *and* $\langle f(\bar{x}), \psi \rangle \in \mathcal{I}_P$, *otherwise* $\varphi_i = true$. *The CR system of a given program the set of all CRs of its functions.*

Example 3. The following is the *CR* of `getBooks` w.r.t the cost model *mem*:

$$getBooks(a,b) = \mathsf{EmptyMap} \qquad\qquad\qquad\{b=1\}$$
$$getBooks(a,b) = dom(a)+in(d,e)+getBooks(a,g) \;\{b=1+e+g, d\leq a, d\geq 1, e\geq 1, g\geq 1\}$$
$$getBooks(a,b) = \mathsf{Pair}+\mathsf{Ins}+dom(a)+in(d,e) \qquad \{b=1+e+g, d\leq a, d\geq 1, e\geq 1, g\geq 1\}$$
$$\qquad\qquad\quad + lookup(a,e)+getBooks(a,g)$$

The first equation can be read as "the memory consumption of *getBooks* is one *EmptyMap* constructor if the size of b is 1". Equations for functions *in*, *lookup* and *dom* are not shown due to space limitations and have resp. constant, zero and linear memory consumptions. Solving the above *CR* results in the UB

$$getBooks(a,b) = \mathsf{EmptyMap}+\mathsf{nat}(\tfrac{b-1}{2})*(\mathsf{nat}(\tfrac{a-1}{4})*\mathsf{Ins}+\mathsf{EmptySet}+ \max(\mathsf{True}, \mathsf{False}))$$

Replacing, for example, EmptyMap, Ins, True and False by 1 results in

$$getBooks(a,b) = 1+ \mathsf{nat}(\tfrac{b-1}{2}) * (2 + \mathsf{nat}(\tfrac{a-1}{4}))$$

4   Deployment Components

Deployment components make quantifiable deployment-level resources explicitly available in the modeling language. A deployment component allows the logical execution environment of concurrent objects to be mapped to a model of physical resources, by specifying an abstract execution context which is shared between a number of concurrently executing objects. The resources available to a deployment component are shared between the component's objects. An object may get and return resources from and to its deployment component. Thus, the deployment components impose a resource-restricted execution context for their concurrently executing objects, but not a communication topology as objects still communicate directly with each other independent of the components.

Resource-restricted deployment components are integrated in the modeling language as follows. Let variables x of type `Component` refer to deployment components and allow deployment components to be statically created by the statement x:=**component** (r) in the main method, which allocates a given quantity of resources r to the component x (capturing the resource constraint of x). Resources are modeled by a data type `Resource` which extends the natural numbers with an "unbounded resource" ω. Resource allocation and usage is captured by resource addition and subtraction, where $\omega + n = \omega$ and $\omega - n = \omega$.

Concurrent objects residing on components, may grow dynamically. All objects are created inside a deployment component. The syntax for object creation is extended with an optional clause to specify the targeted deployment component in the expression **new** $C(\bar{e})$ @ x. This expresses that the new C object will reside in the component x. Objects generated without an @ clause reside in the same component as their parent object. Thus the behavior of an ABS model which does not statically declare additional deployment components can be captured by a root deployment component with ω resources.

Example 4. Consider the book shop model described in Ex. 2 instantiated inside deployment components:

Table 1. The non-trivial cost functions of memory-constrained ABS semantics. All identifiers are the same as in the corresponding rule of Fig. 3, except vp (old value of a variable), $|v|$ (size of term v), P (size of a process), and O (size of an object).

Rule	cost	free
ASSIGN1, ASSIGN2	$cost(e)$	$|vp| - |v|$
READ-FUT	$max(cost(e), |v|)$	0
BIND-MTD	$P + |\overline{v}|$	$-(P + |\overline{v}|)$
ASYNC-CALL	$cost(\overline{e}) + |f|$	0
NEW-OBJECT-CREATE	$O + P + |\overline{v}|$	$-(O + P + |\overline{v}|)$

```
Component c    := component(200);
Database db    := new DataBaseImp(...) @ c;
Agent agent    := new AgentImp(db) @ c;
```

The `Session` objects created and handed out by the `Agent` object will then be created inside `c` as well, without further changes to the model.

The *execution* inside a component d with r resources can be understood as follows. An object o residing in d may execute a transition step with cost c if

- o can execute the step in a context with unbounded resources, and
- $c \leq r$; i.e., the cost of executing the step does not exclude the transition in an execution context restricted to r resources.

After the execution of the transition step, the object may return free resources to its deployment component. Thus, for each transition rule the resources needed to apply this rule to a state t, resulting in a state t', can be characterized in terms of two functions over the state space, one computing the *cost* of the transition form t to t' and one computing the *free* resources after the transition. The allocation and return of resources for objects in a deployment component will depend on the specific cost model $\mathcal{M}$ for the considered resource, so the exact definitions of $cost_{\mathcal{M}}(t, t')$ and $free_{\mathcal{M}}(t, t')$ depend on $\mathcal{M}$.

Example 5. Table 1 shows the $cost_{\mathcal{M}}(t, t')$ and $free_{\mathcal{M}}(t, t')$ functions for the memory cost model of the ABS semantics, using the symbols of Fig. 3. There are some subtle details in these functions – for example, message invocations and future variables are considered to be outside any one deployment component, so the memory required to execute the READ-FUT rule can be larger than evaluating the future variable expression e since the deployment component must have enough memory to accommodate the incoming value v. Also, object creation affects two places, so was split into two rules, similar to method invocation.

Semantics of Resource Constrained Execution. Let $\mathcal{M}$ be a cost model. The operational semantics of $\mathcal{M}$-constrained execution in deployment components is defined as a small-step operational semantics, extending the semantics of ABS given in Sec. 2.1 to resource-sensitive runtime configurations for $\mathcal{M}$. We assume given functions $cost_{\mathcal{M}}(t, t')$ and $free_{\mathcal{M}}(t, t')$.

$$(\text{Context})$$

$$\frac{mycomp(o) = id \qquad cost_{\mathcal{M}}(o\ \overline{msg}, o'\ \overline{msg}'\ \overline{config}') \leq r}{o\ \overline{msg} \longrightarrow o'\ \overline{msg}'\ \overline{config}' \qquad r' = r + free_{\mathcal{M}}(o\ \overline{msg}, o'\ \overline{msg}'\ \overline{config}')}{\{comp(id, r)\ o\ \overline{msg}\ \overline{config}\} \longrightarrow_{\mathcal{M}} \{comp(id, r')\ o'\ \overline{msg}'\ \overline{config}\ \overline{config}'\}}$$

Fig. 4. An operational semantics for resource-constrained deployment components

$$(\text{Assign1-rsc})$$

$$\frac{x \in \text{dom}(l) \quad v = \llbracket e \rrbracket^{\varepsilon}_{(a \circ l)} \quad vp = l(x) \quad cost(e) \leq r \quad mycomp(o) = dc}{dc(r)\ ob(o, C, a, \{l | x := e; s\}, q)}{\rightarrow dc(r + |vp| - |v|)\ ob(o, C, a, \{l[x \mapsto v] | s\}, q)}$$

Fig. 5. Resource-aware assignment rule, with an object ob and deployment component dc. The assignment statement is only executed if e can be evaluated with the current r, which is adjusted afterwards.

Let $\longrightarrow$ denote the single-step reduction relation of the ABS semantics, defined in Sec. 2.1. A resource-constrained run of an ABS model consists of zero or more applications of a transition relation $\longrightarrow_{\mathcal{M}}$, which is defined by the context rule given in Fig. 4. Runtime configurations are extended with the representation of deployment components $comp(id, r)$, where id is the identifier of the component and r its currently available resources. Each object has a field mycomp, instantiated to its deployment component at creation time (we omit the redefined object creation rule). Let $\overline{config}$ denote a set of objects and futures. The context rule expresses how an object o may evolve to o' given a set of invocation messages $\overline{msg}$ in the context of a deployment component with r available resources. Since o may consume an invocation message and create new objects, futures, or invocation messages, the right hand side of the rule returns o' with a possibly different set of messages $\overline{msg}'$ and a configuration $\overline{config}'$.

5   Simulation and Experimental Results

To validate the approach presented in this paper, an interpreter for the ABS language was augmented with a resource constraint model that simulates systems with limited memory. The semantics of this ABS interpreter is given in rewriting logic [18] and executes on the Maude platform [10]. Note that the semantics of Sec. 4, when implemented directly, leads to a significant amount of backtracking in an actual simulation. For this reason, our Maude interpreter was modified to incorporate deployment components and use the costs of Table 1 for the execution of statements. One such modified rule is shown in Fig. 5: An assignment to x can only proceed if the cost of evaluating the right-hand side e of the assignment statement is less than the currently free memory r. In this case, x is bound to the new value v, and r is adjusted using Table 1 (here, the difference between v and the previous value vp). All other transition rules which evaluate expressions are modified in the same way.

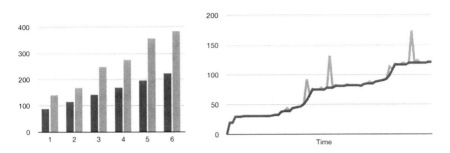

Fig. 6. Final and peak memory use as a function of the size of input (left) and progression of memory use for execution using input size 2 (right)

Simulation results. Deployment component declarations were added to the book shop model described in Ex. 2, restricting the memory available to all objects of type `Database`, `Agent`, and `Session` (i.e., the server part of the model). Cost functions were computed for all functions in the model, as described in Sec. 3 (UBs for all functions in the book shop model can be found in [5]). With this interpreter, creating a deployment component with too little memory leads to the expected deadlock.

To obtain quantitative results, the interpreter was instrumented to record current memory r and peak memory usage $r+\mathrm{cost}(s)$ during the evaluation of its resource-aware rules. This instrumentation yields both *maximum resource usage* and a *time series* of memory usage for a simulation run. Fig. 6 (left) shows the peak intermediate memory usage and memory use at the end of the simulation for various input sizes (i.e., how often to run book orders of constant size). Fig. 6 (right) shows the memory use over time of one single run of the model. The "peaks" in the right-hand side graph occur during evaluation of functions with large intermediate memory usage (the blue line represents memory use between execution steps, when the transient memory has been freed again).

6   Related Work

Static cost inference for sequential programming languages has recently received considerable attention. A cost analysis for Java bytecode has been developed in [2], for C++ in [12], and for functional programs in [13]. Our approach for inferring cost for the functional part of ABS is based on [2], which follows the classical approach of [23]. Inference of worst-case UBs on the memory usage of Java like programs with garbage collection is studied in [4]. The analysis accounts for memory freed by garbage collection, and thus infers more tight and realistic bounds. The analysis supports several GC schemes. The analysis of [13] supports inference of memory usage, and accounts for memory freed by destructive matching. In [16] live heap space analysis for a concurrent language has been proposed. However it uses a very limited model of shared memory. Recently, a cost analysis for X10 programs [9] has been developed [3], which infers

UBs on the number of tasks that can be running in parallel. The concurrency primitives of X10 are similar to ABS, but X10 is not based on concurrent objects.

Formal resource modeling happens mainly in the embedded domain. For example, Verhoef et al. [22] use the timed VDM++ to model processing time, schedulability and bandwidth resources for distributed embedded systems, but their approach is less general and not used for memory consumption. Johnsen et al. modeled processing resources in the context of deployment components in previous work [15], but this work does not use cost analysis methods. There is not much work combining static cost analysis and simulation to analyze resource usage. However, Künzli et al. [17] combine exact simulation and arrival curves to model processing costs, decreasing the needed simulation time by using arrival curves in their simulations to abstract from some of the components in a SystemC model of specific hardware. In contrast, we use cost analysis to generalize simulations on abstract, formally defined object-oriented models.

7   Discussion

Software is increasingly being developed to be configured for different architectures, which may be restricted in the resources they provide to the software. Therefore, it is interesting to capture aspects of low-level deployment concerns at the abstraction level of a software modeling language. In this paper, we have shown how a formally defined executable concurrent object-oriented modeling language can be extended with a notion of deployment component, which imposes a resource-constraint on the execution of objects in the model.

In order to validate the behavior of the resource-restricted model, we propose to combine static cost analysis with simulations. This combination is achieved by applying static cost analysis to the sequential parts of the modeling language, for which practical cost analysis methods exist, while using simulation for the concurrent part, for which static approaches would lead to a state-space explosion. Thus, the complexity of applying static cost analysis to concurrent executions is avoided, and, in addition, we obtain better results than concrete simulations because the sequential parts of the model are simulated by the worst-case bounds. The technique is demonstrated for memory consumption analysis on an example. The analysis of memory consumption considered here could be strengthened by allowing explicit scheduling and garbage collection policies to be included in the model. This is left for future work.

Another interesting issue is how resource analysis carries over from executable models to generated code. A code generator from ABS to Java is under development that translates user defined abstract data types in ABS into object structures. Hence, the symbolic UBs inferred for memory consumption of the ABS models correspond to bounds on the number of objects in the corresponding Java code. Note that it might not be possible to find similar correlations for other cost models such as the number of execution steps. Another line of interesting future work is to set up actual measurements on generated code and use these results to profile our analysis approach for a given cost model.

References

1. Albert, E., Arenas, P., Genaim, S., Puebla, G.: Closed-Form Upper Bounds in Static Cost Analysis. Journal of Automated Reasoning 42(6), 161–203 (2011)
2. Albert, E., Arenas, P., Genaim, S., Puebla, G., Zanardini, D.: Cost analysis of java bytecode. In: De Nicola, R. (ed.) ESOP 2007. LNCS, vol. 4421, pp. 157–172. Springer, Heidelberg (2007)
3. Albert, E., Arenas, P., Genaim, S., Zanardini, D.: Task-Level Analysis for a Language with Async-Finish parallelism. In: LCTES. ACM Press, New York (2011)
4. Albert, E., Genaim, S., Gómez-Zamalloa, M.: Parametric Inference of Memory Requirements for Garbage Collected Languages. In: ISMM. ACM Press, New York (2010)
5. Albert, E., Genaim, S., Gómez-Zamalloa, M., Johnsen, E.B., Schlatte, R., Tapia Tarifa, S.L.: Simulating concurrent behaviors with worst-case cost bounds. Research Report 403, Dept. of Informatics, Univ. of Oslo (January 2011), http://einarj.at.ifi.uio.no/Papers/rr403.pdf
6. Benoy, F., King, A.: Inferring Argument Size Relationships with CLP(R). In: Gallagher, J.P. (ed.) LOPSTR 1996. LNCS, vol. 1207, pp. 204–223. Springer, Heidelberg (1997)
7. Bossi, A., Cocco, N., Fabris, M.: Proving Termination of Logic Programs by Exploiting Term Properties. In: Abramsky, S. (ed.) TAPSOFT 1991, CCPSD 1991, and ADC-Talks 1991. LNCS, vol. 494. Springer, Heidelberg (1991)
8. Caromel, D., Henrio, L.: A Theory of Distributed Object. Springer, Heidelberg (2005)
9. Charles, P., Grothoff, C., Saraswat, V.A., Donawa, C., Kielstra, A., Ebcioglu, K., von Praun, C., Sarkar, V.: X10: An Object-Oriented Approach to Non-Uniform Cluster computing. In: OOPSLA, pp. 519–538. ACM, New York (2005)
10. Clavel, M., Durán, F., Eker, S., Lincoln, P., Martí-Oliet, N., Meseguer, J., Talcott, C.L.: All About Maude - A High-Performance Logical Framework. LNCS, vol. 4350. Springer, Heidelberg (2007)
11. de Boer, F.S., Clarke, D., Johnsen, E.B.: A complete guide to the future. In: De Nicola, R. (ed.) ESOP 2007. LNCS, vol. 4421, pp. 316–330. Springer, Heidelberg (2007)
12. Gulwani, S., Mehra, K.K., Chilimbi, T.M.: Speed: Precise and Efficient Static Estimation of Program Computational Complexity. In: POPL. ACM, New York (2009)
13. Hoffmann, J., Aehlig, K., Hofmann, M.: Multivariate amortized resource analysis. In: POPL, pp. 357–370. ACM, New York (2011)
14. Johnsen, E.B., Owe, O.: An asynchronous communication model for distributed concurrent objects. Software and Systems Modeling 6(1), 35–58 (2007)
15. Johnsen, E.B., Owe, O., Schlatte, R., Tapia Tarifa, S.L.: Dynamic resource reallocation between deployment components. In: Dong, J.S., Zhu, H. (eds.) ICFEM 2010. LNCS, vol. 6447, pp. 646–661. Springer, Heidelberg (2010)
16. Kero, M., Pietrzak, P., Nordlander, J.: Live heap space bounds for real-time systems. In: Ueda, K. (ed.) APLAS 2010. LNCS, vol. 6461, pp. 287–303. Springer, Heidelberg (2010)
17. Künzli, S., Poletti, F., Benini, L., Thiele, L.: Combining simulation and formal methods for system-level performance analysis. In: DATE. European Design and Automation Association, pp. 236–241 (2006)

18. Meseguer, J.: Conditional rewriting logic as a unified model of concurrency. Theoretical Computer Science 96, 73–155 (1992)
19. Plotkin, G.D.: A structural approach to operational semantics. Journal of Logic and Algebraic Programming 61, 17–139 (2004)
20. Pohl, K., Böckle, G., Van Der Linden, F.: Software Product Line Engineering: Foundations, Principles, and Techniques. Springer, Heidelberg (2005)
21. Schäfer, J., Poetzsch-Heffter, A.: JCoBox: Generalizing active objects to concurrent components. In: D'Hondt, T. (ed.) ECOOP 2010. LNCS, vol. 6183, pp. 275–299. Springer, Heidelberg (2010)
22. Verhoef, M., Larsen, P.G., Hooman, J.: Modeling and validating distributed embedded real-time systems with VDM++. In: Misra, J., Nipkow, T., Karakostas, G. (eds.) FM 2006. LNCS, vol. 4085, pp. 147–162. Springer, Heidelberg (2006)
23. Wegbreit, B.: Mechanical Program Analysis. Comm. of the ACM 18(9) (1975)
24. Welc, A., Jagannathan, S., Hosking, A.: Safe futures for Java. In: Proc. OOPSLA 2005, pp. 439–453. ACM Press, New York (2005)

Automatically Refining Partial Specifications for Program Verification[*]

Shengchao Qin[1], Chenguang Luo[2], Wei-Ngan Chin[3], and Guanhua He[1,2]

[1] Teesside University
[2] Durham University
[3] National University of Singapore

Abstract. Automatically verifying heap-manipulating programs is a challenging task, especially when dealing with complex data structures with strong invariants, such as sorted lists and AVL/red-black trees. The verification process can greatly benefit from human assistance through specification annotations, but this process requires intellectual effort from users and is error-prone. In this paper, we propose a new approach to program verification that allows users to provide only partial specification to methods. Our approach will then refine the given annotation into a more complete specification by discovering missing constraints. The discovered constraints may involve both numerical and multi-set properties that could be later confirmed or revised by users. We further augment our approach by requiring only partial specification to be given for primary methods. Specifications for loops and auxiliary methods can then be systematically discovered by our augmented mechanism, with the help of information propagated from the primary methods. Our work is aimed at verifying beyond shape properties, with the eventual goal of analysing full functional properties for pointer-based data structures. Initial experiments have confirmed that we can automatically refine partial specifications with non-trivial constraints, thus making it easier for users to handle specifications with richer properties.

1 Introduction

Human assistance is often essential in (semi-) automated program verification. The user may supply annotations at certain program points, such as loop invariants and/or method specifications. These annotations can greatly narrow down the possible program states at that point, and avoid fixed-point calculation which could be expensive and may be less precise than the user's insight.

However, an obvious disadvantage of user annotation concerns its scalability, since programs to be analysed may be complicated and with significant diversity. Therefore, it may be unreasonable to expect user to provide specification for every method and invariant for every loop when verifying larger software systems. Furthermore, to err is human. A programmer may under-specify with too weak

---

[*] This work is supported in part by EPSRC project EP/G042322 and MoE ARF grant R-252-000-411-112.

M. Butler and W. Schulte (Eds.): FM 2011, LNCS 6664, pp. 369–385, 2011.

a precondition or over-specify with too strong a postcondition. Such mistakes could lead to failed verification, and it may be difficult to distinguish between a real bug or an inappropriate annotation.

To balance verification quality and human effort, we provide a novel approach to the verification of heap manipulating programs, which has long since been a challenging problem. To deal with such programs, which manipulate heap-allocated shared mutable data structures, one needs to keep track of not only "shape" information (for deep heap properties) but also related "pure" proper-ties, such as structural numerical information (size and height), relational numer-ical information (balanced and sortedness properties), and content information (multi-set of symbolic values). Under our framework, the user is expected to provide partial specifications for *primary* methods with only *shape* information. Our verification will then take over the rest of the work to refine those partial specifications with derived (pure) constraints which should be satisfied by the program, or report a possible program bug if the given specifications are rejected by our verifier. This is an improvement over previous works [23], where users must provide full specifications for each method and invariants for each loop. This is also significantly different from the compositional shape analysis [5,9,32]. In spite of a higher level of automation, their analysis focuses on pointer safety only and deals primarily with a few built-in predicates over the shape domain only. Our work targets at both memory safety and functional correctness and supports user-defined predicates over several abstract domains (such as shape, numerical, multi-set).

Our approach allows the user to design their predicates for shapes and relative properties, to capture the desired level of program correctness to be verified. For example, with a singly-linked list structure data node { int val; node next; }, a user interested in pointer-safety may define a list shape predicate (as in [5,9]):

$$\texttt{list}(p) \equiv (p{=}\texttt{null}) \vee (\exists i, q \cdot p{\mapsto}\texttt{node}(i, q) {*} \texttt{list}(q))$$

Note that in the inductive case, the separation conjunction $*$ ([28]) ensures that two heap portions (the head node and the tail list) are domain-disjoint.

Yet another user may be interested to track also the length of a list to analyse quantitative measures, such as heap/stack resource usage, using

$$\texttt{ll}(p, n) \equiv (p{=}\texttt{null} \wedge n{=}0) \vee (p{\mapsto}\texttt{node}(\_, q) {*} \texttt{ll}(q, m) \wedge n{=}m{+}1)$$

Note that unbound variables, such as q and m, are implicitly existentially quan-tified, and $\_$ is used to denote an existentially quantified anonymous variable. This predicate may be extended to capture the content information, to support a higher-level of correctness with multi-set (bag) property:

$$\texttt{llB}(p, S) \equiv (p{=}\texttt{null} \wedge S{=}\emptyset) \vee (p{\mapsto}\texttt{node}(v, q) {*} \texttt{llB}(q, S_1) \wedge S{=}\{v\} \sqcup S_1)$$

where the length of the list is implicitly captured by the cardinality $|S|$. A further strengthening can capture also the sortedness property:

$$\texttt{sllB}(p, S) \equiv (p{=}\texttt{null} \wedge S{=}\emptyset) \vee (p{\mapsto}\texttt{node}(v, q) {*} \texttt{sllB}(q, S_1) \wedge S{=}\{v\} \sqcup S_1 \wedge (\forall x \in S_1 \cdot v \leq x))$$

Therefore, the user can provide predicate definitions w.r.t. various correctness level and program properties, which can be as simple as normal lists or as complicated as AVL trees, depending on their requirements. These predicates are non-trivial but can be reused multiple times for specifications of different methods. We have also built a library of predicates with respect to commonly-used data structures and useful program properties.

Based on these predicates, the user is expected to provide partial specifications for some primary methods which are the main objects of verification. Say, for a sorting algorithm taking x as input parameter that is expected to be non-null, the user may provide $llB(x, S_1)$ as precondition and $sllB(x, S_2)$ as postcondition, and our approach will refine the specification as $llB(x, S_1) \land x \neq null$ for pre, and $sllB(x, S_2) \land S_1 = S_2$ for post. Here we need user annotations as the initial specification, because we reserve the flexibility of verification w.r.t. different program properties at various correctness levels. For example, our approach can verify the same algorithm, but for different refined specifications, such as:

$$
\begin{array}{l}
\texttt{requires } list(x) \quad \land \ x \neq null \ \texttt{ensures } list(x) \\
\texttt{requires } ll(x, n_1) \ \land \ n_1 > 0 \quad \texttt{ensures } ll(x, n_2) \ \land \ n_1 = n_2 \\
\texttt{requires } llB(x, S_1) \land \ x \neq null \ \texttt{ensures } llB(x, S_2) \land \ S_1 = S_2 \\
\texttt{requires } llB(x, S) \ \land \ x \neq null \ \texttt{ensures } ll(x, n) \quad \land \ |S| = n
\end{array}
$$

where the discovered missing constraints are shown in shaded form.

To summarise, our proposal for refining partial specification is aimed at harnessing the synergy between human's insights and machine's capability at automated program analysis. In particular, human's guidance can help narrow down on the most important of the different specifications that are possible with each program code, while automation by machine is important for minimising on the tedium faced by users. Our proposal has the following characteristics:

- *Specification completion*: We discover three types of constraints added into the user-given incomplete specification: constraints in the precondition for memory safety, (relational) constraints in postcondition to link the method's pre- and post-states, and constraints that the method's post-state satisfies.
- *Flexibility*: We allow the user to define their own predicates for the program properties they want to verify, so as to provide different levels of correctness. Meanwhile we aim at, and have covered much of, full functional correctness of pointer-manipulating programs such as data structure shapes, pointer safety, structural/relational numerical constraints, and bag information.
- *Reduction of user annotations*: Our approach uses program analysis techniques effectively to reduce users' annotations. As for our experiments, the user only has to supply the partial specifications for primary methods, and the analysis will compute pre- and postconditions for loops and auxiliary methods as well as refine primary methods' specifications.
- *Semi-Automation*: We classify our approach as semi-automatic, because the user is allowed to interfere and guide the verification at any point. For instance, they may provide invariant for a loop instead of our automated invariant generation, or choose some other constraints as refinement from what the verification has discovered.

```
0 data node2 { int val; node2 prev; node2 next; }
1 node2 sdl2nbt(node2 head,       9        end=end.next; root=root.next;}
              node2 tail)        10  }
2  requires sdlB(head,p,q,S)      11  if (head == root) root.prev = null;
3  ensures  nbt(res,Sres)         12  else root.prev = sdl2nbt(head,root);
4 {node2 root = head;             13  node2 tmp = root.next;
5  node2 end = head;              14  if (tmp == tail) root.next = null;
6  while(end != tail) {           15  else { tmp.prev = null;
7    end = end.next;              16    root.next = sdl2nbt(tmp, tail);}
8    if (end != tail) {           17  root;}
```

Fig. 1. The method to convert a sorted doubly-linked list to a node-balanced tree

We have built a prototype implementation and carried out a number of experiments to confirm the viability of the approach as described in Section 5. In what follows, we will first depict our approach informally using a motivating example and present technical details thereafter. More related works and concluding remarks come after the experimental results.Technical details not covered here can be found in our report [27].

2   Illustrative Example

We illustrate our approach with an example (given in a C-like language). We show how our analysis infers missing constraints to improve the user-supplied incomplete specification, and how it analyses the while loop without user-annotations.

The method sdl2nbt (Fig 1) converts a doubly-linked sorted list into a node-balanced binary search tree, as indicated by the shape-only specification in lines 2 and 3. It first finds the "centre" node in the list (root), where the difference between numbers of nodes to the left and to the right of the centre node is at most one (lines 5-10), as Fig 2 (a) shows. It then applies the algorithm recursively on both list

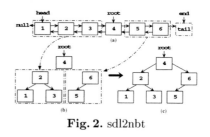

Fig. 2. sdl2nbt

segments to the left and to the right of the centre node, and regards the centre node as the tree's root, whose left and right children are the resulted subtrees' roots from the recursive calls (lines 11-17), as in Fig 2 (b) and (c). As the data structures of doubly-linked list and binary tree are homomorphic (line 0), the algorithm reuses the nodes in the input instead of creating a new tree, making itself in-place. The parameter head in line 1 denotes the first node of the input list, and tail is where the last node's next field points to. When using this method tail should be set as null initially.

The predicate for doubly-linked sorted list (segment) is defined as follows:

$$\mathtt{sdlB}(\mathtt{root}, \mathtt{p}, \mathtt{q}, \mathtt{S}) \equiv (\mathtt{root}{=}\mathtt{q} \wedge \mathtt{S}{=}\emptyset) \vee (\mathtt{root}{\mapsto}\mathtt{node2}(\mathtt{v}, \mathtt{p}, \mathtt{r}) *$$
$$\mathtt{sdlB}(\mathtt{r}, \mathtt{root}, \mathtt{q}, \mathtt{S_1}) \wedge \mathtt{root}{\neq}\mathtt{q} \wedge \mathtt{S}{=}\{\mathtt{v}\} \sqcup \mathtt{S_1} \wedge (\forall \mathtt{x}{\in}\mathtt{S_1}{\cdot}\mathtt{v}{\leq}\mathtt{x}))$$

where the parameters p and q denote resp. the prev field of root and the next field of the last node in the list, and S represents the list's content. And below is the predicate specification for node-balanced binary search trees:

$$\mathtt{nbt(root, S)} \equiv \mathtt{(root{=}null \wedge S{=}\emptyset)} \vee$$
$$\mathtt{(root{\mapsto}node2(v, p, q)} * \mathtt{nbt(p, S_p)} * \mathtt{nbt(q, S_q)} \wedge \mathtt{S{=}\{v\} \sqcup S_p \sqcup S_q} \wedge$$
$$\mathtt{(\forall x{\in}S_p{\cdot}x{\leq}v) \wedge (\forall x{\in}S_q{\cdot}v{\leq}x) \wedge -1{\leq}|S_p|{-}|S_q|{\leq}1)}$$

where S captures the content of the tree. We require the difference in node numbers of the left and right sub-trees be within one, as the node-balanced property indicates.

To refine sdl2nbt's specification, our analysis proceeds in two steps. Firstly, starting from the partial precondition (line 2 of Fig 1), a forward analysis is conducted to compute the postcondition of the method in the form of a *constraint abstraction* [15]. This constraint abstraction is effectively a transfer function for the method, which may be recursively defined (e.g. in this example). Secondly, instead of a direct fixpoint computation in the combined abstract domain (with shape, numerical and bag information), a "pure" constraint abstraction (without heap shape information) is derived from the generated constraint abstraction and the user-given partial postcondition. This pure constraint abstraction is then solved by fixpoint solvers in pure (numerical/bag) domains, such as [24,25].

As for the example, when the forward analysis reaches the while loop at line 6, it discovers that the loop has no user-supplied annotations. In that case, it uses an augmented technique (details follow slightly later) to synthesise the loop's pre- and post-shapes, and invoke the analysis procedure recursively to find additional pure constraints. In this way, we can infer the while loop's postcondition as

$$\mathtt{sdlB(head, null, root, S_h)} * \mathtt{sdlB(root, p, tail, S_r)} \wedge$$
$$\mathtt{end{=}tail \wedge S{=}S_h{\sqcup}S_r \wedge (\forall x{\in}S_h, y{\in}S_r{\cdot}x{\leq}y) \wedge \underline{0{\leq}|S_r|{-}|S_h|{\leq}1}} \quad (1)$$

which indicates that the original list starting from head is cut into two sorted pieces with a cutpoint root. Meanwhile, the essential constraint (the underlined part, saying the list segment beginning with head is at most one node shorter than that with root) to ensure the node-balanced property is derived as well.

When the symbolic execution finishes, it generates the following constraint abstraction as the postcondition of the method:

$$\mathtt{Q(head, p, q, S, res, S_{res})} ::= \qquad\qquad\qquad (\dagger)$$
$$\mathtt{root{\mapsto}node2(v, null, null){\wedge}head{=}root{=}res{\wedge}tmp{=}q{=}tail{\wedge}p{=}null{\wedge}S{=}\{v\}}$$
$$\vee\ \mathtt{head{\mapsto}node2(s, null, root)} * \mathtt{root{\mapsto}node2(v, res_h, null)} \wedge \mathtt{res{=}root} \wedge$$
$$\mathtt{tmp{=}q{=}tail \wedge p{=}null \wedge S{=}\{s, v\} \wedge s{\leq}v}$$
$$\vee\ \mathtt{root{\mapsto}node2(v, res_h, res_r)} * \mathtt{Q(head, p, root, S_h, res_h, S_{res}^h)} *$$
$$\mathtt{Q(tmp, null, tail, S_r, res_r, S_{res}^r) \wedge head{\neq}root \wedge root{=}res \wedge tmp{\neq}tail \wedge}$$
$$\mathtt{q{=}tail \wedge S{=}S_h{\sqcup}\{v\}{\sqcup}S_r \wedge (\forall x{\in}S_h, y{\in}S_r{\cdot}x{\leq}v{\leq}y) \wedge 0{\leq}|S_r|{-}|S_h|{\leq}1}$$

where the first two disjunctive branches are base cases of the method's invocation (where there are only one and two nodes in the returned tree res, respectively), and the last denotes the effect of recursive calls combined into the postcondition (where root's both branches are node-balanced trees). Note that the two Q's in the last branch correspond to the invocations of sdl2nbt in lines 12 and 16.

Constraints of some logical variables (like S_{res}) will not show up until the next step.

In the second step, to derive the definition of the pure constraint abstraction P from the above post-state Q, we use each disjunctive branch of Q to entail the user-given post-shape (with appropriate instantiations of the parameters). During this process, all occurrences of Q are replaced by the post-shape conjoined with the P according to the entailment relation

$$Q(head, p, q, S, res, S_{res}) \vdash nbt(res, S_{res}) \wedge P(head, p, q, S, res, S_{res})$$

The obtained frames (from the SLEEK prover [23]) are used to form (via disjunction) the definition of P:

$$
\begin{aligned}
&P(head, p, q, S, res, S_{res}) ::= \qquad\qquad\qquad\qquad\qquad\qquad\qquad (\ddagger)\\
&\quad head=root=res \wedge tmp=q=tail \wedge p=null \wedge S=S_{res}=\{v\}\\
&\quad \vee\ head{\neq}root \wedge res=root \wedge tmp=q=tail \wedge p=null \wedge S=S_{res}=\{s,v\} \wedge s{\leq}v\\
&\quad \vee\ P(head, p, root, S_h, res_h, S^h_{res}) \wedge P(tmp, null, tail, S_r, res_r, S^r_{res}) \wedge\\
&\qquad head{\neq}root \wedge root=res \wedge tmp{\neq}tail \wedge q=tail \wedge S=S_h{\sqcup}\{v\}{\sqcup}S_r \wedge\\
&\qquad S_{res}=S^h_{res}{\sqcup}\{v\}{\sqcup}S^r_{res} \wedge (\forall x{\in}S_h, y{\in}S_r \cdot x{\leq}v{\leq}y) \wedge 0{\leq}|S_r|{-}|S_h|{\leq}1
\end{aligned}
$$

We then use pure fixpoint solvers to obtain a closed-form formula $p=null \wedge q=tail \wedge S=S_{res} \wedge |S|{\geq}1$ for P, and refine the method's specifications as

$$
\begin{aligned}
&\text{requires } sdlB(head, p, q, S) \wedge\ p=null \wedge q=tail \wedge |S|{\geq}1\\
&\text{ensures } nbt(res, S_{res}) \wedge\ S=S_{res}
\end{aligned}
$$

which proposes more requirements in the precondition, as the head's prev field should be null, and the whole list's last node's next field must point to tail for termination. Meanwhile, there should be at least one node in the list for memory safety. With those obligations, the method guarantees that the result is a node-balanced binary search tree, with the same content as the input list.[1]

Analysis for the while loop. The while loop in sdl2nbt (lines 6-10) discovers the centre node of the given list segment referenced by head. It traverses the list segment with two pointers root and end. The end pointer goes towards the list segment's tail twice as fast as root. When end arrives at the tail of the segment (tail), root will point to the list segment's centre node.

Instead of requiring users to supply the loop invariant, our analysis regards the loop as a tail-recursive method and computes its specifications based on the program state in which the loop starts. Our analysis first synthesises its pre- and post-shapes, and then continues the analysis in the same way as for the main method. The pre-shape can be abstracted from the program state in which the loop starts. The post-shape synthesis is done by checking the symbolic execution result of the loop body (unrolled once) against possible abstracted shapes. For this example, we first generate shape candidates according to the variables accessed by the loop, such as (a) $sdlB(head, p_h, q_h, S_h) * sdlB(root, p_r, q_r, S_r)$, and (b) $sdlB(head, p_h, q_h, S_h) * nbt(root, h_r, b_r, S_r)$. Then the unrolled loop body is symbolically executed to filter out those shapes that are not valid to be an abstraction of postcondition. For this example, executing the loop body yields

---

[1] We will explain how to attach the fixpoint result to both pre and post in Sec 4.

$$\begin{array}{r}\texttt{head} \mapsto \texttt{node2}(v, p, \texttt{end}) \wedge \texttt{head} = \texttt{root} \wedge \texttt{end} = \texttt{tail} \ \vee \\ \texttt{head} \mapsto \texttt{node2}(v_h, p, \texttt{root}) * \texttt{root} \mapsto \texttt{node2}(v_r, \texttt{head}, \texttt{end}) \wedge \texttt{end} = \texttt{tail} \end{array} \quad (2)$$

where (b) is directly filtered out since $(2) \vdash (b) * \texttt{true}$ fails. However (a) remains a candidate, as $(2) \vdash (a) * \texttt{true}$ holds. Therefore, regarding (a) as a possible post-shape, we can employ the same approach to generate a constraint abstraction for the while loop, and solve it to obtain formula (1) in page 373.

3   Language and Abstract Domain

We focus on a strongly-typed C-like imperative language in Fig 3. A program *Prog* consists of type declarations *tdecl*, which can define either data type *datat* (e.g. `node`) or predicate *spred* (e.g. `11B`), and some method declarations *meth*. The language is expression-oriented, so the body of a method is an expression e, where d (resp. $d[v]$) denotes a heap insensitive (resp. heap sensitive) atom expression. We also allow both call-by-value and call-by-reference method parameters (which are separated with a semicolon ;).

Our specification language (in Fig 4) allows (user-defined) shape predicates to specify both separation and pure properties. The shape predicates *spred* are constructed with disjunctive constraints Φ. We require that the predicates be well-formed [23]. A conjunctive abstract program state, σ, is composed of a heap (shape) part κ and a pure part π, where π consists of γ and ϕ as aliasing

$$
\begin{array}{lll}
Prog & ::= tdecl^* \ meth^* & tdecl ::= datat \mid spred \\
datat & ::= \textbf{data} \ c \ \{ \ field^* \ \} & field ::= t \ v \qquad t ::= c \mid \tau \\
meth & ::= t \ mn \ ((t \ v)^*; (t \ v)^*) \ mspec^* \ \{e\} & \tau ::= \textbf{int} \mid \textbf{bool} \mid \textbf{void} \\
e & ::= d \mid d[v] \mid v{=}e \mid e_1; e_2 \mid t \ v; \ e \mid \textbf{if} \ (v) \ e_1 \ \textbf{else} \ e_2 \mid \textbf{while} \ (v) \ \{e\} \\
d & ::= \textbf{null} \mid k^\tau \mid v \mid \textbf{new} \ c(v^*) \mid mn(u^*; v^*) \\
d[v] & ::= v.f \mid v.f{:=}w \mid \textbf{free}(v)
\end{array}
$$

Fig. 3. A Core (C-like) Imperative Language

$$
\begin{array}{lll}
spred & ::= pred(v^*) \equiv \Phi \\
mspec & ::= requires \ \Phi_{pr} \ ensures \ \Phi_{po} \\
\Delta & ::= \textsf{Q}(v^*) \mid \Phi \mid \Delta_1 {\vee} \Delta_2 \mid \Delta{\wedge}\pi \mid \Delta_1 {*} \Delta_2 \mid \exists v{\cdot}\Delta \\
\Phi & ::= \bigvee \sigma^* \qquad \sigma ::= \exists v^*{\cdot}\kappa{\wedge}\pi \\
\Upsilon & ::= \textsf{P}(v^*) \mid \bigvee \omega^* \mid \Upsilon_1 {\wedge} \Upsilon_2 \mid \Upsilon_1 {\vee} \Upsilon_2 \mid \exists v{\cdot}\Upsilon \\
\kappa & ::= \textbf{emp} \mid v{\mapsto}c(v^*) \mid pred(v^*) \mid \kappa_1 * \kappa_2 \\
\omega & ::= \exists v^*{\cdot}\pi \qquad \pi ::= \gamma{\wedge}\phi \\
\gamma & ::= v_1{=}v_2 \mid v{=}\textbf{null} \mid v_1{\neq}v_2 \mid v{\neq}\textbf{null} \mid \gamma_1{\wedge}\gamma_2 \\
\phi & ::= \varphi \mid b \mid a \mid \phi_1{\wedge}\phi_2 \mid \phi_1{\vee}\phi_2 \mid \neg\phi \mid \exists v \cdot \phi \mid \forall v \cdot \phi \\
b & ::= \textbf{true} \mid \textbf{false} \mid v \mid b_1 = b_2 \qquad a ::= s_1{=}s_2 \mid s_1{\leq}s_2 \\
s & ::= k^{\textbf{int}} \mid v \mid k^{\textbf{int}}{\times}s \mid s_1{+}s_2 \mid -s \mid max(s_1,s_2) \mid min(s_1,s_2) \mid |B| \\
\varphi & ::= v{\in}B \mid B_1{=}B_2 \mid B_1{\sqsubset}B_2 \mid B_1{\sqsubseteq}B_2 \mid \forall v{\in}B{\cdot}\phi \mid \exists v{\in}B{\cdot}\phi \\
B & ::= B_1{\sqcup}B_2 \mid B_1{\sqcap}B_2 \mid B_1{-}B_2 \mid \{\} \mid \{v\}
\end{array}
$$

Fig. 4. The Specification Language

and numerical (size and bag) information, respectively. We use SH to denote the set of such conjunctive states. During the symbolic execution, the abstract program state at each program point will be a disjunction of σ's, denoted by Δ. Note that constraint abstractions (e.g. $\mathsf{Q}(v^*)$) may occur in Δ during the analysis. A closed-form Δ (containing no constraint abstractions) can be normalised to the Φ form [23]. Pure constraint abstraction P is analogously defined to Q.

Our memory model is adapted from that of separation logic [28], except that we consider memory cells to be structured records. The detailed model definitions can be found in Nguyen et al. [23]. Meanwhile, for program variables in abstract states, we use unprimed ones to denote their initial values and primed ones for current values [23,27].

4   The Analysis

In this section, we first formulate the main analysis for (primary) methods with given shape specifications. We then show how the analysis is extended to handle auxiliary methods (including loops) without user annotations.

4.1   Refining Specifications for Primary Methods

The algorithm for refinement (CA_Gen_Solve) is given in Fig 5. As illustrated in Section 2, the analysis proceeds in two steps for a primary method with shape information given in specification, namely (1) forward analysis (at lines 1-2) and (2) pure constraint abstraction generation and solving (at lines 3-10).

The forward analysis is captured as algorithm Symb_Exec to the right of Fig 5. Starting from a given pre-shape Φ_{pr}, it analyses the method body e to compute the post-state in constraint abstraction form. Due to space constraints, the symbolic execution rules are given in our technical report [27]. They are similar to

Algorithm CA_Gen_Solve$(\mathcal{T}, mn, e, \Phi_{pr}, \Phi_{po}, u^*, v^*)$	**Algorithm** Symb_Exec
1 $\Delta := \mathsf{Symb\_Exec}(\mathcal{T}, mn, e, \Phi_{pr})$	$(\mathcal{T}, mn, e, \Phi_{pr})$
2 **if** $\Delta = \mathsf{fail}$ **then return** fail **end if**	11 $errLbls := \emptyset$
3 Normalise Δ to DNF, and denote as $\bigvee_{i=1}^{m} \Delta_i$	12 **do**
4 $w^* := \{u^*, v^*, v'^*\} \cup \mathsf{pureV}(\{u^*, v^*, v'^*\}, \Phi_{pr} \vee \Phi_{po})$	13 $(\Delta, l) := [\![e]\!]_{\mathcal{T}}^{mn}(\Phi_{pr}, 0)$
5 $\Delta_\mathsf{P} := \mathsf{Pure\_CA\_Gen}(\Phi_{po}, \mathsf{Q}(w^*) ::= \bigvee_{i=1}^{m} \Delta_i)$	14 **if** $l > 0 \wedge l \notin errLbls$ **then**
6 **if** $\Delta_\mathsf{P} = \mathsf{fail}$ **then return** fail **end if**	15 $\Phi_{pr} := \mathsf{ex\_quan}(\Phi_{pr}, \Delta)$;
7 $\pi := \mathsf{Pure\_CA\_Solve}(\mathsf{P}(w^*) ::= \Delta_\mathsf{P})$	16 $errLbls := errLbls \cup \{l\}$
8 $R := t\ mn\ ((t\ u)^*; (t\ v)^*)\ requires$	17 **else if** $l > 0 \wedge l \in errLbls$
$\mathsf{ex\_quan}(\Phi_{pr}, \pi)\ ensures\ \mathsf{ex\_quan}(\Phi_{po}, \pi)$	**then return** fail
9 **if** $\mathsf{Verify}(\mathcal{T}, mn, R)$ **then return** $\mathcal{T} \cup \{R\}\ \backslash$	18 **end if**
$\{t\ mn\ ((t\ u)^*; (t\ v)^*)\ requires\ \Phi_{pr}\ ensures\ \Phi_{po}\}$	19 **while** $l > 0$
10 **else return** fail **end if**	20 **return** Δ
end Algorithm	**end Algorithm**

Fig. 5. Refining method specifications

symbolic rules used in [23], except for a novel mechanism to derive pure precondition, which we refer to as *pure abduction*.

This pure abduction mechanism is invoked whenever symbolic execution fails to prove memory safety based on the current prestate. For example, if the current state is $ll(x, n)$ (a list that is possibly empty) but $x \mapsto node(\_, p)$ is required by the next program instruction, our pure abduction mechanism will infer $n \geq 1$ to add to the current state to satisfy the requirement. The variable *errLbls* (initialised at line 11) is to record the program locations in which previous pure abductions occurred. Whenever the symbolic execution fails, it returns a state Δ that contains the pure abduction result and the location l where failure was detected, as shown in line 13. If the current abduction location l is not recorded in *errLbls*, it indicates that this is a new failure. The abduction result is added to the precondition of the current method to obtain a stronger Φ_{pr}, before the algorithm enters the symbolic execution loop with variable *errLbls* updated to add in the new failure location l. This loop is repeated until symbolic execution succeeds with no memory error, or a previous failure point was re-encountered. The latter may indicate a program bug or a specification error, or may be due to the possible incompleteness of the underlying SLEEK prover we use.

Back to the main algorithm CA_Gen_Solve, the analysis next builds a heap-based constraint abstraction mechanism, named $Q(w^*)$, for the post-state in steps 3-4. This constraint abstraction is possibly recursive. (Definition † in page 5 is an example of this heap-based abstraction.) We then make use of another algorithm in Fig 6, named Pure_CA_Gen, to extract a pure constraint abstraction, named $P(w^*)$, without any heap property. (Definition ‡ in page 6 is an instance of this pure abstraction.) This algorithm tries to derive a branch P_i for each branch Δ_i of Q. For every Δ_i it proceeds in two steps. In the first step (lines 22-24), it replaces the recursive occurrence of Q in Δ_i with $\sigma * P(w^*)$. In the second step (lines 25-26) it tries to derive P_i via the entailment. If the entailment fails, then pure abduction is used to discover any missing pure constraint σ_i' for $\rho\Delta_i$ to allow the entailment to succeed. In this case, σ_i' is incorporated into σ_i (and eventually P_i). Once this is done, we use some existing fixpoint analysis (e.g. [25]) inside Pure_CA_Solve to derive non-recursive constraint π, as a simplification of $P(w^*)$. This result is then incorporated into the pre/post specifications in line 8, before we perform a post verification in line 9 using the HIP verifier [23], to ensure the strengthened precondition is strong enough for memory safety.

Two auxiliary functions used in the algorithm are described here. The function $\text{pureV}(V, \Delta)$ retrieves from Δ the shapes referred to by all pointer variables from V, and returns the set of logical variables used to record numerical (size and bag) properties in these shapes, e.g. $\text{pureV}(\{x\}, ll(x, n))$ returns $\{n\}$. This function is used in the algorithm to ensure that all free variables in Φ_{pr} and Φ_{po} are added into the parameter list of the constraint abstraction Q. The function $\text{ex\_quan}(\Delta, \pi)$ is to strengthen the state Δ with the abduction result π: $\text{ex\_quan}(\Delta, \pi) =_{df} \Delta \wedge \exists(\text{fv}(\pi) \setminus \text{fv}(\Delta)) \cdot \pi$. It is used to incorporate the discovered missing pure constraints into the original specification. For example, $\text{ex\_quan}(ll(x, n), 0 < m \wedge m \leq n)$ returns $ll(x, n) \wedge 0 < n$.

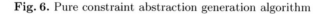

Algorithm Pure_CA_Gen$(\sigma, \mathtt{Q}(w^*) ::= \bigvee_{i=1}^m \Delta_i)$
21 **for** $i = 1$ **to** m
22   Denote all appearances of $\mathtt{Q}(w^*)$ in Δ_i as $\mathtt{Q}_j(w_j^*), j = 1, ..., p$
23   Denote substitutions $\rho_j = [([w_j^*/w^*]\sigma * \mathtt{P}(w_j^*))/\mathtt{Q}_j(w_j^*)]$
24   Let substitution $\rho := \rho_1 \circ \rho_2 \circ ... \circ \rho_p$ as applying all substitutions
      defined above in sequence
25   **if** $(\rho\Delta_i \vdash \sigma * \sigma_i$ **or** $\rho\Delta_i \wedge [\sigma_i'] \rhd \sigma * \sigma_i)$ **and** $ispure(\sigma_i)$ **then** $\mathtt{P}_i := \sigma_i$
26   **else return** fail **end if**
27 **end for**
28 **return** $\bigvee_{i=1}^m \mathtt{P}_i$
end Algorithm

Fig. 6. Pure constraint abstraction generation algorithm

$$\frac{\sigma \nvdash \sigma_1 * \mathbf{true} \quad \sigma_1 \vdash \sigma * \sigma' \quad ispure(\sigma') \quad \sigma \wedge \sigma' \vdash \sigma_1 * \sigma_2}{\sigma \wedge [\sigma'] \rhd \sigma_1 * \sigma_2} \quad \text{(R1)}$$

$$\frac{\sigma \nvdash \sigma_1 * \mathbf{true} \quad \sigma_1 \nvdash \sigma * \mathbf{true} \quad \sigma_0 \in \mathsf{unroll}(\sigma) \quad \mathsf{data\_no}(\sigma_0) \leq \mathsf{data\_no}(\sigma_1)}{\quad (\sigma_0 \vdash \sigma_1 * \sigma' \text{ or } \sigma_0 \wedge [\sigma_0'] \rhd \sigma_1 * \sigma') \quad ispure(\sigma') \quad \sigma \wedge \sigma' \vdash \sigma_1 * \sigma_2 \quad}{\sigma \wedge [\sigma'] \rhd \sigma_1 * \sigma_2} \quad \text{(R2)}$$

$$\frac{\sigma \nvdash \sigma_1 * \mathbf{true} \quad \sigma_1 \nvdash \sigma * \mathbf{true} \quad \sigma_1 \wedge [\sigma_1'] \rhd \sigma * \sigma' \quad ispure(\sigma') \quad \sigma \wedge \sigma' \vdash \sigma_1 * \sigma_2}{\sigma \wedge [\sigma'] \rhd \sigma_1 * \sigma_2} \quad \text{(R3)}$$

Fig. 7. Pure abduction rules

Pure abduction mechanism. We use the SLEEK prover [23] to check Δ_1 entails Δ_2. If the entailment holds it also derives Δ_3 (a.k.a. frame) such that $\Delta_1 \vdash \Delta_2 * \Delta_3$. However, if it fails, we assume that the shape information is sufficiently provided, and use our pure abduction mechanism ($\sigma_1 \wedge [\sigma'] \rhd \sigma_2 * \sigma_3$ in Fig 7) to discover missing pure constraints σ' so that $\sigma_1 \wedge \sigma' \vdash \sigma_2 * \sigma_3$.

Our pure abduction deals with three different cases. The first rule (**R1**) applies when the LHS (σ) does not entail the RHS (σ_1) but the RHS entails the LHS with some pure formula (σ') as the frame; e.g. in $\mathtt{ll}(x,n) \nvdash x{\mapsto}\mathtt{node}(\_,\mathtt{null})$, the RHS can entail the LHS with pure frame n=1. The abduction then checks to ensure $\mathtt{ll}(x,n) \wedge \mathtt{n=1} \vdash x{\mapsto}\mathtt{node}(\_,\mathtt{null})*\sigma_2$ for some σ_2, and returns the result n=1. Note the check $ispure(\sigma')$ ensures that σ' contains no heap information.

In the second rule (**R2**), neither side entails the other but the LHS term could be unfolded. An example is $\sigma = \mathtt{sllB}(x,S)$, $\sigma_1 = x{\mapsto}\mathtt{node}(u,p) * p{\mapsto}\mathtt{node}(v,\mathtt{null})$. As the shape predicates on the LHS are of disjunctive forms (i.e. $\mathtt{sllB}$ in σ), certain branches of σ may entail σ_1. As the rule suggests, to accomplish abduction $\sigma \wedge [\sigma'] \rhd \sigma_1 * \sigma_2$, we first unfold σ and try entailment or further abduction with the results (σ_0) against σ_1. If it succeeds with a pure frame σ', then we confirm the abduction by checking $\sigma \wedge \sigma' \vdash \sigma_1 * \sigma_2$. For the example above, the abduction returns $|S|=2$ (σ') and discovers the nontrivial frame $S=\{u,v\} \wedge u{\leq}v$ (σ_2). Note

Algorithm SynPre	**Algorithm** SynPost $(\mathcal{T}, \mathcal{S}, f, e, \Phi_{pr}, u^*, v^*)$
$(\mathcal{S}, f, u^*, v^*, \sigma, x^*, y^*)$	7 $C :=$ ShpCand$(\mathcal{S}, u^*, v^*)$
1 $C :=$ ShpCand$(\mathcal{S}, u^*, v^*)$	8 $\mathcal{T}' := \mathcal{T} \cup \{f(u^*, v^*) \; requires \, \Phi_{pr} \; ensures \, \mathbf{false} \, \{e\}\}$
2 **for** $\sigma_C \in C$ **do**	9 $\Delta :=$ Symb_Exec$(\mathcal{T}', f, \mathsf{syn\_unroll}(f, e), \Phi_{pr})$
3 **if** $\sigma \nvdash [x^*/u^*, y^*/v^*]\sigma_C$	10 **for** $\sigma_C \in C$ **do**
4 **then** $C := C \backslash \{\sigma_C\}$ **end if**	11 **if** $\Delta \wedge [\sigma] \nvdash \sigma_C$ **then** $C := C \backslash \{\sigma_C\}$ **end if**
5 **end for**	12 **end for**
6 **return** C	13 **return** pair_spec_list(Φ_{pr}, C)
end Algorithm	**end Algorithm**

Fig. 8. Shape synthesis algorithms

that function data_no returns the number of data nodes in a state, e.g. it returns one for x$\mapsto$node(v, p) $*$ ll(p, m). (This syntactic check is important for the termination of the abduction.) The unroll operation unfolds all shape predicates once in σ, normalises the result to a disjunctive form ($\bigvee_{i=1}^{u} \sigma^i$), and returns the result as a set of formulae ($\{\sigma^1, ..., \sigma^u\}$).

In the third rule (**R3**), neither side entails the other and the LHS term cannot be unfolded. e.g., $\sigma = $ x$\mapsto$node(u, p) $*$ p$\mapsto$node(v, null), $\sigma_1 = \exists S \cdot$ sllB(x, S). In this case, the rule swaps the two sides of the entailment and applies the second rule to uncover the pure constraints σ'_1 and σ'. It checks that adding σ' to the LHS (σ) entails the RHS (σ_1) before it returns σ'. For the example, the abduction returns u$\leq$v which is essential for the two nodes to form a sorted list (RHS).

4.2   Inferring Specifications for Auxiliary Methods and Loops

For auxiliary methods[2], we conduct a pre-analysis (Fig 8) to synthesise the pre- and post-shapes before we conduct the refinement analysis from Fig 5. Loops are dealt with by analysing their tail-recursive versions in the same way. This approach alleviates the need for users to provide specification annotations for both loops and auxiliary methods.

The pre-shape synthesis algorithm SynPre (Fig 8 left) takes in as input the set of shape predicates ($\mathcal{S}$), the auxiliary method name (f), its formal parameters (u^*, v^*), the current symbolic state in which f is called (σ), and the corresponding actual parameters (x^*, y^*) of the invocation. The algorithm first obtains possible shape candidates from the parameters u^*, v^* with ShpCand (line 1), then picks up a sound abstraction for the method's pre-shape with entailment, and filter out the ones which fail (line 4). Finally the pre-shape abstraction is returned. While we use an enumeration strategy here, the number of possible shape candidates per type is small as it is strictly limited by what the user provides in the primary methods, and then filtered and prioritised by our system.

To synthesise post-shapes (SynPost, Fig 8 right), we also assign C as possible shape candidates (line 7). We unroll f's body e once (i.e. replace recursive

---

[2] In practice, we treat methods without user-specified shape specifications as auxiliary.

calls to f in e with a substituted e) and symbolically execute it (line 9), assuming f has a specification *requires* Φ_{pr} *ensures* `false` (line 8). The postcondition `false` is used to ensure that the execution only considers the effect of the program branches with no recursive calls (to f itself). We then use Δ to find out appropriate abstraction of post-shape (line 11), which is paired with Φ_{pr} and returned as result. Here we use pure abduction to filter post-shapes to preserve as many shapes that are potentially refinable as possible. The function pair_spec_list(Φ_{pr}, C) forms an ordered list of pre-/post-shape pairs, each of which has Φ_{pr} as pre-shape and a Φ_{po} in C as post-shape.

We illustrate our procedure to generate and confirm candidate shape abstractions (ShpCand) with an example. If we have two parameters x and y with type node, and two compatible shape predicates llB and sllB, then the list of all possible shape candidates for the two variables (C) will be $[$sllB$(x, S) *$ sllB(y, T), llB$(x, S) *$ sllB(y, T), sllB$(x, S) *$ llB(y, T), llB$(x, S) *$ llB(y, T), sllB(x, S), sllB(y, S), llB(x, S), llB(y, S), emp$]$. Elements of this list will be checked against appropriate abstract states (line 3-4 in Fig 8 left and line 11 in Fig 8 right) where unsound elements will be eliminated. For example, in the previous list, only llB$(x, S) *$ llB(y, T) remains in the list and participates in further verification, given $\sigma =$ x$\mapsto$node$(u, p) *$ p$\mapsto$node$(v, $null$) *$ y$\mapsto$node$(s, q) *$ q$\mapsto$node$(t, $null$)$.

The initial experimental results confirm that our shape synthesis keeps only highly relevant abstractions. For the while loop in Section 2, we filtered out 24 (of 26) abstractions. Generally, in case that there are several abstractions as candidate specifications, we employ some other mechanisms to reduce them further. Firstly, we prioritise post-shapes with same (or stronger) predicates as in precondition since it is more likely that the output will have the same or similar shape predicates as the input, e.g. x is expected to remain as sllB (or stronger) if it points to sllB as input. Secondly, we employ a lazy scheme when refining the synthesised pre/post-shapes (to complete specifications). We retrieve (and remove) the pre/post-shape pair from the head of the list, (1) use the refinement algorithm (Fig 5) to obtain a specification for the auxiliary method, and (2) continue the analysis for the primary method. If the analysis for the primary method succeeds, we will ignore all other synthesised pre/post-shapes from the list. These mechanisms help to keep attempts over candidate specifications at a minimum level.

Soundness. Based on the soundness of the following: the entailment prover [23], the abstract semantics (w.r.t. the concrete semantics), the pure constraint abstraction generation, and the fixpoint calculation [24,25], we have

Theorem 1 (Soundness). *Our analysis is sound with respect to the underlying operational semantics.*

The proof and more details can be found in the technical report [27].

5   Experiments and Evaluation

We have implemented a prototype system for evaluation. Our experimental results were achieved with an Intel Core 2 CPU 2.66GHz with 8Gb RAM. The four columns in Fig 9 describe, resp., the analysed programs, the analysis time in seconds, and the primary methods' (given and inferred) preconditions and postconditions. All formulae with a grey background are inferred by our analysis. For some programs, we have verified them with different pre/post shape templates. More results and details are available in the report [27].

The results highlight the refinement of both pre- and postconditions based on user-provided shape specifications, even for complicated data structures such as AVL and red-black trees. Firstly, our approach can compute non-trivial pure constraints for postcondition, e.g. for `delete` we know the content of the result list is subsumed by that of the input list, for list-sorting algorithms we confirm the content of the output is the same as that of the input, and for tree-processing programs (`insert`, `delete` and `avl_ins`), we obtain that the height difference between the input and output trees is at most one. Meanwhile, we can calcu-

Prog.	Time	Pre	Post
List processing programs			
sort_ insert	0.591	$ll(x,n) \land n{\geq}1$	$ll(x,m) \land m{=}n{+}1$
	0.504	$sll(x,n,xs,xl) \land v{\geq}xs$	$sll(x,m,mn,mx) \land xs{=}mn \land mx{=}max(xl,v) \land m{=}n{+}1$
rand_ insert	0.522	$ll(x,n) \land n{\geq}1$	$ll(x,m) \land m{=}n{+}1$
	—	$sll(x,n,xs,xl) \land (fail)$	$sll(x,m,mn,mx) \land (fail)$
delete	1.024	$sllB(x,S) \land |S|{\geq}2$	$sllB(x,T) \land \exists a.S{=}T{\sqcup}\{a\}$
travrs	0.296	$ll(x,m) \land n{\geq}0 \land m{\geq}n$	$ls(x,p,k)*ll(res,r) \land p{=}res \land k{=}n \land m{=}n{+}r$
append	0.512	$ll(x,xn)*ll(y,yn) \land xn{\geq}1$	$ll(x,m) \land m{=}xn{+}yn$
	0.948	$sll(x,xn,xs,xl) \land xl{\leq}ys$ $* sll(y,yn,ys,yl)$	$sll(x,m,rs,rl) \land yl{=}rl \land m{\geq}1{+}yn \land m{=}xn{+}yn$
Sorting (main)		$llB(x,S) \land |S|{\geq}1$	$sllB(res,T) \land T{=}S \quad\quad (\star)$
merge	4.107	$sllB(x,S_x) * sllB(y,S_y)$	$sllB(res,T) \land T{=}S_x{\sqcup}S_y$
flatten	2.693	$bstB(x,S)$	$sllB(res,T) \land T{=}S$
Binary tree, binary search tree, AVL tree and red-black tree processing programs			
insert	1.276	$bt(x,S,h) \land |S|{\geq}1 \land h{\geq}1$	$bt(x,T,k) \land T{=}S{\sqcup}\{v\} \land h{\leq}k{\leq}h{+}1$
delete	0.970	$bt(x,S,h) \land |S|{\geq}2 \land h{\geq}2$	$bt(x,T,k) \land \exists a.S{=}T{\sqcup}\{a\} \land h{-}1{\leq}k{\leq}h$
search	1.583	$bst(x,sm,lg)$	$bst(x,mn,mx) \land sm{=}mn \land lg{=}mx \land 0{\leq}res{\leq}1$
bst_ insert	1.720	$bst(x,sm,lg)$	$bst(x,mn,mx) \land (v{<}sm \land v{=}mn \land lg{=}mx \lor$ $lg{<}v \land v{=}mx \land sm{=}mn \lor sm{=}mn \land lg{=}mx)$
avl_ins	11.12	$avl(x,S,h)$	$avl(res,T,k) \land T{=}S{\sqcup}\{v\} \land h{\leq}k{\leq}h{+}1$
rbt_ins	8.76	$rbt(x,S)$	$rbt(res,T) \land T{=}S{\sqcup}\{v\}$

Fig. 9. Selected Experimental Results

late non-trivial requirements in precondition for memory safety or functional correctness. As an example, the `travrs` method, taking in a list with length m and an integer n, traverses towards the tail of the list for n steps. the analysis discovers m≥n in the precondition to ensure memory safety. Another example is the `append` method concatenating two sorted lists into one. To ensure that the result list is sorted, the analysis figures out that the minimum value in the second list must be no less than the maximum value in the first list.

A second highlight is our flexibility by supporting multiple predicates. Our analysis tries to refine different specifications for the same program at various correctness levels (with different predicates), e.g. `sort_insert` and `append`. For `rand_insert`, which inserts a node into a random place (after the head) of a list, we confirm that the list's length is increased by one, but cannot verify the list is kept sorted if it was before the insertion, as the result indicates.

Another highlight is that we can reduce user annotations by synthesising specifications for auxiliary methods, given raw specifications of primary methods. For example, we have analysed a number of list-sorting algorithms with at least one auxiliary method each. We list two auxiliary methods (`merge` for `merge_sort` and `flatten` for `tree_sort`) and their discovered specifications. Note that these sorting algorithms have the same specification for their primary methods (line ⋆). As another example, `avl_ins` also has some auxiliary (recursive) methods such as calculation of tree's height, which are automatically analysed as well.

We have also tried our approach over part of the FreeRTOS kernel [2]. For its list processing programs `list.h` and `list.c` (472 lines with intensive manipulation over composite sorted doubly-linked lists) it took 2.85 seconds for our prototype to refine all the specifications given for the main functions, which further confirms the viability of our approach.

6   Related Work and Conclusion

Related works. The local shape analysis [9] infers loop invariants for list-processing programs, followed by the SpaceInvader tool to verify larger industrial codes [5,32]. Gulavani et al. [12] propose a stronger bi-abduction algorithm to compute the shape pre/post-condition at the same time. The SLAyer tool [11] implements an interprocedural shape analysis. To infer also size information, THOR [19,20] is armed with additional numerical analysis to gain better precision. Gulwani et al. [13] combine a set domain with its cardinality domain in a general framework. Magill et al. [21] instrument programs with numerical instructions from which pure numerical programs are generated for further analysis. Compared with these, our approach can handle additional data structures with stronger invariants like sortedness, height-balanced and bag-related invariants. Relational inductive shape analysis [6] employs inductive checkers to express shape and numerical information, where they only demonstrate how to analyse a program with one particular shape. Our previous loop invariant synthesis [26] also infers strong loop invariants. Compared with them, this work is inter-procedural and addresses specification refinement with pure properties in both pre- and postconditions in two phases (for shape and pure resp.) with pure abduction.

There are also other approaches to expressing heap-based domains than separation logic. Hackett and Rugina [16] can deal with AVL-trees but is customised to handle only tree-like structures with height property. TVLA [30] can handle complicated data structure properties like sortedness. Bouajjani et al. [3] synthesise list-related invariants over infinite data domains using graph heap representation. Comparatively, separation logic based approach benefits from the frame rule and local reasoning. Meanwhile, our approach aims at full functional correctness including both quantitative and content properties of shapes.

Automated assertion discovery techniques [8,14,31] mainly find numerical program properties. Our work is complementary to them as we focus more on refining specifications for heap-manipulating programs. Semi-automatic approaches [17,29] are also used to infer numerical constraints for given type templates in functional programs, where data structures are mostly immutable.

On the verification side, the HIP/SLEEK verification system [23] supports user-defined shape predicates over a combined domain. The PALE system [22] transforms constraints in the pointer assertion logic (PAL) into monadic second-order logic (MSOL) and discharge them with MONA. JML [4] uses model/ghost fields and model methods to specify/model Java program properties. Jahob [18] also verifies Java and focuses more on heap shape. Spec$^\#$ [1] is for C$^\#$ by enforcing object invariants and method specifications. Havoc [7] is another verification tool for C language about heap-allocated data structures, using a novel reachability predicate. Compared with these works, we can free users from writing whole specifications by requiring only partial specifications, and omit annotations for loops and auxiliary methods.

Concluding remarks. We have reported a new approach to program verification that accepts partial specifications of methods, and refines them by discovering missing constraints for numerical and bag properties, aiming at full functional correctness for pointer-based data structures. We further augment our approach by requiring only partial specification for primary methods. Specifications for loops and auxiliary methods can then be systematically discovered. We have built a prototype system and the initial experimental results are encouraging.

References

1. Barnett, M., Leino, K.R.M., Schulte, W.: The spec$^\#$ programming system: An overview. In: Barthe, G., Burdy, L., Huisman, M., Lanet, J.-L., Muntean, T. (eds.) CASSIS 2004. LNCS, vol. 3362, pp. 49–69. Springer, Heidelberg (2005)
2. Barry, R.: FreeRTOS — a free RTOS for small embedded real time systems (2006)
3. Bouajjani, A., Dragoi, C., Enea, C., Rezine, A., Sighireanu, M.: Invariant synthesis for programs manipulating lists with unbounded data. In: Touili, T., Cook, B., Jackson, P. (eds.) CAV 2010. LNCS, vol. 6174, pp. 72–88. Springer, Heidelberg (2010)
4. Burdy, L., Cheon, Y., Cok, D., Ernst, M., Kiniry, J., Leavens, G., Leino, K.: An Overview of JML Tools and Applications. STTT 7(3), 212–232 (2005)

5. Calcagno, C., Distefano, D., O'Hearn, P., Yang, H.: Compositional shape analysis by means of bi-abduction. In: POPL (2009)
6. Chang, B., Rival, X.: Relational inductive shape analysis. In: POPL (2008)
7. Chatterjee, S., Lahiri, S., Qadeer, S., Rakamaric, Z.: A reachability predicate for analyzing low-level software. In: Grumberg, O., Huth, M. (eds.) TACAS 2007. LNCS, vol. 4424, pp. 19–33. Springer, Heidelberg (2007)
8. Cousot, P., Cousot, R.: On abstraction in software verification. In: Brinksma, E., Larsen, K.G. (eds.) CAV 2002. LNCS, vol. 2404, p. 37. Springer, Heidelberg (2002)
9. Distefano, D., O'Hearn, P.W., Yang, H.: A local shape analysis based on separation logic. In: Hermanns, H. (ed.) TACAS 2006. LNCS, vol. 3920, pp. 287–302. Springer, Heidelberg (2006)
10. Giacobazzi, R.: Abductive analysis of modular logic programs. In: ILPS (1994)
11. Gotsman, A., Berdine, J., Cook, B.: Interprocedural shape analysis with separated heap abstractions. In: Yi, K. (ed.) SAS 2006. LNCS, vol. 4134, pp. 240–260. Springer, Heidelberg (2006)
12. Gulavani, B., Chakraborty, S., Ramalingam, G., Nori, A.: Bottom-up shape analysis. In: Palsberg, J., Su, Z. (eds.) SAS 2009. LNCS, vol. 5673, pp. 188–204. Springer, Heidelberg (2009)
13. Gulwani, S., Lev-Ami, T., Sagiv, M.: A Combination Framework for Tracking Partition Sizes. In: POPL (2009)
14. Gupta, A., Majumdar, R., Rybalchenko, A.: From tests to proofs. In: Kowalewski, S., Philippou, A. (eds.) TACAS 2009. LNCS, vol. 5505, pp. 262–276. Springer, Heidelberg (2009)
15. Gustavsson, J., Svenningsson, J.: Constraint abstractions. In: Danvy, O., Filinski, A. (eds.) PADO 2001. LNCS, vol. 2053, p. 63. Springer, Heidelberg (2001)
16. Hackett, B., Rugina, R.: Region-based shape analysis with tracked locations. In: POPL (2005)
17. Kawaguchi, M., Rondon, P., Jhala, R.: Type-based data structure verification. In: PLDI (2009)
18. Kuncak, V.: Modular Data Structure Verification. PhD thesis, EECS Department, Massachusetts Institute of Technology (February 2007)
19. Magill, S., Berdine, J., Clarke, E., Cook, B.: Arithmetic strengthening for shape analysis. In: Riis Nielson, H., Filé, G. (eds.) SAS 2007. LNCS, vol. 4634, pp. 419–436. Springer, Heidelberg (2007)
20. Magill, S., Tsai, M., Lee, P., Tsay, Y.: THOR: A tool for reasoning about shape and arithmetic. In: Gupta, A., Malik, S. (eds.) CAV 2008. LNCS, vol. 5123, pp. 428–432. Springer, Heidelberg (2008)
21. Magill, S., Tsai, M., Lee, P., Tsay, Y.: Automatic numeric abstractions for heap-manipulating programs. In: POPL (2010)
22. Møller, A., Schwartzbach, M.: The pointer assertion logic engine. ACM SIGPLAN Notices 36(5), 221–231 (2001)
23. Nguyen, H.H., David, C., Qin, S., Chin, W.-N.: Automated verification of shape and size properties via separation logic. In: Cook, B., Podelski, A. (eds.) VMCAI 2007. LNCS, vol. 4349, pp. 251–266. Springer, Heidelberg (2007)
24. Nipkow, T., Paulson, L.C., Wenzel, M.: Isabelle/HOL — a proof assistant for higher-order logic. LNCS, vol. 2283. Springer, Heidelberg (2002)
25. Popeea, C., Chin, W.-N.: Inferring disjunctive postconditions. In: Okada, M., Satoh, I. (eds.) ASIAN 2006. LNCS, vol. 4435, pp. 331–345. Springer, Heidelberg (2008)

26. Qin, S., He, G., Luo, C., Chin, W.-N.: Loop invariant synthesis in a combined domain. In: Dong, J.S., Zhu, H. (eds.) ICFEM 2010. LNCS, vol. 6447, pp. 468–484. Springer, Heidelberg (2010)
27. Qin, S., Luo, C., Chin, W.-N., He, G.: Automatically Refining Partial Specification for Program Verification. Technical Report, Teesside University (2010), `http://www.scm.tees.ac.uk/s.qin/papers/refine.pdf`
28. Reynolds, J.: Separation logic: a logic for shared mutable data structures. In: LICS 2002 (2002)
29. Rondon, P., Kawaguci, M., Jhala, R.: Liquid types. In: PLDI (2008)
30. Sagiv, M., Reps, T., Wilhelm, R.: Parametric shape analysis via 3-valued logic. ACM Transactions on Programming Languages and Systems 24(3), 217–298 (2002)
31. Srivastava, S., Gulwani, S.: Program verification using templates over predicate abstraction. In: PLDI (2009)
32. Yang, H., Lee, O., Berdine, J., Calcagno, C., Cook, B., Distefano, D., O'Hearn, P.W.: Scalable shape analysis for systems code. In: Gupta, A., Malik, S. (eds.) CAV 2008. LNCS, vol. 5123, pp. 385–398. Springer, Heidelberg (2008)

Structured Specifications for Better Verification of Heap-Manipulating Programs

Cristian Gherghina[1], Cristina David[1], Shengchao Qin[2], and Wei-Ngan Chin[1]

[1] Department of Computer Science, National University of Singapore
[2] School of Computing, University of Teesside

Abstract. Conventional specifications typically have a flat structure that is based primarily on the underlying logic. Such specifications lack structures that could have provided better guidance to the verification process. In this work, we propose to add three new structures to a specification framework for separation logic to achieve a *more precise* and *better guided* verification for pointer-based programs. The newly introduced structures empower users with more control over the verification process in the following ways: (i) case analysis can be invoked to take advantage of disjointness conditions in the logic. (ii) early, as opposed to late, instantiation can minimise on the use of existential quantification. (iii) formulae that are staged provide better reuse of the verification process.

Initial experiments have shown that structured specifications can lead to more precise verification without incurring any performance overhead.

1 Introduction

Recent developments of the specification mechanisms have focused mostly on expressiveness [2,1,5] (to support verification for more properties), abstraction [16,18] (to support information hiding in specification) and modularity [14,7,8] (to support more readable and reusable specifications). To the best of our knowledge, there has been hardly any attempt on the development of specification mechanisms that could support better verifiability (in terms of both efficiency and effectiveness). Most efforts on better verifiability have been confined to the verification technology; an approach that may lead to less portability (as we become more reliant on clever heuristics from the verification tools) and also more complex implementation for the verification tools themselves. In this paper, we shall propose a novel approach towards better verifiability that focuses on new structures in the specification mechanism instead.

To illustrate the need for an enhanced specification mechanism, we will make use of separation logic, which allows for a precise description of heap-based data structures and their properties. As an example, consider a data node node2 and a predicate describing an AVL tree that captures the size property via s and the height via h:

```
data node2 { int val; int height; node2 right; node2 left; }
avl⟨root, h, s⟩ ≡ root=null ∧ h=0 ∧ s=0
  ∨ root ↦ node2⟨_, h, r, l⟩ * avl⟨r, h₁, s₁⟩ * avl⟨l, h₂, s₂⟩ ∧ h = max(h₁, h₂)+1
  ∧ − 1≤h₁−h₂≤1∧s=s₁+s₂+1
```

M. Butler and W. Schulte (Eds.): FM 2011, LNCS 6664, pp. 386–401, 2011.

Formula $p \mapsto c\langle v^* \rangle$ denotes a points-to fact of the heap where c is a data node with v^* as its arguments, while spatial conjunction $\Phi_1 * \Phi_2$ denotes a program state with two disjoint heap spaces described by sub-formulae Φ_1 and Φ_2, respectively. These two notations of separation logic allow heap states to be expressed in a succinct manner.

The aforementioned definition asserts that an AVL tree is either empty (the base case root=null $\wedge$ h=0 $\wedge$ s=0), or it consists of a data node (root $\mapsto$ node2$\langle \_, h, r, l \rangle$) and two disjoint subtrees (avl$\langle r, h_1, s_1 \rangle * avl\langle l, h_2, s_2 \rangle$). Each node is used to store the actual data in the val field, and the maximum height of the current subtree in the height field. The constraint $-1 \leq h_1 - h_2 \leq 1$ states that the tree is balanced, while s=s_1+s_2+1 and h=max(h_1, h_2)+1 compute the size and height of the tree pointed by root from the properties s_1, s_2 and h_1, h_2, respectively, that are obtained from the two subtrees. The $*$ connector ensures that the head node and the right and left subtrees reside in disjoint heaps. Our system automatically generates existential quantifiers for local values and pointers, such as r, l, h_1, h_2, s_1, s_2.

Next, we specify a method that attempts to retrieve the height information from the root node of the data structure received as argument. In case the argument has the value null, the method returns 0, as captured by res=0. To provide a suitable link between pre- and post-conditions, we use the logical variables v, h, lt, lr that have to be instantiated for each call to the method. As a first try, we capture both the null and non-null scenarios as a composite formula consisting of a disjunction of the two cases, as shown below:

```
int get_height(node2 x)
    requires x=null ∨ x ↦ node2⟨v, h, lt, lr⟩
    ensures (x=null ∧ res=0) ∨ (x ↦ node2⟨v, h, lt, lr⟩ ∧ res=h);
{if (x = null) then 0 else x.height}
```

This specification introduces disjunctions both in the pre and post-conditions, which would make the verification process perform search over the disjuncts[17]. Basically, each disjunct corresponds to an acceptable scenario of which at least one needs to be proven. However, there are situations when the program state does not contain enough information to determine which of the scenarios applies. For illustration, let us consider that we are interested in retrieving the height information for an AVL tree pointed by x and the program state before the call to the get_height method is avl$\langle x, h_1, s_1 \rangle$. We have to verify that the current program state obeys the method's precondition. However, when verifying the null and non-null scenarios separately, both checks fail as the program state avl$\langle x, h_1, s_1 \rangle$ does not contain sufficient information to conclude neither that x$\neq$null, nor that x=null. We provide the two failing verification conditions in the form of the entailment procedure from [17]: $\Phi_a \vdash \Phi_c * \Phi_r$, where the antecedent Φ_a and consequent Φ_c are given, while the residue Φ_r is to be computed. This entailment finds a subheap in Φ_a that satisfies Φ_c and returns the unused subheap from Φ_a as residue Φ_r. Getting back to the current get_height example, the two failing entailments are given below. As none of the following two entailments succeeds, the verification of the method call fails.

$$\text{avl}\langle x, h_1, s_1 \rangle \vdash (x=\text{null}) * \Phi_{r_1}$$
$$\text{avl}\langle x, h_1, s_1 \rangle \vdash (x \mapsto \text{node2}\langle v, h, lt, lr \rangle) * \Phi_{r_2}$$

As a second try, we write the specification in a modular fashion by separating the two scenarios as advocated by past works [14,7]. In [14], Leavens and Baker proposed for each specification to be decomposed into multiple specifications (where it is called case analysis) to capture different scenarios of usage. Their goal was improving the readability of specifications, as smaller and simpler specifications are easier to understand than larger ones. In [7] multiple specifications were advocated to help achieve more scalable program verification. By using multiple pre/post conditions, we obtain the following specification:

```
int get_height(node2 x)
  requires x=null   ensures res=0;
  requires x ↦ node2⟨v, h, lt, rt⟩   ensures x ↦ node2⟨v, h, lt, rt⟩ ∧ res=h;
```

During the verification process, each scenario (denoted by a pre/post-condition pair) is proven separately [7]. However, neither of the two entailments (for each of the two scenarios) succeeds, causing the verification of the method call to fail.

A possible solution is to perform case analysis on variable x: first assume x=null, then assume x≠null, and try to prove both cases. For soundness, these cases must be disjoint and exhaustively cover all scenarios. Accordingly, the following two provable entailments are obtained, and the verification succeeds:

$$\mathtt{avl}\langle x, h_1, s_1\rangle \wedge x\mathtt{=null} \vdash (x\mathtt{=null}) * \Phi_{r_1}$$
$$\mathtt{avl}\langle x, h_1, s_1\rangle \wedge x\mathtt{\neq null} \vdash (x \mapsto \mathtt{node2}\langle v, h, lt, lr\rangle) * \Phi_{r_2}$$

However, case analysis is not always available in provers, as it might be tricky to decide on the condition for a case split. Traditionally, the focus of specification mechanism has been on improving its ability to cover a wider range of problems more accurately, while the effectiveness of verification is left to the underlying provers. In this paper, we attempt a novel approach, where the focus is on determining a good specification mechanism to achieve better expressivity and verifiability.

Often, a user has an intuition about the proving process. In the current work, we provide the necessary utensils for integrating this intuition in the specification in order to guide the verification. Instead of writing a flat (unstructured) specification, the user can use insights about the proof for writing a structured specification that will trigger different techniques during the proving process:

- **Case analysis** is conventionally captured as part of the proving process. The user typically indicates the program location where case analysis is to be performed [23]. This corresponds to performing a case analysis on some program state (or antecedent) of the proving process. In our approach, we provide a case construct to distinguish the input states of pre/post specifications instead. This richer specification can be directly used to guide the verification process. For the aforementioned get_height method, the case structured specification will automatically force a case split on x:

$$
\begin{aligned}
\mathtt{case}\{x\mathtt{=null} \;&\rightarrow\; \mathtt{ensures\ res=0};\\
x\mathtt{\neq null} \;&\rightarrow\; \mathtt{requires}\ x \mapsto \mathtt{node2}\langle v, h, lt, lr\rangle\\
&\quad\ \mathtt{ensures}\ x \mapsto \mathtt{node2}\langle v, h, lt, lr\rangle \wedge \mathtt{res=h}\};
\end{aligned}
$$

- **Early vs. late instantiations** denote different types of bindings for the logical variables (of consequent) during the entailment proving process. Early instantiation is an instantiation that occurs at the first occurrence of its logical variable, while late instantiation occurs at the last occurrence of its logical variable. While late instantiation can be more accurate for variables that are constructed from inequality constraints, early instantiation can typically be done with fewer existential quantifiers since instantiation converts these existential logical variables to quantifier-free form at an earlier point. We propose to use early instantiation, by default, and only to resort to late instantiation when explicitly requested by the programmer.
- **Staged formulae** allows the specification to be made more concise through sharing of common sub-formulae. Apart from better sharing, this also allows verification to be carried out incrementally over multiple (smaller) stages, instead of a single (larger) stage. The need for early/late instantiations, as well as for staged formulae will be motivated in more details later in Sec 2.

In the rest of the paper we shall focus on the apparatus for writing and verifying (or checking) structured specifications. Sec 2 provides examples to motivate the need for two other aspects of structured specifications. Sec 3 formalizes the notion of structured specifications. Sec 4 formalizes the verification rules to generate Hoare triples and entailment proving for structured specifications, while Sec 5 presents our experimental results before some concluding remarks in Sec 6.

2   Motivating Examples

In the current section we present two more examples that motivate our enhancements to the specification mechanism.

2.1   Example 1

Consider a method that receives two AVL trees, t1 and t2, and merges them by recursively inserting all the elements of t2 into t1. By using the case construct introduced in Sec 1 we may write a case structured specification, which captures information about the resulting tree size when t1 is not null, and about the resulting size and height, whenever t1 is null:

$$\mathtt{case}\{\mathtt{t1} = \mathtt{null} \;\rightarrow\; \mathtt{requires}\; \mathtt{avl}\langle \mathtt{t2}, \mathtt{s2}, \mathtt{h2}\rangle \mathtt{ensures}\; \mathtt{avl}\langle \mathtt{res}, \mathtt{s2}, \mathtt{h2}\rangle;$$
$$\mathtt{t1} \neq \mathtt{null} \;\rightarrow\; \mathtt{requires}\; \mathtt{avl}\langle \mathtt{t2}, \mathtt{s2}, \mathtt{h2}\rangle * \mathtt{avl}\langle \mathtt{t1}, \mathtt{s1}, \_\rangle$$
$$\mathtt{ensures}\; \mathtt{avl}\langle \mathtt{res}, \mathtt{s1} + \mathtt{s2}, \_\rangle\};$$

However, let us note that there is a redundancy in this specification, namely the same predicate $\mathtt{avl}\langle \mathtt{t2}, \mathtt{s2}, \mathtt{h2}\rangle$ appears on both branches of the case construct. After the need for a case construct which was already discussed in Sec 1, this is the second deficiency we shall address in our specification mechanism, that is due to a lack of sharing in the logic formula which in turn causes repeated proving of identical sub-formulae. To provide for better sharing of the verification process, we propose to use *staged* formulae of the form $(\Phi_1 \; \mathbf{then} \; \Phi_2)$, to allow sub-formula Φ_1 to be proven prior to Φ_2.

Though $(\Phi_1 \; \mathbf{then} \; \Phi_2)$ is semantically equivalent to $(\Phi_1 * \Phi_2)$, we stress that the main purpose of adding this new structure is to support more effective verification with the help of specifications with less redundancy. By itself, it is not meant to improve the expressivity of our specification, but rather its effectiveness. Nevertheless, when it is used in combination with the case construct, it could support case analysis of logical variables to ensure successful verification. The same structuring mechanisms can be used by formulae in both predicate definitions and pre/post specifications.

Getting back to the AVL merging example, the redundancy in the specification can be factored out by using a staged formulae, as follows:

```
requires avl⟨t2, s2, h2⟩ then
case{t1 = null  →  ensures avl⟨res, s2, h2⟩;
      t1≠null  →  requires avl⟨t1, s1, _⟩ ensures avl⟨res, s1+s2, _⟩};
```

During the verification process, when reaching a call to the AVL merging method, the current program state must entail the method's precondition. Since the entailment process needs to explore both branches of the specification, the avl⟨t2, s2, h2⟩ node will be proven twice for each method call. By using staged formulae, the second specification will force the common formula to be proved only once. Although the two specifications capture the same information, the second version requires much less proving effort. For this example, there was a 40% reduction in verification time by our system, due solely to the presence of staged formulae.

For the general case, if x denotes the number of heap nodes/predicates that are shared in the consequent formula, and y the number of possible matchings from the antecedent, then the number of redundant matchings that are eliminated is $(x - 1) * y$. An analogy can be made between the use of the staged formula and the use of the binary decision diagram (BDD) as an intermediate representation for SAT formulae to support better sharing of identical sub-formulae [4]. Where applicable, we expect staged formulae to improve the effectiveness of verification.

2.2   Example 2

Parameter instantiation is needed primarily for connecting the logical variables between precondition and postcondition of specifications. Traditionally, manual instantiation of ghost variables has played this role. In this paper, we propose two new mechanisms, early and late instantiations, to support automatic instantiations of logical variables. As an example, consider a data node cell and a predicate cellPred defined as follows:

```
data cell { int val}
cellPred⟨root, i⟩ ≡ root=null ∧ i≤3  ∨  root ↦ cell⟨_⟩ ∧ i>3
```

To highlight the difference between early and late instantiations, we shall consider two separate proof obligations. The first one is given below.

$$p \mapsto \text{cell}⟨\_⟩ \vdash (\text{cellPred}⟨p, j⟩ \wedge j>2) * \Phi_r$$

At this point, we first need to match a heap predicate cellPred⟨p, j⟩ on the RHS with a data node p ↦ cell⟨_⟩ on the LHS to obtain an instantiation for the variable j. A fundamental question is whether the variable instantiation could occur for just the predicate cellPred⟨p, j⟩ (we refer to this as *early instantiation*), or it has to be for the entire formula cellPred⟨p, j⟩ ∧ j>2 (known as *late instantiation*). By default, our system uses early (or implicit) instantiation for variables that are not explicitly declared. In this scenario, early instantiation $j>3$ is obtained when folding with the predicate cellPred$\langle$p, j$\rangle$. This instantiation is transferred to the LHS. Consequently, we obtain a successful proof below.

$$j>3 \vdash (j>2)*\Phi_r$$

Now, let us consider a second proof obligation that will require late instantiation:

$$p=\text{null} \vdash (\text{cellPred}\langle p, j\rangle \wedge j>2)*\Phi_r$$

Similar to the previous case, we will first use a default early instantiation mechanism. After matching cellPred$\langle$p, j$\rangle$, we obtain the instantiation $j\leq3$. However, moving only this binding to the LHS is not enough, causing the proof below to fail.

$$p=\text{null} \wedge j\leq3 \vdash (j>2)*\Phi_r$$

To support late instantiation for variable j, we declare it explicitly using [j] below:

$$p=\text{null} \vdash ([j]\,\text{cellPred}\langle p, j\rangle \wedge j>2)*\Phi_r$$

This time variable j is kept on the RHS until the end of the entailment. As its proof below succeeds, the instantiation for j will be captured in the residue as $\Phi_r = j\leq3 \wedge j>2$.

$$p=\text{null} \vdash (\exists j.j\leq3 \wedge j>2)*\Phi_r$$

Though late instantiation is more general, it may require existential quantifications over a larger formula. Hence, by default, we prefer to use early instantiation where possible, and leave it to the user to manually declare where late instantiation is mandated.

3   Structured Specifications

We shall now focus on the structured specifications mechanism. Fig 1 provides a syntactic description where Z denotes structured (pre/post) specifications, while Q denotes structured formulae that may be used for pre/post specifications, as well as for predicate

Pre/Post. Z ::= $\exists v_1^*{\cdot}Y_1 \ldots \exists v_n^*{\cdot}Y_n$		multiple specs
Y ::= case$\{\pi_1 \Rightarrow Z_1; \ldots; \pi_n \Rightarrow Z_n\}$		case construct
$\mid$ requires $[w^*]$ Φ [then] Z		staged spec
$\mid$ ensures Q		post
Formula Q ::= $\bigvee \exists v^*{\cdot}R$		multiple disjuncts
R ::= case$\{\pi_1 \Rightarrow Q_1; \ldots; \pi_n \Rightarrow Q_n\}$		case construct
$\mid$ $[w^*]$ Φ [then Q]		staged formula
Φ ::= $\bigvee \exists v^* \cdot (\kappa \wedge \pi)$		
Heap formula κ ::= emp $\mid v \mapsto c\langle v^*\rangle \mid p\langle v^*\rangle \mid \kappa_1 * \kappa_2$		
Pure formula π ::= ...		

Fig. 1. Syntax for Structured Specifications

definitions. Apart from multiple specifications, our new syntax includes case constructs and staged formulae.

For structured specification, the `requires` keyword introduces a part of precondition through a staged specification. The postcondition is captured after each `ensures` keyword, which must appear as a terminating branch for the tree-like specification format. We support late instantiation via variables w^*, from `requires` $[w^*]\ \Phi\ Z$ and $[w^*]\ \Phi\ [\textbf{then}\ Q]$ at the end of proving Φ. To minimise user annotations, our system automatically determines the other unbound variables (different from those to be late instantiated) as either existential or to be early instantiated.

Our construct to support case analysis is $\text{case}\{\pi_1 \Rightarrow Z_1; \ldots; \pi_n \Rightarrow Z_n\}$ for specification, and $\text{case}\{\pi_1 \Rightarrow Q_1; \ldots; \pi_n \Rightarrow Q_n\}$ for formula. We impose the following three conditions on $\pi_1, \ldots, \pi_n$:

(i) are *restricted* to only pure constraints, without any heap formula.
(ii) are *exclusive*, meaning that $\forall i, j \cdot i \neq j \rightarrow \pi_i \wedge \pi_j = \texttt{false}$.
(iii) are *exhaustive*, meaning that $\pi_1 \vee \ldots \vee \pi_n = \texttt{true}$.

Condition (i) is imposed since pure formula can be freely duplicated. Condition (ii) is imposed to avoid conjunction over the heap-based formula. If absent, each heap state may have to satisfy multiple case branches. Condition (iii) is needed for soundness of case analysis which requires all scenarios to be considered. To illustrate, consider:

$$[(\texttt{w} : \texttt{t})^*]\ \Phi\ \text{case}\{\texttt{x=null} \Rightarrow Q_1; \texttt{x} \neq \texttt{null} \Rightarrow Q_2\}$$

The first condition holds as the two guards, $\texttt{x=null}$ and $\texttt{x} \neq \texttt{null}$, are pure. Furthermore, our system checks successfully that the guards are exclusive $((\texttt{x=null} \wedge \texttt{x} \neq \texttt{null}) = \texttt{false})$ and exhaustive $((\texttt{x=null} \vee \texttt{x} \neq \texttt{null}) = \texttt{true})$.

3.1   Semantic Model for Structured Formulae

The semantics of our structured formula is similar to those given for separation logic [21], with extensions for the new structured formulae.

To define the model we assume sets *Loc* of locations (positive integer values), *Val* of primitive values, with $0 \in Val$ denoting `null`, *Var* of variables (program and logical variables), and *ObjVal* of object values stored in the heap, with $c[f_1 \mapsto \nu_1, \ldots, f_n \mapsto \nu_n]$ denoting an object value of data type c where $\nu_1, \ldots, \nu_n$ are current values of the corresponding fields $f_1, \ldots, f_n$. Let $s, h \models Q$ in Fig 2 denote the model relation, i.e. the stack s and heap h satisfy the constraint Q, with h, s from the following concrete domains:

$$h \in \textit{Heaps} =_{df} \textit{Loc} \rightharpoonup_{fin} \textit{ObjVal}$$
$$s \in \textit{Stacks} =_{df} \textit{Var} \rightarrow \textit{Val} \cup \textit{Loc}$$

Note that each heap h is a finite partial mapping while each stack s is a total mapping, as in the classical separation logic [21,9]. Function $dom(f)$ returns the domain of function f. The model relation for separation heap formulas is defined below. The model relation for pure formula $s \models \pi$ denotes that the formula π evaluates to `true` in s. Note that $h_1 \perp h_2$ indicates h_1 and h_2 are domain-disjoint, $h_1 \cdot h_2$ denotes the union of disjoint heaps h_1 and h_2. For the case of a data node, $v \mapsto c\langle v^* \rangle$, h has to be a singleton heap. On the other hand, a shape predicate defined by $p\langle v_{1..n} \rangle \equiv Q$ may be inductively defined.

$$
\begin{array}{ll}
s,h \models \mathsf{Q} & \text{iff } \mathsf{Q} = \bigvee_{i=1}^{n} \exists v^* \cdot \mathsf{R}_i \text{ and } s,h \models \bigvee_{i=1}^{n} \exists v^* \cdot \mathsf{R}_i \\
s,h \models \bigvee_{i=1}^{n} \exists v_{i1..im} \cdot \mathsf{R}_i & \text{iff } \exists k \in \{1,..,n\} \cdot \exists \alpha_{k1..km} \cdot \\
& \quad s[v_{k1} \mapsto \alpha_{k1}, .., v_{km} \mapsto \alpha_{km}], h \models \mathsf{R}_k \\
s,h \models [w_{i=1}^{n}] \Phi \text{ then } \mathsf{Q} & \text{iff } \exists h_1, h_2 \cdot h_1 \bot h_2 \text{ and } h = h_1 \cdot h_2 \\
& \quad \text{and } \exists \alpha_{1..n} \cdot s[w_1 \mapsto \alpha_1, .., w_n \mapsto \alpha_n], h_1 \models \Phi \text{ and } s, h_2 \models \mathsf{Q} \\
s,h \models \mathsf{case}\{(\pi_i \Rightarrow \mathsf{Q}_i)_{i=1}^{n}\} & \text{iff } \forall k \in \{1,..,n\} \cdot (s,h \models \pi_k \;\rightarrow\; s,h \models \mathsf{Q}_k) \\
s,h \models \Phi_1 \vee \Phi_2 & \text{iff } s,h \models \Phi_1 \text{ or } s,h \models \Phi_2 \\
s,h \models \exists v_{1..n} \cdot \kappa \wedge \pi & \text{iff } \exists \alpha_{1..n} \cdot s[v_1 \mapsto \alpha_1, .., v_n \mapsto \alpha_n], h \models \kappa \\
& \quad \text{and } s[v_1 \mapsto \alpha_1, .., v_n \mapsto \alpha_n] \models \pi \\
s,h \models \kappa_1 * \kappa_2 & \text{iff } \exists h_1, h_2 \cdot h_1 \bot h_2 \text{ and } h = h_1 \cdot h_2 \\
& \quad \text{and } s, h_1 \models \kappa_1 \text{ and } s, h_2 \models \kappa_2 \\
s,h \models \mathsf{emp} & \text{iff } dom(h) = \emptyset \\
s,h \models p \mapsto \mathsf{c}\langle v^* \rangle & \text{iff } exists\ a\ data\ type\ decl.\ \mathsf{data}\ \mathsf{c}\ \{t_1\ f_1, .., t_n\ f_n\} \\
& \quad \text{and } h = [s(p) \mapsto r] \text{ and } r = \mathsf{c}[f_1 \mapsto s(v_1), .., f_n \mapsto s(v_n)] \\
s,h \models p\langle v_{1..n} \rangle & \text{iff } exists\ a\ pred.\ def.\ p\langle v_{1..n}\rangle \equiv \mathsf{Q} \text{ and } s,h \models \mathsf{Q}
\end{array}
$$

Fig. 2. Model for Structured Formulae

With the semantics of the structured formulae in place, we can provide a translation from a structured formula to its equivalent unstructured formula. This translation is formalised with $\mathsf{Q} \rightsquigarrow_T \Phi$, as shown below:

$$
\frac{\forall i \cdot \mathsf{Q}_i \rightsquigarrow_T \Phi_i}{\mathsf{case}\{\pi_i \Rightarrow \mathsf{Q}_i\}^* \rightsquigarrow_T \bigvee(\Phi_i \wedge \pi_i)} \qquad \frac{\mathsf{Q} \rightsquigarrow_T \Phi}{[w^*]\ \Phi_1 \text{ then } \mathsf{Q} \rightsquigarrow_T \Phi_1 * \Phi}
$$

$$
\frac{\forall i \cdot \mathsf{R}_i \rightsquigarrow_T \Phi_i}{\bigvee \exists v^* \cdot \mathsf{R}_i \rightsquigarrow_T \bigvee \exists v^* \cdot \Phi_i} \qquad \frac{}{[w^*]\ \Phi \rightsquigarrow_T \Phi}
$$

We make use of the semantics for structured formulae Q and for unstructured formula Φ to prove the correctness of the given translation rules.

Theorem 3.1 (Correctness of Translation). *Given Q and Φ such that $\mathsf{Q} \rightsquigarrow_T \Phi$: for all s, h, $s, h \models \mathsf{Q}$ if and only if $s, h \models \Phi$.*

Proof: By structural induction on Q.

4   Modular Verification

The main goal of structured specification is to support a modular verification process that could be carried out efficiently and precisely. In this section, we propose a set of rules to help generate Hoare-style triples for code verification, together with entailment checking to support proof obligations over the structured formulae domain.

4.1   Building Verification Rules

Program verification is typically formalised using Hoare triples of the form $\{pre\}e\{post\}$, where *pre* and *post* are the initial and final states of the program code (e) in some logic. Our verification system uses separation logic, where a Hoare-style specification

$\{pre\}e\{post\}$ is valid, denoted as $\models \{pre\}e\{post\}$, if and only if, for all states (s, h) that $s, h \models pre$, if the execution of e starting from (s, h) does not lead to memory errors and terminates in a state (s_1, h_1), then $s_1, h_1 \models post$.

To better support structured specifications and case analysis, we propose a new triple of the form $\{\!|\Phi|\!\}\, e\, \{\!|Z|\!\}$, with *pre* being an unstructured formula and Z being the structured specification. We use structured specifications in the poststate because our case analysis is guided from the post-states. In contrast, unstructured formulae are used in the prestate since the structured form is unnecessary here. The semantic meaning of this new triple is defined as follows:

Definition 4.1. *The validity of* $\{\!|\Phi|\!\}\, e\, \{\!|Z|\!\}$ *is defined inductively over the structure of Z. That is:*

- *if* $Z \equiv$ ensures Q : $\models \{\!|\Phi|\!\}\, e\, \{\!|Z|\!\} \iff \models \{\Phi\}e\{Q\}$;
- *if* $Z \equiv$ requires Φ_1 [then] Z_1 : $\models \{\!|\Phi|\!\}\, e\, \{\!|Z|\!\} \iff \models \{\!|\Phi*\Phi_1|\!\}\, e\, \{\!|Z_1|\!\}$;
- *if* $Z \equiv$ case$\{\pi_1 {\Rightarrow} Z_1; \ldots; \pi_n {\Rightarrow} Z_n\}$: $\models \{\!|\Phi|\!\}\, e\, \{\!|Z|\!\} \iff$
  $\iff \forall i {\in} \{1, .., n\} {\cdot} \models \{\!|\Phi {\wedge} \pi_i|\!\}\, e\, \{\!|Z_i|\!\}$;
- *if* $Z \equiv (\exists v_1^* {\cdot} Y_1 \ldots \exists v_n^* {\cdot} Y_n)$: $\models \{\!|\Phi|\!\}\, e\, \{\!|Z|\!\} \iff$
  $\iff \forall i {\in} \{1, .., n\} {\cdot} \models \{\!|\Phi|\!\}\, e\, \{\!|\exists v_i^* {\cdot} Y_i|\!\})\square$

Our main verification rules are given in Fig. 3. Note that G records a list of variables (including res as result of the code) visible to the code verifier. Our specification formulae use both primed and unprimed notations, where primed notations represent the latest values of program variables, and unprimed notations denote either logical variables or initial values of program variables.

The verification of method declarations is described by the $[\text{FV--METH}]$ rule. It verifies the method body code against the specification Z, as indicated by the rule. The function $prime(\{v_1, .., v_m\})$ returns the primed version $\{v_1', .., v_m'\}$. The third line of the premise deals with the verification task $G \vdash \{\!| \bigwedge(v'{=}v)^* \wedge \bigwedge(u'{=}u)^* |\!\}$ code $\{\!|Z|\!\}$, where

$$
\frac{\begin{array}{c} [\textbf{FV--METH}] \\ H{=}[(v{:}t)^*, (u{:}t)^*] \\ G = prime(H){+}H + [\textbf{res}{:}t_0] \\ G \vdash \{\!| \bigwedge(v'{=}v)^* \wedge \bigwedge(u'{=}u)^* |\!\}\ \text{code}\ \{\!|Z|\!\} \end{array}}{\vdash t_0\ mn\ ((t\ v)^*, (\textbf{ref}\ t\ u)^*)\ Z\ \{\ code\ \}}
\qquad
\frac{\begin{array}{c} [\textbf{FV--MULTI--SPECS}] \\ \textit{fresh}\ nv^* \\ \rho{=}[(v{\rightarrow}nv)^*] \\ \forall i \cdot G \vdash \{\!|\Phi|\!\}\ \text{code}\ \{\!|\rho Y_i|\!\} \end{array}}{G \vdash \{\!|\Phi|\!\}\ \text{code}\ \{\!|\exists v_1^* {\cdot} Y_1 .. \exists v_n^* {\cdot} Y_n|\!\}}
$$

$$
\frac{\begin{array}{c} [\textbf{FV--REQUIRES}] \\ \{w*\} \cap Vars(G) = \{\} \\ G_1 = G + [(w:t)^*] \\ G_1 \vdash \{\!|\Phi_1 * \Phi_2|\!\}\ \text{code}\ \{\!|Z|\!\} \end{array}}{G \vdash \{\!|\Phi_1|\!\}\ \text{code}\ \{\!|\text{requires}\ [(w:t)^*]\ \Phi_2\ Z|\!\}}
\qquad
\frac{\begin{array}{c} [\textbf{FV--ENSURES}] \\ V{=}PassByValue(G) \\ \vdash \{\Phi\}\ \text{code}\ \{\Phi_2\} \\ \exists prime(V) \cdot \Phi_2 \vdash_{\{\}}^{\text{emp}} Q*S \quad S{\neq}\{\} \end{array}}{G \vdash \{\!|\Phi|\!\}\ \text{code}\ \{\!|\text{ensures}\ Q|\!\}}
$$

$$
\frac{\begin{array}{c} [\textbf{FV--CASE}] \\ \forall i {\in} \{1, .., n\} \cdot G \vdash \{\!|\Phi \wedge \pi_i|\!\}\ \text{code}\ \{\!|Z_i|\!\} \end{array}}{G \vdash \{\!|\Phi|\!\}\ \text{code}\ \{\!|\text{case}\{\pi_1 {\Rightarrow} Z_1; \ldots; \pi_n {\Rightarrow} Z_n\}|\!\}}
$$

Fig. 3. Building Verification Rules for Structured Specifications

the precondition indicates that the latest values of program variables are the same as their initial values. The other rules are syntax-directed and rely on the structure of the specification Z.

The rule $\boxed{\text{FV–MULTI–SPECS}}$ deals with the case where the post-state is a multi-specification. It verifies the code against each of the specifications. Note that the substitution ρ replaces variables v^* with fresh variables nv^*. The rule $\boxed{\text{FV–REQUIRES}}$ deals with the case where the post-state starts with a `requires` clause. In this case, the formula in the `requires` clause is added to the pre-state (by separation conjunction) before verifying the code against the remaining part of the specification in the post-state. The variables for late instantiation (w^*) are also attached to the end of the list G. The rule $\boxed{\text{FV–ENSURES}}$ deals with the case where the post-state starts with an `ensures` clause. It invokes our forward verification rules to derive the strongest postcondition Φ_2 for the normal Hoare triple $\{\Phi\}\text{code}\{\Phi_2\}$ and invokes the entailment prover (described in the next section) to check that the derived post-state Φ_2 subsumes the given post-condition Q (The test $S \neq \{\}$ signifies the success of this entailment proof). Note that V denotes the set of pass-by-value parameters that are not modified by the procedure. Hence, their values (denoted by primed variables) are ignored in the postcondition, even if the program code may have updated these parameters. The last rule $\boxed{\text{FV–CASE}}$ deals with the case where the post-state is a case specification. It verifies in each case the specification Z_i is met when the guard π_i is assumed in the pre-state.

To illustrate the generation of the verification tasks, consider the AVL merging given in Section 2.1. By applying the rules from Figure 3, two Hoare triples are produced.

$$\vdash \{\text{avl}\langle t2, s2, h2\rangle \wedge t1=\text{null}\} \text{ code } \{\text{avl}\langle res, s2, h2\rangle\}$$
$$\vdash \{\text{avl}\langle t1, s1, \_\rangle * \text{avl}\langle t2, s2, h2\rangle \wedge t1 \neq \text{null}\} \text{ code } \{\text{avl}\langle res, s1+s2, \_\rangle\}$$

Theorem 4.1 (Soundness of Verification). *Our verification rules are* sound. *That is, given a program* code, *an unstructured formula* Φ, *and a structured specification* Z, *if our system derives a proof,* $\vdash \{\!|\Phi|\!\}$ code $\{\!|Z|\!\}$, *then we have* $\models \{\!|\Phi|\!\}$ code $\{\!|Z|\!\}$.

Proof: It follows from the soundness of our underlying verification system (i.e. the one without structured specifications) [17], the definition 4.1, and the soundness of the entailment prover enriched with structured formulae (described in the next section).

4.2 Entailment for Structured Formula

Given formulae Φ_1 and Q_2, our entailment prover checks if Φ_1 entails Q_2, that is if in all heaps satisfying Φ_1, we can find a subheap satisfying Q_2.

The main features of our entailment prover are that, besides determining if the entailment relation holds, it also infers the residual heap of the entailment, that is a formula Φ_R such that $\Phi_1 \vdash Q_2 * \Phi_R$ and derives the predicate parameters. The relation is formalized using a judgment of the form $\Phi_1 \vdash_V^\kappa Q_2 * \Phi_R$, which is a shorthand for $\Phi_1 * \kappa \vdash \exists V \cdot (Q_2 * \kappa) * \Phi_R$. Note that κ denotes the consumed heap, while V is a set, $\{v^*, E{:}w^*\}$, containing the existential variables encountered, v^*, together with the variables w^* for late instantiation, .

To support proof search, we have also generalised the entailment checking procedure to return a set of residues S_R: $\Phi_1 \vdash_V^\kappa Q_2 * S_R$. This entailment succeeds when S_R is non-empty, otherwise it is deemed to have failed. The multiple residual states captured in S_R

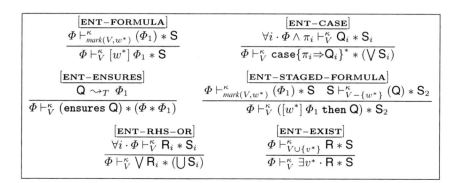

Fig. 4. Entailment for Structured Formula

signify different search outcomes during proving. Our entailment procedure relies on unfolding and folding of the predicate definitions. Unfolding refers to a single inlining of a predicate in the antecedent, while folding is a recursive entailment with the body of a predicate in the consequent. In the current paper, we enhance the entailment proving procedure to handle structured formulae in the consequent. The main rules are given in Figure 4. Take note that we make use of a method $mark(V, w^*)$, which marks the variables to be late instantiated, w^*, by removing them from the existential variables stored in V and adding them as $E : w^*$:

$$mark(V, w^*) = (V - \{w^*\}) \cup \{(E : w)^*\}$$

The rule $\boxed{\text{ENT-FORMULA}}$ makes use of the aforementioned marking method in order to mark the fact that variables w^* are to be late instantiated, whereas rule $\boxed{\text{ENT-EXIST}}$ adds the existentially quantified variables v^* to the set V.

In the rule for staged formula, $\boxed{\text{ENT-STAGED-FORMULA}}$, the instantiation for the variables w^* takes place in the first stage, Φ_1. As instantiation moves the corresponding bindings to the LHS (or antecedent of entailment), the variables w^* must be removed from the set of existentially quantified variables when entailing the rest of the formula, Q. At the end of the entailment proving, the variables that were marked as late-instantiated are existentially quantified in the residue state. The generalised entailment with a set of n formulae in the antecedent is an abbreviation of the n entailments, as illustrated below:

$$\frac{\forall i \in \{1, .., n\} \cdot \Phi_i \vdash_V^\kappa (Q) * S_i}{\{\Phi_1, .., \Phi_n\} \vdash_V^\kappa (Q) * \bigcup_{i=1}^n S_i}$$

The rule $\boxed{\text{ENT-CASE}}$ adds the pure term π_i to the antecedent. This rule requires a lifted disjunction operation defined as $S_1 \vee S_2 \equiv \{\Phi_1 \vee \Phi_2 | \Phi_1 \in S_1, \Phi_2 \in S_2\}$ when applied to two sets of states, S_1, S_2.

While a successful entailment of one disjunct suffices for the entailment of a disjunctive formula, our entailment rule $\boxed{\text{ENT-RHS-OR}}$ facilitates a proof search by trying to entail each of the RHS disjuncts separately. Therefore, the residue state must contain the union of all residues corresponding to the proof search from a set of entailments, $\forall i \cdot \Phi \vdash_V^\kappa R_i * S_i$.

Take note that, at each call site, the forward verification procedure ensures that the method's precondition is satisfied and assumes the method's postcondition. This is achieved by entailing a formula denoting a specification of the Z form. As the corresponding entailment rules are similar to those for the entailment of a structured formula given in Figure 4, we omit them for brevity. The only unusual rule is [ENT–ENSURES] that is needed when entailing the actual postcondition ensures Q. In this case, the postcondition is added to the residual state in unstructured form, immediately after the translation $Q \leadsto_T \Phi_1$ to unstructured form.

Theorem 4.2 (Soundness of Entailment). *Given Φ, Q such that $s, h \models \Phi$, if $\Phi \vdash_V^\kappa Q * \Phi_r$ for some Φ_r, then $s, h \models Q * \Phi_r$. That is, for all program states in which Φ holds if $\Phi \vdash_V^\kappa Q * \Phi_r$ then $Q * \Phi_r$ holds.*

Proof: By structural induction on Q.

5   Experiments

We have built a prototype system using Objective Caml. The proof obligations generated by our verification are discharged using some off-the-shelf constraint solvers (like Omega Calculator [20]) or theorem provers (like MONA [13]). The specification mechanism works with any constraint domain, as long as a corresponding prover for the domain is available. The specific domains that our verifier currently supports, includes linear (Omega Calculator, Z3, CVC-lite) and non-linear arithmetic (Redlog), set (MONA, Isabelle bag tactic) and list properties (a Coq tactic). Though the current paper highlighted mostly simpler specifications, our benchmark included the verification of functional correctness properties, such as sortedness and permutation.

We have conducted preliminary experiments by testing our system on a suite of examples summarized in Figure 5. These examples are small but can handle data structures with sophisticated shape and size properties such as sorted lists, balanced trees, etc., in a uniform way. Methods "insert" and "delete" refer to the insertion and deletion of a value into/from the corresponding data structure, respectively. Method "del_first" deletes the node at the head in a circular list. Moreover, we verify a suite of sorting algorithms, which receive as input an unsorted singly-linked list and return a sorted list. Verification time for each function includes the time to verify all functions that it calls. We compare the timings obtained with and without case analysis.

Take note that for each of the verified methods, in order to compare the results obtained with and without case analysis, we provided specifications with the same level of modularity through specifications with multiple pre/post. FAIL for the "without case" means it did not verify functional correctness (including memory safety). This is due the absence of case analysis that would have been provided by the missing case spec.

Preliminary results indicate that case analysis improves both the completeness and the performance of our system. From the completeness point of view, case analysis is important for verifying a number of examples that would *fail* otherwise. For instance, the method implementing the selection sort algorithm over a linked list fails when it is written with multiple specification instead of the case construct. The same scenario is encountered for the method inserting/deleting a node of red black tree, and for the method appending two list segments. The case construct thus helps our system to verify more examples successfully. Regarding the performance, the timings obtained when using case analysis are smaller, taking on average 21% less computation time than those

| Program | | Timings (in seconds) | | speed |
Codes	LOC	*with* case	*without* case	gain (%)
Linked List		verifies length		
delete	20	0.65	0.89	26
append	14	0.30	0.39	23
List Segment		verifies length		
append	11	0.95	*failed*	-
Circular Linked List		verifies length + circularity		
del_first	15	0.35	0.41	15
insert	10	0.28	0.35	20
Doubly Linked List		verifies length + double links		
insert	18	0.35	0.52	33
delete	29	0.94	1.27	26
Sorted List		verifies bounds + sortedness		
insert	17	0.71	0.96	26
delete	21	0.60	0.68	22
insertion_sort	45	0.92	1.35	32
selection_sort	52	1.24	*failed*	-
bubble_sort	42	1.95	2.92	43
merge_sort	105	2.01	2.53	31
quick_sort	85	1.82	2.47	26
AVL Tree		verifies size + height + balanced		
insert	169	32.27	39.48	19
delete	287	85.1	97.30	13
Perfect Tree		verifies height + perfectness		
insert	89	0.73	0.99	26
Red-Black Tree		verifies size + black-height		
insert	167	5.44	*failed*	-
delete	430	22.43	*failed*	-

Fig. 5. Verification Times for Case Construct vs Multiple Pre/Post

obtained without case analysis. The improvements are due to earlier pruning of `false` contexts with the help of case constructs and optimizations of the case entailment rule.

We also investigated the performance gain that can be attributed to the use of staged formulae. We observed that the timings improved on average by 20%. Noteworthy examples include the AVL insertion (from 32.27s to 22.93s) and AVL deletion (from 85.1s to 81.6s).

We may conclude from our experiments that structured specifications together with case analysis give better precision to our verification system while also improving its performance, when compared to corresponding unstructured specifications.

6   Related Work and Conclusion

Previous works on enhancing pre/post specifications [14,12] were mainly concerned with improving modularity to allow easier understanding of specifications. With this objective, multiple specifications and redundant representations were advocated as the primary machinery. In the context of shape analysis, Chang and Rival [6] make use of `if` notation for defining inductive checkers. However, the conditional gets approximated to disjunction during the actual analysis. Verification wise, the three structured specification mechanisms that we have proposed are not available in existing tools, such as JML [5], Spec# [1], Dafny [15], JStar [8] and VeriFast [10]. The closest relationships may be summarized, as follows. JML supports specification cases, in the form of multiple pre/post conditions, for better modularity and clarity of specifications. Our case constructs also intend to provide better guidance to the verification process. Spec#/Dafny supports ghost variables for manual instantiation (by user) of logical variables. In contrast, our early/late instantiation mechanisms provided two solutions to automatic instantiation of logical variables. Overall, little attempt has been made to add specification structures that can help produce a better verification outcome.

On timings, we did not compare with Spec# and Dafny, since our benchmark on heap-manipulating programs is not properly covered by their specification logic. Regarding JStar, it currently uses logics involving only shapes and equalities, it does not support more expressive properties, like set and numeric properties, needed by our benchmark. Lastly, VeriFast requires more user intervention in the form of explicit unfolding and folding of the abstract predicates through ghost statements.

In a distributed systems setting, Seino et al [22] present a case analysis meant to improve the efficiency of protocol verification, which involves finding appropriate predicates and splitting a case into multiple sub-cases based on the predicates. In order to cover all the possible case splits, they use a special type of matrix. Pientka [19] argues for the need of case analysis in inductive proofs. The potential case splits are selected heuristically, based on the pattern of the theorem. A case split mechanism has been used by Brock et al [3] to guide case analysis during proving. Jhala and McMillan [11] used a temporal case splitting in order to specialize the properties to be proven, so that they depend on only a finite part of the overall state. As opposed to the previous works, our current proposal is to incorporate structured mechanisms within the specification mechanism itself for guiding the case analysis, existential instantiation or staged proving.

Some existing theorem provers use tactics as a way to automate or semi-automate proofs, and our system can take advantage of them through lower-level pure proofs. However, for Hoare-style specification and verification, we have chosen to design a structured specification (rather than another tactic language) for the following reasons:

- It can be provided at a higher-level that users can understand more easily, since it is closer to specification mechanism rather than the (harder) verification process.
- It is more portable, as specification are tied to program codes, while tactic language tend to be prover-specific requiring the invoked prover to understand the relevant commands. Our approach basically breaks down larger (hard) proofs into smaller (simpler) proofs that any prover could more easily and more effectively handle, as confirmed by our experiments.
- Specification can be transformed (or restructured) which allows us to heuristically infer structured specifications from unstructured counterparts. A version of this translation from unstructured formula to structured formula has been implemented in our system. Though this can never be as good as that provided by expert users,

it can nevertheless be used to handle most of the straightforward cases for legacy specifications, leaving the harder unverified examples to be handled by users.

The current paper has pioneered a novel approach towards resolving two key problems of verification, namely better modularity and better completeness through a new form of structured specification. Our proposal has been formalized and implemented with a promising set of experimental results.

Acknowledgement. We thank the anonymous reviewers for their insightful feedback on this work. The work was supported by NUS Grant R-252-000-366-112, MoE Grant R-252-000-444-112 and EPSRC Grant EP/G042322.

References

1. Barnett, M., Leino, K.R.M., Schulte, W.: The spec# programming system: An overview. In: Barthe, G., Burdy, L., Huisman, M., Lanet, J.-L., Muntean, T. (eds.) CASSIS 2004. LNCS, vol. 3362, pp. 49–69. Springer, Heidelberg (2005)
2. Berdine, J., Calcagno, C., O'Hearn, P.W.: Smallfoot: Modular automatic assertion checking with separation logic. In: de Boer, F.S., Bonsangue, M.M., Graf, S., de Roever, W.-P. (eds.) FMCO 2005. LNCS, vol. 4111, pp. 115–137. Springer, Heidelberg (2006)
3. Brock, B., Kaufmann, M., Strother Moore, J.: ACL2 Theorems About Commercial Micro-processors. In: Srivas, M., Camilleri, A. (eds.) FMCAD 1996. LNCS, vol. 1166, pp. 275–293. Springer, Heidelberg (1996)
4. Bryant, R.E.: Graph-based algorithms for boolean function manipulation. IEEE Transactions on Computers 35, 677–691 (1986)
5. Burdy, L., Cheon, Y., Cok, D.R., Ernst, M.D., Kiniry, J.R., Leavens, G.T., Leino, K.R.M., Poll, E.: An overview of JML tools and applications. Software Tools for Technology Transfer (2005)
6. Chang, B.-Y.E., Rival, X.: Relational inductive shape analysis. In: POPL, pp. 247–260 (2008)
7. Chin, W.-N., David, C., Nguyen, H.H., Qin, S.: Multiple pre/post specifications for heap-manipulating methods. In: HASE, pp. 357–364 (2007)
8. Distefano, D., Parkinson, M.J.: jStar: Towards Practical Verification for Java. In: OOPSLA (2008)
9. Ishtiaq, S., O'Hearn, P.W.: BI as an assertion language for mutable data structures. In: ACM POPL, London, pp. 14–26 (January 2001)
10. Jacobs, B., Smans, J., Piessens, F.: A quick tour of the veriFast program verifier. In: Ueda, K. (ed.) APLAS 2010. LNCS, vol. 6461, pp. 304–311. Springer, Heidelberg (2010)
11. Jhala, R., McMillan, K.L.: Microarchitecture verification by compositional model check-ing. In: Berry, G., Comon, H., Finkel, A. (eds.) CAV 2001. LNCS, vol. 2102, pp. 396–410. Springer, Heidelberg (2001)
12. Jonkers, H.B.M.: Upgrading the pre- and postcondition technique. In: Prehn, S., Toetenel, H. (eds.) VDM 1991. LNCS, vol. 551, pp. 428–456. Springer, Heidelberg (1991)
13. Klarlund, N., Moller, A.: MONA Version 1.4 - User Manual. BRICS Notes Series (January 2001)
14. Leavens, G.T., Baker, A.L.: Enhancing the pre- and postcondition technique for more ex-pressive specifications. In: Woodcock, J.C.P., Davies, J. (eds.) FM 1999. LNCS, vol. 1709, p. 1087. Springer, Heidelberg (1999)
15. Rustan, K., Leino, M.: Dafny: An automatic program verifier for functional correctness. In: Clarke, E.M., Voronkov, A. (eds.) LPAR-16 2010. LNCS, vol. 6355, pp. 348–370. Springer, Heidelberg (2010)

16. Parkinson, M.J., Bierman, G.M.: Separation logic and abstraction. In: ACM POPL, pp. 247–258 (2005)
17. Nguyen, H.H., David, C., Qin, S.C., Chin, W.-N.: Automated verification of shape and size properties via separation logic. In: Cook, B., Podelski, A. (eds.) VMCAI 2007. LNCS, vol. 4349, pp. 251–266. Springer, Heidelberg (2007)
18. O'Hearn, P.W., Yang, H., Reynolds, J.C.: Separation and Information Hiding. In: ACM POPL, Venice, Italy (January 2004)
19. Pientka, B.: A heuristic for case analysis. Technical report (1995)
20. Pugh, W.: The Omega Test: A fast practical integer programming algorithm for dependence analysis. Communications of the ACM 8, 102–114 (1992)
21. Reynolds, J.: Separation Logic: A Logic for Shared Mutable Data Structures. In: IEEE LICS, Copenhagen, Denmark, pp. 55–74 (July 2002)
22. Seino, T., Ogato, K., Futatsugi, K.: Mechanically supporting case analysis for verification of distributed systems. In: IJPCC (2005)
23. Zee, K., Kuncak, V., Rinard, M.C.: An integrated proof language for imperative programs. In: PLDI, pp. 338–351. ACM, New York (2009)

Verification of Unloadable Modules

Bart Jacobs, Jan Smans*, and Frank Piessens

Department of Computer Science, Katholieke Universiteit Leuven, Belgium
{bart.jacobs,jan.smans,frank.piessens}@cs.kuleuven.be

Abstract. Programs in unsafe languages, like C and C++, may dynamically load and unload modules. For example, some operating system kernels support dynamic loading and unloading of device drivers. This causes specific difficulties in the verification of such programs and modules; in particular, it must be verified that no functions or global variables from the module are used after the module is unloaded.

We present the approach we used to add support for loading and unloading modules to our separation-logic-based program verifier VeriFast. Our approach to the specification and verification of function pointer calls, based on parameterizing function types by predicates, is sound in the presence of unloading, but at the same time does not complicate the verification of programs that perform no unloading, and does not require callers to distinguish between function pointers that point into unloadable modules and ones that do not.

We offer a machine-checked formalization and soundness proof and we report on verifying a small kernel-like program using VeriFast. To the best of our knowledge, ours is the first approach for sound modular verification of C programs that load and unload modules.

1   Introduction

In statically typed safe programming languages, code is immutable and permanent. That is, both statically bound and dynamically bound routine calls always succeed and are bound to code that satisfies the static type of the call. Also, if an object reference or function value satisfies a given contract at one point in time, it continues to do so forever.

This is not the case in dynamically typed languages and in unsafe languages like C and C++. In C, if at one point during execution at a given address there is a function that satisfies a given contract, this does not mean this will remain the case indefinitely. The module containing the function may be part of a dynamically linked library (DLL, also known as a shared object) that may be unloaded, or the function's code may reside on the stack or in a malloc'ed piece of memory.

Existing verification approaches for C programs (Caduceus/Frama-C [7], HAVOC [5], VCC [4], Smallfoot [1], our own verifier VeriFast [8]) assume that the program is unchanging and is not part of the mutable state. As a result,

---

* Jan Smans is a Postdoctoral Fellow of the Research Foundation - Flanders (FWO).

M. Butler and W. Schulte (Eds.): FM 2011, LNCS 6664, pp. 402–416, 2011.

these approaches cannot be used for sound verification of programs that involve the unloading of code.

In this paper, we propose a separation-logic-based approach for extending a verification approach for C programs to enable verification of the memory-safety, data-race-freedom, and compliance with preconditions, postconditions, and other assertions of programs involving code unloading. Specifically, our contributions with respect to existing verification tools for C are the following features, which none of the existing tools have:

- **Soundness in the presence of unloading.** Verification of an unloadable module checks that when execution of code in the module is attempted, a permission indicating that the code is present is owned by the current thread.
- **Predicate-parameterized function types.** In the absence of unloading, abstract predicate families [11] indexed by function pointer could be used to enable abstraction for function pointer contracts. However, in the presence of unloading, a function pointer no longer immutably refers to a specific function. Predicate-parameterized function types solve this problem, and furthermore allow callers to be agnostic as to whether a function pointer points into an unloadable module or not.
- **Modular support for global variables.** A module, even an unloadable one, may declare global variables. It is checked that these are not used after the module is unloaded.

We implemented the approach in our prototype verifier, VeriFast, and we verified a small server written in C that allows clients to load modules, unload modules, and use services provided by the modules, mimicking operating system kernels that may dynamically load and unload device drivers. Also, we developed a formalization and a machine-checked soundness proof of the approach.

The remainder of the paper is structured as follows. In Section 2, we illustate the problem by means of an example. In Section 3, we formalize the relevant subset of C. In Section 4, we present our approach. In Section 5, we discuss the implementation. Finally, in Section 6, we conclude and discuss related work.

2   Problem Statement

We illustrate the verification challenges addressed by our approach using the example C program shown in Figure 1. The example program adopts some aspects of an operating system kernel that loads and unloads device drivers as kernel modules. It consists of a simple "kernel module", `RamDisk.c`, that implements a file abstraction backed by memory, and a simple "kernel", that loads the kernel module, tests its functionality, and unloads it. Like most kernel modules, the example module uses kernel resources that should be cleaned up properly when the client is done using the module. The example uses a simple byte vector resource (i.e. a growable array of bytes) as backing for its file abstraction. While the example is kept simple on purpose, it contains the essential ingredients of dynamic loading and unloading of modules that offer services to clients and that

```
// Modules.h
struct module;

struct module *load_module
  (char *name,
    void **init, void **exit);
void unload_module
  (struct module *m);
```

```
// KernelModule.h
typedef int read(
  int offset, char *buffer, int count);
typedef void write(
  int offset, char *buffer, int count);

struct file_ops {
  read *read;
  write *write;
};

typedef struct file_ops *module_init();
typedef void module_exit();
```

```
// Kernel.c
#include "Modules.h"
#include "KernelModule.h"

void testOps(struct file_ops *o) {
  o→write(0, "Hello", 6); char b[10];
  int n = o→read(0, b, 10);
  assert(n == 6 &&
    memcmp(b, "Hello", 6) == 0);
}

void main() {
  module_init *init;
  module_exit *exit;
  struct module *m = load_module(
    "RamDisk", &init, &exit);
  struct file_ops *o = init();
  testOps(o); exit();
  unload_module(m);
}
```

```
// ByteVector.h
struct vector;

struct vector *create_vector();
int vector_read(struct vector *v,
  int offset, char *buffer, int count);
void vector_write(struct vector *v,
  int offset, char *buffer, int count);
void vector_dispose
  (struct vector *v);
```

```
// RamDisk.c
#include "KernelModule.h"
#include "ByteVector.h"

struct vector *vector = 0;

int myRead(int o, char *b, int c) {
  return vector_read(vector, o, b, c);
}

int myWrite(int o, char *b, int c) {
  vector_write(vector, o, b, c);
}

struct file_ops o = {0, 0};

struct file_ops *module_init() {
  o.read = myRead;
  o.write = myWrite;
  vector = create_vector();
  return &o;
}

void module_exit() {
  vector_dispose(vector);
}
```

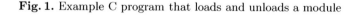

Fig. 1. Example C program that loads and unloads a module

potentially use resources not directly visible to the client in the implementation of these services.

The kernel dynamically loads the `RamDisk` module using an API declared in `Modules.h`. This API assumes each dynamically loaded module exports a function called *module_init* and a function called *module_exit*, and it returns pointers to these functions through its by-reference parameters *init* and *exit*. The client program performs implicit casts of these void pointers to pointers to function types *module_init* and *module_exit*, respectively, declared in `KernelModule.h`.

After loading `RamDisk`, the client program tests its functionality using an assert statement, in function *testOps*. Specifically, it writes the zero-terminated string `"Hello"` to the file and then checks that reading the file yields the same string. If the condition of the assert statement evaluates to false, the program aborts. Finally, the program unloads the module and terminates.

The challenge we take up in this paper is to come up with an approach, suitable for implementation in a semi-automatic program verifier like VeriFast, for verifying modularly that programs that load and unload modules, such as the example program, execute safely. Executing safely is a strong property: it means that the program does not access (i.e., read, write, or execute) unallocated memory and that all assert statements succeed.

Support for unloadable modules introduces additional safety risks, including for instance:

- Programs should not use a function pointer pointing into an unloadable module after this module has been unloaded. For example, if the two final calls in function *main* are swapped, the program is unsafe.
- Programs should not access a global variable declared by an unloadable module after this module has been unloaded. For example, if an access of *o* is added at the end of function *main*, the program is unsafe.

The verification approach should be modular and sound. Modularity implies that:

- Unloadable modules and client programs should be verifiable separately, with minimal assumptions about each other and with proper information hiding. For example, the verification of a client program should not depend on whether a module it loads and unloads declares global variables.
- The verification of code that uses a function pointer should not depend on whether the function pointer points into an unloadable module or into static code. For example, verification of function *testOps* should be agnostic as to whether function pointer *o→write* points to an unloadable module or not.

Soundness in such a modular setting means: If all modules and client programs involved in a run of the system have been verified, then the run is safe (as defined above).

3   Formal Programming Language

We will present our approach in the context of a simple formal programming language that retains only the relevant aspects of C. In this section, we introduce the syntax and the semantics of the programming language. In the next section, we present our specification formalism and proof system.

The formal programming language is an extension of the standard separation logic language [14] with function pointer call and module load and unload commands, and with function values L. The latter are used to represent pieces of code in the heap; they are a higher-level analog of assembly language instructions. The language's syntax is as follows:

$$n \in \mathbb{Z}, x \in \mathrm{Vars}, \tau \in \mathrm{FunTypeNames}$$
$$e ::= n \mid x \mid e + e \mid e - e \qquad\qquad b ::= e = e \mid e < e$$
$$c ::= x := \mathbf{cons}(\bar{e}) \mid x := [e] \mid [e] := e \mid \mathbf{dispose}(e) \mid x := e \mid (c; c)$$
$$\qquad \mid \mathbf{if}\ b\ \mathbf{then}\ c\ \mathbf{else}\ c \mid x := \mathbf{call}\ e(\bar{e}) \mid x := \mathbf{load}\ e\ \mathbf{as}\ \tau \mid \mathbf{unload}(e)$$
$$L ::= \mathbf{lambda}\ (\bar{x})\ c$$

We adopt the standard run-time state of separation logic, consisting of a store s, a total function that maps program variable names to integers, and a heap h, a partial function that maps positive integer addresses to integer values. The domain of the heap coincides with the allocated addresses. In order to be able to store function values in the heap, we assume an injective encoding $\lfloor \cdot \rfloor$ of function values L into integers; this corresponds to the encoding of assembly instructions as byte sequences on real architectures.

To model the loading and unloading of modules, we assume the existence of a module repository *Modules*, which is a finite map from module names to module definitions. A module name is simply an integer. A module definition consists of the module's *contract*, which is a function type name $\tau \in \mathrm{FunTypeNames}$, and a module image. The module image is simply a tuple of one or more integers. The first element of the tuple is the encoded function value for the module's entry point; the other elements may be encoded function values or data (corresponding to global variables in C).

We describe the semantics of the new commands. For a formal big-step semantics of the language, see the extended version of this paper [9].

Function pointer call command $x := \mathbf{call}\ e(\bar{e})$ executes the function value at address e in the heap. Specifically, if at address e there is a function value with parameters $\bar{x}$ and body c, it executes c under a store that binds the parameters to the arguments specified in the call and the variable ip (for *instruction pointer*) to the target address, and it assigns the result of the call, conventionally stored in local variable result by the function, to variable x. The call aborts if address e is not allocated, if the value at address e is not an encoded function value, or if there are more or fewer parameters than arguments. It also aborts if c aborts.

Command $x := \mathbf{load}\ e\ \mathbf{as}\ \tau$, where e is an expression and τ is a function type name, loads the module named e and stores its address in variable x. Specifically, loading a module whose image is $v_1, \ldots, v_n$ means allocating $n + 1$ consecutive addresses, storing the image size n at the first address (used by **unload**), and the image itself at the subsequent addresses. The address x returned by the **load** command is the address where the image size is stored; it follows that the first element of the image is at address $x + 1$.

If there is no module named e in the repository, or if the module's contract is not τ, no module is loaded and the **load** command stores the value zero in x. We do not abort here; this, together with the module contract check, allows us to verify scenarios where the identity of the module being loaded is not known statically, such as when the module name is taken from user input.

Command **unload**(e) deallocates the loaded module at address e. It aborts if address e is not allocated, or if the value n at address e is not positive, or if any of the n subsequent addresses are not allocated; otherwise, it deallocates all of these $n + 1$ addresses.

3.1   Example Program

We illustrate the language by translating the example C program of Figure 1 into it; the result is shown in Figure 2.

The module repository of the example contains a single module, corresponding to module RamDisk of the C example. Its name is 100, its contract is module_init, and its image consists of seven values, the first four of which are the encodings of function values corresponding to functions $module\_init$, $module\_exit$, $myRead$, and $myWrite$, respectively, and the last three correspond to the global variables $vector$, $o.read$, and $o.write$ of the C example.

There are four minor differences between the C example and the formal example. The first is that instead of specifying the specific module RamDisk as the module to be loaded, the formal example uses the value of variable M, whose initial value is arbitrary; imagine it was initialized by the user. If the value of this variable equals 100, the module named 100 in the repository will be loaded; otherwise, the **load** command will return zero and the rest of the program will be skipped. We will verify that the program is safe for arbitrary initial values of the variables; and during verification of the main program, we will make no assumptions about the module repository other than that each module has been verified.

$Modules = \{$
  $(100, (\mathsf{module\_init},$
    $(\lfloor MI \rfloor, \lfloor ME \rfloor, \lfloor MR \rfloor, \lfloor MW \rfloor,$
    $V_0, OR_0, OW_0)))$
$\}$

$main =$
  m := **load** M as module_init;
  if m = 0 **then skip else** (
    init := m + 1; o := **call** init();
    write := [o + 1]; _ := **call** write(42);
    read := [o]; x := **call** read();
    assert(x = 42);
    exit := m + 2; _ := **call** exit();
    unload(m)
)

where
  $MI =$ **lambda** ()
    $[\mathsf{ip} + 5] := \mathsf{ip} + 2; [\mathsf{ip} + 6] := \mathsf{ip} + 3;$
    v := **cons**(0); [ip + 4] := v;
    result := ip + 5
  $ME =$ **lambda** () v := [ip + 3]; **dispose**(v)
  $MR =$ **lambda** () v := [ip + 2]; result := [v]
  $MW =$ **lambda** (x) v := [ip + 1]; [v] := x
  $V_0 = OR_0 = OW_0 = 0$

  skip = x := x
  assert$(b) =$ **if** b **then skip else** $[0] := 0$

Fig. 2. Example program in the formal language

```
// s = {M: 100, ...}, h = ∅
m := load M as module_init;
// s = {m: 1, ...}, h = {1: 7, 2: ⌊MI⌋, 3: ⌊ME⌋, 4: ⌊MR⌋, 5: ⌊MW⌋, 6: 0, 7: 0, 8: 0}
if m = 0 then skip else (
    // s = {m: 1, ...}, h = {1: 7, 2: ⌊MI⌋, 3: ⌊ME⌋, 4: ⌊MR⌋, 5: ⌊MW⌋, 6: 0, 7: 0, 8: 0}
    init := m + 1; o := call init();
    // s = {m: 1, init: 2, o: 7, ...}
    // h = {1: 7, 2: ⌊MI⌋, 3: ⌊ME⌋, 4: ⌊MR⌋, 5: ⌊MW⌋, 6: 50, 7: 4, 8: 5, 50: 0}
    write := [o + 1]; _ := call write(42);
    // s = {m: 1, init: 2, o: 7, write: 5, ...}
    // h = {1: 7, 2: ⌊MI⌋, 3: ⌊ME⌋, 4: ⌊MR⌋, 5: ⌊MW⌋, 6: 50, 7: 4, 8: 5, 50: 42}
    read := [o]; x := call read();
    // s = {m: 1, init: 2, o: 7, write: 5, read: 4, x: 42, ...}
    // h = {1: 7, 2: ⌊MI⌋, 3: ⌊ME⌋, 4: ⌊MR⌋, 5: ⌊MW⌋, 6: 50, 7: 4, 8: 5, 50: 42}
    assert(x = 42);
    exit := m + 2; _ := call exit();
    // s = {m: 1, exit: 3, ...}, h = {1: 7, 2: ⌊MI⌋, 3: ⌊ME⌋, 4: ⌊MR⌋, 5: ⌊MW⌋, 6: 50, 7: 4, 8: 5}
    unload(m)
    // s = {...}, h = ∅
)
```

Fig. 3. An example run of the example program. In this run, the value of M is 100, the module is allocated at address 1, and the "vector" is allocated at address 50.

The second difference is that in the formal example, the *module_init* and *module_exit* functions are at fixed offsets 0 and 1 in the module image, so their addresses can be obtained by adding 1, resp. 2 to the address returned by the **load** command.

The third difference is that in the formal example, for simplicity the contents of a "file" consist of a single integer. Therefore, instead of a byte vector, the module uses a simple memory cell to back its file abstraction. The write function takes the new file contents as its argument, and the read function returns the file contents as its return value.

The fourth difference is that the *testOps* function has been inlined into the main program.

Notice that the functions in the example module use their instruction pointer ip (i.e., the address of the function in memory) to compute the address of the module's other functions and global variables. For example, in the *module_init* function, the address of the global variable *vector* equals ip + 4 since *module_init* is the first element of the module image and *vector* is the fifth element. This is a common technique for achieving position-independent code.

An example run of the example program is shown in Figure 3. The symbols *MI*, *ME*, *MR*, and *MW* refer to the function values defined in Figure 2. Notice that the init call initializes the module's global variables and allocates the "vector" (at address 50). The write call updates the vector, and the exit call de-allocates it.

4   Specification and Verification Approach

In this section, we present an approach for specifying and modularly verifying modules and programs that satisfies the soundness and modularity goals identified in Section 2. The approach is separation logic [14] with abstract predicates [11], extended with

- special built-in abstract predicates **lib**, **module**$_0$, and **module** to allow programs that load and unload modules to reason about loaded modules abstractly, and
- *parameterized function types* and *partial predicate applications* for reasoning about function pointers in a way that allows abstraction over whether a function pointer points into an unloadable module.

We first introduce the specification language and we illustrate it with a specification for the example module. We then define the proof system and outline a proof of the example program.

4.1   Specification Language

As in separation logic and in Hoare logic, a correctness judgment is of the form $\{P\}$ c $\{Q\}$, where c is a command and P and Q are *assertions*, i.e. conditions on the program state. It means: if command c is executed in an initial state that satisfies precondition P, then it executes safely and if it terminates, the final state satisfies Q.

Assertions may contain the usual logical operators $\wedge, \vee, \exists$, and equality between assertion expressions. The assertion expressions include the program expressions as well as *logical variable occurrences*. As in Hoare logic, logical variables are universally quantified across correctness judgments, and serve to connect the precondition and the postcondition.

In Hoare logic, an assertion is interpreted under a store and a logical variable interpretation (a total function from logical variable names to integers). In separation logic, an assertion is interpreted under a store, a logical variable interpretation, and a heap. Separation logic introduces three operators to describe the heap: **emp** states that the heap is empty; the points-to assertion $E \mapsto E'$ states that the heap consists of a single memory cell at address E containing value E'; and the separating conjunction $A * A'$ states that the heap can be split up into two disjoint parts, such that one part satisfies A and the other part satisfies A'.

Abstract predicates (or *predicates* for short) are named, parameterized assertions. They serve to describe a piece of state abstractly, without revealing the details. For example, the predicate $Q(\ell, x)$ defined below describes the resources used by the example module after initialization, when loaded at address ℓ and when the file contents are x:

$$\textbf{predicate } Q(\ell, x) = \ell + 1 \mapsto \lfloor MI \rfloor * \ell + 2 \mapsto \lfloor ME \rfloor * \ell + 3 \mapsto \lfloor MR \rfloor$$
$$* \ell + 4 \mapsto \lfloor MW \rfloor * \exists v \bullet \ell + 5 \mapsto v * v \mapsto x$$

It encompasses the module image (at $\ell + 1$ through $\ell + 7$), plus the vector (at v), minus the memory cells containing the function pointers (at $\ell + 6$ and $\ell + 7$).

To specify function pointers, we introduce *function type definitions* and *function type assertions*. A function type definition associates a function type name with a precondition and a postcondition. A function type assertion $E : \tau$ states that function pointer E may be safely called with the contract associated with function type τ. We allow function types to be parameterized by a list of integer-valued parameters. Therefore, the general form of function type judgments is $E : \tau(\overline{E})$, where $\overline{E}$ are the function type arguments.

For example, consider the function type definition

$$\textbf{funtype } \mathsf{addN}(n)(x) \textbf{ req } \mathsf{P}() \textbf{ ens } \mathsf{P}() \wedge \mathsf{result} = x + n$$

where P is some predicate. It defines a function type addN with one function type parameter n. It applies to functions of one argument. Given this definition, the function type assertion $100 : \mathsf{addN}(5)$ implies that calling the function at address 100 with argument 10, in a state where P holds, returns value 15.

We need to be able to parameterize function types by predicates, in order to abstractly specify the state required by a function pointer. In order to avoid a type system, we assume an encoding of predicate names to integers, and we allow predicate assertions of the form $E(\overline{E})$, where E is the encoding of the predicate name and $\overline{E}$ are the predicate arguments. This way, we can use a predicate name as a function type argument.

For example, we can abstract the function type addN defined above over the predicate P by adding a function type parameter p:

$$\textbf{funtype } \mathsf{addN}'(p, n)(x) \textbf{ req } \mathsf{p}() \textbf{ ens } \mathsf{p}() \wedge \mathsf{result} = x + n$$

Given this definition, we can restate the earlier assertion as $100 : \mathsf{addN}'(P, 5)$.

In general, we wish to instantiate predicate-parameterized function types not just by fixed predicate names, but also by predicate names to which one or more arguments have already been applied. To enable this, we assume an encoding $\lfloor \cdot \rfloor$ of partial predicate applications, of the form $p(\overline{n})$, where $\overline{n}$ are the pre-applied predicate arguments, to integers. The meaning of a predicate assertion $E(\overline{E})$, where E is the encoding of a partial predicate application $p(\overline{n})$ and $\overline{E}$ evaluates to $\overline{m}$, is $p(\overline{nm})$.

For example, we can specify the read and write functions from the example program using the following function types:

$\textbf{funtype } \mathsf{read}(\mathsf{filePred})()$	$\textbf{funtype } \mathsf{write}(\mathsf{filePred})(x)$
$\textbf{req } \mathsf{filePred}(X)$	$\textbf{req } \mathsf{filePred}(\_)$
$\textbf{ens } \mathsf{filePred}(X) \wedge \mathsf{result} = X$	$\textbf{ens } \mathsf{filePred}(x)$

The function types are parameterized by a predicate that describes the resources that implement the file abstraction. The predicate takes as an argument the contents of the file. The contract of read states that it returns the current contents; the contract of write does not care about the old contents (denoted by the underscore, shorthand for $\exists y \bullet \mathsf{filePred}(y)$) and sets its argument x as the new contents.

As we will prove later, the read and write functions of the example module satisfy this contract when instantiated with the predicate Q defined above, partially applied to the location ℓ where the module was loaded. Formally, we will prove $\ell + 3 : \text{read}(Q(\ell))$ and $\ell + 4 : \text{write}(Q(\ell))$. (Remember that if the module is loaded at ℓ, then the *myRead* function is at $\ell + 3$ and the *myWrite* function is at $\ell + 4$.)

Besides parameterized function types and partial predicate applications, we introduce three special built-in abstract predicates to reason abstractly about modules. $\textbf{lib}(E, E')$ describes the memory cell holding the image size of a module named E' loaded at address E. $\textbf{module}_0(E, E')$ describes the memory cells holding the module image of the module named E' loaded at address E, in their initial state. Finally, $\textbf{module}(E, E')$ describes the memory cells that initially held the module image of the module named E' loaded at address E. The latter predicate states only the allocatedness of these cells; it does not describe their contents.

Formally, if $(M, (\tau, (v_1, \dots, v_n))) \in \textit{Modules}$, i.e., there is a module named M with contract τ and whose image consists of the n values $v_1, \dots, v_n$, then we have

$$\textbf{lib}(\ell, M) = \ell \mapsto n$$
$$\textbf{module}_0(\ell, M) = \ell + 1 \mapsto v_1 * \cdots * \ell + n \mapsto v_n$$
$$\textbf{module}(\ell, M) = \ell + 1 \mapsto \_ * \cdots * \ell + n \mapsto \_$$

Using these constructs, we can now specify the *module_init* and *module_exit* functions of the example program:

```
funtype module_init(l, m)()          funtype module_exit(o, filePred, l, m)()
  req module₀(l, m)                     req o ↦ _ * o + 1 ↦ _ * filePred(_)
  ens ∃filePred, r, w •                  ens module(l, m)
    result ↦ r * result + 1 ↦ w * filePred(0)
    ∧ r : read(filePred) ∧ w : write(filePred)
    ∧ l + 2 : module_exit(result, filePred, l, m)
```

The function type module_init serves as the module's contract; the auxiliary function types module_exit, read, and write are referred to in the definition of module_init. As with all function types that serve as module contracts, module_init is parameterized by the address l where the module is loaded and the module name m. The precondition requires the module's image in its initial state. The postcondition states that the return value points to two consecutive memory cells, the first holding a pointer to a read function and the second a pointer to a write function. It further provides the resources filePred(0) that the read and write functions require; the predicate argument 0 indicates the file contents. The module_exit function takes back the memory cells holding the function pointers, as well as the resources denoted by filePred(_), and yields back the module image, in an unspecified state, ready to be unloaded.

4.2   Proof System

Our proof system extends separation logic's assertion logic with rules for deriving function type judgments and for folding and unfolding predicate assertions and

A-FunType
funtype $\tau(\overline{y})(\overline{x})$ **req** P **ens** Q
$$\frac{\vdash P[\overline{v}/\overline{y}] \Rightarrow \ell \mapsto \lfloor \mathbf{lambda}\ (\overline{x})\ c \rfloor * \mathbf{true} \quad \{P[\overline{v}/\overline{y}] \wedge \mathsf{ip} = \ell\}\ c\ \{Q[\overline{v}/\overline{y}]\}}{\vdash \ell : \tau(\overline{v})}$$

A-PredAsn
predicate $p(\overline{y}) = A$
$$\frac{}{\vdash p(\overline{v})(\overline{w}) \Leftrightarrow A[\overline{vw}/\overline{y}]}$$

A-Module-Unfold
$$\frac{(M, (\tau, (v_1, \ldots, v_m))) \in Modules}{\vdash \quad \mathbf{module}_0(y, M) \Rightarrow \\ y + 1 \mapsto v_1 * \ldots * y + m \mapsto v_m}$$

A-Module-Fold
$$\frac{(M, (\tau, (v_1, \ldots, v_m))) \in Modules}{\vdash \quad y + 1 \mapsto \_ * \cdots * y + m \mapsto \_ \\ \Rightarrow \mathbf{module}(y, M)}$$

C-Call
$$\frac{\mathbf{funtype}\ \tau(\overline{y})(\overline{x})\ \mathbf{req}\ P\ \mathbf{ens}\ Q}{\{e : \tau(\overline{y}) \wedge \overline{e} = \overline{z} \wedge P[\overline{z}/\overline{x}]\}\ x := \mathbf{call}\ e(\overline{e})\ \{Q[\overline{z}/\overline{x}, x/\mathsf{result}]\}}$$

C-Load
$$\{\mathbf{emp} \wedge e = y\}$$
$$x := \mathbf{load}\ e\ \mathbf{as}\ \tau$$
$$\left\{ \begin{array}{l} x = 0 \wedge \mathbf{emp}\ \vee \\ x > 0 \wedge \mathbf{lib}(x, y) * \mathbf{module}_0(x, y) \wedge x + 1 : \tau(x, y) \end{array} \right\}$$

C-Unload
$$\{\mathbf{lib}(e, y) * \mathbf{module}(e, y)\}$$
$$\mathbf{unload}(e)$$
$$\{\mathbf{emp}\}$$

Fig. 4. Proof rules

module assertions; and it extends separation logic's program logic with rules for verifying function pointer call and module load and unload commands. The new rules are shown in Figure 4.

Per rule A-FunType, proving a function type assertion $\ell : \tau(\overline{v})$ requires proving a) that the function type's precondition implies that there is some function value with the correct number of parameters at location ℓ, and b) that this function value's body satisfies the function type's contract.

Using this rule and rule A-PredAsn, we can easily prove the assertions $\ell + 3 :$ read$(Q(\ell))$ and $\ell + 4 :$ write$(Q(\ell))$, which express the correctness of the read and write functions of the example module. Indeed, $Q(\ell, X)$ implies $\ell + 3 \mapsto \lfloor MR \rfloor * \mathbf{true}$, and it is a straightforward separation logic exercise to verify the body of MR against the contract $\{Q(\ell, X)\}$ · $\{Q(\ell, X) \wedge \mathsf{result} = X\}$; similarly for the write function.

By additionally using rule A-Module-Fold, we can prove the assertion $\ell + 2 :$ module_exit$(\ell + 6, Q(\ell), \ell, 100)$, where 100 is the name of the example module. This states the correctness of the module exit function of the example module. Finally, using all of these results and rule A-Module-Unfold, we can prove the correctness of the example module: $\ell + 1 :$ module_init$(\ell, 100)$.

This correctness condition, which our proof system imposes on all modules in the module repository, justifies Rule C-Load: it states that the module's entry point satisfies the module's contract, instantiated with the address where the module is loaded and the module's name.

$\{\mathbf{emp}\}$
m := **load** M **as** module_init;
$\{m = 0 \wedge \mathbf{emp} \vee \mathbf{lib}(m, M) * \mathbf{module}_0(m, M) \wedge m + 1 : \mathsf{module\_init}(m, M)\}$
if m = 0 **then skip else** (
    $\{\mathbf{lib}(m, M) * \mathbf{module}_0(m, M) \wedge m + 1 : \mathsf{module\_init}(m, M)\}$
    init := m + 1; o := **call** init();
    $\left\{ \begin{array}{l} \mathbf{lib}(m, M) * \exists p, r, w \bullet o \mapsto r * o + 1 \mapsto w * p(0) \wedge \\ \quad r : \mathsf{read}(p) \wedge w : \mathsf{write}(p) \wedge m + 2 : \mathsf{module\_exit}(o, p, m, M) \end{array} \right\}$
    write := [o + 1]; _ := **call** write(42);
    $\left\{ \begin{array}{l} \mathbf{lib}(m, M) * \exists p, r, w \bullet o \mapsto r * o + 1 \mapsto w * p(42) \wedge \\ \quad r : \mathsf{read}(p) \wedge w : \mathsf{write}(p) \wedge m + 2 : \mathsf{module\_exit}(o, p, m, M) \end{array} \right\}$
    read := [o]; x := **call** read();
    $\left\{ \begin{array}{l} \mathbf{lib}(m, M) * \exists p, r, w \bullet o \mapsto r * o + 1 \mapsto w * p(42) \wedge \\ \quad r : \mathsf{read}(p) \wedge w : \mathsf{write}(p) \wedge m + 2 : \mathsf{module\_exit}(o, p, m, M) \wedge x = 42 \end{array} \right\}$
    assert(x = 42);
    exit := m + 2; _ := **call** exit();
    $\{\mathbf{lib}(m, M) * \mathbf{module}(m, M)\}$
    unload(m)
)
$\{\mathbf{emp}\}$

Fig. 5. Proof outline of the example program

Figure 5 shows a proof outline for the main program. This proof makes no assumptions about the module repository, other than that each module satisfies its contract.

Our proof system is sound: if each module in the module repository and the main program are provably correct, then the main program does not abort.

A full formal treatment of the specification and verification approach is in the extended version of this paper [9]. We developed a mechanically checked proof of its soundness in Coq (see http://www.cs.kuleuven.be/~bartj/unload/).

5   Verification Tool

We implemented the approach in our prototype verifier, VeriFast [8]. VeriFast takes a set of C and Java source files, annotated with preconditions, postconditions, loop invariants, mathematical datatype and function definitions, separation logic predicate definitions, inductive proofs in the form of lemma routines, and in-line explicit proof steps, and then symbolically executes each function in turn, where the symbolic state consists of the symbolic heap, the symbolic store, and the path condition. The symbolic heap is a separating conjunction of *heap chunks* of the form $p(\overline{a})$, where p is a term of first-order logic denoting the name of a separation logic predicate or a partially applied predicate, and $\overline{a}$ are terms denoting the predicate arguments. The symbolic store maps local variable names to terms, and the path condition is a set of formulae that are true on the current execution path. The SMT solver Z3 [6] is used to check boolean conjuncts in assertions, whereas spatial conjuncts, i.e. predicate assertions, are dealt with in the tool itself through simple pattern matching with the symbolic heap.

In order to fit more naturally with the C language, the approach as implemented in VeriFast differs from the formalization in this paper as follows.

Firstly, module assertions unfold to a more abstract representation of the module image. In particular, all code of a module M is represented using a built-in predicate $\mathbf{code}(M)$. For example:

$$\mathbf{module}_0(\mathsf{RamDisk}) = \mathbf{code}(\mathsf{RamDisk}) * vector \mapsto 0 * o.read \mapsto 0 * o.write \mapsto 0$$

Note that a VeriFast module name such as RamDisk denotes both the address where the module was loaded and the module name proper, which identifies its contents.

Secondly, the derivation of a function type judgment $f : \tau(\overline{v})$ for a function f declared in an unloadable module M is split into two steps. In a first step, f is verified with respect to its declared contract, using the following proof rule.

$$\frac{P \Rightarrow [\pi]\mathbf{code}(M) * P' \qquad \{P'\}\, c\, \{Q'\} \qquad [\pi]\mathbf{code}(M) * Q' \Rightarrow Q}{M \vdash \mathbf{fun}\ f(\overline{x})\ \mathbf{req}\ P\ \mathbf{ens}\ Q\ \mathbf{do}\ c}$$

That is, the declared precondition P must imply some fractional (i.e., read-only) permission π for the module's code, and the function's body c is verified against the remainder of the precondition. The removed code fraction is added back to verify the declared postcondition Q.

In a second step, VeriFast simply verifies that the declared contract implies the function type contract:

$$\frac{\mathbf{fun}\ f(\overline{x})\ \mathbf{req}\ P\ \mathbf{ens}\ Q\ \mathbf{do}\ c}{\qquad \mathbf{funtype}\ \tau(\overline{y})(\overline{x})\ \mathbf{req}\ P'\ \mathbf{ens}\ Q' \qquad P'[\overline{v}/\overline{y}] \Rightarrow P \qquad Q \Rightarrow Q'[\overline{v}/\overline{y}]}{f : \tau(\overline{v})}$$

Notice that this latter step does not need to take unloadability into account.

We used the approach of this paper to verify a small multithreaded server that allows clients to concurrently load DLLs, unload DLLs, and use services provided by the DLLs, mimicking operating system kernels that may dynamically load and unload device drivers. Specifically, a loaded DLL can register "devices" with the "kernel", by supplying function pointers that open, read, write, and close the device. Multiple concurrent clients can then access these devices. A reference counting mechanism prevents a module from being unloaded while devices provided by the module are open; furthermore, it is verified that a module unregisters all devices it registered before it unloads. Considering the complexity of this program, the annotation overhead is not excessive: 467 lines of annotations for 245 lines of code. Our tool verifies this program in 0.75 seconds. Website: http://www.cs.kuleuven.be/~bartj/verifast/.

6   Conclusion and Related Work

We presented the first approach for integrating verification of unloadable modules into a semi-automatic verification tool for C. It supports global variables, and its approach to function pointers enables mixing unloadable and non-unloadable code transparently. We reported on verifying a small but complex kernel-like program using our implementation. A formalization, a machine-checked soundness proof, the implementation, and the verified code are available on line.

Cai *et al.* [3] propose a separation-logic-based approach for verifying self-modifying assembly language programs. They formalize a generic target machine in Coq, and instantiate it with x86 and MIPS. They prove a number of assembly programs, including a boot loader, that loads a kernel image from disk and executes it. Their proof rule for well-formedness of a code block with respect to a given precondition is very similar to our A-FUNTYPE rule: the precondition must imply the presence of some code that executes safely. Their soundness proof uses a notion of safety for n steps, very similar to ours. A more recent work in a similar vein is Myreen's [10] on verifying a just-in-time compiler on x86, this time using Isabelle/HOL. Our main contribution with respect to these results is to adapt these ideas to C's system of modules, and to integrate it into a program verification tool for C.

Another, more theoretical, line of work on separation logic for stored code goes under the name of separation logic for *higher-order store* [13, 2, 15]. Instead of representing stored code as an integer-encoded syntactic lambda expression or machine instruction sequence, the authors adopt a higher-order heap: the heap maps addresses to integers and to *semantic commands*, which are themselves relations from heaps to heaps. This recursive domain equation is solved using techniques from category theory and domain theory, leading to a less accessible formalization. Another difference in focus is that the authors attempt not just to abstract over state required by stored code, e.g. using abstract predicates, but to *hide* such requirements, using *higher-order frame rules*. Whereas such hiding is preferable over mere abstraction, there are unsolved problems of modularity [12], and furthermore concurrency is not currently supported. Our contribution here is an instantiation in the context of C's modules, and a simpler formalization.

Acknowledgements

The authors would like to thank Raoul Strackx for helpful comments. This research is partially funded by the Interuniversity Attraction Poles Programme Belgian State, Belgian Science Policy, by the Research Fund K.U.Leuven, and by the EU FP7 project SecureChange.

References

[1] Berdine, J., Calcagno, C., O'Hearn, P.W.: Smallfoot: Modular automatic assertion checking with separation logic. In: de Boer, F.S., Bonsangue, M.M., Graf, S., de Roever, W.-P. (eds.) FMCO 2005. LNCS, vol. 4111, pp. 115–137. Springer, Heidelberg (2006)

[2] Birkedal, L., Reus, B., Schwinghammer, J., Yang, H.: A simple model of separation logic for higher-order store. In: Aceto, L., Damgård, I., Goldberg, L.A., Halldórsson, M.M., Ingólfsdóttir, A., Walukiewicz, I. (eds.) ICALP 2008, Part II. LNCS, vol. 5126, pp. 348–360. Springer, Heidelberg (2008)

[3] Hongxu Cai, Zhong Shao, and Alexander Vaynberg. Certified self-modifying code. In: PLDI (2007)

[4] Cohen, E., Dahlweid, M., Hillebrand, M., Leinenbach, D., Moskal, M., Santen, T., Schulte, W., Tobies, S.: VCC: A practical system for verifying concurrent C. In: Berghofer, S., Nipkow, T., Urban, C., Wenzel, M. (eds.) TPHOLs 2009. LNCS, vol. 5674, pp. 23–42. Springer, Heidelberg (2009)

[5] Condit, J., Hackett, B., Lahiri, S.K., Qadeer, S.: Unifying type checking and property checking for low-level code. In: POPL (2009)

[6] de Moura, L., Bjørner, N.S.: Z3: An efficient SMT solver. In: Ramakrishnan, C.R., Rehof, J. (eds.) TACAS 2008. LNCS, vol. 4963, pp. 337–340. Springer, Heidelberg (2008)

[7] Filliâtre, J.-C., Marché, C.: The why/Krakatoa/Caduceus platform for deductive program verification. In: Damm, W., Hermanns, H. (eds.) CAV 2007. LNCS, vol. 4590, pp. 173–177. Springer, Heidelberg (2007)

[8] Jacobs, B., Smans, J., Piessens, F.: A quick tour of the veriFast program verifier. In: Ueda, K. (ed.) APLAS 2010. LNCS, vol. 6461, pp. 304–311. Springer, Heidelberg (2010)

[9] Jacobs, B., Smans, J., Piessens, F.: Verification of unloadable modules (Extended version). Technical Report CW604, Dept. Computer Science, Katholieke Universiteit Leuven (March 2011)

[10] Myreen, M.O.: Verified just-in-time compiler on x86. In: POPL (2010)

[11] Parkinson, M., Bierman, G.: Separation logic and abstraction. In: POPL (2005)

[12] Pottier, F.: Three comments on the anti-frame rule (July 2009) (unpublished note)

[13] Reus, B., Schwinghammer, J.: Separation logic for higher-order store. In: Computer Science Logic (2006)

[14] Reynolds, J.C.: Separation logic: a logic for shared mutable data structures. In: LICS 2002 (2002)

[15] Schwinghammer, J., Birkedal, L., Reus, B., Yang, H.: Nested hoare triples and frame rules for higher-order store. In: Grädel, E., Kahle, R. (eds.) CSL 2009. LNCS, vol. 5771, pp. 440–454. Springer, Heidelberg (2009)

A Multi-encoding Approach for
LTL Symbolic Satisfiability Checking[*]

Kristin Y. Rozier[1,2,**] and Moshe Y. Vardi[2]

[1] NASA Ames Research Center, Moffett Field CA, 94035, USA
Kristin.Y.Rozier@nasa.gov
http://ti.arc.nasa.gov/profile/kyrozier/
[2] Rice University, Houston, Texas 77005, USA
vardi@cs.rice.edu
http://www.cs.rice.edu/v̄ardi/

Abstract. Formal behavioral specifications written early in the system-design process and communicated across all design phases have been shown to increase the efficiency, consistency, and quality of the system under development. To prevent introducing design or verification errors, it is crucial to test specifications for *satisfiability*. Our focus here is on specifications expressed in linear temporal logic (LTL).

We introduce a novel encoding of symbolic transition-based Büchi automata and a novel, "sloppy," transition encoding, both of which result in improved scalability. We also define novel BDD variable orders based on tree decomposition of formula parse trees. We describe and extensively test a new multi-encoding approach utilizing these novel encoding techniques to create 30 encoding variations. We show that our novel encodings translate to significant, sometimes exponential, improvement over the current standard encoding for symbolic LTL satisfiability checking.

1 Introduction

In *property-based design* formal properties, written in temporal logics such as LTL [31], are written early in the system-design process and communicated across all design phases to increase the efficiency, consistency, and quality of the system under development [34, 36]. Property-based design and other design-for-verification techniques capture design intent precisely, and use formal logic properties both to guide the design process and to integrate verification into the design process [24]. The shift to specifying desired system behavior in terms of formal logic properties risks introducing specification errors in this very initial phase of system design, raising the need for *property assurance* [30, 34].

---

[*] A full version of this paper with appendices is available at http://ti.arc.nasa.gov/m/profile/kyrozier/papers/RozierVardiFM2011.pdf.
[**] Work contributing to this paper was completed at Rice University, Cambridge University, and NASA, was supported in part by the Shared University Grid at Rice (SUG@R), and was funded by NSF under Grant EIA-0216467, NASA's Airspace Systems Program, and a partnership between Rice University, Sun Microsystems, and Sigma Solutions, Inc.

M. Butler and W. Schulte (Eds.): FM 2011, LNCS 6664, pp. 417–431, 2011.
© Springer-Verlag Berlin Heidelberg 2011

The need for checking for errors in formal LTL properties expressing desired system behavior first arose in the context of model checking, where *vacuity checking* aims at reducing the likelihood that a property that is satisfied by the model under verification is an erroneous property [2, 27]. Property assurance is more challenging at the initial phases of property-based design, before a model of the implementation has been specified. *Inherent vacuity checking* is a set of sanity checks that can be applied to a set of temporal properties, even before a model of the system has been developed, but many possible errors cannot be detected by inherent vacuity checking [19].

A stronger sanity check for a set of temporal properties is LTL *realizability* checking, in which we test whether there is an open system that satisfies all the properties in the set [32], but such a test is very expensive computationally. In LTL *satisfiability* checking, we test whether there is a closed system that satisfies all the properties in the set. The satisfiability test is weaker than the realizability test, but its complexity is lower; it has the same complexity as LTL model checking [39]. In fact, LTL satisfiability checking can be implemented via LTL model checking; see below.

Indeed, the need for LTL satisfiability checking is widely recognized [14, 23, 25, 28, 35]. Foremost, it serves to ensure that the behavioral description of a system is internally consistent and neither over- or under-constrained. If an LTL property is either *valid*, or *unsatisfiable* this must be due to an error. Consider, for example, the specification $always(b_1 \rightarrow eventually\ b_2)$, where b_1 and b_2 are propositional formulas. If b_2 is a tautology, then this property is valid. If b_2 is a contradiction, then this property is unsatisfiable. Furthermore, the collective set of properties describing a system must be satisfiable, to avoid contradictions between different requirements. Satisfiability checking is particularly important when the set of properties describing the design intent continues to evolve, as properties are added and refined, and have to be checked repeatedly. Because of the need to consider large sets of properties, it is critical that the satisfiability test be *scalable*, and able to handle complex temporal properties. This is challenging, as LTL satisfiability is known to be PSPACE-complete [39].

As pointed out in [35], satisfiability checking can be performed via model checking: a *universal model* (that is, a model that allows all possible traces) does not satisfy a linear temporal property $\neg f$ precisely when f is satisfiable. In [35] we explored the effectiveness of model checkers as LTL satisfiability checkers. We compared there the performance of explicit-state and symbolic model checkers. Both use the automata-theoretic approach [43] but in a different way. Explicit-state model checkers translate LTL formulas to Büchi automata explicitly and then use an explicit graph-search algorithm [11]. For satisfiability checking, the construction of the automaton is the more demanding task. Symbolic model checkers construct symbolic encodings of automata and then use a symbolic nonemptiness test. The symbolic construction of the automaton is easy, but the nonemptiness test is computationally demanding. The extensive set of experiments described in [35] showed that the symbolic approach to LTL satisfiability is significantly superior to the explicit-state approach in terms of scalability.

In the context of explicit-state model checking, there has been extensive research on optimized construction of automata from LTL formulas [12, 13, 20, 21, 22, 38, 40, 41], where a typical goal is to minimize the size of constructed automata [42]. Optimizing the construction of symbolic automata is more difficult, as the size of the symbolic representation does not correspond directly to its optimality. An initial symbolic encoding of automata was proposed in [6], but the optimized encoding we call *CGH*, proposed by Clarke, Grumberg, and Hamaguchi [10], has become the de facto standard encoding. CGH encoding is used by model checkers such as CadenceSMV and NuSMV, and has been extended to symbolic encodings of industrial specification languages [9]. Surprisingly, there has been little follow-up research on this topic.

In this paper, we propose novel symbolic LTL-to-automata translations and utilize them in a new multi-encoding approach to achieve significant, sometimes exponential, improvement over the current standard encoding for LTL satisfiability checking. First we introduce and prove the correctness of a novel encoding of symbolic automata inspired by optimized constructions of explicit automata [12, 22]. While the CGH encoding uses *Generalized Büchi Automata* (GBA), our new encoding is based on *Transition-Based Büchi Automata* (TGBA). Second, inspired by work on symbolic satisfiability checking for modal logic [29], we introduce here a novel *sloppy* encoding of symbolic automata, as opposed to the *fussy* encoding used in CGH. Sloppy encoding uses looser constraints, which sometimes results in smaller BDDs. The sloppy approach can be applied both to GBA-based and TGBA-based encodings, provided that one uses negation-normal form (NNF), [40], rather than the Boolean normal form (BNF) used in CGH. Finally, we introduce several new variable-ordering schemes, based on tree decomposition of the LTL parse tree, inspired by observations that relate tree decompositions to BDD variable ordering [17]. The combination of GBA/TGBA, fussy/sloppy, BNF/NNF, and different variable orders yields a space of 30 possible configurations of symbolic automata encodings. (Not all combinations yield viable configurations.)

Since the value of novel encoding techniques lies in increased *scalability*, we evaluate our novel encodings in the context of LTL satisfiability checking, utilizing a comprehensive and challenging collection of widely-used benchmark formulas [7, 14, 23, 35]. For each formula, we perform satisfiability checking using all 30 encodings. (We use CadenceSMV as our experimental platform.) Our results demonstrate conclusively that no encoding performs best across our large benchmark suite. Furthermore, no single approach–GBA vs. TGBA, fussy vs. sloppy, BNF vs. NNF, or any one variable order, is dominant. This is consistent with the observation made by others [1, 42], that in the context of symbolic techniques one typically does not find a "winning" algorithmic configuration. In response, we developed a multi-encoding tool, PANDA, which runs several encodings in parallel, terminating when the first process returns. Our experiments demonstrate conclusively that the multi-encoding approach using the novel encodings invented in this paper achieves substantial improvement over CGH, the current standard encoding; in fact PANDA significantly bested the native LTL model checker built into CadenceSMV.

The structure of this paper is as follows. We review the CGH encoding [10] in Section 2. Next, in Section 3, we describe our novel symbolic TGBA encoding. We introduce our novel sloppy encoding and our new methods for choosing BDD variable orderings and discuss our space of symbolic encoding techniques in Section 4. After setting up our scalability experiment in Section 5, we present our test results in Section 6, followed by a discussion in Section 7. Though our construction can be used with different symbolic model checking tools, in this paper, we follow the convention of [10] and give examples of all constructions using the SMV syntax.

2 Preliminaries

We assume familiarity with LTL [16]; For convenience, Appendix A defines LTL semantics. We use two normal forms:

Definition 1. Boolean Normal Form (BNF) *rewrites the input formula to use only* $\neg$, $\vee$, X, U, *and* F. *In other words, we replace* $\wedge$, $\rightarrow$, R, *and* G *with their equivalents:*

$$g_1 \wedge g_2 \equiv \neg(\neg g_1 \vee \neg g_2) \qquad\qquad g_1 \, R \, g_2 \equiv \neg(\neg g_1 \, U \, \neg g_2)$$

$$g_1 \rightarrow g_2 \equiv \neg g_1 \vee g \qquad\qquad G g_1 \equiv \neg F \neg g_1$$

Definition 2. Negation Normal Form (NNF) *pushes negation inwards until only atomic propositions are negated, using the following rules:*

$$\neg \neg g \equiv g$$
$$\neg(g_1 \wedge g_2) \equiv (\neg g_1) \vee (\neg g_2)$$
$$\neg(g_1 \vee g_2) \equiv (\neg g_1) \wedge (\neg g_2)$$
$$(g_1 \rightarrow g_2) \equiv (\neg g_1) \vee g_2$$

$$\neg(X g) \equiv X(\neg g)$$
$$\neg(g_1 U g_2) \equiv (\neg g_1 R \neg g_2)$$
$$\neg(g_1 R g_2) \equiv (\neg g_1 U \neg g_2)$$
$$\neg(G g) \equiv F(\neg g)$$
$$\neg(F g) \equiv G(\neg g)$$

In automata-theoretic model checking, we represent LTL formulas with Büchi automata.

Definition 3. *A* **Generalized Büchi Automaton** *(GBA) is a quintuple* $(Q, \Sigma, \delta, Q_0, F)$, *where:*

- Q *is a finite set of states.*
- Σ *is a finite alphabet.*
- $\delta \subseteq Q \times \Sigma \times Q$ *is a transition relation.*
- $Q_0 \subseteq Q$ *is a set of initial states.*
- $F \subseteq 2^Q$ *is a set of accepting state sets.*

A run of a Büchi automaton A over an infinite trace $\pi = \pi_0, \pi_1, \pi_2, \ldots \in \Sigma$ *is a sequence* $q_0, q_1, q_2, \ldots$ *of states such that* $q_0 \in Q_0$, *and* $\langle q_i, \pi_i, q_{i+1} \rangle \in \delta$ *for all* $i \geq 0$. *A accepts* π *if the run over* π *visits states in every set in F infinitely often. We denote the set of infinite traces accepted by A by* $\mathcal{L}_\omega(A)$.

A trace satisfying LTL formula f is an infinite run over the alphabet $\Sigma = 2^{Prop}$, where $Prop$ is the underlying set of atomic propositions. We denote by $models(f)$ the set of traces satisfying f. The next theorem relates the expressive power of LTL to that of Büchi automata.

Theorem 1. *[44] Given an LTL formula f, we can construct a generalized Büchi automaton $A_f = \langle Q, \Sigma, \delta, Q_0, F \rangle$ such that $|Q|$ is in $2^{O(|f|)}$, $\Sigma = 2^{Prop}$, and $\mathcal{L}_\omega(A_f)$ is exactly models(f).*

This theorem reduces LTL satisfiability checking to automata-theoretic nonemptiness checking, as f is satisfiable iff $models(f) \neq \emptyset$ iff $\mathcal{L}_\omega(A_f) \neq \emptyset$.

LTL satisfiability checking relates to LTL model checking as follows. We use a *universal model* M that generates all traces over $Prop$ such that $\mathcal{L}_\omega(M) = (2^{Prop})^\omega$. The code for this model appears in [35] and Appendix B. We now have that M does *not* satisfy $\neg f$ iff f is satisfiable. We use a symbolic model checker to check the formula $\neg f$ against M; f is satisfiable precisely when the model checker finds a counterexample.

CGH encoding In this paper we focus on LTL to symbolic Büchi automata compilation. We recap the CGH encoding[10], which assumes that the formula f is in BNF, and then forms a symbolic GBA. We first define the *CGH-closure* of an LTL formula f as the set of all subformulas of f (including f itself), where we also add the formula $X(g \mathcal{U} h)$ for each subformula of the form $g \mathcal{U} h$. The X-formulas in the CGH-closure of f are called *elementary* formulas.

We declare a Boolean SMV variable EL_{Xg} for each elementary formula Xg in the CGH-closure of f. Also, each atomic proposition in f is declared as a Boolean SMV variable. We define an auxiliary variable S_h for every formula h in the CGH-closure of f. (Auxiliary variables are substituted away by SMV and do not required allocated BDD variables.) The characteristic function for an auxiliary variable S_h is defined as follows:

$S_h = p$ if $p \in AP$ $S_h = !S_g$ if $h = \neg g$ $S_h = S_{g1}|S_{g2}$ if $h = g_1 \vee g_2$
$S_h = EL_h$ if h is a formula Xg $S_h = S_{g2}|(S_{g1} \& S_{X(g1 \mathcal{U} g2)})$ if $h = g_1 \mathcal{U} g_2$

We now generate the SMV model M_f:

```
MODULE main
VAR
  a: boolean; /*declare a Boolean var for each atomic prop in f */
  EL_Xg: boolean; /*declare a Boolean var for every formula Xg in the CGH-closure*/
DEFINE  /*auxiliary vars according to characteristic function */
  S_h := ...
TRANS /*for every formula Xg in the CGH-closure, add a transition constraint*/
  (S_Xg = next(S_g))
FAIRNESS  !S_gUh | S_h /*for each subformula gUh */
FAIRNESS  TRUE /*or a generic fairness condition otherwise*/
SPEC      !(S_f & EG true) /*end with a SPEC statement*/
```

The traces of M_f correspond to the accepting runs of A_f, starting from arbitrary states. Thus, satisfiability of f corresponds to nonemptiness of M_f, starting from an initial state. We can model check such nonemptiness with SPEC `!(S_f & EG true)`. A counterexample is an infinite trace starting at a state where S_f holds. Thus, the model checker returns a counterexample that is a trace satisfying f.

Remark 1. *While the syntax we use is shared by CadenceSMV and NuSMV, the precise semantics of CTL model checking in these model checkers is not fully documented and there are some subtle but significant differences between the two tools. Therefore, we use CadenceSMV semantics here and describe these subtleties in Appendix C.*

3   A Symbolic Transition-Based Generalized Büchi Automata (TGBA) Encoding

We now introduce a novel symbolic encoding, referred to as TGBA, inspired by the explicit-state transition-based Generalized Büchi automata of [22]. Such automata are used by SPOT [15], which was shown experimentally [35] to be the best explicit LTL translator for satisfiability checking.

Definition 4. *A* **Transition-Based Generalized Büchi Automaton** *(TGBA) is a quintuple* $(Q, \Sigma, \delta, Q_0, F)$, *where:*

- $\delta \subseteq Q \times \Sigma \times Q$ is a transition relation.

- Q is a finite set of states.
- $Q_0 \subseteq Q$ is a set of initial states.
- Σ is a finite alphabet.
- $F \subseteq 2^\delta$ is a set of accepting transitions.

A run of a TGBA over an infinite trace $\pi = \pi_0, \pi_1, \pi_2, \ldots \in \Sigma$ is a sequence $\langle q_0, \pi_0, q_1 \rangle$, $\langle q_1, \pi_1, q_2 \rangle$, $\langle q_2, \pi_2, q_3 \rangle$, $\ldots$ of transitions in δ such that $q_0 \in Q_0$. The automaton accepts π if it has a run over π that traverses some transition from each set in F infinitely often.

The next theorem relates the expressive power of LTL to that of TGBAs.

Theorem 2. [12, 22] Given an LTL formula f, we can construct a TGBA $A_f = \langle Q, \Sigma, \delta, Q_0, F \rangle$ such that $|Q|$ is in $2^{O(|f|)}$, $\Sigma = 2^{Prop}$, and $\mathcal{L}_\omega(A_f)$ is exactly models(f).

Expressing acceptance conditions in terms of transitions rather than states enables a significant reduction in the size of the automata corresponding to LTL formulas [12, 22].

Our new encoding of symbolic automata, based on TGBAs, assumes that the input formula f is in NNF. (This is due to the way that the satisfaction of $\mathcal{U}$-formulas is handled by means of promise variables; see below.) As in CGH, we first define the *closure* of an LTL formula f. In the case of TGBAs, however, we simply define the closure to be the set of all subformulas of f (including f itself). Note that, unlike in the CGH encoding, $\mathcal{U}$- and $\mathcal{F}$- formulas do not require the introduction of new $\mathcal{X}$-formulas.

The set of elementary formulas now contains: f; all $\mathcal{U}$-, $\mathcal{R}$-, $\mathcal{F}$-, $\mathcal{G}$-, and $\mathcal{GF}$-subformulas in the closure of f, as well as all subformulas g where $\mathcal{X}g$ is in the closure of f. Note that we treat the common $\mathcal{GF}$ combination as a single operator.

Again, we declare a Boolean SMV variable EL_g for every elementary formula g as well as Boolean variables for each atomic proposition in f. In addition, we declare a Boolean SMV *promise variable* P_g for every $\mathcal{U}$-, $\mathcal{F}$-, and $\mathcal{GF}$-subformula in the closure. These formulas are used to define fairness conditions. Intuitively, P_g holds when g is a promise for the future that is not yet fulfilled. If P_g does not hold, then the promise must be fulfilled immediately. To ensure satisfaction of eventualities we require that each promise variable P_g is false infinitely often. The TGBA encoding creates fewer EL variables than the CGH encoding, but it does add promise variables.

Again, we define an auxiliary variable S_h for every formula h in the closure of f. The characteristic function for S_h is defined as in the CGH encoding, with the following changes:

$$S_h = S_{g1} \& S_{g2} \text{ if } h = g_1 \wedge g_2$$
$$S_h = next(EL_g) \text{ if } h = \mathcal{X}g$$
$$S_h = S_{g2} | (S_{g1} \& P_{g1 \, \mathcal{U} \, g2} \& (next(EL_{g1 \, \mathcal{U} \, g2}))) \text{ if } h = g_1 \, \mathcal{U} \, g_2$$
$$S_h = S_{g2} \& (S_{g1} | (next(EL_{g1 \, \mathcal{R} \, g2}))) \text{ if } h = g_1 \, \mathcal{R} \, g_2$$
$$S_h = S_g \& (next(EL_{\mathcal{G} \, g})) \text{ if } h = \mathcal{G} \, g$$
$$S_h = S_g | (P_{\mathcal{F} \, g} \& next(EL_{\mathcal{F} \, g})) \text{ if } h = \mathcal{F} \, g$$
$$S_h = (next(EL_{\mathcal{GF} \, g})) \& (S_g | P_{\mathcal{GF} \, g}) \text{ if } h = \mathcal{GF} \, g$$

Since we reason directly over the temporal subformulas of f (and not over $\mathcal{X}g$ for temporal subformula g as in CGH), the transition relation associates elementary formulas with matching elements of our characteristic function. Finally, we generate our symbolic TGBA; here is our SMV model M_f:

```
MODULE main
VAR /*declare a boolean variable for each atomic proposition in f*/
  a : boolean;
  ...
VAR /*declare a new variable for each elementary formula*/
  EL_f : boolean;      /*f is the input LTL formula*/
  EL_g1 : boolean;     /*g is an X-, F-, U-, or GF-formula*/
  ...
DEFINE /*characteristic function definition*/
  S_g = ...
  ...
TRANS /*for each EL-var, generate a line here*/
  ( EL_g1 = S_g1 ) &   /*a line for every EL variable*/
  ...
FAIRNESS    (!P_g1) /*fairness constraint for each promise variable*/
  ...
FAIRNESS    TRUE  /*only needed if there are no promise variables*/
SPEC !(EL_f & EG TRUE)
```

Symbolic TGBAs can only be created for NNF formulas because the model checker tries to guess a sequence of values for each of the promise variables to satisfy the subformulas, which does not work for negative $\mathcal{U}$-formulas. (This is also the case for explicit state model checking; SPOT also requires NNF for TGBA encoding [12].) Consider the formula $f = \neg(a\ \mathcal{U}\ b)$ and the trace a=1, b=0, a=1, b=1, ... Clearly, $(a\ \mathcal{U}\ b)$ holds in the trace, so f fails in the trace. If, however, we chose P_aUb to be false at time 0, then EL_aUb is false at time 0, which means that f holds at time 0. The correctness of our construction is summarized by the following theorem.

Theorem 3. *Let M_f be the SMV program made by the TGBA encoding for LTL formula f. Then M_f does not satisfy the specification !(EL_f & EG true) iff f is satisfiable.*

The proof of this theorem appears in Appendix D.

4   A Set of 30 Symbolic Automata Encodings

Our novel encodings are combinations of four components: (1) Normal Form: BNF or NNF, described above, (2) Automaton Form: GBA or TGBA, described above, (3) Transition Form: fussy or sloppy, described below, and (4) Variable Order: default, naïve, LEXP, LEXM, MCS-MIN, MCS-MAX, described below. In total, we have 30 novel encodings, since BNF can only be used with fussy-encoded GBAs, as explained below. CGH corresponds to BNF/fussy/GBA; we encode this combination with all six variable orders.

Automaton Form. As discussed earlier, CGH is based on GBA, in combination with BNF. We can combine, however, GBA also with NNF. For this, we need to expand the characteristic function for symbolic GBAs in order to form them from NNF formulas:

$$S_h = S_{g1}\&S_{g2}\ \text{if}\ h = g_1 \wedge g_2 \qquad\qquad S_h = S_g\&S_{X_{(Gg)}}\ \text{if}\ h = \mathcal{G}g$$

$$S_h = S_{g2}\&(S_{g1}|S_{X_{(g1\ \mathcal{R}\ g2)}})\ \text{if}\ h = g_1\ \mathcal{R}\ g_2 \qquad S_h = S_g|S_{X_{(\mathcal{F}g)}}\ \text{if}\ h = \mathcal{F}g$$

Since our focus here is on symbolic encoding, PANDA, unlike CadenceSMV, does not apply formula rewriting and related optimizations; rather, PANDA's symbolic automata are created directly from the given normal form of the formula. Formula rewriting may lead to further improvement in PANDA's performance.

Sloppy Encoding: A Novel Transition Form. CGH employs iff-transitions, of the form TRANS (EL_g=(S_g)). We refer to this as *fussy* encoding. For formulas in NNF, we can use only-if transitions of the form TRANS (EL_g->(S_g)), which we refer to as *sloppy* encoding. A similar idea was shown to be useful in the context of modal satisfiability solving [29]. Sloppy encoding increases the level of non-determinism, yielding a looser, less constrained encoding of symbolic automata, which in many cases results in smaller BDDs. A side-by-side example of the differences between GBA and TGBA encodings (demonstrating the sloppy transition form) for formula $f = ((Xa)\&(b \, \mathcal{U} \, (!a)))$ is given in Figures 1-2.

```
MODULE main
/*formula: ((X (a )) & ((b )U (!(a ))))*/
VAR /*a Boolean var for each prop in f*/
  a : boolean;
  b : boolean;
VAR /*a var EL_X_g for each formula (X g) in
    el_list w/primary op X, U, R, G, or F*/
  EL_X_a : boolean;
  EL_X__b_U_NOT_a : boolean;
DEFINE
/*each S_h in the characteristic function*/
  S__X_a__AND__b_U_NOT_a :=
    (EL_X_a) & (S__b_U_NOT_a);
  S__b_U_NOT_a :=
    (!(a )) | (b & EL_X__b_U_NOT_a);

TRANS /*a line for each (X g) in el_list*/
  ( EL_X_a -> (next(a) ) ) &
  ( EL_X__b_U_NOT_a -> (next(S__b_U_NOT_a) ))

FAIRNESS   (!S__b_U_NOT_a | (!(a )))
SPEC       !(S__X_a__AND__b_U_NOT_a & EG TRUE)
```

Fig. 1. NNF/sloppy/GBA encoding for CadenceSMV

```
MODULE main
/*formula: ((X (a ))& ((b )U (!(a ))))*/
VAR /*a Boolean var for each prop in f*/
  a : boolean;
  b : boolean;
VAR /*a var for each EL_var in el_list*/
  EL__X_a__AND__b_U_NOT_a : boolean;
  P__b_U_NOT_a: boolean;
  EL__b_U_NOT_a : boolean;
DEFINE
/*each S_h in the characteristic function*/
  S__X_a__AND__b_U_NOT_a :=
    (S_X_a) & (EL__b_U_NOT_a);
  S_X_a := (next(a));
  S__b_U_NOT_a := ( ((!(a )))
    | (b& P__b_U_NOT_a & (next(EL__b_U_NOT_a)))));
TRANS /*a line for each EL_var in el_list*/
  ( EL__X_a__AND__b_U_NOT_a ->
    (S__X_a__AND__b_U_NOT_a) ) &
  ( EL__b_U_NOT_a -> (S__b_U_NOT_a) )
FAIRNESS   (!P__b_U_NOT_a)
SPEC       !(EL__X_a__AND__b_U_NOT_a & EG TRUE)
```

Fig. 2. NNF/sloppy/TGBA encoding for CadenceSMV

A New Way of Choosing BDD Variable Orders. Symbolic model checkers search for a fair trace in the model-automaton product using a BDD-based fixpoint algorithm, a process whose efficacy is highly sensitive to variable order [5]. Finding an optimal BDD variable order is NP-hard, and good heuristics for variable ordering are crucial.

Recall that we define state variables in the symbolic model for only certain subformulas: $p \in AP$, EL_g, and P_g for some subformulas g. We form the variable graph by identifying nodes in the input-formula parse tree that correspond to the primary operators of those subformulas. Since we declare different variables for the GBA and TGBA encodings, the variable graph for a formula f may vary depending on the automaton form we choose. Figure 3 displays the GBA and TGBA variable graphs for an example formula, overlaid on the parse tree for this formula. We connect each variable-labeled vertex to its closest variable-labeled vertex descendant(s), skipping over vertices in the parse tree that do not correspond to state variables in our automaton construction. We create one node per subformula variable, irrespective of the number of occurrences of the subformula; for example, we create only one node for the proposition a in Figure 3.

We implement five variable ordering schemes, all of which take the variable graph as input. We compare these to the *default* heuristic of CadenceSMV. The *naïve* variable order is formed directly from a pre-order, depth-first traversal of the variable graph. We

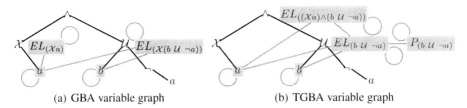

(a) GBA variable graph   (b) TGBA variable graph

Fig. 3. Graphs in (a) and (b) were both formed from the parse tree for $f = ((\mathcal{X}a) \wedge (b\,\mathcal{U}\,\neg a))$

derive four additional variable-ordering heuristics by repurposing node-ordering algorithms designed for graph triangulation [26].[1] We use two variants of a lexicographic breadth-first search algorithm: variants *perfect* (LEXP) and *minimal* (LEXM). LEXP labels each vertex in the variable graph with its already-ordered neighbors; the unordered vertex with the lexicographic largest label is selected next in the variable order. LEXM operates similarly, but labels unordered vertices with both their neighbors and also all vertices that can be reached by a path of unordered vertices with smaller labels. The maximum-cardinality search (MCS) variable ordering scheme differs in the vertex selection criterion, selecting the vertex in the variable graph adjacent to the highest number of already ordered vertices next. We seed MCS with an initial vertex, chosen either to have the *maximum* (MCS-MAX) or *minimum* (MCS-MIN) degree.

5   Experimental Methodology

Test Methods. Each test was performed in two steps. First, we applied our symbolic encodings to the input formula. Second, each symbolic automaton and variable order file pair was checked by CadenceSMV. Since encoding time is minimal and heavily dominated by model-analysis time (the time to check the model for nonemptiness to determine LTL satisfiability) we focus exclusively on the latter here.

Platform. We ran all tests on Shared University Grid at Rice (SUG@R), an Intel Xeon compute cluster.[2] SUG@R is comprised of 134 SunFire x4150 nodes, each with two quad-core Intel Xeon processors running at 2.83GHz and 16GB of RAM per processor. The OS is Red Hat Enterprise 5 Linux, 2.6.18 kernel. Each test was run with exclusive access to one node. Times were measured using the Unix `time` command.

Input Formulas. We employed a widely-used [7, 14, 23, 35] collection of benchmark formulas, established by [35]. All encodings were tested using three types of scalable formulas: random, counter, and pattern. Definitions of these formulas are repeated for convenience in Appendix B. Our test set includes 4 counter and 9 pattern formula variations, each of which scales to a large number of variables, and 60,000 random formulas.

Correctness. In addition to proving the correctness of our algorithm, the correctness of our implementation was established by comparing for every formula in our large benchmark suite, the results (either SAT or UNSAT) returned by all encodings studied here, as well as the results returned by CadenceSMV for checking the same formula as an LTL specification for the universal model. We never encountered an inconsistency.

---

[1] Graph triangulation implementation coded by the Kavraki Lab at Rice University.
[2] http://rcsg.rice.edu/sugar/

6 Experimental Results

Our experiments demonstrate that the novel encoding methods we have introduced significantly improve the translation of LTL formulas to symbolic automata, as measured in time to check the resulting automata for nonemptiness and the size of the state space we can check. No single encoding, however, consistently dominates for all types of formulas. Instead, we find that different encodings are better suited to different formulas. Therefore, we recommend using a multi-encoding approach, a variant of the multi-engine approach [33], of running all encodings in parallel and terminating when the first job completes. We call our tool PANDA for "Portfolio Approach to Navigate the Design of Automata."

Seven configurations are not competitive. While we can not predict the best encodings, we can reliably predict the worst. The following encodings were never optimal for any formulas in our test set. Thus, out of our 30 possible encodings, we rule out these seven:

- BNF/fussy/GBA/LEXM (essentially CGH with LEXM)

- NNF/fussy/GBA/LEXM	- NNF/fussy/TGBA/MCS-MAX
- NNF/fussy/TGBA/LEXM	- NNF/sloppy/TGBA/MCS-MAX
- NNF/sloppy/GBA/LEXM	- NNF/sloppy/TGBA/MCS-MIN

NNF is the best normal form, most (but not all) of the time. NNF encodings were always better for all counter and pattern formulas; see, for example, Figure 4. Figure 5 demonstrates the use of both normal forms in the optimal encodings chosen by PANDA for random formulas. BNF encodings were occasionally significantly better than NNF; the solid point in Figure 5 corresponds to a formula for which the best BNF encoding was more than four times faster than the best NNF encoding. NNF was best much more often than BNF, likely because using NNF has the added benefit that it allows us to employ our sloppy encoding and TGBAs, which often carry their own performance advantages.

No automaton form is best. Our TGBA encodings dominated for R_2, S, and U pattern formulas and both types of 3-variable counter formulas. For instance, the log-scale plot in Figure 6 shows that PANDA's median model analysis time for R_2 pattern formulas grows subexponentially as a function of the number of variables, while CadenceSMV's median model analysis time for the same formulas grows exponentially. (The best of PANDA's GBA encodings is also graphed for comparison.) GBA encodings are better for other pattern formulas, both types of 2-variable counter formulas, and the majority of random formulas; Figure 7 demonstrates this trend for 180 length random formulas.

No transition form is best. Sloppy is the best transition form for all pattern formulas. For instance, the log-scale plot of Figure 8 illustrates that PANDA's median model analysis time for U pattern formulas grows subexponentially as a function of the number of variables, while CadenceSMV's median model analysis time for the same formulas grows exponentially. Fussy encoding is better for all counter formulas. The best encodings of random formulas were split between fussy and sloppy. Figure 9 demonstrates this trend for 140 length random formulas.

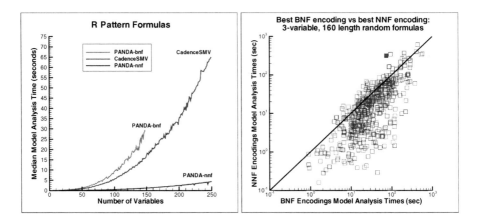

Fig. 4. Median model analysis time for $R(n) = \bigwedge_{i=1}^{n} (\mathcal{GF} p_i \vee \mathcal{FG} p_{i+1})$ for PANDA NNF/sloppy/GBA/naïve, CadenceSMV, and the best BNF encoding

Fig. 5. Best encodings of 500 3-variable, 160 length random formulas. Points fall below the diagonal when NNF is better.

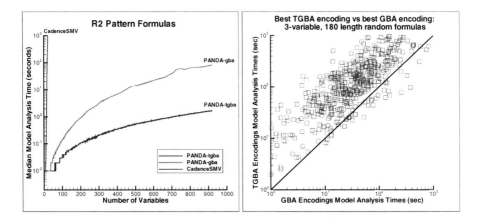

Fig. 6. $R_2(n) = (..(p_1 \; \mathcal{R} \; p_2) \; \mathcal{R} \; ...) \; \mathcal{R} \; p_n$. PANDA's NNF/sloppy/TGBA/LEXP encoding scales better than the best GBA encoding, NNF/sloppy/GBA/naïve, and exponentially better than CadenceSMV.

Fig. 7. Best encodings of 500 3-variable, 180 length random formulas

No variable order is best, but LEXM is worst. The best encodings for our benchmark formula set were split between five variable orders. The naïve and default orders proved optimal for more random formulas than the other orders. Figure 10 demonstrates that neither the naïve order nor the default order is better than the other for random formulas. The naïve order was optimal for E, Q, R, U_2, and S patterns. MCS-MAX is optimal for 2- and 3-variable linear counters. The LEXP variable order dominated for C_1, C_2, U, and R_2 pattern formulas, as well as for 2- and 3-variable counter formulas, yet it was rarely

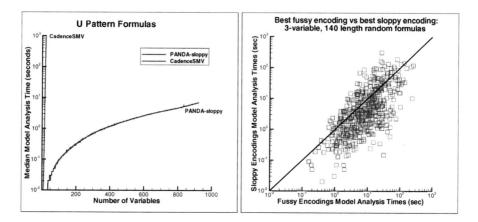

Fig. 8. $U(n) = (\ldots(p_1 \, \mathcal{U} \, p_2) \, \mathcal{U} \, \ldots) \, \mathcal{U} \, p_n$. **Fig. 9.** Best encodings of 500 3-variable, 140 PANDA's NNF/sloppy/TGBA/LEXP scalables length random formulas. Points fall below the exponentially better than CadenceSMV. diagonal when sloppy encoding is best.

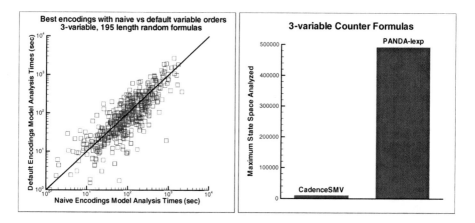

Fig. 10. Best encodings of 500 3-variable, 195 **Fig. 11.** Maximum states analyzed before length random formulas. Points fall above the space-out. CadenceSMV quits at 10240 states. diagonal when naïve variable order is best. PANDA's NNF/fussy/TGBA/LEXP scales to 491520 states.

best for random formulas. Figure 11 demonstrates the marked difference in scalability provided by using the LEXP order over running CadenceSMV on 3-variable counter formulas; we can analyze much larger models with PANDA using LEXP than with the native CadenceSMV encoding before memory-out. We never found the LEXM order to be the single best encoding for any formula.

A formula class typically has a best encoding, but predictions are difficult. While each of our pattern and counter formulas had a best (or a pair of best) encodings, which remained consistent as we scaled the formulas, we found that we could not reliably predict the best encoding using any statistics gathered from parsing, such as operator counts or ratios. For example, we found that the best encoding for a pattern formula was not necessarily the best for a randomly-generated formula comprised of the same temporal operators. We surmise that the best encoding is tied to the structure of the formula on a deeper level; developing an accurate heuristic is left to future work.

There is no single best encoding; a multi-encoding approach is clearly superior. We implement a novel multi-encoding approach: our new PANDA tool creates several encodings of a formula and uses a symbolic model checker to check them for satisfiability in parallel, terminating when the first check completes. Our experimental data supports this multi-encoding approach. Figures 4, 6, and 8 highlight the significant decrease in CadenceSMV model analysis time for R, R_2, and U pattern formulas, while Figure 11 demonstrates increased scalability in terms of state space using counter formulas. Altogether, we demonstrate that a multi-encoding approach is dramatically more scalable than the current state-of-the-art. The increase in scalability is dependant on the specific formula, though for some formulas PANDA's model analysis time is exponentially better than CadenceSMV's model analysis time for the same class of formulas.

7 Discussion

This paper brought attention to the issue of scalable construction of symbolic automata for LTL formulas in the context of LTL satisfiability checking. We defined novel encodings and novel BDD variable orders for accomplishing this task. We explored the impact of these encodings, comprised of combinations of normal forms, automaton forms, transition forms, and combined with variable orders. We showed that each can have a significant impact on performance. At the same time, we showed that no single encoding outperforms all others and showed that a multi-encoding approach yields the best result, consistently outperforming the native translation of CadenceSMV.

We do not claim to have exhaustively covered the space of possible encodings of symbolic automata. Several papers on the automata-theoretic approach to LTL describe approaches that could be turned into alternative encodings of symbolic automata, cf. [4, 18, 20, 37]. The advantage of the multi-encoding approach we introduced here is its *extensibility*; adding additional encodings is straightforward. The multi-encoding approach can also be combined with different back ends. In this paper we used CadenceSMV as a BDD-based back end; using another symbolic back end (cf. [14]) or a SAT-based back end (cf. [3]) would be an alternative approach, as both BDD-based and SAT-based back ends require symbolic automata. Since LTL serves as the basis for industrial languages such as PSL and SVA, the encoding techniques studied here may also serve as the basis for novel encodings of such languages, cf. [8, 9].

In this paper we examined our novel symbolic encodings of LTL in the context of satisfiability checking. An important difference between satisfiability checking and model checking is that in the former we expect to have to handle much larger formulas, since we need to consider the conjunction of properties. Also, in model checking the size of the symbolic automata can be dwarfed by the size of the model under verification. Thus, the issue of symbolic encoding of automata in the context of model checking deserves a separate investigation.

References

1. Amla, N., Du, X., Kuehlmann, A., Kurshan, R.P., McMillan, K.L.: An analysis of SAT-based model checking techniques in an industrial environment. In: Borrione, D., Paul, W. (eds.) CHARME 2005. LNCS, vol. 3725, pp. 254–268. Springer, Heidelberg (2005)
2. Beer, I., Ben-David, S., Eisner, C., Rodeh, Y.: Efficient detection of vacuity in ACTL formulas. FMSD 18(2), 141–162 (2001)
3. Biere, A., Artho, C., Schuppan, V.: Liveness checking as safety checking. In: FMICS, vol. 66(2) (2002)
4. Bloem, R., Cimatti, A., Pill, I., Roveri, M.: Symbolic implementation of alternating automata. IJFCS 18(4), 727–743 (2007)
5. Bryant, R.E.: Graph-based algorithms for Boolean-function manipulation. IEEE TC C-35(8), 677–691 (1986)
6. Burch, J.R., Clarke, E.M., McMillan, K.L., Dill, D.L., Hwang, L.J.: Symbolic model checking: 10^{20} states and beyond. Inform. and Computation 98(2), 142–170 (1992)
7. Cichon, J., Czubak, A., Jasinski, A.: Minimal Büchi automata for certain classes of LTL formulas. In: DepCoS, pp. 17–24 (2009)
8. Cimatti, A., Roveri, M., Semprini, S., Tonetta, S.: From PSL to NBA: A modular symbolic encoding. In: FMCAD (2006)
9. Cimatti, A., Roveri, M., Tonetta, S.: Syntactic optimizations for PSL verification. In: Grumberg, O., Huth, M. (eds.) TACAS 2007. LNCS, vol. 4424, pp. 505–518. Springer, Heidelberg (2007)
10. Clarke, E.M., Grumberg, O., Hamaguchi, K.: Another look at LTL model checking. Formal Methods in System Design 10(1), 47–71 (1997)
11. Courcoubetis, C., Vardi, M.Y., Wolper, P., Yannakakis, M.: Memory efficient algorithms for the verification of temporal properties. In: Clarke, E., Kurshan, R.P. (eds.) CAV 1990. LNCS, vol. 531, pp. 233–242. Springer, Heidelberg (1991)
12. Couvreur, J.-M.: On-the-fly verification of Linear Temporal Logic. In: Woodcock, J.C.P., Davies, J. (eds.) FM 1999. LNCS, vol. 1708, pp. 253–271. Springer, Heidelberg (1999)
13. Daniele, M., Giunchiglia, F., Vardi, M.Y.: Improved Automata Generation for Linear Temporal Logic. In: Halbwachs, N., Peled, D.A. (eds.) CAV 1999. LNCS, vol. 1633, pp. 249–260. Springer, Heidelberg (1999)
14. De Wulf, M., Doyen, L., Maquet, N., Raskin, J.-F.: Antichains: Alternative algorithms for LTL satisfiability and model-checking. In: Ramakrishnan, C.R., Rehof, J. (eds.) TACAS 2008. LNCS, vol. 4963, pp. 63–77. Springer, Heidelberg (2008)
15. Duret-Lutz, A., Poitrenaud, D.: SPOT: An extensible model checking library using Transition-Based Generalized Büchi Automata. In: MASCOTS, pp. 76–83 (2004)
16. Emerson, E.A.: Temporal and modal logic. In: Handbook of Theoretical Computer Science, vol. B, ch. 16, pp. 997–1072. Elsevier, MIT Press (1990)
17. Ferrara, A., Pan, G., Vardi, M.Y.: Treewidth in verification: Local vs. Global. In: Sutcliffe, G., Voronkov, A. (eds.) LPAR 2005. LNCS (LNAI), vol. 3835, pp. 489–503. Springer, Heidelberg (2005)
18. Fisher, M.: A normal form for temporal logics and its applications in theorem-proving and execution. J. Log. Comput. 7(4), 429–456 (1997)
19. Fisman, D., Kupferman, O., Sheinvald-Faragy, S., Vardi, M.Y.: A framework for inherent vacuity. In: Chockler, H., Hu, A.J. (eds.) HVC 2008. LNCS, vol. 5394, pp. 7–22. Springer, Heidelberg (2009)
20. Gastin, P., Oddoux, D.: Fast LTL to Büchi automata translation. In: Berry, G., Comon, H., Finkel, A. (eds.) CAV 2001. LNCS, vol. 2102, pp. 53–65. Springer, Heidelberg (2001)

21. Gerth, R., Peled, D., Vardi, M.Y., Wolper, P.: Simple on-the-fly automatic verification of Linear Temporal Logic. In: PSTV, pp. 3–18. Chapman and Hall, Boca Raton (1995)
22. Giannakopoulou, D., Lerda, F.: From states to transitions: Improving translation of LTL formulae to Büchi automata. In: FORTE (November 2002)
23. Goranko, V., Kyrilov, A., Shkatov, D.: Tableau tool for testing satisfiability in LTL: Implementation and experimental analysis. ENTCS 262, 113–125 (2010)
24. Habibi, A., Tahar, S.: Design for verification of SystemC transaction level models. In: Design, Automation and Test in Europe, pp. 560–565. IEEE, Los Alamitos (2005)
25. Kesten, Y., Manna, Z., McGuire, H., Pnueli, A.: A decision algorithm for full propositional temporal logic. In: Courcoubetis, C. (ed.) CAV 1993. LNCS, vol. 697, pp. 97–109. Springer, Heidelberg (1993)
26. Koster, A.M.C.A., Bodlaender, H.L., van Hoesel, S.P.M.: Treewidth: Computational experiments. ZIB-Report 01–38, ZIB (2001)
27. Kupferman, O., Vardi, M.Y.: Vacuity detection in temporal model checking. STTT 4(2), 224–233 (2003)
28. Merz, S., Sezgin, A.: Emptiness of Linear Weak Alternating Automata. Technical report, LORIA (December 2003)
29. Pan, G., Sattler, U., Vardi, M.Y.: BDD-based decision procedures for K. In: Voronkov, A. (ed.) CADE 2002. LNCS (LNAI), vol. 2392, pp. 16–30. Springer, Heidelberg (2002)
30. Pill, I., Semprini, S., Cavada, R., Roveri, M., Bloem, R., Cimatti, A.: Formal analysis of hardware requirements. In: DAC, pp. 821–826. ACM, New York (2006)
31. Pnueli, A.: The temporal logic of programs. In: IEEE FOCS, pp. 46–57 (1977)
32. Pnueli, A., Rosner, R.: On the synthesis of a reactive module. In: POPL, pp. 179–190 (1989)
33. Pulina, L., Tacchella, A.: A self-adaptive multi-engine solver for quantified Boolean formulas. Constraints 14(1), 80–116 (2009)
34. Roveri, M.: Novel techniques for property assurance. Technical report, PROSYD deliverable 1.2/2 (2004)
35. Rozier, K.Y., Vardi, M.Y.: LTL satisfiability checking. In: Bošnački, D., Edelkamp, S. (eds.) SPIN 2007. LNCS, vol. 4595, pp. 149–167. Springer, Heidelberg (2007)
36. Ruah, S., Fedeli, A., Eisner, C., Moulin, M.: Property-driven specification of VLSI design. Technical report, PROSYD deliverable 1.1/1 (2005)
37. Schneider, K.: Improving automata generation for Linear Temporal Logic by considering the automaton hierarchy. In: Nieuwenhuis, R., Voronkov, A. (eds.) LPAR 2001. LNCS (LNAI), vol. 2250, pp. 39–54. Springer, Heidelberg (2001)
38. Sebastiani, R., Tonetta, S.: "More deterministic" vs. "smaller" Büchi automata for efficient LTL model checking. In: Geist, D., Tronci, E. (eds.) CHARME 2003. LNCS, vol. 2860, pp. 126–140. Springer, Heidelberg (2003)
39. Sistla, A.P., Clarke, E.M.: The complexity of Propositional Linear Temporal Logic. J. ACM 32, 733–749 (1985)
40. Somenzi, F., Bloem, R.: Efficient Büchi automata from LTL formulae. In: Emerson, E.A., Sistla, A.P. (eds.) CAV 2000. LNCS, vol. 1855, pp. 248–263. Springer, Heidelberg (2000)
41. Thirioux, X.: Simple and efficient translation from LTL formulas to Büchi automata. ENTCS 66(2), 145–159 (2002)
42. Vardi, M.Y.: Automata-theoretic model checking revisited. In: Cook, B., Podelski, A. (eds.) VMCAI 2007. LNCS, vol. 4349, pp. 137–150. Springer, Heidelberg (2007)
43. Vardi, M.Y., Wolper, P.: An automata-theoretic approach to automatic program verification. In: LICS, Cambridge, pp. 332–344 (June 1986)
44. Vardi, M.Y., Wolper, P.: Reasoning about infinite computations. Information and Computation 115(1), 1–37 (1994)

On Combining State Space Reductions with Global Fairness Assumptions*

Shao Jie Zhang[1], Jun Sun[2], Jun Pang[3], Yang Liu[1], and Jin Song Dong[1]

[1] National University of Singapore
{shaojiezhang@,liuyang@comp.,dongjs@comp.}nus.edu.sg
[2] Singapore University of Technology and Design
sunjun@sutd.edu.sg
[3] University of Luxembourg
jun.pang@uni.lu

Abstract. Model checking has established itself as an effective system analysis method, as it is capable of proving/dis-proving properties automatically. Its application to practical systems is however limited by state space explosion. Among effective state reduction techniques are symmetry reduction and partial order reduction. Global fairness often plays a vital role in designing self-stabilizing population protocols. It is known that combining fairness and symmetry reduction is nontrivial. In this work, we first show that global fairness, unlike weak/strong fairness, can be combined with symmetry reduction. We extend the PAT model checker with the technique and demonstrate its usability by verifying recently proposed population protocols. Second, we show that partial order reduction is not property-preserving with global fairness.

1 Introduction

In the area of system verification and model checking, liveness means something good must eventually happen. A counterexample to a liveness property is typically a loop (or a deadlock state which can be viewed as a trivial loop) during which good things never occur. Fairness, which is concerned with a fair resolution of non-determinism, is often necessary and important to prove liveness properties. Fairness is an abstraction of the fair scheduler in a multi-threaded programming environment or the relative speed of the processors in distributed systems. Without fairness, verification of liveness properties often produces unrealistic infinite system executions during which one process or event is unfairly favored. It is important to systematically rule out those unfair counterexamples so as to identify real bugs.

The population protocol model has recently emerged as an elegant computation paradigm for describing mobile ad hoc networks [2]. A number of population protocols have been proposed and studied [2,16]. Fairness plays an important role in these protocols. For instance, it was shown that the self-stabilizing population protocols for the complete network graphs only work under *weak fairness*, whereas the algorithm

---

* This research was partially supported by a grant "SRG ISTD 2010 001" from Singapore University of Technology and Design.

M. Butler and W. Schulte (Eds.): FM 2011, LNCS 6664, pp. 432–447, 2011.

for network rings only works under *global fairness* [14]. Different from weak/strong fairness, global fairness requires that a transition (instead of an event or process) must be infinitely often taken if infinitely often enabled. It has been further proved that with only *strong fairness* or weaker, uniform self-stabilizing leader election in rings is impossible [14]. In order to verify (implementations of) those algorithms, model checking techniques must take the respective fairness constraints into account.

In our previous work [27], we developed a unified approach to model checking concurrent systems with a variety of fairness constraints. It was later applied to recently proposed population protocols [19] and previously unknown bugs are detected successfully. Nonetheless, it is limited by the state space explosion problem, like any model checking algorithm. Previous work has identified and solved the problem combining weak/strong fairness with state space reduction techniques like symmetry reduction [12] and partial order reduction [6]. In this work, we examine a combination of model checking with global fairness with symmetry reduction and partial order reduction. The contributions are stated below:

First, we investigate the problem of model checking with global fairness and symmetry reduction. Symmetry reduction is a natural choice to population protocols, or network protocols, which in general often contain many behaviorally similar or identical network nodes. Symmetry reduction has been investigated by many researchers for many years [8,11,3]. In [12,15], it has been shown that combining weak/strong fairness with symmetry reduction is non-trivial. In this paper, we prove that different from weak/strong fairness, symmetry reduction and global fairness can be integrated without extra effort. Adding symmetry reduction slightly changes the algorithm for model checking with global fairness. We present the combined reduction algorithm based on Tarjan's strongly connected component algorithm [29].We extend our home-grown PAT model checker with symmetry reduction and show its scalability by verifying recently proposed population protocols.

Second, partial order reduction is an effective state reduction technique for concurrent systems with independent transitions. It is shown that partial order reduction preserves the behaviors with weak fairness, but not with strong fairness [22,6]. In this paper, we examine the combination of partial order reduction and global fairness, and show that partial order reduction is not property preserving with global fairness.

2   Preliminaries

We present our work in the setting of Labeled Kripke structures (LKS) [7].

Definition 1 (LKS). *An LKS is a 6-tuple* $\mathcal{L} = (S, init, \Sigma, \rightarrow, AP, L)$ *where: S is a finite set of states; $init \in S$ is the initial state; Σ is a finite set of events; AP is a finite set of atomic state propositions; $\rightarrow: S \times \Sigma \times S$ is a transition-labeling relation with events; $L : S \rightarrow 2^{AP}$ is a state-labeling relation with atomic propositions.*

For simplicity, we write $s \xrightarrow{e} s'$ to denote that (s, e, s') is a transition in $\rightarrow$; $s \rightarrow s'$ to denote there exists some e in Σ such that $s \xrightarrow{e} s'$. Figure 1 shows an LKS, where transitions are labeled with event names and states are denoted by numbers, and 0 is the initial state. The dash-lined circles will be explained later.

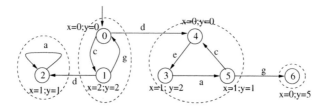

Fig. 1. Labeled Kripke system

We say that $\mathcal{L}$ is finite if and only if S is finite. A run of $\mathcal{L}$ is a finite or infinite sequence of alternating states and events $\langle s_0, e_0, s_1, e_1, \cdots \rangle$ such that $s_0 = init$ and $s_i \xrightarrow{e_i} s_{i+1}$ for all i. Because fairness affects infinite not finite system behaviors, we focus on infinite system runs in this paper. A state s is *reachable* if and only if there exists a finite run that reaches s. Throughout the paper, we assume that LKSs are always *reduced*, *i.e.*, all states are reachable.

We assume properties are stated in the form of state/event linear temporal logic (SE-LTL) formulae [7]. Given an LKS $\mathcal{L} = (S, init, \Sigma, \rightarrow, AP, L)$, an SE-LTL formula ϕ can be constituted by not only atomic state propositions but also events.

$$\phi ::= p \mid a \mid \neg\phi \mid \phi \wedge \phi \mid \mathbf{X}\phi \mid \mathbf{F}\phi \mid \mathbf{G}\phi \mid \phi\mathbf{U}\phi, \text{ where } p \in AP \text{ and } a \in \Sigma.$$

Definition 2. *Let* $\pi = \langle s_0, e_0, s_1, e_1, \cdots \rangle$ *be a run in* $\mathcal{L}$ *and* π_i *the suffix of* π *starting at* s_i. *The path satisfaction relation is defined as follows:*

- $\pi \models p$ *iff* s *is the first state of* π *and* $p \in L(s)$.
- $\pi \models a$ *iff* a *is the first event of* π.
- $\pi \models \neg\phi$ *iff* $\pi \not\models \phi$.
- $\pi \models \phi_1 \wedge \phi_2$ *iff* $\pi \models \phi_1$ *and* $\pi \models \phi_2$.
- $\pi \models \mathbf{X}\phi$ *iff* $\pi_1 \models \phi$.
- $\pi \models \mathbf{F}\phi$ *iff there exists a* $k \geq 0$ *such that* $\pi_k \models \phi$.
- $\pi \models \mathbf{G}\phi$ *iff for all* $i \geq 0$ *such that* $\pi_i \models \phi$.
- $\pi \models \phi_1\mathbf{U}\phi_2$ *iff there exists a* $k \geq 0$ *s.t.* $\pi_k \models \phi_2$ *and for all* $0 \leq j < k, \pi_j \models \phi_1$.

An example is $\mathbf{G}(d \Rightarrow \mathbf{F}(x > 1))$ where d is an event and $x > 1$ is an atomic proposition. The formula states that event d is always followed by a run such that $x > 1$ is eventually satisfied.

3   Model Checking with Fairness

A fairness constraint restricts the set of system behaviors to only those fair ones. Without fairness constraints, a system may behave freely as long as it starts with an initial state and conforms to the transition relation. There are a variety of fairness constraints, *i.e.*, event-level or process-level weak fairness, event-level or process-level strong fairness, global fairness, etc. In the following, we briefly review weak and strong fairness and then focus on global fairness. For simplicity, we focus on event-level fairness.

3.1 Fairness

Event-level weak fairness [17] states that if an event becomes enabled *forever* after some steps, then it must be engaged infinitely often. An equivalent formulation is that every run should contain infinitely many positions at which the event is disabled or has occurred. Given the LKS presented in Figure 1, the run $\langle 0, c, 1, g \rangle^\omega$ where the superscript ω indicates an infinite number of repetitions does not satisfy event-level weak fairness because event d is always enabled (*i.e.*, at both state 0 and 1) but never occurs during the run. The run which loops through state 3, 4 and 5 satisfies weak fairness as no event is enabled forever. Event-level strong fairness states that if an event is *infinitely often* enabled, it must infinitely often occur. This type of fairness is particularly useful in the analysis of systems that use semaphores, synchronous communication, and other special coordination primitives. It has been identified by different researchers [18,14,24]. Given the LKS presented in Figure 1, the run which loops through state 3, 4 and 5 does not satisfy strong fairness because event g is infinitely often enabled but never occurs. It can be shown that strong fairness implies weak fairness. Model checking with weak or strong fairness, or combing weak/strong fairness with state space reduction techniques has been well investigated [10,25,26,27,28].

Definition 3 (Global fairness). *Let $E = \langle s_0, e_0, s_1, e_1, \cdots \rangle$ be a run of an LKS $\mathcal{L}$. E satisfies global fairness if and only if, for every s, e, s' such that $s \xrightarrow{e} s'$, if $s = s_i$ for infinitely many i, then $s_i = s$ and $e_i = e$ and $s_{i+1} = s'$ for infinitely many i.*

Global fairness[1] was proposed by Fischer and Jiang in [14]. It is in fact a restricted form of extreme fairness proposed by Pnueli [23]. Global fairness states that if a *step*[2] (from s to s' by engaging in event e) can be taken infinitely often, then it must actually be taken infinitely often. Many population protocols rely on global fairness [2,14]. Compared to event-level strong fairness, global fairness requires that an infinitely enabled event must be taken infinitely often in *all* contexts, whereas event-level strong fairness only requires the enabled event to be taken in *one* context. Thus, global fairness is stronger than strong fairness. Their difference is illustrated in the following figure.

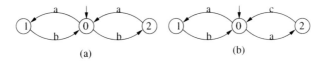

(a)   (b)

Under event-level strong fairness, state 2 in (a) may never be visited because all events occur infinitely often if the left loop is taken infinitely. With global fairness, all states in (a) must be visited infinitely often. Their difference when there is non-determinism is illustrated in (b). Both transitions labeled a must be taken infinitely with global fairness, which is not necessary with event-level strong or weak fairness. *It can be shown that global fairness coincides event-level strong fairness when every transition is labeled with a different event.* This observation implies that we can uniquely label all transitions

---

[1] In [14], it is called strong global fairness and defined for unlabeled transition systems. We slightly changed it so as to suit the setting of LKS.

[2] Step and transition are used interchangeably in this paper.

with different events and then apply model checking algorithm for strong fairness to deal with global fairness. We show however, model checking with global fairness can be solved using a more efficient approach. In contrast to nontrivial combination of strong fairness and symmetry reduction [12], we show that using our approach model checking with global fairness can be straightforwardly combined with symmetry reduction.

3.2 Model Checking with Fairness

Given an LKS $\mathcal{L}$ and a liveness property ϕ, model checking is to search for a run of $\mathcal{L}$ which fails ϕ. In automata-based model checking, the negation of ϕ is translated to an equivalent Büchi automaton $\mathcal{B}$. Model checking with fairness is to search for a system run which is accepting by $\mathcal{B}$ *whilst satisfying the fairness constraints*. In the following, we write $\mathcal{L} \vDash \phi$ to mean that $\mathcal{L}$ satisfies the property (without fairness assumption) and write $\mathcal{L} \vDash_{gf} \phi$ to mean that $\mathcal{L}$ satisfies the property with global fairness, *i.e.*, every run of $\mathcal{L}$ which satisfies global fairness also satisfies ϕ. We define a *loop* in the product of $\mathcal{L}$ and B is a sequence of alternating states/events:

$$\langle (s_0, b_0), e_0, (s_1, b_1), e_1, \cdots, (s_{n-1}, b_{n-1}), e_n, (s_n, b_n) \rangle^\omega$$

such that for all $0 \leq i \leq n$, s_i is a state of $\mathcal{L}$, b_i is a state of $\mathcal{B}$, (s_0, b_0) is reachable, $s_n = s_0$ and $b_n = b_0$. A loop is *accepting* if and only if there exists at least one accepting state of $\mathcal{B}$ in $\langle b_0, b_1, \cdots, b_n \rangle$. Furthermore, we define the following sets for a loop l whose projection on $\mathcal{L}$ is $l_\mathcal{L} = \langle s_0, e_0, s_1, e_1, \cdots, s_{n-1}, e_{n-1}, s_0 \rangle$.

$$
\begin{aligned}
onceStep(l) &= \bigcup_{k=0}^{n-1} enabled(s_k) \\
engagedStep(l) &= \bigcup_{k=0}^{n-1} engaged(s_k, l) \\
enabled(s) &= \{(s, e, s') \mid s \xrightarrow{e} s'\} \\
engaged(s_k, l) &= \{(s_k, e_k, s_{k+1}) \mid \langle s_k, e_k, s_{k+1} \rangle \text{ is a subsequence of } l_\mathcal{L}\}
\end{aligned}
$$

Intuitively, $onceStep(l)$ is the set of steps which are enabled at least once during the loop, and $engagedStep(l)$ is the set of steps which are engaged during the loop. By definition, the proposition follows immediately.

Proposition 1. *Let $E = m(l^\omega)$ be a run in $\mathcal{L}$ where m is a finite run. E satisfies global fairness if and only if $onceStep(l) = engagedStep(l)$.*   □

3.3 Algorithm for Model Checking with Global Fairness

Model checking with fairness can often be reduced to search for strongly connected components (SCC). In graph theory, an SCC is defined as a *maximum* subgraph such that every pair of vertices in the subgraph is connected by a path in the subgraph. A terminal SCC is an SCC such that all of its edges lead to vertices contained in the SCC. Naturally, an LKS can be viewed as a directed graph and therefore the concept of SCC can be extended to LKS. For instance, the LKS presented in Figure 1 contains four SCCs, indicated by dash-lined circles. Among the four, the one containing state 2 is terminal, whereas the one containing state 0 and 1 is not. For simplicity, we refer to a set of states of an LKS as an SCC if the subgraph containing the states and the transitions among them forms an SCC. We write that 'an SCC fails a liveness property ϕ' as equivalent to that a run which reaches any state in the SCC and infinitely often traverses through all states and transitions of the SCC fails ϕ. For instance, the SCC containing state 2 fails the property $\mathbf{G}(d \Rightarrow \mathbf{F}(x > 1))$.

In our previous work [27], we proved that the problem of model checking with global fairness can be reduced to the problem of searching for a terminal SCC which fails the given property. Formally, it can be stated as the following theorem.

Theorem 1. *Let $\mathcal{L}$ be an LKS; ϕ be a property. $\mathcal{L} \models_{gf} \phi$ if and only if there does not exist a terminal SCC S in $\mathcal{L}$ such that S fails ϕ.* □

The theorem implies that we can use a simple procedure to find a counterexample by enumerating all terminal SCCs and then testing each one of them. The approach implemented in the PAT model checker is based on Tarjan's algorithm for on-the-fly identification of SCCs. Its complexity is linear in the number of edges in the graph. Given the LKS presented in Figure 1 with the property $\mathbf{G}(d \Rightarrow \mathbf{F}(x > 1))$, the SCC containing state 2 is identified as a counterexample with global fairness. Note that the SCC containing state 3, 4, and 5 is a counterexample only with no fairness or weak fairness. It is not a counterexample with global fairness because it does not satisfy global fairness, *i.e.*, the step from state 5 to 6 by performing g is enabled infinitely often but never occurs.

4   Model Checking with Symmetry Reduction

Distributed/concurrent systems, especially communicating protocols, often exhibit considerable symmetry. Symmetry reduction aims to explore the symmetry in order to reduce state space. Intuitively, the idea is that states which are symmetric exhibit similar or even identical behaviors and therefore exploring one representative would suffice in proving/dis-proving a property. In the following, we briefly introduce symmetry reduction (refer to Chapter 14 of [9] for details), using the following running example.

Example 1. In [14], a self-stabilizing leader election protocol is proposed for complete networks. The system contains multiple network nodes which interact with each other following a number of simple rules. The system is modeled in the following form.

$$System = Controller \parallel Node(0) \parallel Node(1) \parallel \cdots \parallel Node(N)$$

where *Controller* is a controlling process distinguished from the network nodes; *Node(i)* models a network node with a unique identity i; $\parallel$ denotes parallel composition. A node is marked as either a leader or not. Two nodes can interact according to the rules and start/quit being a leader. For instance, one of the rules states that if two interacting nodes are both leaders, then one of the nodes quits being a leader. The network nodes (*i.e.*, process *Node(i)*) are indistinguishable in the protocol and therefore they are all symmetric. One essential property of the protocol is that all nodes must eventually converge to the correct configuration. That is, eventually always there is one and only one leader in the network, *i.e.*, **FG** *one leader*.

A permutation σ on a finite set of objects is a bijection (*i.e.*, a function that is one-to-one and onto). For instance, a permutation of the process identities in the above example is: $\sigma_0 = 0 \mapsto 1, 1 \mapsto 2, \cdots, N - 1 \mapsto N, N \mapsto 0$ where $0 \mapsto 1$ reads as '0 maps to 1'. A permutation group is a group of permutations. For instance, the group containing all permutation of process identities in the leader election example is a permutation group. Given an LKS $\mathcal{L} = (S, init, \Sigma, \rightarrow, AP, L)$, let G be a permutation group of process identities acting on S. *We first assume any event in Σ is not allowed to be permuted.* A permutation σ is said to be an automorphism of $\mathcal{L}$ if and only if it preserves the transition relation and initial state. Formally, σ satisfies the following condition.

$$(\forall\, s_1, s_2 \in S;\ e \in \Sigma.\ s_1 \xrightarrow{e} s_2 \Leftrightarrow \sigma(s_1) \xrightarrow{e} \sigma(s_2)) \wedge \sigma(init) = init$$

A group T is an automorphism group of $\mathcal{L}$ if and only if every $\sigma \in T$ is an automorphism of $\mathcal{L}$. A permutation σ is said to be an invariance of an SE-LTL formula ϕ if and only if $\sigma(\phi) \equiv \phi$ where $\equiv$ denotes logical equivalence under all propositional interpretations [11]. For instance, given any permutation of process identities in the leader election example, the truth value of proposition *one leader* remains the same and therefore the permutation is an invariance of **FG** *one leader*. A permutation σ is said to be an invariance of $\mathcal{L}$ and property ϕ if and only if it is an automorphism of $\mathcal{L}$ and it is an invariance of ϕ. G is an invariance group of $\mathcal{L}$ and ϕ if and only if every $\sigma \in G$ is an invariance of $\mathcal{L}$ and ϕ.

Given a state $s \in S$, the orbit of s is the set $\theta(s) = \{t \mid \exists \sigma \in G.\ \sigma(s) = t\}$, *i.e.*, the equivalence group which contains s. From each orbit of state s, a unique representative state $rep(s)$ can be picked such that for all s and s' in the same orbit, $rep(s) = rep(s')$. Intuitively, if σ is an invariance of ϕ, states of the same orbit are behaviorally indistinguishable with respect to ϕ. For instance, the states of the 0-node being the only leader and the 1-node being the only leader in the leader election protocol are indistinguishable to the property **FG** *one leader*. Based on this observation, an LKS can be turned into a *quotient* LKS where states in the same orbit are grouped together. Formally, a quotient LKS is defined as follows.

Definition 4. *Let $\mathcal{L} = (S, init, \Sigma, \rightarrow, AP, L)$ be an LKS; G be an automorphism group. The quotient LKS $\mathcal{L}_G = (S_G, init_G, \Sigma, fun_G, AP, L)$ is defined as follows:*

- *$S_G = \{rep(s) \mid s \in S\}$ is the set of representative states of orbits.*
- *$init_G = \{rep(init)\}$ is the initial representative state.*
- *$(r, e, r') \in \rightarrow_G$ iff there exists $r'' \in S$ such that $r \xrightarrow{e} r''$ and $rep(r'') = r'$.*

It has been proved [9] that if G is an invariance group of $\mathcal{L}$ and ϕ, then $\mathcal{L}$ satisfies ϕ if and only if $\mathcal{L}_G$ satisfies ϕ. Formally, it is stated as the following theorem. It is proved by showing that the relation $(s, \theta(s))$ is a bi-simulation relation between $\mathcal{L}$ and $\mathcal{L}_G$.

Theorem 2. *Let $\mathcal{L} = (S, init, \Sigma, \rightarrow, AP, L)$ be an LKS; ϕ be an SE-LTL formula. If G be an invariance group of $\mathcal{L}$ and ϕ, then $\mathcal{L} \models \phi$ if and only if $\mathcal{L}_G \models \phi$.* □

5   Symmetry Reduction with Global Fairness

In the following, we prove that global fairness is orthogonal with symmetry reduction by showing that there is a run which satisfies global fairness and fails ϕ in $\mathcal{L}$ if and only if there is a run which satisfies global fairness and fails ϕ in $\mathcal{L}_G$. For convenience, we fix that ϕ is an $SE\text{-}LTL$ formula to be checked, $\mathcal{B}$ is the Büchi automaton constructed by the negation of ϕ, $\mathcal{L}$ is LKS of the original system, G is invariance group of $\mathcal{L}$ and ϕ and $\mathcal{L}_G$ is LKS of the abstract system after applying symmetry reduction.

Lemma 1. *There exists a run* $p = \langle s_0, a_0, s_1, a_1, \cdots \rangle$ *in* $\mathcal{L}$ *if and only if there exists a run* $q = \langle r_0, a_0, r_1, a_1, \cdots \rangle$ *in* $\mathcal{L}_G$ *such that* $r_i = rep(s_i)$ *for all* i.

Proof. It follows from the proof of Lemma 3.1 in [11]. $\qquad\qquad\qquad\qquad\qquad$ □

Theorem 3. *There exists an accepting loop in the product of* $\mathcal{L}$ *and* $\mathcal{B}$ *which satisfies global fairness if and only if there also exists an accepting loop in the product of* $\mathcal{L}_G$ *and* $\mathcal{B}$ *which satisfies global fairness.*

Proof: (**Sufficient condition**). We first prove the sufficient condition. The proof is divided into two parts. In the first part, we prove (1) if there exists an accepting loop l' in the product of $\mathcal{L}_G$ and $\mathcal{B}$, then there exists an accepting loop l in the product of $\mathcal{L}$ and $\mathcal{B}$. Then we prove (2) if l' satisfies global fairness, so does l.

Let $l' = \langle (r_0, b_0), a_0, (r_1, b_1), a_1, \cdots, (r_{n-1}, b_{n-1}), a_{n-1}, (r_0, b_0) \rangle$ be an accepting loop. Without loss of generality we assume that b_0 is an accepting state. Then there exists in the product of $\mathcal{L}_G$ and $\mathcal{B}$ a path arriving at (r_0, b_0). By Lemma 1 there exists a corresponding path in the product of $\mathcal{L}$ and $\mathcal{B}$ to state (s_0, b'_0) where $r_0 = rep(s_0)$. Because G is the invariance group of L and ϕ, $b'_0 = b_0$ which is also an accepting state. By Lemma 1 again, for l' there exists in the product of $\mathcal{L}$ and $\mathcal{B}$ a path $p^0 = \langle (s_0, b_0), a_0, (s_1, b_1), a_1, \cdots, (s_{n-1}, b_{n-1}), a_{n-1}, (s_0^1, b_0) \rangle$ such that for all i in p^0 we have $r_i = rep(s_i)$. Notice that p^0 is not necessarily a loop. Since $r_0 = rep(s_0^1)$, we can unfold l' again according to Lemma 1, but this time beginning at s_0^1, which will produce the path $p^1 = \langle (s_0^1, b_0), a_0, (s_1^1, b_1), a_1, \cdots, (s_{n-1}^1, b_{n-1}), a_{n-1}, (s_0^2, b_0) \rangle$, and for all i in p^1 we still have $r_i = rep(s_i^1)$. We can repeat this unfolding arbitrary many times which will give us a sequence of path $p^0, p^1, p^2, \cdots$ with the corresponding end states $(s_0^1, b_0), (s_0^2, b_0), (s_0^3, b_0), \cdots$ which are all accepting. As the orbit of the states $s_0, s_0^1, s_0^2, \cdots$ is finite, $s_0^i = s_0^j$ for some i and j. Obviously, the concatenation of the paths p^i to p^{j-1}, say l, is an accepting loop in the product of $\mathcal{L}$ and $\mathcal{B}$.

Because l' satisfies global fairness, $onceStep(l') = engagedStep(l')$. We define a function $recover$ such that given $(s, e, s') \in \rightarrow_G$ and some permutation $\sigma \in G$, $recover((s, e, s'), \sigma) = (t, e, t')$ such that $s\sigma^{-1} = t \wedge t \overset{e}{\to} t'$. Intuitively, $recover$ returns the corresponding transition of (s, e, s') in $\mathcal{L}$ with respect to a specific permutation σ. For $0 \leq m \leq n$, r_m in loop l' corresponds to s_m^t (i.e., $r_m = s_m^t \sigma_m^t$) in each path p^t ($i \leq t < j$). Then

- $enabled(s_m^t) = recover(enabled(r_m), \sigma_m^t)$;
- $engaged(s_m^t, p^t) = recover(engaged(r_m, l'), \sigma_m^t)$.

Thus, $onceStep(l) = \{recover(enabled(r_m), \sigma_m^t), 0 \leq m < n, i \leq t < j\}$ and $engagedStep(l) = \{recover(engaged(r_m, p^t), \sigma_m^t), 0 \leq m < n, i \leq t < j\}$. Since $onceStep(l') = engagedStep(l')$, $onceStep(l') = \{enabled(r_m), 0 \leq m \leq n, i \leq t < j\}$ and $engagedStep(l') = \{engaged(r_m, p^t), 0 \leq m \leq n, i \leq t < j\}$, we have $onceStep(l) = engagedStep(l)$.

(Necessary condition). Let $l = \langle(s_0, b_0), a_0, (s_1, b_1), a_1, \cdots, (s_{n-1}, b_{n-1}), a_{n-1}, (s_0, b_0)\rangle$ be an accepting loop in the product of $\mathcal{L}$ and $\mathcal{B}$. There exists a path arriving at (s_0, b_0). Assume b_0 is an accepting state in $\mathcal{B}$. By Lemma 1 there exists a path in the product of $\mathcal{L}_G$ and $\mathcal{B}$ leading to state $(rep(s_0), b_0)$. By Lemma 1, there exists in the product of $\mathcal{L}_G$ and $\mathcal{B}$ a corresponding loop $l' = \langle(s_0\sigma_0, b_0), a_0, (s_1\sigma_1, b_1), a_1, \cdots, (s_{n-1}\sigma_{n-1}, b_{n-1}), a_{n-1}, (s_0\sigma_0, b_0)\rangle$ such that $\sigma_i \in G$ and $rep(s_i) = s_i\sigma_i$ for all $0 \le i < n$.

Because l satisfies global fairness, $onceStep(l) = engagedStep(l)$. We define a function $twist$ such that given $s \xrightarrow{e} s'$, $twist(s, e, s') = rep(s) \xrightarrow{e}_G rep(s')$. Intuitively, $twist$ returns the corresponding transition in $\mathcal{L}_G$ of (s, e, s'). For all $0 \le i < n$, s_i in loop l corresponds to $rep(s_i)$ in l'. Then

- $enabled(rep(s_i)) = twist(enabled(s_i))$;
- $engaged(rep(s_i), l') = twist(engaged(s_i, l))$.

Thus, $onceStep(l') = \{twist(enabled(s_i)), 0 \le i < n\}$ and $engagedStep(l') = \{twist(engaged(s_i, l')), 0 \le i < n\}$. Because $onceStep(l) = engagedStep(l)$, we have $onceStep(l) = \{enabled(s_i), 0 \le i < n\}$ and $engagedStep(l) = \{engaged(s_i, l), 0 \le i < n\}$. Thus, we have $onceStep(l') = engagedStep(l')$. □

Note that we did not allow the events to be permuted in the definition of permutation given at the beginning of this section, which seems too restrictive. Now we relax the definition of permutation to permute states and events simultaneously. It is proved in [13] that the new definition is equivalent to the one given before. By a simple argument, it can be shown that Theorem 3 still holds.

Based on Theorem 3, we present a practical algorithm for searching the reduced state space for accepting globally fair loops, based on Tarjan's SCC algorithm. Underlining shows the differences compared with the usual algorithm for model checking with global fairness. Assume that G is a permutation group of process identities which is an invariance group of $\mathcal{L}$ and ϕ. Let rep be a function which, given a state, returns a unique representative. Using function rep, we can tell whether two states are in the same orbit or not. Note that identifying an optimal representative function rep can be non-trivial. We adopt the automata-theoretic approach and perform the following. Firstly, a Büchi automaton $\mathcal{B}$ is generated from the negation of ϕ. Next, the synchronous product of $\mathcal{B}$ and $\mathcal{L}$ is computed on-the-fly. Tarjan's SCC algorithm is used to identify SCC in the product along the construction. Note that a state of the product is a pair (s, b) where s is a state of $\mathcal{L}$ and b is a state of $\mathcal{B}$. Assume that the initial state of the product is $(init_s, init_b)$ where $init_s$ is the initial state of $\mathcal{L}$ and $init_b$ is the initial state of $\mathcal{B}$[3].

The detailed algorithm is presented in Figure 2. It resembles the standard Tarjan's SCC algorithm [29]. Note that we use the iterative version of Tarjan's SCC algorithm in the practice implementation for performance reason. Three data structures are used to identify SCCs: *path* is a stack containing states along a path from the initial state to the current one; *index* and *lowlink* are hash tables which assign two numbers to a state. A state is a root of an SCC if and only if the two numbers are equivalent. To apply symmetry reduction, instead of working with concrete states, Tarjan's algorithm

---

[3] For simplicity, we assume there is only one initial state in $\mathcal{B}$.

is applied to representatives of orbits. For instance, *path* contains only $rep(v)$ (line 10) and *lowlink* and *index* map $rep(v)$ to numbers (line 7 and 8). Whenever an SCC is identified (line 17), we check whether the SCC is terminal in $\mathcal{L}$ and accepting. If it is, then we prove existence of at least one counterexample. We skip the details on generating a concrete counterexample. Note that an SCC is terminal in $\mathcal{L}$ if and only if, for every state (s, b) in the SCC, if $s \rightarrow s'$, then there exists (s', b') in the SCC. An SCC is accepting if and only if it contains a state (s, b) such that b is an accepting state in $\mathcal{B}$. The algorithm terminates when all states have been checked. The correctness of the algorithm follows from the theorems presented in previous sections. It is always terminating because the number of un-explored states are monotonically decreasing and the number of states are finite. Its complexity is linear in the edges of transitions in the product of $\mathcal{L}$ and $\mathcal{B}$.

The following claims establish the correctness of the algorithm.

Lemma 2. *In the product of $\mathcal{L}$ (resp. $\mathcal{L}_G$) and $\mathcal{B}$, there exists an accepting loop which satisfies global fairness if and only if there exists an accepting SCC which is also a terminal SCC in $\mathcal{L}$ (resp.$\mathcal{L}_G$).*

Proof: *(Necessary Condition)*. Suppose l is an accepting loop which satisfies global fairness. so $onceStep(l) = engagedStep(l)$. The states in l forms a strongly connected subgraph S in the product and S is a terminal SCC in $\mathcal{L}$. Let S' be the SCC that contains the states in S. Suppose l' be the loop which traverses all transitions in S. Because S is a terminal SCC in $\mathcal{L}$, $onceStep(l') = engagedStep(l') = onceStep(l)$. So S' is also a terminal SCC in $\mathcal{L}$. On the other hand, because l is accepting, there is an accepting state in S'.

(Sufficient Condition). Suppose S is an accepting SCC in the product of $\mathcal{L}$ and $\mathcal{B}$, and it is a terminal SCC in $\mathcal{L}$. Let l be the loop which traverses all transitions in S. We get $onceStep(l) = engagedStep(l)$. so l is a globally fair loop. Since there is an accepting state in l, l is an accepting loop which satisfies global fairness.

Using same argument one can show the lemma holds for product of $\mathcal{L}_G$ and $\mathcal{B}$. □

Theorem 4. *Let ϕ be an SE-LTL formula. If G is an invariance group of $\mathcal{L}$ and ϕ, then $\mathcal{L} \models_{gf} \phi$ if and only if $\mathcal{L}_G \models_{gf} \phi$.*

Proof. By Theorem 1, $\mathcal{L} \not\models_{gf} \phi$ if and only if there exists an accepting SCC in the product of $\mathcal{L}$ and $\mathcal{B}$ which is also a terminal SCC in $\mathcal{L}$. Similarly, $\mathcal{L}_G \not\models_{gf} \phi$ if and only if there exists an accepting SCC in the product of $\mathcal{L}_G$ and $\mathcal{B}$ which is also a terminal SCC in $\mathcal{L}_G$. By Theorem 3 and Lemma 2, there exists an accepting SCC S such that S is a terminal SCC in $\mathcal{L}$ if and only if there exists an accepting SCC S' such that S' is a terminal SCC in $\mathcal{L}_G$, which proves the theorem. □

6   Partial Order Reduction with Global Fairness

In this section, we show that partial order reduction is not property-preserving with global fairness, which means that partial order reduction cannot be applied in our setting.

```
1.          int counter := 0;
2.          stack path := an empty stack;
3.          hashtable index := an empty hash table;
4.          hashtable lowlink := an empty hash table;
5.          TarjanModelChecking((init_s, init_b));

6.          procedure TarjanModelChecking(v)
7.              index[rep(v)] := counter;
8.              lowlink[rep(v)] := counter;
9.              counter := counter + 1;
10.             push rep(v) into path
11.             forall v → v' do
12.                 if (rep(v') is not in index)
13.                     TarjanModelChecking(v')
14.                     lowlink[rep(v)] = min(lowlink[rep(v)], lowlink[rep(v')]);
15.                 else if (rep(v') is in path)
16.                     lowlink[rep(v)] = min(lowlink[rep(v)], index[rep(v')]);
17.                 endif
18.             endfor
19.             if (lowlink[rep(v)] = index[rep(v)])
20.                 set scc := an empty set;
21.                 repeat
22.                     pop an element v' from path and add it into scc;
23.                 until (v' = v)
24.                 if (scc forms a terminal SCC in L and scc is accepting)
25.                     generate a counterexample and return false;
26.                 endif
27.             endif
28.         endprocedure
```

Fig. 2. Tarjan's algorithm with symmetry reduction

We begin by fixing notations and terminology. Given an *LKS* $\mathcal{L} = (S, init, \Sigma, \rightarrow, AP, L)$, the function $\alpha(s)$ returns the set α-successors of s in $\mathcal{L}$. That is, $s' \in \alpha(s)$ iff $s \xrightarrow{\alpha} s'$. Two fundamental relations are first defined for partial order reduction.

Definition 5. *An independence relation $I \subseteq \rightarrow \times \rightarrow$ is a symmetric, antireflexive relation, satisfying the following two conditions for each state $s \in S$ and for each $(\alpha, \beta) \in I$: (1) If $\alpha, \beta \in enabled(s)$, then $\alpha \in enabled(\beta(s))$. (2) If $\alpha, \beta \in enabled(s)$, then $\alpha(\beta(s)) = \beta(\alpha(s))$. The dependency relation is the complement of I.*

Definition 6. *Let $L : S \rightarrow 2^{AP}$ be the function that labels each state with a set of atomic propositions. A transition $\alpha \in T$ is invisible with respect to a set of propositions $AP' \subseteq AP$ if for each pair of states $s, s' \in S$ such that $s' = \alpha(s)$, $L(s) \cap AP' = L(s') \cap AP'$.*

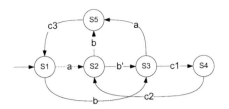

Fig. 3. Model and its reduction

The state space reduction is achieved by only exploring a subset of $enabled(s)$, called $ample(s)$ for any visiting state s. The following conditions on $ample(s)$ are used to preserve properties to be verified [9].

C0 $ample(s) = \varnothing$ iff $enabled(s) = \varnothing$.
C1 Along every path in the full state space starting from s, a transition that is dependent on a transition in $ample(s)$ cannot occur without one in $ample(s)$ occurring first.
C2 If $enabled(s) \neq ample(s)$, then every $\alpha \in ample(s)$ is invisible.
C3 A cycle is not allowed if it contains a state in which some transition α is enabled, but is never included in $ample(s)$ for any state s on the cycle.

It is proved in [9] that when satisfying the above four conditions, the following holds.

Theorem 5. *The original state space and reduced state space are stuttering equivalent.*

Based on Theorem 5, for any globally fair path in the full state space, there is a stuttering equivalent path in the reduced state space. Unfortunately, this path may be not globally fair. Figure 3 shows a part of the full state graph. The transition from $s1$ to $s2$ is not present in the reduced state graph. Let transitions labeled with a and b be independent and all other transitions be mutually dependent. Further let b, b' be invisible and a, c_1, c_2, c_3 visible. For the globally fair path $\lambda = (abc_3 bc_1 c_2 b' ac_3)^\omega$ in the full state space, there is no stuttering equivalent globally fair path in the reduced state space. Because any globally fair path π in the reduced one has to traverse the transition labeled with b from state $s2$ to $s5$, π must include a segment stuttering-equivalent path to $c_2 c_3$ whereas λ does not have such segment.

7   Implementation and Evaluation

In the following, we evaluate the effectiveness of our combined method. We extend the PAT[4] model checker with our algorithms for model checking with global fairness and symmetry reduction.

Previously in [19], PAT has been applied to model checking population protocols with global fairness without symmetry reduction. It is evidenced that only small networks can be checked. In the population protocol model, one protocol consists of N nodes, numbered from 0 to $N - 1$. A protocol is usually described by a set of interaction rules between an initiator u and a responder v. Such rules have conditions on the

---

[4] http://pat.comp.nus.edu.sg

Table 1. Experiment Results

Model	Network Size	Without Reduction		With Reduction		
		States	Time (Sec)	States	Time (Sec)	Gain
two-hop coloring	3	122856	36.7	42182	16.7	54.5%
orienting rings (prop 1)	3	19190	2.27	6398	0.53	76.7%
orienting rings (prop 2)	3	19445	2.23	6503	0.97	56.5%
orienting rings (prop 1)	4	1255754	267.2	313940	70.5	73.6%
orienting rings (prop 2)	4	1206821	267.1	302071	63.6	79.6%
orienting rings (prop 1)	5	11007542	9628.1	2201510	1067.4	88.9%
orienting rings (prop 2)	5	10225849	8322.6	2045935	954.5	88.5%
leader election (complete)	3	6946	0.87	2419	0.51	41.4%
leader election (complete)	4	65468	11.6	16758	5.00	56.9%
leader election (complete)	5	598969	176.1	120021	45.9	73.9%
leader election (odd)	3	55100	6.27	18561	2.56	59.2%
leader election (odd)	5	–	–	6444097	5803.96	×
token circulation	3	728	0.12	244	0.09	25.0%
token circulation	4	4466	0.35	1118	0.19	45.7%
token circulation	5	24847	1.86	4971	0.77	58.6%
token circulation	6	129344	10.7	21559	3.03	71.7%
token circulation	7	643666	77.2	91954	16.2	79.0%
token circulation	8	3104594	740.8	388076	97.1	86.9%

state and the input of the initiator and the responder, and specify the state of the initiator and the responder if a transition can be taken. Interested readers are referred to [19] for protocol details. Note that many of the protocols are designed for network rings. It has been noticed that protocols designed for network rings often require global fairness. All relevant experiment information is provided online [1].

8 Related Work

This work is related to research on combining fairness and symmetry reduction. A solution for applying symmetry reduction under weak/strong fairness was discussed in [12]. Their method works by finding a candidate weak/strong fair path in the abstract transition system and then using annotations of state permutation details for each transition, in order to resolve the abstract path to a threaded structure which then determines whether there is a corresponding fair path in the concrete transition system. A similar approach was presented in [15]. Another close work is a nested depth first search algorithm that combines symmetry reduction with weak fairness [5]. Unfortunately, the combined algorithm cannot guarantee to preserve all behaviors under weak fairness and thus may produce false positives.

We compare our algorithm with the one which handles strong fairness in [12]. Since global fairness can be regarded as a kind of strong fairness, the algorithm is applicable to global fairness. It is the only algorithm for combining strong fairness and symmetry reduction that we could find in literature. First, Theorem 3.11 in [12] shows its time complexity is $O(|\overline{M}| \times n^3 \times |g| \times a)$, where $|\overline{M}|$ is the size of the reduced graph

$\overline{M}$, n is the number of processes, $\mid g \mid$ is the length of the checked property g, and a is the maximum size of the automaton for any basic modality of g. Our algorithm is almost identical to Tarjan's SCC algorithm except for adding line 24, 25 in Figure 2. For a found SCC c the condition checking in line 24 can be implemented in time linear in the number of edges in c. As a result our algorithm can be implemented in time $O(\mid \overline{M} \mid \times \mid g \mid \times a)$. Second, in our approach it is not necessary to record permutations appearing on each path (unless unwinding an abstract counterexample) and to construct threaded structure for each strong connected subgraph B, of which the size is $O(\mid \overline{B} \mid \times n)$. Hence our algorithm outperforms theirs in space and time. Further, an important practical advantage of our algorithm, unlike [12], is that our algorithm reuses the original algorithm for model checking with global fairness with slight changes.

This work is also related to our previous work on combining weak/strong fairness with counter abstraction [28]. The idea is to show that model checking with process-level weak/strong fairness is feasible even if process identities are abstracted away. It is achieved by systematically keeping track of the local states from which actions are enabled/executed within any infinite loop of the abstract state space. Different from the above work, our approach works with global fairness and we show that global fairness and symmetry reduction can be integrated in a relatively easy way. Additionally, this work is remotely related to work on combining state reduction techniques and fairness, evidenced in [20,30,4]. Our work explores one kind of state reduction and shows that it works with global fairness.

Closest to our work on combination of partial order reduction and fairness is that of Peled [22,21] and Brim et al. [6]. Peled proposes equivalence robust property to guarantee that all behaviors under certain fair assumption remain in the reduced state space. However, since only weak fair is equivalence robust, stronger fair assumption need to add more dependency relations to achieve equivalence robustness. In his later work [21], he presents on-the-fly reduction algorithms with/without fairness assumptions. The authors in [6] define two partial order reduction strategies, safe and aggressive reduction, and demonstrate that each weakly fair behavior is preserved in safe reduction but not in aggressive one, while not all strongly fair behaviors are preserved in either reductions.

9 Conclusion and Future Work

The contribution of this work is threefold. First, we show that unlike weak/strong fairness, global fairness can be combined with symmetry reduction. Next, we present a practical fair model checking algorithm with symmetry reduction. Lastly, we prove that classic partial order reduction can not guarantee to preserve properties with global fairness. An interesting line of future work is to identify sufficient condition that allows combination of fairness and abstraction in general. In the current implementation, symmetry relationships are assumed to be known or easily detected. In the future, we plan to develop symmetry detection technique (as well as reduction techniques) for hierarchical complex systems.

References

1. http://www.comp.nus.edu.sg/
2. Angluin, D., Aspnes, J., Fischer, M.J., Jiang, H.: Self-stabilizing Population Protocols. In: Anderson, J.H., Prencipe, G., Wattenhofer, R. (eds.) OPODIS 2005. LNCS, vol. 3974, pp. 103–117. Springer, Heidelberg (2006)
3. Bosnacki, D., Dams, D., Holenderski, L.: Symmetric Spin. In: Havelund, K., Penix, J., Visser, W. (eds.) SPIN 2000. LNCS, vol. 1885, pp. 1–19. Springer, Heidelberg (2000)
4. Bosnacki, D., Ioustinova, N., Sidorova, N.: Using Fairness to Make Abstractions Work. In: Graf, S., Mounier, L. (eds.) SPIN 2004. LNCS, vol. 2989, pp. 198–215. Springer, Heidelberg (2004)
5. Bošnački, D.: A light-weight algorithm for model checking with symmetry reduction and weak fairness. In: Ball, T., Rajamani, S.K. (eds.) SPIN 2003. LNCS, vol. 2648, pp. 89–103. Springer, Heidelberg (2003)
6. Brim, L., Cerná, I., Moravec, P., Simsa, J.: On combining partial order reduction with fairness assumptions. In: Brim, L., Haverkort, B.R., Leucker, M., van de Pol, J. (eds.) FMICS 2006 and PDMC 2006. LNCS, vol. 4346, pp. 84–99. Springer, Heidelberg (2007)
7. Chaki, S., Clarke, E.M., Ouaknine, J., Sharygina, N., Sinha, N.: State/Event-Based Software Model Checking. In: Boiten, E.A., Derrick, J., Smith, G.P. (eds.) IFM 2004. LNCS, vol. 2999, pp. 128–147. Springer, Heidelberg (2004)
8. Clarke, E.M., Filkorn, T., Jha, S.: Exploiting Symmetry In Temporal Logic Model Checking. In: Courcoubetis, C. (ed.) CAV 1993. LNCS, vol. 697, pp. 450–462. Springer, Heidelberg (1993)
9. Clarke, E.M., Grumberg, O., Peled, D.A.: Model Checking. The MIT Press, Cambridge (2000)
10. Delzanno, G.: Automatic Verification of Parameterized Cache Coherence Protocols. In: Emerson, E.A., Sistla, A.P. (eds.) CAV 2000. LNCS, vol. 1855, pp. 53–68. Springer, Heidelberg (2000)
11. Emerson, E.A., Sistla, A.P.: Symmetry and Model Checking. Formal Methods in System Design 9(1-2), 105–131 (1996)
12. Emerson, E.A., Sistla, A.P.: Utilizing Symmetry when Model-Checking under Fairness Assumptions: An Automata-Theoretic Approach. ACM Transactions on Programming Languages and Systems 19(4), 617–638 (1997)
13. Allen Emerson, E., Jha, S., Peled, D.: Combining partial order and symmetry reductions. In: Brinksma, E. (ed.) TACAS 1997. LNCS, vol. 1217, pp. 19–34. Springer, Heidelberg (1997)
14. Fischer, M., Jiang, H.: Self-stabilizing Leader Election in Networks of Finite-State Anonymous Agents. In: Shvartsman, M.M.A.A. (ed.) OPODIS 2006. LNCS, vol. 4305, pp. 395–409. Springer, Heidelberg (2006)
15. Gyuris, V., Sistla, A.P.: On-the-Fly Model Checking Under Fairness That Exploits Symmetry. In: Grumberg, O. (ed.) CAV 1997. LNCS, vol. 1254, pp. 232–243. Springer, Heidelberg (1997)
16. Jiang, H.: Distributed Systems of Simple Interacting Agents. PhD thesis, Yale Uni (2007)
17. Lamport, L.: Proving the Correctness of Multiprocess Programs. IEEE Transactions on Software Engineering 3(2), 125–143 (1977)
18. Lamport, L.: Fairness and Hyperfairness. Distributed Computing 13(4), 239–245 (2000)
19. Liu, Y., Pang, J., Sun, J., Zhao, J.H.: Verification of Population Ring Protocols in PAT. In: TASE, pp. 81–89. IEEE, Los Alamitos (2009)
20. Nitsche, U., Wolper, P.: Relative Liveness and Behavior Abstraction (Extended Abstract). In: PODC, pp. 45–52. ACM, New York (1997)

21. Peled, D.: Combining Partial Order Reductions with On-the-fly Model-Checking. In: Dill, D.L. (ed.) CAV 1994. LNCS, vol. 818, pp. 377–390. Springer, Heidelberg (1994)

22. Peled, D.: All from one, one for all: on model checking using representatives. In: Courcoubetis, C. (ed.) CAV 1993. LNCS, vol. 697, pp. 409–423. Springer, Heidelberg (1993)

23. Pnueli, A.: On the Extremely Fair Treatment of Probabilistic Algorithms. In: STOC, pp. 278–290. ACM, New York (1983)

24. Pnueli, A., Sa'ar, Y.: All you need is compassion. In: Logozzo, F., Peled, D.A., Zuck, L.D. (eds.) VMCAI 2008. LNCS, vol. 4905, pp. 233–247. Springer, Heidelberg (2008)

25. Pnueli, A., Xu, J., Zuck, L.D.: Liveness with $(0, 1, \infty)$-Counter Abstraction. In: Brinksma, E., Larsen, K.G. (eds.) CAV 2002. LNCS, vol. 2404, pp. 107–122. Springer, Heidelberg (2002)

26. Pong, F., Dubois, M.: A New Approach for the Verification of Cache Coherence Protocols. IEEE Transactions on Parallel and Distributed Systems 6(8), 773–787 (1995)

27. Sun, J., Liu, Y., Dong, J.S., Pang, J.: PAT: Towards Flexible Verification under Fairness. In: Bouajjani, A., Maler, O. (eds.) CAV 2009. LNCS, vol. 5643, pp. 709–714. Springer, Heidelberg (2009)

28. Sun, J., Liu, Y., Roychoudhury, A., Liu, S., Dong, J.S.: Fair model checking with process counter abstraction. In: Cavalcanti, A., Dams, D.R. (eds.) FM 2009. LNCS, vol. 5850, pp. 123–139. Springer, Heidelberg (2009)

29. Tarjan, R.: Depth-first Search and Linear Graph Algorithms. SIAM Journal on Computing 2, 146–160 (1972)

30. Ultes-Nitsche, U., James St., S.: Improved Verification of Linear-time Properties within Fairness: Weakly Continuation-closed Behaviour Abstractions Computed from Trace Reductions. Software Testing, Verification & Reliability 13(4), 241–255 (2003)

Author Index